Tapestries for the Courts of Federico II, Ercole, and Ferrante Gonzaga

College Art Association
Monograph on the Fine Arts
Volume LII
Editor, Robert S. Nelson

Clifford M. Brown and Guy Delmarcel

with the collaboration of

Anna Maria Lorenzoni

Tapestries for the Courts of Federico II, Ercole, and Ferrante Gonzaga, 1522–63

Published by

COLLEGE ART ASSOCIATION

in association with

UNIVERSITY OF WASHINGTON PRESS

SEATTLE AND LONDON 1996

Supplemental funding for the color plates was generously provided by the Foundation "The Royal Manufacturers De Wit," Mechelen, Belgium, and the National Foundation Princess Marie-José, Brussels.

Printed in the United States of America

University of Washington Press
PO Box 50096
Seattle, Washington 98145

Library of Congress Cataloging-in-Publication Data

Brown, Clifford M.

Tapestries for the courts of Federico II, Ercole, and Ferrante Gonzaga, 1522–63 / Clifford M. Brown and Guy Delmarcel with the collaboration of Anna Maria Lorenzoni.

p. cm.—(Monographs on the fine arts; v. 52)
Includes bibliographical references and index.
ISBN 0-295-97513-X
1. Tapestry, Renaissance—Belgium—Brussels. 2. Tapestry—Belgium—Brussels. 3. Tapestry, Renaissance—Flanders. 4. Tapestry—Flanders. 5. Gonzaga family—Art patronage. I. Delmarcel, Guy. II. Lorenzoni, Anna Maria. III. Title.
NK3055.B8B76 1996
746.39493′32′09031—dc20 95-25130
CIP

The paper used in this book meets the minimum requirements of the American National Standard for Information Sciences—Permanence of Paper for Printed Library Materials, ANSI Z39.48-1984.

Contents

Illustrations

Color Plates

Figures

Preface

> Very fine and beautiful cloth in plentiful supply in Holland, marvelous tapestries with figures in Brabant, and then there is the music which is undeniably perfect.
>
> —Vincenzo Quirini

According to the Venetian ambassador Vincenzo Quirini, writing in 1506, cloth, tapestries, and music were the principal exports of the Low Countries.[1] By this date tapestry production in what is now Flanders and Brabant had reached a high point of excellence. The Italian nobility had been well acquainted with and greatly appreciative of the craft since its inception in the fourteenth century. Thus, for example, upon the marriage of the future Henry II to Catherine de' Medici in Marseille in 1532, Francis I presented Pope Clement VII, who performed the ceremony, with a tapestry of Leonardo da Vinci's *Last Supper,* now in the Vatican Museum. Paolo Giovio, himself a distinguished collector of tapestries, described this gift as "Belgarum ars suprema," the highest art of the Low Countries, and Lodovico Guicciardini penned a similar appreciation of Flemish skills:[2] "Ma sopra tutto vi è ammirabile et profittevole il mestiere delle tappezerie, che vedrai opera di seta, d'argento et d'oro, per industria e per spesa maravigliose e stupende."[3] Even as late as 1610, the papal nuncio in Flanders, Guido Bentivoglio, who had been entrusted with supervising the weaving of the *Life of Sampson* for Cardinal Scipione Borghese, proclaimed: "per esser questa la città dove meglio che in altro luogo di queste parti si lavora d'arazzi."[4]

The unanimous praise by Italians of northern tapestries is related to an artistic medium they were extremely fond of and that they collected avidly. The northern textile wall hangings were used extensively throughout Europe, and in fact, tapestries have been defined as the "mobile fresco of the North."[5] Tapestries were easily transported and quickly installed. When a court moved from one place to another, the tapestries often preceded them. Mobility and flexibility help to explain why some courts amassed such enormous collections. These large decorations and environments could also be loaned to neighbors and allies. Above all else, however, they were a brilliant reflection of the wealth and prestige of their owners. In this sense they may be considered an essential part of political image making and display.[6]

A great deal of documentation survives regarding the migration to Italy of the northern tapestry weavers. In addition to the repair and maintenance of older weavings, they were responsible for the creation of new tapestries. As Candace Adelson remarked: "Aside from the unusual situation in Ferrara and her close ally Mantua, the history of tapestry weaving in Italy in the fifteenth century essentially boils down to a handful of itinerant northern weavers working for short periods in various cities. Here they found temporary work but not enough patronage to sustain them for any length of time in one place. In the sixteenth century this type of activity seems to have died out. No one could compete with the highly refined organization of Flanders—especially Brussels."[7]

Most of the tapestries owned by the Gonzaga family were made in Brussels. Adelson notes: "Throughout the fifteenth century Italian patrons sent cartoons to Flanders to be woven, and were apparently satisfied with the results. The Este, in fact, persisted in commissioning their largest tapestries in Flanders—as often as not sending designs—even though they contemporaneously had the largest number of tapestry weavers in Italy in their employ."[8] The same is true for the sixteenth century.

At the end of the fifteenth century, Brussels dominated the domestic as well as the foreign market for tapestry production. This was due to superior designs, expert technique, and, in the literal sense of the term, a well-organized "art industry." Only the names of the major entrepreneurs are cited in the few surviving documents related to such transactions. Called "marchand tapissier," they provided funds for the purchase of materials, including the costly gold and silver threads, for the execution of the life-size cartoons, and for the salaries of the weavers. By and large the weavers remain anonymous, although several of their products can be identified thanks to the workshop marks that became compulsory in Brussels after 1528 and in other Flemish centers after 1544. From these marks it is learned that Ercole's *Acts of the Apostles* was woven by Jan van Tieghem and his associates, the Ferrante *Moses* by the Dermoyen company and the Ferrante *Puttini* by Willem de Pannemaker, the purveyor of Charles V, his son Philip II and the Hapsburg regents in the Netherlands. Despite their importance as "art producers," their names are rarely if ever encountered in contemporary documents. Giambattista Lodi (Document 32) refers indirectly to Pannemaker as the author of the *Tunis* series, describing him as "the best master who can be found there [Brussels]." Cardinal Granvelle, writing to Ercole, refers only to the master, the weaver or the merchant (Document 46).

Brussels was the foremost center for tapestry production. In 1545 an agent of Cosimo de' Medici tried to find a Flemish weaver willing to relocate to Florence. He praised the Brussels weavers as outstanding craftsmen, adding that about fifteen thousand people made their livelihood from this industry. With an estimated population of some fifty thousand, this means that almost one-third of the residents of Brussels were engaged in tapestry production.[9]

The trade and financing of the tapestry market, however, was concentrated in Antwerp, which had the largest harbor in Northern Europe and was a crossroads of the financial markets. Until 1551 the tapestry trade in Antwerp had been concentrated in the Predikherenpand, the cloister of the Dominicans, which also functioned as a market for jewelry, paintings, and carved altarpieces. This commercial activity eventually led to the creation of a specific trade market for tapestries, the so-called "tapissierspand," where from July 1554 onward numerous master weavers and dealers from such centers as Brussels, Enghien, and Oudenaarde could rent shops. This explains why there are so many references to the availability of tapestries in Antwerp (Documents 39 and 46).

The history of the collecting of northern tapestries by the Italian courts during the fifeenth and sixteenth centuries is so rich and varied that only the briefest account is possible here. The leading example was probably the papal court. It was after all for Leo X that the *Acts of the Apostles* was woven in Brussels between 1515 and 1519. Designed by Raphael and intended to decorate the Sistine Chapel, this commission served to introduce the High Renaissance to Brussels. The papal collection was also built up from gifts.[10] Thus, for example, in 1423 Philip the Good, Duke of Burgundy, gave Martin V a set of five weavings of the *Life of the Virgin,* which he had acquired from Giovanni Arnolfini, "marchant de Lucques demourant à Bruges." Philip the Good also bought from Italian merchants in Bruges a tapestry of the "historiée de trois hystoires morales du pape, de l'empereur et de la noblesse," which he presented to Eugene IV in 1441–42.[11] It or another edition survives in Tarragona Cathedral, where it is known as *La buena vida,* an impressive allegory on the three social classes—the "oratores," the "bellatores," and the "laboratores."[12] Eugene's nephew was Cardinal Pietro Barbo, who became Pope Paul II in 1464. As early as 1457 Barbo owned an impressive collection of no fewer than one hundred tapestries. The "inventarium pannorum de razio" identifies Arras as the best-known production center of the period. Barbo owned more secular than religious pieces and a great number of "dorsalia," or "spallere," door tapestries and mule covers.[13]

Pope Sixtus IV (1471–1484) added many tapestries to the papal collection, a number of which (the *Old and New Testament,* an *Adoration of the Magi,* the *Life of Samuel,* a *Last Supper,* and the *Jewish Wars under Titus and Vespasian*) bear his coat of arms.[14] Alexander VI (1492–1503) owned a *Credo* series, which is cited in the 1518 inventory.[15] As for Julius II (1503–1513), he apparently ordered a lost *Heliodorus* set, which may have been related to the frescoes in Raphael's stanza of the same name.[16] Julius II also purchased a number of Brussels tapestries that were intended as isolated devotional pieces. Several of these (the *Adoration of the Infant Christ* in the Victoria and Albert Museum, and the *Mystical Grape* in the Vatican) are still preserved.[17] In addition to the *Acts of the Apostles,* Leo X (1513–21) owned the Vincidor *Puttini* and the *Grotesque Gods,* while his successor, Clement VII

(1523–34), ordered the *Life of Christ* (also known as the "Scuola Nuova"), a twelve-piece set woven in Brussels in the workshop of Pieter van Aelst.[18]

Papal patronage in the fifteenth and sixteenth centuries set the tone for Italy's secular courts. The Medicis of Florence were especially active in collecting tapestries through their agents in Bruges and Lyon.[19] Between 1441 and 1455 a set of six *Trionfi* was produced for Giovanni de' Medici in Lille. The Italianate nature of the subject suggests that the preparatory drawings, and perhaps also the cartoons, were produced in Florence. The same anonymous weaver in Lille was entrusted with the creation of "spallere" and "bancalia." The 1492 inventory mentions the older *Trionfi* as well as a large dorsal piece with "una chaccia del duca di Borghogna" and two panels with the story of *Narcissus*.[20] When Cosimo I became duke in 1534, he inherited some seventy *verdure* tapestries, probably "millefleurs," with the Medici arms.[21] It was Cosimo I who brought to Florence in 1545 the Flemish weavers Jan Rost and Nicolas Karcher. By 1553 the two independent Flemish workshops had produced forty-four luxury pieces for the decoration of the Palazzo Vecchio. These were the *Life of Joseph* and the Bacchiacca *Grotesques*. At the time of his death in 1574, Cosimo I owned more than four hundred tapestries, most of them woven in Florence. Nonetheless, he also ordered sets from Brussels, including the *Life of Tobias* and the lavish *Genesis* set, which arrived in Florence in 1551.[22]

Among the other great collectors of the cinquecento was Andrea Doria of Genoa (1466–1560).[22] For him, Piero del Vaga provided designs for the *Furti di Giove*, woven in Flanders between 1532 and 1535, as well as the *Navigazione d'Enea*.[24] Less well documented is the series of *Grotesques with the Gods*, of which three panels bearing the Doria arms have survived. Their designs have been variously attributed to the workshop of Perino del Vaga or to Amico Aspertini and were based on an older set of the same subject designed by Giovanni da Udine for Pope Leo X.[25]

Ferrara was also a major center for the collection and production of tapestries.[26] Duke Ercole II was the near-contemporary of Cosimo I. In 1536 he brought to Ferrara Nicolas Karcher and Jan Rost, whose later work in Florence has already been mentioned. During their eleven years in Ferrara, they produced various impressive series, including the lost *Gigantomachy* (1537–38), based on designs provided by Giulio Romano. Other series include the *Odyssey* by Pordenone (1538–39), the *Hercules* (1542–45), and the *Metamorphoses* (1544–45), based on designs by Battista Dossi. The *Storie di San Giorgio e San Maurelio*, based on cartoons by Luca d'Olanda, was produced between 1550 and 1553 after the workshop was taken over by Giovanni Karcher.[27]

Cardinal Ippolito d'Este, Ercole II's brother, had a wider knowlege of matters, having spent many years at the French court, where he was sent in 1548 as the papal ambassador. The inventory drawn up after his death in 1572 lists some 183 tapestries. In addition to seventy-four *boscaglie, verdure,* and *fogliami,* Ippolito II owned seventeen sets based on stories from mythology and ancient and biblical history. Sets such as the *Life of Scipio,* the *Life of Phaeton,* and the *Romulus and Remus* had been woven from Italian models.[28] In March 1561 he offered a ten-piece set of the "istoria di Nabucho" to one of the "cardinali Gongiaga," possibly Ercole.[29]

Ferrara was linked to Mantua in various ways, both through the marriage of Ercole d'Este's daughter Isabella to the Marquis Francesco II Gonzaga and from the fact that their children, notably Federico II and Ercole, were patrons of Nicolas Karcher, who moved from Ferrara to Mantua in 1539. The tapestries in this book, including the fifty-three surviving panels from the collections of Federico II, Ercole, and Ferrante Gonzaga, are from collections formed by princes who, like Cosimo I de' Medici, Ercole II d'Este, and Federico II Gonzaga, were rulers of city-states; by those like Ippolito II d'Este and Ercole Gonzaga, who were members of the College of Cardinals; and by those like Ferrante, who were servants of the emperor. The fifty-three Gonzaga panels belong to the seven extant sets, the remnants of what had originally been a much larger collection, the scope of which shall be fully explored in the following pages.

Notes

1. Alberi, 1839–63, I, 11–12.
2. Crick-Kuntziger, 1952, 121; Brassat, 1992, 89.
3. Guicciardini, 1588, 75.
4. Hoogewerff, 1923, 212.
5. For a general introduction to techniques and usage, see Bennett, 1992, 3–16; Cavallo, 1993, 17–77; and Adelson, 1994, 1–18.

6. Brassat, 1992, passim.

7. Adelson, 1991, 36–37. The situation in Mantua is best described by Braghirolli, 1879, 7ff.

8. Adelson, 1991, 31–32.

9. Adelson, 1985, 15.

10. Muentz, 1878–82, passim; Smit, 1993, 49–60.

11. Muentz, 1878–82, I, 26, 63.

12. *Brussels 1951*, no. 128.

13. Muentz, 1878–82, I, 278–85.

14. Muentz, 1878–82, III, 263.

15. Muentz, 1878, 178ff. According to Smit (1993, 51), the Vatican series predates the pontificate of Julius II.

16. Smit (1993, 54–55) maintained that they were originally intended for the dado of the Stanza di Eliodoro. It is not longer believed that the Vincidor *Puttini,* with the arms of Leo X, was designed for the Sala di Costantino.

17. See Nello Forti Grazzini's essay in Castelnuovo, 1990, 42 and plates 25 and 67. This study includes many other pre-Renaissance Brussels tapestries now in Italy.

18. For Leo X and Clement VII, see Bombe, 1920, 15–29, and *Vatican 1984*.

19. Muentz, 1888, 20, 27, 39; Grünzweig, 1931, passim, as well as the sometimes unclear synthesis by Schneebalg-Perelman, 1969[A], 19ff.

20. Grünzweig, 1931, 26–94, passim; Gombrich, 1961, 298–99.

21. Muentz, 1888, 59.

22. Adelson, 1991, 6, 10, 18–20, 82.

23. Boccardo, 1983–85, 113ff.; Davidson, 1988, 424ff.; Davidson, 1990, 35ff.

24. For the enlarged edition owned by Ferrante, see under "Aeneas" in the Index to the Major Sets of Figurative Tapestries.

25. Standen, 1985, 100–104; Erkelens, 1962, 131.

26. Forti Grazzini, 1982, 239; Forti Grazzini, 1990, 9–21; and Forti Grazzini, 1991, 53–62.

27. Forti Grazzini, 1982, 60–80.

28. Baratte, 1973, 115–26; Forti Grazzini, 1982, 80, 93 no. 135.

29. Baratte, 1973, 124. The offer is apparently unrecorded in the Gonzaga correspondence files.

Acknowledgments

Although this book is a collaborative effort (one initiated, however, by Guy Delmarcel), the division of labor involved in its organization was straightforward. I compiled the Chronology of the Lives and Art Patronange and Part I, the Documents. Guy Delmarcel compiled the critical comments in the Index to the Major Sets of Figurative Tapestries, wrote the entries for Part II, the Catalogue, and arranged for most of the photographs. Both of us made greater or lesser contributions to each other's sections; Guy Delmarcel provided references to the previously published documents cited in Document 55 and 72, while I made bibliographic suggestions for entries in the Catalogue in addition to serving as coordinator of the project.

Anna Maria Lorenzoni, a treasured friend and a knowledgeable colleague, graciously undertook the time-consuming and arduous task of checking and rechecking the accuracy of the transcriptions of the documents which form the core of the book. Since she did not actually enter the corrections on the computer, she is not responsible for any errors or omissions that inadvertently may have occurred. In addition to our collaboration, now in its twenty-eighth year, the "Lorenzoni touch" has significantly enhanced the research of scholars from Italy and England to Canada and from the United States to Australia. All have been captivated by Anna Maria's wit, charm, and patience in dealing with the linguistic peculiarities of the "stranieri" who spoke Italian with a variety of curious accents. Her unique sensitivity to all aspects of archival research has strenthened innumerable publications dealing with the Gonzaga archives.

While the archival records presented here are remarkably detailed, we have no illusions that they are either complete or definitive. While we have taken every reasonable effort to ensure the accuracy and completeness of the transcriptions of the files included in the seventy-eight sections of the Catalogue, the reader interested in a particular problem would do well to check the published transcriptions against the original documents themselves. Given problems of legibility and also of the complexity of some of the inventories, it is always possible that a useful entry was inadvertently overlooked. Furthermore, new material may always turn up in the Mantua and Parma archives themselves and even among the files that are the subject of individual entries in the Catalogue. Alternatively, discoveries doubtless remain to be made in repositories whose resources could not be systematically explored for this book, as is suggested by a colleague's finding a reference to the Guastalla *Puttini* among the "Mediceo del Principato" papers in Florence (Document 58, note 6).

It is of course both impossible and unrealistic to wait until that illusive "ideal moment" when all that can be found has been accounted for. Indeed in March 1993, just one month after the appearance of my *Our Accustomed Discourse on the Antique,* Paola Barocchi and Giovanna Gaeta Bertelà (*Collezionismo medicio: Cosimo I, Francesco I e il Cardinale Ferdinando,* Modena, 1993, 248) published Ercole Basso's penetrating evaluation of Cesare Gonzaga's holdings.

New and unexpected discoveries will doubtless also emerge regarding the Gonzaga family collections of tapestries. Indeed, one of the original panels from the *Fructus Belli* (Catalogue 3) came to light as recently as several years ago. We hope that some of the new archival and visual information may even see the light of day as a result of the stimulus we provide here. This is as it should be, as each contribution to the literature serves not as an end in itself but as a stepping stone to the next level in the dialogue.

My work in the Mantua State Archives during the past three decades was made all the more productive and pleasurable thanks to the cordiality of those who presided over the *sala di studio* and to the assistance provided by past and present directors: Adele Bellù, Carlo

Marco Belfanti, and Daniela Ferrari. Research in the Parma State Archives was greatly facilitated by the director, Marzio dall'Acqua, who has special knowledge of the Gonzaga of Guastalla files. His staff was especially accommodating and, as in Mantua, were only too happy to bend the rules so as to permit me to accomplish the maximum work in a limited amount of time. The Biblioteca Estense in Modena and the Biblioteca Maldotti in Guastalla were similarly helpful in responding to my research requests.

The matchless holdings of the Avery Fine Arts Library of Columbia University, and the Kunsthistorisches Institut in Florence, provided access to many of the needed bibliographic tools. During the spring terms of 1992 and 1993, when I was an Ailsa Mellon Bruce Senior Fellow at the Center for Advanced Study in the Visual Arts (as well as serving as Distinguished Visiting Professor at George Washington University), I was able to take advantage of the splendid research facilities of the library of the National Gallery of Art. Lamia Doumato, Head of Reader Services, and her staff bent over backward to accommodate even the most obscure requests. Back in Ottawa, the interlibrary loan office of Carleton University was tireless in responding to various eleventh-hour requests, while Erika Fuerst graciously suggested solutions to problematic bibliographic citations.

The Graduate Dean of Carleton University contributed handsomely to the costs related to several research trips to Italy. Generous funds were also made available for various costly incidental expenses, including those involved in having Christina Thiele (Carleton Production Centre, Ottawa), with whom I worked on my previous book, subject this manuscript to a first round of copy editing.

Guy Delmarcel and I used different word-processing systems to prepare our respective sections of the manuscript. Thus it was helpful to be able to rely on the Carleton University Micro Computer Application Support program to convert disks arriving from Belgium. Belonging as I do to the generation that grew up with the typewriter, having composed many of my articles as well as my first book on a second-hand Olivetti portable, purchased in Bologna, it was difficult to make the transition to the computer. Problems related to the mysteries of word processing were patiently and expertly resolved by my friend and companion of twenty-two years, Ronald John Buck, formerly of the Department of Energy, Mines, and Resources of the Government of Canada. Not only did he devise a range of macros to deal painlessly and globally with changes requested to conform with the publisher's rules and regulations, but he also arranged for the dismantling, packing, and reinstallation of our computer system so that the final phase of preparing the copyedited version of the manuscript could be accomplished at our working-holiday address by the shores of the Atlantic Ocean on Hilton Head Island in South Carolina.

Robert Nelson, the editor of the College Art Association monograph series, made suggestions that significantly improved the organization of the manuscript, which also profited from the penetrating analysis provided by Nello Forti Grazzini. Virginia Wageman, Manager of Publications for the College Art Association, expertly attended to the task of shepherding the final manuscript through to publication. Thanks to her, Cherene Holland was chosen as the copyeditor. With exquisite sensitivity and professionalism, she subjected the manuscript to a microscopic examination, thereby ensuring that the reader was spared innumerable infelicities. The authors are of course solely responsible for any errors that may inadvertently have escaped notice. Russell Hassell was responsible for having found a felicitous solution to the design of a complex manuscript and for having suggested interspersing the illustrations throughout the book.

My co-author, Guy Delmarcel, served as an enthusiastic and knowledgeable guide through the maze of complex technical, stylistic, and iconographic problems associated with a book intimately linked with his area of remarkable expertise. Finally, and on a personal note, I owe a special debt of gratitude to my good friend Marek Zubik.

Clifford M. Brown
Ottawa, Canada

Thanks are due three good friends and colleagues: Candace Adelson, Mercedes Viale Ferrero, and especially to Nello Forti Grazzini, who graciously provided a learned critique of the final draft of the manuscript. It is a pleasure to acknowledge the skills, the patience, and the endurance of Isabelle Van Tichelen, my research assistant at the Royal Museums of Art and History in Brussels. Colleagues at the Royal Museums, especially the former directors René De Roo and Herman De Meulenaere, were equally supportive, as was Bert Meijer, Director of the Netherlands Interuniversitair Kunsthistorisch Instituut in Florence.

The private owners and museum curators in charge of the Gonzaga tapestries were helpful in making accessible the relevant materials. Giannino Marzotto generously undertook to subsidize the cost of rephotographing the Ferrante *Puttini,* a task expertly accomplished by Giovetti of Mantua under the supervision of Clifford M. Brown. Others who gave their time and expertise include Rotraud Bauer (Kunsthistorisches Museum, Vienna), Concha Herrero Carretero (Patrimonio Nacional, Madrid), Hervé Oursel (Musée National de la Renaissance, Ecouen), Maria Fernanda Passos Leite (Museu Gulbenkian, Lisbon), Nicole de Reyniès (Inventaire général du Patrimoine, Paris), Anna Maria de Strobel (Gallerie e Musei Pontifici, Città del Vaticano), and Christa Mayer Thurman (The Art Institute of Chicago).

Among the many scholars who were unstintingly thoughtful in communicating important information, the following deserve special mention: Roseline Bacou, Peter Cannon-Brookes, Adolfo S. Cavallo, Dominique and Nicole Chevalier, Wendy Hefford, Hendrik J. Horn, George Hughes-Hartman, Bertrand Jestaz, Yvan Maes, Rolf Quednau, Peter Sarginson, Aurora Scotti, Vincenzo Scuderi, Edith A. Standen, and Bette Talvacchia.

The National Foundation Princess Marie-José (Brussels) and the Foundation "The Royal Manufactory De Wit" (Mechelen) provided generous subventions for the color reproductions, which enhance the book.

A special word of gratitude is due to Clifford M. Brown, whose research in the archives in Mantua and Parma successfully brought to light so much regarding the documentary history of the Gonzaga tapestries. With great patience and tact, he labored diligently to ensure that my needs and concerns were fully represented in this book. Furthermore, not only did he serve as co-author, but he also undertook the full range of time-consuming secreterial chores involved in preparing the computer disks for the publisher.

Guy Delmarcel
Leuven, Belgium

Color Plates

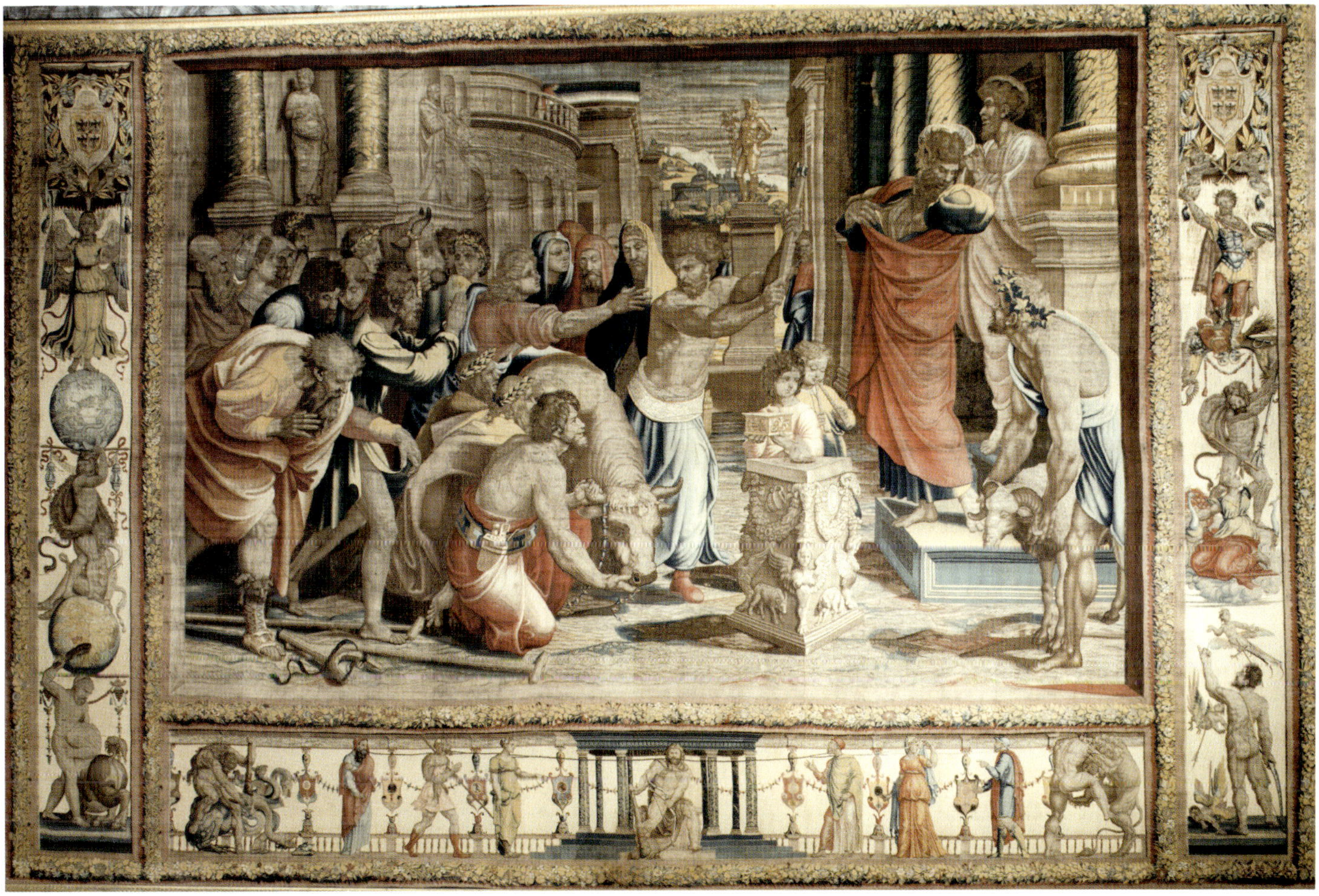

I *Acts of the Apostles: The Sacrifice at Lystra,* Brussels, workshop of Jan van Tieghem and others, before 1557 (see Fig. 35).

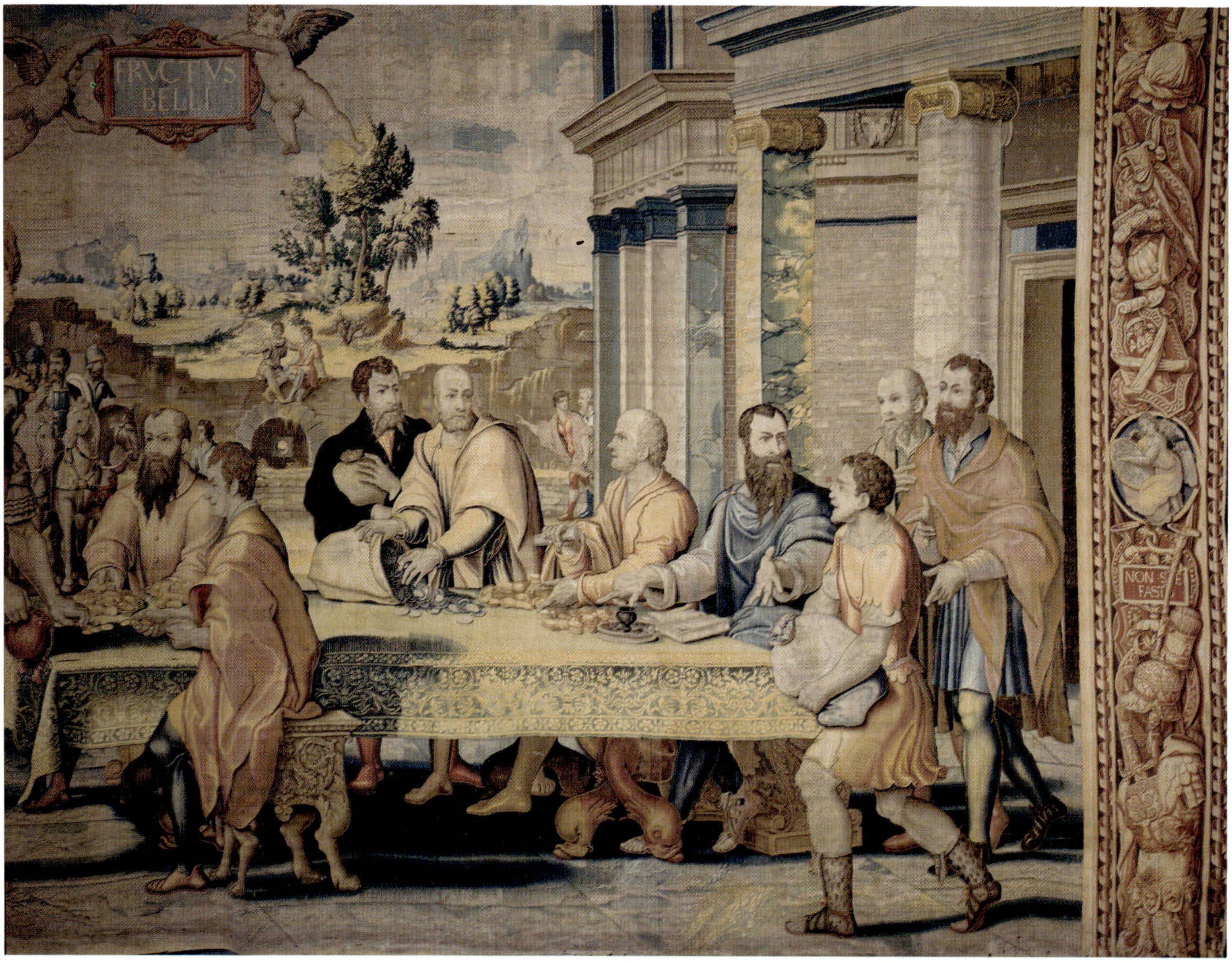

II *Fructus Belli: The Pay of the Soldiers,* detail, Brussels, workshop of Jehan Baudouyn, c. 1545–47 (see Fig. 44).

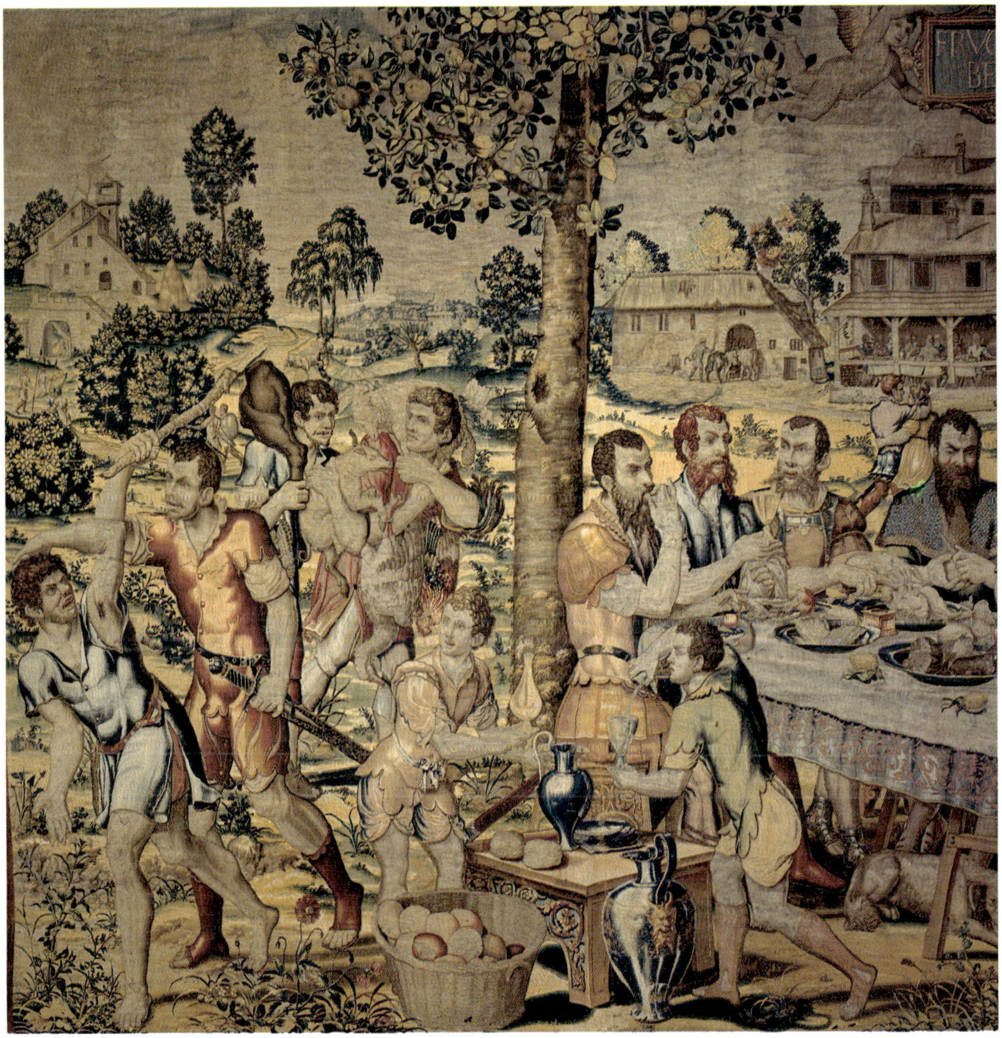

III *Fructus Belli: The Dinner of the Officers,* detail, Brussels, workshop of Jehan Baudouyn, c. 1545–47 (see Fig. 49).

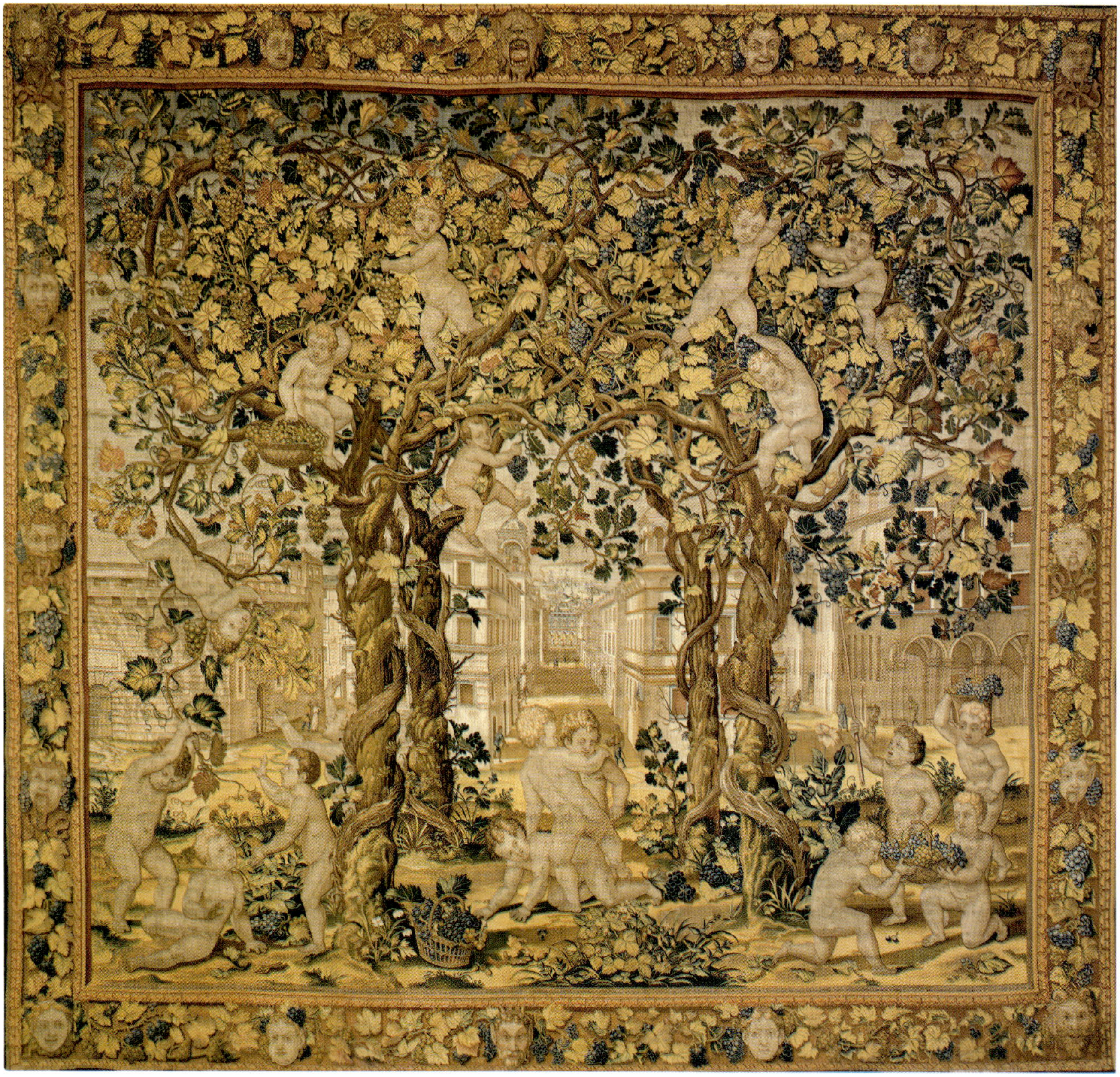

IV *Puttini: The City,* Brussels, workshop of Willem de Pannemaker, 1552–57 (see Fig. 85).

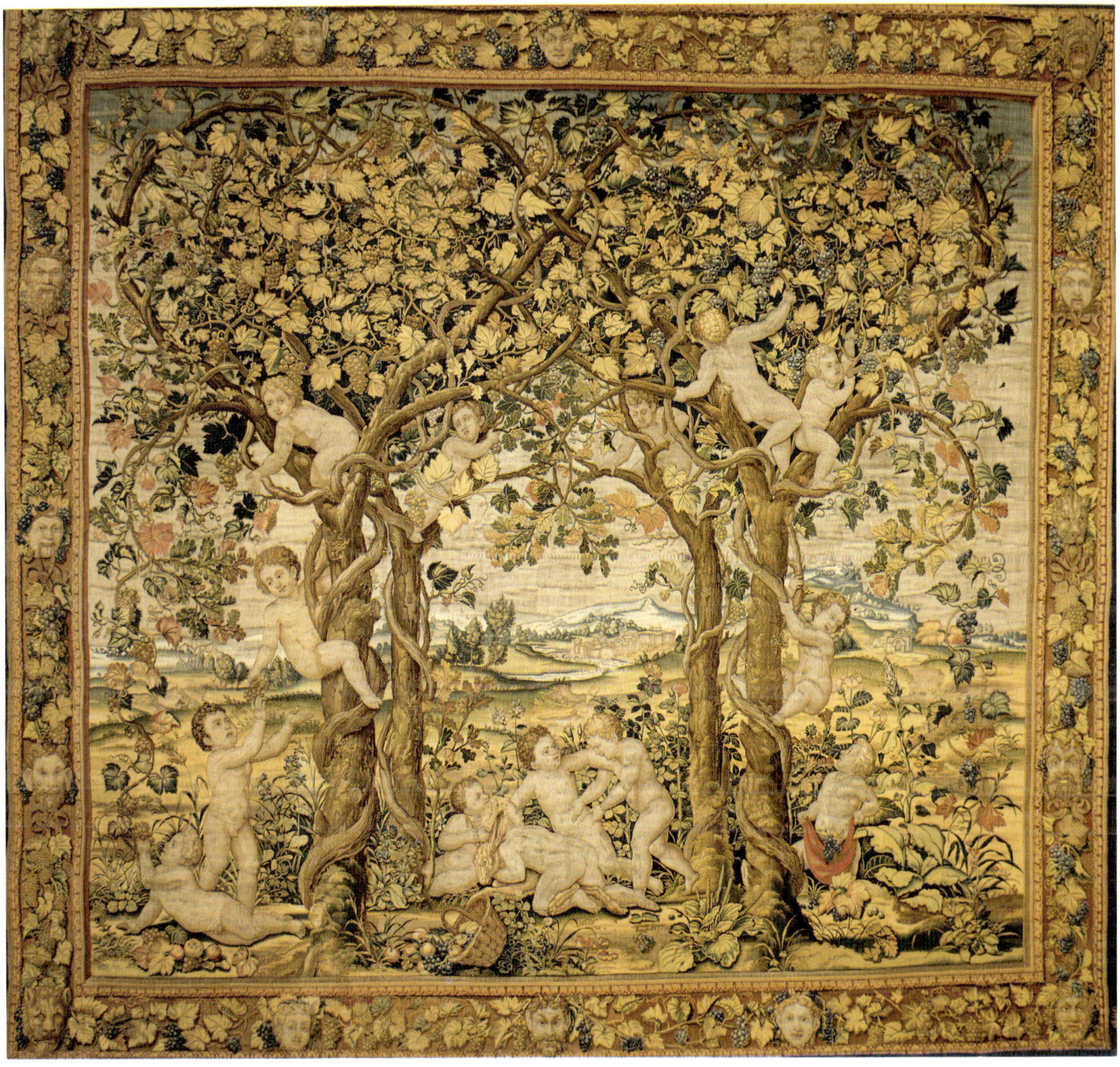

V *Puttini: The Hare,* Brussels, workshop of Willem de Pannemaker, 1552–57 (see Fig. 86).

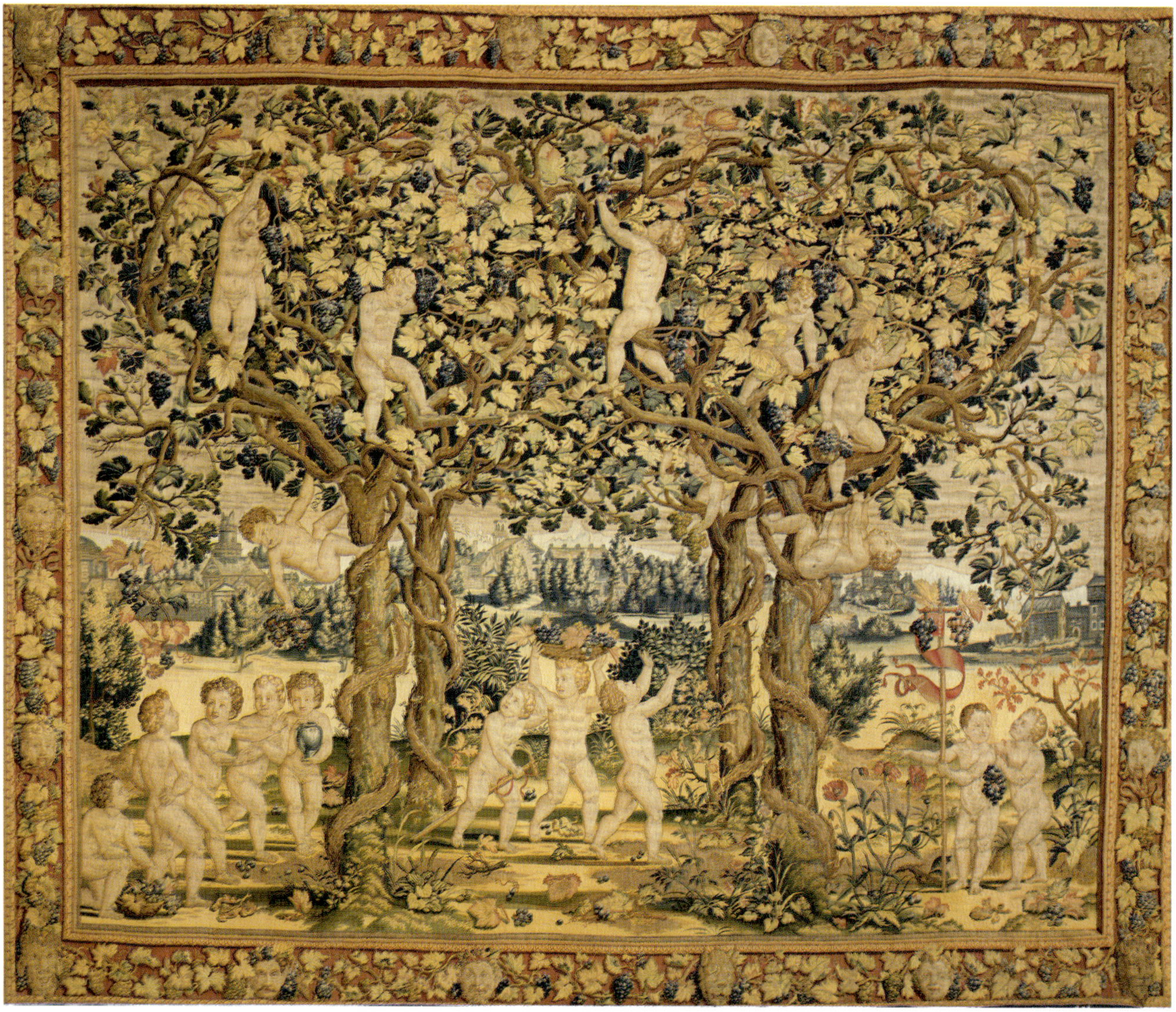

VI *Puttini: The Hobbyhorse,* Brussels, workshop of Willem de Pannemaker, 1552–57 (see Fig. 87).

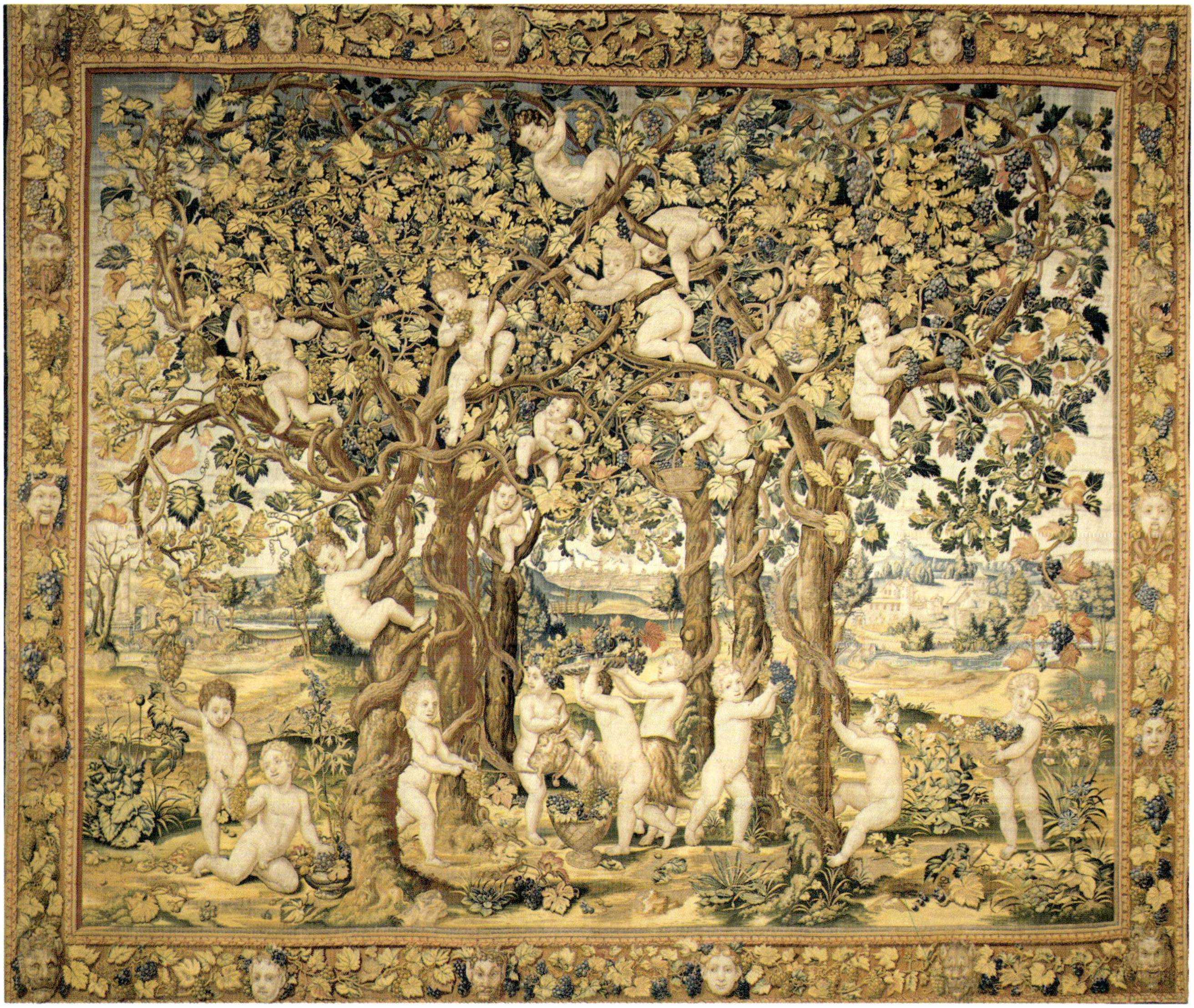

VII *Puttini: The He-Goat,* Brussels, workshop of Willem de Pannemaker, 1552–57 (see Fig. 88).

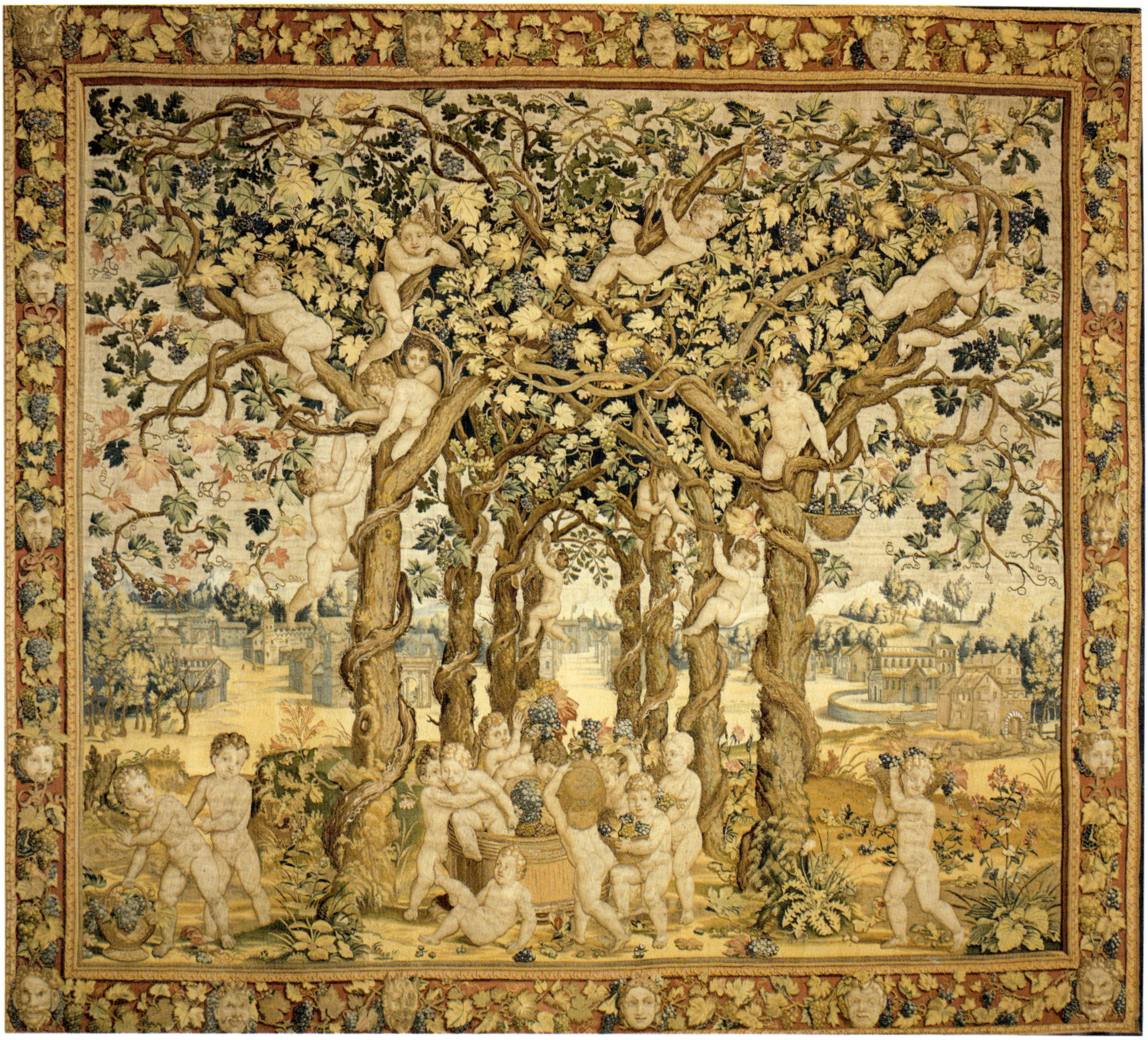

VIII *Puttini: The Winepress,* Brussels, workshop of Willem de Pannemaker, 1552–57 (see Fig. 89).

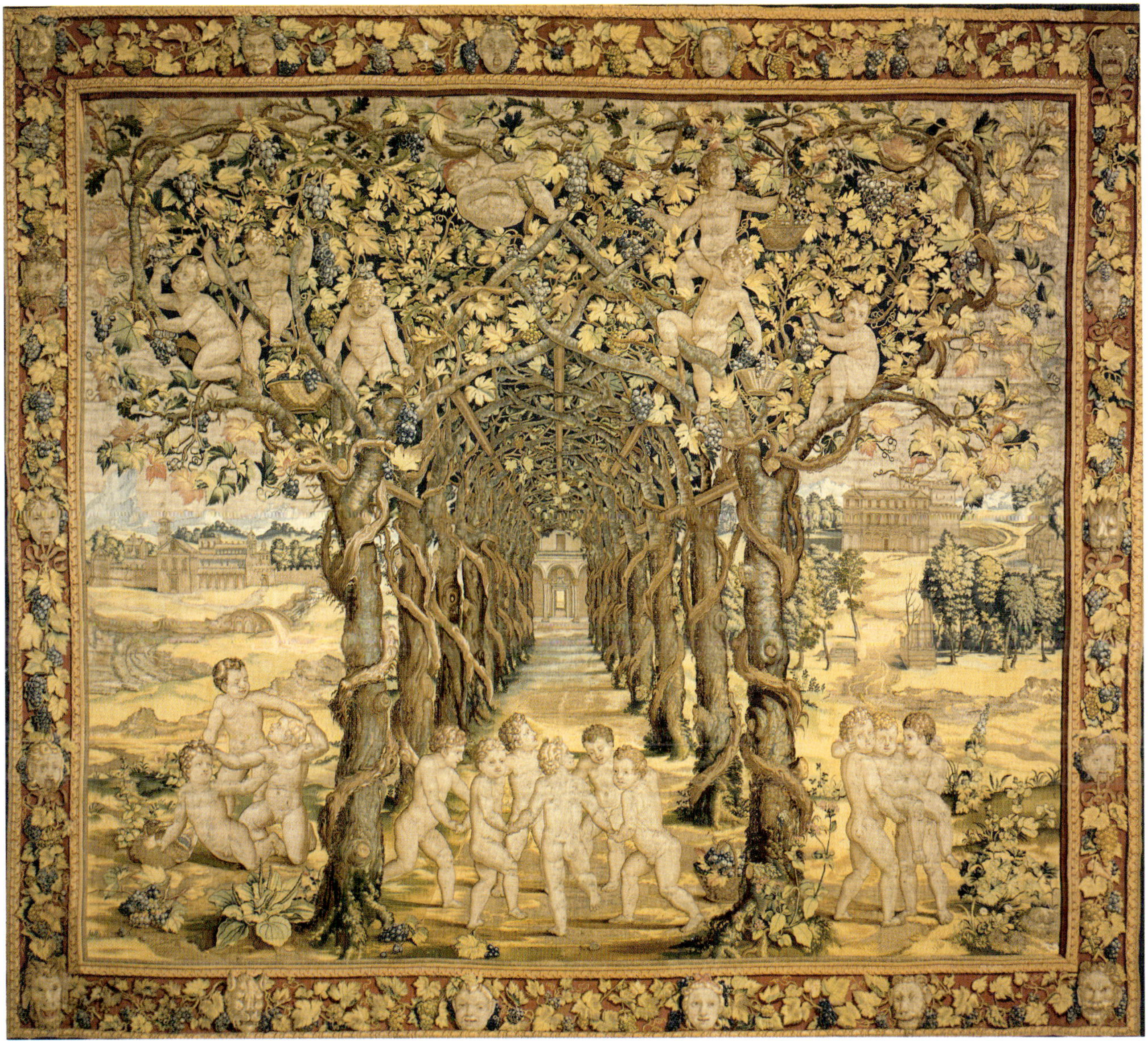

IX *Puttini: The Dance,* Brussels, workshop of Willem de Pannemaker, 1552–57 (see Fig. 90).

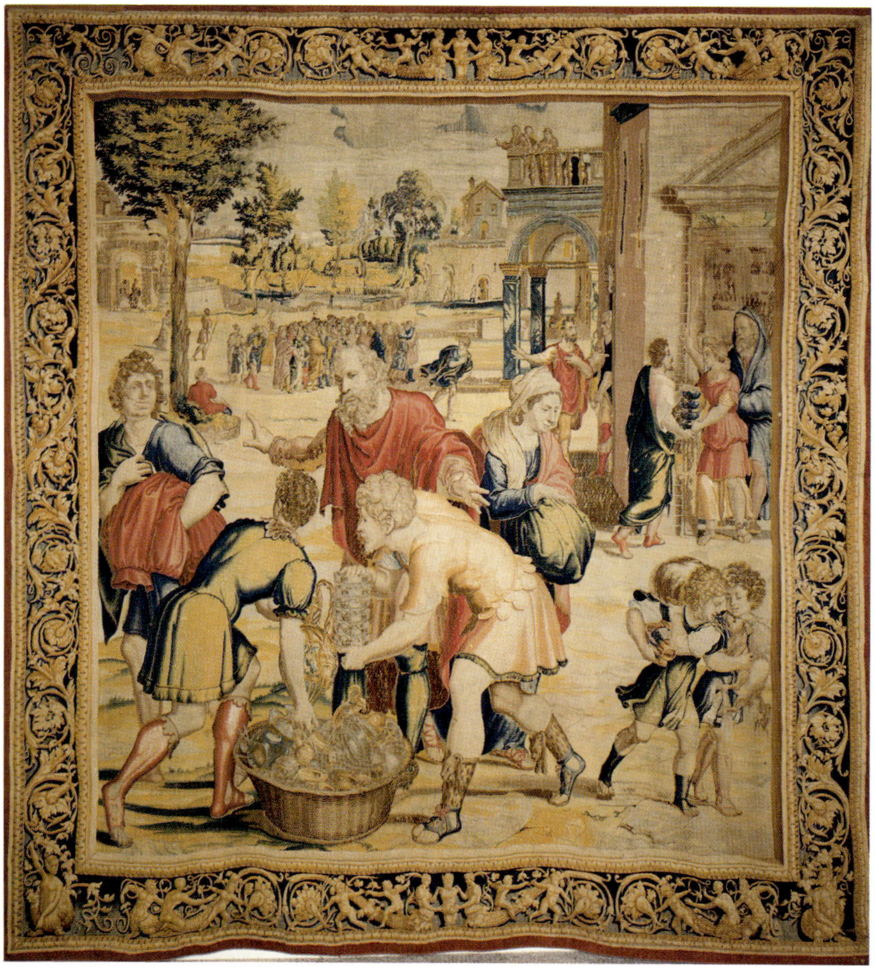

X *Life of Moses: The Israelites Hand Over Their Silver Treasures to Moses,* Brussels, workshop of Willem and Jan Dermoyen(?), 1545–50 (see Fig. 100).

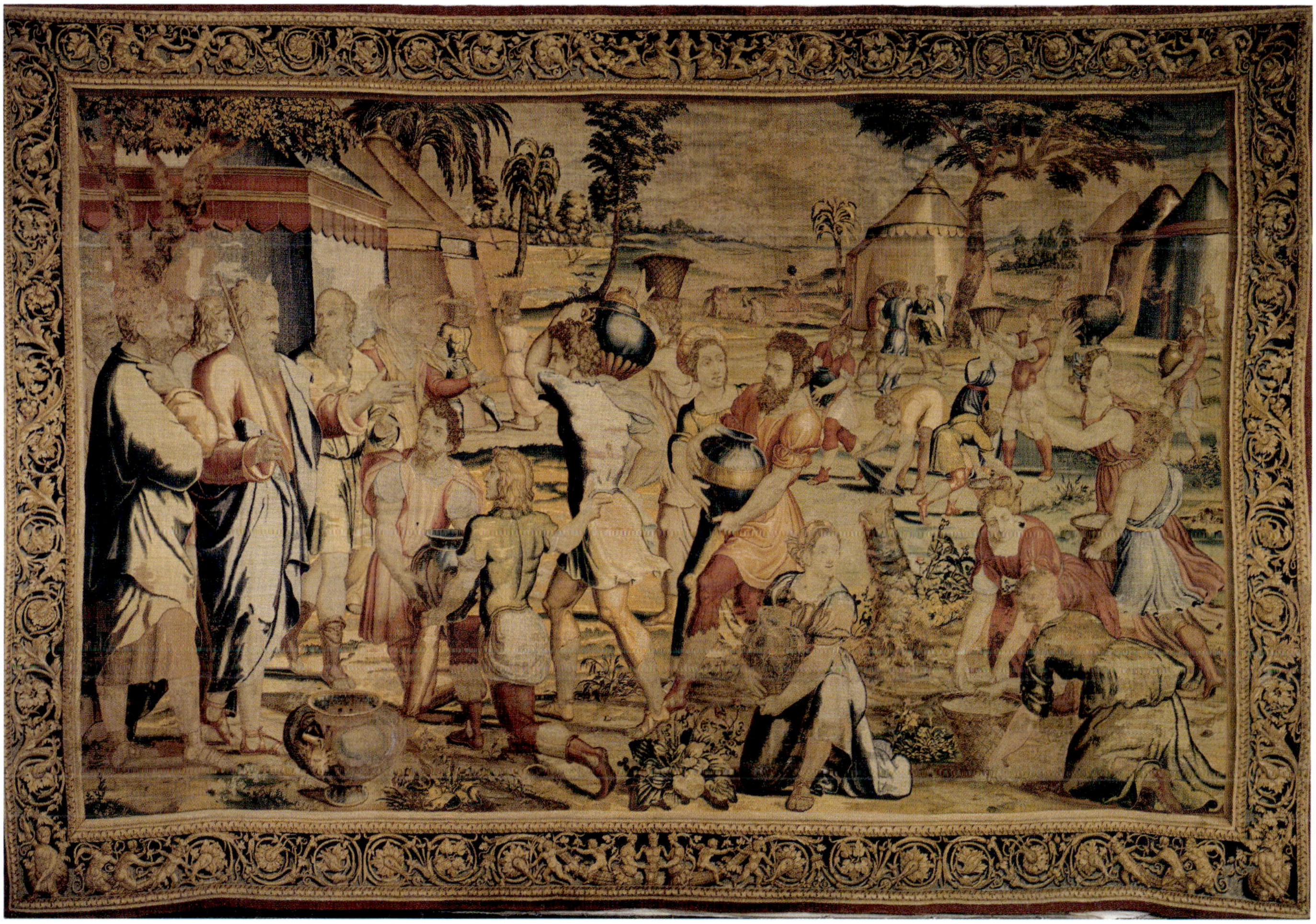

XI *Life of Moses: The Gathering of the Manna,* Brussels, workshop of Willem and Jan Dermoyen(?), 1545–50 (see Fig. 103).

Notes on the Text

Abstract

Abbreviations

b. = busta l. = libro

c. = carte r. = registro

GBM = Guastalla, Biblioteca Maldotti

ASMn = Mantua, Archivio di Stato

AN = Archivio Notarile

RN = Registrazioni Notarili

FP = Fondo Portioli

ASDMn = Mantua, Archivio Storico Diocesano

MV = Mensa Vescovile

ASMo = Modena, Archivio di Stato

MOBE = Modena, Biblioteca Estense

AC = Autografoteca Campori

ASPr = Parma, Archivio di Stato

ES = Epistolario Scelto

RM = Raccolta Manoscritti

Unless otherwise specified, ASMn, ASPr, and GBM always refer to the Gonzaga family files.

Measurements

The Guastalla *braccio* measured 67.10 cm to 68.5 cm and was divided into 12 *once* (Zupko, 1981, 42; Dourstner, 1840, 7). The length of the Guastalla *braccio* is confirmed by comparing the height of the existing tapestry in Brussels of the *Fructus Belli* (479 cm) and of the Marzotto *Puttini* (390 cm) with the dimensions given in the documents. In the Guastalla inventory of 1678 (Document 71), the height of the *Fructus* is given as 7¼ *brazza* and the *Puttini* as 5¾ *brazza*. This gives an average of 67.90 to 68.30 cm.

The Guastalla *braccio* was *smaller* than its Mantuan counterpart. A letter written to Ferrante by Battista da Cantone (Campori, 1866, 25) states: "braza 2. onze 6, a mesure di Guastalla, a mesure di Mantua circa braza 3." This means that 2.5 Guastalla *braccia* are equal to some 3 Mantuan *braccia* or between 55.90 and 56.70 cm. However, Zupko (1981, 44) gives 63.80 cm for the Mantuan *braccio*.

Currency

Guidance on currency is difficult to come by, especially because one must also take into account that a *scudo* is not always a *scudo* but can be a "scuto d'oro in oro." According to Giuseppe Pecorari, references to payment or to values of merchandise in the Mantuan documents that are given in ducats, scudi, lire, and soldi can be converted as follows: 1 ducat = 93 soldi, 1 scudo = 5 or 6 lire, 1 lira = 20 soldi, and 1 soldo = 12 denari.

As was the case with measurements, Mantua and Guastalla assigned a different value to the same denomination. According to the accounting provided in the 1678 inventory of the Guastalla collection (Document 71, no. 2), the *Puttini* was valued at 9,000 Guastalla "ducatoni" or 22,500 Mantuan scudi.

The listing of sums follows the manner in which they are recorded in the documents: thus "libre 9635 - soldi 1 - picoli 3" in Document 15, and "libre 2 - soldi 0 - denari 0" in Document 29. When the second or third denomination is not specifically spelled out, the sums are recorded as follows: lire 741 - 3 (Document 49) or Lire 0 - 15 - 0 (Document 50).

Transcriptions

The texts have been adjusted according to modern practice. This means that all abbreviations have been spelled out and modern punctuation has been added as required. The older habits of placing brackets around noncontroversial missing letters or in employing [*sic*] to highlight legitimate variations in spelling, are both inelegant and unnecessary. The rules governing transcriptions of sixteenth-century documents have been conveniently summarized in *Giulio Romano,* 1992, I, XLIIIff.

Introduction

> [October 1549] We all returned to a group of rooms whose walls were covered with the finest and most beautiful hangings of gold, silver, and multicolored silk threads that depicted—true to life—animals, trees, fruit, and flowers. Only the great Parrhasias and the ingenious Pheidias, the one on canvas and the other in marble, would have been able to rival these depictions of nature. (Document 29)

> On 26 December 1670 the marriage agreement was drawn up in Guastalla between our Duke and the Archduchess, his mother, and by it the Duke of Guastalla set the dowry of the Princess, his daughter, at 200,000 scudi (. . .) in Mantuan currency. It consisted of a great quantity of precious objects, silver, and jewels, as well as the tapestry sets known as the *Fructus Belli,* the *Puttini,* and the *Grotteschi* (. . .).
>
> These deserve to be more precisely described so as to satisfy the curiosity of posterity, which will not be able to see such a collection of unique tapestries of masterly design and embellished with gold and silver. (Federigo Amadei: Document 70)

The quotations above serve to highlight the paramount role played by costly weavings in court ceremonies. The first refers to the rooms assigned to the guests invited to the banquet held by Ercole in the Palazzo Vescovile in Mantua in October 1549 on the occasion of Duke Francesco III's marriage to Catherine of Austria. Across the street, in the Ducal Palace itself (Document 26), the principal rooms were fitted with an impressive array of both fabric and figurative weavings, including an *Aeneas* set on loan from Ercole's brother Ferrante Gonzaga. This was the same Ferrante who earlier that year (Document 24) displayed the *Fructus Belli* (Catalogue 3) in his residence in Milan to honor the emperor Charles V's son, Philip II.

Imitation being the most sincere form of flattery, an original concept by one patron often led to a request for copies. This was as much the case when Cardinal Granvelle borrowed the cartoons for Ferrante Gonzaga's *Puttini* (Document 55 and Catalogue 5) as when Ercole purchased a set of the Sistine Chapel *Acts of the Apostles* (Catalogue 2).

It must have been a remarkable sight indeed to have been in the crowd in the Piazza Sordello in September 1587 when Ercole *Acts* (Fig. 1) was displayed along the facade of the cathedral to serve as a colorful and dramatic backdrop to the procession that accompanied Vincenzo Gonzaga on the occasion of his coronation as the 4th Duke of Mantua (Document 62). The Piazza Sordello served years later, in 1670, when a portion of Anna Isabella Gonzaga's dowry arrived in Mantua on the occasion of her marriage to the 10th and last Duke of Mantua, Ferdinando Carlo (Document 70).

Like the chronicler of that moment, Federigo Amadei, who was concerned with preserving a unique moment for posterity, this book is similarly dedicated to giving further life to an extraordinary group of weavings—weavings that, despite all odds, have survived to the present day and have left remarkable traces among the archival records of the Gonzaga court.

The sets chronicled by Amadei were all woven during the heyday of tapestry production in the 1540s and 1550s. They were commissioned by Ferrante Gonzaga, who was the founder of the Guastalla line of the family. Rather than decreasing in value over time, the *Fructus Belli* (Figs. 44–70) was valued at 75,000 scudi in the 1678 inventory (Document 71). In the same inventory the *Puttini* (Figs. 84–97) was valued at 22,500 scudi, and the *Moses* (Figs. 98–114), "sì per la bontà come per essere paramento raro," at 45,000 scudi. Like the *Fructus* and the *Puttini,* the *Moses* was also the result of Ferrante's patronage, as was the *Grotteschi,* the third tapestry set that came to Mantua with Anna Isabella. Fortunately for posterity, Amadei was overly pessimistic in his appraisal of the situation. Although the *Grotteschi* has indeed disappeared without a trace, the *Puttini* survives intact, as does the *Moses* weaving, while significant portions of the original set, together with several of the original cartoons, and later reeditions of the *Fructus Belli* are still available for study and enjoyment.

Despite their importance, as well as the high value assigned to the acquisition of these tapestries, which occasionally were used as a means of raising funds for the court (Documents 33 and 53), it is to panel painting and frescoes that most scholarly efforts have been directed. Fortunately, in recent years, significant steps have been taken to redress this traditional imbalance, as can be seen by the growing number of publications devoted either to cataloging the holdings of specific museums or to individual sets or certain themes. This book should serve to encourage further a new look at the problem of visual imagery in the life of the Renaissance court.

> Regarding the "spaliere" for the "sala nuova," His Excellency says that he does not own any of a suitable length, i.e. 174 "ale," but that as regards the correct height there are only those of the "historia d'Enea," which were acquired specifically to serve for the arrival [in Milan] of Prince Philip II. (Document 26)

Rather than being all-inclusive, this study focuses on one specific generation of Gonzaga collectors: the children of Francesco II Gonzaga (d. 1519) and Isabella d'Este (d. 1539) (Figs. 9–14). Their son and heir was Federico II Gonzaga, the noted patron of Giulio Romano, who gave Mantua two highly influential creations: the Palazzo Te and the Appartamento di Troia in the Ducal Palace in Mantua. His birth in 1500 was followed in 1505 by that of Ercole, who was destined to be the third Gonzaga cardinal and to serve his family as regent of the state after the deaths of his brother and nephew. With the birth of Ferrante in 1507, the Gonzaga family eventually would have a major player on the international stage. In the name of Charles V, he served both on the battlefield as vice-regent of Sicily and as governor of Milan.

The presence of the Gonzaga arms establishes the provenance of the *Acts of the Apostles* (Catalogue 2), the *Fructus Belli* (Catalogue 3), the *Puttini* (Catalogue 4), and the *Moses* (Catalogue 7). The links between these sets and the Gonzaga brothers are further reinforced by the archival records. As for the remaining sets, their provenance can be established, but by less direct means. The pedigree of the Ferrante *Puttini* (Catalogue 5) can be proven with certainty from the archival evidence, which establishes that the Granvelle set, now in Madrid, was copied from these weavings. The links between Ferrante and the Châteaudun *Moses* (Catalogue 6) are less obvious. Yet the dimensions of the Châteaudun series, as well as the number of panels in the set, link it to the surviving archival records. Furthermore, the two panels that were added to what was traditionally a ten-piece set contain strong links to the style and iconography of the Ferrante *Fructus Belli*. The connection between the Vatican *Cephalus and Procris* (Catalogue 1) and the Gonzaga family is perhaps the most tenuous of all. Given the rarity of the subject and the hints contained in the archival records, it is not unreasonable to suggest a connection. As the possibility is at best remote that the surviving *Aeneas* pieces in Vienna, Milan, and Palermo can be related to Ferrante, they are not given a separate catalogue entry here. Rather, the problem is explored in the appropriate place in the Index to the Major Sets of Figurative Tapestries.

The tapestries that the Gonzaga brothers commissioned or purchased are discussed in the seven catalogue essays in Part II. Other members of the Mantua and Guastalla branches of the family are included in Part I only to the extent that the archival records include tapestries inherited from Federico II (d. 1540), Ercole (d. 1563), and Ferrante (d. 1557). Thus, for example, Document 60 chronicles the wall hangings displayed in the Ducal Palace in Mantua on the occasion of Vincenzo Gonzaga's marriage to Eleonora de' Medici. Four of the sets—the *Puttini, Tobias, Saul,* and *Fortuna*—came to Vincenzo through his father, Guglielmo (d. 1578), who inherited them either directly from the Ercole estate (Documents 48 and 49) or indirectly from that estate through his brother Cardinal Federico (Document 51).

The transcriptions in Document 60 serve a variety of purposes, including providing information about the way tapestries were used in specific rooms on special festive occasions. Document 60 can be studied from this point of view, and also concerning sets that have a different provenance, but its inclusion here was determined solely by its relationship to the generation of Gonzagas who were active during the first half of the sixteenth century. Similarly, what is important in Document 65 are the references to the *Cephalus and Procris, Moses, Fructus Belli, Puttini,* and *Aeneas* sets, all of which were acquired by Ferrante for the Guastalla line of the family.

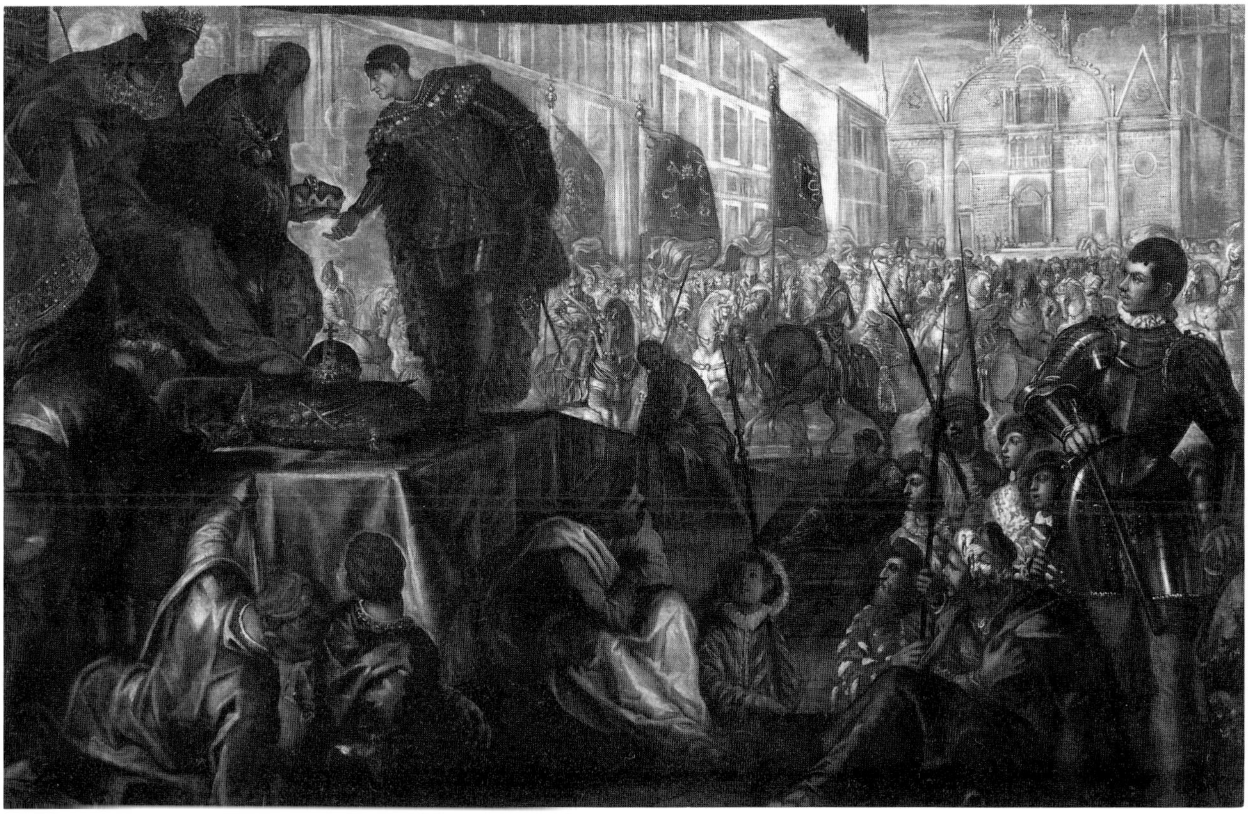

Fig. 1 Jacopo Tintoretto, *The Investiture of Giovanni Francesco Gonzaga as the 1st Marquis of Mantua* (1433), 1579–80. Munich, Alte Pinakothek. In 1587 (Document 62) the facade of the Cathedral (upper right) was covered with the *Acts of the Apostles.*

The archival evidence for the tapestries owned by Federico II, Ercole, and Ferrante is presented chronologically in Part I. The documents are introduced in the Index to the Major Sets of Figurative Tapestries, which has been designed to offer easy access to information regarding specific sets mentioned in the archival records. The extant Gonzaga tapestries themselves are discussed individually in the Catalogue in Part II.

This book appears more than a century after the publication of Willelmo Braghirolli's *Sulle Manifattura di Arazzi in Mantova* (1879). This sequel to Braghirolli's magisterial study on the Mantuan archival sources for Gonzaga wall hangings updates his pioneering research, but primarily only for the first half of the sixteenth century. Given the wealth of documentation for the generation of Federico II, Ercole, and Ferrante, it is surprising to discover how little exists for their successors and how meager the information is for the earlier and later generations of the family.

Although the archival records indicate that tapestries figured prominently in the lives of Federico II, Ercole, and Ferrante's forebears and heirs, few of the weavings owned by that generation have survived to the present day. An *Annunciation* in the Art Institute of Chicago bears the arms of Francesco II Gonzaga (Fig. 2);[1] *verdure* tapestries in the Palazzo Vescovile in Mantua (Fig. 3) may relate to a commission from Isabella d'Este in 1496,[2] while *The Lives of Christ and the Mantuan Saints* was donated to the Duomo in Mantua (Fig. 4) in 1599 by Bishop Francesco Gonzaga.[3] The only other extant family tapestry not accounted for in Part II is the *Allegory of Fortitude* (Fig. 5), an otherwise undocumented dorsal tapestry dated 1528 and containing an inscription that suggests that it was made for Ercole.[4]

Braghirolli provides a particularly useful guide to the records for the fifteenth century. These records are richest, however, for the hangings owned by Cardinal Francesco (d. 1483), which did not become the property

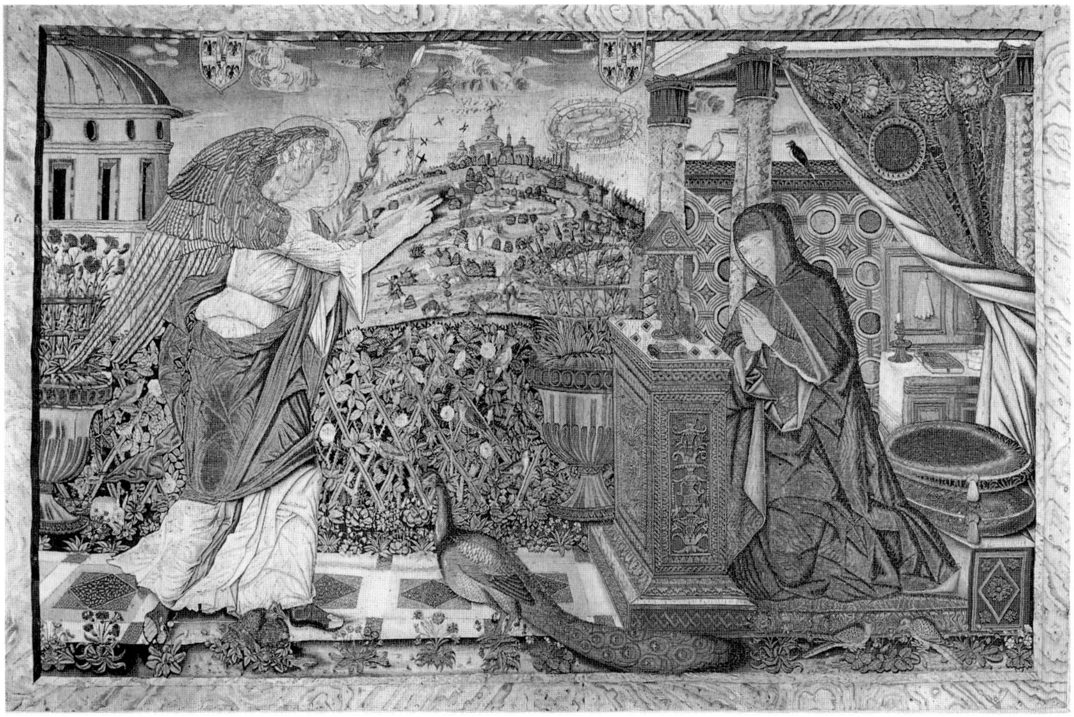

Fig. 2 *Annunciation,* North Italian, c. 1484–1519. Chicago, The Art Institute, Bequest of Mr. and Mrs. Martin A. Ryerson.

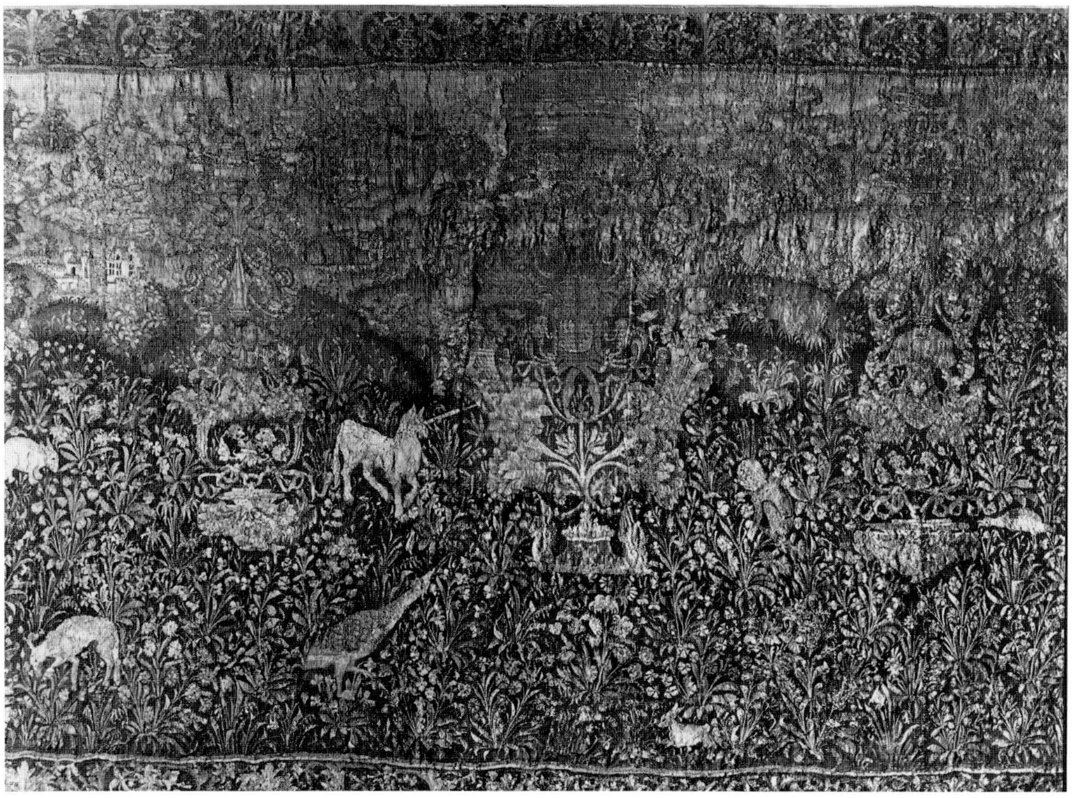

Fig. 3 *Verdure with Animals,* Bruges(?), c. 1496. Mantua, Palazzo Vescovile.

of the heirs of Ludovico II Gonzaga.[5] That Ludovico II (d. 1478), patron of Leon Battista Alberti and Andrea Mantegna, should also have had some interest in the production of figurative tapestries comes as no surprise. It is puzzling, however, that all that remains to document this interest are several enigmatic references to the purchases of silk in 1465 for the tapestry Maestro Maffei was commissioned to execute using designs prepared by Mantegna. In 1469 Mantegna was asked to "ritrarre due galline de India (. . .) perché le voressimo far mettere suxo la tapezaria nostra."[6] Both references may relate to the celebrated Gonzaga "spalliere," which, as late as 1493, was as much a "tourist attraction" as the Camera degli Sposi itself.[7] This in turn may have some connection to the "razzi del Marchese di Mantova del disegno del Mantegna," judged by Marc Antonio Michiel in 1519 to be equal in merit to the "razzi di Alfonso, overo Federico re di Napoli" and the Sistine Chapel tapestries designed by Raphael.[8]

In 1488 Ludovico II's grandson, Francesco II, loaned to Duke Ercole d'Este of Ferrara "coltrine sei grandi da muro cum la historia de Hanibale et Scipione" and "coltrine quattro grandi da muro cum la historia de Lucretia."[9] That they were inherited from the estate of Ludovico II is proven by a document dated 7 February 1469.[10] Beyond this, little is known of the contents of Ludovico II Gonzaga's *guardaroba* or of the additions made to it by his successor, Federico I (d. 1484), or by Francesco II (d. 1519), who purchased a weaving of the *istoria di Rodi* in 1491 and who, according to records of 1516–17, owned "tre coltrine da mur[o] a figuri a istoria de Tirro [Pirro?]," as well as the *Herkenbald* weavings and

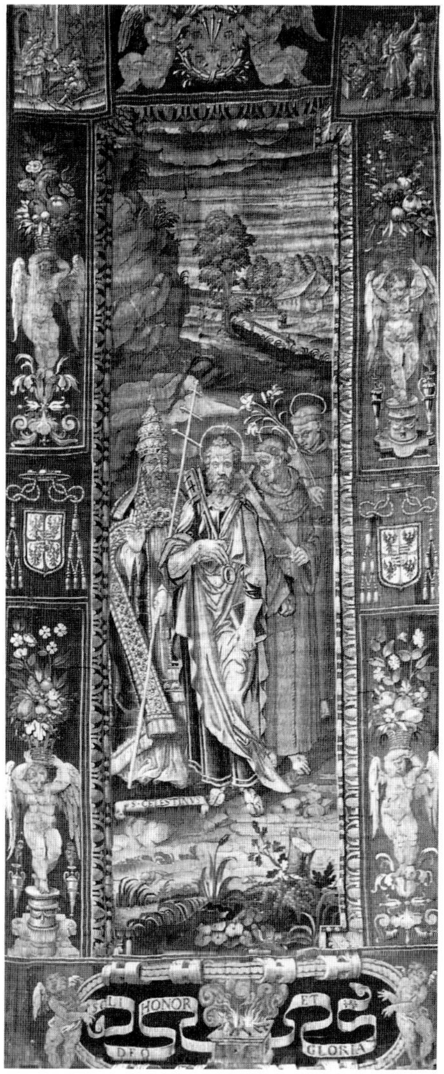

Fig. 4 *Saints Celestinus, Peter, Francis of Assisi, and Antony of Padua,* Bruges(?), c. 1599. Mantua, Palazzo Vescovile.

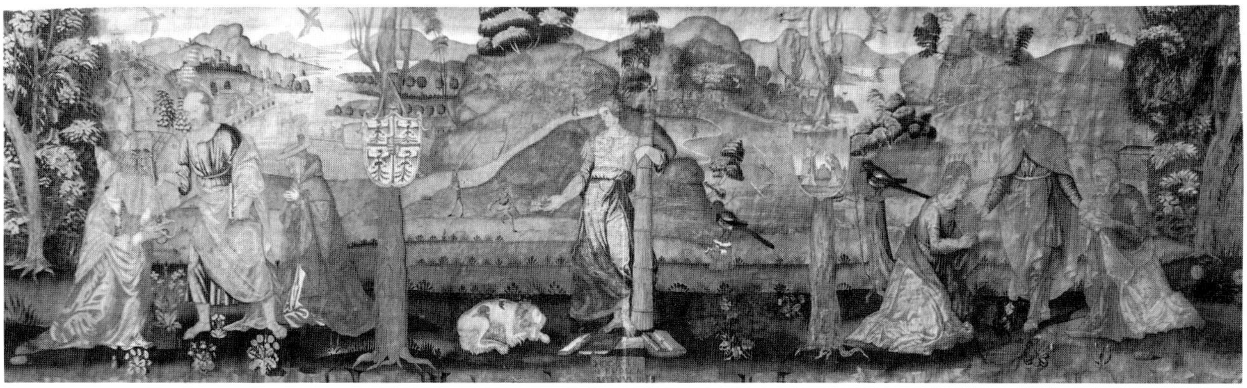

Fig. 5 *Allegory with Fortitude and Saint Peter,* dorsal tapestry, North Italian, 1528. Private collection.

a "spallira a figuri."[11] In the absence of other records, it is not even certain whether all or most of these sets were inherited from his predecessors. As for his wife, Isabella d'Este, who was greeted upon her arrival in Mantua by the celebrated Montefeltro *Troy* tapestries,[12] the principal evidence of her interest in figurative weavings—in this instance a *verdure* tapestry—comes from the order she placed in 1496 for a "raso (. . .) a verdura," which, as noted earlier, may be related to the *verdure* weavings preserved in the Palazzo Vescovile.

As for the generations that followed Federico II, Ercole, and Ferrante, the reigns of Guglielmo (d. 1587) through Ferdinando Carlo (d. 1709), the archival evidence is indeed slender, and few references to such commissions or acquisitions are found in the court correspondence. Those that have surfaced thus far are catalogued primarily in the addenda of Document 66.[13] In addition, of course there was the Guastalla *Trionfo della Fede* series, which, having been based on designs by Rubens, could not have been commissioned until sometime after 1628.

Leaving aside matters that pertain to the quattrocento or to the end of the cinquecento and the opening years of the seventeenth century, let us turn to the man who was born at the beginning of the cinquecento, and was active until just before or just after the midpoint of the century. Federico II is best remembered for his patronage of Giulio Romano and he was also responsible for bringing Nicolas Karcher to Mantua (Document 9). Upon Federico II's death in 1540, the role of regent of the state was assumed by Ercole, who was quick to continue the patronage of Karcher. In addition to a costly "quadro de tappezaria dell'istoria de Moisè" (Document 12), which has not survived, and the *Puttini,* sections of which are in Lisbon and Milan (Catalogue 4), Karcher was also responsible for the *Moses,* now in the Museo del Duomo in Milan (Catalogue 7), which may be related to the commission mentioned in Document 30. It was in Flanders, however, that Ercole acquired a sizable number of weavings of Old Testament subjects (Document 15) as well as the *Acts of the Apostles* (Color Plate I and Figs. 28–43: Catalogue 2), which is displayed in the Ducal Palace in Mantua. Ercole originally intended the *Acts* as a gift to the Duomo (Document 37), but it was eventually bequeathed to the palatine church of Santa Barbara (Document 48).

As for Ferrante, the youngest son, whose collection of tapestries was monumental, much of his life was spent in the employ of Charles V. Sharing similar roots, it is not surprising that the Gonzaga brothers shared a passion common to the age: the acquisition of leather, fabric, and figurative hangings to serve as both ordinary and extraordinary decorations for their residences. Curiously, the records for Federico II's interest in figurative weaving are ungenerous, and, with the exception of the "spalera a figuri de Filomena" and the "dece pecii de tapezaria a figuri de Tiberio e Alexandro Magno" (Documents 9 and 66, no. 27), little reference is made to them in subsequent records, perhaps largely because the major holdings were of *verdure* tapestries, which are notoriously difficult to trace from one archival record to the next. While little is known about the sets recorded in the 1541 inventory (Document 9), one poorly preserved panel, the Zeri *Puttini,* has recently been linked to Federico II's patronage (Catalogue 4). Presumably the Zeri panel and the related, and now lost, pieces were created by Karcher in the brief period between his arrival in the city (1539) and the duke's death in 1540. The work accomplished during this time apparently was extensive: the records refer to the delivery to the palace of "pezi 13" shortly after Federico II's death. Although much of Federico II's collection consisted of fabric rather than figurative weaving, it should be remembered that he was said to have had such extensive holdings that he was able to cover the Castello with tapestries from top to bottom to honor Charles V in 1530, and that among the treasures was a set of "oro, argiento et seda estimata più di diceotto milia ducati."

While Federico II's collection survives in one poorly preserved piece, and in an inventory of limited usefulness (although it documents a total of nearly three hundred individual woven panels), Ercole's interests are attested to by a wide range of archival records, including an especially informative and comprehensive inventory, which catalogues 140 individual panels (Document 49), and through the survival of portions of the *Puttini* set as well as the *Acts of the Apostles* (Catalogue 2 and 4). Although not as extensive as the records for Ercole's collection, a significant amount of primary source material exists for the collection formed by Ferrante and of which there survives not only the Marzotto *Puttini* (Catalogue 5) and original fragments and copies of the *Fructus Belli*

(Catalogue 3), together with three of the original cartoons, but also the Châteaudun *Moses* cycle (Catalogue 6). Lacking a comprehensive inventory of the contents of his *guardaroba,* the 1537 inventory is too early to be significant in making a final calculation (Document 4). Thus no numerical figure can be placed on his holdings, which, however, consisted of several remarkable sets.

The archival evidence for the Gonzaga brothers' collections of tapestries has been grouped into seventy-eight entries. By adding a significant amount of unpublished material to the late nineteenth- and early twentieth-century transcriptions of Braghirolli, Bertolotti, and Luzio, it is possible to present a remarkably detailed picture of the Gonzaga collections of figurative tapestries of the sixteenth century. At the same time, this study takes advantage of recent discoveries by other scholars regarding the *terminus ante quem* for Ercole's acquisition of the *Acts of the Apostles* (Document 37), as well as previously overlooked records of payments to Karcher and to agents who made purchases for him in both 1541–42 and 1549–50 (Documents 12, 13, and 28).

Mindful of the use that will be made of such a source book, and of the occasional ambiguities in archival texts, we have taken care to ensure the accuracy of the transcriptions, although in accordance with modern rules. Interpretative comments have been excluded from Part I because scholars may disagree over the precise importance of various texts. Until the discovery of a reference to the *Atti* in 1557 (Document 37), scholars generally assumed that the coat of arms made by Filippo Orsini in 1559 (Document 40) referred to the inception of that project. The expenditure of more than 8,300 lire in 1549 (Document 28) could relate to the acquisition of the Mantuan *Acts* and thus to Ercole's plans for decorations for the restored Duomo. Given the vagueness of the references, different scholars may put different interpretations on the available evidence, interpretations that in turn may have to be modified on the basis of archival discoveries that will postdate this study. The reader will search in vain for any reference in Document 28 to a possible link to the Mantuan *Acts,* for insofar as possible it is preferable not to interweave speculation with a factual accounting of what the primary sources actually say. Chance conspires with skill in coordinating published and unpublished references, and there is a certain unintended element of interpretation in the mere selection of texts, and the decision as to what and how much of each document to transcribe, without loading the entries with further imponderables.

The Chronology and the Catalogue contain the necessary interpretative information regarding how the texts are to be understood in respect to existing tapestries. There the reader will learn that, in all probability, Giovanni Battista Lodi's letter of 5 February 1552 (Document 32) refers to the commissioning of Ferrante's *Puttini,* which is to be identified with the set now in the Marzotto collection in Trissino, and that the Milan *Moses* in the Museo del Duomo might well be related to the commission that Ercole awarded to Karcher in 1551 (Document 30). Others may view the archival evidence in a different light, for Karcher is also documented as having done a *Moses* weaving in 1542 for Ercole (Document 12), and indeed in 1549 he was paid for the creation of "una carpetta" (Document 27). Thus it is best to separate fact from speculation. For this reason no reference to the Marzotto *Puttini* or to the Milan *Moses* is found in Documents 30 and 32. These entries bear innocuous but factually correct titles.

In several instances—regarding Ferrante's *Puttini,* for example—the results of the archival research presented here are indeed impressive, consisting of correspondence with the patron on the inception of the commission (Document 32) and then moving into the records of his son and heir, Cesare, who, although reluctant to loan such an important set even to so good a friend as Cardinal Simonetta (Document 44), was nonetheless willing to surrender them as collateral against the eventual repayment of a sizable loan (Document 53). From here the documentation passes to the reign of Cesare's son and heir, Ferrante II, who having at first thought to cut his losses, thereby encouraging Duke Guglielmo Gonzaga and the Grand Duke of Tuscany to seek to acquire them (Document 58), eventually changed his mind.

Guglielmo's interest in the Ferrante *Puttini* relates, interestingly enough, to the fact that he had inherited Ercole's version and hoped to use both to create an iconographically interesting suite of decorations in his new rooms in the Corte Vecchia of the Ducal Palace. Loaning the tapestries for his wedding in 1587 (Document 61), Ferrante II subsequently reacquired them since they are included in the 1590 inventory (Document 65). Part of the marriage dowry brought to Mantua by Anna Isabella (Document 69), the *Puttini* subsequently appears in various Gonzaga of Mantua inventories, including the final accounting of 1709 (Document 75). Purchased from the estate of Ferdinando Carlo by the Sagredo family of Venice, it is listed in several of their accountings (Document 77). Although the path from the Sagredo to the Barberigo to the Mocenigo to Donà dalle Rose to the present owner is less well documented, it is fair to say that archival evidence for this set takes us from the moment of its conception to the present day and through a range of different types of archival evidence, from letters and banking records to inventories.

The letters not only serve as a reminder of the role that tapestries woven with threads of silver and gold played in times of financial need, but also of the reason why patrons were reluctant to use too much silver ("perchè in breve divien negro" [Document 32]), as well as circumstances and occasions such as family weddings when the most precious weavings were displayed in the principal ceremonial rooms. The inventories serve not only to provide basic information on the number of pieces in a given set, but they permit one to document the movement of the set within the family and beyond when its use as a dowry meant the removal of the set from its original location.

Although the connection with the Ferrante *Puttini* was not originally made, the text of Lodi's letter of 1552 was actually published in 1924, while Braghirolli was responsible for introducing the 1678 inventory and Luzio for calling attention to the inventory of 1709. By integrating what was previously known with information this is now available, we can learn a great deal about the history of the *Puttini*.

While the present study may legitimately take credit for putting together previously published but unconnected references and in linking them with various unknown texts, it would be exceedingly ungenerous and ungracious not to acknowledge the role played by earlier scholars in pointing the way. Indeed, this indebtedness is not limited simply to leads suggested by published references but also, in the case of Mantuan archival material, to Stefano Davari, whose private notes (ASMn, Schede Davari), which contain a folder regarding tapestries, have been profitably mined by generations of scholars. A major boost to work on Ercole's collection was provided first by archival references in the essay on the *Acts of the Apostles* (*Rome 1984*, 144–45) and then by the detailed research undertaken by Giuseppe Pecorari (1991, 417ff.). Thus the present compilation is as much a tribute to the past as it is a framework for future research.

In assembling the archival transcriptions, our principal aim has been to document the major sets of figurative wall hangings owned by Ercole and Ferrante, and this largely because information on Federico II's holdings is so meager. It is not possible also to provide entries for the numerous references to fabric and leather hangings that survive, especially in Ercole's *carteggio*.[14] Yet if one can picture Cardinal Ercole's residence in the Palazzo Vescovile in Mantua with the installation for the *Puttini* and the *Fortuna* sets, it should also be remembered that walls in other rooms were decorated as well with rare fabrics and tooled leather (Document 49).

Despite the range of archival citations, readers would be misled if they were to assume that all of the Gonzaga sets are as amply documented as the Ferrante *Puttini*. Indeed, far less is known about the other sets associated or associable with Ferrante's patronage. Nonetheless, the crown jewel of the collection, the *Fructus Belli*, can be traced from 1547, when Jehan Baudouyn wrote about the work in progress (Document 19), to its display on the occasion of the visit to Milan of Philip II in 1549 (Document 24). Like the *Puttini*, the *Fructus Belli* was included in the Venetian banking records from 1567 onward, during which time it was used as a pledge against the repayment of a loan to Ferrante's son and heir, Cesare (Document 53). Until 1709, when it was listed in the inventory compiled by the Quarantia Criminale (Document 74), the records for the *Fructus* are identical to those of the *Puttini*. In both cases there is a lacuna in the records between the inventories of 1590 and 1678.

Two other sets, less amply documented but probably related to Ferrante, the *Boschellii* and the *Cephalus and Procris*, are actually not referred to until the 1567 Venetian banking records (Document 53), and then they resurface in the 1590 (Document 65) and 1678 (Document 71) inventories. Like the *Boschellii* (which may be identical to the *Grotteschi,* named as the third set brought to Mantua by Anna Isabella), they remain enigmatic because the precise nature of their subject matter and the circumstances of their acquisition are unknown.

The 1590 inventory of the Gonzaga of Guastalla (Document 65) also records a fourteen-piece *Aeneas* set. Thanks to a passing reference in Ferrante's correspondence of 1549 (Document 26) concerning tapestries he could loan to the Gonzaga court for the wedding of Francesco III, it is possible to connect these tapestries to him and also to learn that they were purchased (rather than commissioned) specifically to decorate the palace for the visit of Philip II (Document 24). Accordingly, something can be learned about sets ordered on the open market as well as those created for a specific patron. Correspondence with Cardinal Granvelle in 1571 (Document 55) concerning the possibility of loaning the cartoons for Ferrante's *Puttini* sheds valuable light on the prerogatives of patrons who retained the cartoons to protect their "copyright." The Viron-Granvelle correspondence is also important because it documents another set, the still-enigmatic "bois de Soignes ou il y a dedans des personnaiges de Poesies comme Orpheus et deesses."

Except for letters from Baudouyn and Lodi and the reference to the purchase of the *Aeneas,* little can be learned from Ferrante's records of the circumstances surrounding the commissioning or the acquisition of individual items. As the financial registers do not survive or survive only in a highly fragmentary form, information regarding prices is also scarce. Indeed, what is known of Ferrante's collection derives primarily but not exclusively from the banking records and the inventories of the later members of the Guastalla family, and then from the Gonzaga of Mantua records regarding those items traceable to Ferrante that became the property of Ferdinando Carlo.

A passing reference in the file of 1549 (Document 26) refers to the quantities of silk, fabric, and leather hangings in Ferrante's collection, hangings he was reluctant to part with because he had acquired them in preparation for an anticipated visit to Milan by Charles V. Although a single document, dating to 1547 (Document 18), deals with the creation of cartoons for "spaliere" for Ferrante's suburban Milanese villa, little is actually known about his various residences in South Italy, in Milan, or in Mantua, and thus little can be said of how his collection was displayed for ordinary use or on special occasions. As shall be seen shortly, this is the same problem one encounters, with several notable exceptions (Documents 14, 20, and 22), when trying to interprete the even more ample documentation for Ercole's collection. It is in fact only on those occasions, in 1580 (Document 59) and 1584 (Document 60), when the Duke of Mantua used pieces inherited either directly from Ercole or indirectly through his brother Cardinal Federico, that enough documentation exists about how figurative weavings were used. Weddings were certainly occasions for bringing out the family's precious tapestries, and Ercole himself is known to have decorated rooms in the Palazzo Vescovile for a banquet he hosted in 1549 (Document 29), as did Ferrante II many years later (Document 61).

Inventories rather than correspondence files are the principal means by which information about Ferrante's holdings has been preserved, and inventories are equally important in documenting Cardinal Ercole's possessions, many of which were intended for display in his rooms in the Palazzo Vescovile (Fig. 6). In fact, it is rather remarkable to be able to locate year to year and owner to owner pieces traceable to Ferrante and Ercole. Ferrante's tapestries are traceable largely in the inventories of the Gonzaga of Guastalla, at least until 1670, when a portion of the collection was ceded to the Gonzaga of Mantua (Documents 69 and 71). Since Ercole divided his collection between his Guastalla and Mantua nephews (Documents 48–49, 51–52), the records of both branches need to be consulted from the very beginning in order to trace the provenance of his holdings. This raises the question of whether the transcriptions of the later Guastalla and Mantua inventories should be limited solely to references to Ferrante and Ercole's possessions or if every mention of tapestries should be included. It would have been a fairly simple matter to have presented heavily edited transcriptions of these texts. To have done so, however, would have been inelegant, and at the same time this procedure would have diminished the usefulness of these transcriptions for scholars working on other aspects of the Gonzaga family tapestries. Reproduced as an integrated whole, the records of the wall decorations placed in various rooms on the occasion of the arrival in Mantua of Eleonora de' Medici in 1584 (Fig. 7) provide a unique insight into how tapestries were used in the

Ducal Palace on special occasions (Document 60). The fact that many of the tapestry sets came from Ercole's collection of course explains why this text can be included in the catalogue, for, without a link to that collection or to Ferrante's or even Federico's, there would be no justification for including it here. And so, by accident rather than by design, this study also chronicles the sum total of the holdings of figurative weavings of the Gonzaga of Guastalla and of Mantua of the latter sixteenth as well as of the seventeenth century.

More is known about Ercole's sets of tapestries than of Ferrante's because his correspondence provides a great deal of information on the circumstances surrounding their acquisition on the open market and thus something of the criteria employed in accepting or rejecting them. For example, writing to an agent in 1561 (Document 42), Ercole cautioned his agent Cavriana to exercise care in ensuring that the tapestries he purchased were not "quelle ordinarie che hanno visi bruttisimi et il resto assai goffo." Had he been disappointed in the purchases made earlier by Bassano Cortese (Documents 13, 15, and 28)? Was this the reason, "altre volte rimaso ingannato," he was reluctant to acquire the *historia d'Anniballe* in 1561 without first seeing a sample of the workmanship (Document 43)? This being impossible, Ercole let Cardinal Granvelle serve as his surrogate, which was a wise decision, for on a subsequent occasion Granvelle spoke critically of the weaver's skills: "La megliore ch'io veddi fu de la historia d'Alessandro Magno, e pur non mi contenta troppo (. . .) che'l borde non sia bello, et la campagna, ma non mi danno satisfactione li personaggi. Qui si lavora molto meglio di paessaggi (. . .) dove non

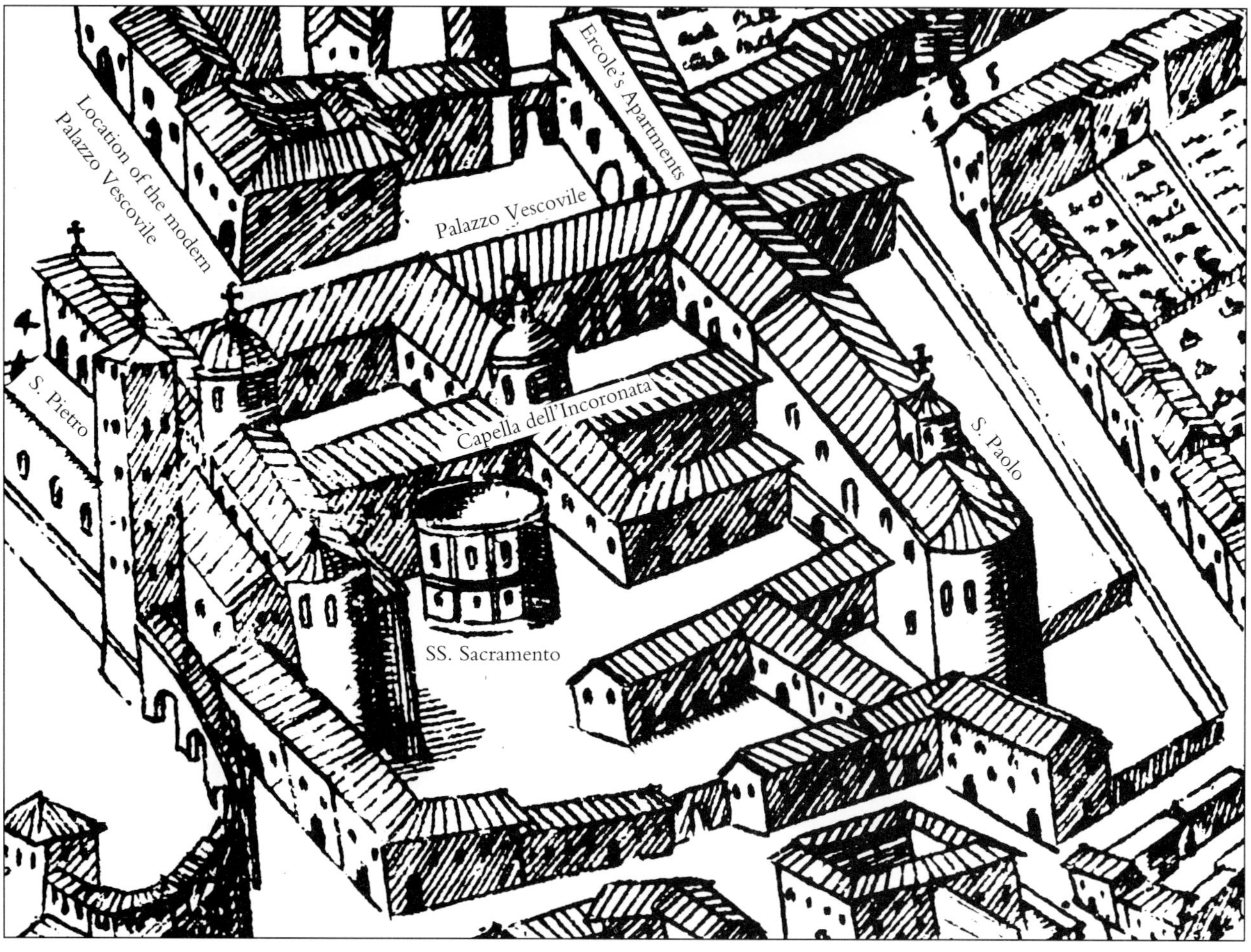

Fig. 6 Gabriele Bertazzolo, *Plan of Mantua*, 1628, detail. Mantua, Biblioteca Comunale. Shows the area around the Duomo and the Palazzo Vescovile, including Ercole Gonzaga's apartments. The superimposed labels highlight the main points of interest.

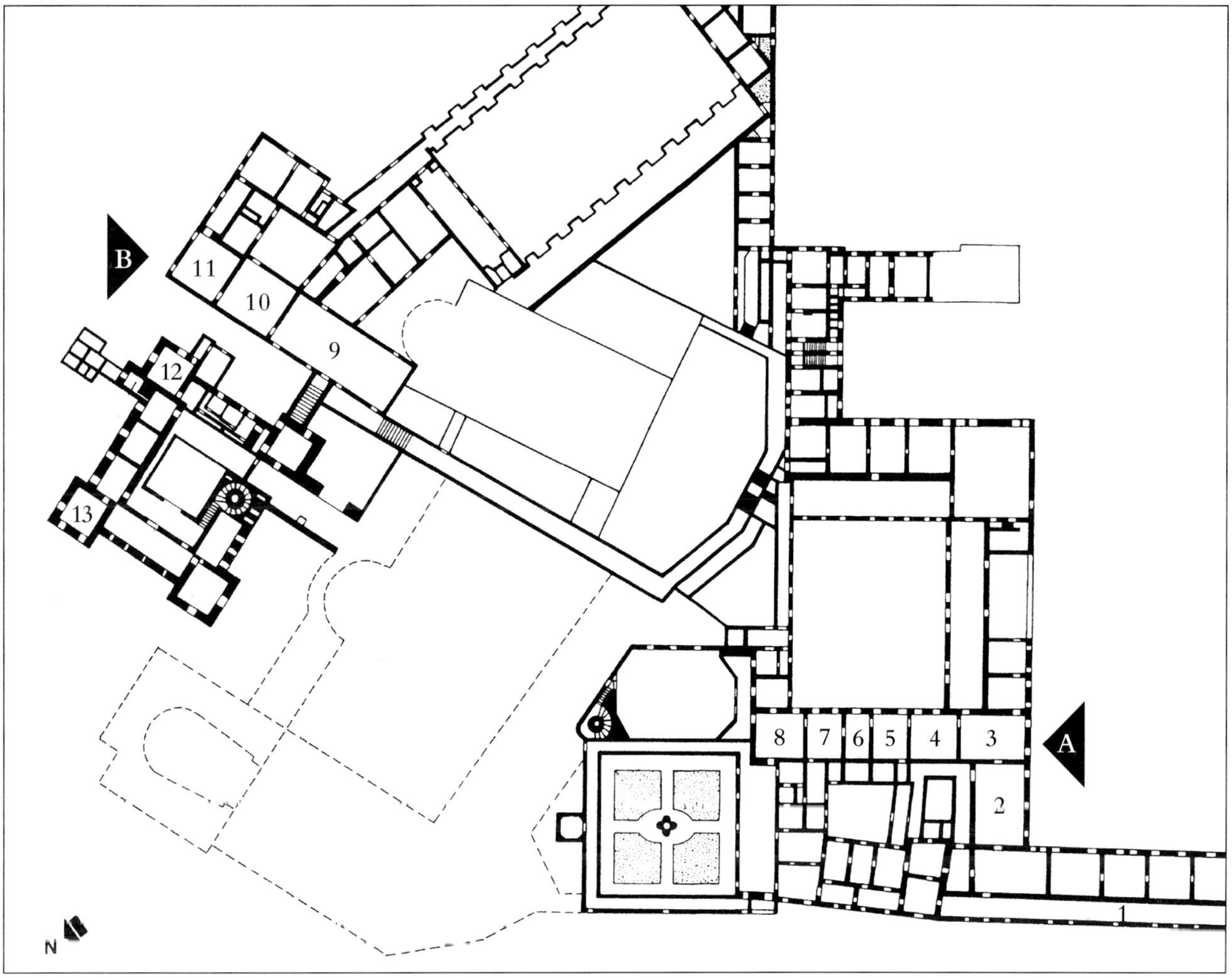

Fig. 7 Mantua, Plan of the Palazzo Ducale.

A. Corte Vecchia (no. 2 = Sala del Pisanello). In 1580 (Documents 58, 59) Ercole's *Puttini* was displayed in no. 7 (Camera dell'Aquila). Beyond the "anditello" (no. 6), the Camera del Leone (no. 5) was reserved for the Ferrante *Puttini* and the *Suzanne* was in the Camera del Cani, the present Sala dello Zodiaco (no. 8). The *Saul*, the *Tobia vecchia*, and the *Fortuna* were displayed elsewhere.

B. Corte Nuova (no. 9 = Salone di Manto; no. 13 = Camera degli Sposi in the Castello). In 1584 (Document 60) the *Puttini* was displayed in the Sala dei Capitani (no. 10), the *Tobia Nuovi* in the Sala dei Marchesi (no. 11), and the *Suzanne* in the Camera delle Armi (no. 12) of the Castello.

vi fossero persone, o ben poche" (Document 46). Yet, given that Ercole had once cautioned his brother (Document 36) that "non contenessero favola o cosa lasciva, ma qualche historia della scrittura et del Testamento Vecchio," thus subjects "conveniente al grado et professione mia," it is surprising to learn that he also considered acquiring themes more suitable to the profession and lifestyle of a Ferrante Gonzaga. Be this as it may, thanks to the preservation of a substantial amount of Ercole's correspondence, we known something about his attitudes and tastes.

Indeed, the correspondence between two important cardinals is so detailed that one gets a vivid idea of the tapestry trade in Flanders and of the relationships between the tapestry weavers and their customers. First, it is remarkable how individuals of the rank of Cardinals Gonzaga and Granvelle were in direct and extended cor-

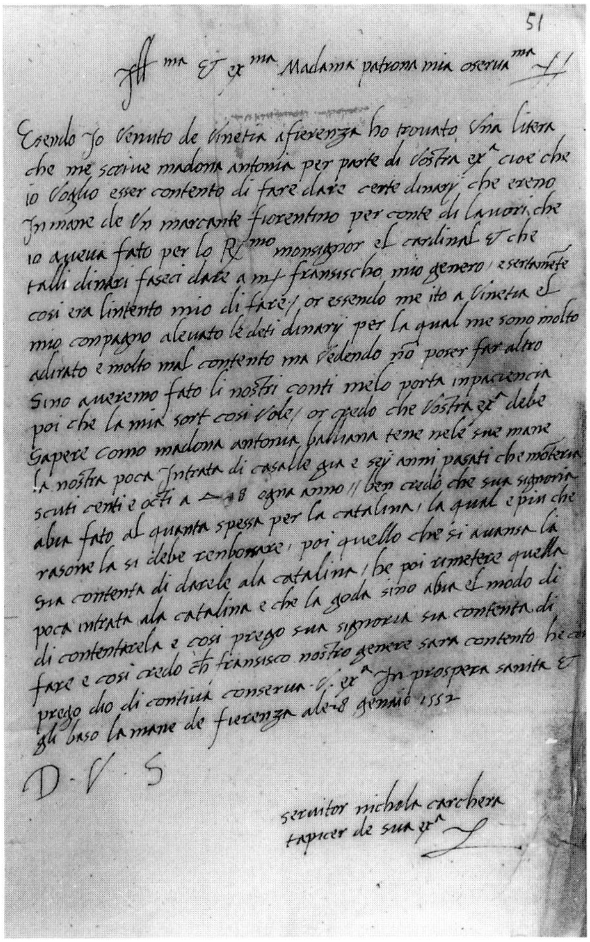
51

Ill.ma et Ex.ma Madama patrona mia oseruan.ma

Esendo Jo venuto de Vinetia a fierenza ho trouato una litera
che me scriue madona antonia per parte di vostra ex.a cioe che
io voglio esser contento di fare dare certe dinary che ereno
Jn mane de un marcante fiorentino per conte di lauori che
io aueua fato per lo R.mo monsignor el cardinal et che
talli dinari fasci dare a m. fransischo mio genero / esertamete
cosi era lintento mio di fare / or esendo me ito a Vinetia el
mio conpagno aleuato le deti dinary per la qual me sono molto
adirato e molto mal contento ma vedendo no poter far altro
sino averemo fato li nostri conti melo porta inpacienzia
poi che la mia sort cosi vole / or credo che vostra ex.a debe
sapere como madona antonia palliana tene nele sue mane
la nostra poca Jntrata di casalle gia e sey anni pasati che molterà
scuti centi e octi a 48 ogna anno // ben credo che sua signoria
abia fato al quanta spessa per la catalina / la qual e piu che
rasone la si debe renborsare / poi quello che si auansa la
sua contenta di darele ala catalina / he poi rimetere quella
poca intrata ala catalina e che la goda sino abia el modo di
di contentarcela e cosi prego sua signoria sia contenta di
fare e cosi credo ch fransisco nostro genere sara contento he c…
prego dio di contiua conserua v. ex.a Jn prospera sanita et
gli baso la mane de fierenza ale 28 genaio 1552

D. V. S

seruitor nichola carchera
tapicer de sua ex.a

Fig. 8 Nicolas Karcher to Margherita Paleologa, 28 January 1552 (Document 31). Mantua, Archivio di Stato.

respondence about such acquisitions, which thus meant so much to them. As Ercole had been cheated on a previous, similar case, he asked the merchants for a sample (letter of 12 July 1561). But Ercole apparently could not convince the merchant to send him one, and so he relied on Cardinal Granvelle, who was the principal adviser to Margaret of Parma, regent of the Netherlands and a reputed connoisseur and a collector himself. Gonzaga asked him to judge the qualities both of the design and the weaving: "si contenti di dargli un'occhiata et parendole che'l dissegno sia bello e ben lavorato." From the later documents, it is clear that Granvelle himself could not convince the weaver to send a sample to Italy, as the weaver argued that the sale of the *Hannibal* set was already in negotiation with a Spanish merchant and that the sample tapestry would not be back in time. Thus these documents prove the economic strength and independence of such Brussels weaver-merchants, bargaining with foreign merchants in Antwerp, the place of trade, as well as with powerful cardinals, and not being intimidated by them. In the end, Ercole Gonzaga missed this set and the tapestries were sold to someone else (letter of Granvelle, 12 October 1561).

Unfortunately, less is known regarding how the individual sets recorded in the 1563 inventory (Document 49) were displayed. Ercole's inventory provides a fixed location "per il studiolo" only for the "tapezerie a fogliami." That wall hangings, although not specifically figurative weavings, were the dominant decoration is made clear by Ercole's instructions in 1542 regarding the creation of a frieze to fill in the space on the walls of his dining room left blank by the dimensions of the tapestries (Document 14). Similarly, in his instructions in 1558 to Bernardino Pia concerning work then under way to prepare the Roman palace for his arrival, Ercole refused to spend money repainting walls that would be covered by hangings, and he ordered Pia to select "delle più belle tapezzarie" for the decoration of the "camera principale" (Document 38). As early as 1522 (Document 1) and then again in 1539 (Document 8), the documents stress the importance of both figurative and fabric hangings.

Ercole acquired certain sets with specific ecclesiastical needs in mind, as, for example, the unspecified set(s) loaned annually to decorate the Duomo on the Feast of Corpus Christi (Document 11). As well, Ercole could hardly have ordered the *Acts of the Apostles* (which he left to the Duomo according to the terms of his 1557 testament, but to the palatine Church of Santa Barbara in his third and final testament) without having a clear idea of how they would be used. The documentation for Ercole's collection begins with several general references (Documents 1 and 3). The first reference suggests the extent to which he was accustomed to fabric-covered walls from his student days, and the correspondence of 1537 (Document 6) suggests a clear preference for tapestries over paintings. Although Ercole clearly had a collection by 1531 (Document 3) sufficiently large enough to be recorded in his testament, it is only after the death of Federico II and Ercole's return to Mantua as regent, with his residence in the Palazzo Vescovile, that he seems to have begun to collect with a vengeance. Thus, in 1541–42, Nicolas Karcher was kept busy on his behalf (Document 12), the records being the only ones in the corpus to trace the payments on a weekly basis for a specific commission. At the same time, an agent was authorized to spend more than 9,000 scudi on weavings of unspecified Old Testament subjects (Document 15). Like the *Aeneas* of Ferrante, these weavings were purchased on the open market rather than designed to his specifications. Similar large purchases were made in 1549–50 (Document 28), when Ercole reassumed the role of regent and once again had Karcher working for him (Documents 27 and 30). That these major commissions and acquisitions coincide with the inception of Ercole's two terms as regent clearly is not without significance.

One would greatly wish to know more of the message Giovanni Carlo Borromeo carried with him to Florence in 1551 and thus about the commission Ercole gave to Nicolas Karcher at this time (Document 30). One is grateful nonetheless for the record of his response to Ferrante's offer to purchase tapestries in Brussels because it contains the important reference to Ercole's preference for subjects "conveniente al grado et professione mia" (Document 36). Thus it is not surprising to find that among the 130 individual panels catalogued in the 1563 inventory (Document 49), those that do not have a religious theme are largely *verdure* weavings. As for the cartoons provided to Ercole in 1549 by a minor member of Giulio Romano's shop, Anselmo Guazzi (Document 25), for tapestries to be woven in Flanders, they are certainly less interesting than the mass of documentation that has surfaced on Nicolas Karcher, the man who was also responsible for founding the Grand Duke of Tuscany's tapestry works in Florence (Fig. 8).

NOTES

1. Inv. no. 1937, 1099 (117 × 183 cm). The design for this panel is related to the style of Andrea Mantegna. Originally, therefore, it could have been created for Ludovico II Gonzaga (d. 1478), for it is known that Mantegna did drawings of a cock and a peafowl for tapestries in 1469 (Hunter, 1914; Goebel, 1924, 589–90; Mayer, 1969, 29–30 and pl. 11; Thornton, 1991, 47, no. 51). The use Francesco II made of these designs dates the weaving to the period between 1484 and 1519.

2. In 1496 Isabella d'Este ordered some *verdure* tapestries, giving precise instructions that animals and birds be included (Brown and Lorenzoni, 1973, 97–122: docs. 2, 27, and 41). These might be related to the large and heavily restored hangings (measuring 218 × 674 cm and 154 × 608 cm) in the Palazzo Vescovile that were probably created in the Bruges workshops (*Mantua 1972*, 26–35, entries 16–18; Adelson, 1985[A], 253, no. 42, where the Mantuan hangings are said to be of the 16th century). The tapestries can be compared to the *verdure* hangings of Paolo Giovio and of Matthias Lang, Bishop of Salzburg. Delmarcel and Duverger, 1987, 192–203.

3. The six tapestries in this set were given by Francesco Gonzaga in 1599 to the Duomo in Mantua, where they are still preserved. The documents refer to them either as French or Flemish, although in all likelihood they were woven in Bruges (reproduced in Patricolo, 1904; *Mantua 1974*, 107, no. 133 (measuring 520 × 220 cm). See also the pamphlet by S. Sicoli (*Mantova, Basilica di S. Barbara: Gli Arazzi di Francesco Gonzaga* [Soprintendenza per i Beni Artistici e Storici per le Provincie di Brescia, Cremona, Mantova], Mantua, 1987). The scale of the wine-red and green-blue dyes is similar to what is found there, as are the designs of the inner border, which can be related to those found in a *Life of Christ* made in Bruges between 1607 and 1644 for the Church of Saint Vincent in Rouen (Delmarcel and Duverger, 1987, 294–305, nos. 29–32). The models for both sets appear to have been Flemish engravings.

4. This dorsal tapestry, in a private collection, displays the Gonzaga arms as well as an inscription, which reads: "HOC. OPUS. F. FE [or EE] DE. CA. MDXXVIII." It may be interpreted as: "Hoc opus f(ieri) fe(cit)" E(rcole) deca(nus) 1528" (Sotheby's London, 9 December 1969, no. 11 [5 feet 9 inches high by 19 feet 3 inches wide]). Accordingly, this *spalliera* could be the oldest surviving tapestry ordered by Ercole, one commissioned within a year of his having become "Cardinalis Decanus." The lettering is not entirely clear. Braghirolli (1879, 100) knew a companion piece, the *Creation of Eve,* and he read the inscription as: "hoc. opus. f. fe. de. ca. MDXXVIII." For Ercole's title, see *Dictionnaire,* 21, 1986, 621 (title granted on 3 May 1527).

It depicts Fortitude in the center with Saint Peter giving the keys to a pope on the right and with Moses with the Tablets of the Law on the left.

5. According to Francesco's testament, the tapestries were to be distributed to various members of his household or to be sold to provide them with a financial bequest. For the entire inventory, see Chambers, 1992, 142ff.

6. Braghirolli, 1879, 33.

7. Braghirolli, 1879, 33; Signorini, 1985, 249, 301.

8. Golzio, 1936, 103–4.

9. ASMn, b. 2434, c. 280; 2903, l. 132, cc. 54r–v; 1184 (4 July and 7 August). According to a letter written by Calandra on 2 September 1488, the tapestries that Ercole wanted to honor the visiting members of the Milanese court were returned to Mantua in poor condition. This may explain why they are not referred to thereafter in the archival records. Braghirolli, 1879, 39; Bertolotti, 1888, 1035.

10. ASMn, b. 1182. Signorini, 1985, 301. See also ASMn, b. 2890, l. 62, c. 32 r–v and 38. The two sets measured "braccia 130."

11. ASMn, b. 2904, l. 138, c. 65; l. 139, c. 45r and b. 1433, cc. 200, 206. On 17 January 1501 Bishop Ludovico Gonzaga (ASMn, b. 1801; Rossi, 1889[A], 308, no. 1) requested the loan from Francesco II of "lo paramento grando di brocato, più coperte di brochato, et lo panno di razo di Rodi." In 1495, during the Battle of Fornovo, Francesco II captured "quatro pezi del apparamento de Re de Franza" (ASMn, b. 1447, c. 293, b. 2110 cc. 103, 197), and in 1502 reference is made to the acquisition in France of "tre balle de tapezarie et panni nostri." See also ASMn, b. 629, c. 348. For the records from 1516 to 1517, see ASMn, Libri dei Mandati, no. 27, cc. 136–40. The *Herkenbald* tapestry is listed as "una coltrina da mur[o] a figuri a istoria de uno che taglio la testa a uno suo nepote." Reference is also made to the "spallira a figuri," which was located in Francesco II's rooms in the Palazzo di San Sebastiano.

12. Concerning the request that Federico da Montefeltro loan the *Troy* tapestries to the Gonzaga court, see note 2 in the Epilogue.

13. Understandably, references to other types of wall hangings owned by the later Gonzagas are not included and, similarly, the reader will not find mention of figurative weavings other than tapestries. The most fascinating account was a letter written to Duke Vincenzo by A. Catherina Lecca Cantona from Milan on 31 August 1600 (ASMn, b. 1724): "Haverà forsi memoria Vostra Altezza Serenissima come gli anni passati le vennero alle mani alcune opre mie fatte all'ago di seta et d'oro, delle quali, secondo mi fu riferito, ella restò assai gustata. Hora le fo sapere come per lasciare qualche notabile memoria de'fatti miei, io mi sono deliberata di far un opra di non poco momento, che sarà un intero addobamento da letto, et da tavolino, fatto tutto a punti d'ago, pur d'oro et seta, senza mischiarvi alcuna sorte di drappo. Il fondo è di fogliami diversi et d'uccelli. Nel mezzo del cielo, della coperta, delle cortine et del tavolino, sono compartite sette historie romane bellissime. Ne'freggi sono diverse historie greche et romane, le quali arrivaranno al numero di nonanta in circa. Quelle della prima cortina, et suoi pendeni, saranno essempi d'amore fra padri et figliuoli. Quelle della seconda essempi d'amore fra marito e moglie. Quelle della terza essempi di singolare honestà di donne illustri. Quelle della quarta, essempi d'opre segnalate delle donne. Ciascuna di queste historie, oltra quello che se ne vedrà dai gesti delle figure di lunghezza d'un palmo geometrico et più, sarà dichiarata con poche parole latine, scritte in un cartello d'argento con lettere maiuscole romane (. . .)."

14. ASMn, r. 6511, c. 32 (to Carlo Borromeo); ASMn, b. 6513, c. 9 (to Cesare Gonzaga); ASMn, b. 1930 (Ludovico Tridapali: 26 April and 1, 3, and 15 May). Some of the leather and fabric hangings are catalogued in the 1564 inventory. Occasionally references to other types of hangings are found in the entries; for example, the "apparamenti di seta o (. . .) corami," which Ferrante acquired in 1549 in preparation for the anticipated arrival in Milan of Charles V (Document 26). The same document also describes the purchase of the *Aeneas* tapestries to honor Philip II. Furthermore, and as, was frequently the case, wall hangings used on special occasions featured a combination of tapestries and fabric and leather hangings, as, for example, when the Ducal Palace in Mantua was decorated to receive Henry III in 1574 (Document 56). Given the state of preservation of the records of his chancery office, and in the absence of a comprehensive inventory of Ferrante's possessions, it is difficult to be precise about the contents of his *guardaroba*.

Chronology

The Lives and Art Patronage of Federico II, Ercole, and Ferrante Gonzaga

This chronological guide is selective rather than all-inclusive, and related facts have been gathered together under the date of the most significant example. In order to provide a useful overview, a balance has been sought between biographical references and those pertaining to art patronage.

As the *primogenito* and heir to Mantua, which became a duchy during his reign, affairs of state naturally were uppermost in Federico II's mind. The striking mark on the city-state left by his years in office, one that is still clearly in evidence, owes much to his enlightened patronage of Giulio Romano. Cinquecento Europe would have been greatly impoverished without the existence of the Palazzo Te and the Appartamento di Troia in the Ducal Palace. His decision to bring Nicolas Karcher to Mantua set the tone for the subsequent patronage of Federico II's brother Ercole.

As fate would have it, Ercole's career as a cleric was less important perhaps than his role as regent both after the death of Federico II and then after the untimely demise of his nephew. In addition to carrying on where his brother left off as a patron of Giulio Romano and Nicolas Karcher, it is thanks to Ercole than Mantua still boasts the important version of the Raphael *Acts of the Apostles* tapestries. Ercole was aided in his duties as co-regent by his brother Ferrante, who enhanced the prestige of his family through his close relationship with Charles V.

Ferrante's role as a patron of architecture would be better known if the Villa Simonetta outside Milan were better preserved. Nonetheless, it is clear that, in the service of the emperor, Ferrante continued Federico II's interest in the civic architectural projects that were created in Milan in the name of Charles V.

Federico II (1500–1540)

5th Marquis and 1st Duke of Mantua

FIGS. 9, 10

For the reign of Federico II (1519–40), see *Mantova, La Storia,* II, 1961, 269ff. His patronage of Giulio Romano has been explored by Hartt, 1958; *Mantua 1989;* and *Giulio Romano,* 1992.

17 MAY 1500

Born and baptized with the name of his grandfather (Federico I: d. 1484).

1503

Began his studies with Francesco Virgilio (Luzio and Renier, 1903, 86ff.).

JULY 1510

Date of the Francia portrait (Metropolitan Museum of Art: Luzio, 1887, 59–60). In August 1512, Julius II asked Raphael to add Federico II's features "in una camera che fa depinze" (Golzio, 1936, 24). In 1512 he was depicted on a medal with Mars and the Three Graces (Verheyen, 1977, fig. 26). Other portraits (lost) include one by Bonsignori (1503) (Brown, 1979, 81–82, 85–87). A drawing in Vienna relates to his *Last Supper* of 1506–7 (Schmitt, 1961, 124). Federico II was also included in a fresco by Costa (Vasari-Milanesi, 1878, III, 134–35).

AUGUST 1510–FEBRUARY 1513

Federico II resides at the court of Julius II (Luzio, 1886, 509ff.). Shortly after his arrival in Rome, Federico II "ha cavalcato al Capitolio, al Coliseo, et ad veder molte altre antiquità." He was on the

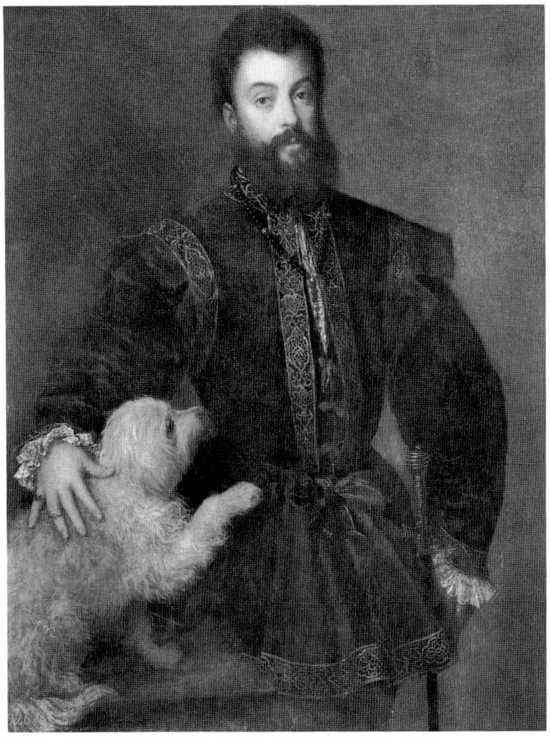

Fig. 9 Titian, *Portrait of Federico II Gonzaga,* c. 1523. Madrid, Museo del Prado.

Capitoline (July 1511) for Plautus's comedy and he accompanied the pope to dinner in Agostino Chigi's villa and then to Ostia for the hunt.

In January 1512 Federico II examined the porphyry sarcophagus in Santa Agnese as well as the Tiberius statue recently unearthed near Santa Maria sopra Minerva. The same year, Caradosso made Ippoliti a "scudo per portar su la baretta" depicting *Hercules and Cacus,* and Federico II sought permission regarding the commissioning of "uno Laoconte d'oro di tutto relevo con li figlioli e serpi."

22 OCTOBER 1515

Met Francis I in Milan and accompanied him to France. See the study by Tamalio (1994) as cited in Knecht, 1994, 109, 113 (and also 124, 425). The conversations between Federico II and Francis I not infrequently touched on matters pertaining to the arts. On 13 February 1516 it is learned: "Hozi ragionando la Maestà de Re con il signor Federico di molte picture e con messer Rozon, lui ha referto tute le belle cose che tien Vostra Signoria [Isabella d'Este] (. . .)." Federico II noted the similarity between one of the garden fountains at Blois and its counterpart in the Palazzo di San Sebastiano (Smith, 1989, 307ff.). While in France, he remained in contact with the court painter Costa (Brown, 1970, 109).

1517

The betrothal to Maria Paleologa (d. 15 September 1530) was annulled in 1529. He was subsequently promised to Giulia of Aragona but eventually married Maria's sister Margherita (Davari, 1891). These negotiations had an impact on his long-standing liaison with Isabella Boschetti (*Mantua 1989,* 442).

29 MARCH 1519

Named as Francesco II's heir, with the emperor confirming him as the 5th Marquis of Mantua on 7 April 1521.

MAY 1519

Asked Castiglione to obtain drawings by Michelangelo and Raphael for the tomb of Francesco II (Morrogh, 1992, 145, 147–48, fig. 8).

1 JULY 1521

Named captain general of the papal forces, an event commemorated in a canvas by Costa now in Prague (Schaeffer, 1908, 162ff.).

1521

Publication of Equicola's *Istoria di Mantua.* Benevoli compiled the *Monumentum Gonzagium* (c. 1520–25: Rostagno, 1899, 135ff., 186ff.). A history commissioned from Aretino remained unfinished (Luzio, 1888, 18ff.). In 1515 Lelio Manfredi began work on the translation of the *Tirante il Bianco* and subsequently composed the *L'ordine di cavaglieria* (Kolsky, 1994, 51–52).

1521–22

Redesigned the ground floor of the castle, laying the foundation for a *studiolo* and library (Brown, 1988, 315ff.). The frescoes in the Sala dello Zodiaco provide visual evidence for Leonbruno's collaboration with Mario Equicola (Lippencott and Signorini, 1991, 244ff.).

The 1542 inventory refers to 95 "retratti de varii signori, signore et capitanei christiani et infideli" in the *camerino davanti al Studio* (which also housed a collection of 179 books). The Studio dalle Antiquità contained antique coins, marble and bronze heads, statuettes, fragments, lamps, and animals.

The first acquisitions for the *studiolo* were purchased by Castiglione. On 24 March 1526 antique marbles and the "volumi de Hippocrate" were shipped from Rome to Mantua. On 28 October 1526 Giulio Romano advised on the arrival of antiquities from Rome, perhaps the collection he had purchased from the Ciampolini heirs (Fusco and Corti, 1991). The previous year, negotiations were under way to acquire Penni's portion of the Ciampolini collection.

1522

Participated in the defense of Pavia, an event commemorated in several medals (Hill, 1930, 68, 170). The Tintoretto cycle (1580) for the Corte Nuova (Ducal Palace) included three pictures devoted to his exploits (1521–22) the taking of Parma, the battle for Milan, and the siege of Pavia (Eikemeier, 1969, 97–104).

10 SEPTEMBER 1522

Castiglione wrote concerning the "disegno di Marmirolo," the first indication of plans for a major addition to the old fortress-palace complex and of Giulio Romano's involvement in the project. Payment for the "modello de Marmirolo" is dated 20 March 1523. The following year Castiglione ordered "corami dorati e inargentati" with the Mount Olympus device. At the same time, the duke sought works from several painters, including Sebastiano del Piombo (Shearman, 1991, 295–96; Luzio, 1913, 28; Hirst, 1981, 158). Leonbruno painted in the loggia a fresco depicting of the *Battle of Pavia* (Gamba, 1906, 68).

Razed to the ground in the eighteenth century, Marmirolo was one of the marvels of Europe (*Mantua 1989*, 520–21). Ulloa (1563, 156, 248–49) described the lavishness of the appointment of the rooms on the occasion of a visit by Philip II in 1549 (for which, see also Calvete de Estrella, 1930, I, 112–13). A fresco depicting the Battle of Tunis (1535) might have been based on the "disegno di Tunici" sent by Ferrante, which is perhaps related to a painting recorded in Ercole's 1563 inventory (Brown, 1991, 220).

22 AUGUST 1523

Named captain general of the papal and Florentine forces with a three-year salary of 30,000 ducats.

29 AUGUST 1524

Castiglione learned of his anxiety regarding Giulio Romano's departure from Rome. Upon arriving he undertook to supervise work on the villa at Marmirolo. On 5 June 1525 Giulio was made a Mantuan citizen, and on 30 August 1526 he was appointed "capomaestro" of all construction in the city. That October he provided designs for "una bella sepoltura di marmore con un epitaphio" for a favorite dog (*Giulio Romano,* 1992, I, 177), and, shortly thereafter, he became involved with plans for the creation of the Palazzo Te.

Correspondence between November 1525 and March 1526 survives regarding the creation of a "salera" at a cost of 69 "ducati d'oro larghi" (*Giulio Romano,* 1992, I, 106ff.), but in February 1526 (*Mantua 1989,* 456) Federico II announced that "havemo deliberato farli fare in Mantua al nostro aurifice." Thereafter, Giulio provided designs (Strahov codex) for a wide range of luxury items for the duke's table (*Mantua 1989,* 464–65). See also *Giulio Romano: Designs for Mantua,* Oxford, Christ Church Picture Gallery, 1995.

1525

Loaned Clement VII the Gonzaga family copy of Eustathius's commentary on Homer (Bertolotti, 1884, 9; Meroni, 1966, 68). Received from Fabio Calvo (his former tutor in geometry and Greek) "un ellephante di metallo cum un Hannibale a cavallo, antiquo" (Brown, 1988, 221 n. 12).

1527–34

Work on the construction and decoration of the Palazzo Te. Drawings of this project, as well as of the Appartamento di Troia in the Ducal Palace (1536–39), were sent by Jacopo Strada to the Duke of Bavaria in 1567 (*Mantua 1989,* 392ff.).

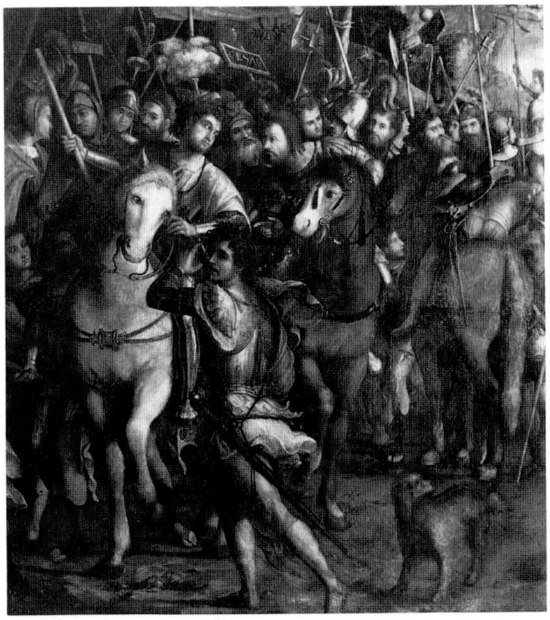

Fig. 10 Lorenzo Costa, *Triumph of Federico II Gonzaga,* 1522, detail. Prague, National Gallery.

22 FEBRUARY 1527
Initiated negotiations for a work by Michelangelo for the Palazzo Te (Luzio, 1913, 246–51). Federico II was also unsuccessful in his negotiations with Maramoldo for antiquities from the Sack of Rome.

1528
Commissioned a *Hercules* seal from Benvenuto Cellini (Plon, 1883, 192).

21 SEPTEMBER 1529
Named captain general of the imperial forces in Italy.

FEBRUARY AND MARCH 1530
Correspondence with Titian related to the *Madonna and Child with Saint Catherine and a Rabbit* (Paris, Louvre). Titian was also asked to execute a portrait of Cornelia Malaspina for Francesco de los Cobos. Earlier, in 1527, Federico II received Titian's portrait of Pietro Aretino and Girolamo Adorno (Wethey, 1969–75, I, 105–6; II, 77, 201).

25 MARCH 1530
Arrival in Mantua of Charles V (Document 9), who especially admired the astrological cycle in the Sala dei Venti of the Palazzo Te.

8 APRIL 1530
Elevated by Charles V to the rank of duke.

19 MARCH 1531
Sought out a collection of Flemish pictures for the Appartamento di Troia and was offered the possibility of commissioning a series of "gli sette peccati mortale, figurati da sette favola de Ovidio magiore" (Brown, 1992, 18–19). In May 1535 he acquired 120 Flemish pictures (Brown, 1981, 53ff.).

3 OCTOBER 1531
Federico II arranged for the display of pictures by Mantegna, Titian, Giulio Romano, and Leonardo in Margherita Paleologa's rooms in the Castello (Brown, 1981, 53). For her Giulio also built the "Palazzino di Paleologa" (*Mantua 1989,* 385ff.).

CIRCA 1531–40
A number of historiated majolica plates (one of which bears the date 1533) survives from a service executed by Nicolò da Urbino sometime after Federico II's marriage to Paleologa. The dish in the Victoria and Albert Museum with Federico II's *impresa* of Mount Olympus belongs to such a set (*London 1981,* 198–201). On 3 December 1533 Valerio Belli advised that he would be unable to undertake work for Federico II (Bertolotti, 1888, 1041). Belli's skills were known to Federico II certainly as early as October 1529 (Aretino, 1551, 17–18).

9 NOVEMBER 1532
During a second visit to Mantua, Charles V admired "alcune armature" that maestro Franceschino had made for the duke (Bertolotti, 1885, 103–4). Years later, on 28 February 1577 (ASPr, b 50/1), Ferrante's widow gave the Archduke Charles "un armatura del signor Ferrando." Ferrante was shown wearing a "waisse halbe Rüstung sambt seinem hemblin" on a portrait mannequin displayed at Ambras in the gallery of Ferdinand II of the Tyrol (Sanvito, 1993, 187–88) (Fig. 14).

Perhaps it was in 1532 that Federico II presented the emperor with four pictures by Correggio of the *Loves of Jupiter.* It is not known precisely when Federico II commissioned the *Danaë* (Rome, Galleria Borghese), the *Leda* (Berlin), and the

Ganymede and the *Io* (Vienna). The date of the commission, and whether the *Io* and *Ganymede* were ordered by Federico II for a specific site and then offered to Charles V with the promise of additional works, remains uncertain (Gould, 1976, 130ff.).

10 MARCH 1533
Birth of his *primogenito,* Francesco III (d. 1550). In 1536 Benedetto Lampridio was hired as a tutor (Luzio and Renier, 1903, 247).

11 SEPTEMBER 1534
Ludwig of Bavaria sent his court painter to Mantua to study with Giulio Romano (Brown, 1994, 23–25).

1536–
Giulio Romano creates the Appartamento di Troia, a suite of rooms beyond the Castello. For these rooms Titian was commissioned to paint portraits of the Caesars (Wethey, 1969–75, III, 235–36). The Gabinetto di Cesare, as it is known from the drawings commissioned by Jacopo Strada, originally contained a handsome collection of small-scale antique and all'antica bronzes, including Andrea Sansovino's *Apollo.* Other antique works, heads, statuary (including the *Venus Genetrix,* now in Vienna), and reliefs were displayed in the Loggia di Marmo. When Cardinal Granvelle requested a drawing of the *Battle of the Amazons* relief, Giovanni Battista Scultori was reluctant to provide him with one because he believed it to be of poor quality (Brown, 1992[A], 28).

3 NOVEMBER 1536
Invested by Charles V with the Duchy of Monferrato.

1538
Birth of Guglielmo (d. 1587), the future 3d Duke of Mantua.

1539
Birth of Ludovico, founder of the Nevers branch of the Gonzaga family. Death of his mother, Isabella d'Este, on 13 February 1539.

8 OCTOBER 1539
Established a tapestry factory in the Borgo San Giorgio under the direction of Nicolas Karcher (Document 9).

28 JUNE 1540
Died at his palace at Marmirolo. A team of co-regents headed by Ercole Gonzaga was appointed for the seven-year-old Francesco III. Navagero (Segarizzi, 1912–16, I, 52) commented on Federico II's passion for horses and architectural projects: "Le spese solevano esser al tempo del duca morto molto grandi, perché Sua Eccellenza spendeva assai nelle stalle, assai nelle fabbriche e molto in tener gran corte."

Giovio (1558, 352–53) contrasted the interests of the Marquis Francesco II ("ma sopra tutti gli altri signori di quel tempo, senza dubbio s'acquistò egli gloria grande di gran quantità, di bellezza et diversità di cavalli (. . .): percioche egli manteneva le mandre delle cavalle per accrescere la razza") with those of his son Federico II: "dove si vide poi, che il signor Federigo suo figliuolo era per rifare in qualche parte l'ordine di queste mandre, osservando i frutti di differente matrimonio et di diversa razza: se allettato dall'insatiabile desiderio di edificare, non havesse speso in altro."

12 JULY 1540
Payment to Giulio Romano for Federico II's catafalque (*Mantua 1989,* 568–69).

Ercole (1505–1563)

Cardinal and Regent of Mantua

FIGS. 11, 12

For an overview of Ercole's life, with detailed bibliography, see *Dictionnaire* (XXI, 1986, 620–28) and in Brunelli (1986, 101–16). A summary of the contents of his chancery office is provided by Segre (1912, 3–15). Affò's study (Parma, Biblioteca Palatina, b. 1207) remains unpublished. Discussions of Ercole's art patronage focus primarily on his involvement with Giulio Romano (Hartt, 1958, and *Mantua 1989*). Recently, attention has been paid to his collection of tapestries and paintings (*Rome 1984,* 144–45; Brown, 1991, 203ff.).

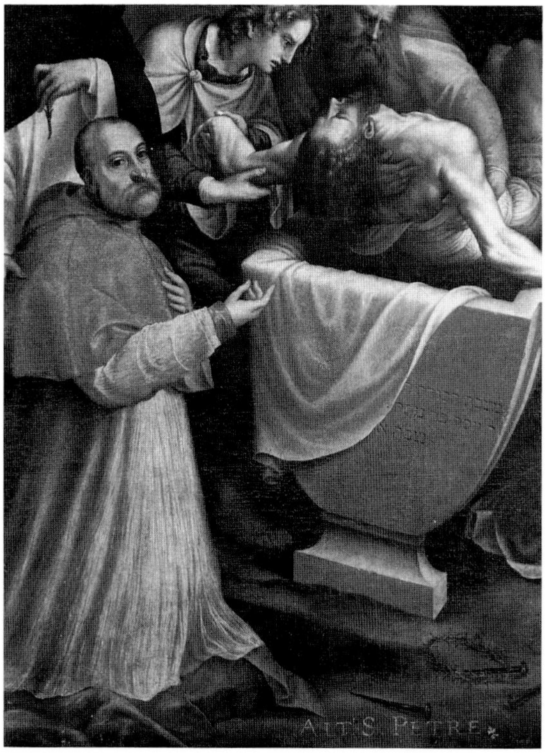

Fig. 11 Circle of Giulio Romano, portrait of Ercole Gonzaga from the *Deposition of Christ*. Mantua, Church of Sant'Egidio.

NOVEMBER 1505

Born and baptized Luigi in honor of the king of France. He was renamed Ercole in memory of Isabella d'Este's father (Kolsky, 1991, 116).

1508

Began his studies under Francesco Virgilio.

10 MAY 1521

Replaced his uncle (Cardinal Sigismondo) as Bishop of Mantua, by which date he was also commander of the abbey at Felonica.

19 JULY 1522

Isabella d'Este expressed the desire for Trissino to meet Ercole "quale se deletta mirabilmente del studio delle lettere et mostra un bon ingegno et quel che ne piace molto in lui et havemo per un bon segno è ch'el se deletta della conversatione de letterati" (ASMn, b. 2997, l. 37, n.p.).

1522–25

Enrolled in Pompeo Pomponazzi's school in Bologna (Luzio, 1886[A], 374ff.). His regular tutor, however, was Lazzaro Buonamici, to whom Isabella d'Este confided: "Verrei meno ai miei doveri di madre se non cercassi con ogni mezzo e per ogni via di far raggiungere a mio figlio le alte vette della cultura" (Jedin, 1972, 501). Despite his profession, it was not until about 1535 that Ercole's studies included sacred writings. He unsuccessfully negotiated with Prospero Colonna (January 1523) for possession of the "più singulare libraria de libri greci et latini che si trovassi in Italia." His subsequent efforts in 1529 to acquire another collection, one that he feared might leave Italy for England, likewise came to naught.

3 MAY 1527

Isabella d'Este went to Rome in March 1525 with the intent of obtaining a cardinal's hat for Ercole. On the eve of the Sack, he was given the papal bull ordaining him a cardinal deacon. In it Ercole was referred to as "eximia ingenii claritate ac litterarum scientia et morum integritate nec non singulari prudentia et in arduis magnanimitate" (Luzio, 1908, 31ff.).

1528

Commissioned several seals from Benvenuto Cellini (Plon, 1883, 187ff.).

8 JULY 1528

Date of an inscription in Isabella d'Este's copy of the 1501 Aldus Manutius *Virgil* (Rhodes, 1954, 377–80), which also refers to the Bishop of Verona, Giovanni Matteo Giberti, whose own ecclesiastical reforms were to serve as a model for those Ercole subsequently effected in Mantua. At the time, Ercole was in Quingentole, the seat of the villa of the Bishops of Mantua, which was subsequently decorated for Ercole by Giulio Romano (*Mantua 1989*, 524–25). Featured in the entrance corridor was Ercole's *impresa* "Sic Repugnamus," in which two swans are shown attacking an eagle.

CIRCA 1530

Cardinal Ippolito de' Medici presented Ercole with the Parmigianino portrait of Charles V (Brown, 1991, 212).

26 DECEMBER 1531

Payment recorded for the transport of a "mappamondo." The 1563 inventory, with its high proportion of maps of specific areas of Europe and the Near East, documents Ercole's strong interest in geography and in major military campaigns (Brown, 1991, 217–20). The "assedio di Perono" refers to the siege of Péronne in 1536 by Charles V, while the "retirade di Lucimborgo" may relate to the 1536 siege of St. Dizier, in which Ferrante participated.

1535

Inspired by Giberti, Ercole began a reform of the clergy and instituted pastoral visits (Rezzaghi, 1986, 25ff.). Out of this concern grew the Leonardo de Marini *Catecismo* (1555) and the *Breve ricordo di Monsignore illustrissimo et Reverendissimo Monsignor Hercole Gonzaga (. . .) delle cose spettanti alla vita de Chierici, al governo delle Chiese, et alla cura delle Anime di questo suo Vescovato di Mantova* (1561).

16 JUNE 1537

In one of many letters to Cardinal Gasparo Contarini (Friedensburg, 1899, 168–70), Ercole described his progress in theological studies:

> non mancherò di dirle come ogni giorno ordinariamente faccio venire il lettore qui di San Domenico [Pietro Bertano] a leggere nella mia saletta una lettione dell'epistole di san Pavolo, alla quale sempre, oltra quelli di casa mia, si truova buon numero de preti et molti gentilhuomini di questa città, quali sì per tenermi compagnia, sì ancho per udire il detto lettore, che veramente è persona dottissima, et di gran valore.

A useful listing of the wide range of books purchased by Ercole in 1537–38 is provided by Rezzaghi (1968, 56ff.). From 1539 there survives a payment for the books bound for Ercole by "Zoan Petro libraro" (Brown, 1991, 223–24 n. 12). In addition to Bede's commentaries on the Epistles of Saint Paul and "supra Salamone," these included a "comentari filosofie moralie," "una tabula de le opere de Santo Tomaso," "uno Apiano Alesandrino," and "uno Terentio."

2 JANUARY 1538

Ercole advised Cardinal Contarini of his plans for a general reform of his churches, plans that included annual pastoral visits (begun in 1535). In 1558 Ercole published *Constitutioni per la chiesa cathedrale di Mantova* (Rezzaghi, 1986, passim). In these as in other matters pertaining to the church, Ercole was strongly influenced by the leaders of reform within the Catholic church, among them Contarini, Giberti, Reginald Pole, and Giovanni Pietro Carafa.

1539

Date of the publication of the first of a group of motets by Jacquet of Mantua dedicated to Ercole (Fenlon, 1980, 68ff.).

AFTER 13 AUGUST 1540

Navagero's *Relatione* (Segarizzi, 1912–16, I, 54–56) provides a vivid description of the cardinal's physical appearance:

> Si ritrova ora d'anni 35, proportionatissimo di corpo, grande di statura, di colore tra il bianco ed il rosso. Ha nella faccia una certa dolcezza congionta con una infinita e mirabil gravità; dal che nasce che al primo aspetto ognuno si li affeziona, ma però talmente che, insieme con quell'affezione, lo conosce degno di esser riverito. Ha movimenti d'occhi e di tutto il resto molto gravi, e tutti da principe; e finamente ogni suo parte, quanto al corpo, dimostra esser nato alle grandezza.

Navagero also wrote at length about his personality and his academic abilities:

> oltre l'esatta intelligenza della lingua greca et latina e la cognizione di diverse scienze e un mirabil giudizio di tutte le cose, è poi d'una innocentissima vita e di purissimi e candidissimi costumi (. . .). E abbondantissimo nelle lemosine.

Few portraits survive and all date from his mature years, including the medal struck during the time he served as president of the third sitting of the Council of Trent (Pollard, 1984, III, nos. 843 and 1441), as well as a 1563 Venetian engraving (and related paintings) of the sitting itself (*Trent 1993*, 114–19, 127–28) (Fig. 5). A full-length portrait (after an original by Ippolito Andreasi [?], is located over his coffin in the sacristy of the Duomo in Mantua (another version is located in the Ducal Palace [*Trent 1993*, 130–31]), and he appears kneeling on the lower left of the San Egidio *Burial of Christ* (*Mantua 1989*, 450; Grassi, 1993, 44ff.), which is based on a design

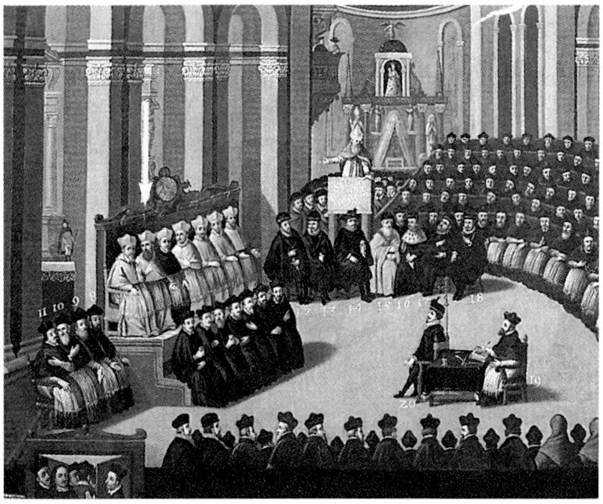

Fig. 12 Anonymous, *Ercole Gonzaga Presides over the Meeting of the Council of Trent in the Church of Santa Maria Maggiore,* mid-17th-century copy, detail. Trent, Castello del Buonconsiglio, Monumenti e collezioni provincali. The superimposed arrow points to Ercole Gonzaga.

of Giulio Romano's. For the medal of the young Ercole, see Hill (1930, 65, no. 285). It had been Ercole's intention in 1528 to commission a portrait from Sebastiano del Piombo (Brown, 1991, 218).

1540–49
Principal of the triumvirate of co-regents (together with Margherita Paleologa and Ferrante) of Mantua during the minority of Francesco III. On 8 October 1540, Ercole received a letter of support and encouragement from Jacopo Sadoleto (published in *Epistolarum Libri Sexdecim* [edition consulted, Cologne, 1608, 579–87, and also 22–25, 58–61]). In his "Relatione," Navagero commented on the speed with which Ercole initiated measures to improve the precarious financial condition of the court (Segarizzi, 1912–16, I, 52).

1540
Giulio Romano remodels his apartments in the Palazzo Vescovile (Piva, 1985, 9–17; Brown, 1991, 223 n. 6).

19 NOVEMBER 1541
Date of the first of several letters from Sernini regarding a copy of Michelangelo's *Last Judgment* (Brown, 1991, 221, n. 3). Other evidence survives showing the extent to which Ercole was attracted to Michelangelo's late works, an interest that can be traced back to 1533, when, according to Vasari, he spoke highly of *Moses* for the tomb of Julius II: "che dal cardinal di Mantova fu detto che quella sol figura bastava a ornare papa Giulio."

31 JANUARY 1542
Established a school in Mantua for the "Dottrina Cristiana" and subsequently (toward 1558) one for clerics to provide instruction in "le lettere humane" (Rezzaghi, 1968, 34ff.), as well as funds for further studies in law, philosophy, and medicine. Ercole's plans for a school run by the Jesuits (1561), for which he left an endowment of 4,000 scudi, were not realized in his lifetime.

25 FEBRUARY 1542
Capilupi's letter (*Giulio Romano,* 1992, II, 947–48) describes the "moresca" staged for carnival, in which the participants were "vestiti a guisa di pastori col dissegno di messer Giulio Romano." This was followed by a production of "i *Captivi* di Plauto." Ercole's interest in theater resulted in his commissioning Bertani (1549) to build a permanent structure (Fabbi, 1974, 18ff.; Carpeggiani, 1992, 67ff.).

1543
Provided new statutes for the production of silk.

15 APRIL 1545
Commissioned Giulio Romano to rebuild the Duomo (*Giulio Romano,* 1992, II, 1027–28).

12 MAY 1546
Ercole is offered Cardinal Pole's version of the Colonna drawing of "un Cristo di mano di Michelangelo (. . .) in forma di pietà," thus either the Isabella Stewart Gardner Museum drawing or a variant. The following year, on 30 April 1547, Fermo Ghisoni was paid by Ercole for three paintings, one of them based on the Colonna *Pietà*. Ghisoni's "Cristo vivo" was based on the British Museum drawing that had been shown to members of Ercole's entourage (Brown, 1991, 203, 210).

7 NOVEMBER 1546
Announced the death of Giulio Romano (*Giulio Romano,* 1992, II, 1168–69):

> Perdessimo il nostro Giulio Romano con tanto mio dispiacere, che in vero mi pare d'haver perduta la mano destra (. . .) che la morte di questo raro huomo mi haverà almeno giovato a spogliarmi dell'appetito del fabbricar, degli argenti, delle pitture et cetera, perchè infatti non mi basteria l'animo di far alcuna cosa di queste senza il disegno di quel bello ingegno, onde finite questi poche, i disegni de'quali sono appresso di me, penso di sepelir con lui tutti i miei desiderii come ho detto.

The reference to "argenti" refers to designs that Giulio produced for table service, such as the one for a "brocca" in the Victoria and Albert Museum, and the design for a "scaldaletto" in Oxford, which is documented in a letter of 6 February 1546 (*Mantua 1989*, 462–64).

13 DECEMBER 1548

Writing to Cardinal Granvelle, Scultori spoke of the pleasure Ercole received in observing the creation of a "istoria molto copiosa de figure e de diverse altre varietà, et ancora de dodeci sfoglii reali a doi sfoglii per pezzo" (Brown, 1992[A], 25–26).

14 MAY 1549

On his advice Francesco III issued a patent appointing Bertani as "capomaestro" of all work in the Duchy (D'Arco, 1857–59, 154–55).

1550–56

Principal of the co-regents of Mantua during the minority of Guglielmo.

24 JANUARY 1551

Issued a decree against "superflue et eccessive pompe" (Luzio, 1912, 65–78).

1552

By this date five of the nine altarpieces (commissioned from Ghisoni, Brusasorzi, Farinati, del Moro, and Veronese) for the Duomo had been completed (Wojno Kiefer, 1987, 34ff.).

26 DECEMBER 1556

Wrote in anticipation of the gift of a portrait of Cosimo de' Medici by the "eccellente maestro" Angolo Bronzino (Brown, 1991, 214–15).

1 NOVEMBER 1557

The *Acts of the Apostles* tapestries (Document 37) were bequeathed to the Cathedral in Mantua and 2,000 ducats set aside for the construction of two memorial chapels dedicated to Saints Thomas and Domenic. In addition to bequests to various retainers and family members (including the disposition of territories under his control), Scipione Gonzaga received all of Ercole's books, except for the theological and philosophical texts, which went to the monastery of San Domenico. Provision was made for "Soris Annae eius filiae naturalis." Other illegitimate children included Isabella, who was married to Federico Maffei, and Camillo (Brown, 1991, 218). A fourth child is cited in the 1576 "Minuta d'informazione del Senato di Mantova fatto di instanza d'Isabella Petrozani" (ASMn, b. 418).

1558

Bertani dedicated to Ercole his *Gli oscuri et dificili passi dell'opera ionica di Vitruvio*. The frontispiece contains his arms above the head of a depiction of his namesake, Hercules (Sheard, 1979, 98–99; *London 1982*, 204–5). A medal showing "Cardinale Hercule et un'Idra" on the other is recorded in his inventory (Brown, 1991, 209). The Hercules references are interesting especially because Ercole pointedly rejected a similar reference in the decoration of his palace in Rome (Document 38).

1559

Lost the papal tiara to Pius IV (Giovan Angelo de' Medici). The matter of his candidacy was considered after the death of Paul III (Farnese) in 1550 and the pros and cons discussed in a letter by Ferrante (ASMn, b. 1920: 29 January 1550).

1560

Composed the *Avvertimenti* to provide his nephew Cesare Gonzaga with an understanding of Rome and the Romans (Zamponi, 1872; Brown, 1985, 49ff.). Two years earlier, and in his role as foster father to various members of the extended family, Ercole also attended to the educational needs of the sixteen-year-old orphaned son of the Lord of San Martino dall'Argine, Carlo Gonzaga (ASMn, 1945, l. 5, cc. 23–24). Together with his brother Ferrante, and by decree of Charles V, Ercole also served as regent to the young Vespasiano of the Sabbioneta line of the family after the death of Ludovico (1540).

14 FEBRUARY 1561

Pius IV named Ercole and Cardinal Puteo as papal legates to the Council of Trent. Pius IV agreed to a marriage into the family by Ferrante's son Cesare (1560) and to the elevation of Ercole's nephews (Francesco and Federico) to the College of Cardinals.

13 SEPTEMBER 1561

Date of a letter from Titian regarding the "effigie del Gran Sultano a cavallo" requested by Ercole (Brown, 1991, 214). Several years before, Titian had appealed to Ercole for assistance regarding his "beneficio di Medoli."

9 MAY 1562

Tintoretto announced the completion of a "battaglia turchesa," perhaps depicting the Battle of Tunis (Brown, 1991, 220).

2 MARCH 1563

Ercole drew up a new testament in which he modified some of the bequests recorded in his testament of 1 November 1557 and added new beneficiaries (among them the Jesuit order, which was left 4,000 scudi for the founding of a college in Mantua, and the Monte di Pietà, which was left "sei milla scudi"). The *Acts of the Apostles* and the *Puttini* were left to Duke Guglielmo Gonzaga (Document 48).

3 MARCH 1563

Died in Trent: his remains were transported to Mantua for burial in the Duomo.

1 APRIL 1563

Date of the "Inventarium bonorum quondam illustrissimi et reverendissimi domini domini Herculis Gonzaga cardinalis Mantue" (Document 49). In related texts there is also a detailed listing of the contents of Ercole's 1,500-volume library (Brown, 1991, 223–24 n. 12), which included 140 Lutheran items that can be linked to Ercole's collection of "ritratti de signori Todeschi et Luterani, numero 29."

1564

The Accademia degli Invaghiti publishes *Componimenti (. . .) in morte di Monsignore Hercole Gonzaga (. . .) con la vita del medesimo* (G. Castellani).

Ferrante (1507–1557)

Duke of Ariano, Prince of Molfetta and Lord of Guastalla, Vice-Regent of Naples and Governor of Milan

FIGS. 13, 14

Ferrante was the subject of two biographies: Ulloa (1563) and Gosellini (1574). For his formative years, see Tamalio (1991). The surviving fragments of his chancery office (ASPr) were catalogued by Costa (1889), while Sorbelli (1937) listed those in the BMG. For related material, see the "Documenti Campori" and the "AC" in MOBE. Still unpublished is the Vatican manuscript Codici Ottoboniani no. 2213: *Discorsi e Ragionamenti dell'Illustrissimo e molto Reverendo Monsignore lo Vescovo di Pavia [Gian-Girolamo Rossi] fatti in quattro dialoghi, dove intervengono il signor Don Ferrante Gonzaga (. . .) e l'Autore* (Affò, 1789–1833, IV, 94–95).

28 JANUARY 1507

Born and held at the baptismal font by the future Leo X.

1513

His role as cleric was reassigned to Ercole (Luzio, 1906, 99, 120).

3 MAY 1523

Departed for Spain, where he remained until 1526.

10 JUNE 1524

Ercole praised his academic diligence (Luzio, 1886[A], 374 n. 2), whereas in 1553 Novelli (Segarizzi, 1912–16, II, 62), took Ferrante to task for his undervaluing letters and for his unwillingness to permit his sons to obtain a humanistic education:

> uno figlio [i.e., Francesco], ch'è prete, sta a Mantoa col reverendissimo cardinal suo zio, e questo solo dà opra alle lettre. Gli altri non vuole il padre ch'attendino ad altro che alla disciplina militare, stimando Soa Eccellenza molto più che riescano buoni soldati che homini litterati, conciosiach'essa ancora abbi fatto 'l medesimo. Ma invero questo suo proposito èbiasmato generalmente da tutti, perché alla professione dell'armi conviene benissimo la cognizione delle lettere.

In 1542 Sernini wrote that "gli gran Capitani antichi tutti erano letterati; né so perché Vostra Eccellenza tenga in sì poco l'imparare" (Tiraboschi, 1822–26, VII/1, 91). Gosellini (1574, 439) drew different conclusions: "per huomo non letterato, egli havesse honesta cognitione, et de le attioni di questo, et di quel Capitano più celebrato, discorresse à le volte, dandone le ragioni, et riducendole a la pratica de'suoi tempi." Under the initials "F.G.," Ortensio Lando (1553) roundly condemned Ferrante's attitude, his preference for German rather than Latin, and his unwillingness to patronize men of letters or to have his children study literature, except those training for the priesthood. And yet Ferrante does not appear to have opposed the cultural inclinations of his *primogenito,* Cesare.

1527

After the death of Carlo of Borbone, Ferrante assumed command (as general of the Light Calvary) of the imperial forces during the Sack of Rome, at which time he took possession of several of the papal tapestries (Document 2).

CIRCA 1529

Date of Titian's *Portrait of a Young Man [Ferrante?] in Armor* in the Armand Hammer Museum, Los Angeles (*London 1981,* 184ff.). All other portraits (except perhaps the circa 1523 *Portrait of Youth [Ferrante?] with a Glove,* Louvre: Hope, 1980, 64) date from his maturity. These include the Leone Leoni medal and statue and the Vermeyen drawing (Horn, 1989, 38 and pl. A116). The Ambras copy of a lost original (by Ghisoni?: Gosellini, 1574, 437) dates from around the same time (Amadei and Marani, 1980, 79), as does the depiction included in the lower left of the Santa Maria delle Grazie *Assumption of the Virgin* (Margonari and Zanca, 1973, fig. 39).

Vivid descriptions were penned by both of his biographers. Ulloa (1563, 171) contrasted the man Ferrante once was—of good stature, heavy, robust, and strong—with the prematurely old man he became:

Fu Don Ferrante huomo di buona statura, piutosto grande che picciolo, corpulente, robusto, et di natura fortissima. Haveva la barba folia et i capegli crespi, ancora che per la su natura calida, et anco per il continuo uso della celata fosse divenuto calvo. Il corpo suo era gagliardo, e molto forte, sano et gran sopportatore delle fatiche, benche in ultimo per cagione de'continui travagli della guerra cominciasse a decrepitare, et a mancargli le forze; per la qual cosa dopo che a Mantova s'era ritirato a vita quieta e tranquilla non potendo caminare per la importunità et molestia delle gotte se faceva condurre in chiesa ad ascoltare i divini ufficii in una sedia portata da dui huomini.

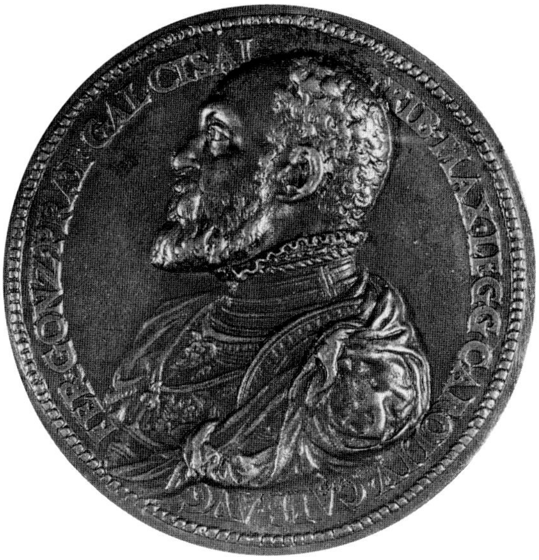

Fig. 13 Leone Leoni, portrait medal of Ferrante Gonzaga, c. 1555. Antwerp, Museum Vleeshuis.

Gosellini (1574, 436–37) preferred to remember Ferrante at the height of his powers:

Fù Don Ferrando di corpo in altezza più che commune, quadrato, et ad ogni fatica, et destrezza, et di cavaleria, et militare, attissimo, et infaticabile. Di fattezza proportionate, et virili bellissimo. Al volto, à la barba folta, à l'occhio grande et nero, pleno di certa gravità, anzi maestà, di che non pure l'aspetto, mà tutte le sue maniere, l'habito, e i portamenti erano composti; che i riguardanti ad armarlo et à riverirlo sforzavano.

1529–30

Participated in the siege of Florence. After the death of the Prince of Orange, he assumed command of the forces (August 1530).

1530

Named governor of Benevento by Clement VII.

DECEMBER 1531

Named to the Order of the Golden Fleece. A drawing in the Victoria and Albert Museum is for one of the links (*London 1980,* 114–15). A majolica service, from which a dish is in the same museum (*London 1981,* 202), dates from this time.

1532

Participated in the Hungarian campaign at the head of a three-thousand-strong calvary. Named Duke of Ariano by Charles V, whom he accompanied on his visit to Mantua. On this occasion Ferrante may have presented to the emperor the inlaid cabinet decorated with scenes from the story of Gideon now in the Victoria and Albert Museum (Thorpe, 1951, 24–28, 56).

1533

Commissioned the Ubeda *Pietà* from Sebastiano del Piombo (Hirst, 1972, 585ff.) as a gift for the secretary of Charles V, Francesco de los Cobos. The following year Federico II communicated Ferrante's wish to have from Titian "due quadri da camera di pittura (. . .) quali vorria mandar a donare in Spagna" (Gaye, 1839–, II, 251–252). The subject matter of one of these was specified as being "il ratto di Proserpina."

1533–46

Served as vice-regent of Sicily:

> Tipica figura di principe-condottiere del Rinascimento, magnifico campione di un'umanità "virtuosa" nel senso machiavelliano, don Ferrante era nato troppo tardi perché le sue doti potessero avere quel felice coronamento pratico, che avevano avuto un secolo prima le doti di uomini del suo stesso stampo, di un Francesco Sforza, ad esempio: ora, egli doveva servire. Ma come ne'rapporti con i propri subordinati, cosí anche nei rapporti con l'imperatore emergevano doti rare di sicurezza di sé, rivelantisi nel franco e schietto eloquio, e un bisogno di agire, di veder ampio d'attorno a sé che lo muovevano, spesso, ad uscire dal confine d'Italia per consigliare a Carlo V le direttive da seguire nella lotta in Germania o contro il Turco e che infondevano nei suoi rapporti con l'imperatore un tono di assoluta e talora anche rude sincerità, un senso di dignità personale per vero non comune. (Chabod, 1971, 168)

Gosellini (1574, 12–13) spoke of his civic projects in the following terms:

> Ridusse à la presente fortezza il castello di Messina (. . .). L'istessa città ampliò, et cinse di mura; col giuditio, et con l'arte le infinite difficoltà superando di quel sito, per l'adietro da ogni altro, come incapace di ogni fortezza, intentato. Et feccevi un altro castello su'l colle, detto il Gonzaga, conservatore de la città, et de la memoria de l'autore di opera così grande. Rinovò in Palermo, et feccelo meglio inteso, et più forte, il castello, che è guardia del Molo. Fortificò in parte Palermo, Trapani, Melazzo, Catania, Siracusa, e'l castello d'Agosta, et stavasi disegnando di fortificare Lentini, come luogo à difender quel Regno da le Turchesche armate.

Ulloa (1563, 180) summed up Ferrante's architectural accomplishments with a reference to his love of agriculture: "et di questa sua inclinatione lascio honorati testimonii come un giardino a Palermo di molte diversità di piante e di arbori di soavissimi frutti adorno." He also made reference to Ferrante following in his father's footsteps in breeding horses.

1534

Married Isabella of Capua (for a portrait medal, see *Milan 1977,* 144–45), thereby becoming Prince of Molfetta. In honor of his marriage, Ferrante may have acquired the *Cephalus and Procris* hangings (Catalogue 1).

JUNE 1535

Fought alongside Charles V at the Battle of Tunis. In a diploma signed by the emperor on 3 May 1540 Ferrante was rewarded for his participation with the alum mining rights in Sicily (Affò, 1780, 51).

17 JANUARY 1535

Birth of Ippolita (d. 1563; for portrait medals, see *Milan 1977,* 140, 145). Ferrante lavished great care on her marrriage to Fabrizio Colonna. For it Luca Contile composed his "La Cesarea Gonzaga," which was performed in Milan on 22 January 1550 (Affò, 1787–1833, 95–133).

1536

Served as captain general of the imperial forces in the reconquest of Piedmont. In November his *primogenito* was born. Cesare (d. 1575) founded an academy as well as a noted collection of Greco-Roman art (Brown, 1993, passim).

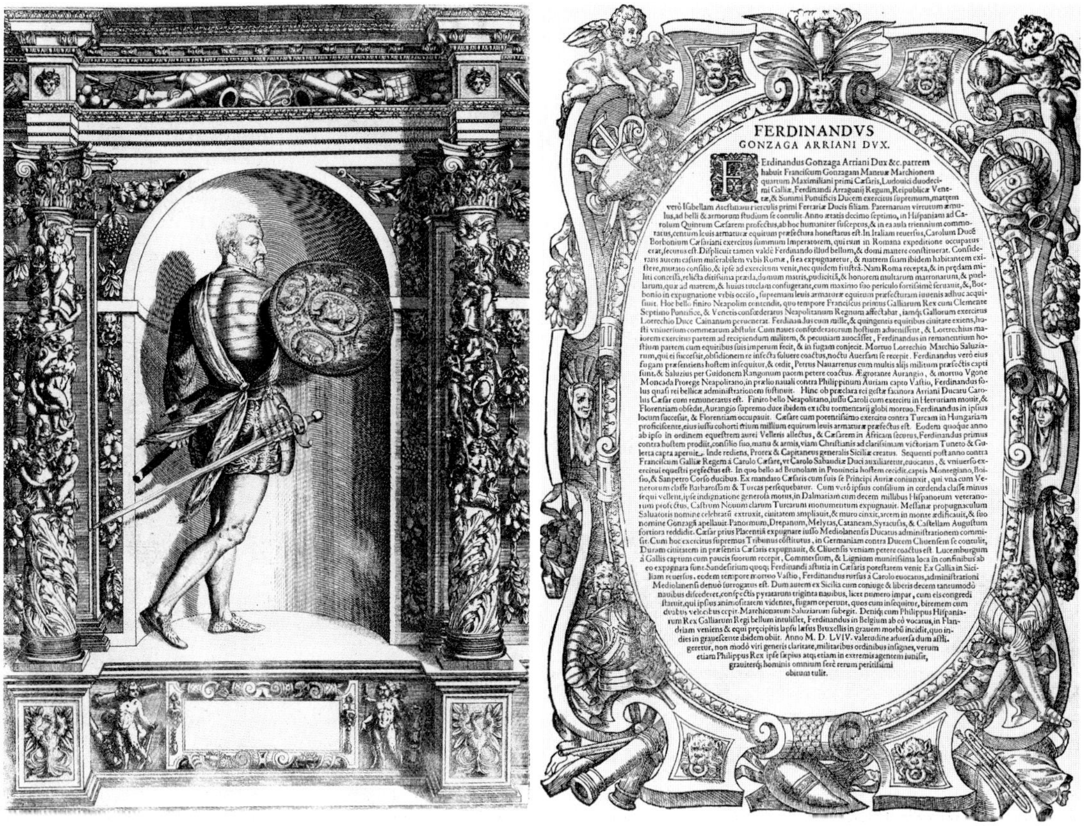

Fig. 14 Domenicus Custos, *The Ambras "Rüstkammer" Portrait of "Ferdiandus Gonzaga Arriani Dux.,"* engraving. From Schrenck von Nozing, *Augustissimorum imperatorum (. . .)*, 1601.

1537

Birth of Francesco (d. 1566), who was named cardinal in 1561.

3 OCTOBER 1539

Ferrante acquired Guastalla (dall'Acqua, 1985, 35ff.). On 23 August 1549 Giunti began the fortification of the city.

8 OCTOBER 1539

Ferrante removed from Rome to Sicily "unam tabulam marmoream depictam, cum diversis ornamentis in sex capsis existentibus" (Jestaz, 1963, 420, 451, no. 5). He was later named by H. Golzius as one of the collectors of antique coins known to him in Brussels (*Julius Caesar sive historiae imperatorum Cesarumque romanorum [. . .]*, Bruges, 1563, unpaginated listing).

28 SEPTEMBER 1540

Birth of GianVincenzo (d. 1591), who was named cardinal in 1578.

APRIL 1541

In a letter to Leone Leoni, Aretino spoke of the "tazza d'oro che fate al gran Ferrante Gonzaga" (D'Arco, 1857–59, II, 131; Aretino, 1957, II, 159–60).

1541

Participated with Charles V in the ill-fated "impresa di Algeri."

24 FEBRUARY 1542 (–1546)

On 24 February 1542 (ASPr, ES, b. 19), Giulio Romano wrote regarding "il desegno del boccale et bacino." In a letter of 21 October 1545 he referred to the "caldarino d'argento," while three letters dated 6 February, 23 June, and 15 September 1546 dealt with work in progress by Ettore Donati in working from his designs, and with the "candelieri" and the "candeliere e un caldarino da altare" (*Giulio Romano,* 1992, II, 947, 1035, 1144, 1150, 1162–63). A number of his designs survive in Chatsworth and Oxford (*London 1981,* 195–97, and *Mantua 1989,* 461–63). When he met Francis I, having negotiated the Treaty of Crepy (1544), Ferrante was presented with "pretiosi vasi d'oro, et d'argento in gran quantità" (Gosellini, 1574, 39–40). Table service belonging to Ferrante, containing his arms as well as the collar of the Order of the Golden Fleece, is recorded in the 25 February 1575 inventory of silver owned by his son Cesare (ASPr, b. 5). This included "tazze," "coppe," "salere" (with the motto "Nec Spe, Nec Metu"), "tondi," "piatti," and "bacile."

1543
Was part of Charles V's entourage when he met Paul III at Busseto.

1544
In conjunction with Henry VIII, Ferrante negotiated the treaty of Crépy (18 September) with the representatives of Francis I after the recapture of Luxembourg and the siege of St. Dizier (north of Troyes).

Enrolled Roland de Lassus, who later became famous as the composer Orlando di Lasso, for his choir.

12 JANUARY 1545
Advised the Messina senate of Francis I's desire for copies of the Hannibal and Scipio statues (La Farina, 1840, 84–85; Guasti, 1881, 41).

19 JUNE 1546
Triumphal entry into Milan (where he replaced Alfonso d'Avalos as governor), an event celebrated in a booklet by Verità Landolfo. Domenico Giunti undertook a range of civic projects for Ferrante, but much of the work of refortifying the city (begun on 22 March 1549) and its surrounding territories was done under the direction of the "Capitano de l'Artiglieria Giovanni Maria Oligato ingegnero." In July 1546 Oligati was authorized to undertake a tour of inspection in Piedmont, while that August authorization was granted for work to continue at Pavia. In October, Oligati received funds for his trip to Cremona and Lodi, and the following month he submitted a detailed report on the state of the fortifications there and at Alessandria. "Mirabilmente piaciuta" were the words Philip II used to describe his reaction to what he saw in 1551 (Leydi, 1989, 19ff., 83–86). For work on the fortress at Piacenza, see Soldini, 1991, 11ff. A succinct statement of Ferrante's work on the fortifications is provided by Gosellini (1574, 59–59):

> Milano si può dire esser edificato di nuovo (. . .). Et se vi s'aggiunge il gran numero de le chiese, ò ristorate, ò nuovamente edificate, per la sollecita cura di Carlo Borromeo (. . .). Il Palagio ducale, stanza de'Governatori, amplio etiandio, et rinovo don Ferrando di sale, e stanze, et loggie magnifiche (. . .). Fortificò similmente, et di mura in gran parte, Pavia, Novara, Alessandria, et altre frontiere de lo Stato di Milano, et del Piemonte.

At the same time, Giunti saw to the construction of a suburban villa (Tarchi, 1953). Known from a seventeenth-century engraving, the surviving portion displays fragments of landscape frescoes created by the Flemish artists brought to Milan especially for this purpose (Borsieri, 1619, 59–60) as well as his special *impresa,* the compass surrounded by the motto "Nec Spe, Nec Metu" (Gosellini, 1574, 440). For the "Alias Devorat Una Mea[s]" *impresa,* see Praz in *London 1981,* 70.

31 JULY 1546
Compiled a "relatione c'havete a far a Sua Maestà delle cose di Sicilia" (Carreri, 1896).

1 NOVEMBER 1546
Date of the first of many communications from Leone Leoni (Ronchini, 1865, 23). In a letter to Pietro Aretino (1551, 267) of 6 November 1546 Ferrante advised: "ho letto il prologo della vostra horatia et nella parte che a me ne tocca vi ho conosciuto più cortese, che giudicioso; ma et della cortesia vi ringratio, et di coretto giudico mi godo."

26 JULY 1547
Letter to Giovio documenting Ferrante's visit to his museum in Como. On 22 July 1547 Giovio solicited his portrait from Domenico Giunti. In December of that year (and again on 19 October 1549), Giovio

praised Ferrante's villa Gualtiera (Simonetta), and he composed the text for the inscription for the entrance to the complex: "Ferdinandus Gonzaga a Carolo V Imp. Aug. Max. / Cisalpinae Galliae Praefectus / Quum ex Bellicis atque civilibus curis meritam / Non ignobilis ocii requiem quaereret / Nymphaeum Suburbani Secessus / Honestae voluptati dedicavit" (Fig. 95). In August 1551 Giovio sent a copy of the "libro delli Elogii per passatempo in questi fieri caldi" (Ferrero, 1956–, II, 92, 117, 145–47, 200, 254 n. 12).

10 SEPTEMBER 1547
Ferrante's role in the assassination of Pierluigi Farnese soured relations between the two families (Brown, 1985, 57 n. 5).

1 JANUARY 1549
Hosted a banquet for Philip II in Milan, at which time the *Fructus Belli* was displayed together with the *Aeneas* weavings (Documents 24 and 26). This was followed by the elaborate festivities staged on the occasion of the marriage of Ippolita Gonzaga to Fabrizio Colonna.

15 AUGUST 1549
Leone Leoni offered Ferrante casts from the models made for Francis I of Roman antiquities for the villa Gualtiera (Ronchini, 1865, 26–27).

8 SEPTEMBER 1549
Titian's letter (ASPr, ES, b. 19) dealt primarily with the pension he had been awarded by Charles V, but he accompanied his request for assistance with "il ritratto dello Imperatore."

2 MAY 1550
Ferrante's wife asks for works from Bernardino Campi, who was subsequently referred to as "famigliare" of the family by Ippolita (*Cremona 1985*, 154).

1552
Commissioned the *Puttini* tapestries (Document 32) and compiled a "relazione" for Charles V in defense of the ring of bastions begun under his administration three years earlier (Beltrami, 1897).

16 APRIL 1552
As executor of the estate of Luigi Alessandro Gonzaga (Lord of Castelgoffredo), Ferrante ordered the drawing up of a comprehensive inventory (GBM, 91/1).

1553
In his *Relatione* (Segarizzi, 1912–16, II, 61), Novelli observed that Ferrante "non ha fama di principe liberale come aveva il quondam signor marchesa Del Guasto, anzi d'esser ristretto nel spender e molto avido al guadagno." When required, however, Ferrante was willing to spend lavishly, as, for example, on his remarkable collection of figurative wall hangings. Nonetheless, the simple fact of the matter was that he was short of funds most of his life, so much so that he bequeathed to his heirs mainly debts. In 1535 (ASMn, b. 1904, c. 306), he lamented that the governorship of Benevento had cost him more than the income he derived, while in 1541 (ASMn, b. 1911: 10 June [Mozzarelli, 1985, 27 n. 28]), he confessed that "sono molti tempi ch'io non penso in altro che in levarmi di debiti et disimpegnar le cose mie di costì." For Ferrante's financial obligations to Tommaso de Marini see ASPr, b. 49. When in 1557 Ferrante offered to acquire tapestries (Document 36), he was reminded that Ercole was short of funds because the loan to his brother had not been repaid.

1554
Publication of *Il terzo libro delli madrigali a quattro voci*, which Hoste da Reggio published in honor of Ferrante. The first volume (1547) had been dedicated to Ercole. For Ferrante, Hoste created a cantorial group, training Orlando di Lasso, who served Ferrante in Milan, publishing his own *Il primo libro di Madrigali a cinque voci* the year after Ferrante left his post. The role that music played in Ferrante's life is further documented by the motet sent to him in 1547 by Nicolas Gombert, master of the Chapel of Charles V: "sachant que v.re noble esprit se delecte en la musique" (Fenlon, 1980, 32–33; *Milan 1977*, 171, 177).

MARCH 1554
Under a cloud of suspicion, Ferrante left Milan and traveled to Brussels. By imperial decree, dated 10 June 1555, he was absolved of any administrative mismanagement. By that date he had returned to

Italy. The theme of "invidia" over which Ferrante triumphed appears in the iconography of the Leoni medal and the life-size bronze statue.

CIRCA 1555–56

Commissioned a portrait medal from Leoni, the reverse of which showed Hercules overcoming envy (*Milan 1977,* 142). A letter of 13 June 1556 indicates that Leoni was also commissioned to create a monumental life-size statue similar to the one of Charles V. The commission, carried forward by Cesare Gonzaga (d. 1575), was brought to completion for his son Ferrante II in 1594, when it was set on a pedestal in Guastalla in the Piazza Maggiore, facing the Ducal Palace (Plon, 1887, 182ff., 393–94).

2 AUGUST 1555

At Philip II's request, Ferrante returned to the north and to active duty. The following year Ferrante was offered, but rejected, a commission from the Venetian Republic.

14 NOVEMBER 1556

Writing from Venice (ASPr, ES, b. 19: *Grandi Artisti,* 1990, 28), Antonio Pola referred to both the death of Pietro Aretino and to dealings with Titian, from whom he acquired certain unspecified paintings:

> Al gionger mio qui in Venetia, ho trovato che quel mascarone del Aretino ha reso l'anima al diavol, la qual morte credo non dispiacerà a nessuno, et in special a voi altri signori, perché non sentiranno più fastidio et gabella di quel pecorone, per il che non ho possuto così particularmente intender d'ove nacque la discortesia di Ticiano anchor, per quanto m'ha detto il Carnisecca il detto Ticiano si scusa sopra quella felice memoria, la qual gl'havea inviato a dir che Vostra Eccellenza havea domandato che si apparechiasse da desinar in casa sua et, vedendo che, passata l'hora, non compareva gl'officiali a far da mangiar, che lui tenne che Sua Eccellenza quel dì non havessi più a venir et con questo resoluto andò a far suoi negotii. Ma siase come si voglia, fra il sudetto Carnisecca et me penso che li avanzaremo un mezzo centenar de scudi in comprar quelli quadri che Sua Eccellenza desidera haver da questo huomo discortese.

15 NOVEMBER 1557

Participated with Emmanuel Philibert at the Battle of St. Quentin (10 August 1557). Shortly thereafter, his health seriously impaired, he returned to Brussels. Here, "in Brusselles, terra dil ducato di Brabantia, in casa di Monsignore di Javeche," Ferrante compiled his testament on 15 November 1557 (ASMn, b. 333. cc. 258ff.). He died the following day. Named as universal heir was his *primogenito,* Cesare, who was recommended to Philip II, whom he begged would provide him with an income of 5,000 scudi for five years so as to be able to repay debts owed to Tommaso de Marini. Without royal assistance Ferrante feared that his household would be reduced "ad extrema ruina et perditione" (see also Pilati, 1993, 337). As this was a "cedula" to an earlier, still-to-be-discovered testament, no reference was made to other matters, such as his final resting place.

Ferrante planned to be buried in Santa Maria delle Grazie, outside Mantua. He paid for the restoration of the choir and for the high altarpiece, the *Assumption of the Virgin* (Donesmondi, 1613–16, I, 183). Although the tombs were never realized, Ercole left instructions in his testament for burial chapels off the choir of the Duomo in Mantua, where both he and Ferrante were to be interred (Brown, 1991, 225–26). In the end both were placed in the sacristy of the Duomo (*London 1981,* 11), where Cardinal Sigismondo had been buried (*Mantua 1989,* 567).

1561

Giulio Gabrielli da Gubbio composed a "Laudatio Ferdinandi Gonzagae" (in *Plutarchi Libellus,* 41–83). His *Oratione funebre* appeared in 1568.

1563

Ulloa published his biography (ASPr, ES, b. 21 and GBM, b. 15, c. 29). Four years later, Giuseppe Betussi (ASPr, ES, b. 3) wrote for information to be incorporated in his study "delle cose illustri d'Italia." A biographical account accompanied the engraved portrait of Ferrante (see under Federico II: 9 November 1532) in the Schrenck von Nozing publication of 1601 (Fig. 14).

1574

Gosellini published his biography.

Index to the Major Sets of Figurative Tapestries

Thanks to the remarkable preservation of the chancery records of the Gonzaga court, it is possible to trace the movement the figurative tapestries of Federico II, Ercole, and Ferrante.

Gonzaga of Mantua

Federico II: d. 1540—5th Marquis and 1st Duke of Mantua (Document 9).

Ercole: d. 1563 (Documents 1, 3, 5–8, 11–17, 20–22, 25, 27–31, 36–43, 45–49, 51–52, 54, 57, 59–60, 62, 66–68, 74). His holdings were divided among the children of Federico II (Guglielmo and Cardinal Federico) and Ferrante (Cardinal Francesco). Guglielmo inherited the *Acts of the Apostles* and the *Puttini* (Documents 48 and 49). The remainder of the collection was divided between Cardinal Federico of the Mantuan branch of the family and Cardinal Francesco of the Guastalla line (Documents 51 and 52). Upon Federico's death in 1565, the estate (including the *Tobias,* the *Saul,* and the *Fortuna* sets) passed to Guglielmo and thus to the Mantuan branch. Upon Francesco's death in 1566, the estate (including the *David* set) passed to Cesare and thus to the Guastalla branch.

Francesco III: d. 1550—2d Duke.

Guglielmo: d. 1587—3rd Duke (Documents 56–58). Inherited Ercole's *Acts of the Apostles* and *Puttini* (Document 48) and obtained other tapestries from the estate of his brother Cardinal Federico (Document 51).

Ludovico: d. 1585—Duke of Nevers, Count of Rethel. Younger brother of Guglielmo, who founded the branch that became the dukes of Mantua with Carlo I (Document 66, Addenda B).

Vincenzo I: d. 1612—4th Duke (Documents 59–60, 62).

Francesco IV: d. 1612—5th Duke.

Ferdinando I: d. 1626—6th Duke (Document 66).

Vincenzo II: d. 1627—7th Duke (Document 67). With his death, the main line of the family became extinct.

Carlo I: d. 1637—8th Duke. The son of Ludovico, Duke of Nevers, and the first ruler of Mantua from this branch of the family.

Carlo II: d. 1665—9th Duke (Document 68).

Ferdinando Carlo: d. 1708—10th Duke (Documents 69–71, 73–75). With his death, the Nevers line of the family became extinct. Upon his marriage to Anna Isabella Gonzaga of Guastalla, the *Fructus Belli, Puttini,* and *Grotteschi* were moved to Mantua. In 1678 Ferdinando Carlo also assumed the title of 4th Duke of Guastalla.

Gonzaga of Guastalla

Ferrante: d. 1557—Duke of Ariano, Prince of Molfetta, and Lord of Guastalla (Documents 2, 4, 10, 18–19, 24, 26, 32–33, 36, 44, 53, 55, 58, 61, 63–65, 69–78).

Cesare: d. 1575—Duke of Ariano, Prince of Molfetta, and Lord of Guastalla. Inherited Ferrante's tapestries as well as a portion of Ercole's collection from the estate his brother Cardinal Francesco (Document 52).

Ferrante II: d. 1630—1st Duke of Guastalla (Documents 58, 61, 63–65).

Cesare II: d. 1632—2d Duke.

Ferrante III: d. 1678—3d Duke (Documents 69 and 70). Three sets of tapestries were part of Anna Isabella's dowry when she married Ferdinando Carlo Gonzaga (*Fructus Belli, Puttini,* and *Grotteschi*). Ferrante III's estate was divided between Anna Isabella and her sister, the Duchess of Guastalla (wife of Vincenzo), who was given the *Cephalus and Procris, Aeneas,* and *Moses* sets.

Ferdinando Carlo: d. 1709—10th Duke of Mantua and 4th Duke of Guastalla (Documents 69–71, 73–75).

Vincenzo: d. 1714—5th Duke.

Antonio Ferdinando: d. 1729—6th Duke.

Giuseppe: d. 1746—7th Duke (Document 76). With his death, the Guastalla line of the family became extinct.

The listing at right takes into account both the tapestry sets owned by or inherited from Federico II, Ercole, and Ferrante and their heirs as well as the sets that belonged to other members of the Gonzaga of Mantua and Guastalla. This is the case because the later inventories do not distinguish between what was inherited from Federico II, Ercole, and Ferrante and what derived from other sources.

Reference is not made to armorial and *verdure* hangings or of those merely called "tapezzarie di Fiandra." Such imprecise designations make it difficult to trace these sets from document to document. Given the lack of clarity of the designation, no separate listing is provided for the ten-piece set, the "apparamento di tapezaria con oro et argento et setta a figura delli Acitoni [?]," recorded only in the 1627 inventory (Document 67, no. 22). Entries are provided for the following sets:

Achilles - Gonzaga of Mantua
Acts of the Apostles - Ercole
Adam, l'historia de - Gonzaga of Mantua
Aeneas - Ferrante
Alberi - Gonzaga of Mantua
Alexander the Great - Gonzaga of Mantua
Alexander the Great - offered to Ercole
Bois de Soignes - Ferrante
Boschelli - Ferrante
Cephalus and Procris - Ferrante
Caccia - Gonzaga of Mantua
Cesare, congiura fatto contra - Gonzaga of Mantua
Cyrus - Gonzaga of Mantua
David - Ercole
Diana and Niobe - Gonzaga of Mantua
Dido (and Aeneas?) - Francesco Gonzaga of Guastalla
Donne Francese - Gonzaga of Guastalla
Elijah - Gonzaga of Mantua
Fabrica - Gonzaga of Guastalla
Filomenia, spalera a figuri de - Federico II
Fortuna condotta da quatro Aquile - Ercole
Fortuna - Gonzaga of Mantua
Fructus Belli - Ferrante
Giardin d'amore - Gonzaga of Mantua
Gideon - Gonzaga of Mantua
Grottesche altre volte nominato Astrologia - Gonzaga of Mantua
Grotteschi - Gonzaga of Guastalla
Hannibal - offered to Ercole
Hercules - Gonzaga of Mantua
Isach et Jacob, historia d' - Gonzaga of Guastalla
Joseph - Ercole
Joseph - Gonzaga of Mantua
Libro di Re - Gonzaga of Guastalla
Moses - Ercole
Moses - Ferrante
Moses - Gonzaga of Mantua
Phaeton - Gonzaga of Mantua
Philomela - see *Filomenia*
Puttini - Ercole
Puttini - Federico II
Puttini - Ferrante
Saul - Ercole
Spozalizio - see *Cephalus and Procris*
Susanna - Gonzaga of Mantua
Tiberius - Gonzaga of Mantua
Tobias - Ercole
Tobia nuovi - Gonzaga of Mantua
Tobia vecchi - Ercole
Trionfo della Fede - Gonzaga of Guastalla
Troy - Ercole
Troy - Gonzaga of Mantua

Achilles

Gonzaga of Mantua

This eight-piece set is first documented in the 1668 inventory (Document 68, no. 8). It was attributed to Rubens in the 1709 listing (Document 74, no. 7).

The last reference to a full set, one woven with gold thread by Daniel Eggermans, is found in the 1852 records of the estate of King Louis-Philippe. Four of these panels are now in the castle of Vila Viçosa (Portugal).[1] None of the some twenty-five sets woven before 1668 survives intact.[2] The original sketches and cartoons were purchased in 1653 from Rubens's brother-in-law, Pierre Fourment, by the Brussels workshop of Gerard van der Strecken and Jan van Leefdael. It is possible that this shop wove the Gonzaga set sometime between the 1665 inventory (in which it is not mentioned) and the 1668 inventory (in which it is listed).[3] Most of the recorded sets were sold by Antwerp dealers, who exported them to Spain. In October 1657, the Antwerp dealer Louis Malo sent a set of eight to Venice, perhaps the very one acquired by the Gonzaga.[4] By 1665 two sets are documented in the collection of the Dukes of Savoy.[5]

1. Haverkamp-Begemann, 1975, 81.
2. Ibid., 82–88.
3. Duverger, 1971, 158.
4. Haverkamp-Begemann, 1975, 84.
5. Ibid., 86–87.

Acts of the Apostles

Ercole

COLOR PLATE I AND FIGS. 28–43

See also Catalogue 2

This nine-piece set, measuring 7 *ale* in height, is first mentioned in the 1557 testament and then in the 1563 inventory (Documents 37 and 49, no. 2). It was bequeathed to Duke Guglielmo "per honorare la chiesa di Santa Barbara," the palatine church of the Ducal Palace (Document 48). Originally, however, the set had been left to the Duomo (Document 37). The *terminus ante quem* for the commission is usually set in 1559 on the basis of a payment for Ercole's arms (Document 40). As he already owned a set, it is clear that Ercole would not have acted on Cardinal Granvelle's suggestion in 1562 (Document 46). Donated by Guglielmo to the palatine church of Santa Barbara in 1569 (Document 54), the *Acts* was used to embellish the facade of the Mantua Cathedral in 1587 on the occasion of the coronation of Duke Vincenzo (Document 62).

Adam, l'historia de

Gonzaga of Mantua

This nine-piece set "fodrato di tella turchini con oro et seta," measuring 5 1/3 *braccia* in height and a total 66 3/4 *braccia* in width, is recorded only in the 1614 inventory (Document 66, no. 5).

On 20 April 1591 the widow of Erik of Brunswick wrote to Duke Vincenzo Gonzaga to dispute his claims to "una stanza di tapezzaria di Fiandra." Vincenzo held these tapestries to ensure the success of his claims against Erik's estate for the return of the money his father, Guglielmo, had allocated for the purchase of the Vendramin-Calergi palace. Included among the tapestries, according to the 1588 inventory was "pezzi nove di tapezzaria de Fiandra di seta et oro con sopra l'historia de Adam." The 1587 inventory indicates that silver threads were also employed and that the cycle opened with "la Creatione d'Adamo nel Paradiso terrestro" and concluded with "la cessatione del diluvio, col sacrifico che fece Noè a Dio" (Document 66, Addenda E). As Vincenzo apparently did not keep the Brunswick set, the Gonzaga tapestries may have been similar, but not identical, to the Brunswick series. The Gonzaga *Adam* is first recorded in 1614. Thus it was most likely acquired by Vincenzo. The Brunswick and Gonzaga sets may have looked like the surviving panels from the *Genesis* set woven for Duke Cosimo I de' Medici by 1551[1] and the Wawel Castle series completed by 1548.[2]

1. Adelson, 1983, 915 n. 47; Meoni, 1989.
2. Szablowski, 1972, 457–59.

Aeneas

Ferrante

Documented as a new acquisition in 1549 (Document 26), the *Aeneas* is described as a fourteen-panel set measuring a total of 6 *ale* in height and 100 *ale* in length. The *Aeneas* is first recorded in the 1590 inventory (Document 65, no. 14) and then in the 1678 inventory (Document 71, no. 7; the notary original refers to "una portiera"), and finally in the 1749 "Rinoncia" (Document 76, nos. 8 and 13–14), by the terms of which the Duke of Modena was given title to the Guastalla tapestries. One panel from the set is recorded in the 1771 inventory of the possessions of the Duke of Modena (Document 78).

Although no fourteen-piece *Aeneas* survives from the sixteenth century, connections exist between Ferrante's lost series and some existing tapestries. It is likely that Ferrante acquired an extended reedition of the set that was woven in Flanders between 1531 and 1536 for Andrea Doria after designs by Perino del Vaga. From this lost set of six weavings, two autographed drawings by Perino for the *Banquet of Dido and Aeneas* were recently related to two Brussels tapestries, now in Vienna and Madrid.[1] The Madrid panel (Fig. 15) belongs to a set of seven tapestries, woven in Brussels in the 1540s or later, probably in the workshop of Cornelis de Ronde.[2] Another group of five tapestries is preserved in the Fondazione Whitaker in Palermo, four of which have subjects identical to the Madrid series.[3] At least four other subjects, now remaining as isolated pieces from scattered sets, can be added to the eight subjects in Madrid and Palermo, thus enlarging to twelve the original cycle of six *Doria* tapestries.[4] Previously unnoticed is the beautiful *Meeting of Aeneas and Dido,* now in the Castello Sforzesco in Milan, and *Dido Preparing Herself for Suicide,* now in the Whitaker Foundation in Palermo (Villa Malfitano), the last one belonging to a group of five pieces in this collection.

All of these tapestries, as well as the *Banquet* in Vienna (Museum für Angewandte Kunst), have the same borders and originally formed the same set.[5] Thus, it is not impossible that the series actually consisted of fourteen panels. It is not possible, however, to determine which set was actually owned by Ferrante. The tapestry

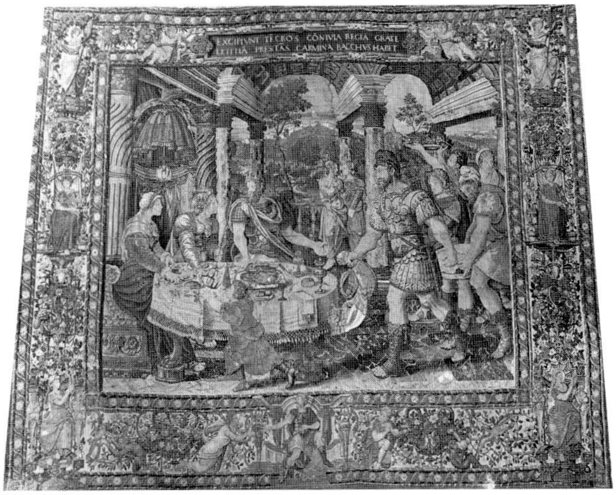

Fig. 15 *The Banquet of Aeneas and Dido,* Brussels, workshop of Cornelis de Ronde after a design by Perino del Vaga, c. 1540. Madrid, Patrimonio Nacional.

of *Aeneas Killing the Stag,* now in the Victoria and Albert Museum in London, is, however, of the same dimensions as Ferrante's set, and this is also the case both with the *Aeneas before Dido* (sold at the Hôtel Drouot in Paris as lot 176 on 10 March 1978 and as lot 821 by Sotheby's Monaco on 23 February 1986) and *Aeneas and Dido as Lovers* (private collection). The design of these contemporary but later editions of Perino's *Aeneas* set from around 1530 was strongly influenced by details and figures borrowed by the Brussels cartoon designs from the early editions of Giulio Romano's *Scipio* tapestries.[6] It may be that these modifications were introduced at the request of Ferrante Gonzaga or another Italian customer, as similar sets can be traced in the collection of the Este in Modena and the Trivulzio in Milan. Ferrante's set was six *ale* in height. Accordingly, a fragment of this group might be found in the *Aeneas and Achates Hunting,* now in the Victoria and Albert Museum in London, and among related pieces.[7]

1. Davidson, 1990, 41–43; for the Madrid series 116, see Junquera, 1986, 1, 325–32.
2. Delmarcel and Dumortier, 1986, 54–56.
3. Forti Grazzini, 1993, 99–146; Scuderi, 1993.
4. Hefford, 1986, 80–81.
5. Compare Davidson, 1990, 43, fig. 7, and Forti Grazzini, 1984, 88, fig. 22.
6. Forti Grazzini, 1993, 137.
7. Hefford, 1986, 83–84, and independently by Delmarcel and Dumortier, 1986, 54.

Alberi
Gonzaga of Mantua

This seven-piece set, measuring 5 *braccia* in height and 51 *braccia* in width, is first mentioned in 1584 (Document 60, no. 15). In the 1627 inventory (Document 67, no. 19), it is described as "li Alberi a figure, boscaglie et catie" and its height is given as $5\frac{2}{3}$ *braccia* (see also Document 66, no. 29).

If it was manufactured in Brussels, the Gonzaga set may have resembled the six hunting scenes with the arms of the Vidoni family (Rome, Palazzo Venezia: circa 1575–1600).[1]

1 Versyp, 1971.

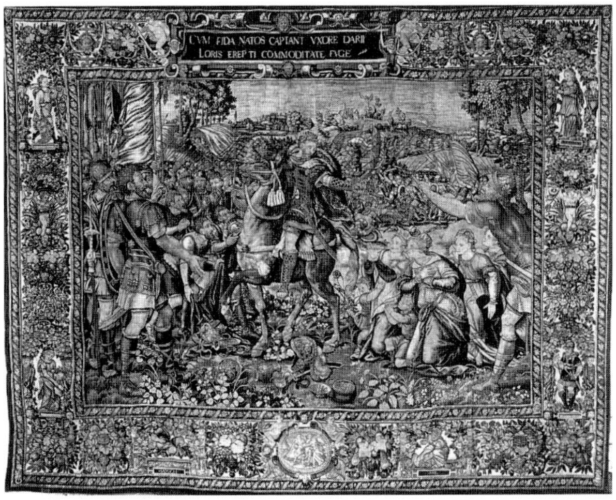

Fig. 16 *Alexander and the Family of Darius,* Brussels, workshop of Cornelis de Ronde, c. 1560. Vienna, Kunsthistorisches Museum.

Alexander the Great
Gonzaga of Mantua

This thirteen-piece set, measuring $6\frac{1}{3}$ *braccia* in height and 92 *braccia* in length, is first recorded in the 1627 inventory (Document 67, no. 3). Nine pieces, described as "usato," are recorded in the 1665 inventory and then in the 1668 listing (Document 68, nos. 5 and 10).

The dimensions of some 3.50 meters in height and a total width of 51.50 meters suggest a comparison between the lost Gonzaga set and the *Alexander* weavings signed by Jan Raes and Jacob Geubels.[1] It was only after 1627 that Jacob Jordaens designed the celebrated version, editions of which belonged to Cosimo II de' Medici (after 1658) and Cardinal Flavio Chigi (before 1668).[2]

1. Böttiger, 1928, 44–46.
2. Nelson, 1983, 205–7.

Alexander the Great
Offered to Ercole

Writing in January 1562, Cardinal Granvelle provided an evaluation of the merits, as well as the failings, of a set he had seen depicting "la historia d'Alessandro Magno" (Document 46). In view of his generally negative appraisal ("che, come dico, non mi contenta"), as well as his preference for the *Acts of the Apostles,* Ercole would not have been interested in acquiring the *Alexander* set.

If Granvelle referred to the Brabant "ell" used by the Brussels tapestry weavers, then the *Alexander* set fulfilled Ercole's requirements for a maximum height of 5 *ale* or *elles,* that is, circa 3.48 meters. The nine pieces by Cornelis de Ronde (d. 1569), now in Vienna (Fig. 16),[1] or the various sets made by Frans Geubels (active c. 1546–85), one of which is in Boston,[2] are of similar dimensions. The Vienna series, filled with figures and with elaborate floral borders, corresponds closely to Granvelle's appraisal of the set he had recommended to Ercole.

1. Delmarcel and Dumortier, 1986, 55–57.
2. Duverger, 1969, 157.

Bois de Soignes
Ferrante

Writing on 16 July 1571 to Cardinal Granvelle, Viron refers to Ferrante's Ovidian set in the bois de Soignes (Document 55). The series measured 240 "aulnes" and contained figures "une aulne" in height.

Located near Brussels, the Soignes forest, subsequently owned by Charles V, was originally the property of the Dukes of Brabant. Ferrante's tapestries and their iconography point to direct links with the court, as was the case with the famous *Hunts of the Emperor Maximilian* set, now in the Louvre. Evidently of great importance, the *Soignes Metamorphoses* remains an enigmatic set, for it is neither described nor catalogued in the records of the Gonzaga family. If recorded anywhere in the documents, it may be identified with the "Boschellii, peci numero 11" that was given as collateral for the repayment of a loan in 1567 (Document 53). Alternatively, it might be identified with the ten-piece set of the *Terra de Fiandra,* recorded in the 1590 inventory (Document 65, no. 7).

A *Metamorphoses,* based on Ovid's stories, including the story of Orpheus, had been woven in Brussels in the second quarter of the sixteenth century, thus at the time when Ferrante presumably ordered his set. Prior to 1542, Francis I acquired a Brussels "espallière" of between 2.20 and 6.60 meters, which included the scene of Orpheus taming the animals with his music.[1] A *Metamorphoses,* combined with the *Aeneid,* was included in the thirty-piece set made for Cardinal Erard de la Marck between 1532 and 1538.[2]

1. Schneebalg, 1971, 290, no. 284.
2. Steppe and Delmarcel, 1974, 44.

Boschellii

Ferrante

Together with the *Fructus Belli,* the *Puttini,* and the *Cephalus and Procris,* Cesare Gonzaga pledged an eleven-piece set called the *Boschellii* in 1567 (Document 53). Like the others, so too the *Boschellii* appears to have been owned by Ferrante, although nothing relevant is found in the 1590 inventory (Document 65). If it is mentioned anywhere in the 1678 inventory (Document 71, no. 3), it is with respect to the *Grotteschi,* which, however, is listed as consisting of twelve pieces.

The designation "Boschellii" may have been another way of referring to the *Soignes Metamorphoses* (see above). If this is not the case, then one must imagine a large set with woods and landscapes. Such sets, containing forest landscapes and wild animals, woven in Brussels around 1550, survive in the Wawel Castle in Kraków.[1]

1. Szablowski, 1972, 191–286.

Cephalus and Procris

Ferrante

FIGS. 21–27

See also Catalogue 1

The notary copy of the 1678 Guastalla inventory clarified the meaning of the term "Spozadici" through the addition of the phrase "di Cefalo e Procre." First recorded in 1567 (Document 53), the "Spozadici," also called the "Sponsalitio," is described as a six-piece set measuring 33 *braccia* or 165 *ale.* The 1590 inventory (Document 65, no. 11) described the set as being 5 *ale* in height and its total length (in "braccia di Guastalla) was given as 30.5 × 65.5 = 20.89 meters. The six pieces in the Vatican measure 21.78 meters in length, a figure comparable with this. According to the 1678 inventory (Document 71, no. 8), its value was said to be 5,250 scudi. This value is far less than the *Fructus Belli* and the *Puttini,* which, together with the "Spozadici," had been pledged as collateral back in 1567. In the 1749 "Rinoncia" (Document 76, no. 9), the *Spozalizio* is valued at 11,250 lire.

Caccia

Gonzaga of Mantua

Recorded only in the 1614 inventory (Document 66, no. h), this two-piece set of "spalliere" depicted armed men and ladies with hunting dogs.

Cesare, congiura fatto contra

Gonzaga of Mantua

This set measures 5 1/3 *braccia* in height and 36 1/6 *braccia* in width (and woven with wool "con figure grande"). The 1614 inventory (Document 66, no. 10), however, does not record the total number of pieces.

The *Caesar* series may have been similar in shape and design to the four pieces of the *Triumph of Vespasian,* now in Santa Maria Maggiore in Bergamo.[1] Caesar's assassination is represented in an impressive Brussels tapestry, dated 1549, now in the Vatican Museum. Two contemporary pieces from the collection of the Grand Dukes of Tuscany are still in Florence. Fragments of a larger set, they were woven in Brussels.[2]

1. Dhanens, 1953, 337–39, pls. II–IV.
2. *Florence 1980*, 69–70, nos. 113, 114.

Cyrus

Gonzaga of Mantua

This twelve-piece set, measuring 80 *braccia* in width, is recorded in the 1614 inventory (Document 66, no. 21).

After 1550 several large *Cyrus* sets were woven in Brussels from Italianate designs, probably from cartoons by the workshop of Michiel Coxcie. The most famous of these, a set of ten panels, now in Madrid, was woven by Jan van Tieghem and Jan Ghieteels (?). They were owned by Philip II by 1560 and were displayed at the funeral of Francis II. The series was rewoven, with variants, on at least four occasions between 1550 and 1600. Isolated pieces survive in San Francisco and Saint Louis.[1]

1. Junquera, 1986, 1, 279; Bennett, 1976, 139; *Ghent 1987*, 84.

David

Ercole

This four-piece set, five *alle* in height and 26 *alle* in width (for a total of 130 "alle quadro"), is first recorded in the 1563 inventory (Document 49, no. 5). It next appears in the 1566 inventory (Document 52, no. 6), and then in the 1590 inventory (Document 65, no. 1).

Numerous sets of this subject were produced in Brussels, Oudenaarde, and Enghien during the first half of the sixteenth century. Ercole's weavings, probably bought between 1540 and 1560, were reduced in height. A similar-size set, 5 *ale* or 3.40 meters in height, was woven in Brussels around 1520, and of this, three pieces are preserved in Madrid.[1] A second set, signed by Pieter Coecke van Aelst, is now in the collection of the Princes Hohenzollern of Sigmaringen.[2] Similar dimensions are given for a fully Italianate set of six pieces woven around 1550 and now in Vienna.[3] The two *David* pieces in the Zaragoza Cathedral date from the 1520s, but they are more than 1 *ala* higher than the set owned by Ercole,[4] and the same is true for the *David* set woven during the 1530s in the style of the Orley workshop, now in Burgos Cathedral.[5]

1. Junquera, 1986, 1, 9, series 3.
2. Crick-Kuntziger, 1936, 193–97.
3. Birk, 1884, 183 (series LXIX); Standen, 1974, 220–21.
4. Torra de Arana, 1985, 199.
5. Beauvois-Faure, 1969, 29–39.

Diana and Niobe

Gonzaga of Mantua

This eight-piece set, woven with gold thread, is first mentioned in the 1665 inventory (Document 68, no. 6), in which it is described as "usato." Listed also in the 1668 inventory (Document 68, no. 9), it is recorded again in 1709 (Document 74, no. 4) with an attribution to Giulio Romano. A "historia di Diana" (in eight pieces, with a height of 5 Flemish *ells*) is recorded as part of the dowry brought to Mantua in 1609 by Margherita of Savoy (Document 66, Addenda J).

This subject became popular in tapestries through the Parisian workshop editions of the first half of the seventeenth century, which were based on models created by Toussaint Dubreuil. The Mantuan set, however, was presumably of Flemish manufacture, and as it was described as "usato" in 1665, it must have been acquired years earlier. A Flemish tapestry of about 1525–30, showing Niobe and her children attacking the worshipers of Latona, is in the Museum of Lamego (Portugal).[1] The composition cannot be assigned to Giulio Romano, to whom the Mantuan set is attributed. Indeed no designs by Giulio related to the Niobe iconography are now known, although drawings such as the Louvre *Birth of Apollo and Diana* (inv. 3500) for the Hampton Court painting might have been reused as models for tapestries.[2]

1. Mendonca, 1983, 100, and Castelnuovo, 1990, 100.
2. *Mantua 1989*, 427.

Dido (and Aeneas?)

Gonzaga of Guastalla

The single panel of the "historia di Didone," 4 *ale* high and 12 *ale* wide, is recorded in the 1566 (Document 52, no. 11) and 1590 (Document 65, no. 5) inventories. This panel has nothing to do with the Ferrante *Aeneas* (see above) series, although it was probably the remainder of an old series. If it was woven during Cardinal Francesco's lifetime, it might have resembled a lavish work such as the *Meeting of Dido and Aeneas* in the Castello Sforzesco in Milan.[1] Its precise connection to Ercole's six-piece "historia di Troia" (see below) remains uncertain.

1. Forti Grazzini, 1984, 22–25, no. 8; Forti Grazzini, 1993.

Donne Francese

Gonzaga of Guastalla

Listed only in the 1566 inventory of the holdings of Cardinal Francesco Gonzaga (Document 52, no. 9), in which it is described as consisting of two pieces, 5 *ale* in height and a total of 68 *ale* in width.

Elijah

Gonzaga of Mantua

This eight-piece set with "dui antiporti" is documented in the 1565 inventory (Document 51, no. 2). Presumably it was acquired by Margherita Paleologa, for it was recorded in the 1567 inventory (Document 66 Addenda B, no. 3).

Sets woven in Oudenaarde and Brussels in the sixteenth century were devoted to prophets and heroes of the Bible. The story of Elijah and Elisha is represented in a set of five Brussels tapestries in the Castello Sforzesco in Milan that dates to around 1550–60.[1] This series can be compared with the set in seven pieces, now lost, which was described in 1580 at the Este court in Ferrara. Perhaps Cardinal Federico's set was similar to the Este version. In his inventory reference is made to a *Saul* set (see below) inherited from Ercole. The Milan *Elijah Elisha* series bears the same unidentified weaver's monogram that appears on the contemporary *Saul* series (see below) now in Cuenca. The same Brussels workshop may have delivered such biblical series to both Ercole and Cardinal Federico. In 1564 Cardinal Bernardo Salviati purchased a three-piece set of this subject.[2]

1. Forti Grazzini, 1984, 21.
2. Hurtubise, 1980, 258.

Fabrica

Gonzaga of Guastalla

This eight-piece set is recorded only in the 1590 inventory (Document 65, no. 3).

Filomenia, spalera a figuri de

Federico II

The "spalera a figuri de Filomena" is first recorded in the 1541 inventory (Document 9). The "favola di Filomena" is subsequently listed in the 1614 inventory (Document 66, no. 1), where it is said to be 2¾ *braccia* in height and 11 *braccia* in width.

This dorsal tapestry, 149 by 616 cm, contained a story previously unknown in figurative weavings of the Renaissance. If "Filomenia" does not refer to the heroine of some late medieval romance, then she is Philomela, the sister of Procne, who was transformed into a nightingale. If this is indeed the case, then the *spalliera* of Filomena is yet another example of the Ovidian "poesie" represented in tapestry *(Metamorphoses,* VI, 447–670).

Fortuna condotta da quattro Aquile

Ercole

FIGS. 82–83

See also Catalogue 4

This twelve-piece set is described as the "spaliere della Fortuna condotta da quatro Aquile" in the 1563 inventory (Document 49, no. 10), but as "portiere" in the *Divisio,* measuring "alle 72" with six "portiere," one "soprauscio," and a "sopraportiera." After being listed in the 1565 inventory of Cardinal Federico (Document 51, no. 9), it next surfaces in 1584, when it was used to decorate one of the rooms in the Ducal Palace at the marriage of Vincenzo Gonzaga (Document 60, no. 8). On this occasion the total width of the twelve pieces was given as 39 *braccia* (circa 60 feet) and the height as 4¼. After being listed in the 1614 inventory (Document 66, no. 28), from which we learn that two of the pieces were "fodrati [di] tella turchina," the set is last recorded in the 1627 inventory (Document 67, no. 16).

According to Delmarcel and Brown, the "Fortuna condotta da quatro Aquile" can be related to the Teylers Museum *modello* by Giulio Romano, as well as to the variant drawing in the collection of Chatsworth House.[1] Forti Grazzini has suggested, however, that the format of both *modelli* better relates to overdoor designs, and he raises the possibility that these designs might be connected with the "sopraportere" or with the "portiere" for the *Puttini* (see below).[2] It seems more logical to maintain that the Haarlem drawing was a *modello* for the twelve *Fortuna* "spalliere." According to the 1584 and 1627 records, these "spalliere" measured 2.41 to 2.55 meters in height with a total width of 22.12 to 24.88 meters (for 1 "braccio di Mantova" = 56.7 or 63.80 cm), which means an average width of only 1.85 to 2.07 meters for each of the twelve. Their dimensions were therefore those of a vertical rectangle rather than a horizontal one, as is more traditional for *spalliera* tapestries. Perhaps the term "spalere" is actually used here in the sense of an armorial set such as the "reposteros" in Spain. The proportions of the Spanish "reposteros" were of 1:1.3 (average), while those of the Haarlem and Chatsworth drawings are 1:1.48.

1. Delmarcel and Brown, 1988, 112.
2. Forti Grazzini in *Mantua 1989*, 479.

Fortune

Gonzaga of Mantua

Measuring 5 *braccia* in height, this "spalera con una Fortuna in mezo" is mentioned only in the 1614 inventory (Document 66, no. 46bis).

Fructus Belli

Ferrante

PLATES I–II AND FIGS. 44–70

See also Catalogue 3

This set is discussed in Jehan Baudouyn's letter in 1547 (Document 19), and two years later the *Fructus Belli* is mentioned in a description of the rooms in which Philip II was received by Ferrante in Milan (Document 24). In 1561 Cesare Gonzaga excluded the *Fructus* from the sets available to Cardinal Simonetta in 1561 (Document 44), but they were included in the shipment to Venice in 1567, where they served as collateral against the repayment of a loan (Document 53). Here the eight-piece set was said to measure 7 *braccia* in height and 90 *braccia* in width (circa 139 feet). Loaned back to the family on the occasion of Ferrante II's marriage in 1587 (Document 61), the *Fructus* is listed in the 1590 inventory (Document 65, no. 12), at which time the height was given as "ale otto." Part of the marriage dowry of Anna Isabella (Documents 69 and 70), the tapestries in the *Fructus,* measuring 99 *braccia* by 7¼ "braccio di Guastalla," are listed individually in the 1678 inventory (Document 71, no. 1), in which their value was far in excess of any other similar set.

Attributed to Giulio Romano in the 1709 inventory (Document 74, no. 2), the tapestries are mentioned by Anna Isabella's relatives in Guastalla, who attempted to retrieve them after the death of Ferdinando Carlo (Document 75). Shortly, therefore, the *Fructus Belli* left Italy and was recorded in the 1747 inventory of Jean-Baptiste Colbert de Torcy (1665–1746), who had served as minister of foreign affairs to Louis XIV until 1715. The set remained in the Colbert de Torcy family until 1805, when the tapestries were divided among the children of Henriette Bibienne Colbert (1727–1805). The *Pay of the Soldiers* and the *Dinner of the Generals* went to Antoinette de la Porte de Riantz and were bought in 1991 by the Musée National de la Renaissance, Ecouen.[1] Four of the other six were dispersed during the nineteenth century. Three of them, the *Artillery,* the *Battlefield,* and *Reward and Punishment,* were purchased in May 1892 by the James family at the Leyland sale and are now part of the collection of the E. James Foundation,

West Dean, Chichester.[2] The *Triumphal Cortege* was acquired from a private collection in 1977 by the Royal Museums of Art and History in Brussels.

Unlike the cartoons for the *Puttini,* which were retained by Ferrante (see below), those for the *Fructus Belli* remained in Brussels. They are referred to in 1692 (Document 72), when their use was recommended to the Duke of Savoy.

1. Guilbault and Lambert in *Ecouen 1992*, 30–31.
2. Information provided by Peter Sargison, principal of West Dean College, from the handwritten records of William James.

Giardin d'Amore

Gonzaga of Mantua

Recorded only in the 1614 inventory (Document 66, no. g), it measured 6 by 7 *braccia*.

Gideon

Gonzaga of Mantua

This five-piece set is recorded first in Cardinal Federico's inventory (Document 51, no. 3) and subsequently in Margherita Paleologa's (Document 66, Addenda B, no. 4).

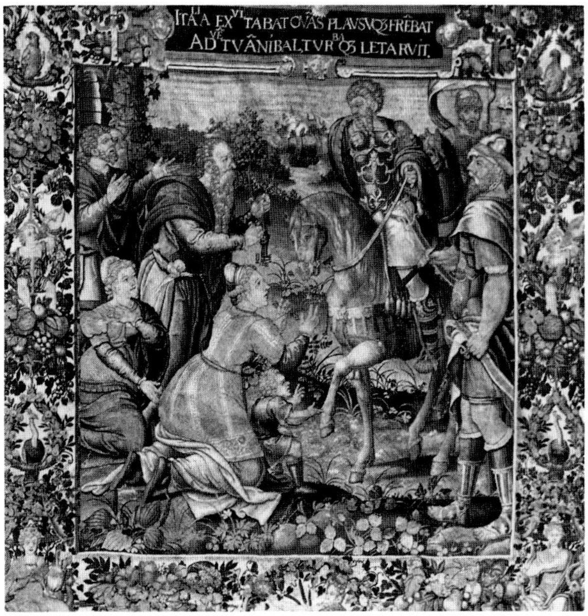

Fig. 17 *The Life of Hannibal,* Brussels, c. 1560. Zamora, Cathedral Museum.

As noted above under "Elijah," many biblical sets were produced by the Brussels workshops during the sixteenth century. Four *Gideon* tapestries, surrounded by a palm trunk border and datable to the 1530s, are now at Châteaudun. A set of seven subjects, woven by Frans Geubels (end of the sixteenth century), and designed in the style of Michiel Coxcie, is preserved in the Cathedral of Albarracin,[1] while an eleven-piece set, with similar borders but different subjects, is in Hardwick Hall. Furthermore, three pieces in the style of the Albarracin series found in Florentine collections come from the collection of Cosimo I de' Medici.[2]

1. Duverger, 1969, 120; Rabanos Faci, 1978, 32 and fig. 16.
2. *Florence 1980*, 68–69, nos. 109–11.

Grotteschi

Gonzaga of Guastalla

Recorded together with the *Fructus Belli* and the *Puttini* on the occasion of the arrival in Mantua of Anna Isabella (Document 70). In the 1678 inventory (Document 71, no. 3), the set is noted as having twelve pieces and is valued at 4,500 scudi. See also under "Boschellii."

Grotesche altre volte nominato Astrologia

Gonzaga of Mantua

Consisting of three pieces and measuring 16⅔ *braccia* in width, this set is recorded only in the 1614 inventory (Document 66, no. 17).

Hannibal

Offered to Ercole

Referred to by Cardinal Granvelle, it appears that Ercole passed up this option (Document 43).

The Cathedral of Zamora owns a five-piece Brussels *Hannibal* set (Fig. 17), dating to the 1560s, the dimensions of which (c. 3.50 meters) correspond to the five "ane" required by Ercole. These tapestries were designed in the style of Coxcie and were woven by a hitherto unidentified workshop that created other *Hannibal* tapestries.[1] To the same period, however, one must also relate

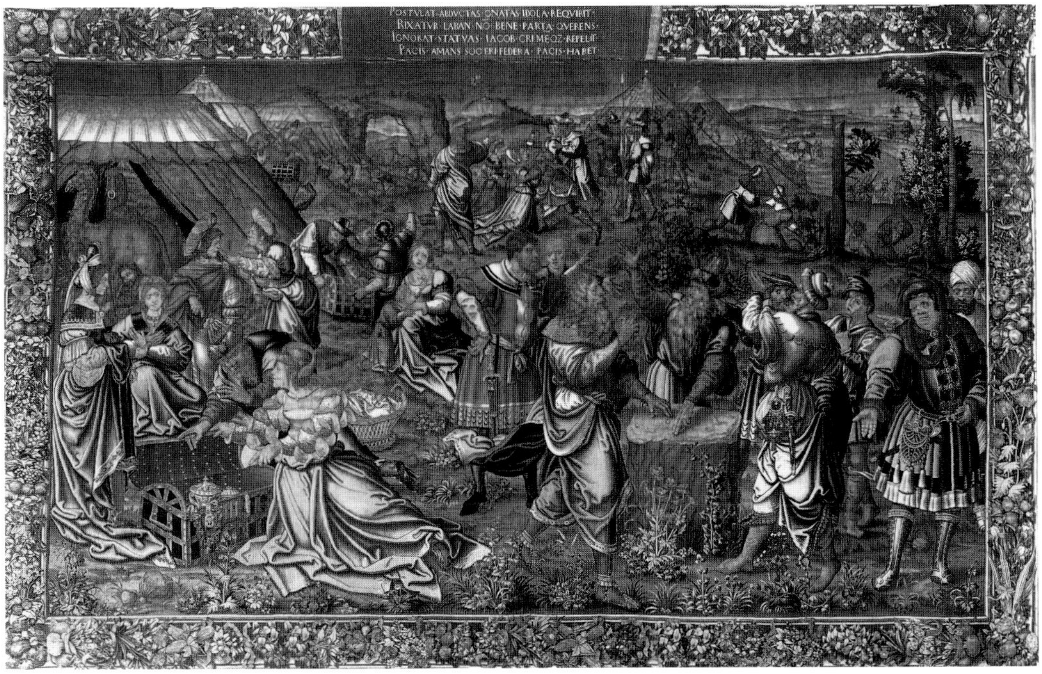

Fig. 18 *Reconciliation of Jacob and Laban,* Brussels, workshop of Willem de Kempeneer after designs by Bernard van Orley, c. 1535. Brussels, Royal Museums of Art and History.

the two *Hannibal* sets (now in Munich and Florence) produced in Brussels by Cornelis de Ronde. They are surrounded by the same allegorical borders that decorate Ercole's *Acts of the Apostles*.[2] The *Alexander* set (see above), also recommended to Ercole, was probably woven in the de Ronde workshop; Cardinal Granvelle may have had this shop in mind when he wrote about the *Hannibal*.

1. Asselberghs, 1964, 171–85; 1971.
2. Delmarcel and Dumortier, 1986, 56–61.

Hercules

Gonzaga of Mantua

The "boscaglia con forze d'Ercole," in seven pieces, measuring 4¼ *braccia* in height and 40½ *braccia* in width, is recorded first in 1614 (Document 66, no. 15) and then in the 1627 inventory (Document 67, no. 11).

Hercules series in a landscape or *verdure* setting are fairly common. The length of 4.25 *braccia* (some 2.41 to 2.71 meters) is rather small, and this suggests that the Gonzaga series was a *spalliera*. It is not known if the three "forze d'Hercule" "spaliere" (three "brazza" in height and varying in length from four to six to nine "brazza") listed in the 6 April 1552 inventory of Luigi Alessandro Gonzaga (Lord of Castelgoffredo, who was the son of Rodolfo [1461–1495]), was comparable to the "boscagli con fattiche d'Hercule."[1]

1. GBM, b. 91/1.

Isach et Jacob, historia d'

Gonzaga of Guastalla

This three-piece set is first recorded in the 1590 inventory (Document 65, no. 4). These panels may be identical to the three *Joseph* tapestries owned by Ercole and then by his nephew Cardinal Francesco, described above. In several known examples, the life of Joseph is indeed inserted at the end of that of his father, Jacob, such as in the last two weavings of the *Jacob* set by Willem de Kempeneer and Bernard van Orley in Brussels (Fig. 18).[1] Some remnants of this, or of the *Joseph* sets cited above, may have survived in Mantua until the nineteenth century. In 1879 Braghirolli referred to "due arazzi di grande dimensioni rappresentanti Labano che nella tenda di Giacobbe in Galaad cerca i proprii idoli nascosti da Rachele e Giuseppe venduto."[2] This description corresponds with panels 6 and 7 of the van Orley set now in Brussels,[3] and also with a fragmentary set in the Uffizi.

1. Crick-Kuntziger, 1956, 46–47, nos. 32 and 33.
2. Braghirolli, 1879, 99.
3. Crick-Kuntziger, 1956, plates 38 and 41.

Joseph
Ercole

This three-piece set, "et più una peza della medesima sorte con una dea," is listed in the 1563 inventory (Document 49, no. 6). According to the *Divisio,* three of the pieces were 5 *alle* in height and 18 in length, or 90 *alle* square; the fourth was 4½ *alle* in height and 3 in length, or 14 *alle* square. Ercole's set is recorded in Cardinal Francesco's inventory of 1566 (Document 52, no. 7), in which the measurement is given as 90 *ale.*

These weavings, doubtless of Joseph in Egypt, were frequently represented as symbols of chastity and of good government. The theme became famous from the twenty-piece set woven in Florence for Cosimo I de' Medici by Jan Rost and Nicolas Karcher between 1546 and 1553.[1] The three pieces listed in Ercole's inventory were probably woven in Flanders because many pieces of several Brussels sets from this period can still be traced back to the same area. The best example is the group of two Brussels *Joseph* pieces of a very Italianate design, datable to c. 1548–55, formerly in the Rospigliosi collection in Rome. One of these, depicting *Joseph Ruler of Egypt,* is now in the Minneapolis Institute of Art.[2] Other examples are the three *Joseph* tapestries (circa 1530–40) with floral borders in a private collection in Pau (France), two weavings with a palm tree border from the same period, sold at Christie's (London: 8 December 1988, nos. 222 and 223), and an impressive *Sons of Jacob Meeting Joseph,* which was woven by Frans Geubels and is now in the Dayton Art Institute.[3]

1. Adelson in *Florence 1980,* 50–60.
2. Adelson, 1994, 122–30, no. 11.
3. For another *Joseph* weaving by Geubels, with a different border, see Duverger, 1969, 115.

Joseph
Gonzaga of Mantua

This eight-piece set, with two "antiporti," is recorded only in the 1566 inventory of Cardinal Federico (Document 51, no. 1).

Libro di Re
Gonzaga of Guastalla

This ten-piece set, 5 *ale* in height and 310 *ale* in width, is first recorded in the 1566 inventory of the collection of Cardinal Francesco (Document 52, no. 8). Five of the pieces are listed in the 1590 inventory (Document 65, no. 2).

Moses
Ercole

The account books of Ercole for 1541–42 (Document 12) specify that Nicolas Karcher was paid for "quatro portiere" as well as for "un quadro de tappezaria dell'istoria de Moisè." It is not known if the *portiere* were related to this *quadro* or whether the commission was limited to a single panel or was part of a larger suite.

The designation "quadro de tappezaria" points to small pieces, objects that could be framed and thus used as woven paintings. Ercole owned a small number of such woven pictures (Document 49), including a "quadro di seta, oro et argento di Moisè nel deserto," which, according to the *Divisio,* measured "alle 16 per quadro." This comes close to the "alle de Fiandra 17 quadrato" recorded in the payment to Karcher (Document 12). Did Ercole order such a set as a sample for a larger project? Was the larger project the Guglielmo *Moses* mentioned below?[1] Perhaps not, since these tapestries, measuring 17 Flemish *ells,* are much larger.

1. Pecorari, 1991, 418.

Moses

Ferrante

PLATES IX–X AND FIGS. 98–114

See also Catalogue 6

Not recorded until 1590 (Document 65, no. 15), the *Moses* was described as a "paramento raro" in the 1679 inventory (Document 71, no. 5), and it is last recorded in the 1749 listing, according to which the title to the Guastalla tapestries was vested in the Duke of Modena (Document 76, nos. 1, 2). Only two pieces are recorded in the 1749 inventory, however, in which reference is also made to "altri due piccioli pezzi d'arazzi per soprausci." These are part of the "portiere numero 4" recorded in the notary copy of the Guastalla inventory. According to the 1678 inventory, the set consisted of twelve panels, 79¼ "braccia di Guastalla" in length and 5⅓ "braccia di Guastalla" in height. In the 1590 inventory the height alone was given as "ale cinque." Minus the overdoors, the series survives intact at Châteaudun.

Moses

Gonzaga of Mantua

FIGS 115–122

See also Catalogue 7

In 1568 an agent of Duke Guglielmo referred to the possibility of repurchasing from Cardinal Carlo Borromeo "quelle belle tapezzarie che l'Illustrissimo et Eccellentisimo signor Duca nostro gli mandò a donare" (Document 66, Addenda C). The "tapezzarie" can be securely identified with the *Moses* series in the Museo del Duomo, which bears the arms of Duke Guglielmo.

Until a fire in 1906 destroyed three of the six tapestries, the *Moses* series survived intact in the Museo del Duomo, to which it had been bequeathed in 1569 by Carlo Borromeo. The tapestries bear the arms of Guglielmo Gonzaga and are believed to have been woven by Nicolas Karcher between 1550 and 1555—in short, at a time when Mantua was ruled in Guglielmo's name by Ercole Gonzaga. If this set was actually commissioned by Ercole, then his letter to Karcher of 1551 (Document 30) may well refer to this.

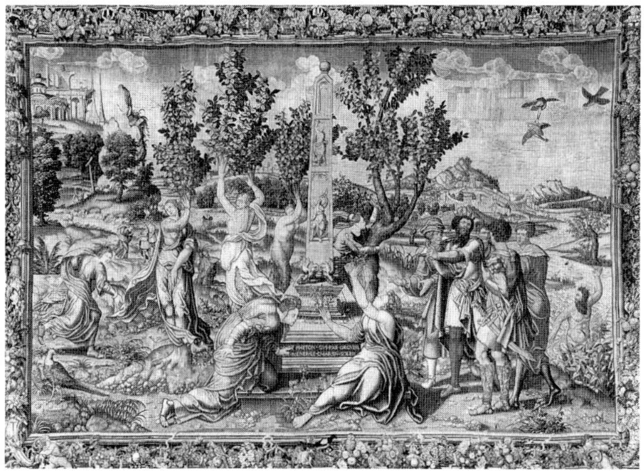

Fig. 19 *The Tomb of Phaeton,* Brussels, c. 1535. Ecouen, Musée National de la Renaissance.

Phaeton

Gonzaga of Mantua

This six-piece set was described as "usate," and therefore already old, in the 1665 inventory (Document 68, no. 4). Listed in the 1668 inventory (Document 68, no. 7), it is described in 1709 (Document 74, no. 6) as "grandi" and having been designed, "senza oro," by Giulio Romano.

A set already worn by 1665 and subsequently attributed to Giulio Romano clearly refers to Italianate weavings. Indeed, at least four pieces of a lavish Brussels series (Fig. 19), woven around 1530–40, once belonged to the Toperczer collection.[1] Three of them, namely, the *Departure of Phaeton,* the *Fall of Phaeton,* and the *Metamorphosis of the Heliads* were purchased in 1994 by the Musée de la Renaissance in Ecouen. The cartoons for this set were adapted and rewoven in Brussels with Baroque borders by Provost and Andries van den Dries (Vienna, series LXXXVI), by Jan Raes (private collection, Palma de Mallorca), and by Jan Leyniers (Kansas City, Nelson-Atkins Museum of Art). The *Fall of Phaeton* from the Toperczer set was rewoven in Enghien after 1550 and is now in Munich.[2]

As with other mythological sets woven in Brussels during the second quarter of the sixteenth century (such as *Vertumnus and Pomona* and *Venus and Vulcan*), the original *Phaeton* series presents figures and landscapes in a design that is close to sketches by Giulio Romano and his shop, such as the *Death of Adonis,* the *Calydonian Boar Hunt, Cephalus and Procris,* and *Hylas and the Nymphs.*[3] Finally, it should be recalled that Cardinal Ippolito d'Este bought four *Phaeton* tapestries in Flanders before 1560, a set that he presented in 1565 to Cardinal Altemps.[4]

1. Crick-Kuntziger, 1951. The three Toperczer pieces were sold at Christie's in London on 2 June 1959 and the pieces reappeared there on 13 December 1979 (nos. 74 and 175) and 4 December 1980 (no. 152). A fourth piece was sold at Sotheby's in London on 4 November 1977 (no. 5).
2. Delmarcel, 1980, 64–65, no. 28.
3. Hartt, 1958, I, 22; II, fig. 475; *Mantua 1989*, 425.
4. Baratte, 1973, 119, 124; Forti Grazzini, 1982, 93, no. 135.

Philomela

Federico II

(See under "Filomenia, spalera a figuri de")

Puttini

Ercole

FIGS. 73–83

See also Catalogue 4

The *Puttini,* consisting of ten panels, two "sopraportere," and three "portiere," was bequeathed to the Duke of Mantua (Document 48) and is listed in the 1563 inventory (Document 49, no. 1). According to the *Divisio,* the *portere* contained Ercole's arms as well as "foglie di lauro di oro." Used in the decoration of the Ducal Palace in 1580 (Document 59), the series served in a similar capacity in 1584 (Document 60, no. 1). Writing on 12 January 1629 regarding the sale of the Gonzaga art treasures to Charles I, G. C. Zavarelli mentioned the possibility of purchasing "doi fornimenti de razzo, un de Putini" (Luzio, 1913, 159). Recorded in the 1614 inventory (Document 66, no. 3), the *Puttini* is subsequently listed in 1648 (Document 68, no. 1) and then again in 1709 (Document 74, no. 3). The surviving panels from this series are in Lisbon and Milan.

Puttini

Federico II

FIGS. 71–72

See also Catalogue 4

Although not recorded in the documents, one panel survives (Mentana [Rome], Zeri collection) from the set commissioned by him from Nicolas Karcher.

Puttini

Ferrante

PLATES III–VIII AND FIGS. 84–97

See also Catalogue 5

According to the 1679 inventory (Document 71, no. 2), each panel in this six-piece set measured 5 3/4 "braccia di Guastalla" by 39 1/6 *braccia* for a total width of 225 *braccia.* The *Puttini* is mentioned as not being available for loan to Cardinal Simonetta in 1561 (Document 44), and in 1567 it is listed as collateral against the repayment of a loan (Document 53). The cartoons for the *Puttini* were requested by Cardinal Granvelle in 1571 (Document 55), while the tapestries themselves were loaned back to Ferrante II in 1587 (Document 61). Three years later they are listed in the 1590 inventory (Document 65, no. 13); the six panels are also recorded in the 1678 inventory (Document 71, no. 2). Part of the dowry Anna Isabella brought with her to Mantua (Documents 69 and 70), the *Puttini* is listed among the items Ferdinando Carlo took with him to Venice in 1707 (Document 74, no. 1). Acquired after the death of Ferdinando Carlo by the Sagredo family, the series is referred to in a number of that family's documents (Document 77). In the 1749 inventory (Document 76, no. 5), mention is made of four small *Puttini* tapestries "che servono per soprausci." As these are not mentioned early, they may have nothing to do with Ferrante's set.

Lodi's letter of 1552 (Document 32) probably documents the commission. The entire set is preserved in the Marzotto collection.

Saul

Ercole

Together with the *Tobias* (see below), the *Saul* was displayed in 1547 on the occasion of the Cardinal of Trent's visit to Mantua (Document 22). Both may have been included among the Old Testament tapestries acquired by Bassano Cortese in 1542 (Document 15). A seven-piece set, 6 *ale* in height, it is recorded in the 1563 inventory (Document 49, no. 4). According to the *Divisio*, the set was 6 *ale* high and 53 *ale* long, "danno in tutto alle 318." Inherited by Cardinal Federico (Document 51, no. 7), the set passed into the possession of the Gonzaga of Mantua. It is mentioned for possible use for the decoration of the Ducal Palace in 1580 and again in 1584, when its total measurements are given as 6¼ *braccia* in height and 56 *braccia* in length (Documents 59 and 60, no. 13). It is last recorded in the 1614 inventory (Document 66, no. 26), at which time it was called "vecchio."

This set belongs to the same group of biblical tapestries owned by Ercole and/or his nephews: *David, Elijah, Gideon, Moses,* and *Tobias.* Having a height of 6 to 6½ Mantuan *braccia* (× 63.8 cm = 382 to 414 cm), the *Saul* weavings were probably from the cartoons that served for the set preserved in Cuenca Cathedral,[1] or from the partially preserved set of three in Munich.[2] The Cuenca set, comprising five of the original eight weavings, is designed in the style of followers of Bernard van Orley, such as the *Abraham* series (Vienna, Hampton Court, and Toledo) with scenes surrounded by large vegetable borders. Woven around 1550, the Cuenca set bears the marks of Frans Geubels (active c. 1540–85) and of the unidentified workshop whose sign also appears on the *Elijah* series now in Milan (see above), as well as on the *Hercules* series in Brussels.[3]

1. Junquera, 1973, 2–8.
2. Duverger, 1969, 134–141.
3. Crick-Kuntziger, 1956, plates 44–47.

Spozalizio

Ferrante (see under *Cephalus and Procris*)

Susanna

Gonzaga of Mantua

This seven-piece set, 5½ *braccia* high and 45 *braccia* in width, is first recorded in 1580 (Document 59), at which time it was deemed not large enough to cover the walls of the Camera dei Cani in the Corte Vecchia of the Ducal Palace. It was used to decorate the Camera delle Armi on the occasion of the wedding of Duke Vincenzo in 1584 (Document 60, no. 4). The full set is recorded in Casale in 1627 (Document 67, no. 23), but only one panel was recorded in the 1661 inventory (Document 68, no. 2).

Susanna and the Elders is a subject that had been variously represented in figurative weavings. Agnes Sorel (d. 1450) bequeathed a six-piece "histoire de la chaste Suzanne" to the church of Loches, and a set of five tapestries was owned by Anne de Bretagne before 1495. Prior to 1580, only two existing sets are known. Both of them were woven during the first quarter of the sixteenth century. They are the three pieces related to the Tournai workshop of Arnould Poissonnier, now in the Musée Marmottan in Paris[1] and an isolated Brussels weaving of the *Stoning of the Elders* (c. 1520), formerly at Heilbronner.[2] The Susanna story was, however, the subject of weavings made in minor centers toward the end of the century. In 1577 King Frederick II of Denmark ordered a five-piece *Susanna* set at Helsingor, where weavers from Brussels and Oudenaarde were active.[3] Finally, no fewer than three *Susanna* sets were produced in Oudenaarde between 1587 and 1622.[4] A *Susanna* tapestry is to be found today in the Oudenaarde museum.

1. Joubert, 1987, 159.
2. Goebel, 1928, II, pl. 378.
3. Goebel, 1934, II, 227.
4. Duverger and Versyp, 1951, 270.

Tiberius

Gonzaga of Mantua

This ten-piece set is recorded in 1584 (Document 60, no. 16), and it is mentioned again in the 1614 inventory (Document 66, no. 27). Presumably the set was inherited from Federico II, for in the 1541 inventory (Document

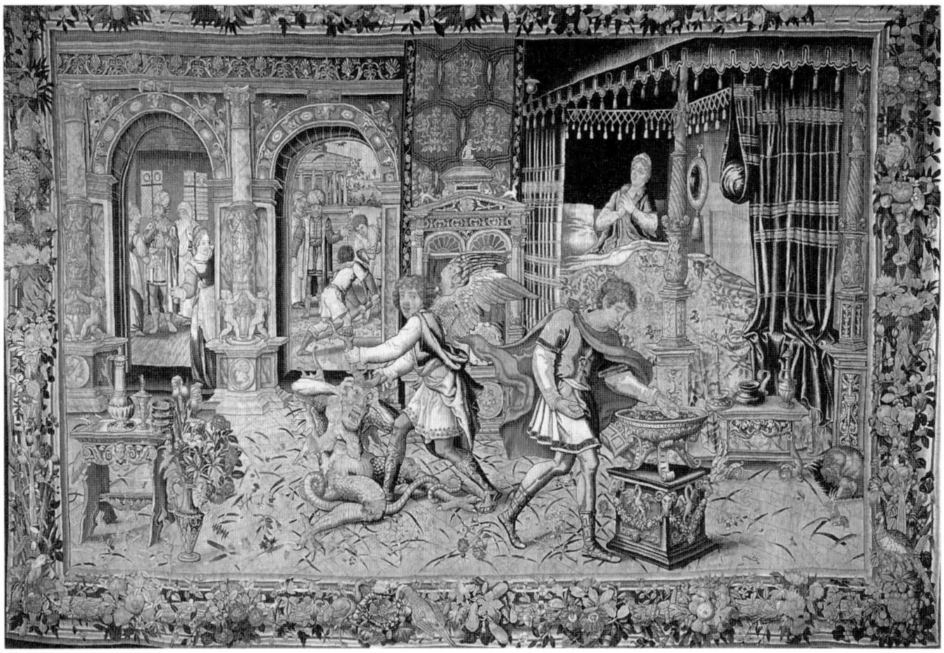

Fig. 20 *Tobias's Wedding Night,* Brussels, after a design by the Master of the Prodigal Son, c. 1540. Gaasbeek, Castle Museum.

9) mention is made of "dece pecii de tapezaria a figuri de Tiberio e Alexandro Magno." For additional comments, see under *Alexander* above.

Tobias

Ercole

This twelve-piece set, together with six *sopraportiere* with Ercole's coat of arms, is first recorded in 1547 (Document 22). It may have been purchased together with the *Saul* (see above) in 1542 (Document 15). It next appears in the 1563 inventory (Document 49, no. 3). According to the *Divisio,* the set measured 85 *alle* in length. It subsequently appears in the 1565 inventory of Cardinal Federico (Document 51, no. 6), before passing into the collection of the Duke of Mantua. The "Tobie, del Cardinale, pezzi numero 12" is recorded in 1584, at which time the measurements are given as 5 1/3 *braccia* (height) by 89 1/2 *braccia* (length) (Document 60, no. 2, and Document 66, no. 24). By 1584, however, the Gonzaga family owned two *Tobias* sets—"Del Cardinale" and the "Tobia nuovi overo le boscaglie che erano dell'Arrivabene" (see below). Document 60, no. 6, and Document 66, no. 26bis, make reference to a third set, one in sixteen pieces and measuring 91 1/2 *braccia,* which is called the "Tobia vecchi." Given that the "Fugre di Tobia" recorded in the 1668 inventory consisted of twelve pieces (Document 68, no. 12), it is probable that they are to be identified with the "Tobie del Cardinale" in the 1614 inventory (Document 66, no. 24). It is uncertain which of the two *Tobias* sets is referred to in the 1709 inventory of Ferdinando Carlo's possessions since the listing refers only to three pieces (Document 74, no. 8). For additional comments, see under "Tobia nuovi" below.

Tobia nuovi

Gonzaga of Mantua

This ten-piece set, 5 1/3 *braccia* in height and 62 *braccia* in width, is first recorded in 1584 (Document 60, no. 3), where it is also called the "Tobia nuovi overo le boscaglie che erano dell'Arrivabene." The *Tobia nuovi* is listed in the 1614 inventory (Document 66, no. 23).

The story of Tobias was a favorite theme in Flemish tapestry, in part because it was used as an allegory of marriage and thus for wedding presents. The episodes represented on textiles are indeed focused on Tobias's journey to his niece Sarah, who had lost seven husbands during her wedding nights because of the evil curse by the devil Asmodeus. Tobias succeeded in exorcizing the devil and was thus able to marry Sarah. During the second quarter of the sixteenth century, two different sets of cartoons were used by various Brussels workshops, which produced at least seven editions of them. Of those extant, none can be related to the Gonzaga collection, although it is probably true that the sets mentioned from 1564 to 1627 were similar to these two Brussels editions. By combining the various episodes, represented in the partially preserved sets, it is clear that there were indeed twelve different episodes, as was the case with Ercole's weavings. The height of the Gonzaga series (5 1/3 *braccia*) corresponds with the average height of 3.70 to 4.30 meters of the existing tapestries.

Eight tapestries have been preserved in one series of each group. The first, and probably the oldest, is the Vienna series (IV), which relies on cartoons designed in the style of Bernard van Orley and thus with a pronounced Italianate style in the architecture.[1] Later adaptations of these cartoons can be found in Madrid (series 34), where only six of the eight subjects are preserved,[2] in the four pieces formerly at Bisham Abbey and now in the Winnipeg Art Gallery,[3] and in at least three tapestries in the Cathedral of Palma de Mallorca. The second group of cartoons is more mannerist in style, reminding one of the style of Pieter Coecke van Aelst. These cartoons have been convincingly attributed to the anonymous "Master of the Prodigal Son," who was active in Antwerp from 1530 to 1560.[4] The largest edition of these, consisting of eight pieces, is preserved at Tarragona Cathedral,[5] while the Museum of Gaasbeek, near Brussels, owns a five-piece reconstruction based on at least two different editions (Fig. 20).[6]

1. Baldass, 1920, 4–5, nos. 9–16.
2. Junquera, 1986, 241.
3. Sold by Sotheby's, London, 17 March 1967.
4. Volckaert, 1987.
5. Battle Huguet, 1946, 41–49, plates XVI–XXIII.
6. *London 1965*, no. 11. At least one piece in Gaasbeek belongs to the set once preserved in the castle of Crevin (France) and of which other weavings are now in Mons and on the art market.

Trionfo della Fede

Gonzaga of Guastalla

This eight-piece set, 6 "braccia di Guastalla" in height and 45 *braccia* in width, is first recorded in the 1678 inventory (Document 71, no. 6). The notary original states that "in luogo di fregio vi sono i colonnati." The *Trionfo* was displayed on the occasion of the dedication of the convent of the Santissimo Crocifisso in 1673:

> Fu magnificamente addobbata la Chiesa, aggiugnendovi al di fuori un grand'atrio, che teneva tutto il piazzale che le sta innanzi, in cui si entrava per un gran portone di vaghissima architettura ornata di verdeggianti festoni, emblemi, ed iscrizioni addatte. Al detto atrio conduceva il resto della via, ornato a foggia di sala tutta coperta di arazzi rappresentanti il trionfo della Fede.[1]

The title suggests that the tapestries were based on the Rubens series of the *Triumph of the Eucharist* and thus were probably acquired during the reign of Ferrante III (1632–78). The first edition of the series, made between 1625 and 1628, for the Archduchess Isabella Clara Eugenia, was composed of twenty-two subjects. Most later editions, including the Guastalla set, were reduced to eight weavings. The Guastalla series was probably woven by Frans van den Hecke (d. 1675) or by his son Jan-Frans (active 1662–1700), who obtained the copyright to the cartoons after the completion of the *editio princeps*. A set of eight pieces was delivered in 1673 to Count Harrach in Spain; a set of ten, acquired in 1665 by Carlo Emmanuele of Savoy, is still preserved in Turin. In addition, there are the eight *Triumphs* now in Cologne Cathedral, which were acquired in 1678 or 1688 by Cardinal Wilhelm Egon von Fürstenberg.[2] In all the documents referring to these and other *Eucharist* tapestries by Rubens, the set is always described as the "Triumph of the Church" ("Triompho della Chiesa") and never as "Faith." However, no other allegorical set with the same subject can be traced during the seventeenth century. Thus it is likely that the Guastalla set was indeed woven after Rubens's cartoons.

1. Affò, III,1785–87, 175, and *Tempo*, 1985, 115–16, no. 31.
2. De Poorter, 1978, 239–46.

Troy

Ercole

First recorded in Ercole's collection in 1547 (Document 20), this six-piece set is next listed in the 1563 inventory (Document 49, no. 12), in which it is described as "usate." The 1566 inventory (Document 52, no. 12) refers to one piece. In 1584 Ferrante II loaned Duke Vincenzo Gonzaga a *Troy* set of uncertain provenance to decorate the "sala grande" (Document 60, note 2).

A series of *Troy* tapestries described as worn in 1564 was probably the remnants of an eleven-piece edition of the Tournai tapestries from the second half of the fifteenth century and of which at least four editions were made between 1472 and 1493.[1] However, it not impossible that reference is made here to a series woven in Brussels around 1520. In 1522 Pieter Coecke van Aelst was paid for a set of seven tapestries, the *History of Troy,* which he delivered to the young emperor, Charles V.[2] Two of these weavings were brought from Spain to Italy in the eighteenth entury by Cardinal Alberoni and are kept in the Collegio Alberoni in Piacenza.[3]

1. Asselberghs, 1970, 84.
2. Saintenoy, 1921, 6.
3. *Brussels 1935*, nos. 613–14, pl. CXLII.

Troy

Gonzaga of Mantua

The 1614 inventory (Document 66, no. 8) records a ten-piece set measuring 5 1/3 *braccia* in height and 62 2/3 *braccia* in width. Nine of them are recorded in the 1707 inventory (Document 74, no. 5). Described as the "Incendio di Troia," they were considered to be old but of good design.

After the Tournai and Brussels editions, which were woven before 1525, the subject reappeared in tapestry around the middle of the sixteenth century. In 1560 King John III of Sweden bought a thirteen-piece *Troy* set in Antwerp. Described in the 1563 inventory, they are now lost, but several individual pieces of at least four different sets document their style.[1] A representative example of *Troy* tapestries from the turn of the century are the four panels woven in Brussels in the shop of Geubels-Aerts-Raes from 1615 to 1620. They were acquired by the Soprintendenza alle Gallerie di Piemonte (Turin) from the collection of Ferrero di Ventimiglia. They had been owned by this family as early as 1680.[2] The Gonzaga set may have been similar to this one.

1. Delmarcel and Dumortier, 1986, 5; Stettler, 1973, 229ff.
2. Ferrero Viale, 1981.

Part I

The Documents

The documents are arranged chronologically in seventy-eight sections. Each entry deals with a specific document (an individual letter or an inventory) or with group of related texts, as, for example, with the various correspondence from 1549 (Document 29) concerning the tapestries displayed on the occasion of Francesco III's marriage. In one instance (Document 69), several inventories have been grouped together under a single heading. Unlike other similar texts, which are both lengthy and detailed, these are not sufficently weighty to merit individual listings.

Together, the seventy-eight entries contain the sum total of what is known at present about the tapestries owned by Federico II, Ercole, and Ferrante Gonzaga as well as the fate of their tapestries as recorded in the later records of the Mantuan and Guastalla branches of the family. The comments that accompany the documents are largely descriptive and factual. Matters of speculation and interpretation are noted in the Index to the Major Sets of Figurative Tapestries and in the Catalogue.

Various types of archival records from the chancery records of the Gonzaga brothers' courts are relevant to the documentation of their tapestry collections. These include correspondence, records of payment, testaments, and inventories. Correspondence includes letters directly commissioning a specific tapestry set (Document 32), asking for funds to complete a project well under way (Document 19), or requests for cartoons from which the weavers would work (Document 18). Documents regarding the creation of cartoons are also found in the account books of the court (Document 25), which also record payments to agents for the acquisition of various types of figurative weavings (Documents 13, 21, and 28). On occasion, the account books even document the precise breakdown of costs involved in the production of these weavings (Document 12). In this instance it is work commissioned by the noted weaver Nicolas Karcher, whose activities are further documented in an impressive array of letters (Documents 12, 23, 27, 30–31, and 34–35).

Inventories are perhaps the most important and informative of the documents because they provide the most comprehensive overview, which is otherwise known only fragmentarily by the accidental preservation (or lack thereof) of letters and records of payment. There are two types of inventories, beginning with those drawn up immediately upon the deaths of Federico II and Ercole (Documents 9 and 49). Unfortunately, no similar accounting has surfaced for Ferrante. Thus his holdings have to be reconstructed from the 1590 inventory (Document 65), the one drawn up for his grandson. On the other hand, various documents from Ferrante's life, primarily letters, concern either the commissioning of specific sets (Documents 19 and 32) or document the display and the loan of his tapestries (Documents 10, 24, and 26). As for the clauses in testaments, they say a great deal about the value the original owner placed on his prized weavings (Documents 37 and 48).

With what is known from records that survive from the lives of the three principals, it is relatively easy to distinguish in the later inventories of the various members of the Mantuan and the Guastalla branches of the Gonzaga family those weavings that originally belonged to Federico II, Ercole, and Ferrante. Remarkably, the paper trail left by these tapestries survived for decades after the deaths of the original owners. Invariably the sets that were the pride and joy of their original owners are similarly treasured by subsequent generations, as was most emphatically the case with Ferrante's *Fructus Belli, Puttini, Grotteschi,* and *Moses,* which were distributed among the daughters of Ferrante III of Guastalla, who died in 1678, thus 120 years after the death of their original owner (Document 71).

Rather than the present ordering of the documents, based on chronology, some readers might have preferred a fourfold division, one that was related to ownership. Such an arrangement might have made it easier for the reader to focus on Federico II, Ercole, or Ferrante, with texts dealing with the subsequent history of their individual holdings relegated to a fourth and final section. Since the documents are preceded by an index that indentifies the personalities concerned, it should not be too difficult to pull together the references relevant to the collections formed by the three principals.

Thus, for example, the reader is directed primarily to Document 9 for Federico II, although the single set unquestionably associated with him, the *Tiberius,* is subsequently referred to in the 1614 inventory (Document 66, no. 27). The paper trail for the later history of Ercole and Ferrante's collections is much richer. Since Ercole left his tapestries to both the Mantua and the Guastalla branches of the family (Document 49), they are recorded in both sets of inventories. Since Ferrante's tapestries came to Mantua when Anna Isabella Gonzaga married Ferdinando Carlo (Document 69), it is not only the Guastalla inventories that record the subsequent fate of his holdings. Some of the relevant specifics are highlighted in the index that follows, where, for example, the reader will find specific reference to the presence of Ercole's *Puttini, Fortuna, Saul,* and *Tobias* in Mantua on the occasion of Eleonora de' Medici's arrival in Mantua in 1584 (Document 60) and of Ferrante's *Fructus Belli, Puttini,* and *Grotteschi* in 1671 (Document 70).

As for the history of the tapestries during the life of the owners, the index serves to direct the reader to the various references to Ercole's holdings, begining with 1522 (Document 1) and ending with the 1563 inventory (Document 49). Along the way, there are references to commissioning tapestries (Documents 5, 12–13, 15, 21, 25, 27–28, 30, 36, and 41–42) as well as to files concerning the hanging of various sets (Documents 1, 7–8, 11, 14, 16, 20, 22, and 29). Ercole's relationship with Nicolas Karcher is the subject of Documents 12, 17, 23, 27, and 30. As for Ferrante, his name first occurs in connection with tapestries in 1527 in the matter of the acquisition of several of the Raphael weavings from the Sistine Chapel (Document 2). The commissioning of the *Fructus Belli* and their display in his residence in Milan are dealt with in Documents 19 and 24, while the loan of the Ferrante *Aeneas* to the court in Mantua is discussed in Document 26.

30. 1551: Work commissioned by Ercole from Karcher.
31. 1551–52: Karcher misappropriates funds from Ercole intended for his daughter's dowry.
32. 1552: The commissioning of a set of tapestries for Ferrante.
33. C. 1555: Ferrante pawns a portion of his collection.
34. 1555: A decree by Guglielmo in favor of Karcher.
35. 1556: An appeal to Mantua concerning Karcher and his acquisition of property at Sermide.
36. 1557: Ercole responds to Ferrante's offer to provide tapestries.
37. 1557: The Second Testament of Ercole and the *Acts of the Apostles*.
38. 1558: Ercole responds to Bernardino Pia concerning the placement of tapestries in the Roman palace.
39. 1559: Ercole rejects a set of tapestries sent from Antwerp but accepts a replacement.
40. 1559: Ercole orders a cartoon for his coat of arms and fabric for friezes for tapestries.
41. 1561: "Spaliere a la grotesche" and "dui portieri" repaired by Karcher.
42. 1561: Ercole seeks to acquire "qualche bella tapezzerie (. . .) fatta a figure."
43. 1561: Granvelle offers to purchase a *Hannibal* set for Ercole.
44. 1561: Cesare Gonzaga agrees to the loan of tapestries, excluding the *Puttini*, the *Verdure*, and the *Fructus Belli*.
45. 1562: Karcher appeals to Ercole for funds.
46. 1562: Granvelle comments on tapestries, including the "Historia d'Alessandro Magno," and recommends the *Acts of the Apostles* to Ercole.
47. 1562: The "Registro Necrologico" Account of Karcher's death.
48. 1563: The Third Testament of Ercole.
49. 1563: The inventory of Ercole's tapestries.
50. 1563: The loan of tapestries from Cesare Gonzaga for the Chapel of the Madonna in the Duomo.
51. 1565: Ercole's tapestries recorded in Federico Gonzaga's inventory.
52. 1566: Ercole's tapestries recorded in Francesco Gonzaga's inventory.
53. 1567–84: Records concerning Ferrante's tapestries pledged by Cesare Gonzaga.
54. 1569: Guglielmo Gonzaga donates the *Acts of the Apostles* to the Church of Santa Barbara.
55. 1571–74: Granvelle negotiates the loan of Ferrante's *Puttini* cartoons.
56. 1574: Guglielmo Gonzaga displays Ercole's *Puttini* on the occasion of the state visit of Henry III.
57. 1578: Ercole's *Tobias* set in the Gonzaga palace at Revere.
58. 1579: Guglielmo Gonzaga attempts to acquire the Ferrante *Puttini*.
59. 1580: Ercole's *Puttini, Saul, Tobias,* and *Fortuna* used on the occasion of Vincenzo Gonzaga's marriage to Margherita Farnese.
60. 1584: Ercole's *Puttini, Fortuna, Saul,* and *Tobias* used on the occasion of the arrival in Mantua of Eleonora de' Medici.
61. 1587: Ferrante II arranges for the loan of the *Fructus Belli* and the *Puttini*.
62. 1587: Ercole's *Acts of the Apostles* displayed on the occasion of the coronation of Vincenzo Gonzaga.
63. 1588: Ferrante II orders the shipment of the *Boscaglie* tapestries.
64. 1590: Ferrante II loans tapestries to the Accademia degli Invaghiti.
65. 1590: Ferrante's tapestries recorded in the Gonzaga of Guastalla inventory.
66. 1614: Ercole's armorial tapestries, his *Puttini*, the *Tobias, Saul,* and *Fortuna* recorded in the Gonzaga inventory.
67. 1627: Ercole's tapestries recorded in the inventory of the palaces in Mantua and Casale.
68. 1648–68: Ercole's tapestries in the later inventories of the Gonzaga family.
69. 1670: Ferrante's tapestries in Anna Isabella Gonzaga's dowry.
70. 1671: Ferrante's *Fructus Belli, Puttini,* and *Grotteschi* displayed on the occasion of the arrival in Mantua of Anna Isabella.
71. 1678: Ferrante's tapestries recorded in the inventory dividing the Guastalla collection among Ferrante III's daughters.
72. 1692: The cartoons for Ferrante's *Fructus Belli*.
73. 1704: Ferrante's tapestries in Anna Isabella Gonzaga's inventory.
74. 1709: Ferrante and Ercole's tapestries in the inventory of Ferdinando Carlo's estate.
75. 1709: The Gonzaga of Guastalla claim Anna Isabella Gonzaga's portion of Ferrante's tapestries.
76. 1749: The final disposition of the Gonzaga of Guastalla tapestries.
77. 1755–63: The Ferrante *Puttini* in the Sagredo family inventories.
78. 1771–72: Ferrante's *Aeneas* tapestry in the inventory of the Duke of Modena.

1. 12 DECEMBER 1522
Tapestries in Ercole's Quarters in Bologna

On 12 January 1522 Ercole described the decoration of his student quarters in Bologna.[1] The walls of one of his rooms were covered "con le tapezzarie che ho mandato qui." Thus we know that Ercole already had certain resources of his own, although it is not known if these "tapezzarie" were actually figurative weavings. Others were clearly fabric hangings, such as the "tela d'oro et veluto cremosino." It is not surprising that the seventeen-year-old youth, whose rooms were lavishly appointed with hangings, grew up to become the cardinal-regent whose inventory (Document 49) records a vast quantity of figurative, fabric, and tooled leather hangings:

> Gionsi alla stantia mia, dove ritrovai che l'Aliprando, mio maestro di casa, haveva fatto fare, ne l'intrar di la casa, una porta tutta ornata di verdura con soi festoni et nove arme poste in tre strene a tre arme per strena, ornatissime al possibile.
>
> (. . .) Licentiati tutti quelli gentilhomini et scolari, smontai da cavallo et andai alle mie stantie, quale mi piaceno summamente. Ne l'intrare, primo vi è uno salotto bellissimo, in volta, apparato con le tapezzarie che ho mandato qui con alcuni cornisoni di pictura, che stanno molto bene, et vi è un letto con l' apparamento mio di damascho cremosino con le letteree recamate. De quel loco s'intra in uno camarotto, pur in volta, ornato di tapezzarie d'alto a basso con due lettére, una con la trabacha di panno d'oro, l'altra con uno sparavero di tela. Vi è anche, doppo questo, un'altra camera, anchor in volta, apparata medemamente di tapezzarie da alto a basso, con un'altra lettéra con l'apparamento di tela d'oro et veluto cremosino, nel qual loco io farò il studio mio et senza dubio harò boni alloggiamenti.

1. ASMn, b. 1149, cc. 244–45; Luzio, 1886, 375–76.

2. 16 MAY 1527
Ferrante and the Sistine Chapel Tapestries

Although Ferrante profited little from the Sack of Rome,[1] he was nonetheless responsible for appropriating several of the Sistine Chapel *Acts of the Apostles* tapestries. On 16 May 1527 Isabella d'Este learned how the tapestries (identified in later documents as the *Conversion of Saint Paul* and the *Saint Paul Preaching at Athens*) were to be transported to Mantua:

> Io ho fatto parlar allo Archivescovo di Capua per Pandolpho [Pio da Carpi] de li panni che io ho fatto reddimere de mani de soldati, et perché gli ha detto de li denari ch'io ho sborsato per haverli, esso gli ha resposto che, se ben San Pietro fusse prigione, non haveriano il modo de riscoterlo (. . .). Et pertanto, parendomi non poter portare con me detti panni senza guastarli, ho iudicato essere meglio mandarli a Vostra Excellentia con pregarla che sia contenta farli condure con le robbe sue et ordinare che in quelli dui de la Capella siano posto dui linzola con uno legno groso in mezo come è uno subio da telaro, et così involtarli sopra quello, perché altramente dicono che se tagliano come se fusseno tagliati da uno coltello.

Ferrante also stated that "se io havesse il modo farebbe ogni opera per haver li altri pezzi, quali penso che andaranno in malhora."[2] This statement adds weight to Isabella's own subsequent reference to "li quatro pezi di la tapezaria."[3]

1. Marino Sanudo, as quoted by Luzio, 1908, 100–101.
2. ASMn, b. 875, c. 381v; Luzio, 1908, 89. For Isabella's letter to Sigismondo Fanzino da la Torre of 7 October 1527, justifying her involvement in the removal of the "dui pezi di tapezaria di la capella di Sua Santità redempti da le mani de Spagnoli per il signor Don Ferrante, nostro figliolo, con soi denari," see ASMn, b. 2999, l. 47, cc. 28–29v; Luzio, 1908, 93.
3. Isabella's reference to "li quatro pezi di la tapezaria del Papa" is found in a letter of 19 May 1528 to Pico Maria della Mirandola (ASMn, b. 1999, l. 47, cc. 73–76r; Luzio, 1908, 387–88). See also the mention of "li quatro pezzi de la bella tappezaria che era dil Papa" in a letter to Sestola of 25 April 1528 (ASMn, b. 2999, l. 47, cc. 68r–v). On the removal of the papal tapestries, see Shearman, 1972, 140–41.

3. 18 NOVEMBER 1531
The First Testament of Ercole

In the first of three testaments, Ercole bequeathed to the Cathedral of Mantua silver valued at "scutorum mille auri," vases with statues of Peter and Paul, as well as wall hangings worth 500 gold scudi.[1] The modest value of the hangings suggests that Ercole had not yet begun to form the collection for which he was subsequently famous (Document 49), but his letter of 12 December 1522 suggests otherwise (Document 1). Perhaps the remainder of the figurative and fabric hangings were included in the general reference to "bonis mobilibus et inmobilibus" bequeathed to Federico II: "Item, reliquit et legavit prefatae ecclesiae cathedrali [Mantuae] tot de bonis mobilibus ipsius reverendissimi domini testatoris prout sunt tapezariae et alia huiusmodi quot capiet valor scutorum quingentorum auri."

1. ASMn, b. 333, cc. 220–23; *Rome 1984,* 144 n. 14. The needs of the cathedral figured prominently in Ercole's thinking. Not only did he provide for the rebuilding of the structure after the fire of 1545 and commission for it a series of altarpieces (Kiefer, 1987, 34ff.), but he traditionally loaned figurative hangings for the feast of Corpus Christi (Document 11). Furthermore, in his Second Testament (Document 37), the Duomo was bequeathed the *Acts of the Apostles*.

4. 9 MAY 1537
Listing of Ferrante's Verdure *Tapestries*

This sheet, dated 9 May 1537, contains a listing of the contents of the "palazzo del Illustrissimo signor don Ferrante de Gonzaga," including various types of *verdure* hangings, some with festoons and one with *puttini.* This is not a definitive accounting of all that Ferrante owned, since the list apparently deals with only one locale. According to Sernini, the residence in Messina contained "tapezzarie infiniti" (Document 10).[1]

The inventory records a small number of individual *spalliere.* It is difficult to establish a connection between the *verdure* catalogued in 1537 and those recorded in the 1590 inventory (Document 65), which lists various figurative sets (*Fructus Belli, Puttini, Sponsalitio, Aeneas, Grotteschi*) inherited from Ferrante's estate. The commissioning of the first of these great figurative sets, the *Fructus Belli,* dates from 1544–45, the *Aeneas* was acquired in 1549, and the *Puttini* was ordered in 1552, thus the years when Ferrante exchanged his position of vice-regent of Sicily (1535–46) for that of governor of Milan (1546–54). And yet, Sernini's letter proves, by the beginning of the year 1540 Ferrante was already in possession of a sizable collection.

1. una spalera a verdura cum lo marchesato rusata, de braccia 4½.
   "Marchesato" probably refers to the Gonzaga coat of arms as it existed before 1530, at which time the family was elevated to the rank of Duke.
2. una spalera a verdura similla de braccia 10.
3. una spalera a verdura similla de braccia 6.
4. una spalera similla de braccia 10 vel circa.
5. una spalera a verdura cum festoni, de braccia 8.
6. una spalera similla de braccia 10.
7. una spalera similla de braccia 8.
8. uno razetto a verdura cum uno festono, de braccia 4.
9. uno razetto simil de braccia 5.
10. uno razetto simil de braccia 5.
11. uno razetto simil de braccia 4.
12. uno celono a figure tuto strazato.
13. una spalera a verdura, vechia e rotta, de braccia 12.
14. una spalera a verdura cum lo marchesato e putini, vechia e rotta, de braccia 10.
15. uno celono a verdura, rotto.

1. BMG, b. 10: "Spese private ed inventari dei beni mobili: 1515–1552." The palace in question is probably one of Ferrante's many residences in South Italy, but not necessarily the one in Messina.

5. 8 APRIL–19 MAY 1537
A Tapestry Version for Ercole of a Painting by Raphael

In reporting on the *Pietà* commissioned from Sebastiano del Piombo, Sernini referred to delays in shipping a painting by Raphael that had to remain in Rome until the completion of the cartoon ordered by Ercole.[1] Sernini's letter documents both a painting acquired by Ferrante and one of the earliest tapestry commissions that can be associated with Ercole. More likely an embroidery, it probably can be identified with either the "quadretto della Madonna" or the "quadretto della Madona in bagno," both of which are recorded in the 1563 inventory (Document 49, nos. b–c), rather than with Nicolas Karcher's "Moise nel deserto" (Document 12 and Document 49, no. a).[2]

A. Nino Sernini to Ferrante Gonzaga, Rome, 8 April 1537 (MOBE, AC, "Sernini": no. 32):

> Havevo ragionato con quel dipintore che ne fece vendere il quadro dipinto da Rafaello, sopra il quale esso ha ricavato un disegno in cartone da mandarlo in Fiandra a requisione del Cardinale nostro, per haverlo poi in tapezzeria, et l'ha cavato tanto bello che non si può disiderare meglio et ragionando con lui, mi ha detto che gli basta l'animo farne uno tanto simile che non si conosciarà l'un da l'altro.

B. Nino Sernini to Ferrante Gonzaga, Rome, 3 May 1537 (MOBE, AC, "Sernini," no. 10)":

> Come già scrissi a Vostra Excellentia, il Cardinale haveva in cartone fatte ricavare le figure del quadro che si comperò quando essa fu qui per mandarlo poi in Fiandra per farlo in tapezzerie. Il maestro l'ha ritratto benissimo ma non l'ha possuto finir se non dipoi le feste, ch'è stato in su la partita del Cardinale. Volendo mò io mandare il quadro, secondo l'ordine datomi da Vostra Excellentia, non mi pare molto sicuro il farlo per essere il tempo troppo atroce[?] et il mare mal sicuro per le fuste, però pensavo che fusse necessario fuggire questo periculo o valersi d'una occasione d'un passaggio di galere o lassare passare la state et, a dir il vero, mi parrebbe troppo perdita, poiché con dinari non se ne pò più havere un simile. Il mandarlo a Napoli per muli è cosa difficile perché, ogni volta che sarà messo in casse che gli si conviene, un mulo non lo potrà, et più non vagliono aportarlo; pure non mi è sovenuto questo pensiere si non mò scrivendo, ma me ne chiarirò perché, partendomi di Roma, vorrei pure prima mandarlo, ma però per via sicura.

C. Nino Sernini to Ferrante Gonzaga, Rome, 19 May 1537 (MOBE, AC, Sernini, no. 34b):

> Et se io lo potrò accordare, vedrò di mandare il quadro comperato di mano di Rafaello a Civitavecchia o a Napoli, benché in l'uno et l'altro luogo, come ho scritto, lo mando per mare mal volentiere rispetto alle fuste, et per terra è troppo grave a mandarlo che un mulo non lo potrebbe ogni volta che sarà incassato come ha da stare perché non si guasti, et quando ci risolvessimo di farlo ricavare dal dipintore non si potrebbe mandare perché bisogna che lo tenga avante. Il cartone certamente ha fatto benissimo et ha satisfatto al Cardinale il quale l'ha portato con lui, et quando bene fusse qui per fare cosa che stesse bene, bisognarebbe havere il propio quadro per li colori.

1. Documents A and C were published by Hirst, 1972, 588–90.

2. The painting on which the cartoon was based might be identified with the *Madonna della Gatta* in the Museo di Capodimonte in Naples. Actually by Giulio Romano, it was attributed to Raphael by Vasari (1878–, VI, 489), who saw it in the collection of Ferrante's son. For more information on the *Madonna della Gatta,* generally thought to have been acquired by Federico II (in which case, how precisely did it come into the hands of Cesare Gonzaga?), see *Rome 1984,* 94–96.

6. 1537
Ercole Asked to Arrange for "Luca Fiamingho" to Provide Cartoons

Several undated letters from Alfonso d'Este, traditionally assigned to the year 1537, request Ercole to intervene with Giulio Romano so that "Luca fiamingho" could come to Ferrara to prepare tapestry cartoons.[1] These letters were doubtless written prior to 27 January 1538, the day Federico II issued a patent in which he agreed to the departure from Mantua of "maestro Luca nostro carissimo."[2]

> Havendo io bisogno per un mese di maestro Luca fiamingho, qual si ritrova in Mantua, per fargli fare un carthone da far fare tapezzarie, né potendolo havere, per havere lui alcuni lavorieri in quella città, ho voluto col mezzo di questa mia, pregare Vostra Signoria Reverendissima, come ben di core la prego, che voglia essere contenta vedere che messer Iulio Romano, al qual haveva da lavorare si contenti che per il predetto mese mi venghi a servire che me ne farà singular piacere.

The Duke of Ferrara's second letter responds to four from "vostra signoria reverendissima." In it reference is made to:

> quelle pitture de paesi dati al mio c[apitano] della guardia de'Lanzichenech da quel Fiamengo et [. . .] a messer Giulio Romano, rispondo che havendo fa[tto] dir questa cosa al prefato mio capitanio, ha risposto esser vero c[he] da un maestro Luca li fu dato un poco di charta dipint [. . .] la penna, la qual si bagnò con alcune littere che egli havea [nel] suo ritorno in qua, et dice haverlo scritto ad esso [maestro] Luca et che scrisse anco il tutto ad esso messer Giulioa.

The duke's wish for the services of "Luca fiamingho" may be connected with work undertaken at this time in Ferrara by the Karcher brothers, since, on 29 September 1536, Gerolamo Sestola advised the court in Mantua that Alfonso d'Este had brought to Ferrara "fiaminghi a lavorare di tapezarie per li alogiamenti nuovi."[3] It may be significant that he wrote to Ercole rather than to Federico II, for whom Luca is known to have worked. Perhaps Luca had executed cartoons for tapestries for him, which was why the request was directed to Ercole.

1. ASMo, Arazzi e tappezerie, b. 21. First published by Forti Grazzini (1982, 89 n. 64). He believed that the letter was addressed to Federico II by Ercole II d'Este. A second letter is from ASMo, Archivio per materie—Arti Belle—Pittori, busta 15, fasc. (*Giulio Romano,* 1992, II, 1182).

2. ASMn, b. 3001, l. 2, c. 96r; *Giulio Romano,* 1992, II, 749 (January 27 1538).

3. ASMn, b. 1251. "Luca fiamingho" is to be identified with the Luca Todescho who worked as a painter of landscapes in the Appartamento di Troia under Giulio Romano between 1536 and 1537 (Hartt, 1958, I, 164, 166, 171 n. 2, 217, 260). He was subsequently involved in the creation of two "belli paesi" for Marmirolo. Shortly before Giulio's death in 1546, Luca (better known as d'Olanda) moved to Ferrara, where he worked for Duke Ercole II on cartoons for tapestries (Forti Grazzini, 1982, 67–68). In *Mantova 1989* (p. 446) he is identifed as Luca Cornelisz. According to Forti Grazzini, 1991, 10, Luca may have been comissioned in 1537 to prepare the cartoons for the borders of Giulio Romano's *Gigantomachia.*

7. 12 DECEMBER 1537
The Transfer of Tapestries from Ercole's Roman Residence

On 26 January 1538 reference is made to unspecified tapestries that were transported from Rome to Mantua:[1]

> — e per di nolo per dui forcieri e uno fagotto da Ferrara a Mantova con tapezzarie e un aparamento da leto mandato da Roma.

1. ASDMn, MV, Entrate e Uscite, b. 18, c. 127.

8. 31 OCTOBER–3 DECEMBER 1539
The Arrangment of Tapestries in Ercole's Roman Palace[1]

Sernini's communications of 3 October and 3 December[2] are part of a group of letters written during the course of 1539 concerning repairs to Ercole's residence on Via Alessandrina in Rome.[3] Although Sernini was primarily concerned with fabric decorations (it is not clear if the phrase "tapezzerie" refers to figurative weavings), his are the most extensive discussions of wall coverings prior to Ercole's decision to focus on the Palazzo Vescovile in Mantua. In a sense, Sernini's letter forms a logical sequel to the document of 1522 concerning the decoration of Ercole's rooms in Bologna (Document 1).

From the letter of 31 October, Ercole learned how hangings were used by Cardinal Ippolito d'Este.[4] The *sala* and its *anticamera* were completely covered with "bellissime tapezzerie." Most of the doors in the various rooms were covered with "portiere di velluto racamate d'oro." Sernini's letter of 3 December responds to a query from Ercole regarding the "portiera" and, based on what Ippolito d'Este had done, he makes a range of suggestions also regarding the fabric for the *letto.*

A. Nino Sernini to Ercole Gonzaga, Rome, 31 October 1539 (ASMn, b. 1909, cc. 256–57):

> Giovedì che fummo alli XXIII del presente andai in su le poste fino a Bolsena a incontrare il cardinale di Ferrara (. . .). La domenica di sera alloggiò al Populo, et cenato ch'ebbe, andò sconosciuto in palazzo et prima visitò il cardinale Farnese (. . .) et andò a basciare il pié a Sua Santità (. . .). Li cardinali [vennero a (. . .) compagnarlo] a casa, dov'era la porta ornata secondo l'usanza, di dentro (. . .) a questo modo: la sala prima è tutta parata di bellissime tapezzerie, dove per lo lungo è una tavola che vi mangiano accomodatamente venti persone; l'anticamera, cioè quella del paramento, è pure aparata del medesimo modo, l'anticamera poi, di quel paramento di velluto cremesi et broccato [et non] gli essendo piaciuto quella parte dove è il camino scoperta, ha voluto che del medesimo s'appare tirando sopra le fenestre et il camino il medesimo fregio d'oro et di velluto con le sue francie pur d'oro et di seta. Et fra il camino e le fenestre vi sono messi li teli che vi bisognono. In questa stanza vi è un bel letto di velluto cremesi, con racami tessuti d'oro et di seta; la camera dove dorme è parata di raso pavonazzo, con certe trine larghe tre dita, d'oro et d'argento, et il letto del medesimo con una tavoletta coperta di velluto cremesi con le francette d'oro che l'ho fatta fare io. In queste due ultime stanze stanno otto sedie di velluto (. . .); a la porta dil salotto et a quella di la camora dil paramento stanno portiere di scarlatto racamate di velluto del medesimo colore, le quali sono riuscite molto belle, ma la seconda sera se ne abrusciò mezzo una, che vennero certi a fare certa moresca, né si seppe come si ataccassse il fuoco, pure si remediarà. Alla porta di l'anticamora et de la camora vi sono le portiere di velluto racamate d'oro, che sono riuscite bellissime et vaghe, né v'è cosa più bella. S'è aparata ancora la capella essendovi avanzate delle tapezzerie, in la sala grande et nel salotto si tiene la sera l'intorce bianche. Il tinello si fa dove tenevamo la dispensa, l'havemo fatto imbiancare et riesce delli belli di Roma, et così è fatta bianca la camora rincontro alla cucina dove si fa il tinello [secreto] et tutto viene benissimo. La spesa che fa questo signore è grossissima, et tutta la corte pensa che s'habbia a ritirare parendo impossibile che vi possa durare (. . .). Il cardinal

Farnese volse pur vedere le portiere di velluto, et è vero, secondo [mi ha detto il recamatore, ch'à mandato a Lucca] per velluto di diversi colori per aparare tre stanze, et ha ordinato un fregio d'oro per essi paramenti con fogliami (antichi), ma per ancora non si lavora non essendo venuto il drappo (. . .).

B. Nino Sernini to Ercole Gonzaga, Rome, 3 December 1539 (ASMn, b. 1902, cc. 296–300):

Ancorché Vostra Signoria Illustrissima non scriva parola di portiera, se n'è pur tra noi ragionato, et ancor che si sia pensato che quella harà dato ordine si faccino insieme con le tapezzerie, et che siano più ricche et vistose con la sua arme, non di meno è stato concluso che non si possa fare senza una portiera racamata per la sua camora, quando non fussi mai per altro, per posserla mutare. Et volendo fuggire gli stremi et acostarse all'honesto, s'è ragionato che sia di panno rosato con un fregio bellissimo di velluto, et in certi loghetti secondo ricercherà il racamo, et questa è stata inventione di messer Curtio, vi si mettano certe puntette d'oro et d'argento che afferma tornerà cosa vaga et bella; in mezzo poi una bella arme grande, come s'usa, ornata di tela d'oro et argento, v'andaranno drento palmi nove di panno come il sopradetto del tavolino. Il velluto non lo vorrei cremesi, ma più tosto verdino, di quella sorte che facessimo il saio [a Lelio?] ch'è più vistoso, et chi volesse cavare il lavoro un de l'altro bastarebbono sette palmi, ma con questa industria l'opera non riesce poi come io vorrei, ancor che l'habbi fatta fare in le portiere di panno di Ferrara, ma non sono puoi in consideratione rispetto a quelle di velluto, però per fare il fregio bello ve n'andranno 14 palmi; la ricamatura costarà circa 12 scudi et altri tanti gli profili che vanno a torno al ricamo; l'arme con le sue telette varrà un 15 scudi, di modo che in tutto una portiera varrà in ogni modo cinquanta scudi, ma sarà bella, honesta et honorevole (. . .). Io ho proposto che a Vostra Signoria Illustrissima non è mai piaciuto che si [alunghe?] la tavola et ho considerato che'l cardinale di Ferrara si serve di quella nostra grande che noi operavamo alle volte et con la giunta di sei palmi, et non di meno non fa più di tre piatti et vi mangiono fino a vinti persone (. . .). Certo è che al piatto che si fa in casa è male non vi possono sempre mangiare, quando accadesse, dodeci o quatrodeci persone, et quando Vostra Signoria Illustrissima si risolvesse a farlo, si manderia la misura del tappeto che a Veneti(a) s'haverebbe con più vantaggio. Mi pare ancora che siamo assai sforniti di coperte da muli, né havemo cosa buona: si potrebbe dare ordine si facessono insieme con le tapezzerie, mandando qualche disegno che piacesse; quelle del cardinale di Ferrara, che n'ha fatte fare trenta, costa l'una [...] undici scudi, non ne portò più di vinti, ma X n'haveva mandate a fare in Fiandra; mi pare che n'habbiamo necessità (. . .). S'è fra di noi ragionato ancora del letto di tabi, et tutti tre li consultori inclinavano se ne facessono dui, acompagnandone uno con raso o damasco, et l'altro con velluto, che parescono d'estate et d'inverno, et li colori piacevono turchino et verde, che sarebbono molto allegri et vaghi; non è dubbio che riuscirebbono, perché questi colori con oro riescono mirabilmente (. . .). A me piaceria l'anticamora di Vostra Signoria Illustrissima stesse senza letto, benché Ferrara vi lo tenga, et quella si ne servisse di quella stanza quando le piacesse, senza restringersi in quel suo camerino ch'à del malanconico, et così usa Ferrara et non sta male; vi si può bene tenere una tavoletta mezzana, che vi sta benissimo et serve a più bisogni (. . .).

---

1. Several years after reporting on the tapestry hangings of Cardinal Ippolito d'Este, Sernini reported (10 June 1542) on those employed by Pope Paul III (Solmi, 1908, 38): "Nostra Signore a buon hora al solito andò in processione, et si fece portare in la sedia, secondo l'usanza, et perchè la notte era piovuto, la mattina fu molta fresca. Furono messe fori molte belle tapezzarie, ma non furono considerati se non cinque pezzi di Cornaro. Li quali sono divini, essendo il disegno di Rafaello sopra l'istoria d'Anibale et Scipione, o per dir meglio delli fatti d'esso Scipione. Li panni sono piú alti et lunghi di l'ordinario, non v'è oro, et per quanto ho inteso costono vicino a 2000 ducati, vi stette sempre tanta gente a vedergli che non si posseva passare, et il Cardinale vi si fece portare, ma a casa sua non ha dove servirsene per la lor grandezza. Ho visto ancora gli corami del Reverendissimo Borgos, che sono bellissimi, ma mi paiono piccoli, et il disegno è pure di Rafaello, fatto a lavori grotteschi et in li fregi sono figure et storiette diverse. Le pelli sono messo per il traverso et non per il lungo, si come si usa, et si fussono più alti riuscirebbono mirabilmente per esser molto vaghi et ricchi."

2. Transcriptions of the legible passages in these letters, in which the ink has badly corroded the paper, were laboriously executed by Daniela Ferrari and Anna Maria Lorenzoni.

3. ASMn, b. 1909, cc. 256–57 (9 October). Further information on the "fabrica" is contained in letters written by Plotis and Sernini in 1540 (ASMn, b. 1910, cc. 13, 15, 17, 19, 21, 25, 82–84, 103–4, 107, 111, 434). The little-studied question of Ercole's residence in Rome deserves further research. For additional information on Ercole's residence in Rome, see Document 38.

4. On Ippolito's collection, see Baratte, 1976, 115ff.

9. 8 OCTOBER 1539–28 MAY 1540

Karcher in the Service of Federico II and the Ducal Inventory of Wall Hangings

On 28 May 1540 Margherita Paleologa requested that Karcher be permitted to return from Casale as soon as possible in order that he might finish the "lavorieri che fa per el signor illustrissimo et nostri." This might relate—but then again it might not—to the payment made by Ercole after the death of Federico II for the transport to the castle of a thirteen-piece set.

Karcher is first mentioned in a letter to Federico II of 12 January 1539. On 8 October 1539 Karcher was granted tax concessions in exchange for the work he had undertaken in Mantua in his shop in the Borgo San Giorgio together with his eleven assistants.[1]

> Havendo noi condutto in questa terra Nicola Carcher di Burselles, maestro di tappezarie, perché l'habbia da tessere per la corte nostra tappezzarie, secondo gli disegni che gli faremo dare, volemo che l'habbia l'essentione da tutti gli datii per lui et quelli che pigliarà a lavorare seco, che seranno in tutto undeci bocche, acciò che facilmente el possa aver delli operari et lavorare con maggiore commodità sua. Però lo esentamo et liberamo dal datio della macina, dal datio del vino et di qualunque altra cosa ch'el comprarà o condurà a Mantova per il vivere delle dette undeci bocche per tutto il tempo che a tale effetto el starà qui, commandando alli spectabili maestri delle entrate, alli datiarii et altri officiali nostri, alli quali spetta o spettaria, che osservino et faciano osservare inviolabilmente la presente essentione al predetto Nicola per tutto il tempo ch'el starà qui per lavorarci, non obstante ordine alcuno perché così volemo havendolo noi condotto a posta per noi.

On 14 November 1539, Grossino advised that Karcher had begun work on the friezes: "in questa matina ho parlato con maestro Nicollò tapezero, et m'à deto aver comenzato a lavorar in la tapezeria perhò in li frissi."[2]

There is one certain reference and a second possible reference to Karcher's work for Federico II, who died on 28 June 1540. The first is found in the correspondence of his wife, Margherita Paleologa, who wrote on 28 May 1540 to both Anna Paleologa and Sigismondo Fanzino expressing concern that Nicolas might be delayed in Casale, where he had gone to raise money on behalf of his brother in Ferrara, and therefore would be unable to complete certain works in time.[3]

> Maestro Nicolò Carchera, tapezzier, viene a Casale per scoder da messer Princivale Calorio, advocato in Monferrato, i denari de certe terre venduteli per sodisfar al debito per el qual el fratello è a Ferrara, come dovete sapere. Et perché desideramo ch'el gli habbia senza perdimento di tempo importandoli, come fa, la liberatione del fratello et sua oltre che per li lavorieri che fa per el signor illustrissimo et nostri, bisogna ch'el sia qua presto, lo havemo voluto acompagnare con la presente per la quale ne imponemo che, in caso che gli bisogni favore o aiuto per imedimento che si cercase contro il dovere de interponere alla sodisfatione, non li manchate faciendo di maniera che ben espedito et senza bisognare far lite del suo et se ne possi ritornar presto in qua che, quanto più presto et meglio espedito lo havemo qua, ne sarà tanto più caro.

The work in progress was presumably finished only in March 1541, when Cardinal Ercole's account books refer to the payment of "soldi dici per far portar le tapezarie del Signor Duca, numero pezi 13, in Castello."[4] If the transport was from Karcher's shop, and this is by no means certain, then whatever he and his eleven assistants were working on consisted of a set of thirteen panels.

The "inventario de la tapezaria de la corte de lo Illustrissimo signor Duca [Federico II]" (ASMn, Estensioni Notarili, K. 10, c. 68v: 1 January 1541) contains no identifiable reference to work by Karcher.[5] What is more disappointing, however, is the vagueness of Odoardo Stivini's descriptions, which form the earliest surviving inventory of the possessions of the Gonzaga of Mantua. Two sets, the *Tiberius and Alexander the Great* and the *Philomela,* are, however, clearly identifiable in subsequent inventories (Documents 57, note 2 and 66, no. 1):

- — nove coltrini de colocuti a figuri, boni.
- — sei coltrini a figuri di colocuti, vechie.
- — sette pezii de tapezaria a figuri cum arbori e cazze.
- — [*Tiberius and Alexander the Great*] dece pecii de tapezaria a figuri de Tiberio e Alexandro Magno.
- — quindece pecii de tapezaria a verdura cum animali, usi.
- — vintisei pecii de tapezaria a verdura, zalda, parte cum animali e parte senza.
- — sei pecii de tapezaria a figurini, usi.
- — dece pecii de tapezaria a figuri, alte brazza 5, usi.
- — sette pecii di tapezaria a verdura, schietti, alti brazza 5, usi.
- — una spalera a figuri cum oro e seda, longa brazza 19.
- — uno pezo piccolo de tapezaria a figuri cum oro e seda, longo brazza dui e mezo.
- — quatro spalere fine cum seda cum vasii.
- — vintiquatro spalere a verdura de più sorte.
- — sei spalere a figure da le Povesie, alte brazza 4.
- — [*Philomela*] una spalera a figuri de Filomena.
- — ottantadue spalere a verdura, alti brazza 3, vechie e usate e parte strazate.

— vintisette spalere a barcho, alti brazza 3 l'una.
— sette spalere a barcho, alti brazza dui e mezo l'una.
— tredece spalere a figure, alti brazza dui e mezo.
— vintiquatro spalere a verdura, alti brazza dui e mezo.
— dece petii de spalera zalda a imprese de Madama bona memoria, videlicet sei piccoli.
— sei pecii de spalera de panno leonato, videlicet 5 piccoli.
— trentacinque razi a verdura, schietti.
— dece pezi de tapezaria a verdura schietti.
— vintiquatro pecii de tapezaria a barcho, videlicet parte boni e parte rotti.

The 1541 inventory demonstrates the importance of figurative weavings to the court of Federico II, and further confirmation is found in other sections of the comprehensive inventory Odoardo Stivini undertook in the years immediately following the duke's death. Literally hundreds of "spalere a verdure" were catalogued in various locations, but only a small number was "a figuri." Presumably those "a verdure" were floral, although they might have been fabric, the duke owning a certain number of these, such as the "spalera a listi de lana morella e ranza (. . .) due spalere a brocha fine."[6]

By 1530, if not earlier, Federico II owned a lavish collection, largely of fabric hangings, for in this year the contents of the *guardaroba* were emptied to honor Charles V. The walls of the great circular staircase by which one ascended to the *piano nobile* were completely covered with hangings, and hangings enlivened all eighty rooms. The finest hangings were reserved for the rooms assigned to Charles V, which were covered with "brocato d'oro":

> Poi tutto il Castello era apparato da ogni banda da alto a basso di finissime tapizerie (. . .) et tutta la scala grande da ogni banda apparata pur di tapizerie, et quante sale et camere vi sono nel Castello, che sono a numero forsi ottanta, tutte erano apparate di varie sorte di bellissime tapezerie con bellissimi paramenti da letto (. . .) et le camare dedicate per lo alloggiamento di Sua Maestà Cesarea, cioè per la sua persona, quali erano cinque con quattro camarine, erano apparate tutte da alto a basso di brocato d'oro tirato et brocato d'oro riccio, con una tapezeria in di camarini di oro, argiento et seda estimata più di diceotto milia ducati, li quali paramenti et tapizerie tutte sono dil signor Marchese di Mantua, che pur non tolse in prestito uno pezzo al mondo, che veramente era bellissima cosa a vedere esso Castello così adornato com'era, cosa non mai più fatta altra volta.[7]

One can only speculate on the set woven with gold, silver, and silk threads and said to have been worth more than 18,000 ducats.

Somewhat curiously, given what was available to Federico II by 1530, his correspondence files reveal little about the acquisition of figurative weavings, although rather more is known about the fabric and leather hangings. To begin with, there is the correspondence in 1524 with Baldassare Castiglione in Rome regarding the creation of "spallere di coramo" containing the "impresa nostra del Monte Olimpo," a project that began small but resulted in the commissioning of that vast quantity of "corami dorati e inargentati" for the "camerini et sale et salette" of the residence at Marmirolo.[8] Several years thereafter, on 11 February 1527, Federico II wrote to Francesco Gonzaga about the creation of the "corami per l'aparamento del nostro palazzo del Te [...] et accio che intendiati meglio la mente nostra, dicemovi che li apparamenti del salotto et del camarotto hanno ad esser di coramo rosso in tutti li spatii volemo che siano indorati, ma li frisi et collonelle o compartimenti d'essi spatii volemo che siano indoratti, et quelli delli dui camarini volemo che siano in questo modo, che nel primo siano di coramo bertino nelli spatii et che medemamente li frisi et colonelle sieno dorate, nel secondo sieno di coramo d'argento con li frisi et colonelle ut supra."[9] Passing over the correspondence from Francesco da le Arme for the "spaliere de oro et de corame," ordered in 1529,[10] a particularly interesting file exists from 1531 for the Palazzino Paleologa, for whose three principal rooms the duke wished "paramenti di corami adorati della sorte che forno quelli che ultimamente ne facesti fare in Roma, e voressimo che fossero lavorati como quelle, de oro e de color turchino se tutte se posseno far di tal colore il quale ni piaceria sopra ogni altro colore, pur, quando non si potessero havere de turchino, se contentaressimo d'altro pur che cadauna stanza havesse l'apparamento d'un colore et una sorte sola." To this was added the commission for "cinquanta tondi di coramo con dentro lavorata l'arma della casa nostra et quella di Monferrato ligati insieme, li quali siano di grandezza che si potessano mettere tra le colone et li fregi delle spalere."[11]

According to the ASMn Schede Davari, Grossino

wrote from Mantua on 20 December 1531 regarding "il comprare tappezzerie a Ferrara." The poor state of preservation of ASMn, b. 2516 (the right-hand half of each page is missing), makes it virtually impossible to clarify this citation. Thus it is indeed fortunate that Braghirolli cited the key phrase "le tapezzerie che se sono mandate a tor a Ferrara saranno presto qui che importano ducati 408."[12] In and of itself, the reference to "tapezzerie" need not refer to figurative wall hangings. Several years later, on 29 September 1536, Gerolamo Sestola wrote from Ferrara concerning "fiamengii" the Duke of Ferrara had brought "a lavorare di tapezarie per li alogiamenti nuovi."[13] The reference is of course to the arrival of the Karcher brothers in Ferrara.[14]

---

1. Karcher's letter of 12 January 1539 is cited by Adelson, 1990, 487, no. 4. For the decree of September 1539, cf. ASMn, Libro dei Decreti, 41 56r; Luzio, 1891; 1914, 109–10; Luzio, 1919, 34; Adelson, 1990, 494, no. 6; *Giulio Romano,* 1992, II, 825–26). Presumably Duke Federico II first became aware of Karcher from a reference in Gerolamo Sestola's letter (ASMn, b. 1251). It is not known, however, when Federico II actually saw the work of the Karcher brothers or the nature of the negotiations with Nicolas Karcher.

2. ASMn, b. 2527; Luzio, 1919, 34 n. 1. Included in the catalogue of documents by Adelson, 1990, 495, no. 7; see also *Giulio Romano,* 1992, II, 829.

3. ASMn, b. 3001, l.3, cc. 148r–v.; Giulio Romano, 1992, II, 845–46. Both letters contain more or less the same wording, and the transcription is from the one written to Franzoni. The document was discovered by Lorenzoni. See ASMn, b. 1952, c. 251, for Anna Paleologa's letter of acknowledgment ("ho receputa la lettera che Vostra Illustrissima Signoria me ha scritto in recomandatione de maestro Nicolò tapezero . . ."). Unfortunately nothing more illuminating has survived. That Karcher owned property in Casale is not surprising since it was in this city that his father "Luigi Carchiera, arazziere," who is first documented there in September 1526, wrote his testament (Adelson, 1990, 487, no. 3). See also Baudi di Vesme, 1982, 1229, for the complete text of the 21 June 1526 testament: "In civitate Casalis (. . .). Ibidem cum sit quod magister Carcheria de Brusellis in Brabant tapicerius et incola civitatis Casalis quoddam suum testamentum noncupativum (. . .) fecerit, in quo inter cetera, post multa legata et disposita per eum, suos heredes universales (. . .) sibi instuit Nicolaum et Joannem eiusdem magistri Aluysii filios legitimos et naturales equis portionibus (. . .), constando [?] de ipso testamento publico instrumento rogato nunc quondam egregio Emanuelli Gallono olim notario publico et civi Casalensi, ad quod opportuna relatio haberi voluit et vult; sitque quod exinde aliud condiderit testamentum quod, ut asserit, fecit et condidit potius ad suggestionem et seductionem nonnullorum faventium predicto. Nicolao, quam quod valere voluerit et vellit idem magister Aloysius, prout de ipso testamento constat publico instrumento rogato quondam egregio Jacobo de Nigris olim notario publico Casalensi, ad quod relatio haberi voluit, in quo inter reliqua disposita et ordinata, in eo suum universalem heredem instituit et nominavit dictum Nicolaum alterum ex dictis eius filis, factis quibusdam particularibus legatis predicto Joanni alteri filio, et prout et sicutin eo contineri dicatur, animo et intentione id revocandi et annullandi; hinc est quod predictus magister Aloysius Carcheria, sanus Dei gratia sensu et intellectu licet aliquantulum corpore languens, volens de rebus suis disponere (. . .), confirmat dictum primum testamentum receptum per quondam Emanuellem notarium, ita quod suum sortiatur affectum in omnibus et singulis in eo dispositis."

4. ASMn, FP, b. 6 (31 March 1542).

5. ASMn, Estensioni Notarili, K. 10, c. 68v; Ferrari, 1994, 104.

6. ASMn, Estensioni Notarili, K. 10 passim. See Ferrari, 1994, 110–11, for references to wall hangings scattered about in various rooms in the Ducal Palace, such as the six "spalere a verdura" in "le camere dove aloza messer Zaffardo in Castello," the "quatro spalere a figure" in the "due camare in Corte, dove aloza el detto messer Zaffardo quando ge piace, et per bisogne de forestieri," or those "a verdura" and "a figuri cum il 'marchesa'" in the "secundo camerotto da le Colone per forestieri."

7. Romano, 1892, 244–45.

8. See ASMn, b. 2966, l. 28, c. 41v, as cited by Luzio, 1913, 28. See Castiglione (26 April; 4, 13 May; 31 July; 27 August 1524); ASMn, b. 868, cc. 183–84, 194, 206, 289–99, 313; also the documents added to the corpus by Shearman (1991, 296), who correctly relates this commission to the reference to the "corami dorati e inargentati tra grandi e piccoli," recorded in the 3 November 1540 inventory. The commission continued in 1525, when, on 8 March, the duke wrote to Francesco Gonzaga (ASMn, b. 2967, l. 32, c. 45) that he required "per adornare un loco nel nostro pallazo de Marmirolo dui peci di coramo dorato longo dece braza et ⅔ et ½ per cadauno et alti braza 6 et ¾, a braza da panno alla mesura mantuana, et dui altri pezzi longhi braza 7 et ½ et altri braza 6 et ¾ per cadauno, però volemo che voi li faciati fare lì che siano ben designati a qualche bella foggia." For Francesco's letters of 17 March and 4 September, see ASMn, b. 869, cc. 127, 406.

9. ASMn, b. 2931, l. 290, c. 22. For the letters from Francesco Gonzaga, see ASMn, b. 873, cc. 142–43, 154v, 212.

10. ASMn, b. 1152 (letters from Francesco da le Arme, 4, 19 January; 4 March; 4, 27 April; 13, 18 June 1529).

11. ASMn, b. 2926, l. 46, cc. 4v–5, 20, 25r–5, 44r–v, 67. For the letters from Francesco Gonzaga, see ASMn, b. 880 (25, 31 May; 5, 11, 15, 24 June; 3 July; 8 August). Related material exists for the years 1534–35 (ASMn, b. 1156: Francesco da le Arme) and 1537 (ASMn, b. 2525: Grossino). There are also scattered references to these matters in the *copialettere* of Federico II himself.

12. Braghirolli, 1879, 44. The ASMn, Schede Davari, also provides a transcription for one of three letters written in Mantua (4, [?], 12 October 1531) signed by Carlo (Bologna?). There it is learned that "le tapezarie de Basano sono gionte (. . .); non sono ancora gionte le mostre de quelle da Ferrara, ma le aspetto de hora in hora (...), ma per quanto intendo non sono dite tapezarie de messer Octaviano Dada, ma de Romano Tonbeso." The last-named letter also contains a reference to the "veluti de fare le spallere de 2 camarini."

13. ASMn, b. 1251.

14. Archival citation as above, note 1. Forti Grazzini, 1982, 61.

10. 11 MAY 1540
Tapestries in Ferrante's Residence in Messina

On 11 May 1540 Sernini wrote to Ercole regarding his recent visit to Ferrante and in the course of describing Ferrante's residence he commented on the "tapezzarie infinite":[1]

> Dil resto, la casa sua è così ben fornita di quello che bisogna a un suo pari che se ne può contentare, havendo letti et tapezzerie infinite et ogni cosa bellissima et, se io non l'havessi veduto, non l'harei creduto: ha più di vinti letti che se ne può servire in ogni honorata foresteria et del continuo ne fa lavorare et pur hoggi mi ha mostrate certe pezze di taffetta di Levante di diversi colori et mi ha detto che Vostra Signoria Illustrisima ne vole per tre letti, et credo ne restarà contenta non essendo di molta spesa et honesti da potersene servire in ogni occorrenza.

1. ASMn, b. 1910, cc. 420–21.

11. 18 JUNE 1541
Ercole Loans Tapestries to the Duomo for the Feast of Corpus Christi

It is difficult to say precisely when Ercole began the custom of loaning tapestries to the Duomo. The registers for 1540 say nothing, and it is only on 18 June 1541 that an entry reads: "Alli tappezarie del signore Illustrissimo per fare apparare la Giesa il dì dil Corpo di Cristo." A similar entry is found under 1 July.[1] The volume for 1542 contains a related reference (but adds the phrase "spalere grande") and in June 1544 payment was made: "per fare portare le tapezerie dalla corte del Cardinale per apparare la giesa per la solenità del Corpo di Nostro Signore."[2]

Among the payments relevant to the Duomo is one dated 20 June 1545 for "braccia vintitre di travello grosso per unze ⅔ per agiungere in chiesa per apparare le tapezzarie el dì del Corpo di Cristo."[3]

1. ASDMn, Massaria, r. 2981–82 (1540); r. 2983, c. 87 (18 June), c. 87v (1 July). References in earlier volumes, as, for example, r. 2972, c. 87, "for tapestries hung on festive occasions," appear to refer to church property rather than to objects personally owned by Ercole.
2. ASDMn, Massaria, r. 2984 (1542), cc. 112v–113; r. 2986 (1544), c. 106. Successive years have not been checked, but the indication is that the records never specify which set or sets were involved in the transaction.
3. ASDMn, Fondo Capitolo della Cattedrale, c. 85v, as published by Piva, 1988, 148.

12. 9 JANUARY–31 DECEMBER 1542
Karcher in the Service of Ercole and the "quadro de tappezaria dell'istoria de Moisè"

Although the record of payments comes from the volume for 1542, it refers to work begun in 1541. Indeed, in November 1542 Karcher was given 890 libre, 15 soldi, 6 picoli "posto in credito a lui nel precedente libro dell'anno 1541." On 3 July 1541 Sernini advised Ferrante Gonzaga of the tapestries commissioned by Ercole:[1]

> Di le tapezzerie che'l Cardinale ha disegnato fare a Mantova, non gli scriverò altramente il parere di Vostra Eccellenza, sì perché ècredibile che lo sappia et lo debbia fare per suo passatempo, poi Sua Signoria Illustrissima non me n'ha scritto, ma ne sono stato avisato da servitori di casa, et non so poi come l'intendesse né vorrei che giudicasse che io mi voglia intrometere in quello che non mi tocca.

Sernini's reference to work undertaken in Mantua can be related to payments that survive in the Fondo Portioli of the Archivio di Stato di Mantova for supplies delivered to Karcher's shop in the Borgo San Giorgio:[2]

> (A) Adì 31 de marzo 1542—E più soldi 0, piccoli 9, dati al fachino chi à portà lana tenta per le tapezarie che fano fare il prefato Reverendissimo a Santo Gorgo [sic].
> (B) Adì di 30 [aprile 1542] per chiodi numero 36 (. . .) per 'doperare da Santo Gorgo per il tapezero.
> (C) Adì 20 de novembre 1542: Maestro Bartolomé marango[n] de' havir da la corte del Reverendissimo et Illustrissimo signor Cardinale nostro libre una, soldi otto per lizaroli numero 28 per li tapezeri de Santo Gorgo.

The full significance of these references is revealed by the payments (9 January through 31 December) in the volume for 1542 in the Archivio Storico Diocesano.[3] The payments can be subdivided into various categories, including references to payments of the nearly 600 libre for the purchase of supplies:

(a) libre 45 paid on 28 January for "libre cinquanta de lana."
(b) libre 71, soldi 13, picoli 6 paid to Bassano Cortese on 6 June for "Libre 35 de lana tenta compre in Fiandra per fare tappezerie" (see under Document 13, n. 2).
(c) libre 60 given to messer Bartolomeo Brasilio on 18 June "per comprar lana per le tappezarie,"

(d) libre 133, soldi 4 and libre 193, soldi 14 for the purchase on 25 September by Ottaviano d'Adda of "libre tre de argento filato di brocato (. . .) comprato (. . .) in Milano per bisogno de far tapezzarie per Sua Signoria Reverendissima,"
(e) libre 26, soldi 15 paid to Karcher on 17 August "per comprar robba per far tappezaria," and
(f) libre 160, soldi 10 paid to Karcher on 4 November "per comprar seda a Verona per far tappezaria," while
(g) he received 72 libre on 19 December "per comprar lana."

On two occasions the records specify the precise nature of the work for which payment was given: for example, on 24 January 1542 Karcher received lire 545, soldi 14 "per la fattura de un quadro de tappezaria dell'istoria de Moisè, d'oro e seda alle de Fiandra 17, quadrato," while on 28 January 1542 he was paid 45 libre toward the cost of "quatro portiere."

A number of cumulative summaries of money owed and monies paid to Karcher are provided, including the reference under 4 November to the 890 libre "posto in credito a lui nel prececedente libro dell'anno 1541." During the course of 1542, payments to Karcher are recorded in the following amounts: libre 545, soldi 14; libre 938, soldi 9; libre 1,041, soldi 5; and libre 2716, soldi 17, picoli 6. This adds up to a total of libre 5240.

cc: 37*v*–38

— Maestro Nicolò contrascritto de'haver libre cinque cento quaranta cinque e soldi quatordeci posti a spesa in libro Venere a carta 49 per la fattura de un quadro de tappezaria dell'istoria de Moysè, d'oro e seda, alle de Fiandra 17 quadrato, a raggione de scuti [. . .] per alla, vigor bullette sott'il, dì 24 de gennaro 1542 in filo n. 16—libre 545 - soldi 14.
— E più libre trecento novanta doi, soldi quindeci posti in debito a lui in questo a carta 79—libre 392 - soldi 19. Libre 938 - 9 - 0.

[January]
— Maestro Nicolò Carchier tappezero de'dar a dì 9 genaro 1542 scuti sette d'oro contati a lui al conto delle fature che lui fa in far tappezarie per Sua Signoria Reverendissima—libre 37 - soldi 9.
— E più a dì 14 del soprascritto scuti sette d'oro contati a lui al conto soprascritto—libre 37 - soldi 9.
— E piu a dì 21 detto scuti sete d'oro contati a lui al conto soprascritto—libre 37 - soldi 9.
— E più a dì 28 detto libre quaranta cinque contante a lui a render raggione di libre cinquanta de lana d'esser compra per lui a soldi 18 la libra per far quatro portiere per sua signoria reverendissima—libre 45.
— E più a dì detto scuti sette contati a lui al conto soprascritto—libre 38 - soldi 9.

[February]
— E più a dì 6 di febraro 1542 scuti sette contati a lui al conto soprascritto—libre 37 - soldi 9.
— E più a dì 11 detto scuti sette contati a lui al conto soprascritto—libre 37 - soldi 9.
— E più a dì 18 detto scuti sette contati a lui al conto soprascritto—libre 37 - soldi 9.
— E più a dì 27 detto scuti sette contati a lui al conto soprascritto—libre 37 - soldi 9.

[March]
— E più a dì 4 de marzo 1542 scuti dette contati a lui a conto soprascritto—libre 37 - soldi 9.
— E più a dì 11 de marzo 1542 scuti sette contati a lui al conto soprascritto—libre 37 - soldi 9.
— E più a dì 20 detto scuti sette contati a lui al conto soprascritto—libre 37 - soldi 9.
— E più a dì 27 detto scuti sette contati a lui al conto soprascritto—libre 37 - soldi 9.

[April]
— E più a dì 3 de aprile 1542 scuti dicie d'oro contati a lui al conto soprascritto—libre 53 - soldi 10.
— E più a dì 8 detto scuti dicee d'oro contati a lui al conto sopracritto—libre 53 - soldi 10.
— E più a dì 15 detto scuti sette contati a lui al conto soprascritto—libre 37 - soldi 9.
— E più a dì 22 detto scuti sette contati a lui al conto soprascritto—libre 37 - soldi 9.
— E più a dì 29 detto scuti sette contati a lui al conto soprascritto—libre 37 - soldi 9.

[May]
— E più a dì 6 de maggio 1542 scuti sette d'oro contati a lui al conto soprascritto—libre 37 - soldi 9.
— E più a 13 detto scuti sette d'oro contati a lui al conto soprascritto—libre 37 - soldi 9.
— E più a dì 20 detto scuti sette contati a lui a conto soprascritto—libre 37 - soldi 9.
— E più a dì 27 detto scuti sette contati a lui a conto soprascritto—libre 37 - soldi 9.

[June]
— E più a dì 3 de giugno 1542 scuti sette d'oro contati a lui al conto soprascritto—libre 37 - soldi 9.
— E più a dì 10 detto scuti sette contati a lui al conto soprascritto—libre 37 - soldi 9.

cc. 49v–50

— Messer Zanibono Andreaso controscritto d'haver libre seicento venti, soldi tredeci et picoli quatro, posti a spesa in Libro Venere a carta 49 per il precio de varie robbe compre da lui per far un pezzo de tappezaria per bisogno di Sua Signoria Reverendissima vigore bullette sotto il dì di 24 gennaro 1542 in filo numero 15—libre 620 - scudi 13 - 4.

— Et più d'havere libre quatrocento diece, soldi desnove, picoli sei, posti a spesa in Libro Venere a carta 58 per il precio de varie robbe compre da lui per far tappezarie per Sua Signore Reverendissima vigore bullette de dì 19 de settembre per tutto dì ottobre 1542 in filio numero 100—libre 410 - soldi 19 - 6.

— Messer Zanibono Andreaso merzadro de'dar adì 25 de febraro 1542 libre ottocento novanta una, soldi quatro et picoli tre contate a messer Bartholameo del Zucha agente suo al conto delle robbe che lui ha datto per il bisogno de Sua Signoria Reverendissima—libre 891 - scuti 4 - 3.

— Et più a dì 20 de Maggio 1542 scuti cento d'oro contati a lui al conto soprascritto—libre 535.

— Et più a dì 22 de decembre 1542 libre seicento novanta otto, soldi quatordeci et picoli diece contate a lui al conto soprascritto—libre 698 - soldi 14 - 10.

— Et più de' dar libre cento sette, soldi quatro posti in credito a lui in questo a carta 123—libre 107 - soldi 4.

cc. 78v–79

— Maestro Nicolò contrascritto d'haver libre mille quaranta'una e soldi cinque, posti in debito a lui in questo a carta 92—libre 1041 - soldi 5.

[June]

— M[a]estro Nicolò Charchier, tappezero de'dar libre trecento novanta due e soldi quindeci posti in credito a lui in questo a carta 38—libre 392 - soldi 15.

— E più a dì 17 di zugno 1542 scuti sette d'oro contati a lui al conto delli fatturi che lui fa in far tappezzaria per sua Signoria reverendissima—libre 37 - soldi 9.

— E più a dì 23 detto scuti sette d'oro contati a lui al conto soprascritto—libre 37 - soldi 9.

[July]

— E più a dì primo di luglio 1542 scuti sette d'oro contati a lui al conto soprascritto—libre 37 - soldi 9.

— E più a dì 12 detto scuti sette d'oro contati a lui al conto soprascritto—libre 37 - soldi 9.

— E più a dì 15 detto scuti sette d'oro contati a lui al conto soprascritto—libre 37 - soldi 9.

— E più a dì 18 detto libre sesanta contate a lui per man de messer Bartolomeo Brasilio per comprar lana per le tappezarie di sua signoria reverendssima et a render raggione—libre 60.

— E più a dì 22 detto scuti sette d'oro contati a lui al conto soprascritto—libre 37 - soldi 9.

— E più a dì 29 detto scuti sette d'oro contati a lui al conto soprascritto—libre 37 - soldi 9.

[August]

— E più a dì 5 agosto 1542 scuti sette d'oro contati a lui al conto soprascritto—libre 37 - soldi 9.

— E più a dì 12 detto scuti sette d'oro contati a lui al conto soprascritto—libre 37 - soldi 9.

— E più a dì 17 detto scuti cinque d'oro contati a lui per comprar robba per far tappezaria—libre 26 - soldi 15.

— E più a dì 19 detto scuti sette d'oro contati a lui al conto soprascritto—libre 37 - soldi 9.

— E più a dì 26 detto scuti sette d'oro contati a lui a conto soprascritto—libre 37 - soldi 9.

[September]

— E più a dì 3 de settembre 1542 scuti sette d'oro contati a lui al conto soprascritto—libre 37 - soldi 9.

— E più a dì 12 detto scuti sette d'oro contati a lui al conto soprascritto—libre 37 - soldi 9.

— E più a dì 16 detto scuti sette d'oro contati a lui al conto soprascritto—libre 37 - soldi 9.

— E più a dì 23 detto scuti sette d'oro contati a lui al conto soprascritto—libre 37 - soldi 9.

cc. 91v–92r

— Maestro Nicolò contrascritto d'haver libre dua millia settecento sedeci soldi desette e picoli 6, posti a spesa in libro Venere a carte 64 per sua mercede et fattura et denari spesi in setta e lana per varii pezzi di tappezarie per lui fatti, vigore bullette sotto il dì ultimo di dicembre 1543, in filo numero 148—libre 2716 - soldi 17 - 6.

— Maestro Nicolò Carchier tapezzeri de'dar libre mille quarant'una e soldi cinque posti in credito a lui in questo a carta 79—libre 1041 -soldi 5.

— E più a dì ultimo di settembre 1542 scuti sette d'oro contati a lui al conto delle fatture che lui fa in far tappezzaria per sua signoria reverendissima—libre 37 - soldi 9.

[October]

— E più a dì 7 de ottobre 1542 scuti sette d'oro contati a lui al conto soprascritto—libre 37 -soldi 9.

— E più a dì 14 detto scuti sette d'oro contati a lui al conto soprascritto—libre 37 - soldi 9.

— E più a dì 21 detto libre quaranta contate a lui al conto soprascritto—libre 40.

— E più a dì 27 detto libre quaranta contate a lui al conto soprascritto—libre 40.

[November]

— E più a dì 4 de novembre 1542 scuti trenta d'oro contati a lui per comprar seda a Verona per far tappezaria ut supra et a render ragione—libre 160 - soldi 10.

— E più a dì detto libre quaranta contati a lui al conto delli fattura ut supra—libre 40.

— E più de' dar libre ottocentonovanta soldi quindeci e picoli sei posti in credito a lui nel precendente libro dell'anno 1541, signato Sole, a carta 113 per vigore del presente reporto—libre 890 - soldi 15 - 6.

— E più de'dar a dì 11 detto libre quaranta contate a lui al conto soprascritto—libre 40.

— E più a dì 18 detto libre quaranta contate a lui al conto soprascritto—libre 40.

— E più a dì detto libre quaranta contate a lui al conto sopradetto—libre 40.

[December]

— E più a dì 2 di dicembre 1542 libre quaranta contate a lui al conto soprascritto—libre 40.

— E più a dì 9 detto libre quaranta contate a lui al conto soprascritto —libre 40.

— E più a dì 19 detto libre settanta due contate a lui per comprar lana per il sopradetto bisogno—libre 72.

— E più a dì detto libre quaranta contate a lui al conto sopradetto—libre 40.

— E più a dì 23 detto libre quaranta contate a lui al conto soprascritto—libre 40.

E più a dì 30 detto libre quaranta contate a lui al conto soprascritto—libre 40.

cc. 103v.-104

— Il magnifico messer Ottaviano d'Adda de'dare libre centonovanta tre et soldi quatordeci poste in credito a lui in seguenti Libro segnato Jove a carta 64—libre 193 - soldi 14.

— 25 Settembre, Il magnifico messer Ottavino d'Adda (. . .) d'haver libre centotrentatre et soldi quatro posti a spese in Libro Venere a carte 58 per il precio de libre tre et soldi quatordeci per oncia, comprato per lui in Milano per bisogno de far tappezarie per sua Signoria Reverendissimo vigore bullette sott'il dì 25 de settembre 1541 in filo numero 101—libre 133 - soldi 14.

Whatever the problems these payments raise, they are the most complete surviving set that documents one aspect of Ercole's patronage of Karcher and the only one to provide a day-by-day accounting of the range of expenses incurred. It is important to note that at the same time that Karcher was working for Ercole in the Borgo San Giorgio, his agent in Flanders, Battista Cortese, the son of Bassano Cortese, was spending 1,547 libre on the acquisition of a ready-made set of *portiere,* as well as 9,635 libre on tapestries depicting subjects from the Old Testament (Documents 12–13 and 15). Between these and the monies given to Karcher, Ercole spent a small fortune (no less than a total of 1,547, 9,635, 1,082, and 1,909 libre) on figurative weavings between 1541 and 1542.

---

1. MOBE, AC, "Nino Sernini," no. 21a (addressed to Ferrante Gonzaga).

2. ASMn, FP, b. 6; Luzio, 1919, 34 n. 3, with the exception of no. C. See Document 9 for the transcription of the passage from the payment of 31 March 1542 concerning work by Nicolas for the ducal court itself.

3. ASDMn, MV, Amm, anno 1542 (libro Marte), cc. 37v–38, 49v–50, 78v–79, 91v–92r. 104, 110; Pecorari, 1991, 426–28; *Giulio Romano,* 1992, II, 962–64, 979–81, 993–95. ASDMn, MV, Amm. lacks the volume ("libro Venere") for 1541.

13. 3 MARCH 1542

Payment from Ercole for the Acquisition of "dodeci portiere"

As with the Old Testament series that Battista Cortese acquired (Document 15), the purchase of the twelve *portiere* refers to a commission undertaken in 1541 but only paid for in the following year. The Cortese family figures prominently in commercial transactions with Ercole, including "Santino Cortese da Lodi mercante in Roma and Bassano suo fratello in Mantua."[1]

According to Ercole's account books, a payment was made to Battista Cortese on 3 March 1542 in the amount of libre 1,547 "soldi duoi" "per il precio di dodece portiere di lana fina compre da lui":[2]

> Battista Cortese de'havere libre mille cinquecento quarantasette, soldi duoi, posti a spesa in libro Venere a carta 60 per il precio de dodece portiere di lana fina compre da lui per bisogno di Sua Signoria Reverendissima, computando altre spese et precio d'altre robbe (. . .) sotto il dì 3 de marzo 1542.

Nothing is known of the subject matter of these *portiere.* The payment should be seen in relation to the money paid to the same Cortese on 31 December 1542, but representing a debt actually incurred during the preceding year for the acquisition of tapestries depicting scenes from the Old Testament (Document 15).

1. As cited in ASDMn, MV, Spese, b. 22, c. 2. For various transactions conducted by Bassano de Cortese, see ASMn, Repertori Notarili, Cizzoli (1511–57) under the following dates: 20 February 1537, 2 January 1538, 26 March 1539, 27 February 1540, and 4 April 1549. See ASDMn, MV, Carteggio, b. 1, c. 185, for Ercole's letter to his factotum of 3 February 1537 concerning the need to "conservare il credito con messer Bassano," and a related letter from Francesco Andreasi of 22 January 1537 (ASMn, b. 1906, c. 652).

2. ASDMn, MV, Amm., 1542, cc. 109v–110, 115. Pecorari, 1991, 428, no. 3. On c. 110 reference is made to the following: "et più de'haver libre settant'una, soldi tredeci et picoli sei posti in spesa in Libro soprascritto [Venere] a carta 60 per altri tanti spesi in libre 35 de lana tenta compra in Fiandra per far tapezzaria (. . .) sott'il dì 6 de zugno 1542—libre 71 - soldi 13 - 6." The acquisition of wool at this time would seem to relate to work undertaken by Karcher (Document 12, under c. 110).

14. 28 December 1542
Tapestries for Ercole's Dining Room in the Palazzo Vescovile

After 1540, when he became co-regent, Ercole devoted more attention to his residence in Mantua in the Palazzo Vescovile (Fig. 6). Between 1540 and 1542 Giulio Romano and his team undertook various repairs and created a range of friezes and related decorative paintings.[1]

A payment dated 28 December 1542 concerns work done by Pompeo in the Palazzo Vescovile in Mantua. Pompeo was required to create a frieze only in the Camera di Mezzo, a room that served as the cardinal's dining room, since the remainder of the wall surface was to be covered with tapestries.[2] Conceivably this document is to be read in conjunction with the commission given in 1541 and thus with Documents 13 and 15:

> La corte de lo Reverendissimo et Illustrissimo signor Cardinale de Mantoa de' dar a maestro Ponpio pittor e li conpagni quali àn lavorato in Vescovado a ragiongere un freso over alargarlo ni la Camera di Mezzo dove magna soa reverendissima signoria fatto per rispetto de le tapaciarie che non agiongevan su le banche, qual agionta di freso monta de soa fatura e suo colore libre una, soldi sedici, cioè libre 1, soldi 16.

Given his future role as adviser to Ercole in matters pertaining to the purchase of tapestries (Documents 43 and 46), it is important to note that Antoine Perrenot, the future Cardinal Granvelle, was among the first to see the tapestries in the Camera di Mezzo when he dined in the Palazzo Vescovile in January 1543.[3] As for the hangings involved, they presumably relate to the payments to Cortese for the acquisition of *portiere* as well as for "varie istorie del Testamento Vechio" (Documents 13 and 15). Alternatively these payments might relate to work commissioned from Nicolas Karcher (Document 12).

1. Piva, 1985, 15–17. For references to overlooked payments, largely from 1542, see Brown (1991, 222 n. 5). See the latter also for a discussion of the surviving plan of the old Palazzo Vescovile and the location of Ercole's apartment.

2. ASMn, FP, busta 6.

3. MOBE, AC, under Ippolito Capilupi (6 January 1543, addressed to Ferrante).

15. 31 December 1542
Payment to Battista Cortese for Ercole's Acquisition of Old Testament Tapestries

Although recorded under 1542, the expenses actually refer back to 1541 and thus are related to the same campaign that resulted in Ercole acquiring a group of *portiere* tapestries (Document 13). The column "de' dar" in the account book for 1542 breaks down the money owned to Battista Cortese into two portions of libre 3,129, soldi 15 and libre 6,505, soldi 6, picoli 3.[1]

> — (c. 99v) Battista Cortese de'dar libre tre millia cento venti nove e soldi quindeci posti in credito a lui nel precedente libro dell'anno 1541 signato Sole a carta 58 per vigore del presente reportato—libre 3129 - soldi 15.
>
> — (c. 100) Messer Battista contrascritto de'havere libre tre millia cento venti nove et soldi quindeci posti in debito a messer Bassano Cortese, suo padre, in questo a carta 117 ut supra—libre 3129 - soldi 15.

Under the date 31 December 1542,[2] payment in the amount of libre 9,635, soldi 1, picoli 3 is recorded to Bassano Cortese for expenses incurred by his son Battista: "in Fiandra in varii et diversi pezzi de tappezzaria di lana e seda fina fatti in varie istorie del Testamento Vechio."

> — (c. 117) Messer Bassano Cortese de'haver libre nove millia seicento trenta cinque, soldi uno et picoli trei posti a spesa in Libro Venere a carta 62 per altri tanti che messer Battista suo figliolo à spesi in Fiandra in varii et diversi pezzi di tappezzaria di lana et seda fina fatti in varie istorie del Testamento vechio vigore bullete sotto il dì ultimo decembre 1542 in filo numero 135—libre 9635 - soldi 1 - picoli 3.

The breakdown for these expenses as given in the "de' dar" column (c. 116v) is as follows:

— messer Bassano controscritto de'dar libre tre millia cento vinti nove e soldi quindeci posti in credito a messer Battista Cortese, suo figliolo, in questo a carta 100—libre 3129 - soldi 15.
— Et più de'dar libre sei millia cinquecento cinque, soldi sei e picoli trei posti in credito a messer Francesco Andreaso, fattor, in questo a carta 128, per tanti che lui ha fatto credito a esso messer Battista nel suo libro Vulcano a carta 4 et debitor mi Pietro Sivello nel medemo libro a carta [. . .]—libre 6505 - soldi 6 - picoli 3.[3]

It is clear from the records that Cortese had made the purchases the preceding year, thus about the same time that he had acquired the "dodeci portiere" (Document 13). The size and magnitude of the purchases Ercole authorized suggest that it was at this time that he acquired some or all of the Old Testament series (*Tobias, Saul, David,* and *Joseph*) recorded in the 1563 inventory (Document 49). The *Tobias* and the *Saul* are specifically mentioned as being in Ercole's possession when the Cardinal of Trent was entertained in Mantua in 1547 (Document 22). Francesco inherited the *David* and the *Joseph* and his inventory (Document 52, nos. 6–7). Unfortunately, his inventory does not provide any indication of their worth. Federico's inventory (Document 51, nos. 6 and 7) claims that the *Tobias* was worth 787½ scudi, while the *Saul* was valued at 397½ scudi, for a total of 1,185 scudi.

1. ASDMn, MV, Amm. 1542, cc. 99v–100r. Pecorari, 1991, 428, no. 3; Giulio Romano, 1992, II, 998–99. The "volume dell'anno 1541 signato Sole" does not exist. It should be noted that on cc. 114v–115 funds were provided to Bassano Cortese for his trip to Flanders.

2. ASDMn, MV, Amm., 1542, cc. 116v–117r.; Pecorari, 1991, 428, no. 3; *Giulio Romano,* 1992, II, 995–96.

3. c. 128 reads: "Il spettabile messer Francesco Andreaso, fattore, de'haver (. . .) et più de'haver libre sei milla cinquecento cinque et soldi sei posti in debito a messer Bassano soprascritto in questo a carta 117 per tanti che esso ha fatto creditor esso messer Bassano in suo libro Vulcano a carta 4 et debitor mi Pietro Sivello nel medemo libro a carta 104—Libre 6505 - soldi 6."

16. 16 April 1543
Ercole Responds to a Loan Request from Ippolito d'Este

On 16 April 1543 Cardinal Ippolito II d'Este wrote from Ferrara regarding the need for "razzerie et coltrinaggi alti et senza arme per apparare salle et stantie grandi" in order to honor certain visiting "forastiere."[1] Through his sister-in-law, Margherita Paleologa, Ercole responded that it was difficult to find suitable hangings in Mantua in part because much had been sent to San Benedetto Po in anticipation of the arrival of Paul III.[2]

> Non si è mancato, secondo l'ordine lasciatomi da Monsignor nostro Illustrissimo et Reverendissimo nel partir di Sua Signoria per Viadana, di far cercare di razzarie et coltrinaggi alti senza arme, secondo il bisogno di Vostra Excellentia, non solo in casa, ove poche tapezzarie sono rimaste per essersi mandato a San Benedetto ciò che vi era di buono per el bisogno medemo che essa le vorrebbe, ma anco tra li mercadanti et hebrei che ne sogliono vendere et in effetto non si è truovato cosa al proposito, di che mi increscе summamente per lo desiderio in che sono di vederla sodisfatta in ogni cosa dove bisogna che la si habbi per iscusati se di qua non se gli ne manda. Partita che sia Sua Santità di Santo Benedetto, penso che Monsignor Reverendissimo, conoscendo che possi essere a tempo, non restarà di farle avisare di subito cio che vi sarà al proposito.

1. ASMn, b. 1207 bis.

2. ASMn, b. 2940, l. 328, c. 126. Paul III met Charles V at Busseto. The pope traveled to San Benedetto Po, while the emperor went to Canneto, in order to invest Francesco III Gonzaga with title to both Mantua and Monferrato. As noted by Piva, 1988, 119 n. 85, the 1592 *Cronica della vera origine (. . .)* of B. Luchino refers to the tapestries Ercole provided to accommodate the pope.

17. 10 November 1544
A Gift from Ercole to Karcher

Although in itself insignificant, the gift of two birds for the feast of Saint Martin serves to fill the gap that otherwise exists in what is known of Ercole's relationship with Karcher between 1542 and 1549.[1]

> Item a dì detto [lo Novembre 1544] a mastro Nicolò Carchier tappezer per comprar due oche grasse per la festa di san Martino—Libre 1 - soldi 10.

1. ASDMn, MV, Amm., b. 20, c. 171v. Pecorari, 1991, 430, no. 8.

18. 24 MARCH 1547
Cartoons for Spalliere *for Ferrante's Milanese Residence*

On 24 March 1547 Ferrante learned from Domenico Giunti of the progress that was being made by the "poveri mastri" who had been charged with the creation of "cartoni delle ispalliere":[1]

> Li cartoni delle ispalliere si fanno, però li poveri mastri non ànno mai posuto avere un soldo del servito dalla Camera di quello sono restati per istima d'accordo, con dire che non c'è danari; però li tratengo con dire che quella alla sua venuta subito li farà pagare, altrimenti non volevano lavorare.

1. Baroni, 1968, 483, no. 1122.

19. 31 AUGUST 1547
A Letter to Ferrante from Jehan Baudouyn Concerning the Fructus Belli

Jehan Baudouyn's letter of 31 August 1547 turned up "presso un negoziante d'autografi" at the end of the nineteenth century.[1] In clear and unequivocable terms, it justifies the costs involved in the weaving of the set ("trois ducas d'or pour chacune alune" and "deux cens cincquante carlus d'or ou environ" for the commission itself), which is identified in the first sentence as the "histoire du Fructus Belli." Presumably the set had been commissioned by the end of 1544 or the beginning of 1545, since only the eighth and final piece remained to be woven in the summer of 1547. The *Fructus Belli* was displayed in Ferrante I's Milanese residence on the occasion of the arrival of Philip II in Milan in 1549.

In addition to the letter written from Brussels on 31 August 1547 in an attempt to obtain additional funding, Baudouyn is known to have communicated with Ferrante on 15 June and 2 August 1547.[2] The information contained in these letters is largely the same as what is found in the letter published by Rossi, although mention is made of a certain Giovanni Balbani, who was to evaluate the set together with Giovanni Battista Lodi.[3] Presumably Balbani was related to Tomasso, a Lucchese merchant in Antwerp who rented a shop in Antwerp in 1546 for a period of six years.[4] As for the "Anthoine Marco" who provided funds to Baudouyn, he is to be identified with Ferrante's secretary (ASPr, b. 41, c.1) and not with the painter Antonio Moro:[5]

> Illustre vertueulx et Mag.me Princie
> Comme ainsy soit que je Jehan Baudouyn povre serviteur et tappissier de Vostre Excellence a Bruxelles en Brabant en faisant l'histoire du Fructus Belli, me treuve grandement et tellement agravé que tout ce que ma vie durant j'ay peu amasser, je y ay employé et encoires, ce ne suffisant, je y suis au derrière plus que la somme de deux cens ducas d'or pour honnorablement et fidélement servir vostre noble excellence comme j'ay faict, et encoires entendz fer jusques à la fin et totalle perfection de l'ouvraige de Vostre Excellence, esperant que Vostre Noblesse tiendra et observera de sa part les bonnes promesses que Vostre Magnificence, estant ensemble ses nobles en ma povre maison, lors me feist quant en desvelopant l'ouvraige de Vostre Seigneurie de l'hostieu, en voyant le quel, je me complaindiz grandement et remonstroys a Vostre Noblesse que ne me seroit nullement possible le continuer et parachesver sy richement et de telle finesse d'estouffes comme je l'avoys encommenché pour le pris quil estoit contraicté, sy je ne me vouloys en tout destruire et ruyner.
>
> A quoy Vostre Excellence lors me va respondre, maistre Jehan Baudouyn, continuez et parachesvez mon ouvraige selon la bonté et finesse encommenchée et je suis content que ce que maistre Jehan Baptiste painctre et autres marchans bien entenduz diront et jugeront que vous aurez plus merité que le contract, je le vous feray payer reallement et de faict. Sur la quelle bonne promesse et totale confidence de Vostre Illustre Magnificence, j'ay continué la besoingnie et ay sy honnorablement servy Vostre Excellence, comme les bons marchans d'Anvers et autres partout journellement disent, que j'ay bonne confiance que Vostre Illustre Magnificence ne vouldroit permettre ny desirer que je povre tapissier de Vostre Magnificence seroys perdu et destruict à vous bien et fidelement servir. Car je vueil tenir bon que je y ay merité en finesse d'estoffes et en manifacture de bon ouvraige le valeur de trois ducas d'or pour chacune aulne et que plus est je presente à faire mon serment solempnel que journellement en Anvers s'en vent a trois ducas l'aulne qui n'est à beaucoup pres sy fin d'estouffe, ne le bordures sy bien estoffées comme est l'ouvraige de Vostre Excellence. Parquoy, o vertueulx et illustre Prince, je suis content que Vostre Excellence jouysse de fruict de mon labeur et diligence sans que en riens je y proffite, mais il plaira à

Vostre Illustre Magnificence me oster hors de la tres grande charge ou je me trouve et me secourrir de quelque bonne somme de déniers pour pouvoir parachever et parfaire l'ouvraige de Vostre Excellence encommenchée. Dont ne reste á faire que une seulle pièche.

Il est bien vray que Anthoine Marco m'a furny oultre la calculation contractée la somme de deux cens cincquante carolus d'or ou environ, parquoy il ne veult plus riens debourser ni advancher plus d'argent et quant à ma part, je n'ay pas la puissance de povoir parfaire l'ouvraige de Vostre Excellence sans provision de nouvelle assistence, car je y ay employé tout ce que j'avoys au monde vaillant pour le reduire en l'estat auquel presentement il est. Pour la quelle cause en toute humilité a Vostre Illustre Excellence je supplie que vostre bon plaisir soit me pouveoir et furnir d'aultant de deniers que je puisser achesver vostre dicte ouvraige et honnorablement je satisferay a Vostre Illustre Excellence et si lors à Vostre Illustre Excellence en chose qui concerne mon art aulcunement je puisse servir, Vostre Illustre Magnificence me trouvera tousjours pour vostre loyal serviteur à tousjours et jamais, ce scait Dieu le créateur, au quel je prie que à vous, illustre, vertueulx et magnanime Prince, donner et octroyer l'accomplissemente de voz tres nobles et vertueulx desirs.

De Bruxelles ce derrenier jour du moys d'aoust 1547.

De Vostre Seigneurie

humble serviteur
Jehan Baudouyn tappissier
à Bruxelles en Brabant.

1. Rossi, 1889, 252–53. The original document is no longer traceable.

2. Hymans, 1910, 23–25.

3. Giovanni Battista Lodi was also involved in commissioning the *Puttini* (Document 32).

4. Donnet, 1897, 82.

5. Hymans, 1910, 23–25.

20. 30 SEPTEMBER 1547
Ercole's Troy *Tapestries in the Palazzo Vescovile*

Among the expenses incurred during the course of 1547 is a reference to the *Troy* tapestries, which, together with certain leather hangings, were moved from the ground floor to the rooms on the *piano nobile* of the Palazzo Vescovile (Fig. 6):[1]

— per far portar le tapezarie di Troia et distachar li corami et locarli et transportar la robba dalle camere di sotto alle camere di sopra in facchini et in chiodi—Libre 2 - 10.

1. ASDMn, MV, Amm., b. 18, c. 381.

21. 6 OCTOBER 1547
Ercole Orders Payment for "una spalera a fogliami grandi"

On 6 October 1547 Ercole authorized the payment of 176 libre to Bassano Cortese for a "spalera a fogliami" measuring 12 *alle* in length and 3 *alle* in width:[1]

> de'dare alla botega de Basano Cortexe per una spalera a fogliami grandi, fina, longa alle 13 e alta alle 3 in toto sono alle 39 a ¾ de ducato per alla de primo costo in Anversa, monta Libre 157, soldi 10 e de' dare per la condutta d'Anversa a Mantova provisione, datio et altre spexe, in tutto Lire 18 - soldi 10—Libre 176 - soldi 9.

1. ASDMn, MV, Entrate e Uscite, b. 18, c. 412.

22. 30 NOVEMBER 1547
Ercole's Saul *and* Tobias *Hung in the Palazzo Vescovile*

On 30 November payment is recorded for cleaning the *Saul* and the *Tobias* tapestries, which had been placed in the rooms reserved for the visiting Cardinal of Trent (Fig. 6).[1] Both sets are recorded in the 1563 inventory (Document 49). Based on the 1547 reference, a *terminus ante quem* can be established for their acquisition:[2]

> In facchini, chiodi et brochette per parar et disparar le camere alla venuta di monsignor reverendissimo di Trento et più per far sbatter le tapezarie di Saul et di Tobia et governar—libre 3 - 4.

1. ASDMn, MV, Amm., b. 18, c. 433. Pecorari, 1991, 430, no. 9. On another occasion (ASMn, FP, b. 7, 30 August 1559), Ercole ordered "per far portar sei somme di corami da casa del signor Don Cesare [Gonzaga] in vescovato et per far apparare le camare alla venuta della signora Duchessa di Urbino."

2. ASDMn, MV, Amm, b. 18, c. 433, under the heading "Henrico Hollonio debbe havere dalla corte di monsignor illustrissimo et reverendissimo di Mantova per altri tanti spesi per bisogno della camera et in servizio del signor Francesco et suoi pagi." The previous month, on

20 September 1547 (ASMn, b. 410b), reference is made in the economic records of Duke Francesco III Gonzaga to payment for having "portavisse de Curia in Castro et converso in diversis vicibus, tapezarias, apparamenta, mataracios, piumacios(. . .) et aliis rebus pro usu illustrissimi domini nostri et pro forcieri et casse et aliis rebus que portavise de curia ad navem conductendam ad Reverem et hoperi due facti per Antonio et Gobbo in batendo et squasando tapezarias de castro." Under the same year other references are found to "maestro Jacomo tapezerio per sua mercede in repezando sex spaleria a verdure" as well as to "maestro Francesco tapezerio." It is not clear whether the loan from Ercole included figurative tapestries.

23. 9 JUNE–17 OCTOBER 1548
Karcher Expected Back in Mantua for His Daughter's Wedding

On three separate occasions (9 June, 19 September, and 6 October), the Mantuan court sent urgent communications to Karcher requesting that he return for his daughter Catherina's wedding:[1]

> A maestro Nicola Carchero: Maestro Nicola mio carissimo, Vi scrissi fin alli XVIII del passato come si stava aspettando la venuta vostra per concludere il matrimonio di vostra figliola Catherina, mia creata, el che non mi parea di fare senza la presentia vostra, et non ne ho mai inteso altro. Et perché al giovane sono proposti, come vi fu scritto, de gli altri partiti di maggior dote quali si è cercato fin hora di fare escludere, si manda hora vostro figliolo a posta acciò c'habbia da cavar ferma rissolutione, che andando di questa maniera la cosa alla longa, li potrebbe parrere d'essere burlato, et potria pigliarsi ad altro partito. Così ve aspetto con ferma rissolutione.

In response to these messages, Karcher (who had left Mantua to take up residence in Florence in October 1545) wrote to Margherita Paleologa on 30 September and then again on 17 October 1548.[2] The first letter explained the reasons Karcher was unable to leave Florence: he was in the middle of a legal suit against one of his financial backers.

While the second letter largely repeats what was said previously, it does hold out the possibility of Karcher undertaking work for Paleologa—specifically the creation of "alquanti cosine de tapiceria per la camera," and he asked that "me manderà el disigno" and requested Paleologa to write on his behalf to "signor Maiordome messer Peter Fransisco Rizo" to enlist his support with regard to Karcher's legal problems. It is not known if Margherita commissioned new work or if she contacted Rizzo. As for the letter of 30 September, the entire text reads:

> Ho ebuto una di Vostra Excellentia che me portò Rafel, fiollo di messer Iule Romane, et ho vedute quanto Vostra Signoria me fa instancia del venire a Mantua, la qual cossa al presente non m'è posibile che io me posso partire perché sono intrato in uno conpromesso contro uno fiorentino, il qual volle la mità di quanto io posso fare in Fierenza et questo è per causa de una promessa che me aveva promesso di non amancarmi de quater overo sei mille scuti, se seria stato di bisogno, he non à mai trovato un quatrino, siché adesso sono a le mane stretamente per cavarmi forra di questo obligo. Spero in la Excellentia del signor Duca mio patrono et nel suo maiordomo me caverano fora di tanti afani. Considerando adonca questa cossa e non potendomi partire, mandovi el mio fiollo Gulielmo[3] in loco mio, el qual è informato de la menta mia con litera di procura he tuto quello ch'el farà in questo ato del matrimonio del Catalina sarà ben fato, he così prego Dio gli consede la sua santa benedicione che poseno far bene in sino al fino. Non starò a recomandarvi la Catalina perché è Vostra creata e vostra serva, credo che semper vi sia recomandata, he tuto quello che ò promesso ne le mane de messer Ioan Carlo, el qual à la scrita ne le sue mane, non amancherò he farò più che non ho promesso he tanto presto quanto poterò me troverò in Mantua he se mancherà quelche cossa, io non amancherò, he se posso qualche cossa per Vostra Excellentia, lo farò più che volontiere. Io poso lavorare a chi ben mi vene, siché averò di gratia che Vostra Excellentia me comanda. Io et la mia consorta, vostri servitori, con tuto el cor si recomandemo a Vostra Excellentia, pregando di continue Dio la prospera con tuti li soi carri fiolli.

Regarding Karcher's failure to pay his portion of the marriage dowry, see Document 31.

1. ASMn, b. 2941, l. 333, c. 72v, c. 86, c. 90.
2. ASMn. b. 1962, cc. 345, 378. See Adelson (1990, 512–13, no. 32) for the letter from Pier Francesco Riccio to Cosimo I de' Medici announcing Karcher's arrival from Mantua.
3. "Magistro Guielmo filio quondam magistri Nicolai tapezerii" was one of the artisans involved with the preparation of Ercole's funeral catafalque in May 1563. See ASMn, AN, notaio Agostino Ragazzolo, pacco 7566.

24. 1 JANUARY 1549
The Fructus Belli *in Ferrante's Residence in Milan*

In his account of Philip II's visit to Milan in 1549, Juan Cristobal Calvete de Estrella described the banquet Ferrante had held in his honor on 1 January 1549.[1] While referring only in passing to the "riquísima tapicería," he specifically identified those in the "sala" as the *Fructus Belli.*

> El siguiente día, que fué de Año nuevo, de mil y quinientos y cuarenta y nueve, fué el Príncipe a cenar en casa de don Hernando de Gonzaga (. . .). Estaba la posada de don Hernando de Gonzaga en orden y muy adereçada de riquísima tapicería que había harto que ver en ella. Estaba el patio cubierto de un entrecielo por causa de sereno, todo cercado de muchas hachas encendidas que hacían el patio tan claro como si fuera de día. Había debajo de los soportales del patio hechos tres ricos estrados, y el de medio y más alto para la real persona del Príncipe, y el de la mano derecha para la Princesa de Molfeta y su hija y damas, y también en el de la siniestra estaban muchas señoras y hermosas damas muy ricamente vestidas y de muchas joyas adornadas. Los Caballeros dançaron con ellas al uso de la tierra. Dançó el Principe con la hija de don Hernando, esposa de Fabricio Colona, y el Duque de Alba con la Princesa y los Señores y Caballeros cada uno como iba tomando por la mano las damas, que casi no quedó ninguno que no dançase, y en esto se entretovo el Príncipe buena pieça.
>
> Luego entraron a cenar en la sala por una puerta que había junto a los estrados. Era la sala para solo aquel efecto hecha y labrada de nuevo y adornada de muy ricos paños de tapicería, en los cuales se podían ver historiados por muy sutil arte y gran artificio todos los hechos de la milicia y arte de la guerra, y lo que a un Príncipe guerrero y gran Capitán en ella suele acaecer. Detúvose el Príncipe un poco en mirarlo, en tanto que la Princesa y su hija con todas aquellas Señoras y damas entraban.

1. Calvete de Estrella, 1930, 1, 79–82.

25. 7 MAY–31 DECEMBER 1549
Ercole Authorizes Payment to Anselmo Guazzi for Cartoons

"Anselmo di Guazi dipintor" was one of the painters involved in the redecoration of the Palazzo Vescovile in the fall of 1549; he had also been involved in the project in 1540, when Giulio Romano was in charge.[1] One of the few works attributed to Guazzi is the decorative frieze with *putti,* swags, and eagles that survives from the 1540 project. Various documents link him to work under the supervision of Giulio Romano at the Palazzo Te and in the Ducal Palace, and his hand has recently been identified with certain frescoes at San Benedetto Po.[2] Given Guazzi's modest skills, it may be presumed that the designs prepared for Ercole's tapestries were largely decorative rather than monumental figural compositions.

According to Ercole's records, Guazzi received 151 libri on 31 December 1549 for work undertaken between 7 May and 3 August on the production "de cartoni che lui fa per la tappezzaria che se deve fare in Fiandra."[3] It remains to be determined if any connection exists between this payment and money provided, beginning on 21 September 1549, to Bassano Cortese for the tapestries produced in Flanders (Document 28):

> — Maestro Anselmo controscritto de'haver libre cento cinquanta una et soldi quattro posti a spesa in libro signato Tonsone a carta 142 per haver depincto cartoni quattro per far fare tappezzaria (. . .) sotto il dì ultimo de dicembre 1549—Libre 151 - soldi 4.
> — Maestro Anselmo Guazo depintor de'dar a dì 7 di maggio 1549 scuti quatro d'oro contanti a lui a conto de cartoni che lui fa per la tappezzaria che se deve fare in Fiandra et a render ragione—Libre 21 - soldi 12.
> — e più de'dar a dì 29 detto scuti quattro d'oro contanti a lui al conto soprascritto—Libre 21 - soldi 12.
> — e più de'dar a dì 19 di zugno 1549 scuti cinque d'oro contanti a lui al conto soprascritto—Libre 27.
> — e più de'dare a dì 5 di luglio 1549 scuti diece d'oro contanti a lui al conto soprascritto—Libre 54.
> — e più de' dare a dì 3 d'agosto 1549 scuti cinque d'oro per lui (. . .)—Libre 27

1. Piva, 1985, 9ff.
2. Tanzi, 1989, 137–38; Berzaghi, 1981, 299–300.
3. ASMn, FP, b. 5, cc. 89v–90.

26. 16 AUGUST–26 SEPTEMBER 1549

The Loan of Ferrante's Aeneas *for the Marriage of Francesco III*

Writing from Milan on 16 August 1549, Annibale Litolfi communicated Ferrante's response to Sabino Calandra's memorandum of 7 August 1549 regarding the decoration of the rooms in the Castello for the forthcoming marriage of Francesco III.[1] Ferrante approved of the plan for the manner in which the rooms were to be covered with hangings: "gli adornamenti et apparati delle stanza nuove et vecchie si come hanno del necessario et del magnifico così sumamente piacciono a Sua Eccellenzia"; he nonetheless suggested that a second set of hangings be used, at least for the room of Catherine of Austria:

> si pensi alla provisione di qualche seconda sorte d'apparati, almeno per le stanze della Serenissima sposa, perché non converebbe di tenervi al continuo quelli delle nozze et perciò serà di mistiero havere qualche tapezzaria da mettere in luogo di quelle che si levassero et lauderia che si circasse d'haverne di Fiandra.

The "brevità dil tempo," Ferrante admitted on 16 September, "tolto il potere fare far nuove tapezzarie."

In this same letter of 16 September, Luzzara also spoke of Ferrante's willingness to loan to Mantua his *Aeneas* set for the *sala nuova,* which was perhaps one of the rooms in the Appartamento di Troia, the suite created adjacent to the Castello by Giulio Romano between 1536 and 1539. The *Aeneas* was identified as one that had been purchased specifically to honor Philip II:

> Ho letto la lettra vostra al signor Don Ferrando Illustrissimo la cui Eccellenza come amorevolissima che è, offerisse in generale spagliere, argenteria et ciò che altro è in poter suo, ma venendo al particolare d'essa vostra lettra dirò tutto quel che di parte in parte mi fu risposto nel leggierla.
>
> Quanto alle spagliere per la sala nuova, Sua Eccellenza dice che non ne ha che tirino tanto in longo, come si ricercano, di 174 ale, ma ne ha ben che di altezza aggiongono alle sei, et queste sono quelle della Historia d'Enea, de quali non si è servito se non alla venuta dil Principe di Spagna et, avenga che non siano tanto longhe come bisognarebbono, non dimeno le darà molto volontieri potendosi provedere alla longhezza con aggiongerne un pezzo all'altro et sono in tutto da xiiii pezzi.

The *Aeneas* consisted of fourteen pieces, six *ale* in height but somewhat shy of the desired 174 *ale* in length (see also under the Index of the Major Sets of Figurative Tapestries). We know from Giovanni Maria Luzzara's letter 23 September 1549 that the "spagliere dell'historia d'Enea (. . .) ponno essere in tutto da cento ale."[2] Although he was willing to ship the *Aeneas* set from Milan, Ferrante was less well disposed to part with the contents of his storage rooms, which Luzzara examined and which contained hangings, silk fabric, and leather rather than figurative tapestries, reserved for an anticipated visit of Charles V:

> Et perché messer Gioanni le disse che sarebbono tanto buoni gl'apparamenti di seta o qualche corami di che Sua Eccellenza ne èbenissimo fornita, secondo che egli et io habbiamo visto hoggi nella sua salvarobba che ci ha mostrata il Zaffardo. Rispuose che tutti questi apparamenti ella gli ha fatti fare per la venuta dell'Imperatore, la quale potrebbe essere l'estate che viene, et però non li lasciarebbe vedere imperoché allhora non sarebbono puoi tenuti per nuovi.

On 18 September 1549 Ferrante was advised that Giovanni Colla had left for Milan to accompany the shipment to Mantua of the objects loaned "per le mie nozze."[3] In the end, however, Colla did not take the fourteen pieces in the *Aeneas* set from Milan for, on 26 September 1549, Luzzara referred to the loan from Ferrante of "otto di quelli dell'Historia di Enea, et cinque d'un'altra sorte." Furthermore, he was also given by Barbara Trivulzio "tredeci pezzi di tapezzaria molto bella."[4] The possibility of tapping the Trivulzio resources had first been raised by Luzzara in his letter of 16 September. Lacking the personal resources to provide "tapezzarie almeno per quattro stanze," Ferrante suggested that the Duke of Mantua turn for assistance to either the "signora Barbara madre dil già Conte Giovanni Trivultio o dal Conte Francesco dalla Somaglia."

The thirteen-piece Trivulzio set is not otherwise identified in the correspondence. As for Ferrante's "cinque d'un altra sorte," it is conceivable that they were from the set of six mentioned by Luzzara in his letter of 16 September 1549. There, in addition to offering the *Aeneas* tapestries, mention was made of "un altro apparamento di sala di certe tapezzerie, le quali sono da sei pezzi et fanno assai bel vedere, ma sono hormai vecchie et da lei usate spesso."[5]

1. ASMn, b. 199, cc. 106–21 (7 August); Intra, 1896, 41ff. ASMn, b. 1669 (16 August). Regarding the wedding itself, see *L'Entrata*, 1549. The anonymous author says nothing about the manner in which the rooms were appointed. The booklet does, however, refer to the wall hangings that Ercole placed in the Palazzo Vescovile (Document 29). For the letter written on Ferrante's behalf by Giovanni Maria Luzzara on 16 August 1549, see ASMn, b. 1669.

2. ASMn, b. 1669 (23 September).

3. See also ASMn, b. 2973, l. 62, c. 116v (18 September 1549) for Francesco III's letter announcing Colla's departure from Mantua. ASMn, b. 1669 (Luzzara to Francesco III: 26 September).

4. ASMn, b. 1669 (Luzzara to Litolfi: 26 September). Luzzara added that "il Conte Francesco non ha tapezzarie," and as for Barbara Trivulzio he stated that "quando morse il Conte suo figliolo elle erano di già state imprestate via et però non ne sapea ben render conto, ma se le havrebbe fatte restituire."

5. On 11 December 1549 (ASMn, b. 2942, l. 338, c. 31), Francesco III wrote "alla Signora" that "si rimanda a Vostra Signoria le spaliere che la si contentò di servire in queste nozze." See also ASMn b. 1919, c. 371 for the 4 October 1549 letter from the Bishop of Reggio to Ercole regarding the loan "de le tapezzerie et paramenti pontificali ch'lla mi ricerca per queste sue nozze."

27. 5 September 1549
Payment to Karcher for Ercole's "Carpetta" Made in Florence

On 5 September 1549 Ercole authorized payment to Karcher of 615 libre to cover the cost of the manufacture of a carpet. Of this amount, 320 libre was for the purchase of silk and gold threads.[1]

— Maestro Nicolò controscripto de'haver libre seicento quindeci et soldi dodeci posti in debito a lui nel seguente libro signato Acteon a carta 125—Libre 615 - soldi 12.

— Maestro Nicolò Caricher tappezzer de'dar a dì 5 di settembre 1549 scuti sesanta d'oro conti a messer Achille da Covo per tanti fatti pagar a lui in Firenze per comprar seda et oro per far una carpetta per Sua Signoria Reverendissima et a render ragione—Libre 320.

— e più de'dar libre ducento nonantauna e soldi dodici posti in credito al spectabili messer Francesco Ceppo fattor in questo a carta 170 per tanti conti a messer Achille da Covo suprascripto—Libre 291 - soldi 12.

Presumably the money referred to in this transaction was what Karcher was to have sent to Mantua to cover his share of Catherine's dowry (Document 31). In addition to receiving the *Acts of the Apostles* and the *Puttini* from Ercole's estate (Document 48), Guglielmo Gonzaga was also assigned "una carpetta di seta, oro, et argento, granda in campo verde, longa braccia 13."[2] Might this be the carpet made by Karcher? Under the rubric "carpetta" in the 1563 inventory, one first finds reference to two of "veluto" and two of "panno verde." There is, however, also reference to "una carpetta da tavola de seda verde nova, con un friso alla morescha d'oro et d'argento et sette de diversi colori," as well as to "una carpetta di lana fina et seda, d'un quadrono, nova, con il friso," to four more of various types of "veludo," and a miscellaneous group of an additional seven, including the "carpetta" for the "studiolo di panno verde, trista."

As a sequel to the Gonzaga commission, and between 1550 and 1553, Karcher wove a "carpita alla moresca" for Cosimo de' Medici. The Medici "carpita" has survived and is now found in the family villa at Poggio a Caiano.[3]

1. ASMn, FP, b. 5, c. 134v–135.

2. ASMn, RN, Agostino Ragazzolo, pacco 7566 (13 July 1563). See Document 49, nos. 1, 2, and 14, for the remainder of the bequest to Guglielmo.

3. Adelson and Landini, 1990, 54, fig. 2. This reference was kindly provided by Nello Forti Grazzini.

28. 21 September 1549–1553
Tapestries Ordered in Antwerp for Ercole

Payments made in 1549 and 1553 provided Bassano and Battista Cortese with a total of 9190 libre. On 21 September 1549 Cardinal Ercole authorized 1,620 libre to be given to Bassano Cortese as a partial payment for a set of tapestries whose creation he was overseeing in Flanders:[1]

— Messer Bassano Cortese de'dar a dì 21 de settembre 1549 scuti trecento d'oro conti a messer Ambroso di Arsago, suo agente, sotto dì 29 d'agosto 1549 per parte de precio de tappezzarie che lui fa fare in Fiandra et a render ragione—Libre 1620.

— Messer Bassano controscritto de'haver libre millesei-centoventi poste in debito a lui nel seguente libro signato Acteon a carta 172.

This payment was preceded on 20 August 1549 by one in the amount of libre 804 - 2 - 6 "per il precio de tappezzarie.[2] There is every reason to believe that this payment in the ASMn is to be related to those recorded in the account books in the ASDMn of 1553, which refer back, however, to 1550:[3]

— Messer Battista contrascritto de'haver libre seimillia settecento sessantasei et soldi quattro, posti a spesa in Libro signato Andromeda a carta 147 per il precio di più pezzi di tappezzarie vigore bullette sott'il dì 10 di decembre 1553 in filo n. 1—Libre 6766 - soldi 4 (c. 176).

The breakdown of this amount is found on c. 175v:

— Messer Battista Cortese de'dar libre tremillia cinquecento trentasei et soldi dodeci, posti in credito a lui in questo a carta 141 [Messer Battista Corte de'haver libre tremillia cinquecento trentasei et soldi dodeci posti in debito a lui in questo a carta 176—Libre 3536 - soldi 12].
— Et più de'dar scuti trecento sette et mezzo d'oro, posti in credito a Bettino Focarino in questo a carta 158 [Messer Bettino Focarino (. . .) de'dar scudi trecentosette e mezzo d'oro posti in debito a messer Battista Cortese in questo a carta 176 per tanti fatti pagar a lui in Anversa per conto di tappezzarie sotto l'anno 1550—Libre 1660 - soldi 10] per tanti pagati a suo fratello Gierolamo in Anversa a conto tappezzarie - Libre 1660 - soldi 10.
— Et piu de'dar a dì 23 di decembre 1553 scudi cinquanta d'oro contati al signor Maestro di casa per dar a lui al conto soprascritto—Libre 270 - soldi [. . .]
— Et più de' dar a dì 29 detto scudi cento d'oro contati al soprascritto al conto soprascritto—Libre 540 - soldi [. . .]
— Et più de'dar libre settecento cinquantanove et soldi dui, posto in credito a lui nel seguente Libro signato Paride a carta 73—Libre 759 - soldi 2.
Libre 6766 - soldi 4.

The relationship between these payments and the payments for cartoons to Anselmo Guazzi (Document 25) remains somewhat of a mystery.

1. ASMn, FP, b. 5, cc. 134v–135.
2. ASMn, FP, b. 5, cc. 109r–v.
3. ASDMn, MV, Amm., anno 1553, cc. 140v–141, 158, 175v–176; Pecorari, 1991, 429, no. 6.

29. OCTOBER 1549
The Hangings in the Palazzo Vescovile on the Occasion of the Wedding of Francesco III

The reference to the fabric and the figurative hangings displayed in the Palazzo Vescovile on the occasion of the marriage of Francesco III is the only published description of the interior of Ercole's residence:[1]

Finita la messa (. . .) li prefati illustrissimi signori sposi (. . .) se ne tornorno adietro riducendosi a desinar (. . .) nel Vescovato ad un banchetto preparatogli da monsignor Reverendissimo nostro: il quale, per li molti varii delicati cibi et preciosissimi vini et ordini tenuti da gentilhuomini riccamente vestiti che alle mense serviano, fu di tanta magnificentia ornato et degno di tanta commendatione, che volendovi spiegar in queste carte tutte le qualità sue, sarebbe un voler asciugar con un picciol vaso l'ampio letto del mar Adriano over accogliere nelle nodose reti i freddi spiragli di Borrea et di Aquilone: però, traslasciando ciò che ne potrei dire, conchiudovi in due parole che fu un convito pontificale (. . .). Si ritirorno tutti insieme in alcune camere tappezzate di finissimi et bellissimi drappi d'oro, d'argento et di seta di piú colori, maestrevolmente contesti, nei quali tanti diversi animali, alberi, frutti et fiori al vero conformi dentro vi si scorgeano, che'l gran Parasio et l'ingegnoso Fidia, l'uno in tela et l'altro in marmo a gran pena gli havrebbe potuti piú alla maestra natura verisimili dimostrare."

Payments on 4 and 25 January 1549 for "chiodi numero 100 da vaso per atacare le tapezarie" might be connected with these hangings.[2] The payment in August 1549 to Girolamo Ferrar "per un canon de lata per mandar un carton in Fiandra per tapezzaria" refers, however, to a commission that could not have been finished in time for this event.[3]

On 29 November 1549 payment was made for a range of work, unspecified repairs to the cardinal's collection of wall hangings, by "Jeronimo sarto," doubtless for the wedding.[4]

— Item, per haver fodrato dui pezi di tapeceria per il camerino di Sua Signoria Reverendissima—Libre 2 - soldi 0 - denari 0.
— Item, per haver fornito peze numero 66 de tapecarie et pezi numero III de curamo adorate per le camare et le altre tapecarie di Fiandra a soldi 6 per pezo, et come le corde di sopra - Libre III - soldi 16 - denari 0.

1. *L'Entrata*, 1549, 5v–6.
2. ASMn, FP, b. 6.
3. ASMn, FP, b. 6, no. 46.
4. ASMn, FP, b. 6. It should also be noted that on 4 October 1549 (ASMn, b. 1912, c. 371) the Bishop of Reggio wrote to Ercole regarding the "tapezzerie et paramenti pontificali ch'ella mi ricerca per queste sue nozze." It is not clear if Ercole requested the "panni et paramenti" for his own use or on behalf of the court (Document 26).

30. 6 MAY 1551
Work Commissioned by Ercole from Karcher

Ercole wrote to Karcher on 6 May 1551 to advise him that Giovanni Carlo Borromeo "mercante fiorentino"[1] would be in Florence and that he was charged with providing a response to Karcher's letter regarding work in progress for Ercole.[2] Unfortunately, no folder of correspondence survives in the Mantua archives from Florence for this year:[3]

> A maestro Nicolò Carcieri: Maestro Nicolò, alli dì passati havemmo una vostra lettera, nella quale mostravate di disiderare di sapere la mente nostra intorno al dare compimento di coteste cose che fate per noi et, tra per la nostra indispositione et altre occupatione che habbiamo havute, non vi habbiamo mai puotuto rispondere, ne farvi sapere quel che vogliamo che facciate. Hora che se ne viene a Firenze maesser Giovanni Carlo Borromei, habbiamo voluto scrivervi questa nostra per dirvi che circa alle dette cose habbiamo aperta la mente et voluntà nostra allui, acciò che, giunto ch'egli sia, vi venga a ritrovare et chiarirvi per vostra sodisfattione di quanto vogliamo che facciate et di ciò che desideramo da voi intorno al proseguire l'opera già incominciata per noi. Voi, pertanto, sentirete quello ch'esso messer Giovanni Carlo vi dirà da parte nostra et farete appresso ciò che dal lui vi serà ordinato, perché tutto è secondo il voler nostro, et ci rimettiamo alla relatione di lui, facendo voi certo che, essequendo quanto vi dirà, ci sarà tutto grato et accetto et state sano.

1. ASMn, b. 1112, for many letters from Florence from Giovanni Borromeo (1537) and from his son Carlo. See also ASDMn, MV, Amm., registro anno 1542, cc. 51v, 10lv. In the former he is called "mercante in Mantua"; in the latter he is referred to as "mercante fiorentino."

2. ASMn, b. 2942, l. 337, c. 120v (6 May 1551).

3. Ercole's letter to Karcher is found in a volume of *copialettere* belonging to Guglielmo rather than among his personal *registri* and could relate to the *Moses* series in Milan (Catalogue 7). The tapestries were probably not commissioned specifically for Cardinal Carlo Borromeo, for his arms are not included in the borders. They might have been presented to Carlo toward 1560, when his sister Camilla married Guglielmo's cousin Cesare, the son of Ferrante. The gift to Carlo is recalled by Bernardino Pia in 1568, when Guglielmo was advised of the possibility of purchasing "quelle belle tapezzarie che l'Illustrissimo et Eccellentissimo signor Duca nostro gli mandò a donare" (ASMn, b. 900, c. 905, 7 February). On the *Moses* series, see Forti Grazzini (1982, 189ff.) and Catalogue 7.

31. 26 NOVEMBER 1551–28 JANUARY 1552
Karcher Misappropriates Funds from Ercole Intended for His Daughter's Dowry

In September 1549 Ercole provided Karcher with 615 libre to cover the cost of the manufacture of a carpet (Document 27). Conceivably these were the funds Karcher referred to as having been claimed by his partner in his absence, thus leaving him without funds to send to Mantua to cover his portion of his daughter's marriage dowry.

On 26 November 1551, Margherita Paleologa wrote to remind Karcher of his obligations, pointing out that the court had paid its share of the dowry:[1]

> A mastro Nicolò Carchieria. Mastro et cetera. Voi sapete che quando si maritò la Catarina, vostra figliuola, acciò che ne havesse da seguire l'effetto si fece per me promessa al marito che egli per conto della dote sarebbe intieramente satisfatto, così di quel ch'io intendeva che ella dovesse havere da me per la servitù fattami, come di quanto le era per voi constituito in dote. Da me al tempo in che si restò egli è stato intieramente satisfatto, ma da voi non ha già per anchor potuto havere cosa alcuna con tutto che di tanto sia passato il termine che si prese, per il che non posso fare di non raccordarvi che dobbiate satisfare a quanto sete tenuto, che, havendovi io intromessa la mia parola, non potrei mancare di mantenerla a tutto mio potere, et così vi piacerà di fare senza mettervi più tempo in mezo, che, oltre che farete quel che potra il debito vostro, sarà anco a me di piacere et sodisfattione.

Karcher was not in Florence when Paleologa's letter arrived. In his response, dated 28 January 1552 (Fig. 8), he lamented that while in Venice his colleague has taken the money deposited with an unnamed Florentine merchant by Ercole and he offered instead to transfer to Catherina the income from the "intrata di Casalle" (Document 23).[2]

> Esendo io venuto de Vinetia a Fierenza, ho trovato una litera che me scrive madona Antonia per parte di Vostra Excellentia, cioè che io voglio esser contento di fare dare certe dinari che ereno in mane de un marcante fiorentino per conte di lavori che io aveva fato per lo Reverendissimo Monsignor el Cardinal, et che talli dinari faseci dare a messer Fransischo mio genero e sertamente così era l'intento mio di fare; or essendome ito a Vinetia, el mio conpagno à levato le deti dinari, per la

qual me sono molto adirato e molto mal contento, ma, vedendo non poser far altro sino averemo fato li nostri conti, me lo porta inpaciencia poiché la mia sort così vole. Or credo che Vostra Excellentia debe sapere como Madona Antonia Balliana tene ne le sue mane la nostra poco intrata di Casalle, già è sei anni pasati, che monteria scuti cento e octi a Lire 18 ogna anno. Ben credo che Sua Signoria abia fato alquanta spessa per la Catalina, la qual è più che rasone la si debe renborsare, poi quello che si avansa la sia contenta di darele a la Catalina he poi rimetere quella poca intrata a la Catalina e che la goda sino abia el modo di di [sic] contentarela, e così prego Sua Signoria sia contenta di fare e così credo che Fransisco nostro genero sarà contento he prego Dio di contiva conserva Vostra Excellentia in prospera sanità e gli baso la mane.

1. ASMn, b. 3002, l. 7, c. 91.
2. ASMn. b. 1967, c. 51.

32. 9 FEBRUARY 1552
The Commissioning of a Set of Tapestries for Ferrante

On 5 February 1552 Giovanni Battista Lodi wrote to advise Ferrante about the options that existed in Brussels for the weaving of a set of tapestries.[1] Dated MDLI "ab incarnatione," the year is to be corrected to conform to the modern calendar, in which the new year begins on 1 January rather than on 25 March.[2]

All'Illustrissimo et Eccellentissimo Signore il Signore Don Ferando Gonzaga, Capitan Generale di Sua Maestà et Governatore del Stato di Milano et cetera, Signor mio osservandissimo.

Illustrissimo et Eccellentissimo Signor mio Signor osservandissimo,
Hauta la commissione di Vostra Eccellentia sopra le tapezzarie da farse subito, il Nicola et io andassimo a Brusselles dove, fatta ogni diligenza, al fine habbiamo fra tutti gli altri trovato uno sufficiente con molti et buoni lavoranti, accomodato di fine sete d'ogni colore, il quale per la Cesarea Maestà riduce in tapezzaria d'oro l'impresa di Tunis. Gli mostriammo l'opera con buon modo. Egli domanda per l'ultimo prezzo, a farle ricche d'oro et di finissime sete, quatuordeci fiorini per ala. E con che ci assottigliassimo assai, non si puotè tirar a manco. Ma volendoli dar noi l'oro, le farà, per otto fiorini l'ala, di sete finissime, e l'oro gli daremmo promette lealmente et bene metter ne l'opera.

Egli ha fama del miglior mastro che ivi si trove, et per tale l'habbiamo riputato noi a le opere sue. Se sarà il nobil piacere di Vostra Eccellentia farle espedire per lui, la suplico humilmente farne avertire qual de duo modi più le agrada.

Non mi pare se gli debba mettere argento, perché in breve divien negro et disdice assai. Nientedimanco la volontade di Vostra Eccellentia sia fatta, a la cui, come buono et humil servitore che le sono, inchinevole mi rimetto per sempre. Et pregando Idio per la felicitade di Vostra Eccellentia, le bascio con tutta riverenza le illustrissime mani.

Da Lira a li V di Febraro MDLI ab incarnatione - Di Vostra Eccellentia - Humilissimo servitore - Battista Lodi pittore.

1. ASPr, ES, b. XVIII. Orbaan, 1923–24, 252–53; Delmarcel and Brown, 1988, 120–21.
2. Given the date and the reference to gold and silver, this letter doubtless documents the commission for the *Puttini* (Delmarcel and Brown, 1988, 116–17). See also Catalogue 5.

33. CIRCA 1555
Ferrante Pawns a Portion of His Collection

In 1557 Camilla Borromeo stated that Ferrante had raised 1,000 scudi for the fortifications of Guastalla by pawning tapestries valued at between 3,000 and 4,000 scudi.[1] She maintained that the losses to the family should be covered by the emperor because by fortifying Guastalla, Ferrante had protected one of the flanks leading to Milan.[2]

Quando, in tempo del cardinale di Trento et del marchese di Pescara, si diede principio a la fortificatione di questa terra per servigio di Sua Maestà, il che fu la salvatione de lo stato di Milano, il signor Don Ferrando di gloriosa memoria, ricercato da detti signori, prestò loro alcune tapezzarie le quali essi impegnarono per molti scudi da servirli in detta fortificatione et da l'hora in qua, che debbono essere poco men de venti anni, sono state sempre pegno in man de giudei. Il signor mio consorte [Cesare], che sia in gloria, supplicò a Sua Maestà che fosse servita farle disimpegnare et ella ordinò al governatore di Milano che s'informasse et facesse relatione. Questa relatione è stata mandata da Milano non è molto et sarà costì in poter del signor Contadore Vargas o di alcuno di quei altri signori segretarii. Vi prego a fare ogni diligenza per tolerarla et per procurare che Sua Maestà la intendi et ordini quel che più le sia servigio, che non è honesto, che per mille scudi spesi in servigio di Sua Maestà questo figliolo ne

> perdi tre o quattro mila, quanti vagliano le dette tapezzarie. Siate contento non mancare in questo de la diligenza che di voi mi prometto, dandomi con le prime avviso del seguito.

According to this text, Ferrante had acted on behalf of the Cardinal of Trent and the Marchese of Pescara. The date specified by Camilla, "poco men de venti anni," sets the event to the very year of Ferrante's death, in 1557. Conceivably, therefore, Camilla meant to say "poco più," which would mean that the loan using tapestries as collateral could have been made shortly after Ferrante was relieved of authority as governor of Milan, and thus to the years 1555–56, when he was back in Guastalla. This date appears correct also because the Cardinal of Trent replaced Ferrante as governor of Milan in 1556.[3]

---

1. ASPr, b. 50/1 (1 January, 12 March 1577).
2. Ercole referred in October 1557 to his having loaned Ferrante "mille [scudi] prestati per la fortificatione di Guastalla" (ASMn, r. 6512, cc. 79v–80v). See ASMn, b. 1945, l. 4, cc. 3r, 48, 60–62, 74–75, 82–83, for references in letters from Ercole to Cesare Gonzaga of 1558 regarding the need to "finire la fortificatione."
3. In Ferrante's *ristretto* for 1557 (ASPr, b. 44), there is the copy of a letter written to Don Alvero di Sandi on 10 July requesting that "nel suo passaggio per lo stato, parlò al Cardinale di Trento de gli avanzi suoi con gli quali si dovevano disimpegnare gli argenti di Sua Eccellenza." See ASPr, b. 44 (18 July: to Mauro), which refers to "gli argenti impegnati per il signor Cesare," and which furthermore identifies the pieces as those pawned to Isach as well as to the "giudeo di Lodi."

34. 25 JULY 1555
A Decree by Guglielmo in Favor of Karcher

The decree signed by Duke Guglielmo, perhaps on orders from Ercole, who was still regent, reaffirms privileges originally granted by Federico II in 1539 (Document 9), especially and specifically with regard to twelve members of his shop:[1]

> Gulielmus et cetera. Considerantes votis magistri Nicolae Carcherae de Brusselle, tapetum curiae nostrae confector[is], qui a nobis petendum curavit ut exemptionem sibi concedere velimus pro duodecim operariis, quos exercet in dictis tapetis conficiendis, tenore presentis decreti, vigore nostri arbitrii et absolutae potestatis, quibus publice fungimur in hac nostra civitate Mantuae totoque eius dominio, ducatu et districtu, ex certa quoque nostri scientia et animo bene deliberato, concedimus dicto Nicolae pro dictis duodecim operariis, seu operariis ipsis, per id tempus quo prefatae curiae nostrae serviet, immunitatem et exemptionem macinae datii vini pro parte ipsi seu ipsis spectante et gabellarum eumque sive eos immunem sive immunes facimus ab omnibus aliis datiis et gravaminibus quibuscunque per dictum tempus ita ut duodecim operariis sive prefatus Nicolas possit singulis annis dicti temporis molere seu moli curare illud omne frumenti seu cuiuscunque grani et emere vinum ac conducere Mantuam, quod opus fuerit pro usu dictorum duodecim operariorum, libere et impune et sine solutione macinae et datiorum quorumcumque, sed teneatur dictus Nicolaus accipere bullettam debitis temporibus dictam immunitatem a magnificis magistris Intratarum nostrarum, qui magistri curent ne dictus magister Nicolas gaudeat iis immunitatibus nisi pro operariis duodecim, qui re ipsa hanc artem exercebunt. Mandantes ipsis magistris Intratarum, officialibus ad datium vini, ad quos spectat vel in futurum spectabit, ut immunitatem hanc per id tempus quo curiae nostrae serviet, dicto magistro Nicolae observent et observari faciant (. . .). Datum Mantuae sub fide nostri maioris sigilli, die XV iulii MDLV.
>
> A dì XV di ottobre 1555 fu fatta una dichiaratione che la sovrascritta essentione s'intendi intiera sì per la parte spettante a maestro Nicola et suoi operari, come per quella delli venditori da' quali comprerà robbe per uso suo et d'essi operari.

---

1. ASMn, Libri dei Decreti, vol. 44 (1553–56), fol. 220. Bertolotti, 1889, 1041; Luzio, 1914, 110–11; Luzio, 1919, 34.

35. 1 DECEMBER 1556
An Appeal to Mantua Concerning Karcher and His Acquisition of Property at Sermide

Endimio Calandra's letter from Venice of 1 December 1556 is addressed to the custodian of the Ducal Palace, Pietro Martire Cornacchia.[1] By this date Guglielmo Gonzaga had obtained the age of majority and Ercole no longer ruled Mantua as co-regent. Nonetheless, and in view of the fact that Karcher has served Ercole, it may be that his influence was expected in convincing Karcher to honor his commitment to Giovanni Mocenigo. Karcher's involvement with commissions in Venice may date back to his 1551 trip (Document 31):

Scrissi di Padova a messer Giovanni Mocenigo per maestro Niccolò tappezziero, ma mai hebbi risposta da Sua Signoria. Poiché son venuto qui mi ha parlato et s'è doluto molto della scortesia usatagli da maestro Niccolò al qual dice che ha mandato doe volte et che ad un gentilhuomo fece la più impertinente risposta del mondo. Io me son maravigliato che maestro Niccolò che suole essere la dolcezza et amorevolezza del mondo sia diventato così terribile. L'ho escusato ch 'el male et la necessità lo dovevano stringere et ho cercato di placarlo. Et m'ha detto che aspettava di veder se gli osserva quello che gli ha promesso, di portargline doi pezzi a questo Natale; caso che non, che cercarà di provedervi per altro mezzo. Però pregate maestro Niccolò che non manchi di venire et osservare la sua parola, che, se acquista un puoco di credito, qui non gli mancarà di lavorare; io l'ho scritto molte volte, ma a me pare che non l'intenda. Io fo l'ufficio anco per questa volta et se non giova, non potendo tener più questo gentilhuomo, lasciarò che faccia ciò che vorrà. Se porta questi doi pezzi di tapezzaria haverà denari et ciò che vorrà che darà ardire che si possa parlare per lui, ma, in tanto tempo, non vedendosi opera alcuna, mal si può parlare.

Predating this letter by many months is a notary act of 5 February 1556.[2] With it Karcher used the dowry provided by his son Anselmo's wife, Catherina, to acquire property "in villa Carbonariae potestariae Sermidi":

> Ibique magnificus dominus Federicus, filius quondam magnfici domini Johannis Francisci, cognominati Grossini de Grossis, nobilis Mantuae de contrata predicta Aquilae, per se et cetera, iure proprio et in perpetuum (. . .) dedit, vendidit et traddidit magistro Nicolao, filio quondam Alovisii Carcherae, tapezario, civi Mantuae, habitatori in Burgo Sancti Georgii, suburbio Mantuae, ibi presenti, ementi et acquirenti pro se et cetera et de denariis dotis honestae mulieris dominae Catherinae, eius nurus, uxoris Anselmi, eius filii, et pro cautione et bona securitate dictae dotis adeo quod aliquis creditor ipsius magistri Nicolai quantumcumque anterior et quamcumque pretendens ipothecam etiam anteriorem et quomodocumque privilegiatam non preferratur dictae dominae Catherinae sed ipsa omnibus sit anterior et ita ipse magister Nicolaus dixit et declaravit ac expresse prothestatus fuit, cui declarationi et prothestationi prefatus dominus Federicus consensit unam petiam terrae arativae et salicivae bobulcarum septem sitam in Villa Carbonariae potestariae Sermidi, in contrata Pizoni, penes viam communis a primo latere, dominum Vincentium de Andreasiis a secundo, dominum Julium Agnellum a tercio et ipsum dominum venditorem a quarto, salvis et cetera (. . .). Et hoc pro precio et finito mercato inter ipsas partes facto, firmato et concluso scutorum centum auri, scilicet et ratione librarum quinque et soldorum octo parvorum Mantuae pro singulo scuto. Quod precium seu quos scutos centum prefatus dominus Federicus ad instantiam dicti magistri Nicolai presentis, stipulantis et acceptantis pro se (. . .), dixit et confessus fuit se habuisse et recepisse (. . .) a dicto magistro Nicolao (. . .) prout constat publico instrumento rogato per me notarium paulo ante stipulationem presentis instrumenti (. . .) Ego Hieronymus, filius quondam domini Johannis Baptistae de Cizolis, notarius, rogatus et cetera.

1. ASMn, b. 1489; Luzio, 1914, 111; Luzio, 1919, 35.
2. ASMn, AN, notaio Gerolamo Cizzoli, pacco 784.

36. 13 OCTOBER 1557
Ercole Responds to Ferrante's Offer to Provide Tapestries

On 13 October 1557 Federico Maffei wrote from Brussels about the notable decline in the price of tapestries.[1]

> L'altro giorno (. . .) [il signor don Ferrando] (. . .) mi disse anchora ch'io dovessi scrivere a Vostra Signoria Illustrissima se la pensasse di fornirsi la casa di tapezarie, che ora hé il tempo, perché quello che già valea dodeci, hora non val otto, maxime qui non vole tapezarie di molta finezza.

Maffei had written earlier on this matter. On 2 October 1557 Ercole wrote to thank him for Ferrante's offer to find tapestries.[2] Despite the drain on his funds for other needs, Ercole advised that he was willing to consider spending between 1,500 and 2,000 scudi for tapestries, provided that they depicted scenes from either the Old or the New Testament. Specifically eliminated from consideration were tapestries depicting "favola o cosa lasciva," as such subjects were not "conveniente al grado et profession mia:"

> Ho ricevuta la vostra lettera di del presente nella quale d'ordine et in nome del signor Don Ferrando mi ricordate che questo sarebbe appunto tempo da fornirmi di tapezzerie havendo io bisogno, o voluntà di comperarmene. A che vi rispondo che voi havete fatto bene a scriverlomi sì come anco Sua Eccellenza ha, secondo il suo solito, fatto amorevolmente a darmene questo ricordo, ma ella non ha già mostrato d'havere in memoria che non mi sono mai stati restituiti quei VI mila scudi di

sempre, né anco gli altri mille prestati per la fortificatione di Guastalla, i quai danari insieme con dell'altre spese che mi è convenuto fare da alcuni mesi in qua mi fanno pensar ad altro in questo tempo che a fornirmi di tapezzarie. Tutta volta non lascierò di dirvi che questa così buona occasione che Sua Eccellenza me ne dà trovandosi in cotesti paesi, potrebbe farme venir voluntà di comperarne alcuni pezzi quando si trovasse cosa a proposito mio, ma io non ne haverei bisogno per più che per un paio di camere, et queste vorrei che fossero di bellissima sorte, et havessero dentro della seta et un poco d'oro et d'argento, et che insieme fossero di cosa conveniente al grado et profession mia, cioè che non contenessero favola o cosa lasciva, ma qualche historia della scrittura et del Testamento Vecchio (. . .). Havendo sopra tutto l'occhio a questo, che io non voglio nelle dette tapezzerie spender più che millecinquecento fin in duemila scudi (. . .). Le tapezzarie che dico di sopra non vorrei che passassero v ale di Fiandra et fossero di varii pezzi, non molto larghi per poterle meglio accommodar nelle camere.

Ferrante died the following month, and it is therefore doubtful if he was able to find what Ercole required: a set composed of various pieces, suitable for placing in various rooms and not exceeding 5 *ale* in height

1. ASMn, b. 1929, c. 457; *Rome 1984*, 145 n. 25.
2. ASMn, r. 6512, cc. 79v–80v; *Rome 1984*, 145 n. 26.

37. 1 NOVEMBER 1557
The Second Testament of Ercole and the Acts of the Apostles

On 1 November 1557 the notary Gerolamo Cizzoli drew up the second of the three surviving testaments (Documents 3 and 48).[1] In it provision was made for endowing the Duomo in Mantua with the "aulea sua actuum apostolorum." Except for extraordinary circumstances, the marriage of the *primogenito,* or to honor a particularly distinguished visitor, the authorities were forbidden from removing the tapestries from the premises. Ercole subsequently changed his mind (Document 48) and in the end the *Acts* was given to Duke Guglielmo for use in the palatine church of Santa Barbara:

> Item, reliquit et legavit praedictae Ecclesiae cathedrali aulea sua actuum apostolorum, quae aulea non vult unquam asportari ab ipsa ecclesia, neque mutuo dari aliquibus nisi in casu quo illustrissimus dominus Dux Mantuae duceret uxorem et opus esset ornare aliquam ecclesiam in celebratione missae pro ipsis nuptiis seu alia quacumque gravi re, quae accideret et pertineret ad decorem et honorem et commodum praefati illustrissimi principis et Ducis pro tempore existentis.

In the absence of other evidence, the 1557 reference to the *Acts* provides a secure *terminus ante quem* for its acquisition and proves that the payment to Orsini in March 1559 (Document 40) for the design of the cardinal's coat of arms had nothing whatsoever to do with the purchase of the *Acts.* Furthermore, it is clear that Ercole had no need to act on the offer of a set made by Cardinal Granvelle in 1562 (Document 46).

Having established the *terminus ante quem* for the Mantuan series of the *Acts,* it remains to be determined when precisely the set was purchased. In the absence of other evidence (the *registri economici* in the ASDMn lack many of the relevant years, while the *registri* preserved in the ASMn begin only with 1552), this task might have been made easier if Cizzoli had kept a copy of Ercole's testament of 19 December 1554.[2] For if Ercole owned the *Acts* by that date, he surely would have made special provision for its disposition. Cizzoli did retain the 26 March 1555 "Codicillus," which, however, is not relevant here.[3] The *Repertori Notarili* (Gerolamo Cizzoli) for 1555 records under the date 7 November 1555 yet another "Testamentum Reverendissimi et Illustrissimi Domini Cardinalis Mantuae." Unfortunately, Cizzoli annotated his index with the phrase "cancellatum et conbustum fuit," the same phrase one reads under 5 December 1555: "Testamentum Reverendissimi et Illustrissimi Domini Domini Cardinalis Mantuae." Where these testaments should be found in the *minute,* Cizzoli left the note in the first instance, "Hic cadit Testamentum Reverendissimi et Illustrissimi Cardinalis cassum et non repertum in filcia licet sit in inventario," and in the second, "Hic cadit Testamentum Reverendissimi et Illustrissimi Domini Cardinalis cassum et combustum prout fit mentio in inventario."[4]

Given that testaments of 1554 and 1555 were withdrawn, it has not been deemed necessary to refer to them otherwise and thus to leave the 1557 and 1563 testaments as Ercole's second and third, although they were actually his fifth and sixth. It is difficult to understand why Ercole felt it necessary first to draw up and then cancel two testaments, especially when he left intact until 1563 his 19 November 1557 testament, which made certain provisions for his brother Ferrante, who had actually died on 16 November.

1. ASMn, AN, notaio Gerolamo Cizzoli, pacco 784; Pecorari, 1989, 429–30, no. 7.

2. ASMn, Repetori Notarili, Girolamo Cizzoli, b. 27 (1554), "Testamentum Reverendissimi et Illustrissimi Domini et cetera—19 Decembris 1554 (non est in filcia suprascriptum testamentum)."

3. ASMn, AN, notaio Cizzoli, pacco 784, 1555, no. 23 (26 March 1555).

4. ASMn, AN, notaio Cizzoli, pacco 784, 1555, nos. 68 and 78. Merely to complete the picture, although it has no bearing on the tapestries, Ercole compiled a codicil on 17 September 1558, the only known copy of which is found in ASPr, RM, b. 129.

38. 11 AUGUST–15 SEPTEMBER 1558

Ercole Responds to Bernardino Pia Concerning the Placement of Tapestries in the Roman Palace

The residence in question appears to be the "Palazzo di Portogallo" referred to in Giuliano Cesarino's letter of 11 May 1558,[1] rather than the residence on Via Alessandrina (Document 8). In his letter of 9 April 1558, Bernardino Pia reported that "sono finiti i cinque piani fatti in strada alla facciata in contro la scala grande de questa casa di Portogallo, et si è agiustata et accomodata tutta la facciata in modo che pare che si sia fatto di novo una gran fabrica et di molta spesa. Si fano hora quelli di dentro per sostegno della scala."[2] Few of Bernardino Pia's letters survive. Thus one must rely entirely on the responses from Mantua to reconstruct the decoration of Ercole's residence.

On 11 August 1558 Ercole responded to Pia's report on work accomplished.[3] The "camera principale" was to be decorated with the "più belle tapezzarie che mi truovi," so that it would be suitable to receive "ogni persona honorata che venga per corteggiare o per parlarmi":

> Ho havute le vostre di XXX del passato et III del presente et visto quanto mi scrivete, et massimamente da parte del signor Giuliano[Cesarini], intorno al rifare del solaio della camera principale, poi che così la chiamate, o pur farvi solamente i fregi. A questo vi rispondo che se per camera principale voi intendete quella che è in capo alla saletta, son risoluto che, dovendo andare ornata delle più belle tapezzarie che mi truovi et affermarsi in essa ogni persona honorata che venga per corteggiare o per parlarmi, si faccia anco bello il solaio a giudicio del signor Giuliano et costi ciò che vuole; ma se la camera non è quella che dico io, disidero che vi facciate prima ben intendere perché io non ho danari da spendere, se non in cose che sieno necessarie, o per honore, o per commodo mio. Et per questa cagione vi scrissi a questi giorni passati, che io non mi curavo che per hora si facesse quella camera sopra il volto della porta poi che non si faceva per necessità, il che vi replico di nuovo, quantunque tenga per certo che a quest'hora habbiate ricevuto quelle lettere mie.
>
> Del dipingere la sala grande, mi piace il partito preso dal signor Giuliano di far prima consultare molto bene la spesa che vi anderebbe, perché, se stesse male una salaccia di quel modo deserta et brutta per ingresso a camere belle et adornate, potrebbe anco importar tanto il dipingerla, essendo grande et le pitture care, che mi risolverei di non entrare per hora in quella spesa benché certo è di gran consideratione il potere poi colle pitture fare senza le tapezzarie in quel luogo che ne richiede tante. Veggansi adunque prima i disegni et la spesa et poi ci risolveremo a quel che potremo fare.

On 16 August 1558 Ercole acknowledged receipt of the "due disegni fattisi per la pittura da fare nella Sala Grande." One of the two pleased him, but he left the final decision to "signor Giuliano" and he indicated that the anticipated costs were rather high:[4]

> è il vero che dugento scudi mi pare un gran pagare, considerando massimamente et la qualità dei colori che sono di pochissimo momento et che il solaro ha da dipingersi colle stampe che è manifattura et ordinaria et facile da farsi.

Pia was cautioned that

> i lavori sieno ben fatti et in bellezza habbiano corrispondenza al resto delle pitture gia fattesi poi che il maestro è eccellente secondo lo scrivere vostro, et il pagamento è tale che molto ben corrisponde a quelli che si sono fatti per le pitture dell'altre stanze.

On 17 August 1558 Ercole wrote regarding the "cielo della Capella," which[5]

> per giudicio mio non può essere altro che un volto di canne bianco o con un poco di ornamento come piacerà al signor Giuliano, overamente un solaio di tavola con alcune rosette dipinto; qual di questi due piacerà più al signor Giuliano.

On 22 August 1558 the correspondence returned to the matter of the decoration of the "sala Grande":[6]

> Son andato pensando et risolvendomi che la pittura, che si ha da fare costì nella sala grande, si faccia di colori et non di chiaro et scuro solamente, come vi scrissi per l'altre, et benché io pensi che con li dugento scudi quel maestro possa indursi a dipingerla di colori, ricordandomi che questa mia qui, che deve essere poco meno della metà di cotesta di Roma, non mi costò più che quaranta scudi, non di meno mi contenterò che si paghino, oltra li dugento, altri venticinque scudi et crederò che'l pittore non habbia da ricusarne l'offerta, tuttavolta, quando pure lo facesse, veggasi che con questi danari la sala si dipinga a colori, se non tutta, una buona parte, talmente divisata et compartita a giuditio del signor Giuliano che riesca bella di vista et vaga più che sia possibile.

On 26 August 1558 Pia was cautioned against the proposed plans for a frieze depicting the Triumph of Hercules. Approval was given for a frieze depicting the "giuochi di quei Puttini," which Ercole believed would work well with the tapestries that would cover the remainder of the wall surface.[7]

> Ho veduto i fregi cioè i disegni mandatimi per quello che nella medesima camera haverà da farsi et vi dico che non voglio per niente questo che ha lo "Trionfo d'Hercole," perché sarebbe cosa da dare con molta ragione da dire a Pasquino con questa vanità di trionfare in pittura; l'altro mi sodisfa assai et laudo che si faccia perché haverà convenienza con le tapezzerie che vi anderanno attaccate sotto et, facendosi variato di parte in parte quanto ai giuochi di quei puttini, doverà riuscire assai vago et vistoso.

Various miscellaneous matters were addressed in the letter of 6 September 1558,[8] and on the 15th Pia was reminded that it would be a waste of money and time to devote too much attention to the painting of wall surfaces that would be hidden by tapestry hangings:[9]

> Io non credo che si sia fatto questo errore di smaltare di fresco le camere mie ove si sono fatti li fregi, dalli detti fregi in giù, perché oltre che la spesa sarebbe stata buttata via andando tutti quei muri coperti di tapezzarie, sotto le quali non importa che'l muro sia bianco o nero, ne nascerebbe questo inconveniente che tutte quelle stanze per la humidità delle smaltature sarebbono inhabitabile per un gran pezzo

In addition to a letter of 22 September, a final letter exists, one addressed to Pia on 17 December 1558.[1]

---

1. ASMn, b. 1930.
2. ASMn, b. 1930. Earlier correspondence with Pia regarding the matter of wall hangings is shown by ASMn, b. 1945, l. 4, cc. 82–83 (2 April 1558). On that occasion Ercole addressed himself to the question of the "misure delle stanze per fare fare i corami che havete mandate." Ercole required that Pia provide "di nuovo (. . .) le dette misure con un filo a facciata per facciata et la misura di ciascuna facciata sia poi mandata in qua in una carta nella quale sia scritto che facciata è quella, di maniera che tante sieno le carte col filo quante le misure et se in una facciata di camera o sala saranno più finestre fate che similmente che si pigli la misura di ciascuno spatio che sia fra una finestra et l'altra et si discerna l'un dall'altro appartatamente. A questo modo credo che intenderemo tutti, però usatemi di gratia intorno tutta la diligenza che potete acciò che non vi si habbia a tornare più et io me ne possa servire come disidero."
3. ASMn, r. 6514, cc. 16–17.
4. ASMn, r. 6514, cc. 21–22.
5. ASMn, r. 6514, cc. 24–25.
6. ASMn, r. 6514, cc. 30r–v.
7. ASMn, r. 6514, cc. 37r–v.
8. ASMn, r. 6514, cc. 53–54.
9. ASMn, r. 6514, cc. 61–62; *Rome 1984*, 145 n. 24.
10. ASMn, r. 6514, cc. 66r–v. ASMn, b. 1945, l. 5, cc. 29v–31, acknowledges receipt of Pia's letter of 7 December and expresses great pleasure at the results of work "nella casa mia di Roma," especially since it had met with the approval of "monsignore Illustrisismo Camerlengo che è signore intendente et di buon giudicio." Ercole was distressed to learn, however, that the "pittore s'ingannò nel mercato che tenne con voi per conto della sala grande onde s'haverà da dargli un quindeci o 20 scudi di più per cortesia et mercede, vi rispondo che tanto si faccia quanto vorrà il signor Giuliano [Cesarini] che per essere Sua Signoria il principale architetto in cotesta fabrica mi contenterò di tutto quello ch'essa giudicherà che sia honesto et ragionevole."

39. 14 March–12 September 1559
Ercole Rejects a Set of Tapestries Sent from Antwerp but Accepts a Replacement

Gerolamo Piperario was paid on 14 March 1559 for travel from Antwerp to Mantua, and back, with "più pezze di tappezzarie" that had not met with Ercole's approval.[1]

> Il Magnifico messer Jeronimo Piperaro de'havere dalla corte de l'illustrissimo et Reverendissimo signor Cardinale nostro di Mantova, scuti settantasette e uno quarto d'oro in oro per più spese fatte in condur da Anversa a Mantova più pezze di tappezzarie et ricondute da Mantova in Anversa non essendo alla sustiffatione di Sua Signoria Illustrissima e Reverendissima -scuti 77¼.

Evidently Piperario was able to find a suitable substitute, for on 30 June 1559 Ercole wrote:

> Ho ricevuto la vostra lettera et m'è stato caro intendere per essa che m'habbiate incaminate le tapezzerie, tanto più havendomi detto il Conte Federigo [Maffei] ch'elle riescon molto belle, et che sarano a mia sodisfattione. Starò adunque aspettando di vederle, et, fra tanto, haverò caro che si facciano quei pezzi più piccoli, del prezzo de'quali non accade ch'io vi dica altro perché mi rimetto liberamente a voi che gli paghiate qual che s'haverano a pagare.[2]

The following month, on 24 July 1559, Ercole wrote to Giulio della Valla that he had not yet received the tapestries:[3]

> Messer Carlo Peveraro, che mi ha comperato alcune tapezzerie in Fiandra, mi scrisse una sua lettera alli X del passato, facendomi sapere che erano già quindici dì ch'esso me le haveva inviate sotto la condotta di Matteo Ledere, il qual gli haveva promesso che in cinquanta giorni me le farebbe havere: il qual termine, come si può farne il conto, vien ad essere finito alli xv di questo. Nondimeno, non solamente non ho io veduto ancora queste tapezzerie, ma non ne ho sentito pure una parola al mondo. Disiderando pertanto di saperne novella et d'intendere se sono in Venetia o altrove, et quando io possa aspettarle d'haverle di qua, ricerco et priego voi con la presente che vogliate farne costì un poco di diligenza et avisarmi di quello che ne haverete trovato, che me ne farete molto disiderato piacere.

Evidently della Valla was successful in his inquiries because on 12 September 1559 payment is recorded to Jacomo Valvarde for the expenses incurred in transporting from Antwerp to Mantua "balle due di tappezarie" that had been acquired by Piperario.[4]

> L'Illustrissimo et Reverendissimo signor Cardinale di Mantova de'dare a Iacomo Valverda, mercante in Verona, scudi diecenove d'oro in oro et soldi nonantasette e mezo di moneta di Verona, che sono di Mantova scuti 19 d'oro in oro et soldi 49, per la condutta d'Anversa a Mantova di balle due di tappezarie di conto di Sua Signoria Illustrissima, mandate dal Magnifico Gerolamo Piperaro d'Anversa per la condutta di Matheo Lederi e compagni et per il Magnifico Piperaro di Mantova consignate alli aggenti di Sua Signoria Illustrissima alli 12 di settembre 1559 in Mantova—scuti XIX d'oro - soldi 49.

At the same time that tapestries were being carried back and forth from Antwerp, payment is recorded on 10 June 1559 for the acquisition of 359 *brazza* "di raso figurato," intended to be made into "spaliere da camera."[5]

> A dì 10 di Giugnio 1559—Messer Francesco d'Arrona, detto Pessano, de'havere dalla corte de l'Illustrissimo et Reverendissimo signor Cardinale nostro di Mantova libre duamillia cinquecento undeci e soldi dieci di moneta di Millano per altri tanti per lui spesi in brazza trecento cinquantanove di raso figurato di più collori a missura di Millano, compro per lui per far spaliere da camera per Sua Signoria Illustrissima in ragione ciovè libre cento cinquantatre de quatro colori a libre 8 il braccio et braccia ducento e seii di tre colori a libre seii, soldi cinque a libra di quella moneta, il quale, misurato alla missura di Mantova, resta braccia ducento nonantacinque et le quali libre 2511, soldi 10, danno scuti 436 de oro in oro et soldi ottanta a soldi 115 per scuto et reduti a nostra moneta in ragion de soldi 113 per scudo danno Lire 2437 - soldi 8.

---

1. ASMn, FP, b. 7; Luzio, 1919, 36; *Rome 1984*, 145 n. 22. For the 1559 mandate "pro Hieronimo Piperario cive et mercatore," see ASMn, Libri dei Mandati, vol. 52, c. 42v.
2. MOBE, 1. 619, d.G. 2.6. cc. 61v–62.
3. ASMn, r. 6515, 94v–95; Campori, 1866, 34.
4. ASMn, FP, b. 7, c. 174; Luzio, 1919, 36; *Rome 1984*, 145 n. 22. Together with the payment to Orsini for the cartoon for the cardinal's arms (Document 40), these texts have traditionally been associated with the acquisition of the *Acts of the Apostles*. See Document 46 for Granvelle's offer of the *Acts* in 1562.
5. ASMn, FP b. 7.

40. 22 MARCH–26 APRIL 1559
Ercole Orders a Cartoon for His Coat of Arms and Fabric for Friezes for Tapestries

Under the date 22 March 1559, payment is recorded to Filippo Orsini for the cartoon of two coats of arms, which were sent to Flanders:[1]

> Lo illustrissimo et Reverendissimo signor il signor Cardinale di Mantua de'dar a me Phillippo Orsone pictore in Mantua per haver fatto due arme in carta per mandar in Fiandra (. . .) montano libre 2, soldi 10.

The following month "maestro Julio di Ferrari vellutar" received payment for fabric "per far frisi su tappezarie."[2]

de'havere dalla corte de l'Illustrissimo et Reverendissimo signor Cardinale nostro di Mantua libre cento due et meggia per la fatura de braccia quarantadua et quarte tre di velluto gialdo cum il fondo di argiento per far frisi su tappezarie di Sua Signoria Illustrissima—Libre 102 - soldi 12 - denari 0.

1. ASMn, FP, b. 7, c. 37r. Luzio, 1919, 36; *Rome 1984*, 145 n. 22. Together with the reference to the transport of tapestries of 1559 (Document 39), this text has traditionally been related to the acquisition by Ercole of the *Acts of the Apostles*, for which see Document 37; *Rome 1984*, 145 n. 22, also refers to a payment on 1 April 1559 (ASMn, FP, b. 7) to Giovanni di Fiandra "per l'andata sua di Fiandra." It is not certain if this refers to the transport of the cartoon or to some other matter. It is clear, however, that Piperario, not Giovanni di Fiandra, was responsible for the transport of the tapestries referred to in Document 39.

2. ASMn, FP, b. 7 (26 April 1559); Luzio, 1919, 36.

41. 12 APRIL–8 JULY 1561
"Spaliere a la Grotesche" and "dui portieri" Repaired by Karcher

In March 1561 Ercole referred to his tapestries in the context of the shipment of various possessions to Trent.[1] Entries in the *Registri Economici* from 12 and 21 April, 12 May, and 8 July appear, however, to refer to the Palazzo Vescovile in Mantua.[2] On 21 April, reference is made to the "soldi otto per avir portato a casa del signor Cezer pezi 13 de spalleri grandi et poi portata a casa del filiolo di Issacho da Porto." Then under 21 April, payment is recorded to "Bernardino et compagno, fachini, per aver desparato le camari di Rusalemo ch'è sta' pezi 15 de spaleri a la grotesche." On 12 May 1561, payment was made to the "fachini chi à portato tapezarie per aparare le camari di Rusalemo."[3] Especially notable is the payment on 8 July 1561 "al fachino chi àportato dui portieri a maestro Nicholò tapezero in Santo Gorgio."

1. ASMn, r. 6516, cc. 39r–v (4 March 1561, al Rettori di Verona): "e perciò dovendo io andare presto a Trento è de bisogno che si mandino hora molte de le mie robbe innanzi per provedermi la casa, massimamente frumento, materazzi, tapezzerie, et altre cose simili."

2. ASMn, FP, b. 7.

3. This suite of rooms is first mentioned on 20 November 1542 (ASMn, FP, b. 6). Yet rather than dating from the reign of Ercole, a "Jerusalem" room is already recorded during the reign of Bishop Antonio degli Uberti. Pecorari, 1985, 28 n. 26.

42. 5 MAY 1561
Ercole Seeks to Acquire "qualche bella tapezzerie (. . .) fatta a figure"

On 5 May 1561 Ercole wrote from Trent to ask Cavriana to purchase suitable tapestries, taking special care to avoid the ordinary ones.[1] Although other letters from Cavriana, dated in Vienna, survive for this year, his response to Ercole's request is not among them:

> Aggiungo questo all'altro che vi ho scritto poco fa per dirvi che siate contento d'avisarmi se di costà se trovasse qualche bella tapezzeria fina de lana et seta fatta a figure, ma, a figure belle garbate et ben fatte, et non di quelle ordinarie che hanno visi bruttissimi et il resto assai goffo. L'altezza d'esse tapezzerie haveria da essere di cinque ale o poco più. Fatemi sapere, in caso che ve ne siano, le qualità loro tutte cioè la finezza, la bellezza, l'historia, il numero delle pezze et il costo in ragion d'ala acciò che, informato di tutto, possa risolvermi et avisarvi della mia risolutione.

At the same time that Ercole ordered figurative tapestries, he wrote to Tridapali on 6 May concerning the "mostre di quei corami che voi fate fare a messer Giulio Aliprando." Finding the samples satisfactory, Ercole ordered Tridapali to commission "settecento tra le pelli intere, colone et fregi."[2]

1. ASMn, b. 1945, l. 6, cc. 30 r–v.

2. ASMn, b. 1945, l. 6, 31v–33 (6 May) and cc. 33 r–v (to Aliprando), 46r–v for the letter to Tridapali of 13 May 1561. When the matter was first raised with Tridapali on 19 April 1561 (cc. 2v–3), Ercole had specified that he required about 500 "pelle con i fregi" for the decoration of two or three rooms. For Tridapali's letters from Venice of 26 April and 3 May, see ASMn, b. 1936.

43. 12 JULY–12 OCTOBER 1561
Granvelle Offers to Purchase a Hannibal Set for Ercole

Ercole wrote from Trent on 12 July 1561 of his willingness to acquire a *Hannibal* set,[1] but he refused to pay before seeing a sample of the workmanship. In the enclosure to Cardinal Granvelle, he specified that the set in question was to be purchased "in Anversa":[2]

> La risolutione mia intorno a tutte quelle sorti di tapezerie che sono notate nella vostra lettera è questa: ch'io piglierei quelle dell'historia d'Anniballe, ogni volta ch'io

potessi vederne un pezzo, et che la qualità et garbo, delle figure mi sodisfacesse, et questo perché sapend'io quai mostacci si facciano per l'ordinario in Fiandra, et essendone delle altre volte rimaso inganato, non sono in nissuna maniera per comperare hora queste se non me ne chiarisco di propria vista. Vedete pertanto se il mercatante di cui sono vuol contentarsi di lasciarne venire un pezzo in qua, pertanto ch'io gli dia una vista, et o me lo ritenga, piacendomi, et vi rescriva che comperiate il resto, o, non mi piacendo, ve lo faccia subito rimandare (. . .). Ma quando neanco di questo modo lo possiate havere, alhora vorrei che vi contantaste di andare a trovare Monsignor Illustrissimo di Granvela et gli deste l'alligata lettera mia, nella quale ricerco che Sua Signoria Reverendissima voglia interporre l'autorità sua col detto mercatante, acciò che lasci venire un pezzo della detta tapezzeria.

On 2 September 1561 Ercole wrote to Cardinal Granvelle regarding the question of the shipment of a sample of the *Hannibal* set, a sample that had not yet arrived.[3] Thinking that it might never be sent, Ercole resolved to rely on Granvelle's judgment:

et per me lo consideri, perché se ella, che ha dissegno, me le loderà, le piglierò senza curarmi altramente di vederle io, confidandomi più del giudicio di lei che del mio istesso. Priego adunque Vostra Signoria Illustrissima che per amor mio si contenti di dargli un'occhiata et parendole che'l dissegno sia bello et ben lavorato, me lo faccia sapere, perché mi risolverò subito o di torle o di lasciarle, secondo che sarà il parer di lei.

Cardinal Granvelle was not remiss, and on 30 September Ercole wrote to acknowledge receipt of Granvelle's letters of 7 and 14 September:[4]

ho inteso quanto cortesemente ella si pigliasse fatica di trattare con quel mercatante acciò che io fossi accommodato di potere vedere un pezzo di quelle tapezzerie, et l'instanza et offerta ch'essa gli fece perché fossero le mie quando egli non le havesse già vendute, come disse che haveva.

Among the letters Ercole received during 1561, four from Cardinal Granvelle deal with the purchase of the *Hannibal* set.[5] On 24 August 1561 he wrote:

Quanto al tapitiero, essendomi occorso andar in Anversa per alcune cose mie et dandomi ivi il signor Cavriana le lettere di Vostra Signoria Illustrissima, io feci cercar quel huomo in Anversa et non lo trovai, che già era ritornato qua, et venendo io qua, lo feci cercare, et egli era di nuovo ito in Anversa, ma, subito che fu ritornato, lo feci chiamare da me et gli feci grandissima instantia perché consentisse che un pezzo di quella tapetieria, che Vostra Signoria Illustrissima desidera havere, si portasse a spese soe a Trento, offerendogli la sigurtà et partiti che egli stesso potesse domandare; ma stette fermo con dire che in questo vi saria troppo grande pregiuditio suo perché, fra tanto che quel pezzo restasse in viaggio, che non saria meno di doe o tre mesi, restaria impedito di non poter vender il resto, et particularmente mi nominò un mercante spagnuolo con il quale diceva havere poco mancho che convenuto per vendergli tutti li pezzi, et che non sapeva se, da poi la soa partita d'Anversa, il suo fattore havesse concluso il mercato, et aggiongeva che, quando fusse certo che Vostra Signoria Illustrissima, visto quel pezzo, dovesse comprar il tutto, potria far quel che Vostra Signoria Illustrissima domanda con meno danno suo. Io gli replicai che, con questa conditione d'esser obligato a comprar il tutto, non havea di bisogno Vostra Signoria Illustrissima di far portare un pezzo costà, poiché già saria presa la risolutione et, venendo là, li vederia tutti, ma che chi compra vuole contentare li occhi, et piace molte volte a uno quel che dispiace a un altro, et che forse quel mercante spagnuol o non haveria comprato, o non con quel ventaggio che da Vostra Signoria Illustrissima potrebbe cavare quando quella si contentasse del pezzo che havesse visto, et di più che, non havendo anchora fatto compra quel mercante spagnuolo, forse vorria anchora farlo vedere da quelli da chi havesse comissione da comprare, et che non era la distributione delle tapitierie adesso tanto buona che fusse bene per un poco di porfidia perder l'occasione della compra che Vostra Signoria Illustrissima gli vuol fare; replicò che sapeva che era al settembre che d'ordinario si fa vendita di simil robba, et che nanzi al settembre non ritornarebbe quel pezzo. Pur io instai tuttavia a premerlo et offerirgli tutta quella sigurtà che volesse, et finalmente prese per resolutione di che lunedì prossimo andarebbe in Anversa et ivi saperebbe se era fatta la vendita o non et che fra tanto pensarebbe anchora quello che potesse fare, aggiongendo che, se qualcheduno gli parlasse in Anversa, gli direbbe quel che, dapo d'havervi pensato, potria fare, mostrando di desiderare di volermi far piacere, et io, col mezzo del contraroleur di Madama nostra, ne ho fatto advertire il signor Cavriana perché, venendo in Anversa, li facia parlare per haverne la risolutione, la quale desidero sommamente sia di sodisfar a Vostra Signoria Illustrissima.

A duplicate copy of this letter was dispatched from Brussels on 7 September 1561. On 14 September 1561 Granvelle acknowledged Ercole's letter of 3 September. Stating that Ercole, "si fida pur troppo del mio occhio, intendendomi io così poco di simili cose," Granvelle nonetheless promised to examine the sample "et avisarò Vostra Signoria Illustrissima di quel che me ne parrà." When the matter is last referred to (12 October 1561), it was to console Ercole about the failed negotiations:

> Per la mia precedente [not preserved], haverà Vostra Signoria Illustrissima inteso qualmente quella tapezzeria fu venduta ad altri, nanzi ch'io la potessi vedere, che, per ubedire al commandamento di Vostra Signoria Illustrissima (. . .), havea subito scritto a messer Ottaviano Palma et reiterato anchora un'altra volta acciò che mi facesse portare la detta tapezzeria, ma in fine egli mi rispose quello che Vostra Signoria Illustrissima haverà visto per la soa lettera, la quale mandai domenica passata insieme con la mia, et certamente mi rincresce infinito che Vostra Signoria Illustrissima non sia stata servita et compiaciuta in questo, benché non già per colpa mia, et la supplico che, se in altro io la posso servire mi comandi alla libera, come sa che può come a tanto affettionato servitor suo et di tutta la casa.

1. ASMn, r. 6516, cc. 43–44 (12 July).
2. ASMn, r. 6516, cc. 44r–v (12 July).
3. ASMn, r. 6518, cc. 12v–13 (2 September).
4. ASMn, r. 6518, cc. 12v–13 (3 September) and 39r–v (30 September).
5. ASMn, b. 1938 (24 August, 7 and 14 September, 12 October).

44. 11 OCTOBER–19 NOVEMBER 1561
Cesare Gonzaga Agrees to the Loan of Tapestries, Excluding the Puttini, *the* Verdure, *and the* Fructus Belli

Cesare Gonzaga wrote on 11 October 1561 that he was willing to loan Cardinal Simonetta a group of tapestries, but not the *Puttini,* the *verdure* tapestries, and the *Fructus Belli:*[1]

> Che mandando il Cardinale Simonetta a pigliar tappezzerie per fornir un paro di camere, se consegnino a quel tante, riservando li Puttini, Verdure, et Fructus Belli, et pigliando ricevuta de la consegna.

The following month, on 19 November, Aldegatto was advised:[2]

> Che al Cardinal Simonetta accomodi due stanze in casa per la persona sua, a la quale non se mancherà di cosa che habbi bisogno, facendole condur, se sarà de bisogno, quelle tapezzerie che Sua Eccellenza gli ha prestate fin a Trento.

1. ASPr, b. 46 (to Aldegatto). This letter proves that these sets had not yet been shipped to Venice to serve as collateral for a loan (Document 53). Other sets, of unspecified subject matter, had already served to obtain cash (Document 53). On 2 November 1565 Cesare agreed to send to Venice certain unspecified tapestries for use by Monsignore d'Aranto: "Rallegrandosi dell'arrivo suo a Roma, et dandoli aviso de come Sua Eccellenza manderà a Vinegia le tapezzerie et letto che desidera."
2. ASPr, b. 46. Francesco and Agostino d'Aldegatto are described as Mantuan citizens and merchants to whom the estate of Luigi Alessandro Gonzaga, Lord of Castelgoffredo, owed a great deal of money. Guastalla, Biblioteca Maldottiana, b. 91 "Inventarii," 6 April 1552, cc. 61, 70.

45. 2 JANUARY 1562
Karcher Appeals to Ercole for Funds

On 2 January 1562 "maestro Nicolò tapezier servitore affettionatissimo" appealed for funds from Ercole to provide for his daily needs and for his daughter's dowry:[1]

> L'animo generoso di Vostra Signoria Illustrissima conosciuto da tutto il mondo et provato da molti, et la innata et real bontà, qual sempre è solita Vostra Signoria Illustrissima usar verso di tutti quelli che a lei ricorrono massimamente verso gli suoi servitori ne'lor bisogni, mi ha fatto sempre, dall'hora in poi ch'io fui fatto degno di servirla in questa mia arte, star con ferma speranza che la non mi dovesse mai negar cosa alcuna honesta ch'io li chiedesse né abandonar nella mia necessità et travaglii, et hora mi dà ardire et baldanza di ricorrere nelle sue braccia per un mio bisogno et negotio pio et importante, il qual'è questo.
>
> Io ho, come sa Vostra Signoria Illustrissima, tre figlie, le quali già dovrebbono esser maritate, et non ho cosa al mondo che più mi travaglii et prema l'animo di questa vedendomi non havere il modo di darli la dote. Hora di novo mi è comparso un bonissimo et honesto partito, et son per far contratto di una di loro. Sol la povertà m'impedisce et mi è per impedire se non son aiutato da qualche banda, però ricorro a Vostra Signoria Illustrissima et la prego non dirò per qual si voglia servitù ch'io li habbia fatto, ma sì ben per il buon animo ch'io ho di servirla con dispendio della vita propria, et per la sua solita benignità et magnificentia che, in questo mio bisogno pio et honesto, si degni soccorremi et supplir con l'aiuto suo ove mancano le mie forze, acciò possi far tanta dote a questa mia figlia, serva di Vostra Signoria Illustrissima quanta basti a locarla honestamente et non mi lasciar fugir questa occasione, la quale non tornerà poi Dio sa quando.

> Spero che Vostra Signoria Illustrissima non permetterà ch'io sii defraudato della speranza con la quale a lei son ricorso, et con questo starò aspettando la man larga di Vostra Signoria Illustrissima, alla quale basciando le sacrate mani et pregando Nostro Signore che ci dii gratia di basciarli in breve gli santissimi piedi, mi li offero et ricomando.

Ercole's response is known from a reference to the authorization of a gift of 50 scudi in Francesco Galvagno's letter of 21 April 1562: "Non mancherò di far l'ufficio, con mastro Nicolò tapezzero, che ella mi commanda circa li cinquanta scudi per maritar la lui figliuola."[2]

1. ASMn, b. 1941, c. 202. Luzio, 1891; 1919, 35. For the marriage in 1548 of another daughter, see Document 23.
2. ASMn, b. 1940, c. 346.

46. 12 JANUARY 1562

Granvelle Comments on Tapestries, Including the "Historia d'Alessandro Magno," and Recommends the Acts of the Apostles *to Ercole*

Given Ercole's requirements for the height of his hangings, Granvelle recommended the *Alexander the Great* series rather than the *Acts of the Apostles.*[1] Granvelle admitted that while the manufacture of the *Alexander* series was good, the design of the figures left something to be desired. Eighteen months would be required if Ercole were to opt for commissioning the *Acts,* a set measuring 7 *ale* in height as opposed to the 5 *ale* preferred by Ercole. All things considered, he felt that Ercole would do better commissioning hangings with the designs of animals and landscapes because the figural compositions were less successfully executed:

> Io parlai in Anversa a Ottaviano Parma, il quale mi parlò come, avendo commissione di lei e del signor Cavriana sopra la tapizzeria, et ne veddi parechi pezzi et dico liberamente che a me non mi piacevano quelle che io veddi di personaggi, essendo così che se li patroni non se li mandono d'Italia in queste bande, poche volte si fanno cose che di là dieno contento. La megliore ch'io veddi fu de la historia d'Alessandro Magno, e pur non mi contenta troppo: doi o tre panni sono molto pieni di figurre, sariano meno mali, la stoffa è buona et secondo la tapizzeria al presente è cara, si converrebbe agevolmente del pretio.Et se non fosse che credo Vostra Signoria Illustrissima la vorrà per servirsene in quel luogho, crederia seria bene farne far una aposta. Et si volessi haver quella delli Atti delli Apostoli, che li patroni si fecero in Italia, s'obligarebbe il maestro di farli in 18 mesi: è ben vero che sarebbe al meno che sette ane d'alteza, et Vostra Signoria Illustrissima, a quello che mi vien detto, ne vorebbe solamente di cinque d'altezza, et di questa misura non ho visto nissuna meglior di questa che dico di Alessandro, che, come dico, non mi contenta: non già che'l borde non sia bello, et la campagna, ma non mi danno satisfactione li personaggi. Qui si lavora molto meglio di paesaggi, et credo che Vostra Signoria Illustrissima faria ottima elettione di contentarsi che si facessi scelta di paesaggi et animali in essi, dove non vi fossero persone, o ben poche, et più presto picole che grandi.

1. ASMn, b. 1943, c. 415 (12 January 1562). Unfortunately Ercole's "registri," the volumes in ASMn, end on 8 December 1561 and thus his response cannot be documented. The letters written to Cardinal Granvelle (12, 21, and 28 April) and preserved in Simancas do not refer to the tapestries. *Colección de Documentos inéditos para la Historia de España,* tomo IX: Noticia de los Españoles que asistieron al Concilio de Trent, D. Pedro Sainz de Baranda, Madrid, 1846, 119–20, 132–33, 138–40.

47. 31 OCTOBER 1562

The "Registro Necrologico" Account of Karcher's Death

On 31 October 1562 the "Registro Necrologico" notes Karcher's death: "Nicolò de Carchar, tapezir in del borgo de San Zorzo, morto di febra et pasion di stomacho infermo dui mesi de età de anni 64."[1]

1. ASMn, Registro Necrologico, 7, c. 174v. Luzio, 1914, 112; Luzio, 1919, 35.

48. 2 MARCH 1563

The Third Testament of Ercole

According to the terms of Ercole's third testament, "tutta et ogni sorte della suppeletile" were to be divided equally between his two nephews, Cardinal Federico and Cardinal Francesco.[1] Federico died in 1565 and his portion was inherited by the Gonzaga of Guastalla, whereas upon Francesco's death (1566) the Gonzaga of Mantua was the beneficiary. Notwithstanding this provision, two sets of tapestries were otherwise disposed of: the *Acts of the Apostles* to the palatine chapel of Santa Barbara and the *Puttini* to the Duke of Mantua.

> Item, lascia all'Illustrissimo signor Cardinale di Monferrato et all'Illustrissimo signor Cardinale Gonzaga, suoi nepoti, tutta et ogni sorte della suppeletile di argenti, paramenti et simili cose, le quali si habbia a dividere egualmente tra essi signori Illustrissimi nel modo che detto Illustrissimo signor testatore, vivendo, dividerà, overo, piacendo a Dio che moia, si divida egualmente tanto argento, paramenti, letti et simili cose habbino l'uno quanto l'altro et per portione giusta, eccetto alcuni argenti, quali si divideranno dal Reverendissimo Monsignor di Nola, qual sa l'intentione d'esso Illustrissimo signor testatore.
>
> Item, lascia all'Illustrissimo et Eccellentissimo signor Duca di Mantova le tapezzarie nominate delli Atti delli Apostoli per honorare la chiesa di Santa Barbara, novamente da Sua Eccellenza erretta, et similmente le tapezzarie nominate delli Putini, per servirsene come meglio parerà a Sua Eccellenza.

---

1. ASMn, b. 333, cc. 267ff. *Rome 1984*, 144.

49. 1 APRIL 1563
The Inventory of Ercole's tapestries

The "Registrazioni notarili" contains a detailed copy of the "Inventarium bonorum quondam illustrissimi et reverendissimi domini domini Herculis Gonzaga cardinalis Mantue."[1] This is complemented by various notary acts (9 June, 9 and 13 July 1563) and the *Divisio,* all of which record the transfer from Ercole's estate to his various beneficiaries.[2]

Separated from the "Descriptione Tapezzarie" is a group of entries concerning "quadri di seta, oro et argento" (or "lana"). Clearly these are framed small-scale pictures, possibly embroidery or small tapestries and include:

(a) [*Moses in the Wilderness*] un quadro di seta, oro et argento di Moise nel deserto.
Divisio—Federico: "Un razo de tapezaria de Moyse, d'oro et setta, de alle 16 per quadro."

(b) [*Madonna*] un quadretto della Madonna di seta, lana et oro.
Divisio—Francesco: "tapezzaria della Madonna, Lire 48–12."

(c) [*Madonna in bagno*] un quadretto della Madonna in bagno.
Divisio—Francesco: "un quadro di tapezaria de lana della Madona in bagno, Lire 12."

(d) [*Three Magi*] un quadretto di tre Magi d'oro, argento, seta et lana. *Divisio* - Francesco: "un quadro de tapezaria d'oro et setta delli tre Maggi de alle 5 per quadro—Lire 270."

(e) [*Mary and Saint Elizabeth*] un quadro di Santa Maria et Santa Helisabet di seta, oro et argento.
Divisio—Francesco: "un razo de tapezaria d'oro et setta di Santa Elisabet d'ale 8 per quadro, Lire 345 - 12."[3]

The *Divisio* records that Cardinal Francesco was given the "quadro de tapezaria d'oro et setta della Madonna con Santa Catherina et altra figura d'ale 2½ per quadro, Lire 162," which is seemingly not listed in the inventory itself.

Among the works assigned to Cardinal Federico in the *Divisio* but not easily related to entries in the inventory are the following:

(a) Un razo a barcho de alle 20 in tutto per quadro a Lire 3 l'alla—Lire 60.

(b) Un razo de lana fina d'alle 20 in tutto per quadro a Lire 36 l'alla—Lire 36.

(c) Un razo rotto della prima sorte, vale Lire 6.

(d) Un fornimento da scrana in tapezaria con oro, argento, et setta, Lire 41 - 13.

(e) [*Armorial*] Due arme da tapezaria, vale Lire 16 - 4.

Among the works assigned to Cardinal Francesco in the *Divisio* but not easily related to entries in the inventory are the following:

(a) [*Forest*] "Undeci pecci di tapezarie a boscalia alte alle 6, longhe in tutto alle 69, danno alla quadra alle 414, a Lire 13 - 10 l'alla, vale—Lire 5589.

(b) Cinque sopraportiere della soprascritta tapezaria, che sono alte alle 27 a Lire 10 l'alla, vale Lire 270.

(c) [*Figural*] Sei pecci di tapezaria a figure, anticha, smarita di colore, in tutto alle 134½ a soldi 50, Lire 336 - 5.

(d) [*Foliage*] Tredeci pecci di tapezarie a fogliami alte alle 3, usate et parte rotto, longhe in tutto alle 90 per quadro danno alle 273 a soldi 54 l'alle—Lire 737 - 2.

(e) [*Foliage*] Pecci 14 de tapezarie a fogliami alte alle 3 usate et parte rotte, longhe in tutto alle 91½, danno al quadro alle 274½ a soldi 54 l'alle, montano—Lire 741 - 3.

In addition to figurative tapestries, Ercole owned a sizable number of fabric hangings and a vast assortment of tooled leather panels:

> *Fabrics:* (a) *portiere*: eleven ("scarlatto," "panno rosso (con/senza l'arma)," "panno morello," "veluto verde recamate pontificalmente." (b) *spalliere:* twenty ("veluto de rosa secha," "veluto verde," "damasco figurato," "ormesino gialdo (. . .) con le colone di veluto gialdo"). *Leather:* 3,000 (panels, "colone," and "frisi").

Although not extensive, the documentation for the acquisition of nonfigurative wall hangings should not be entirely overlooked. Thus, for example, on 19 November 1557 Ercole authorized his nephew, Cesare Gonzaga, to provide him with leather panels suitable to decorate four or five rooms:[4]

> Et accioché in questa parte sappiate ancora come sodisfarmi, i corami haveranno da essere lavorati, et non di colore alcuno, ma ò d'oro solo, o d'oro et argento insiemme, et non tutti d'una sorte o d'una stampa, ma havendosene, come dire, da apparare quattro o cinque camere, se ne può pigliare di diversi lavorieri sì come saranno diverse le camere purché non sieno di colore ma d'oro et d'argento et oro, com'è detto. Ben vorrei che le foggie fossero delle più belle, delle più vaghe et delle più moderne che si facessero, et non havendo di questo voi tutta la cognitione che bisognerebbe, potrete similmente parlarne con Monsignore Nuntio et con altri che ne hanno vedute assai per potermi col parere di diversi amici et più intelligenti di voi maggiormente sodisfare.

The preceding year, correspondence was initiated with Cardinal Borromeo regarding "il disegno d'un nuovo drappo che io vorrei farmi fare perché in un apparamento da camera che si farà il damasco turchino havesse da servire per fregio."[5] Years earlier, in January 1549, payment was recorded for a "spalere de corame," including the cost for making the "folii d'arzento per li soprascritti corami."[6] From a later period (1561) letters from Ludovico Tridapali exist regarding the acquisition in Venice of "pelli di corami per fare spaliere" and also an "apparamento da camera che la pensa di fare di damasco."[7]

Descriptione Tapezzarie

1. [*Puttini*] tapezzaria de Putini, pezzi diece di lana, seta, oro et argento; sopraportere della medema sorte doi, portiere tre de lana, seta et oro, fatte a folie di lauro con l'arma di Monsignore Illustrissimo in meggio.
   Divisio—Duke Guglielmo: Dieci pezzi de tapezaria de lana fina, seta, oro et argento, nominate li Putini; tre portere di lana fina con l'arma de Monsignor Reverendissimo felice memoria con foglie di lauro di oro; Due sopraportere di tapezaria della sorte delle di Putini di sopra.
2. [*Acts of the Apostles*] tapezzarie di Atti Apostolici, le quali sono alte ale sette, sono numero nove, di lana et filisello.
   Divisio—Duke Guglielmo: Nove pezzi di tapezaria delli Atti Appostolici di lana fina e fulusello, alta ale 7.
3. [*Tobias*] tapezarie della Historia di Tobia numero dodeci, di lana fina, sopraportere per la detta historia numero sei con l'arma in meggio.
   Divisio—Cardinal Federico: Dodeci peci di tapezarie della historia de Tobbia d'alteza de alle 5 et largheza de alle 85 danno per quadro alle 425 a lire 10 l'alla, monta lire 4250. Sei sopraportiere correspondenti al sudetto ornamento con l'arma in meggio, de alle 42 estimata a libre 10 l'alla, in tutto Lire 420.
4. [*Saul*] tapezarie della historia de Saul, alte ale sei, numero sei, di lana fina.
   Divisio—Cardinal Federico: Pecci sei di tapezarie della historia di Saul, alte alle 6, et longhe alle 53, danno in tutto alle 318, a libre 8 l'alla, monta libre 2575 - 16.
5. [*David*] tapezarie della historia de David, alte ale cinque, numero quatro, di lana.
   Divisio—Cardinal Francesco: Quatro pecci de tapezaria della historia de David, alte alle 5, longhe in tutto alle 26, danno al quadro alle 130 a libre 4, [soldi] 10 l'alla—libre 585.
6. [*Joseph*] tapezarie della historia de Joseph de lana fina et seda, numero 3 et più una peza della medesima sorte con una dea.
   Divisio—Cardinal Francesco: Tre pecci de tapezaria de l'historia de Joseph, alta alle 5, longhe in tutto alle 18, danno al quadro alle 90, libre 4 l'ala, vale—Libre 360; un pezo de tapezaria a figura, alto alle 4½, longo alle 3, in tutto alle 14, a Libre 4, l'alla, libre 56.
7. [*Foliage*] tapezarie di lana et terzarolo a fogliami grandi a verdura con bestie diverse, numero 16.[8]

As noted in the introductory, various *verdure* tapestries are recorded in the *Divisio* under Cardinal Francesco and they may relate to this entry as well as to those that follow.

8. [*Foliage*] tapezerie a fogliami per il studiolo, numero 6, di lana et terzarolo.
9. spaliere basse di ale 3 numero 26, di lana della terza sorte.
10. [*Fortuna*] spaliere della Fortuna condotta da quatro Aquile, numero xii di lana.
    Divisio—Cardinal Federico: Sei portiere de alle 12 in tutto alla quadra a libre 7 l'alla danno alle 72 con la Fortuna tirata da l'aquila, estimata—libre 504. Sei altri simili portiere come le sudette—libre 504. Un soprauscio della predetta della Fortuna, de alle 2 alla quadra a libre 7 l'alla, vale libre 14; Una sopraportiera della Fortuna, estimata libre 14.
11. tapezerie fatte a [. . .], alte ale sei, di lana fina et fulicello, numero xi.
11a. sopraportiere cinque della medesima sorte.
12. [*Troy*] tapezzarie della historia di Troia de lana della terza sorte, pezi sei, usate.

Although not recorded in the *Divisio,* it is listed in the subsequent inventory of Cardinal Francesco (Document 52, no. 12).

13. [*Shepherds*] una tapezaria d'un pezo con una fontana et pastori, vechia.
    Divisio—Cardinal Federico: un razo usato a fontana d'alle venti in tutto a libre 2 l'alla, vale—libre 40.
14. [*Armorial*] Quatro arme da tapezarie nove.[9]
15. pezzi dua de tapezarie, usati, figurati.

1. ASMn, RN, Agostino Ragazzola, pacco 7566. For the copy made in 1564 for Ludovico Gonzaga, see Ragazzola, pacco 7567, and the ASMn, RN, anno 1564, which was cited in *Rome 1984,* 145, where it was incorrectly maintained that it took nearly a year for the inventory to be compiled.
2. ASMn, RN, Agostino Ragazzola, pacco 7566.
3. One or more of these might be identified with two references to an "ancona de tapezzaria" recorded in the inventory of Cardinal Francesco.
4. ASMn, b. 1945, l. 3, cc. 7–9v.
5. ASMn, r. 6515, cc. 32–32v.
6. ASMn, ASMn, FP, b. 5, cc. 64v–65.
7. ASMn, b. 1936.
8. Perhaps the very set displayed in the Palazzo Vescovile in 1549 on the occasion of the banquet held in honor of the marriage of Francesco III (Document 29).
9. Numbers 14 and 15 are not part of the "Descriptione Tapezzarie" but are recorded elsewhere in the inventory. According to the *Divisio* (as above in note 1) and in addition to the "carpetta" (Document 27) and the *Puttini,* Guglielmo also was given "tre portere di lana fina con l'arma di Monsignore Reverendissimo felice memorie con foglie di lauro."

50. 27 DECEMBER 1563
The Loan of Tapestries from Cesare Gonzaga for the Chapel of the Madonna in the Duomo

Payment is recorded in the documents of the Duomo for the expenses incurred in transporting unspecified tapestries from the palace of Cesare Gonzaga to adorn the chapel of the Madonna on the occasion of a mass held in honor of several visiting princes.[1] It is not possible to determine if these were fabric or figurative hangings or whether the objects selected were among those inherited by Cesare from the estate of his father, Ferrante. On other occasions Cesare had made similar loans (Document 44):

— a dui che aiuttorno aparare la capella della Madona dentro e fora quando vi venero a messa li principi Ernesto et Ridolfi d'Austria con li Illustrissimi et Reverendissimi il Cardinale di Augusta et Mantua et l'Eccellentissimo signor Duca nostro di Mantova—Lire 0 - 15 - 0.

— et a fachini che portorno et riportorno tapezzarie da casa del illustrissimo signor Cesare alla chiesa per tal servitio—Lire 0 - 8 - 0.

1. ASDMn, Massaria, r. 3004.

51. 7 MARCH 1565
Errcole's Tapestries Recorded in Federico Gonzaga's Inventory

The fourth son of Duke Federico II, Federico was born in 1540. He was named cardinal in 1563 and after the death of Ercole he became head of the Mantuan diocese. Federico died *ab intestato* at the age of twenty-five on 21 February 1565, which meant that his possessions were divided between Duke Guglielmo and Ludovico Gonzaga de Nevers.[1] On 7 March 1565 an inventory was compiled of Federico's possessions.[2] It records a large collection of tapestries, including the "Moyse con oro, seta et argento" and six figurative sets, three of which—the *Fortuna,* the *Tobias,* the *Saul,* and the "tapezzarie (. . .) a cardi"—came from the estate of Ercole. Since Cardinal Federico's *Joseph* consisted of eight pieces, it cannot be identified with the set of three owned by

Ercole, which, in any event, became the property of Cardinal Francesco. Like the other sets owned by Federico, the *Fortuna,* the *Tobias,* and the *Saul* series were inherited by the Gonzaga of Mantua, for they are recorded as having been used for the decoration of the Ducal Palace in 1580 and 1584 (Documents 59 and 60 nos. 2, 8, and 13).

1. [*Joseph*] Primo, otto pezzi de tapezzaria di Fiandra della Historia di Giuseppe con dui antiporti di essa historia—lire 934.
2. [*Elijah*] Otto pezzi di tapezzaria di Fiandra con dui antiporti della historia de Elia—lire 920. [Recorded in Margherita Paleologa's inventory (Document 66, Addenda B no. 3).]
3. [*Gideon*] Cinque pezzi de tapezzaria di Fiandra della historia di Gedon—lire 573 - 15. [Recorded in Margherita Paleologa's inventory (Document 66, Addenda, B no. 4).]
4. Deci pezzi di tapezzaria fina di Fiandra a verdura—scuti 192.
5. Sei pezzi di tapezzaria a verdura, grossi. Un pezzo di tapezzaria della detta verdura—scuti 126 ⅔.
6. [*Tobias*] Dodeci pezzi di tapezzaria di Fiandra della Historia di Tobia con sei soprapontieri [sic] di detta historia—scuti 787½. [Inherited from Ercole.]
7. [*Saul*] Sei pezzi di tapezzaria di Fiandra della Historia di Saullo—scuti 397½. [Inherited from Ercole.]
8. Sei pezzi di tapezzaria di Fiandra con dui sopraportieri a cardi—scuti 69, soldi 48. [Although not mentioned in Ercole's inventory, they are recorded in the *Divisio* of 1563 as "sei pecci di tapezarie a carde d'alle 88, in tutto alle quadra [. . .] a lire [. . .] l'alle—Libre 440.]
9. [*Fortuna*] Dodeci pezzi di tapezzaria di Fiandra a Fortune—scuti 158, soldi 76. [Inherited from Ercole.]
10. [*Foliage*] Deci pezzi di tapezzaria a fogliazzi grossi—scuti 132, soldi 104.
11. Quatro antiporti a figure, di Fiandra—scuti 20.
12. [*Moses*] Un pezzo di tapezzaria di Moyse con oro, seta et argento. [Inherited from Ercole.]

1. For the act regarding the division of the estate, see ASMn, RN, Extensione, XXVI, fol. 35, and ASMn, Magistrato Camerale Antico, Bb II, under the date 5 November 1571. More work would be required to determine if any of the tapestries not recorded in subsequent Gonzaga of Mantua inventories went to France as part of Ludovico Gonzaga de Nevers's settlement.

2. ASMn, b. 333, 290ff. (7 March 1565). Not included in the transcription are the references to the "razo a porto di Fiandra," "razo a Fortuna di Fiandra," "razo di lana fina," and "razo vecchio, rotto."

52. 10–13 JANUARY 1566

Ercole's Tapestries Recorded in Francesco Gonzaga's Inventory

Ferrante's son Francesco was born in 1537 and he died at the age of twenty-nine in 1566. On 21 January 1566, an inventory was compiled, one that included various items from the estate of Ercole, including the "retratti de lutterani numero quattordici," as well as ten paintings and a good number of tapestries.[1] Excluded from the transcription are the six "paramenti da camera," fashioned from various types of fabrics, as, for example, the "paramento da camara di domasco carmosino non finito, pezzi numero 6 di altezza 43, alto brazza sei," or the "paramento da camera di ormesino giallo pezzi numero sei con fiame negre d'ormesino e frangie [di] seda gialda de altezza 25 e mezzo in tutto et alto braccia 3⅓." Immediately before the listing of *tappezaria* (c. 13) are recorded a vast quantity of "corami adorati," 802 pieces in all.

The various "ancona di tapezzaria" and two sets of figurative tapestries, the *David* and the *Joseph,* can be identified with pieces coming from Ercole's estate. With the possible exception of the *"Boscalie"* (see 5 below) and the *Troy* piece (see 12 below), which may also have come from Ercole's estate, the provenance of the remainder of his collection, as, for example, the "historia di Re," cannot yet be determined. As noted by Pecorari, whereas his cousin Cardinal Federico had little disposable income, Francesco was able to count on considerable funds because by 1557 Ercole had appointed him abbot of Felonica.

1. una ancona di tapezzaria vechia.
2. un'altra ancona de tapezzaria con oro et argento.
3. un'altra ancona di velluto carmosino con una Madonna in meggio fatta de tapezzaria di oro et de seta.
4. [*Armorial*] due arme Gonzaga fatte de tappezzaria nove.
5. [*Forest*] tappezzaria fatta a boscalia con animali, pezzi quindeci, computati cinque portieri, sono numero ale 380, usate. E più un altro pezzo de medemo, ale 48.
6. [*David*] tappezzaria de la instoria di Davide, pezzi 4, ale per numero 130. [Inherited from Ercole.]
7. [*Joseph*] tappezaria del la historia di Josepho pezzi 3, ale 90. [Inherited from Ercole.]
8. [*Libro di Re*] tappezaria de Libro di Re, pezzi numero 10, alta ale cinque, ale per numero 310.

9. [*Donne Francese*] tappezzaria de Donne Francese, pezzi 2, alte ale 68.
10. tappezzaria di verdure alta ale 5, pezzi 10, ale 255.
11. [*Dido*] tappezzaria de historia di Didone, alta ale 4, ale 12.
12. [*Troy*] tappezzaria di Troia, alta ale 4, pezzo 1, ale 12.
13. tappezaria de foliami, alta ale 3, pezzi 17, ale 373.

---

1. ASPr, RM, b. 123. A more accurate copy, however, is to be found in ASMn, AN, Petrozanni Cinzio, pacco 6909.

53. 1567–1584

Records Concerning Ferrante's Tapestries Pledged by Cesare Gonzaga

On occasion Cesare Gonzaga did not hesitate to use gems, silver, and tapestries as collateral for the loan of cash.[1] References to such transactions occur not only during Ferrante's life (Document 33), but also are found in Cesare's papers for the years 1561–62.[2] What distinguishes the transaction of 1567 is that on this occasion Cesare offered as collateral the finest items from his collection: the *Fructus Belli*, the *Puttini*, the *Spozalizio*, and the *Boschellii*.

The records relevant to this transaction date from September 1567 to 1584, although the tapestries were not redeemed until shortly after 1587.[3] Over the years the Guastalla silver, gems, and tapestries remained in the hands of the Venetian bankers Marco Bono, Bartolomeo Bontempelli del Calice, and Pirro Calvi. Renewed annually (see, for example, the letter of agreement between Calice and Camille Borromeo of 31 March 1584 and the notary act of 1578), the yearly interest on the loan was calculated on one sheet at 388 Venetian ducats.[4]

The silver ("argenti dorati" and "argenti bianchi") was valued at 2,891 scudi and the gems at 7,100 scudi. The tapestries, which measured 1,230 *braccia*, were valued at 3,171 ducats.[5] This brought the total of the objects pledged to more than 13,000.

At the end of the "Nota d'argenti ch'erano in Venezia in poter del Signor Pirro Calvi per ducati milleottocentocinquanta," reference is made to the "pezi sei de tappezzarie de *Puttini* con oro, argento et seta."[6] A more detailed accounting, but one that failed to mention the *Puttini*, is found on the undated page entitled "copia della estima delle gioie fate in Venecia et tapeciarie."[7]

— [*Cephalus and Procris*] Spozadici pecci numero sei, in tuti braccia 33 di questa misura de ali numero 5 et sono alle numero 165—estimate ducati tre l'ala.
— [*Forest*] Boschellii peci numero 11, in tuti braccia 67 di questa misura de alle numero 6 che sono alle numero 402—estimati ducati 3 l'ala.
— [*Fructus Belli*] Fructus Belli pecci numero 8 di questa misura braccia 96 de alle numero 7 che sono in tuti alli numero 672—estimati ducati 3 l'ala.
Suma in tuti braccia 196, alle numero 1239—ducati 3171.

In a statement dated 15 December 1580 Bartolomeo del Calice noted that he had in his possession "gioie, argenti et tapezzarie (. . .) et dette per cautione mia per le ottomiliaotto ducati et otto grossi da Lire 6, soldi 4."[8] Among these were the "otto pezzi de razzi a figure con il motto *Fructus Belli*, sei pezzi chiamati li *Puttini* con oro, argento, seda et lana" and "sei pezzi chiamati dello *Sponsalitio*."

---

1. In addition to such obvious precedents as the 1496 agreement between Piero de' Medici and Agostino Chigi (Cugnoni, 1879, 114–16), there is the letter Cardinal Ippolito d'Este sent to his sister Isabella on 29 August 1512, in which using tapestries as collateral to ensure access to cash was clearly spelled out (ASMn, b. 1194), and for related material from this file, including a letter of 30 September 1512 (Forti, 1982, 55): "Domane partirà di qui una nave carica de robbe di la Serenissima signora Regina de Napoli per venire a Mantua, fra le quale sonno anchora alcune balle de tapeciarie del signor Duca nostro fratello che si mandano fuori perché in ogni bisogno più facilmente potriasse retrovare denari sopra epse, essendo fuora, cha non se le retenessimo qui."

2. Among other references are the following, all from ASPr, b. 46: On 28 July 1561 Cesare wrote to Mauro regarding the need to "trovar le fede de le tapezzerie che sono a Casalmaggiore impegnate." The same tapestries are referred to by Cesare in his letter to Aldegatto of 31 August 1561: "De le robbe che Sua Eccellenza ordina che se mandino in qua [to Rome], procurando che, quando non si possino haver le tapezzerie che sono a Casalmaggiore impegnate, se ne impegneno altrettante di quelle costì et si rescuotteno quelle." "[T]apezzerie, che sono in poter del figliolo di Isac di Porta" are mentioned in Cesare's letter to Aldegatto of 20 September 1561 and again in a letter to him of 25 October 1561. On 2 January 1562 Cesare asked Marni to provide him with "le fedi de le tapezzerie," and, on 21 March 1562, Marni was advised that "Che se per conto del valor de le tapezzerie impignate si potesse haver tanta artiglieria, Sua Eccellenza la pigliarebbe."

3. GBM, b. 23, cc. 36–55. See Document 61 for the loan to Ferrante II of the *Fructus Belli* and the *Puttini* and Document 65 for the record of these tapestries in the 1590 inventory of the possessions of the Gonzaga of Guastalla.

4. GBM, b. 23, cc. 36, 38.

5. GBM, b. 23, c. 37.

6. GBM, b. 23, c. 42.

7. GBM, b. 23, c. 43.

8. GBM, b. 23, c. 50.

54. 3 MAY 1569
Guglielmo Gonzaga Donates the Acts of the Apostles *to the Church of Santa Barbara*

Although not named specifically, it is known that the *Acts* was included among the furnishings donated to Santa Barbara on 3 May 1569.[1] First, the set was bequeathed to Guglielmo by Ercole for this precise purpose, and second, it is documented here in later papers:[2]

> Legavit ecclesiae S. Barbarae (. . .) omnia et quaecumque bona et res quascumque auri et argenti, quamvis in eis existant lapides preciose, de quibus omnibus fieri voluit diligentem descriptionem, destinatas et destinata ad usum Ecclesiae ecc.

Donesmondi, writing at the beginning of the seventeenth century, described in detail the gifts Duke Guglielmo gave to his palatine church and stated:

> Nelle feste di Capella s'appara la parte superiore del Coro d'arazzi finissimi di seta, con l'istorie intessute de gli atti Apostolici, e l'inferiore di velluti, con fregi grandi di broccato: Eccetto nella Domeniche d'Avento e di Quaresima, che s'adoperano tapezzarie di lana.

1. ASMn, b. 330 (testament of Duke Guglielmo Gonzaga). Luzio, 1914, 73 n. 1.
2. Document 48 for Ercole's testament and Luzio, 1913[A], 82, for the reference to the *Acts* in a text of 1776.
3. Donesmondi, 1613, 214.

55. 1571–1575
Granvelle Negotiates the Loan of Ferrante's Puttini *Cartoons*

Letters written by Viron, treasurer to Cardinal Granvelle, between 16 February 1571 and 4 July 1575 document the negotiations for the loan of the cartoons for Ferrante's *Puttini.*[1] At the same time the correspondence also refers to a second set of Ferrante's, an Ovidian cycle set in the forest of Soignes.[2] The first reference to a commission for copies of the *Puttini* is found in Viron's letter of 16 February 1571, which revealed that Pannemaker no longer had the cartoons in his possession:

> Touchant la tappisserie des Vignes j'ay escript que ledict Pannemaker n'en avoit aulcung patron et qu'il seroit besoing en avoir ung vidimus ou recouvrer les patrons et les ayant ici, je ferai le debvoir que V. I. S. sera servie comme il desire.

On 24 February 1571 it is learned that Pannemaker had located the cartoons for a portion of the borders:

> Et quant a la tappisserie du Vignoble de don Fernand de Gonzaga, ledict Pannemaker a tant sercher par ses papiers qu'il a trouve une piece du bordz d'icelle que va icy aussy joinctement et du surplus il le fauldroit sercher a ceulx qui l'ont emportez avec ladicte tappisserie et en prendre vidimus, comme j'ay adverty V. I. S.

Although not otherwise mentioned in the correspondence, Viron's letter of 16 July 1571 refers to another set of Ferrante's, one with scenes from an Ovidian set in the forest of Soignes near Brussels, measuring 240 *aulnes* and containing figures "une aulne" in height:

> Il y a encoire une autre tappisserie de verdure aussi bien fine du bois de Soignes ou il y a dedans des personnaiges de Poesies comme Orpheus et deesses d'une aulne de haulteur qu'ilz ont aussez bonne grace et a este fete l'ordonnance par don Fernando de Gonzaga qui fit fere la premiere tappisserie. Il y en a II cent XL aulnes au pris de IV florins VII patars l'aulne. Nous voudrions volontiers scavoir vostre volonte avant qu'elle fut vendue laquelle nous attendons.

On 29 June 1572 Viron reported on the progress that was being made on one set and on the location of the cartoons for the *Puttini:*

> Je sollicite Pannemaker de vos ouvraiges, lesquels se avancent fort mesme les pilliers et les visite toutes les sepmaines. De celle de la Vigne et Petitz Enfant, j'ay avertir V. S. I. ou sont les patrons dont je tiens se pourront recouvrer par V.S. des Goncages.

The matter of the whereabouts of the cartoons for the *Puttini* was more fully described in Viron's letter of 11 February 1573:

> Et quant a l'aultre tappisserie de don Fernando de Gonzaga je suis este devers ledict Pannemaker qui dit n'a les patrons d'icelle et que les heritiers dudict don Fernando les ont emporte, mais qui en pourroit avoir ung petit vidimus, l'on pourroit dresser les patrons qu'est tousjours plus de despence et reformer ce que ne se trouveroit agreable suyvant que l'escripvez.

Finally, on 1 October 1573, Viron was able to report that Cesare Gonzaga had agreed to the loan or sale of the cartoons at a cost of between 400 and 500 scudi:

> J'ay receu la lettre du seigneur Cesar de Gonzaga en vertu de laquelle le marchant nomme Nicole m'a accorde me delivrer les patrons, combien qu'il dit l'on luy est redevable de IV ou V cent escuz et que pour ce il ne veult fere difficulte de maniere que je tiens pour ceste heure estre es mains de Malpas. Et vient bien a propos pour mettre en besoingne Pannemaker pour besoingne et emploie les soies de Grenade, car il n'a nul ovraige sinon les IV pieces de voz armes. Je ensuyvray precisement le contenu de vostre rescription et ayant les patrons, je verray combien il y aura de pieces dont je avertira V. I. S. et treuve au propoz de y avoir des oiseaux au vifz, faiz par More, que j'ay en main. Et quant àvoz armes l'on les pourroit mettre en hault au milieu de chascune piece et le Durate en bas. Et tiendray la main que le tout voyse suyvant vostre intention. Certes la tappisserie des galleries sont bien fines, et belles.

After a brief mention in his letter of 9 January 1574 ("J'ay escript que les tappisseries de la Vigne seront de cinques aulnes et demie et seront six pieces selon les patrons"), and again on 31 May 1574 ("La tappisserie de la Vigne est sur le mestier et icy va joinctement la copie du marche; elle sera belle comme j'espere et Pannemaker ne si fera riche, car toutes choses sont trop chieres"), Viron was able to report the completion of the set in his letter of 4 July 1575:

> J'ay pieça avertir V.S. de l'envoie de la tappisserie de la Vigne et par qui la reste n'est livree sinon la derniere piece pour celle qu'est envoie et du surpluz en useray comme m'escripvez. Il vous plaira me mander si je les dois garnir de canevas pour estre prestes quant le manderez. Le tappissier Pannemaker se tient bien oblige a V. I. S., la suppliant avoir tousjours souvenance de luy et mesme envers ses seigneurs comme le marquis de Mendoza a sa venue

1. Besançon, Bibliothèque, Mss. Granvelle, vols. 18, 29, and 101 as published by Piquard, 1950, 121–25.

2. See under "Bois de Soignes" in the Index to the Major Sets of Figurative Tapestries.

56. 24 JULY 1574

Guglielmo Gonzaga Displays Ercole's Puttini *on the Occasion of the State Visit of Henry III*

On 24 July 1574, Teodoro di San Giorgio wrote to advise Guglielmo about the hangings to be used to decorate the rooms that had been set aside for Henry III.[1] In addition to great quantities of fabric and leather hangings, two sets of figurative tapestries were used, including Ercole's *Puttini* for the Camerone de' Capitani and an otherwise unidentified set of "tapezzaria di Fiandra" of Cesare Gonzaga, which was reserved for the Sala Grande.[2]

> — La Sala Grande: tapezzarie di Fiandra del signor Cesare.
> — Il Camarone de' Capitani, per mangiare: li Puttini con baldachino si sono provati et sarà le vedriate.

1. ASMn, b. 2592. Published in Mantua 1979, 204, but first mentioned by Cottafavi, 1936 (1963), 28–29. The text of the letter is very detailed, listing all of the rooms reserved for the royal visitor and his entourage as well as the decorations, mainly leather and fabric. Accordingly, this document forms an interesting contrast to the texts from 1580 and 1584 (Documents 59 and 60) when rooms were hung primarily with figurative weavings. See also ASMn, b. 389, cc. 220ff.

2. The Sala Grande is to be identified with the Sala di Manto, one of the larger rooms in the palace complex (Fig. 7, no. 9). Therefore, Cesare's set must have been of considerable width. Perhaps the set involved is to be identified with the twenty-one pieces in the set of "tapezzaria fatta a grotthesca," recorded in the 1590 inventory (Document 64). On the other hand, Cesare may have provided a fabric hanging similar to the "tapezzaria di veluto et raso verde," which Ferrante II provided in 1584 for the same Sala Grande (Document 60).

57. 1578

Ercole's Tobias *Set in the Gonzaga Palace at Revere*

A memorandum of 1578 dealing with the decorations of the Gonzaga palace at Revere refers in general terms to the "tre stanze di tappezzarie di Fiandra."[1] One of the rooms in Guglielmo's private suite was hung with "historia della Tobia, l'altra delle Tiberi."[2]

1. ASMn, b. 389.

2. According to the documents of 1584 (Document 60, nos. 2–3), the Gonzaga actually owned more than one set of the Tobias story: the "Tobie, del Cardinale," as well as the "Tobia nuovi overo le Boscaglie," which was a gift from the Arrivabene family. The *Tiberius* can be identified with the set first recorded in the 1541 inventory of the holdings of Federico II (Document 9).

58. 1579
Guglielmo Gonzaga Attempts to Acquire the Ferrante Puttini

On 26 September 1579, Paolo Moro wrote of the arrival in Venice of Ferrante II Gonzaga.[1] Apparently Ferrante II had decided he could raise cash by selling part of the collection that his father Cesare had pledged back in 1567.[2] And thus it was on 4 October 1579 that Guglielmo gave instructions to Giovanni Ceresara and Giovanni Carlo del Re concerning "Modone hebreo," who was being sent to Venice on his behalf.[3] In the letter to Ceresara it is specified that:

> il signor nostro serenissimo manda Modone hebreo a Vinegia per haver certe tapezzarie per guarnire la camera nuova che è oltre quella dell'Aquila. Perciò Vostra Signoria sia contenta di far prendere la misura delli pezzi che vanno intorno alla detta camera et di darla ad esso Modone.

Not only did Modone require the precise measurement of the wall surface in the "camera nuova," but he was also to carry with him to Venice one panel from Ercole's *Puttini*.[4] The reason for this was the need to compare Ercole's *Puttini* with the set from Ferrante that Cesare Gonzaga had given as a pledge against the repayment of a loan in 1567, as is known from the undated "Instrutione a Modone hebreo di quanto ha da fare a Venezia per servigio di Sua Altezza":[5]

> Primeramente ha da vedere se la tapezzaria che ha collà l'Eccellentissimo Signor Don Ferrante Gonzaga, chiamata delli Puttini, si confà con quella di Sua Altezza che chiamano del medesimo nome, della quale n'havrà un pezzo da portar seco et, trovandola tale et che sia in tanta quantità che basti ad apparare la camera della quale li sarà data la misura dal signor Giovanni Ceresara, procurerà con quelli migliori mezzi che saprà, di tirarla al più basso et avantagioso prezzo che si possa per servigio di Sua Altezza. Et quando havrà inteso l'ultimo prezzo, procurerà di farsene dar un pezzo da portar seco a far vedere a Sua Altezza acciò ch'ella possa rissolvere se le piacerà la tapezzaria et il mercato.

A copy of the report Modone wrote upon the completion of his mission does not survive. Modone appears to have failed since in the end Ferrante II decided against selling the set, perhaps because he was not satisfied with the price others were willing to pay. Guglielmo Gonzaga was not, however, the only collector who learned about the possible sale of the *Puttini*. On 9 January 1579, the Tuscan ambassador in Venice, Ottavio Abbioso, notified the Grand Duke Francesco de' Medici that:[6]

> Qui si trovano sei pezzi di bellissimi razzi, quali non mai usati, di setta et oro, lunghi braccia XL, et alti V et più sono lavorati a figure de putti ignudi che fanno giuoco intorno a viti; furono fatti fare da Don Ferrante Gonzaga et hoggi il suo nipote, figlio di don Cesare vorebbe venderli; per esser io stato ricercato di far intendere a Vostra Altezza Serenissima tutto questo, fuor che il padron d'essi, che ciò non mi è parso dover osservare, ho voluto darlene, aggiugnendo che, dando io parola di stare ad ogni pericolo, mi daria la via di haverne un pezzo per mandarlo a Vostra Altezza Serenissima acciò che quella potesse veder se fosse cosa di suo gusto.

The room for which Guglielmo wanted the Guastalla *Puttini,* the "Camera del Leone," also known as the "camera nuova," was located near the "Camera dell'Aquila." Together they formed part of his private rooms in the Corte Vecchia, which were under construction and decoration between 1575 and 1582. (Fig. 7) While in part reconstructable from both documentary and archaeological evidence, major changes occurred in the eighteenth century to provide for the present Appartamento degli Arazzi.[7] In the end, and while Guglielmo did indeed place the Ercole *Puttini* in the Camera dell'Aquila, other arrangments had to be made for the decoration of the Camera del Leone.[8] Had the original idea been realized, then one would have linked the two rooms by a common theme, a theme made all the more vivid by the painted decorations for the "anditello" that separated the Camera del Leone from the Camera dell'Aquila, where Lorenzo Costa the Younger painted frescoes depicting dancing *putti* playing a variety of musical instruments (Document 59). As projected, the visitor to the Corte Vecchia rooms of Guglielmo would have walked through the Camera dei Papi (no. 3) in order to gain access to the Camera delle Imperatrici (no. 4). From these symbols of Church and State, he would have passed into the Camera del Leone (no. 5), whose lower surfaces were covered with the Ferrante *Puttini*. The designation for the room doubtless reflects the dominant motif in the decorative frieze below the ceiling. The "anditello" (no. 6), as already noted, has the Costa fresco of the *Playing Puttini,* while the Camera dell'Aquila (no. 7) derives its name from the eagles presumably depicted in the decorative frieze. The final room in this sequence, the Camera dei Cani (no. 8), retains, with modifications, its original zodiac ceiling. From these more public rooms, limited access was possible to the private areas, which included a chapel and a study (no. 10).

---

1. ASMn, b. 1511, c. 107.
2. Document 53.
3. ASMn, b. 2953, l. 385, cc. 74r–v. Delmarcel and Brown, 1988, 121.
4. ASMn, b. 2953, l. 385, c. 75 (5 October 1579), from which Ceresara learned that "Oltre alle misure che io scrissi hieri a Vostra Signoria ch'ella dovesse dare a Modone, bisogna anco darli un pezzo delli Puttini da portar seco a Vinegia."
5. ASMn, b. 1407. Delmarcel and Brown, 1988, 121.
6. Archivio di Stato (Florence), Mediceo del Principato, 2987, cc. 7r–11r (10v–11r). Discovered by Martha McCrory.
7. Regarding Guglielmo's rooms in the Corte Vecchia, see Cottafavi, 1939, 203ff. The room near the Camera dell'Aquila is probably to be identified with the Camera del Leone (also called the "camera nuova)." Although other options may exist, it might have been for this suite of rooms that Ippolito Andreasi made designs for tapestries to be woven in Venice in 1579, as is known from a letter to "Salomone Levi hebreo" of 28 August 1579 (ASMn, b. 2953, l. 385, cc. 46r–v; Bertolotti, 1879, 1043). At the time of Modone's mission, Guglielmo was also preoccupied with the completion of Tintoretto's decorations for the Sala dei Marchesi and the Sala dei Duchi of the Corte Nuovo (see the letter to Paolo Moro of 6 October 1579: ASMn, b. 2953, l. 385, c. 75v; Eikenmeier, 1969, 75ff.). For more information, see Berzaghi, 1985, 43ff. For further information, see Document 59. Although it postdates by some years the reign of Duke Guglielmo, the 1614 inventory (Document 66) provides some insight into how the wall surfaces were normally covered. The Camera del Leone had "un apparamento de fette numero ventitre di cendal de Napoli verde ranzo riccamato argentino" the anditello was covered with "sei pezzi; di corame d'oro argento et color verde con colonne a vista d'oro argento," and the Camera dell'Aquila had "un apparamento de fette numero nonantaotto di ormesino basso gialo con fregi."
8. Berzaghi, 1985, 52.

59. 6–8 October 1580

Ercole's Puttini, Saul, Tobias, *and* Fortuna *Used on the Occasion of Vincenzo Gonzaga's Marriage to Margherita Farnese*

The preceding year, 1579, Guglielmo Gonzaga sought to obtain the Ferrante *Puttini,* which he intended to hang together with the set he had inherited from Ercole in two adjacent rooms—the Camera del Leone and the Camera dell'Aquila, located in the Corte Vecchia beyond the "Sala del Pisanello" (Fig. 7).[1] In the letters of 1580, no further reference is made to the Camera del Leone. Ercole's *Puttini* was reserved for the Stanza dell'Aquila and his *Saul* for the Camera dei Cani, as is known from a letter written by Federico Donato on 6 October 1580:[2]

> Ho hauto tutte le lettere del Signore. Li Puttini apareranno la stantia dell'Aquila, le Susane non bastano per quella de Cani et sbalzeriano un brazzo et mezzo, dove che siamo in pensiero di quello che habbiamo che fare. Dicono questi superiori alla draparia che sariano boni quelli Sauli che s'adoperano aparare la saletta del signor Principe Serenissimo.

Additional information is provided by Donato's letter of 9 October 1580, in which reference is made to Ercole's *Tobias* and his own *Fortuna* sets:[3]

> Nella camera delle armi ho fatto mettere li Tobbia vecchi, che sono però belli et proprii a detta camera. Le altre stantie hano tapezarie a figure et boscaie, tolti fuori et li più vaghi si son messi nella terza camera ove si mangierà. Poi ho fatto preparar 5 altre camere nell'appartamento che era delle done di Madama Serenissima, et la camera ultima ho fornita della tapezzaria de Fortuna.

Although she did not arrive in Mantua until March 1581, it might be suggested that these decorations were intended to honor the bride of Duke Vincenzo, Margherita Farnese.

---

1. Document 58. Related to the present file may be the letter of 2 October 1580 (ASMn, b. 2210), which discusses the return to Venice of "li due pezzi di tapezzaria," which Bartolomeo dal Calice has acquired. At the same time (4 October 1580: ASMn, b. 2612), Federico Donato dealt with various fabric hangings: "veluti gialli (Sole)," "veluti gialli (Leone)," "paramento novo (Cani)," and "veluti di Madama (Aquila)."
2. ASMn, b. 2612. The Camera dei Cani is identified by Berzaghi (1985, 44) with the present Stanza dello Zodiaco (no. 8) in the Corte Vecchia and thus with the room just beyond the Camera del Leone (no. 5), the *anditello* (no. 6), and the Camera dell'Aquila (no. 7).
3. ASMn, b. 2612. Berzaghi (1985) does not deal with the location of the *camera delle armi,* which, like the "altre stantie" and the "appartamento che era delle done di Madama Serenissima," is not so easy to locate.

60. 1584

Ercole's Puttini, Fortuna, Saul, *and* Tobias *Tapestries Used on the Occasion of the Arrival in Mantua of Eleonora de' Medici*

Eleonora de' Medici entered Mantua as the second bride of Vincenzo Gonzaga on 25 April 1584.[1] From the texts concerning the hangings selected for the decoration of the rooms in the bridal suite, a great deal can be learned about the tapestries and other hangings owned by the family. Four sets, the *Puttini,* the *Tobie del Cardinale,* the *Saul,* and the *Fortuna,* came to the court from the estate of Cardinal Federico, who had received them as a bequest from Cardinal Ercole.[2] As for the references to *Fogliazze,* they must refer in part to the "tapezzerie a foiazzi" mentioned by Paolo Moro in his letters of 4 and 26 February 1581.[3] Of the rooms mentioned in the documents, the *Camera de Capitani* (no. 10) is the modern Sala dei Capitani, which gives access to the Camera de Marchesi (i.e., the Sala dei Marchesi [no. 11] for which Tintoretto painted four of his "fasti gonzagheschi" in 1580). The other rooms, the Sole, Cappe, and Armi (no. 12), are on the *piano nobile* of the Castello in the area originally occupied by Isabella d'Este (Fig. 7).

The transcriptions that follow include information found in various lists housed in ASMn, b. 204, cc. 193–96, 205, 252–53, 267, 277. Small discrepancies in the listings are not always taken into account, although under no. 1 carte 193 records the number of pieces in the *Puttini* set as being ten (carte 253, however, refers only to eight pieces).

The first item in the transcription is always from carte 193, which provides information on the number of pieces and the size of each set. This is followed by information primarily gleaned from carte 194, which lists the tapestries by location under two headings: "per apparar ordinariamente" and "per le nozze."

Not all of the rooms were decorated with tapestries. The full listing of rooms recorded in carte 194 is as follows: *Per Apparar Ordinariamente:* 1. Camera dell'Armi (*Susane*), 2. Camera delle Cape ("fogliazze"), 3. Camera dell'udienza ("fogliazze"), 4. Camera del Sole ("fogliazze"), 5. Camera di sopra vicino alla stuffa ("fogliazze"), 6. Camera de Capitane (*Tobia Vechi*), 7. Camera de Marchesi (*Tobia nuovi*), 8. Camera delli Duca (*Sauli*), 9. Camera apresso, 10. Camera delle Virtù, 11. Nel Studiolo. *Per le Nozze:* 1. Camera dell'Armi ("tapezzeria di Madama Serenissima"), 2. Camera delle Cape ("brocati"), 3. Camera dell'udienza, 4. Camera del Sole ("li Palii di Fiorenza"), 5. Camera di sopra vicino alla Stuffa. 6, Camera de Capitani (*Puttini*), 7. Camera de Marchesi ("Brocati d'oro et argento"), 8. Camera delli Duca, 9. Camera apresso, 10. Camera delle Virtù, 11. Studiolo.

1. Gli Puttini sono pezzi numero 10, apparano brazza 66 ½, alte brazza 6 ¼.
   c. 194. Per le nozze—nella camera de Capitane: li Puttini. c. 253. un fornimento alto 5 [alle] longo 43 [alle] a Putini cioè un de 7, un de 7, un de 6, un de 6, un de 5, un de 4, un de 4, un de 4.
2. Tobie, del Cardinale, pezzi numero 12, apparano brazza 89½, alte brazza 5⅓.
   c. 194. Per apparar ordinariamente—nella camera de Capitani, li Tobia Vechi.
3. Tobie novi, pezzi numero 10, apparano brazza 62, alte brazza 5⅓.
   c. 194. Per apparar ordinariamente—Nella camera de Marchesi, li Tobia Nuovi overo le Boscaglie che erano dell'Arrivabene.[4]
4. Susanne pezzi numero 7 apparano brazza 45, alte brazza 5½.
   c. 194. Per apparar ordinariamente—nella camera dell'Armi, le Susane.
5. Boscaglie pezzi numero 8, apparano brazza 46, alte brazza 5⅓.
6. Tobie Vecchi pezzi numero 16, apparano brazza 91, alte brazza 5⅓.
7. Fogliazze pezzi numero 10 apparano brazza 49, alte brazza 4¼.
   c. 194. Per apparar ordinariamente—nella camera del Sole, fogliazze pezzi numero 10, alte brazza 4.
8. Fortune, pezzi numero 12, apparano brazza 39, alte brazza 4¼.
9. Coltrine pezzi numero 9 apparano brazza 84 alte brazza 6⅔.
10. Fogliazze pezzi numero 7, apparano brazza 42, alte brazza 5½.
    c. 194. Per Apparar ordinariamente—Nella camera di sopra vicino alla stuffa, il restante delle soprascripte fogliazze.
11. Fogliazze pezzi numero 8, apparano brazza 31, alte brazza 4.
    c. 194. Per apparar ordinariamente—Nella Camera dell'Udienza, Fogliazze pezzi numero 8, alte brazza 4.
12. Fogliazze pezzi numero 5, apparano brazza 30, alte brazza 3¾.
    c. 194. Per apparar ordinariamente—Nella

Camera delle Cape, Fogliazze pezzi numero 5, alte brazza 3¾.

13. Sauli pezzi numero 6, apparano brazza 56, alte brazza 6½.

c. 194. Nella Camera delli Duca—Li Sauli. c. 253 refers to "un fornimento a figura storia Saul, alto 6, longo 40 cioè un pezo 4/5/6/7/8/10.

14. Fogliazze pezzi numero 10, apparano brazza 52, alte brazza 4¼.

c. 194. Per apparar ordinariamente—Nella Camera del Sole, Fogliazze pezzi numero 10, alte brazza 4.

15. Gli Alberi pezzi numero 7, apparano brazza 51, alte brazza 5.

16. Tiberi pezzi numero 10, apparano brazza 50. alte brazza 5.[5]

---

1. Amadei, 1955, II, 846–47.

2. See ASMn, b. 204, c. 277, for reference to loans to the court from other sources; to the "paramenti se ne prende in prestito dal signor Vespasiano [et] dal signor Don Ferrante [II Gonzaga]." From the latter, in addition to various "tapezzarie di veluto, raso, damasco" and "molti tapeti da tavola," Duke Vincenzo obtained "una tapezzaria di veluto et raso verde che appara la sala grande," as well as "una [tapezzarie] di lana con l'historia di Troia per la medesima sala." The *Troy* set is presumably to be identified with one from Ercole's collection that was inherited by the Gonzaga of Guastalla. The loan from Ferrante II may be from the same hangings previously used in 1574 (Document 56).

3. ASMn, b. 1512. Letters from Paolo Moro of 4 and 26 February 1581. Beginning with the letter of 11 March 1581, the discussion turns to the matter of "corami." ASMn, b. 204, c. 253, records five groups of "boscaglie," a total of twenty-eight pieces, all of them 5 *braccia* in height.

4. Reference is found in ASDMn, Massaria, b. 3003, anno 1562, c. 263, to the "spalere Arrivabene," presumably a gift to the Duomo.

5. To be identified with the entry in the 1541 inventory of Federico II's tapestries (Document 9).

61. 11 MARCH–5 JUNE 1587

Ferrante II Arranges for the Loan of the Fructus Belli *and the* Puttini

On the occasion of the arrival of Vittoria Doria in Guastalla, Ferrante II sought to provide suitable decorations for the palace. In addition to the "due paramenti novi," these included the *Fructus Belli* and the *Puttini,* which Cesare Gonzaga had left in Venice as collateral in 1567 (Document 53). Although the transaction is not documented, it is clear from the reference to these sets in the 1590 inventory that Ferrante II arranged payment of the loan, thereby redeeming these sets (Document 65):

A: Bernardino Marliani to Ferrante II Gonzaga, 11 March 1587:[1]

> Ho scritto al Moro a Venetia che faccia opera col Calice che si abbiano le tapezzarie dei Puttini et quelle di Fructus Belli per valercene in questa occasione, che poi se gli restituiranno, subito o si riscoteranno se vi sarà commodità di denari, et fra tanto se gli è proveduto di sicurtà in Venetia per mezo di Messer Girolamo Costa, mercante di Mantova.

B: Ferrante II Gonzaga (from Genova) to his *fattore,* 8 April 1587:[2]

> Dalla lettera vostra ho veduto il discorso fatto intorno alla mia venuta (. . .). Farò parimente che, finiti i due paramenti, siano incaminati per metterli con li *Puttini* et *Fructus Belli* in questa maniera, cioè *Fructus Belli* nella Sala, i due paramenti novi nelle due prime stanze et li *Puttini* nell'altra.

C: Ferrante II Gonzaga to Paolo Moro, 5 June 1587:[3]

> Havendo io bisogno di valermi delle tapezzarie che mi ha prestate messer Bartolomeo del Calice, et non potendo per hora ricuperarle col restituire li denari per li quali esse erano pegno, ho eletto di mandare a messer Bartolomeo le gioie che vederete, le quali doveranno essere di valore equivalente

---

1. ASPr, b. 49.

2. ASPr, b. 50/2, cc. 40v–42.

3. ASPr, b. 50/2, cc. 55r–v. See also cc. 55v–56 for the letter to Bartolomeo de Calice (5 June 1587) thanking him for the loan of the "tapezzarie dei Puttini et di Fructus Belli per l'occasione della venuta di mia moglie."

62. 22 SEPTEMBER 1587

Ercole's Acts of the Apostles *Displayed on the Occasion of the Coronation of Vincenzo Gonzaga*

From the account of the ceremony accompanying the coronation of Duke Vincenzo Gonzaga on 22 Septemer 1587,[1] it is learned that the Gothic facade of the Cathedral of Mantua (Fig. 1) was covered by the *Acts:*

> E si haveva a fare nella chiesa di San Pietro, cathedrale di questa città, conforme all'uso antico. Et però inanzi la porta d'essa chiesa, si era da mastri di legname, per ordine de'signori sopra ciò deputati, preparato un palco

grandissimo alto non più d' un braccio e mezo da terra, il quale si stendeva in larghezza da ottanta braccia su la piazza cominciando alle basi de'leoni che sostentano le colonne della porta maggiore della chiesa, e di larghezza teneva la facciata della soddetta, dall'una porta picciola sino all'altra, serrandovisi in mezo la maggiore. Si alzavano poi a' piedi d'essi leoni, tre gradi, sopra de'quali era un piano che occupava tutto'l spatio qual è da un leone all'altro. Sotto la volta della porta, qual è tutta di marmo, vi era un ricchissimo baldochino di veluto turchino et brocato d'oro. Le colonne sostentate da leoni erano coperte dello stesso veluto et brocato. Era il palco tutto anch'esso coperto ad alto di panni bianchi per ripararsi dal sole, quali erano sostentati da altissimi travi, perché non impedissero la vista del popolo, del quale era non solo piena a suo tempo la chiesa ma la piazza e le finestre tutte e tutti i tetti ancho delle case, et essi travi erano circondati tutti di panni di color giallo.

La facciata della chiesa era apparata delle tapezzarie pretiosissime, nelle quali sono descritti gli Atti delli Apostoli, con figure tanto vaghe, che paiono a punto esser vive. Il piano sotto il baldochino era coperto anch'egli di finissimi tapeti Alessandrini.

1. Follino, 1587.

63. 10 JANUARY 1588
Ferrante II Orders the Shipment of the "Boscaglie" Tapestries

The loan agreement with Bartolomeo del Calice in 1587 concerned only two of the four sets that had been sent to Venice as collateral in 1567: the *Fructus Belli* and the *Puttini* (Documents 53 and 61). Presumably it is the third set, the *Boschellii,* which is referred to in the "Notta delle robe che si hanno da mandare di Guastalla alla Serra Capriola," which was drawn up on 10 January 1588.[1] In addition to "trabacche," the "panni da tavola o tepeti," the "cosini di veluto," the "refrescatorio d'argento," and the "candellieri," Ferrante also requested: "Tutte le tappezzarie a boscaglia con le sue portiere, et se non le hanno, si mandano altre portiere d'altra sorte ma non già di brocato."

1. ASPr, b. 50/2.

64. 2 FEBRUARY 1590
Ferrante II Loans Tapestries to the Accademia degli Invaghiti

On 2 February 1590, Ferrante II wrote:

> Me scrive il Marliani che gli academici Invaghiti voriano il mercordì di caranevale prossimo recitare certe orazione nella sala grande del palazzo mio di Mantova, e che desideranno tapezzerie per ornarlo, mi sono contento di piacere loro, però gli farete consegnare qualche cosa per tal effetto avvertendo che vi sia gente che n'habbia cura acciò non si guastino.[1]

Presumably Ferrante II provided the academy with the same "tapezzerie vecchie a grotteschi e fogliazza" he had loaned it the previous year.[2]

The history of loans of tapestries to the Invaghiti dates back to at least 1571, when an appeal was made to Cesare Gonzaga to "ordinar di nuovo che ella sia tapezzata et proveduto di foco al solito."[3]

1. Mantua, Biblioteca Comunale (MnBC), ms. 995, copied from a document in the ASPr, c. 119 and c. 126, for the reference in August 1590 to the fact that: "e se non vi fossero di quelle basse, trovate qualche altra cosa di meno valore che vi sia e dategliela."
2. MnBC, ms. 995, 118 (12 June 1589) and c. 115 (Marliani: 11 June 1589).
3. MnBC, ms. 995, c. 103 (1 November 1571).

65. 29 NOVEMBER 1590
Ferrante Gonzaga's Tapestries Recorded in the Gonzaga of Guastalla Inventory

A comprehensive inventory survives of the contents of the Ducal Palace in Guastalla. The "Inventarium bonorum mobilium Illustrissimi et Excellentissimi Ferdinandi Gonzagae Malphetae Princips, Guastallaeque Domini et cetera" opens with a detailed listing of sets of tapestries and then proceeds to catalogue a vast assortment of *paramenti.*[1]

The tapestries fall into three categories, the first of which consists of sets inherited from Ferrante: *Sponsalitio, Moses, Fructus Belli, Puttini,* and *Aeneas.* The second category consists of sets received as part of the estate of Cardinal Francesco and includes the *David, Historia del Re, Isaac and Jacob, Dido,* the "arme Gonzaga da Cardinale," and the panels of the *Madonna* and the *Resurrection.* This category of course includes items that

Cardinal Francesco himself received from the estate of Ercole, such as the *David* series. Finally, there are the other sets, such as the *Fabrica* and the *Terra di Fiandra,* about which nothing is known.

1. [*David*] Tapezzaria dell'Historia de David, pezzi quatro [Document 52, no. 6].
2. [*Historia del Re*] Tapezzaria dell'Historia del Re, pezzi cinque [Document 52, no. 8].
3. Tapezzaria della Fabrica, pezzi otto.
4. [*Isaac and Jacob*] Tapezzaria dell'Historia d'Isach et Jacob, pezzi tre.
5. [*Dido*] Tapezzaria di Didone, pezzo uno [Document 52, no. 11].
6. [*Foliage*] Tapezzaria bassa a spalere, alta ale tre a fogliami, pezzi diecesette.
7. [*Terra de Fiandra*] Tapezzaria della Terra de Fiandra, alta ale tre, pezzi dieci.
8. [*Foliage*] Tapezzaria a spalere fatta a fogliami, alta ale due e mezza, pezzi numero ventisei.
9. [*Foliage*] Tapezzaria a spalere fatta a fogliami, alta ale tre, pezzi duoi.
10. [*Grottesques*] Tapezzaria fatta a grotthesca, alta ale cinque e mezza, pezzi ventiuno.
11. [*Cephalus and Procris*] Tapezzaria dell'historia del *Sponsalitio*, alta ale cinque, pezzi sei.
12. [*Fructus Belli*] Tapezzaria de *Fructus Belli,* alta ale otto, pezzi otto.
13. [*Puttini*] Tapezzaria delli *Puttini* con oro et argento, alta ale cinque, pezzi sei.
14. [*Aeneas*] Tapezzaria dell'historia d'Enea, alta ale sei pezzi quattuordici.
15. [*Moses*] Tapezzaria dell'Historia de Moyse, alta ale cinque, pezzi duodeci.
16. [*Armorial*] Tapezzaria vecchia con arma Gonzaga, alta ale tre, pezzi numero quattro.
17. [*Landscapes*] Tapezzaria vecchia a paesi qual serve per invoglio, alta ale tre, pezzi due.
18. Tapezzaria simile alla sodetta, pezzi cinque.
19. [*Armorial*] Tapezzaria per coperta de muli con arma Gonzaga, pezzi cinque.
20. Tapezzaria vecchia da invoglio.
21. Tapezzaria del barcho che soleva servire nel tempo di Sua Eccellenza di felice memoria per porre sopra la nave armata dove egli andava dentro, pezzo uno.
22. Portere di tapezzaria a figura pezzi numero cinque.
23. [*Armorial*] Due arme Gonzaga da Cardinale di tapezzaria attacate insieme [Document 52, no. 4].
24. [*Madonna*] Una Madonna de tapezzaria d'oro et seta et lana [Document 49, no. C].
25. [*Resurrection*] Ressurettione di Nostro Signore d'oro, seta et lana di tapezzaria.
26. [*Madonna*] Un'altra Madonna di tapezzaria d' oro, seta et lana.
27. [*Madonna*] Una Madonna di tapezzaria d'oro, seta et lana posta in un pezzo di veluto cremesino con il freggio de tela d'oro atorno.

Doubtless more can be learned about the collection of tapestries during the years when they were under the custodianship of Ferrante II, in particular any additions that were made to the holdings. Thus, for example, the register of letters for the years 1612–14 reveals the following letter written to Carderina on 7 March 1614:[2]

> Ho visto quello che mi scrivete delle tapezzarie, ma li pezzi mi paiono un poco difficili per accomodare in una stanza, tuttavia, quando il prezzo sia honesto, mi risolverò forsi di pigliarle et mi pare non doverebbono passare nove lire l'ala, parendomi di ricordarmi che mi diceste qui ch'erano honestamente usate. Perciò desidero che mi rimettiate in memoria le qualità di dette tapezzarie, cioè se son fresche ancora et se sono a boscaglia o a figure et se il dissegno èragionevole. Desidero anco che mi mandiate la misura giusta d'un pezzo, perché, se bene me ne scrivete assai chiaramente, al calcolo che fo io vi è di non so che di differenza, e di gratia sia con la prima occasione, che sabato poi ve ne darò risolutione quando io sappia che habbiate stabilito il contratto, manderò poi il resto dell'ordine che sarà necessario che è quanto m'occorre dirvi per risposta di detta vostra lettera.

1. ASPr, b. 5. In the same "busta," but under the 23 February 1575 inventory of "argenti" owned by Cesare Gonzaga, reference is made to "uno quadro de tappezaria de fiandra con una Madona."
2. ASPr, b. 54 bis.

66. 1614
Ercole's Armorial Tapestries and His Puttini, Tobias, Saul, *and* Fortuna *Recorded in the Gonzaga Inventory*

A vast assortment of tapestry sets (as well as leather and fabric hangings) is recorded in the 1614 Gonzaga inventory.[1] The figurative tapestries were catalogued in the *guardaroba* under the date 18 August 1614 and it proceeds by "armario." The valuation of the "spaliere e tapezzarie" was undertaken by Girolamo de Romani and Francesco Arrigoni. The sets from Ercole's estate include the armorial tapestries (no. 2), the *Puttini* (no. 3), the

Tobias (no. 24), the *Saul* (no. 26), and the *Fortuna* (no. 28). In addition to the special collections of figurative sets and fabrics housed in various "casse lunga," there were also hangings found in various rooms. Thus, for example, one room was decorated with "un apparamento di corame dell'istoria della casa di Austria (. . .) alto brazza sei 1/4 in pezzi numero disnove di giro braza centonoventiquattro e mezzo,"[2] as well as "un apparamento simile con figure grande d'oro et diverse colori in pezzi numero sette, alte braza cinque 1/3."

The 1614 inventory is the first comprehensive accounting of the possessions of the Gonzaga of Mantua after that compiled in 1540–41 (Document 9). This seems an appropriate place, therefore, to refer to some of the surviving documentation that does not relate to Ercole's private holdings. Curiously the items are sparce regarding the main line of the family.

In addition to the few letters and the inventory dating from the lifetime of Duke Federico II, and the material from the lifetime of Dukes Guglielmo and Vincenzo that has already been discussed (Documents 56–59 and 62), the remainder of the relevant items are catalogued in the Addenda at the end of this entry.

Embroidery or Small Tapestries

a. [*Passion of Christ*] Uno pezzetti di spalera con oro, argento et seta con la Passione di Nostro Signore—scudi 200.

b. [*Saint George*] Un pezzetto di spalera con oro, argento et seta con un Santo Giorgio—scudi 50.

c. [*Serpente Eneo*] Un pezzetto di spalera con oro, argento et seta con l'istoria del Serpente Eneo—scudi 400.

d. [*Figure delli signori*] Uno pezzo di spalera bassa a figure delli signori della casa, con oro, argento et seta—1000 scudi.

e. [*Madonna and Child*] Un pezzo di spalera con oro, argento et seta con la Nostra Dona con il Fanciul Jesù in braccio qual preme un grappo d'uva et lettere che dicono "ex latere Christi credit [crevit?] aeclesia [?]"—scudi 500.

f. [*Madonna and Child with the Magi*] Un pezzetto di spalera con oro, argento, et seta con sopra una Madonna et il Bambino con li Tre Maggi—scudi 50 [See Document 49, no. D for reference in the 1563 inventory of Ercole's possessions, to his "quadro di tri Magi d'oro, argento, seta, et lana," which, however, was inherited by Ferrante's son, Cardinal Francesco, and thus by the collatorial branch of the family].

g. [*Giardin d'amore*] Un pezzo di spalera fina con seta, detto il giardin di amore, alto brazza 6½ et longo braza sette ¼—scudi 15.

h. [*Hunt*] Due pezzi di spalera fina con ramo di rose, con huomini armati con l'arma Gonzaga et donne c'hanno cani a lasso a mano alti brazza tre cioè uno lungo brazza otto et l'altro brazza tre ¼—scudi 12.

i. [*Christ on the Road to Emmaus*] Un quadretto di spalera fina con seta et oro, con Nostro Signore et due peregrini che andavano in Emaus con di sopra lettere di oro che dicono: Sanctus [?] Lucas evangelista [?] XXIIII—scudi 5.

Large-Scale Figurative Tapestries

1. [*Philomela*] Un pezzo di spalera fina con seta, della favola di Filomena, longo brazza undeci ⅔, alta brazza due ¾—scudi 18 [To be related to the "spalera a figuri de Filomena" recorded in the 1541 inventory (Document 9)].

2. [*Armorial*] Sedeci arme Gonzaga di tapezzaria vecchie, con il capello da cardinale quali erano della felice memoria del signor Cardinale Ercole—scudi 2.

3. [*Puttini*] Un apparamento di tapezzaria con oro, argento et seta a figure delli Putini in pezzi numero dieci, alto brazza sei ¼, di giro brazza sessantasei—a scudi 10 l'alla quale cresce di brazza ½ quarto.

3a. Tre portiere che l'accompagnano [i.e., the *Puttini*]—scudi 180.

3b. Due sopraportiere similmente compagne [i.e., the *Puttini*]—scudi 80.

3c. Un pezzetto simile di pittura fatto sopra la tella per mettere in un cantone—scudi 8.

4. Un apparamento di tapezzaria di Fiandra in pezzi numero otto, alto brazza sei ¼, di giro brazza cinquantadue e un terzo, venuto da Casale—scudi 1500.

5. [*Adam*] Un apparamento di spalera di lana con oro et seta dell'istoria d'Adamo fodrato di tella turchina con oro e seta, alto brazza cinque ⅓ in pezzi numero nove, di giro brazza sessanta ¾—scudi 4275.

6. [*Forest*] Un apparamento di boscalia fina con figure et animali, fodrato di tella turchina in pezzi numero sei, alto brazza tre ¾, di giro brazza trentaquattro ⅓—a lire 15 l'alla.

7. Un apparamento di tapezzaria di Fiandra di lana et seta in pezzi numero otto, alto brazza cinque e mezo, di giro brazza quarantasei ⅓—a scudi 8 l'alla.

8. [*Troy*] Un apparamento di tapezzaria parte di lana et parte di seta dell'istoria di Troia, fodrato di tella turchina, alto brazza cinque ⅓, in pezzi numero dieci, di giro brazza sessantadue ⅔—a scudi 8 l'alla.

9. [*Forest*] Un apparamento di boscalia fina con figure et animali, fodrato di tella turchina, in pezzi numero

sei, di giro brazza trentauno ¾—a lire 15 l'alla.

10. [*Julius Caesar*] Un apparamento di tapezzaria di lana fina con figure grande della congiura fatta contro Cesare, fodrato di canevazza, alto brazza cinque ⅓, di giro brazza trentasette ⅙—a scudi 7 l'alla.

11. [*Foliage*] Un apparamento di fogliazza, fodrata di canevazza, alto brazza cinque ⅞, in pezzi numero quindeci di giro brazza nonantadue e mezo—a lire 9 l'alla.

11a. Una portiera simile fodrata di tella turchina.

11b. Una sopraportiera simile - scudi 16 [including 11a].

12. [*Forest*] Un apparamento di boscaglia della seconda sorte, alto brazza quattro ⅓, in pezzi numero dodeci, de giro brazza sessanta ¾—a lire 6 l'alla.

13. [*Foliage*] Un apparamento di fogliazze, alto brazza quatro ¼, in pezzi numero dieci, di giro brazza quarantaotto ¾—a lire 3 l'alla.

14. Un apparamento di tapezzaria fina, figurata, alto brazza cinque ¼, in pezzi numero sei, di giro brazza trentaquattro et un quarto, venuto da Casale—a scudi 4 l'alla.

15. [*Forest with Labors of Hercules*] Un apparamento di boscaglia con forze d'Ercole, alto brazza quattro ¼, in pezzi numero sette, di giro brazza quaranta ½—a lire 9 l'alla.

16. [*Foliage*] Un apparamento di fogliazze della seconda sorte, alte brazza tre ¼, fodrati di canovazzo, in pezzi numero tredeci, di giro brazza sessantatre ¾—a lire 4 l'alla.

17. [*Grotteschi*] Un apparamento a Grotesche, altre volte nominato Astrologia, in campo rosso, alto brazza due ½, in pezzi numero tre, de giro brazza sedeci ⅔—a lire 6 l'alla.

18. [*Foliage*] Un apparamento di fogliazza, novo, della seconda sorte, con figure et animali, alto brazza cinque ¼, in pezzi numero otto, di giro brazza quarantasette ½—a lire 9 l'alla.

19. [*Forest*] Un apparamento di boscaglia, nuovo, della seconda sorte, alto brazza cinque ¼, in pezzi numero otto, di giro brazza quarantacinque ½—a lire 12 l'alla.

20. [*Foliage*] Un apparamento di fogliazza fodrata di canovazzo, alta brazza sei ⅞, in pezzi numero dodeci, di giro brazza sessantasei—a lire 9 l'alla.

21. [*Cyrus*] Un apparamento di tapezzaria fina a figura dell'istoria di Ciro, alta brazza sei ¼, in pezzi numero undeci, di giro brazza ottanta ¾—a scudi 8 l'alla.

22. [*Forest*] Un apparamento de boscaglia, alta brazza cinque ⅓, in pezzi numero otto, de giro brazza quarantatre—a scudi 3 l'alla.

23. [*Tobia novi*] Un apparamento delli Tobia novi in pezzi numero dieci, alti brazza cinque ¾, de giro brazza sessanta.

24. [*Tobia del Cardinale*] Un apparamento delli Tobia del Cardinale in pezzi numero dodeci, alti brazza cinque, un terzo, di giro brazza ottantanove ⅔—scudi 2 l'alla.

24a. [*Armorial*] Sei sopraportiere simile con l'arma del Cardinale e putini—scudi 24.

25. [*Forest with Figures and Animals*] Un apparamento di boscaglia fine con gran numero di figure picole et diverse sorte di animali, in pezzi numero dodeci, alte brazza cinque ⅓, di giro brazza settantatre e ⅓—a scudi 4 l'alla.

26. [*Saul*] Un apparamento di tapezzaria dell'Istoria di Saul, vecchio, alto brazza sei ½ in pezzi numero sei, di giro brazza cinquantasei ¼—a scudi 2 l'alla.

26 bis. [*Tobia vecchi*] Un apparamento di Tobia vecchi in pezzi numero sedici, alta brazza nonantauno ½—a lire 6 l'alla.

27. [*Tiberius*] un apparamento dell'istoria di Tiberio alto brazza cinque ⅔, in pezzi numero dieci di giro brazza cinquanta ⅓—a lire 3 l'alla [To be related to the "Tiberio e Alexandro Magno" set recorded in the 1541 inventory of Federico II (Document 9)].

28. [*Fortuna*] Un apparamento delle Fortune, in pezzi numero dodeci alto brazza quattro ¼, due de' quali fodrati [di] tella turchina, di giro brazza trentanove—a scudi uno l'alla.

29. [*Trees with a Hunt*] Un apparamento di tapezzaria degli Alberi, a figure, boscaglia et caccie in pezzi numero sette alti brazza cinque ⅔, di giro brazza cinquantauno—a lire 3 l'alla.

30. [*Forest with Figures and Animals*] Un apparamento di Boscaglia a figure et animali, alti brazza tre ¼, in pezzi numero cinque, di giro brazza trentauno et un quarto—a lire 5 l'alla.

31. [*Forest*] Un apparamento di Boscaglia della seconda sorte, con caccie, alti brazza tre ⅔, in pezzi quattro, di giro brazza ventidue—a lire 5 l'alla.

32. [*Forest*] Un apparamento di Boscaglia della seconda sorte, alte brazza 4¼, in pezzi numero 6, di giro brazza 37⅓—a lire 5 l'alla.

33. [*Armorial*] Un apparamento di spaliera a figura con l'arme sopra delle quatro aquile vecchie, alte brazza 3½, in pezzi numero 10, di giro brazza 58 ⅙—scudi 25.

34. Un apparamento di spalera a figura, vecchio, strazzato, alte brazza 2⅔, scompagnate, in pezzi numero 7—scudi 10.

35. [*Poesie*] Un apparamento delle Poesie, alte brazza 3⅙, una delle quali è in due pezzi, di giro brazza 56.

36. [*Foliage*] Un apparamento di fogliazze, alte brazza 4,

in pezzi numero 7, vecchie, di giro brazza trenta et uno ottavo.

37. [*Foliage*] Un apparamento di fogliazze vechie, alte brazza 3¼, in pezzi numero 6, due de'quali sono scavezzi, di giro brazza 23—a lire 3 l'alla.
38. [*Foliage*] Un apparamento di fogliazze vecchio, alto brazza 4⅞, in pezzi numero cinque, di giro brazza ventisette—scudi 15.
39. [*Foliage*] Un apparamento di fogliazze vechie, alto brazza 3⅞, in pezzi numero tre, fodrato di canevazzo, di giro brazza 20.

39a. Un altro pezzo che accompagna, alto brazza 3¾, longo brazza 6.

39b. Un altro pezzo alto brazza 4 fodrato di tela turchina, longo brazza 7½.

40. [*Foliage*] Un apparamento di fogliazze vecchio, strazzato, alto brazza 2½, in pezzi numero otto, di giro brazza 29¼.
41. Due portiere picole con una figura in piedi che accompagna—scudi 1.
42. [*Sampson*] Due sopraportiere di tapezzarie con Sansone.
43. [*Foliage*] Due portiere a fogliazze fodrate di tela turchina, larghe brazza 3¼ per cadauna.
44. [*Armorial*] Una portiera di tapezzarie con l'arma delle 4 Aquile.
45. [*Forest with Hercules and the Nemean Lion*] Una portiera di tapezzaria a boscaglia con Ercole con un leone, fodrata di tela turchina —scudi 10.
46. [*Juno and Peacock*] Una portiera di tapezzaria con una Giunone et un pavone, fodrata di tela turchina.

46bis. [*Fortune*] Un pezzo di spalera con una Fortuna nel mezo, alto brazza cinque, largo sei, strazzatissimo.

47. Un pezzo di spalera con due figure et lettere gialle nel friso di sopra, alto brazza 3¾, longo brazza 6, strazzatissimo.
48. Un pezzo di spalera a figura, alto brazza 3, longo tredeci [brazza], strazzatissimo.

---

1. ASMn, b. 400, cc. 459ff. (especially cc. 476–81). As with other similar inventories, an extensive accounting is also given of fabric and leather hangings. Beginning on c.523v is the listing of the specific rooms as opposed to the contents of the *guardaroba*. Each of the rooms had its own special wall hangings (see under Document 58, note 7).
2. Perhaps this is to be identified with the "corrami d'oro con figure in piedi della Serenissima Casa d'Austria" recorded by Ottavio Piccolomini in his 24 January 1631 "Relatione" as being in the private apartments of Carlo I Gonzaga (d. 1637). Meroni, 1976, 33.

ADDENDA

A. 1554: Tapestries offered by "Rigo di Schotti fiamengo in Venezia al ponte di Barreleri."

The correspondence files refer to various sets, including the "Forze d'Hercule," the "historia de Isaia," the "historia di David," and the "Ystoria de Jacob." The file, which was noted by Bertolotti, 1889, 1042–43, consists of a letter from Benedetto Agnello of 1 January 1554 (with an enclosure by Rigo di Schotti), as well as Angello's letter of 16 January 1554 (ASMn, b. 1486). Full details on the measurements of the series are provided.

B. 1567: Testament of Margherita Paleologa (ASMn, b. 332).
This document records two groups of *verdure spalliere* totaling nineteen pieces, one of which was bequeathed to Ludovico, the founder of the Nevers branch of the family. Paleologa's collection was actually more extensive, as can be learned from the 15 April inventory (ASMn, Magistrato Camerale Antico, B. b. II). The reference to the *Elijah* and the *Gideon* tapestries is particularly interesting since apparently Paleologa inherited these from her son, Cardinal Federico (Document 51).

1. [*Foliage with Birds*] una spallera in undeci pezzi di tapezzaria di Fiandra fra grandi et piccioli, fatta a fogliazzi con varii uccelli, la quale spallera è dell'Illustrissimo et Eccellentissimo Duca di Nevers.
2. [*Landscape with Animals*] Una spallera di Fiandra in otto pezzi di tapezzaria fatta a paesi con figure et animali de diverse sorti et li pezzi sono parte grandi et parte piccioli.
3. [*Elijah*] Otto pezze di spalliere di Fiandra figurate et istoriate con la storia di Elia con duoi antiporti.
4. [*Gideon*] Cinque altre pezze di spalliere di Fiandra figurate con le istorie di Gedeon.

C. 1567: The Carlo Borromeo tapestries (ASMn. b. 900, c. 905).
On 7 February 1568 the court in Mantua learned from Bernardino Pia of Carlo Borromeo's intention to sell all of his possessions in order to raise funds for pious works. Accordingly, Pia wrote of the possibility of purchasing back "quelle belle tapezzarie che l'Illustrissimo et Eccellentissimo signor Duca nostro gli mandò a donare." As is noted in the Index to the Major Sets of Figurative Tapestries (see under *Moses* [Gonzaga of Mantua]), this set is to be identified with the *Moses* cycle partially preserved in the Museo del Duomo in Milan.

D. 1579: A letter from Paolo Moro in Venice dated 22 August (ASMn, b. 1511, cc. 87–88).
In his letter to Paolo Moro requesting information on

behalf of the Patriarch of Aquilea concerning the possible arrival in Mantua of objects stolen from Cesare Caraffa, including "due fornimenti d'razzi a figure alte brazza cinque che son in numero 12 pezzi."

E. 1587: The Erik of Brunswick collection of tapestries.
The extensive files for the litigations with the heirs of Erik II of Brunswick and Luneburg (1528–84) record a remarkable collection of tapestries, none of which, however, seems to have ended up in the hands of the Gonzaga of Mantua. The material can be summarized as follows. On 28 October 1583 Guglielmo Gonzaga agreed to pay 50,000 ducats for a palace on the Grand Canal in Venice, which had been acquired in 1581 from Alvise Loredano by "Enrico duca di Bransuich e Lunerburch e Conte de Claramonte." This amount had been reduced by 6,000 ducats prior to Guglielmo's death on 14 August 1587, but ownership of the palace, better known as the Vendramin-Calergi, was challenged by Andrea Doria, who claimed that it formed part of the dowry he was promised when he married Catherina on 17 February 1580. The negotiations for and the dispute over the Brunswick residence in Venice fill four ample boxes of documents (ASMn, b. 350–53) and there are related texts in the court correspondence with Milan. Among the latter is an undated sheet (filed with material from 1587) that records the "tapezzarie che erano del già Duca Enrico di Bransvich."

On 20 April 1591 (ASMn, b. 712, c. 240), Erik's widow wrote to Duke Vincenzo to protest his refusal to give up claims to "una stanza di tapezzaria di Fiandra." According to the Milan inventory of 1588 (ASMn, b. 1706), Erik of Brunswick owned four "tapezzaria de Fiandra a boschaia con caccia," a nine-piece set depicting "l'historia de Adam," from the Creation through the Flood, eleven armorial *verdure* tapestries, and a miscellaneous collection of forty-nine Flemish tapestries, including those depicting "le historie de Troia et de' peccati morali." The Milan inventory, also of 1587, is even more detailed. From it one learns that the seven-piece set of the *Deadly Sins* measured "cinque ale" in height, while the *Troy* set consisted of ten pieces, "alta cinque ale et un terzo, di giro ale 55 in circa che concerne tutta la guerra di Troia con figure mezane et piccole, et boscaglia belissima." The nine-piece *Adam* set (see under "Adam" in the Index to the Major Sets of Figurative Tapestries), woven with "oro, argento et seta," measured five and half *ale* in height and its total length was 50 *ale*. As for the listing of 1584, which records possessions kept in Pavia rather than in Milan, we learn something of Erik's total holdings, but the description of the tapestries is vague.

F. 1590: The offer of a set of tapestries.
"David di Cervo hebreo" wrote from Milan on 23 January 1590 to offer Duke Vincenzo a set of *verdure* tapestries ("cosa rara et bella et nuova") measuring 52 *ale* (ASMn, b. 1711; Bertolotti, 1889, 1044).

G. 1593: Tapestries for the Ducal Palace.
Luigi Rogna wrote on 17 November 1593 concerning the tapestries ordered in Venice for various rooms in the Ducal Palace. While important because they specify measurements and locations, the references to the "apparamento di tappezzerie" are too general to permit identifications (ASMn, b. 2660; *Mantua 1979*, 211).

H. 1600: Tapestries ordered by Vincenzo Gonzaga.
A group of informative letters written by Francesco Marini from Antwerp to Vincenzo Gonzaga documents negotiations for the acquisition of tapestries "sendomi parse per la qualità loro bellissime" (ASMn, b. 575, cc. 6, 8, 15–16, 30–31, 2, 9. 29 June, 7 July, 2 and 9 September 1600; ASMn, b. 2251 to Marini: 10 August 1600). Unfortunately, nothing is said in the letters about the subject matter of the weavings, although on 9 June Marini wrote at length:

> conforme a quanto da Vostra Altezza mi fu comandato qua di presenza, comessi le tapizzerie per le due sale secondo la fattura. E recommandai al tapizzero la bontà, e prestezza. Quando me n'hanno portato alcuni pezzi ch'erano forniti, mi sono accorto che havevano un diffetto di non poca qualità et era che sendosi serviti del patrone o sie dissegno fatto per tapizzerie di altezza solamente di anne cinque, quel sopra più non era ben ripartito, ma si vedeva molto chiaro che era una gionta fatta alla detta altezza senza haver agiustato il dissegno a proportione; così non ho voluto ricceverle, et havendo fatto instanza al detto maestro acciò le facci fare sopra un novo disegno di quella altezza, m'ha detto che, bisognandoli far la spesa del detto disegno aposta, non è possibile che le possa dare a quel pretio ma che almeno bisognerà si paghino un scuto et ¼ l'ana, sendo massime cresciuta parimente di prezzo la roba che vi va dentro. E

non havendo pagato Vostra Altezza quelle altre se non un scuto l'ana, non ho voluto rissolvermi a spender di vantagio senza darline aviso, e tanto più che, bisognandovi al meno otto mesi a finirle, in ogni modo non seranno più in tempo per questo inverno che viene e per l'altro vi è ancor tempo assai. Serà donche Vostra Altezza servita d'avisarmi quello comanderà ch'io facci che tanto eseui[rò] prontamente.

On 10 August 1600 (ASMn, b. 2251), Vincenzo wrote to approve the arrangements.

I. 1605: Tapestries available from Venice.
Antonio Costantini wrote from Venice to Duke Vincenzo on 26 June 1605 (ASMn, b. 1537: Bertolotti, 1889, 1043) concerning "certe tapezzerie di singolar bellezza et ricchezza," which he had seen in the Ghetto.

J. 1609: Tapestries brought to Mantua by Margherita of Savoy.
Two sets of tapestries, the "Historia di Scipione et Annibale" and the "Historia di Diana," formed part of the dowry agreed to by the Dukes of Mantua and Savoy on the occasion of the marriage of Margherita to Francesco IV Gonzaga (ASMn, b. 205, cc. 54v–55; Braghirolli, 1879, 101). The eight pieces in the *Diana* set are presumably to be identified with an entry in the 1668 Gonzaga inventory (Document 68, no. 6).

K. 1617: The Montalto tapestries.
On 18 November 1617 (ASMn, b. 1013), Raniero Bissolati wrote concerning the proposed sale of the contents of the *guardaroba* of Cardinal Montalto. The inventory promised by Bissolati on 25 November 1617 does not survive (see also his letters of 2 and 23 December 1617). Thus, little can be learned about the "tapezzarie fatte in Firenze," which, in any event, were presumably never acquired by the Mantuan court.

L. Circa 1713–14: Christina of Sweden's collection.
A Mantuan provenance for this collection is found in the "Descrizione degli Arazzi della Regina Cristina di Svezia, provenienti dal Sacco, prima di Mantova, poi di Praga, portati in Roma dalla medesima, ed in sua morte comprati e posseduti presentemente da Sua Eccellenza il signor Principe domino Livio Odescalchi." A copy of the version in the Biblioteca Apostolica Vaticana (Bibl. Cicognara, Miscellanea n. 5) is found in ASMn, Schede Davari, no. 8, cc. 861–67. The tapestries named in this text, "Storia d'Augusto e Cleopatra con Marc'Antonio," "Istoria di Giulio Cesare," "Istoria d'Elena e di Paride," and the "Trionfi del Petrarca," have no known connection with the Gonzaga family, having never been named in any of the inventories. Nordenfalk (1966, 266ff.) established the provenance of some of these sets as either having been inherited from Gustavus II Adolphus or acquired directly by Christina herself.

67. 1627
Ercole's Tapestries Recorded in the Inventory of the Palaces in Mantua and Casale

Folio XI of the comprehensive 1627 inventory contains an extensive listing of tapestries.[1] In addition to this listing of the contents of the Ducal Palace, there is a second inventory of 9 January 1627 dealing with the palace at Casale Monferrato.[2] The former inventory records two sets formerly in the collection of Ercole: the *Saul* and the *Fortuna.*

Part of the reason for this comprehensive inventory was the preparation for the sale to Charles I of England of many of the treasures of the Ducal Palace. For whatever reason, tapestries and other wall hangings do not figure in these transactions.[3] Shortly after the sale, Mantua was subject to a massive asault by the imperial troops. Although it is clear from the evidence that survives that the 1630 sack of the palace had some effect on the collection of wall hangings, precise information is lacking.[4] It may be, however, that two sets described in the Este inventory of 1638 as "arazi di Mantova" came to Modena as a result of the dispersal of the Gonzaga collection by the imperial troops.[5] One of these sets, "a boscalia," featured swans. If intended as an *impresa,* the swans could identify the set as having been designed for Ercole.

Contents of the Ducal Palace in Mantua

1. [*Forest*] Un apparamento di boscaglia della Camera di Marchesi, alto bracia 5⅓, in pezzi numero 8, di girro brazza 43, estimato Lire 3690.
2. Un apparamento di tapezaria di lana fina et setta, nova, in pezzi numero 10, alto brazza 5¼, di girro brazza 46⅓, estimato Lire 920.
3. [*Alexander the Great*] Un'apparamento di tapezaria di lana, della seconda sorte, de l' Historia d'Allesandro Magno, alta brazza 6⅓, in pezzi numero 13, di girro brazza 92, estimato Lire 12672.

4. [*Julius Caesar*] Un apparamento di tapezaria di lanna fina fatta contro Cesare, fodrata di canevazo, alto brazza 5⅓, in pezzi numero 6, di girro brazza 37⅛, estimato Lire 3600.
5. [*Frieze with Figures and Animals*] Un apparamento di foiaza nova della seconda sorte con Figure et Animali, alto brazza 5¼, in pezzi numero 9, di girro brazza 47¼, estimato Lire 2700.
6. [*Foliage*] Un apparamento di foiaza nova della seconda sorte, fodrato di canevazzo, alto braza 6⅞, in pezzi numero 12, di girro brazza 66, estimatto, Libre 4464.
7. [*Foliage*] Un apparamento di foiaza della seconda sorte, alto brazza 3¼, in pezzi numero 7, di girro brazza 40, estimatto Lire 3033.
8. [*Foliage*] Un apparamento di foiazza alto brazza 3⅛, in pezzi numero 3, et un altro pezzo che accompagna, alto brazza 3¾, tutti quattro pezzi fodrati di canevazzi et un altro pezzo alto brazza 4 che accompagna, fodrato di tella turchina, sí che sono in tutto pezzi numero 5 di giro brazza 33⅓, estimatto Lire 3025, 10.
9. [*Forest with the Hunt*] Un apparamento di Boscaglia della seconda sorte con cacce, alto brazza 3⅔ in pezzi numero 4, di girro brazza 22, estimato Lire 367,10.
10. [*Poesie*] Un apparamento della Povesie di tapezaria, alto brazza 5⅚, di girro brazza 56, in pezzi numero 7, estimatto Lire 728.
11. [*Forest with the Labors of Hercules*] Un apparamento di Boscaglia con Fattiche d'Hercule, alto brazza 4¼ in pezzi numero 7, di girro brazza 40½, estimatto Lire 2340.
12. [*Saul*] Un apparamento di tapezaria de l' Historia di Saulo, alto brazza 6½, in pezzi numero 6, di girro brazza 56¼, estimatto Lire 6048.
13. [*Forest with Figures and Animals*] Un apparamento di Boscaglia fina con figure et animali, fodrato di tella turchina, alto brazza 3¾, in pezzi numero 6, di giro brazza 34⅓, [estimatto] Lire 1428.
14. [*Forest with Figures and Animals*] Un apparamento di boscaglia fina con figure et animali fodrato di tella turchina, alto brazza 3⅜, in pezzi numero 6, di girro brazza 31¾, estimatto Lire 1260.
15. [*Foliage*] Un apparamento di Foiaza della seconda sorte fodrato di canevazzo, alto brazza 3¼ in pezzi numero 13 di girro brazza 63¾ cioè pezzi numero 6 che sono in detta Camera et pezzi numero 7 nella stanza dove mangiano li signori Cavaglieri di Sua Altezza Serenissima, estimatto Lire 1080.
16. [*Fortuna*] Un apparamento di tapezaria detto le Fortune in pezzi numero 12, alto brazza 4¼, di giro brazza 39 [estimatto] Lire 1036.
17. [*Forest with Figures*] Un apparamento di Boscaglia fina con gran numero di figure piccole et varie sorti d'animali in pezzi numero 12, alto brazza 5⅓ di girro brazza 37½, estimatto Lire 6300.
18. Un apparamento di tapezaria fina di Fiandra, alto brazza 6¼ in pezzi numero 8 di girro brazza 52⅓, [estimatto] Lire 10800.
19. [*Forest with a Hunt*] Un apparamento di tapezaria detto Li Alberi, a figure, boscaglie et catie, in pezzi numero 7, alto brazza 5⅔, di girro brazza 51, estimatto Lire 4080.
20. [*Forest*] Un apparamento di Boscaglia della seconda sorte in pezzi numero 10, di girro brazza 45½, estimatto Lire 2580.
21. [*Tobias*] Un apparamento di tapezaria delle Tobie, nova, in pezzi numero 10, alto brazza 5¾ di girro brazza 60, estimatto Lire 7372.
22. [*Acitoni*] Un apparamento di tapezaria con oro et argento et setta a figura delli Acitoni [?] in pezzi numero 10, di giro brazza 66, estimato sesantadue l'alla, Lire 26352.

From the "Descriptio bonorum hereditariorum allodialium sitorum in dominio Montisferrati—datum in Casale

23. [*Susanna*] pezzi sette di tapezzaria di Fiandra di seta et lana, alta braccia 5⅔ che rappresenta l'historia di Susanna et tira braccia 185, estimati scudi 370.
24. [*Forest*] altri pezzi sette di tapezzaria di Fiandra fatta a boscaglia d'altezza di braccia 3½, et tira in tutto braccia 133, estimati scudi 133.
25. altri pezzi cinque di tapezzaria di Fiandra fatta a brochette, d'altezza di braccia 3, vecchia, tira in tutto braccia 54, estimati scudi 24.
26. un altro pezzo di tapezzaria di Fiandra, rotta, vecchia, di braccia sei, estimato scudi 3.
27. [*Foliage*] una portiera di tapezzaria di Fiandra fatta a fogliami, di lana e seta, fodrata di sangallo, estimata scudi 10.
28. [*Foliage*] altri quattro pezzi di tapezzaria di Fiandra di lana, detta le Fogliazze, alta braccia 4⅓, tira in tutto braccia 57, estimati scudi 57.
29. quattro pezzi di tapezzaria di Fiandra fatti a figura con seta et lana con fregi atorno di figure grandi, di altezza di braccia cinque, in tutto tirano braccia 119, estimati scudi 80.
30. quattro pezzi di tapezzaria simile alla prossima sudetta della medema altezza, di braccia in tutto 80, estimati scudi (?) il braccio scudi 54 - 4.

1. ASMn, b. 330, cc. 1090–93.
2. ASMn, b. 330, cc. 524ff.
3. The documentation in Mantua and in London for the sale has been published by Luzio (1913, passim).

4. Moscardo (1668, XII, 486) refers to the shipment to Trent by Galasso of paintings, jewels, vases, rock crystal, and "tapezzerie" (as cited by Quazza, 1926, II, 149 n. 2). There is also the reference in Marco Dardani's letter from Brescia of 4 September 1634 (ASMn, b. 1567: Luzio, 1913, 82) to furniture, cabinets, baldachins, and wall hangings ("alcuni razzi vecchi") scattered about Northern Italy by Aldringhen's troops. Unfortunately the sole document regarding the postsack situation in Mantua, Ottavio Piccolomini's letter to the emperor of 23 Janury 1631 (Siena, Biblioteca Comunale, Ms. B.V. 2, 17–23; Meroni, 1976, 33–36), refers in general terms mainly to fabric hangings.

5. ASMo, Cam. duc., Arazzi e Tappezzerie: "Pezzi numero 7 d'arazi a boscalia con varii annimalli nominati 'della balena,' e detti gli arazi di Mantova, alti alle 6." "Pezzi numero 5 d'arazi a boscalia con varii animali e particolarmente cigniare, detti parimente gli arazi di Mantova, alti alle numero 6." Further references in subsequent inventories confuse rather than clarify matters. In the "inventario della Guardarobba della Razzeria" of 19 December 1662, the "Whale set" is described as "un altro paramento di razzi simili detti [razzi] di Mantova, fati a boscaglia con figure di animali grandi nel mezo, in uno de'quali vi è la gran ballena, sono alti ale 6, diviso in pezzi numero 7 con frigio che nella cima di sopra ha ne'cantoni figure a grotesche et nel mezo un'altra figura con un pavone, giro tutto ale 51, pezzi numero 7." A second listing, one that actually immediately precedes this entry, refers to "un paramento di razzi a boscaglia mezi fini, detti li razzi di Mantova, con figure et animali diversi et huomini a cacia, alti ale 6, diviso in pezzi numero 7 con frigi che sopra vi è Mercurio, e di sotto una figura in ginochio, et a mezo due figure che suonano, gira in tutto ale 34⅙, pezzi numero 7." Given this description and the fact that the set consisted of seven pieces, it cannot be identified with the "Swan" series.

See also the 1664 "Misure delli Razzi," which refers to the "paramento di razzi di Mantova a boscaglia," measuring 6½ *braccia* in height and divided into two groups of six, each of varying length (between 5 and 20¼ *braccia,* with one set measuring 47¼ in length, the other 45½ in length). Several undated listings, such as the "Notta distinta," refer to the "pezzi numero 12 detti di Mantova," while the "Arazzi di Sua Altezza" refers to the first group of six as measuring 6½ *braccia* and being 46 *braccia* in length, while the second was said to be 45 *braccia.* Similar information is contained in the "Inventario dell'Arrazzeria." Yet the "Notta delli Araggi" refers to "pezzi nove araggi detti di Mantova." Finally, in 1772 (ASMo. Cam. duc., Casa, Guardarobba, reg. 301, c. 389), reference is found to "un arazzo mezzo fino, usato, logorato ed affumicato, detto li Mantovani, con piccole figure ed animali [altezza] 6⅓, [lunghezza] 5¾."

68. 1648–1668

Ercole's Tapestries in the Later Inventories of the Gonzaga Family

Four inventories between 1648 and 1668 help us to trace the history of the Gonzaga family collection of tapestries. Included among them are the *Puttini* of Cardinal Ercole, which is catalogued in 1648 and again in 1668, as well as the twelve-piece *Tobias* set mentioned in 1668.

1648[1]

1. [*Puttini*] pezzi dieci di spaliera chiammati li Putini.

1661[2]

2. [*Suzanna*] pezzo di tapezzaria di Fiandra detta la Susanna, numero 1.
3. [*Foliage*] apparamento di Fiandra detto delle fogliazze in pezzi sette, numero 7.

1665[3]

4. [*Phaeton*] pezzi sei spaliere di Fiandra con la favola di Fettone, usate.
5. [*Alexander*] pezzi nove spaliere da razzo con l'istoria dei fatti d'Alessandro il Grande, usate.
6. [*Diana and Niobe*] pezzi otto spaliere a razzo tessuto d'oro, con la favola de Diana e Niobe, usato.

1668[4]

7. [*Phaeton*] sei pezzi di Fettonte, cioè figure.
8. [*Achilles*] otto pezzi d'Achile.
9. [*Diana*] otto pezzi di Diana.[5]
10. [*Alexander the Great*] pezzi nove, Fatti dal Magno Allessandro.
11. [*Puttini*] dieci pezzi di Putini.
12. [*Tobias*] dodeci pezzi con sopra Le fugre [*sic*] di Tobia.

---

1. ASMn, b. 400, c. 611v.
2. ASMn, b. 400, cc. 650ff. Braghirolli, 1879, 49. This listing, however, is of the "Guardarobba di Sua Altezza Serenissima in Casale." The *Susanna* is recorded again in an undated inventory (post-1708?). ASMn, b. 400.
3. ASMn, b. 332.
4. ASMn, b. 400, cc. 664ff.; Braghirolli, 1879, 49.
5. Possibly to be identified with a Savoy set (Document 66, Addenda J).

69. 12 AUGUST 1670

Ferrante's Tapestries in Anna Isabella Gonzaga's Dowry

On 12 August 1670, Ferrante III of Guastalla came to an agreement with the Duke of Mantua regarding the terms of the dowry that Anna Isabella would bring with her to Mantua, an agreement that was finalized on 26 December 1670.[1] Territories aside, the dowry consisted of 2,000 gold scudi worth of jewelry, silver, and tapestries. Among the latter were the *Fructus Belli* and the *Puttini.*[2]

> Il signor Duca di Guastalla, suo Padre, darà in conte di dote e per dote della medesima signora Principessa Anna Isabella, sua figlia, alla celebratione del matrimonio scudi

ducentomilla da lire sei per ciascun scudo, valuta di Mantova, e questi in tante supellettili dalle più pretiose, come sono li apparati nominati Fructus Belli, e li Putini, gioie, argenti et altre mobilie per servitio d'essa Signora Principessa.

1. ASMn, b. 214, cc. 258–61.
2. As is known from the 1678 inventory (Document 71), Anna Isabella also brought with her to Mantua the *Grotteschi* tapestries.

70. 7 APRIL 1671
Ferrante's Fructus Belli, Puttini, *and* Grotteschi *Displayed on the Occasion of the Arrival in Mantua of Anna Isabella*

The marriage of Ferdinando Carlo to the daughter of Ferrante III, Duke of Guastalla, took place in Mantua on 7 April 1671. In his eighteenth-century manuscript *Cronaca,* Federigo Amadei recorded the tapestries displayed on this occasion, all of them sets from Guastalla that formed part of Anna Maria's dowry:[1]

> A tenore pertanto a questi preliminari furono estesi, sotto il giorno 26 dicembre, in Guastalla li capitoli matrimonali, stati sottoscritti dal nostro Duca e dall'Arciduchessa, lui madre, ed in essi il Duca di Guastalla costituì in dote alla Principessa sua figlia la somma di ducento mila scudi da lire sei l'uno, valuta mantovana, in tante preziose suppellettili consistenti in arazzi denominati Fructus Belli, altri denominati li Puttini ed altri li Grotteschi, con inoltre vari argenti e gioie da consegnarsi nell'atto della celebrazione del matrimonio. Venendo poi a morire il Duca di Guastalla, in tal caso egli per allora costituiva adesso alla figlia in dote la metà di tutt'i suoi beni liberi ed allodiali, con facoltà alla medesima figlia di potere liberamente disporre per il valsente di scudi cento mila mantovani, da estraersi dalli detti allodiali, intendosi che questa somma fosse estradotale e perciò a libera disposizione sua.
>
> Per appagare la curiosità de' posteri, li quali non potranno vedere gli arazzi tutti rari e per lo disegno e per la bellezza del ricco lavoriero misto d'argento e d'oro, degna cosa è da sapersi che que' denominati Fructus Belli erano otto pezzi del giro di 99 braccia di misura in tutto, alti braccia 7 ed un quarto per cadauno; onde a calcolarsi in un sol corpo erano braccia 276. Il primo pezzo rappresentava la paga, che si dà a' soldati in campagna; il secondo la marcia di un esercito; il terzo l'incendio di una città; il quarto l'assidio di una fortezza batuta dal canone; il quinto una battaglia campale; il sesto un convito alla militare, il settimo un trionfo, e l'ottavo il premio e la pena dei soldati. E tant' era la bellezza di questi pezzi che apprezzavansi più di mille doppie l'uno.
>
> Gli arazzi denominati li Puttini erano tessuto d'argento, oro e seta, e consistevano in sei pezzi del giro di braccia 39 e mezzo, dell'altezza ciascuno di braccia 5 e tre quarti, che in tutto per quadro erano braccia 225.
>
> I Grotteschi consistevano in dodici pezzi alti braccia 5 e mezzo per ciascuno; giravano braccia 77, e per quadro erano in tutto braccia 368 e mezzo.

1. Amadei, 1955, IV, 24–25; Braghirolli, 1879, 50–51.

71. 25 AUGUST 1678
Ferrante's Tapestries Recorded in the Inventory Dividing the Guastalla Collection among Ferrante III's Daughters

From the marriage agreement of 1670 it was learned that Anna Isabella was to bring with her to Mantua certain sets of tapestries, notably the *Fructus Belli* and the *Puttini.* Her part of the Guastalla artistic patrimony also consisted of the set known as the *Grotteschi,* as is learned from the 1679 copy of the 1678 inventory.[1] This 115-page listing records objects under the name of the individual to whom the item was to be bequeathed. Margherita d'Este Gonzaga, the widowed Duchess of Guastalla, and her two daughters, Anna Isabella, wife of the Duke of Mantua, and Maria Vittoria, who became Duchess of Guastalla through marriage to her father's cousin Vincenzo. Maria Vittoria was given "gioie, argenti, biancherie, tapezzarie et altre suppelettili," valued at "doicentomilla moneta pure di Mantova." Anna Isabella, wife of Ferdinando Carlo, Duke of Mantua, was assigned objects of roughly the same value. Her portion included several sets originally owned by Ferrante, although Maria Vittoria received Ferrante's *Sposalizio* and the *Aeneas* as well as the *Moses,* which was valued at twice that of the *Puttini* "sì per la bontà come per essere paramento raro."[2]

The main entries in the transcription that follows are taken from the copy in the ASMn made in 1679. It is not always identical to the notary version that was registered the preceding February; the notary copy does not contain information on the value assigned to each object or set. Significant variant wordings found in the ASMn,

Atti notarile copy of the document are set in brackets at the appropriate point in the transcription.

Property of Anna Isabella and then of Ferdinando Carlo, Duke of Mantua

1. [*Fructus Belli*] Un paramento d'arazi detto il Fructus Belli in pezzi otto, di giro in tutto di brazza 99 misura di Guastalla, et d'altezza brazza 7¼, che sono brazza in quadro settecentoventisei, quali pezzi otto sono li seguenti, cioè: (a) La paga dei soldati, (b) La marchia dell'esercito, (c) L'Incendio di una città, (d) Una batteria, (e) Il fatto d'armi, (f) Il Convitto, (g) Il Trionfo, et (h) Il Premio et pena. Quali pezzi tutti sono stati stimati, come per fede appare, doppie diecimila, che fanno ducatoni trentamila che danno [scudi] di Mantova da Lire 6, dico scuti settantacinquemille—scuti numero 75,000.
2. [*Puttini*] Un altro paramento d'arazzi detto li Puttini con oro et argento in pezzi sei, di giro brazza 39⅙, altezza brazza 5¾ misura soddetta, che è in tutta brazza in quadro duecentoventicinque et un quarto, stimato in corpo ducatoni novemille che danno scudi da Lire 6 di Mantova ventiduemilacinquecento, dico—scuti numero 22,500.
3. [*Grotteschi*] Un paramento d'arazzi detto li Grotteschi in pezzi dodici [tutti contornati di fregi], alto brazza 5½, di giro brazza 67, che in tutto sono brazza in quadro 368½, consegnato alla detta Serenissima Signora Duchessa nelle divisioni, stimato ducatoni milleottocento, che danno scuti numero 4500.
4. [*Madonna and Child with Saint John*] Un quadro d'arazzi con oro, con sopra la Madonna, il Bambino, e San Giovanni, alto brazza 3, largo brazza 2⅔, stimato ducatoni centoottanta—scudi numero 450. Tutti li detti arazzi sommano ducatoni 40.980 [che danno] scuti numero 102.450.

Property of Maria Vittoria and then of the Duke of Guastalla

5. [*Moses*] Un paramento d'arazzi detti li Mosè in pezzi dodici [contornati di fregio], di giro brazza 79¼ [79 e tre quatri misura di Guastalla], d'altezza brazza 5⅓, sono in tutto brazza in quadro quattrocentoventuno e mezzo, il tutto computato sì per la bontà come per essere paramento raro, stimato ducatoni dieciottomila, che danno scudi da lire 6 l'uno di Mantova numero 45.000. [Portiere numero 4 compagne pure dell'istesso paramento contornate di fregi d'altezza di brazza tre, larghezza brazza due e mezo, due delle quali sono fodrate di tela turchina.]
6. [*Triumph of Faith*] Un paramento d'arazzi detto Il Trionfo della Fede in pezzi numero 8, [in luogo di fregio vi sono i colonnati] alto brazza 6, giro brazza 45, in tutto brazza in quarto ducentosessanta, stimato ducatoni 4500, che danno scuti come sopra di Mantova numero 11.250.
7. [*Aeneas*] Un paramento d'arazzi detti li Enea in pezzi numero 14 [tutti contornati di freggi], d'altezza brazza sei, di giro brazza 91, in tutto brazza in quadro 546, stimato ducatoni 9000, che danno scudi 22.500. [Una portiera compagna dell'istesso paramento con fregi intorno, alta brazza 4 e un quarto, larga brazza 3.]
8. [*Cephalus and Procris*] Un paramento d'arazzi detti il Sposalizio [di Cefalo e Procre] in pezzi sei, alti brazza 5, di giro brazza 30½ che sono in quadro brazza 152½, stimato ducatoni 2100 che danno scudi numero 5250. [Due portiere compagne del medesimo paramento contornate di fregi fodrate di tela, sono alte brazza due e mezo per una e così anche di larghezza.]
9. [*Todeschi*] Un detto nominato li Todeschi in pezzi otto [tutte contornati con fregi], alti brazza 6.1, giro brazza 58, con una portiera simile, stimato in corpo ducatoni 450, che danno scudi numero 1125. [Una portiera compagna contornata di freggi, alta brazza 4, larga brazza 2 e mezo.]
10. [*Foliage*] Un paramento d'arazzi detti le Fogliazzi [grandi] in pezzi 6 [tutti contornati di fregi], alto brazza 5⅓, di giro brazza 30⅔, stimato ducatoni 240 che danno scudi numero 600.
11. [*Foliage*] Un detto, detto li Fogliazzi Bassi in pezzi sei [tutti contornati di fregi], alti brazza 4, di giro brazza 23 stimato ducatoni 90 che danno scudi numero 225.
12. [*Hunt*] Un paramento d'arazzi a Caccia in pezzi 6 [tutti contornati di fregi], alti brazza 5⅓ di giro brazza 31, inclusi due soprausci simili [con suoi fregi sono per chiaschuno d'altezza brazza 2, giro brazza due e mezo], stimato ducatoni 135 che danno scudi numero 337/3.
13. [*Hunt*] Un detto [chiamato pure le Caccie] in pezzi sei [tutti contornati di fregi], alti brazza 5⅙, di giro brazza 32, stimato ducatoni 90 che danno scudi numero 225.
14. [*Hunt*] Un detto a Caccia più basso, cioè a Caccia di Cervi in pezzi sei, alto brazza 4, di giro brazza 28, stimato ducatoni 75 che danno scudi numero 187/3.
15. [*Persian Figures*] Due pezzi di arazzi chiamati Le Figure [vestite] alla Persiana, alti brazza 5⅔ di giro brazza 13, stimati ducatoni 45 che danno scudi numero 112/3.
16. [*Figures all'antica*] Tre pezzi d'arazzi annessi alli detti con figurine vestite all'antica, alti brazza 5, di giro brazza 8⅔, stimati ducatoni sessanta che danno scudi numero 150.
17. [*Hunt*] Un paramento d'arazzi a Caccia in pezzi 4

[contornato di fregi], alto brazza cinque, di giro brazza 19½, stimato ducatoni 90 che danno scudi numero 225.

18. [*Figures alla Tedesca*] Un pezzo d'arazzi con Figure alla Tedesca [con fregio contornato], alto brazza 4, di giro brazza 8, stimato ducatoni 15 che danno scudi numero 37/3.
19. Un paramento d'arazzi per il bucintoro [tutti contornati di fregi] d'altezza brazza 3, giro brazza 49, in pezzi numero 10, stimati ducatoni 210 che danno scudi numero 525.
20. [*Foliage*] Un paramento d'arazzi detti li Fogliazzi [vecchi e] bassi in pezzi numero 4, alti brazza 2⅔, di giro brazza 24, incluse tre portiere usate, stimato in tutto ducatoni trenta che danno scudi numero 75.
21. [*Resurrection*] Un quadro d'arazzi con oro detto la Rissurrezione del Signore, alto brazza 2, e longo brazza 3, in tutto brazza 6 in quadro, stimato ducatoni 150 [che danno scudi] numero 375.
22. [*Cain and Abel*] Un quadro di arazzo detto il Sacrificio d'Abel con oro, alto brazza 2¼, e largo brazza 3, in tutto brazza 7 in quadro, stimato ducatoni 150 che danno scudi numero 375.
23. [*Madonna and Child*] Un quadro d'arazzi con la Madonna et il Bambino, largo brazzo 1, e longo brazza 1, sopra il pallio di veluto cremosino contornato di tela d'oro, stimato ducatoni 45 che danno scudi numero 112/3.

Tutti le detti arazzi sommano ducatoni 35520 che danno scudi 88,900.

1. (1679) ASMn, b. 214, folio 367, cc. 7–9, 27v–30. Braghirolli, 1897, 92–94. This version was based on an inventory drawn up by Ottavio Mazzi on 25 February 1678. ASMn, AN, notaio Ottavio Mazzi, pacco 5594 (under the date 9 August 1678. Items 1–3, the *Fructus, Puttini,* and *Grotteschi,* had left Guastalla for Mantua in 1671 (Document 70). Curiously, only the last named is included in Mazzi's listing, although all three are recorded in the 1679 copy.

2. The inventory records numerous fabric hangings, including the twelve "paramenti" that went to Mantua and that were made of "velutto cremesino a opera, che forma l'arma Gonzaga, con fondo tela d'argento, e l'altro tela di damasco cremesino." Among the "paramenti" that remained in Guastalla was one "di damasco cremesino di paragone riccamato con festoni di frutti e fiori et ucelli con fondo di tela d'oro contornato di cordoncino d'oro."

72. 15 OCTOBER 1692
The Cartoons for Ferrante's Fructus Belli

On 15 October 1692, Philibert Sallier de la Tour received from an unidentified Brussels weaver a list of tapestries suitable for purchase by Duke Vittorio Amedio II of Savoy.[1] At the same time, Vittorio was provided with a list of cartoons from which tapestries could be woven, one of them being the *Fructus Belli:*

> Que si l'on veut avoir une histoire pour la première tenture, il faudra faire un nouveau dessein, car tout ce qu'il y en a chez les maistres tapissiers ne son point du goust d'aujourd'huy. Ceux de Rafael, de Jules Romain, et autres grands maistres sont tous perdus, mutilez et gastez, pour avoir esté fabriquez trop souvent et raccomodez par des meschans peintres, à la réserve d'un seul, qui est de la main de ces deux grands maistres Rafael et Jules Romain. C'est le Fructus Belli ou fruict de la guerre en huict pièces, qui est encore tout entier pour n'avoir esté fabricqué que deux à trois fois, mais les figures en sont si grandes, qu'il conviendroit mettre la tenture à sept aulnes de hauteur, et pour ce sujet on a commencé à réduire ce beau dessein en plus petitte forme en sorte que les plus grandes figures n'ont que six pieds de hauteur au lieu de sept et demy, comme elles sont dans l'original, ou l'architecture, perspectives et paysages tenans trop du goticque, on les a remis en plus bel ordre, ce qui en augmente la beauté de beaucoup; de façon que l'on pourroit faire une tenture sur six aulnes, ou sur cincq et demye, aussy belle qu'il y en auroit en Europe et qui surpasseroit mesme celle, qui est parmy les meubles du Roy de France, à qui le Cardinal Mazarin l'a légaté, et qui l'avoit receu en présent du Roy d'Espagne à la paix des Pirénées; et qui en avoit payé soixante mil ducats au Duc de Medina las Torres, car sa Majesté ne voulut pas donner la sienne, qui est du mesme dessein, et qui est encore en Espagne, mais il faudroit en payer vingt escus de l'aulne, et vingt cincq si on voudroit l'avoir avec de l'or, et il faudroit attendre deux ans pour l'avoir à cause qu'il y a des pièces de douze aulnes de longueur et que tout est extrêmement remply d'ouvrages et d'ornemens.

1. Archivio di Stato (Turin), Lettere Ministri, Olanda, mazzo 2. Ferrero Viale, 1968, 813.

73. 26 JANUARY 1704
Ferrante's Tapestries in Anna Isabella Gonzaga Inventory

On 26 January 1704, a comprehensive inventory was drawn up of the "robbe assente proprie del Duca di Mantova, ritrovate nell'eredità della defonta Duchessa Anna Isabella."[1] On Tuesday, 12 February, the contents of the "camerino contiguo, et annesso da una parte alla camera della Guardaroba" were catalogued.

1. [*Fructus Belli*] Un apparamento d'arazzi detto il Fructus Belli, di pezzi otto, cioè la paga de' soldati, la marchia dell'essercito, l'incendio d'una città, la batteria, il fatto d'Armi, il convito, il trionfo et il premio e pena.
2. [*Puttini*] Un altro apparamento d'arazzi detto li Putini, con oro, et argento in pezzi sei.
3. [*Grotteschi*] Un altro aparamento d'arazzi detto li groteschi di pezzi dodici.
4. [*Armorial*] Tredici scudetti d'arazzi con lo stema della Serenissima casa Gonzaga.

With the exception of the "scudetti d'arazzi" (Document 74, note 2), the listing merely repeats information already gleaned from the 1678 inventory (Document 71).

1. ASMn, Magistrato Camerale Antico, Rogiti, Istrumenti, Jurium (1558–1704), B. b. II. As cited by Braghirolli, 1879, 51 n. 2.

74. 1709

Ferrante's and Ercole's Tapestries Recorded in the Inventory of Ferdinando Carlo's Estate

Ferdinando Carlo left for Venice in January 1707, taking with him much of the artistic patrimony of Mantua. The best documentation of what precisely was removed remains the inventory, discussed below, that was drawn up after his death. Closer in date to the removal from Mantua is the *Ristretto di tutti li mobili della Corte di Sua Altezza Serenissima di Mantova che di suo comando si sono mandati a Venetia l'anno mdccvii ricavato per alfabetto dall'inventario generale:*[1] The reference in this alphabetical summary taken from the now-lost *inventario generale* is disappointingly brief:.

— Arme d'arazzo di Guastalla tredici—numero 13.
— Aparamenti di Fiandra tra pretiosi et ordinarii, ponendone questi in ragione di pezzi, sono pezzi ottantacinque—numero 85.

Of the eighty-five individual pieces, only fifty-two can be identified in the 1709 inventory.[2]

Ferdinando Carlo died in Padua on 5 July 1708. The following January a Venetian court, the Quaratina Criminale, drew up a detailed inventory of the contents of the Palazzo Michele delle Colonne.[3] In the listing of the tapestries, reference is found not only to Ferrante's *Puttini* and the *Fructus Belli* but also to Ercole's *Puttini.*

1. [*Puttini*] Pezzi di arazzi grandi numero 6 instoriatti con Putini, tessuti con oro, disegno di Raffael.
2. [*Fructus Belli*] Pezzi di arazzi grandi numero otto instoriati con figure grandi al natural, disegno di Giulio Romano.
3. [*Puttini*] Pezzi di arazzi grandi numero dieci compresovi in questi numero quattro che dissero esser nella camera principale del palazzo del soler secondo, instoriati con Putini tessuti con oro, disegno di Giulio Romano.
4. [*Diana*] Pezzi di arazzi grandi numero otto instoriatti con figure, disse rappresentar la Diana, tessuti con oro, disegno della scola di Giulio Romano.
5. [*Troy*] Pezzi di arazzi grandi numero nove istoriatti con figure, rappresenta l'Incendio di Troia, antichi, di buon disegno, schietti senza oro.
6. [*Phaeton*] Pezzi di arazzi grandi numero sei, istoriatti con figure rappresenta Fetonte, disegno di Giulio Romano, senza oro.
7. [*Achilles*] Pezzi di arazzi grandi numero otto instoriatti con figure rappresenta gli Achilli, tenuti con poco oro, disegno del Rubens.
8. [*Tobias*] Pezzi di arazzi numero tre, detti i Tobbia, senza oro, disegno di Raffael.

1. ASMn, Fondo D'Arco, b. 102.
2. As for the "arme d'arazzo di Guastalla," these are doubtless to be identified with the "tredici scudetti d'arazzi" recorded in the 1704 inventory of Anna Isabella's possessions (Document 73).
3. Archivio di Stato, Verona, ms. 609, già 48. We consulted a copy made in 1912 (ASMn, b. 400) for the present publication. Luzio, 1913, 85–86, 316–18. The inventory also refers to "numero vintiuno pezzi di arazzi piegatti, vecchi."

75. 1709

The Gonzaga of Guastalla Claim Anna Isabella Gonzaga's Portion of Ferrante's Tapestries

Upon the death of Ferdinando Carlo, various individuals presented petitions to the Quarantia Criminale in Venice regarding ownership of all or a portion of the estate. Among these was the Duke of Guastalla, who based his claim on a provision in the testament of Ferdinando Carlo's first wife, Anna Isabella, who died in 1703. Although Anna Isabella had named Ferdinando Carlo as her heir, she nonetheless requested that "ch'esso man-casse senza figliuoli maschi, prego la bontà dell'Altezza Sua a restituire tutta et intiera la mia heredità sudetta alli signori Principi Antonio e fratello, miei nipoti di sorella ugalmente e con portioni uguali, overo alli loro descendenti maschi."[1] Because of the fact that Anna Isabella's marriage did not produce children, the Guastalla branch of the family could claim its due after the death of Ferdinando Carlo. This explains the pamphlet the Guastalla branch printed in January 1709, which reviewed every facet of the marriage agreement, beginning with the text of 1670 and ending with the "inventario solenne di tutti li beni mobili, immobili (. . .) lasciati nella heredità della fu Serenissima Signora, Signora Anna Isabella Gonzaga, Duchessa di Mantova," which had been drawn up in January and February 1704. This inventory includes a detailed accounting also of three sets of tapestries: the *Fructus Belli,* the *Puttini,* and the *Grotteschi.*[2] In the end, however, the Guastalla claims were rejected by the Quarantia Criminale, which awarded to Leopoldo I d'Lorraine title to all of Ferdinando Carlo's possessions, including what he had received from Anna Isabella.

1. ASPr, b. 20, cc. 32–33.
2. ASPr, b. 20, cc. 63ff.

76. 1749
The Final Disposition of the Gonzaga of Guastalla Tapestries

With the death of Giuseppe Maria, in 1746 Guastalla passed briefly into the hands of the Hapsburg rulers, only to become part of the Bourbon empire in 1751. Before this occurred, however, in 1749 there was drawn up a "Nota delle tapezzarie di qualche prezzo riguardevole, di ragione del patrimonio allodiale dell'ultimo defunto Signor Duca di Guastalla, Giuseppe Maria Gonzaga, che si sono escorporate dall'Inventaro Generale, ed incassate per spedirle, come si fa, a Milano, d'ordine del Regio Ducale Consiglio inesivamente a'superiori comandi di Sua Eccellenza il Signor Conte d'Harrach, Governatore dello Stato di Milano e General Comandante della Lombardia Austriaca."[1]

A related document is the "Rinoncia, possesso, cessione e rilascio de'beni e ragioni dell'eredità del fu Serenissimo Signor Duca di Guastalla, Giuseppe Maria Gonzaga, fatta per parte della Regia Ducal Camera di Sua Maestà l'Augustissima Imperatrice Regina d'Ungheria e Boemia, al Serenissimo Signor Duca di Modena."[2] Both documents contain identical listings of tapestries—tapestries that were awarded to Francesco III d'Este, Duke of Modena.

1. [*Moses*] undici pezzi d'arazzi chiamati li Moisè, maggior parte delli dodici pezzi marcati nell'Inventario generale sotto il numero 375, e stimati Lire 180.000.
2. Un pezzo d'arazzo, compimento delli sudetti dodici pezzi, marcati sotto il suddetto numero 375 nell'Inventario generale, con altri due piccioli pezzi d'arazzi per soprausci, spettanti alla suddetta istoria.
3. [*Foliage*] Cinque pezzi d'arazzi detti li Sfoiazzi, cioè tre grandi, e due piccioli, marcati nell'Inventario sotto il numero 377, e stimati Lire 2400.
4. Cinque piccioli pezzi d'arazzi che servono da soprausci, quattro de'quali istoriati, ed uno con animali, marcati nell'Inventario al numero 379, e stimati Lire 1500.
5. Due piccioli pezzi d'arazzi con sopra rame di fiori, marcati nell'Inventario sotto il numero 381, e stimati Lire 24.
6. [*Puttini*] Quattro piccioli pezzi arazzi chiamati li Puttini, belli e buoni, che servono per soprausci, e marcati nell'Inventario sotto il numero 380, e stimati Lire 960. Tre de'quali pezzi per essere fuori della Guardaroba in tempo della confezione dell'Inventario, si credono per sbaglio duplicati sotto il numero 240, mentre non ve ne sono altri che li suddetti primi quattro pezzi.
7. Un pezzo arazzo grande, istoriato, uso, e marcato nell'Inventario sotto il numero 378, stimato Lire 1200.
8. [*Aeneas*] Due pezzi arazzi, parte delli quatordici pezzi istoriati Enea, marcati sotto il numero 54 [see also nos. 13 and 14].
9. [*Cephalus and Procris*] Sei pezzi d'arazzi intitolati il Sposalizio, e marcati nell'Inventario sotto il numero 376, del valore di Lire 11.250. Si avverte che questi sono stati per sbaglio duplicati sotto il numero 239 di detto Inventario, mentre quelli citati sotto detto numero non vi sono, né vi sono mai stati.
10. [*Foliage*] un pezzo d'arazzo picciolo Sfoiazzo marcato nell'Inventario al numero 245, del valore Lire 300.
11. [*Triumph of Faith*] Cinque pezzi arazzi istoriati La Fede, parte delli otto pezzi, marcati nell'Inventario sotto il numero 146, e stimati Lire 12.000.
12. [*Triumph of Faith*] Tre pezzi d'arazzi istoriati la Fede,

resto delli otto pezzi marcati nell'Inventario sotto il numero 146.

13. [*Aeneas*] Cinque pezzi arazzi, parte delli quattordici chiamati gli Enea [cf. no. 8 above and no. 14 below], marcati nell'Inventario al numero 54.
14. [*Aeneas*] Sette pezzi d'arazzi, resto delli quattordici pezzi rappresentanti l'Istoria d'Enea, marcati nell'Inventario generale al numero 54 e stimata tutta l'opera Lire 12,500.

---

1. ASPr, b. 14, no. 19.
2. ASPr, b. 14, no. 14. A version of the *Rinoncia* was discovered by Daniela Ferrari among the Peyri papers of the Cavriani Archives, now deposited in the ASMn. The reasons for the existence of this copy remain unclear and the Peyri claim to all or some of the Guastalla possessions remains to be determined.

77. 1755–63
The Ferrante Puttini *in the Sagredo Family Inventories*

Four inventories and evaluations survive of the possessions of the Sagredo family, and in each of them reference is made to the *Puttini,* originally owned by Cecilia Grimani Calergi and then by her daughter Caterina Sagredo, who married Gregorio Barbarigo.[1] The earliest mention occurs on 16 September 1755, when reference is made to the "Fornimento di arazzi con oro, istoriati con Puttini, di giro brazza quaranta, alti braza 5, quarte 3—Lire 2450."[2] On 10 October 1762, A. Dini valued at 590 zecchini "pezzi sei arazzi fini con oro rappresentanti scherzi di Puttini, paesaggi," and in a related evaluation Domenico Grandi referred to the "pezzi sei di arazzi di Raffael d'Urbino tessuti d'oro con Baccanali di puttini che distaca uva e scherza tra loro indica l'Autunno."[3]

Finally, on 30 March 1763, in the "Nota delli arazzi appresi in pagamento di dote e stimati da noi sottoscritti ["Francesco Fontebasso pittor," "Pietro Longhi pittor," "Giuseppe Garbato strazarol," and "Marco Dorigo strazzarol"], one reads: "Fornimento d'arazzi con oro, figurati baccanali, boscherecci, pezzi numero 6 in giro di brazza 38 1/2, in altezza di braccia cinque crescenti, sono braccia 214, il material stimato dai sottoscritti strazzaroli —Lire 300, più per stima fatta dalli suddetti arazzi della materia spettante a noi sottoscritti pittori—Lire 1100. [Totale] Lire 1400."[4]

---

1. The *Puttini* appears to have formed part of the dowry of Caterina Sagredo. She and her sister Marina, widow of Andrea Pisani, were the children of Gerardo Sagredo and Cecilia Grimani Calergi. Upon her death Cecilia's property was equally divided between Caterina and Marina (Venice, Correr, MssPd C. 2755: 3 March 1763).
2. Venice, Correr, MssPd C. 2753, VIII.
3. Both texts, neither of which seems now to be locatable, were first published by Lorenzetti and Planiscig, 1934, 69–70.
4. Venice, Correr, MssPD C. 2755, II.

78. 1771–1772
Ferrante's Aeneas *Tapestry in the Inventory of the Duke of Modena*

According to the orders issued by Maria Theresa, Francesco III, Duke of Modena, was given the possessions of the last duke of Guastalla (Document 76). The only indication that this gift was indeed received is found in the 1771–72 Modena inventory, in which reference is made, however, only to Ferrante's *Aeneas* set.[1]

The inventory refers to the provenance in the entry that reads: "un arazzo mezzo fino usato detto gli Enea di Guastalla che seguito agli sudetto di Reggio, altezza 6 1/3, lunghezza 7 1/4."[2] According to this entry, the palace in Modena contained one piece from a set, the remainder of which was in Reggio Emilia. The preceding entry refers to "un arazzo mezzo fino usato ed in parte logorato, detto gli Enea, pure di seguito a quello in opera nel suddetto Ducale Palazzo di Reggio, altezza 6 1/2, lunghezza 7 1/4."[3]

---

1. Valenti, 1986, 95; 1986a, 58.
2. ASMo, Camera Ducale, Casa Guardarobba, r. 301, II, c. 389.
3. The Este family owned its own five-piece *Aeneas* set (6 *ale* in height), which is recorded in the 1638 inventory (ASMo, Cam. duc., Arazzi e Tapezzerie). That set actually consisted of thirteen pieces (6 1/2 *braccia* high and 92 *braccia* in length), as is known from the 1664 "Misura delli Razzi." Referred to in the 1674 inventory, and elsewhere (ASMo as above), these listings must be distinguished from the 1772 inventory, which specifies a Guastalla provenance for the second set.

Part II

Catalogue

The seven catalogue entries that follow deal with the surviving sets of tapestries that were owned by Federico II, Ercole, and Ferrante Gonzaga. These include the *Cephalus and Procris* (Vatican), the *Acts of the Apostles* (Mantua), the *Fructus Belli* (Brussels, West Dean, and Ecouen), the *Life of Moses* (Châteaudun), and the *Puttini* (Trissino). They were all woven during the heyday of tapestry production in Brussels. Others, including the *Puttini* (Lisbon and Milan as well as the fragment in Mentana) and the *Life of Moses* (Milan), belong to those created at a time when work shops run by the Flemish master Nicolas Karcher flourished in Mantua and Florence.

The interest shown in tapestries by the Gonzaga brothers parallels the patronage of the Hapsburgs both in the Netherlands and in Spain (Charles V, Mary of Hungary, and Philip II) as well as their principal adviser, Cardinal Granvelle, for whom reeditions were woven of the *Acts of the Apostles,* the *Fructus Belli,* the *Puttini,* and the *Moses.* This demonstrates the preeminent role played by the Gonzaga vis-à-vis courts elsewhere in Europe.

With the exception of Ferrante's and Ercole's *Puttini,* it is difficult to establish a precise chronology for the other sets. In the essays that follow, a compromise has been made between a discussion based on chronology and one based on iconographic parallelism. A discussion based on iconography has the advantage of grouping similar sets together, as, for example, the Federico II, Ercole, and Ferrante *Puttini* or the Ferrante and the Ercole/Guglielmo *Life of Moses.*

The oldest of the surviving sets appears to be the *Cephalus and Procris,* which may celebrate Ferrante's marriage in 1534. During the following decade Ercole and Ferrante acquired the sets most intimately linked with their names: the *Acts of the Apostles* and the *Fructus Belli.* The *Acts* relates to the ecclesiastical beliefs and aspirations of Ercole, while the *Fructus* gave visual form to Ferrante's philosophy as a soldier in the service of Charles V. With differences in the iconographic thrust as it related to their specific station in life, all three brothers commissioned sets of *Puttini.*

Absent from the catalogue are the surviving fragments in the Victoria and Albert Museum of an *Aeneas* set, which Nello Forti Grazzini thinks might have originally belonged to Ferrante. Since the evidence for ownership is not sufficiently clear, the matter of the provenance of the *Aeneas* is discussed only in the Index to the Major Sets of Figurative Tapestries.

1. Ferrante's *Cephalus and Procris*

Città del Vaticano, Musei e Gallerie Pontificie
Inv. nos. 3834–39
Marriage of Cephalus (inv. 3838): 355 × 355 cm (Fig. 21)
Wedding Banquet (inv. 3837): 355 × 400 cm (Fig. 22)
Abduction of Cephalus (inv. 3834): 355 × 344 cm (Fig. 23)
Cephalus Tests Procris's Fidelity (inv. 3839): 354 × 334 cm (Fig. 24)
Reconciliation (inv. 3836): 355 × 401 cm (Fig. 25)
Death of Procris (inv. 3835): 353 × 344 cm (Fig. 26)

Comparative Illustration
Giulio Romano, *Death of Procris,* drawing, 1530 (Fig. 27)

A six-piece set that is documented from 1567 until 1749, the *Cephalus and Procris,* now in the Vatican collections, is either identical to or related to the series acquired by Ferrante probably in 1534. The story of Cephalus and Procris became popular in art only in the seventeenth century, which makes the Gonzaga set all the more unusual. The Vatican tapestries have an average height of 355 centimeters. Their Italianate style dates the series to the second quarter of the sixteenth century.[1]

Ovid's account of the story of Cephalus and Procris was popularized by Niccolò da Correggio, whose play was performed in Ferrara in 1487. The Gonzaga family was doubtless familiar with Niccolò's *Cefalo,* which was published in 1521.[2] As a cautionary tale against marital jealousy, it was ideal for performing at weddings.[3] Indeed Ferrante's set was actually referred to as the "Spozalizio" or "Sponzalizio" in later documents.

The design of the tapestries and the ornamentation of the borders suggest that the Vatican set, or the model on which it was based, was purchased by Ferrante in 1534 on the occasion of his marriage to Isabella of Capua.[4] Alternatively, the *Cephalus* might have been acquired to celebrate the marriage of their daughter, Ippolita Gonzaga, to Fabrizio Colonna, which took place on the eve of Philip II's arrival in Milan in 1549.[5] Shortly thereafter, Luca Contile's *Agia* was performed (1551) and in it Ippolita was identified with Giana, Cesare Gonzaga with Enio, Ercole with Cephalus, and Ottavio with Phaeton.[6]

The first two panels (Figs. 21–22) depict the *Marriage of Cephalus and Procris* and the *Wedding Banquet.* Following Ovid *(Metamorphoses,* VII, 672), the first scene shows Cephalus accompanied by his father, Aeolus, while Venus contemplates the scene from the clouds. Prominence is given to Bacchus and to the powers of wine in the *Wedding Banquet,* which also shows musicians (Orpheus or Apollo). The details of the marriage scene were not actually described, although they were mentioned both by Ovid and by Hyginus in the *Fabulae.*[7]

The third panel (Fig. 23) depicts the *Abduction of Cephalus by Aurora.* According to Ovid *(Metamorphoses,* VII, 700–704), this happened while Cephalus was hunting a deer. The burning torch held by Aurora derives from a passage in the *Theogony* of Hesiod, and this permitted later mythographers to claim that Aurora was the sister of the Sun and Moon, the figures who are in fact depicted next to her in this panel.[8] Appearing twice in this tapestry, Aurora is also shown surrounded by the sun's rays, attempting to remove Cephalus from the earth.

The fourth panel (Fig. 24) is a representation of *Cephalus Tests Procris's Fidelity.*[9] Disguised as a merchant bringing presents, Cephalus is shown in a well-appointed interior reminiscent of those seen in other Brussels tapestries.[10] Realizing that Cephalus is uncertain about her fidelity, Procris flees to Diana, but the Goddess sends her back with two presents, a hunting dog and an unerring spear. Without recognizing her, Cephalus encounters his wife, who, after revealing herself, offers him these

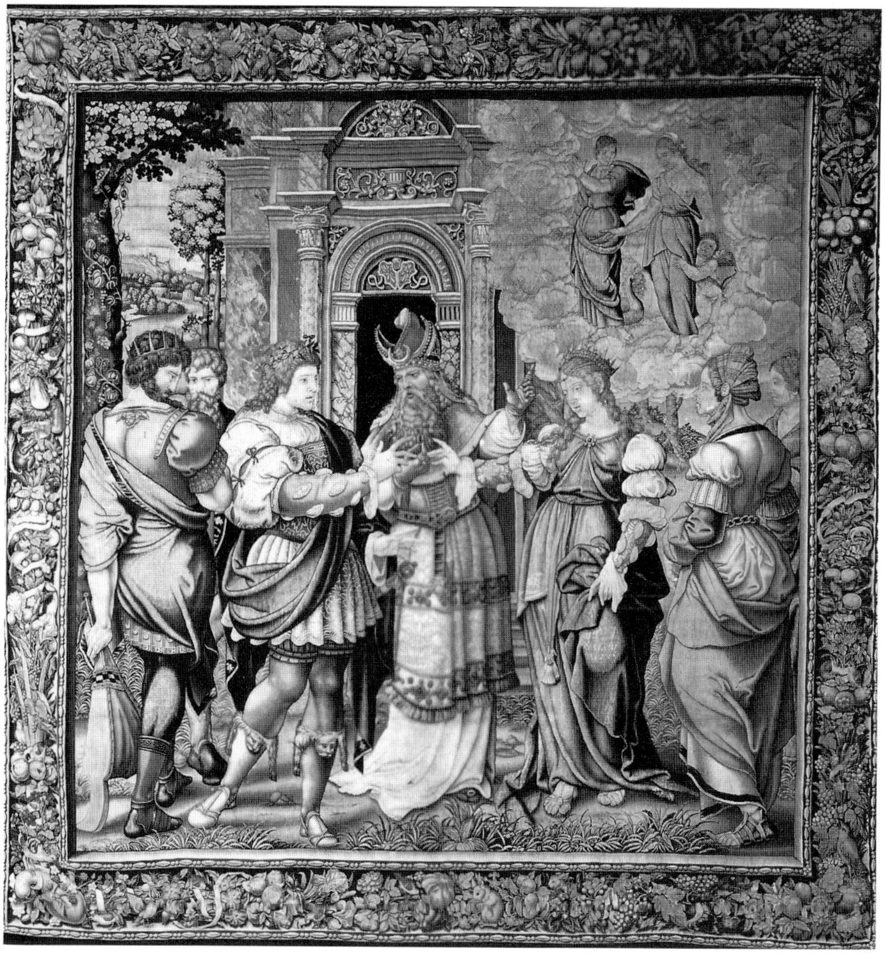

Fig. 21 *Cephalus and Procris: The Marriage of Cephalus and Procris,* Brussels, c. 1530. Vatican, Musei e Gallerie.

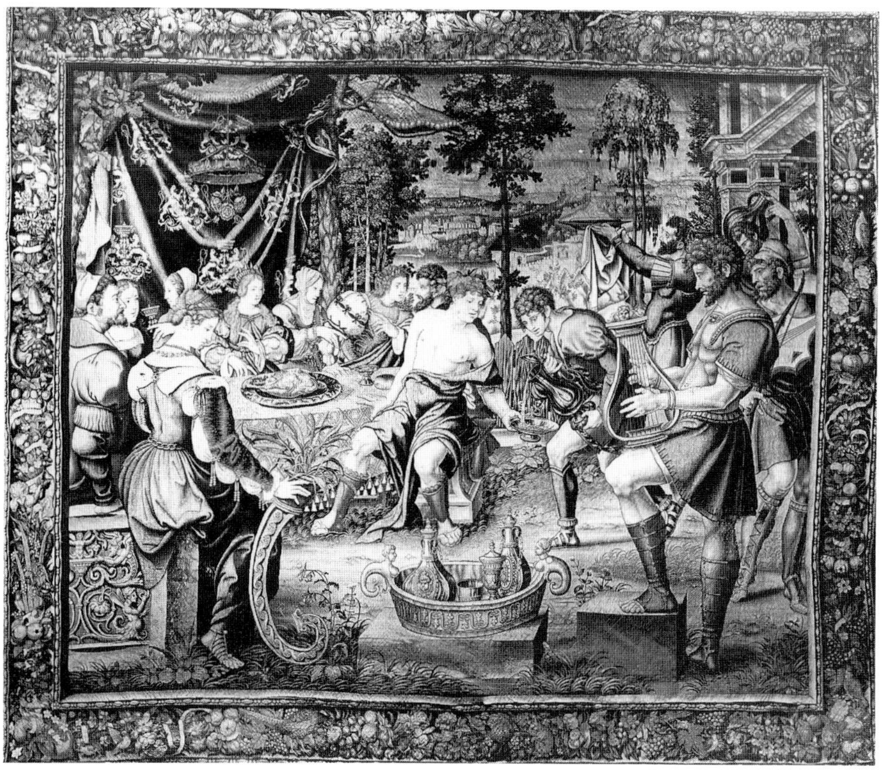

Fig. 22 *Cephalus and Procris: The Wedding Banquet of Cephalus and Procris.* Brussels, c. 1530. Vatican, Musei e Gallerie.

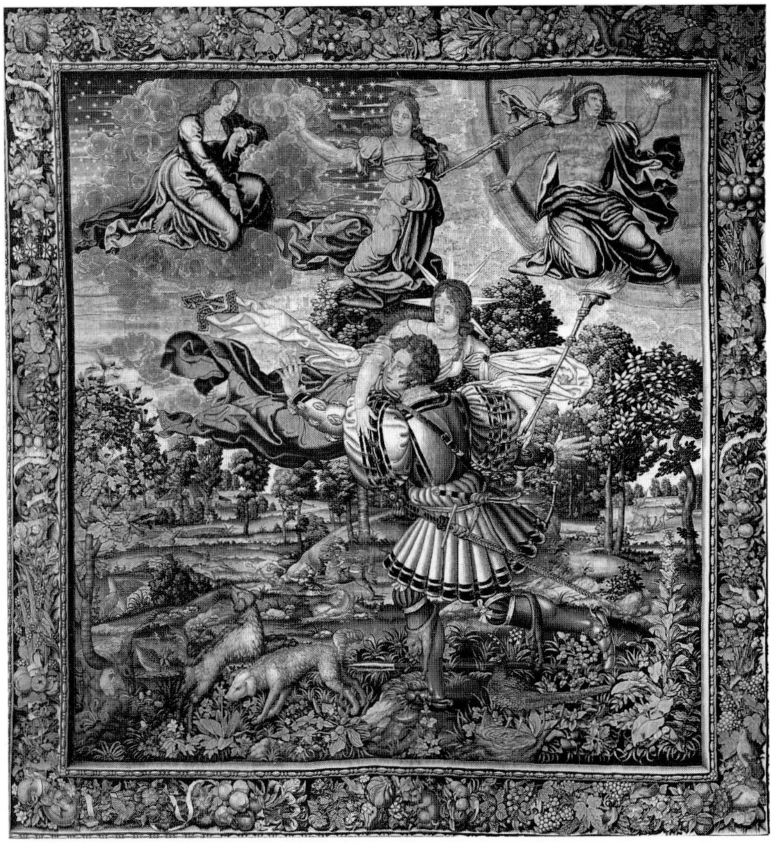

Fig. 23 *Cephalus and Procris: The Abduction of Cephalus by Aurora.* Brussels, c. 1530. Vatican, Musei e Gallerie.

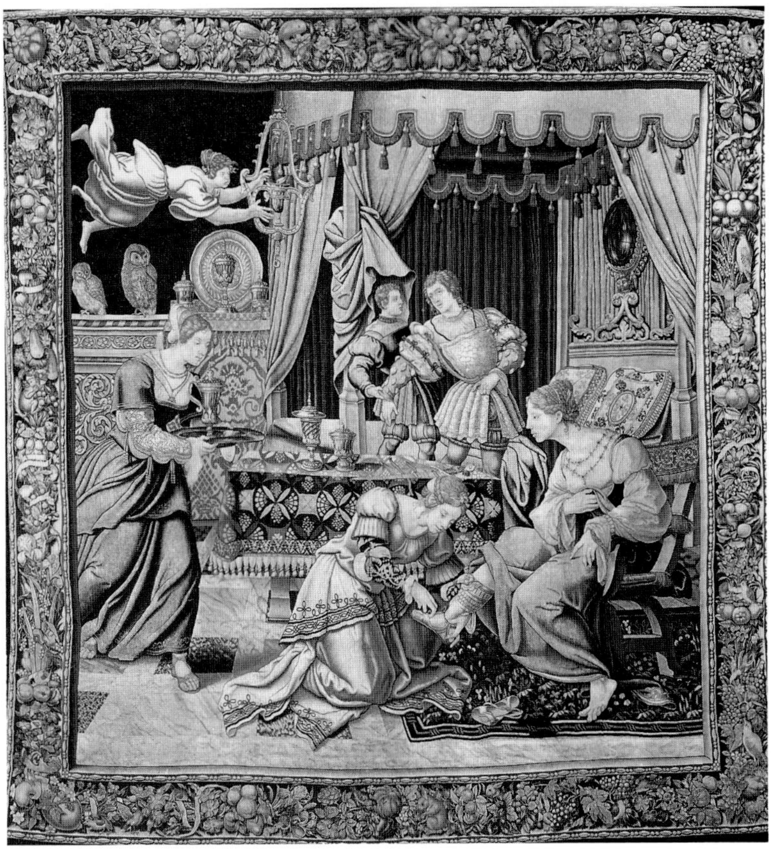

Fig. 24 *Cephalus and Procris: Cephalus Tests Procris's Fidelity.* Brussels, c. 1530. Vatican, Musei e Gallerie.

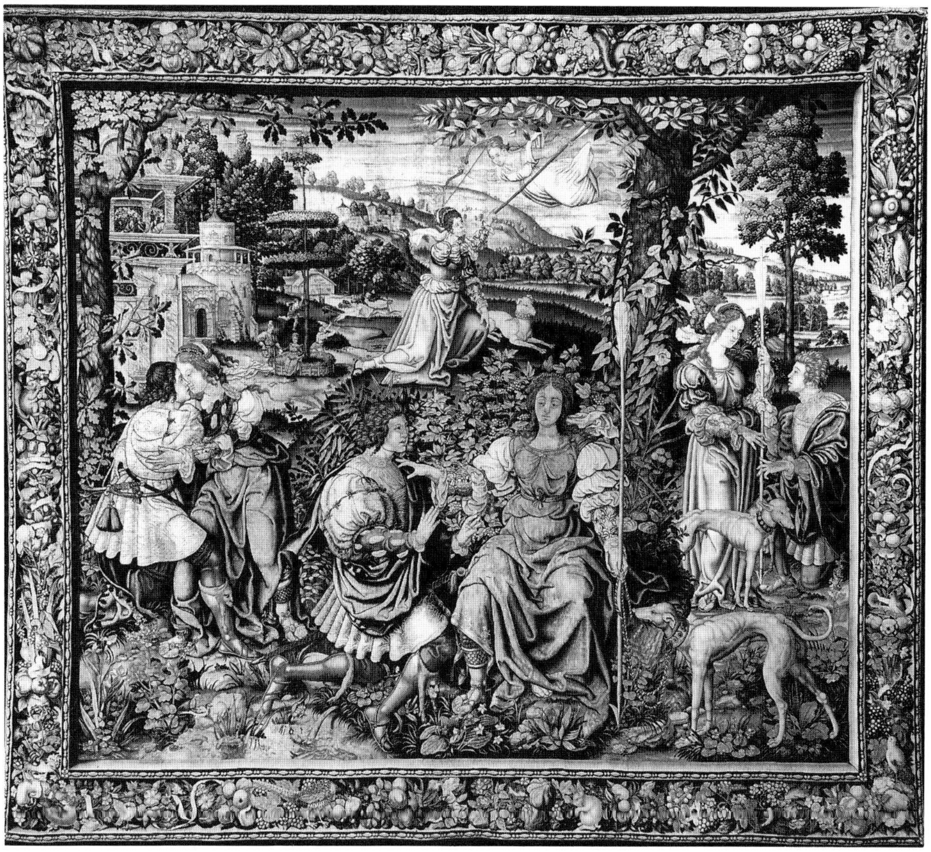

Fig. 25 *Cephalus and Procris: The Reconciliation of Cephalus and Procris.* Brussels, c. 1530. Vatican, Musei e Gallerie.

presents (Fig. 25). This is depicted on the fifth tapestry.[11]

The last scene (Fig. 26) portrays the tragic end of the story when Procris, maddened by gossip, spies on Cephalus. Mistaking the noise, he releases the spear, thereby killing his wife (Ovid, *Metamorphoses,* VII, 820–86).

The Vatican set compares favorably with the *Hunts of the Emperor Maximilian* (Louvre, Paris), which was woven in Brussels between 1528 and 1533 after designs by Bernard van Orley.[12] The borders, filled with floral elements and birds held together by ribbons, are reminiscent of those on the Blumenthal *Crucifixion* in the Metropolitan Museum of Art (New York) and the *Spheres* series in Madrid, both of which date to between 1520 and 1530.[13] Given the correspondence between the Vatican set and what is known of the Gonzaga tapestries regarding the number of panels, the dimension, and the style, it is reasonable to maintain that the former set is either identical to or at least similar to the one owned by Ferrante. If Ferrante actually commissioned the Vatican set or its prototype, then the sketches and models would have been sent to Brussels, where they would have been enlarged under the supervision of someone such as Tommaso Vincidor da Bologna. If they were commissioned or purchased for his marriage to Isabella of Capua, then the *Cephalus* would represent one of Ferrante's earliest acquisitions.

A drawing by Giulio Romano of the *Death of Procris* (Fig. 27; Frankfurt am Main) is generally dated to 1530.[14] It is traditionally believed to be related to other depictions of the hunt, such as the *Death of Hylas,* the *Death of Adonis*, and *Meleager and the Erymanthian Boar.*[15] Although Oberhuber was less certain of this, Hartt maintained that these were studies for frescoes in the destroyed palace at Marmirolo. It is important to note, however, that Giulio's *Procris* was actually used for a Brussels tapestry of roughly the same date as the *Sposalizio.*[16] The lavish borders of this tapestry are identical to those found in several other

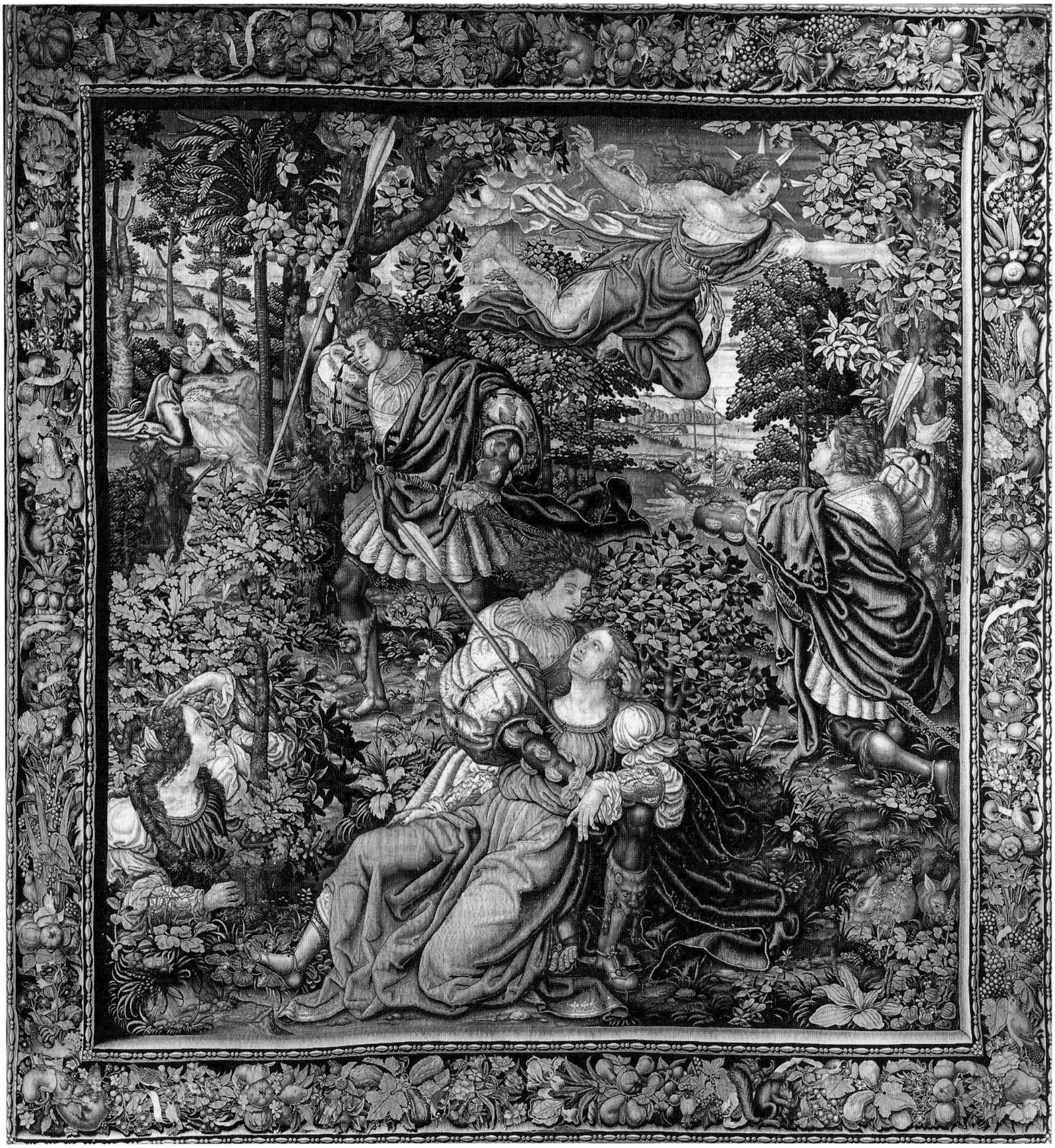

Fig. 26 *Cephalus and Procris: The Death of Procris.* Brussels, c. 1530. Vatican, Musei e Gallerie.

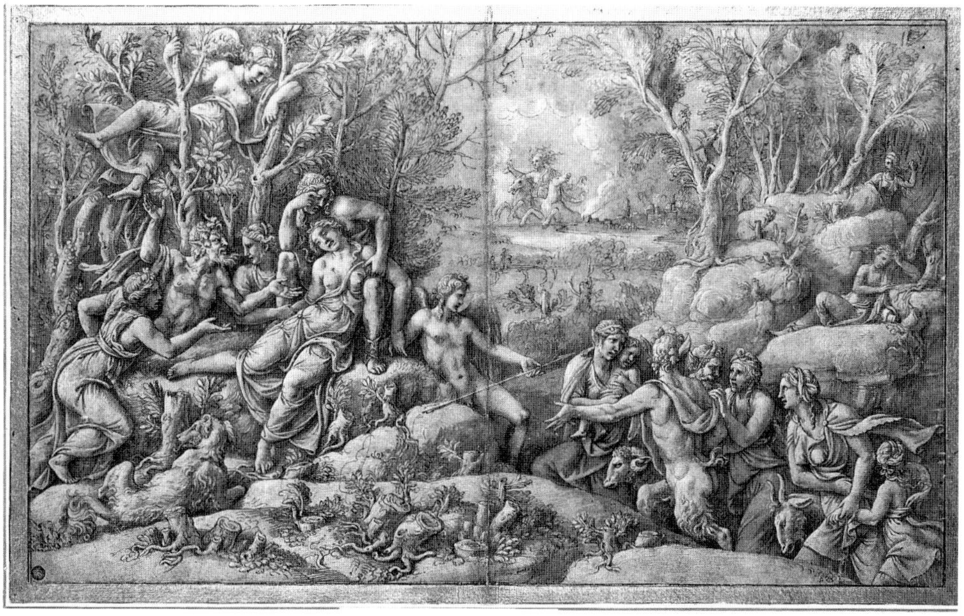

Fig. 27 Giulio Romano, *The Death of Procris,* drawing, c. 1530. Frankfurt, Staedelsches Kunstinstitut.

Brussels pieces that are remnants of a larger set, the *Abduction of the Sabine Women,* attributed to Giulio Romano.[17] If Ferrante owned a Brussels *Cephalus* set around 1530, it could have been based on designs by Giulio. Although the Vatican *Cephalus* cannot be attributed to him, the figurative style does point to the influence of an Italian artist.

NOTES

1. The *Death of Procris* was reproduced by Goebel (1923, I–II, pl. 392) and by Baldass, (1928, pl. XIV) together with the *Wedding.*

2. Lavin, 1954, 266–68.

3. Lavin, 1954, 270. A strong link exists between the Gonzaga of Guastalla and the Cephalus theme, since a staged version (in seven scenes) of the tragedy of "Procri" was composed by Cesare II Gonzaga. The principal participants are Diana, Jealousy, Procris, Cephalus, the nymphs of Diana, a chorus of hunters, and choruses of infernal and celestial deities. A copy of the text, transcribed by Carlo Gavani in 1826, is preserved in the BMG, where it is incorrectly attributed to Ferrante II (Affò, 1787, III, 149).

4. *London 1981,* 182, no. 147. For the borders see Delmarcel, 1981 [A], 228.

5. *London 1981,* 182, no. 148.

6. Salza, 1903, 113ff.

7. Ovid, *Metamorphoses,* VII, 695–96; Hyginus, *Fabulae,* chap. 189: "Procris Pandionis filia, hanc Cephalus Deionis filius habuit in coniugio."

8. Comes, 1627, 545. This is based largely on late medieval and early Renaissance traditions. Seznec, 1961, 226, 279.

9. Ovid, *Metamorphoses,* VII, 738–40; Hyginus, *Fabulae,* chap. 189, 1.3: "atque dat munera speciosa quae Procri deferret"; and Comes, 1627, 546: "s'en alla trouver sa femme en forme d'un bon homme d'affaires," and this according to Boccaccio (*Genealogia Deorum,* XIII, chap. 65).

10. See the *Banquet of Tobias,* Vienna, Kunsthistorisches Museum, series IV/3. Baldass 1928, pl. 14.

11. Mentioned briefly by Ovid *(Metamorphoses,* VII, 753–56), whereas Hyginus *(Fabulae,* par. 5–9) describes the reconciliation in full detail.

12. Baldass (1928, 259) attributed it to van Orley and compared it to the *Tobias* set in Vienna. For illustrations of the *Hunts of the Emperor Maximilian,* see Balis, De Jonge, and Delmarcel, 1993, 39. The date of the set was established by Delmarcel, 1984, and Delmarcel, 1991, 122–23.

13. New York, see Standen, 1985, I, 61, entry 5. Madrid, series 15, see Junquera, I, 1986, 101ff. which is also reproduced by Goebel (1923, II, pls. 113–14). For the border type see Delmarcel, 1981 [A], 228.

14. Frankfurt am Main, Staedel Institut, inv. 4336, 333 by 560 mm. See Hartt, 1958, catalogue no. 292, Fig. 473; *Mantua 1989,* 425; *Vienna 1989,* 174 and entries 85 and 90.

15. Hartt and Oberhuber in *Vienna 1989* (as in note 14); for *Hylas,* see also Bacou in Paris, 1983, entry 77, and the drawing of Giulio, worked up by Rubens, in the Fondation Custodia, Paris, in *Brussels-London 1972,* 98, entry 72. Nello Forti Grazzini has suggested a possible connection between these designs and the set of "poesie" recorded in the 1541 inventory of Federico II's holdings (Document 9).

16. Sold at auction, Palais Galliera, Paris, 10 June 1966, entry 140 (present whereabouts unknown). See Delmarcel, in press.

17. Four Brussels tapestries of the sixteenth century can now be traced. Those with the same border as the *Death of Procris* weaving are: *Battle between Romulus and the Caenini* (Brussels, Royal Museums of Art and History, inv. Tp. 1), *The Meeting of the Roman and the Sabine Women* (Monuments Historiques, Castle of Azay-le-Féron), and the *Sabine Women Pleading for Their Families* (Brussels, Town Hall). A fourth piece, with the *Treason of Tarpeius's Daughter and the Capture of Rome* (London, collection D. Franses), has a different border. See Asselberghs in *Culan 1971,* 16–17; Delmarcel in *Brussels 1974* and idem, 1979, 8, pl. 17; *Paris 1965,* entry 27; and Jarry, 1966, 19, Fig. 22; Franses, 1986, 18, entry 4. This *Sabine Women* set, rightly attributed to Giulio Romano by Félibien, is discussed by Delmarcel, in press.

2. Ercole's *Acts of the Apostles*

Mantua, Palazzo Ducale, Soprintendenza per i Beni Artistici e Storici
The Miraculous Draught of Fishes: 495 × 610 cm (Figs. 28–30)
The Charge to Peter: 495 × 740 cm (Figs. 31–32)
The Healing of the Lame Man: 498 × 765 cm (Fig. 33)
The Death of Ananias: 495 × 745 cm (Fig. 34)
The Sacrifice at Lystra: 495 × 772 cm (Color Plate I; Figs. 35–37)
The Stoning of Stephen: 495 × 581 cm (Fig. 38)
The Conversion of Saul: 495 × 745 cm (Figs. 39–40)
The Conversion of the Proconsul: 495 × 777 cm (Fig. 41)
Paul Preaching in Athens: 495 × 645 cm (Figs. 42–43)

With the exception of the *Life of Christ and the Mantuan Saints* (Fig. 20), the *Acts of the Apostles* is the only Gonzaga tapestry set still in Mantua. Ercole made special provision for the *Acts* in his second testament (1557), in which the nine panels were bequeathed to the Duomo (Document 37). They were donated to the palatine chapel of Santa Barbara in his third and final testament of 1563 (Document 48).[1] His coat of arms is located in the upper corner of each panel. That they are not integral to the original design proves that they were acquired from an edition already available in the workshop.[2] This assumption is confirmed by the existence of the edition in Madrid, which is identical to the Mantua set, even down to the unadorned shields in the upper corners.[3]

The Mantua and Madrid sets are among the earliest of the reeditions of Raphael's *Scuola Vecchia.* The original cartoons were created by Raphael between 1514 and 1516, and they were woven in the workshop of Pieter van Aelst between 1516 and 1519–21.[4] The Mantua and Madrid sets were produced by the same team of Brussels weavers, whose marks are inserted in the selvedges. One of the monograms belongs to Jan van Tieghem (Fig. 28), the second is composed of the letters FNVG, and the third, found only on the Mantua set, remains to be identified. The Brussels city mark (compulsory after May

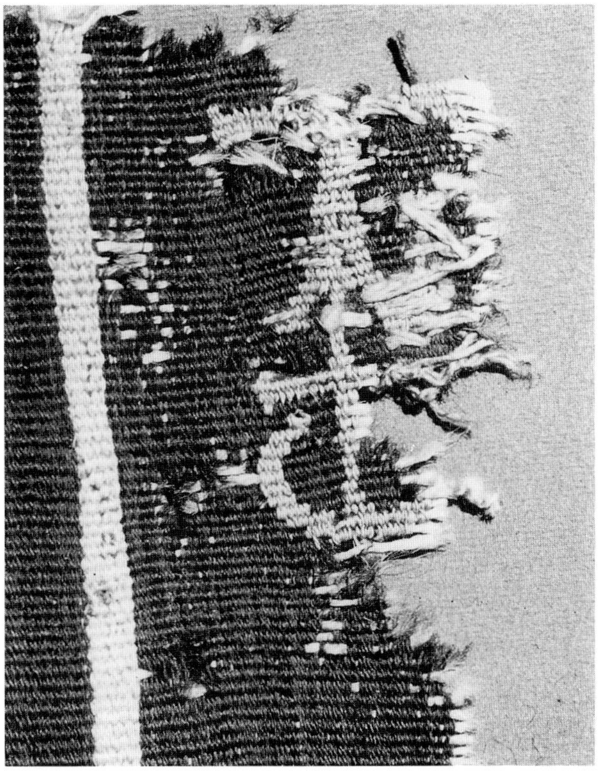

Fig. 28 Detail of the weaver's mark of Jan van Tieghem from *The Miraculous Draught of Fishes* (Fig. 30).

1528) in the selvedges of the Mantua pieces provides a *terminus post quem*. Unfortunately, nothing is known about the date or the circumstances under which Ercole acquired his set, which must, however, have occurred prior to 1557.

The original edition of the *Acts* was destined for the Sistine Chapel, in which new popes were elected. No set better symbolizes Ercole's ecclesiastical aspirations, which were nearly realized at the conclave of 1559.[5] Despite this, the *Scuola Vecchia* tapestries may have been intended to refer to the delegation of apostolic power to Ercole, first as a cardinal and then as papal legate to the Council of Trent. By adding his coat of arms to an edition in stock (Fig. 29), and then by bequeathing them to the Gonzaga palatine church, Ercole clearly intended these tapestries to serve as a palladium of his career.

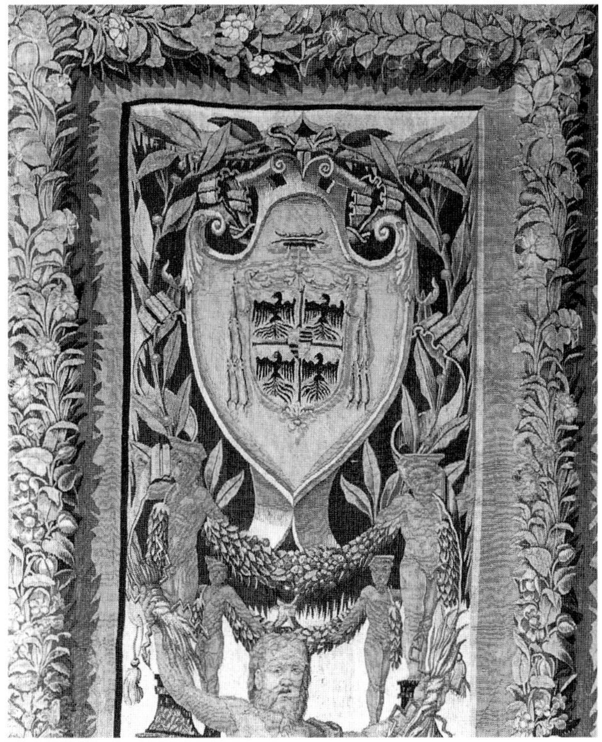

Fig. 29 Detail of the coat of arms of Ercole Gonzaga from *The Miraculous Draught of Fishes* (Fig. 30).

Ercole was intimately involved in the Santa Barbara project. Construction of the palatine church was well under way by February 1563, and in October of that year the altars and the crypt were consecrated. With its elaborate liturgy, organized by a chapter of canons, and possessing its own music chapel, Santa Barbara was planned, like the Sistine Chapel, as a private chapel as well as a state church.[6] No set of tapestries could better fit such a program than the *Acts of the Apostles*. Ercole may ultimately have been motivated to acquire the *Acts* by an event that occurred years earlier. In 1527 his brother Ferrante had removed several of the original *Scuola Vecchia* tapestries from Rome (Document 2). The boat transporting them to Mantua was, however, hijacked by pirates.[7] It may be entirely coincidental, but Ferrante's scheme was actually realized, several decades later, by his older brother.

It may be possible to determine the date of the weaving of the Mantua set by examining what is known about related sets. Pieter van Aelst appears to have kept the cartoons in his workshop after delivering the Vatican tapestries in 1519–21. Apparently he made no further use of them between then and his death in 1532 or 1533. In 1534 Francis I purchased three pieces in a sale negotiated by Daniel and Antoon Bombergen and Willem Dermoyen.[9] Lost since the French Revolution, this set was surrounded by a border of "enigmatic and grotesque figures" framed by floral garlands that were apparently identical to the borders woven by van Tieghem for the Mantua and Madrid sets.[10] Unfortunately, it is not known if the Francis I panels were woven as a joint venture or if Bombergen and Dermoyen were merely acting as traders for an edition produced by van Tieghem.[11]

Van Tieghem's origins and his beginning as a tapestry weaver are not documented. It is generally believed that he was active in the 1540s, at which time he wove an edition of the *Acts*, which is to be identified with the Berlin set (destroyed) whose nine panels had an inner frieze with floral garlands identical to those in the Mantua and Madrid sets, which he actually signed. The Berlin set originally belonged to Henry VIII and it is mentioned in his 1549 inventory.[12] Presumably the Mantua and Madrid sets had been woven by this date. Since such sets represented a major outlay of funds for the merchant-weaver, they were normally sold as soon as possible. Lacking a coat of arms, the Madrid set is no better datable than the Mantuan one. Bearing the marks of Brussels, of Jan van Tieghem, and of the workshop FNVG, it may have been acquired either by Charles V or Philip II after 1555.[13] Van Tieghem's reputation as an

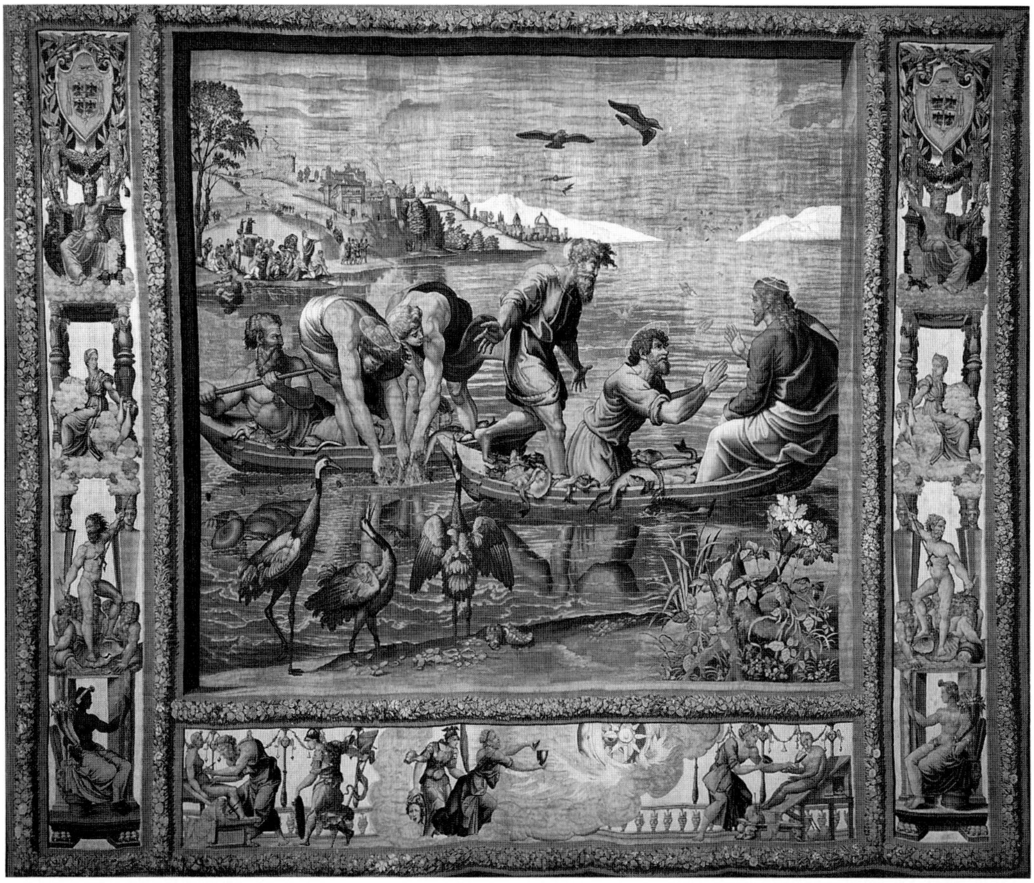

Fig. 30 *Acts of the Apostles: The Miraculous Draught of Fishes,* Brussels, workshop of Jan van Tieghem and others, before 1557. Mantua, Palazzo Ducale.

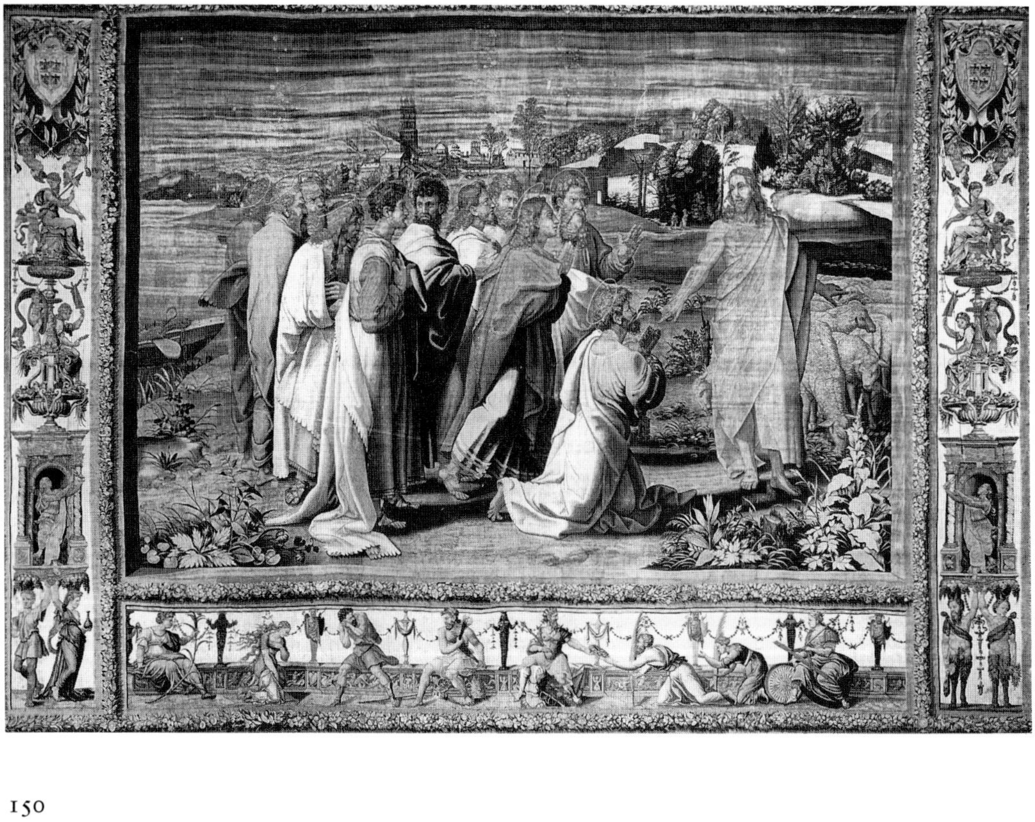

Fig. 31 *Acts of the Apostles: The Charge to Peter,* Brussels, workshop of Jan van Tieghem and others, before 1557. Mantua, Palazzo Ducale.

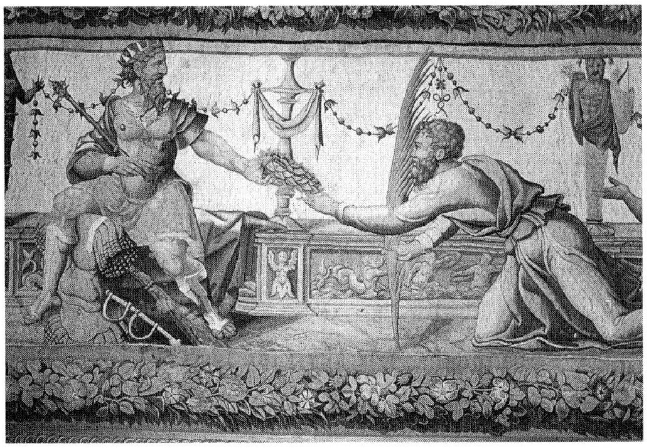

Fig. 32 Detail of *Good Government* from the lower border of *The Charge to Peter* (Fig. 31).

outstanding weaver must therefore have been established long before 1551 since his mark appears on the *Genesis* now in Florence, which was delivered to Cosimo I de' Medici in June of that year. The material and aesthetic quality of this set presupposes an elaborate workshop and a large investment from this entrepreneur.[14]

The other two weavers' marks in the Mantua set are more difficult to identify. The FNVG monogram probably belongs to Frans Ghieteels.[15] The third monogram consists not of letters but of a geometric design. The subject of various fanciful theories, he can be referred to as the "Geometric Master."[16] The same marks as those found on the Mantua *Acts* are also woven on editions of a *Moses* series, including Ferrante's *Moses* at Châteaudun, although instead of Frans the initials are of his father, Jan. The Madrid *Moses* woven from the same cartoons is signed by the Geometric Master, whereas the Vienna *Moses* was signed by Jan van Tieghem and the Geometric Master.[17] On the other hand, the Madrid *Acts* was signed by van Tieghem and FNVG. As van Tieghem was Jan Ghieteels's son-in-law, FNVG, if identified as Frans Ghieteels, may have been his brother-in-law. Accordingly, one is probably faced with a joint venture of weavers related by family ties. These entrepreneurs had the dominant position in the production of tapestries delivered from 1548 onward to Sigismund II Augustus of Poland. Many of these sets, described in the 1553 inventory, are still preserved in Wawel Castle in Kraków.[18] Ercole bought his *Acts* from those Brussels weavers who also provided sets to his brother Ferrante, as well as to the Hapsburgs in the Netherlands and Spain, to Duke Cosimo I de' Medici, and to the King of Poland.

Much has been written, especially by Shearman, about the iconography and the historic value of the Vatican edition of the *Acts,* but little has been written about the meaning of the borders. Compared to the earlier sets, the ornamentation of the borders of the Leo X edition of the *Acts* was both original and innovative. Instead of surrounding the central composition with the customary swags of flowers, fruit, and birds, Raphael designed historical and allegorical scenes. The lower horizontal borders are conceived as fictive bronze-colored bas-reliefs of events in the life of Leo X. Each tapestry had a single vertical border, woven at the left or right side. They bear the Medici arms, below which are depicted the triumph of Virtue over Opportunity or Fortune, the Cardinal and Theological Virtues, the Fates, Time, the Seasons, the Liberal Arts, and the Labors of Hercules.[19]

In the Mantua series van Tieghem and his associates replaced the lower relief scenes with allegories in the same style as those on the vertical borders.[20] It is not yet possible to determine if the borders are the result of a coherent iconographic program, although it is clear that some scenes were taken from the existing vertical series.[21]

1. *The Miraculous Draught of Fishes* (Fig. 30): The lateral borders depict the Four Elements: Jupiter-Fire, Juno-Air, Neptune-Water, Ceres-Earth. The lower frieze portrays the creation of man by Prometheus, who stole fire (one of the four elements) from heaven.
2. *The Charge to Peter* (Fig. 31): The lateral borders depict the Fates with the thread of life, while the lower frieze portrays Justice or Good Government distributing rewards and punishments (Fig. 32).
3. *The Healing of the Lame Man* (Fig. 33): The Hours (left) and the Seasons (right) are depicted on the lateral borders as symbols of the changing time. The lower border is apparently a depiction of an allegory of Fortune giving or denying wealth.[22]
3. *The Death of Ananias* (Fig. 34): The lateral borders depict the Muses,[23] who are partially repeated and partially completed in the lower frieze.[24]
8. *The Sacrifice at Lystra* (Color Plate I and Fig. 35): The

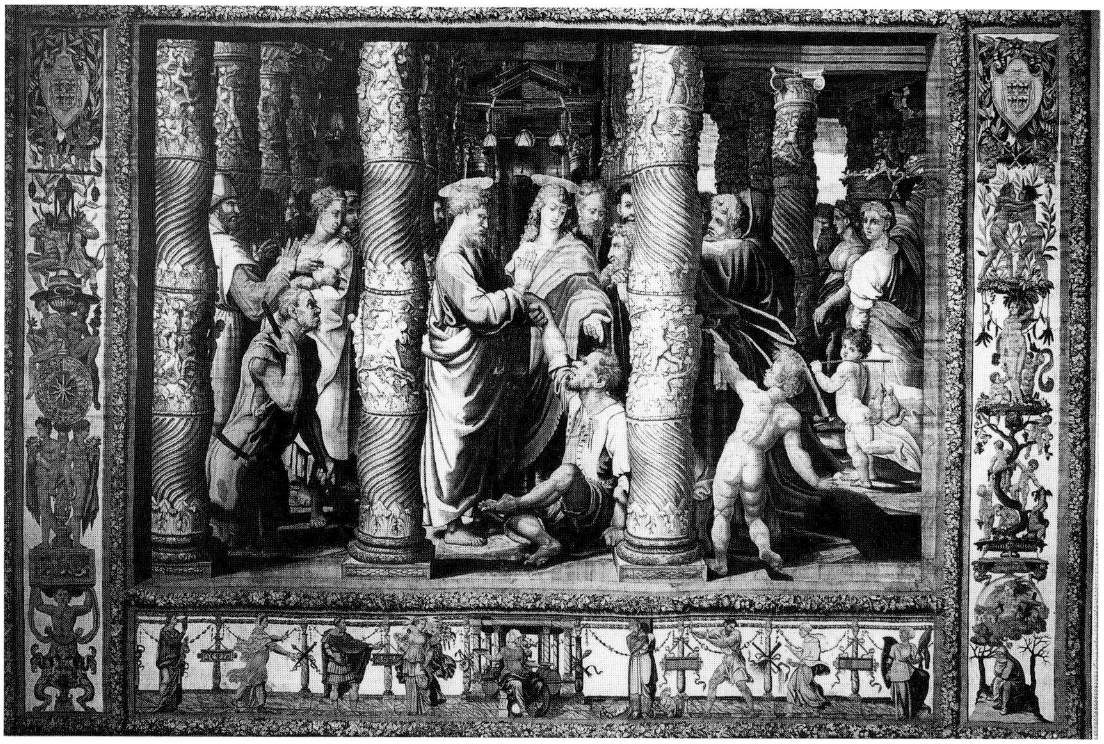

Fig. 33 *Acts of the Apostles: The Healing of the Lame Man,* Brussels, workshop of Jan van Tieghem and others, before 1557. Mantua, Palazzo Ducale.

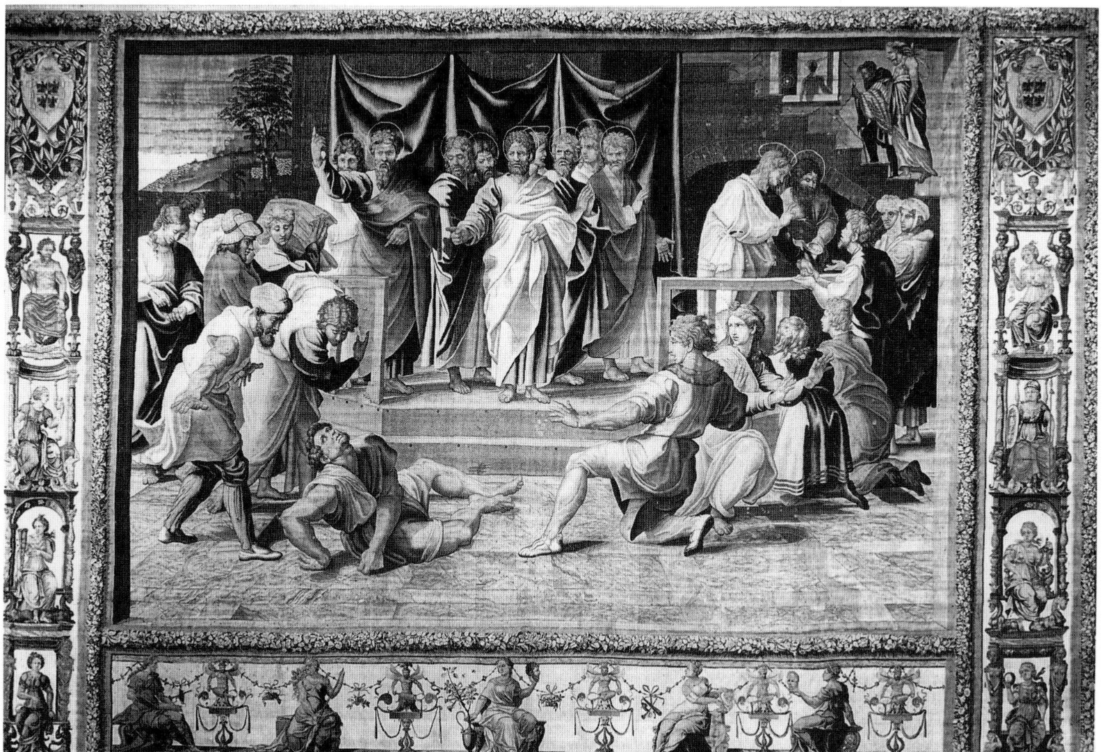

Fig. 34 *Acts of the Apostles: The Death of Ananias,* Brussels, workshop of Jan van Tieghem and others, before 1557. Mantua, Palazzo Ducale.

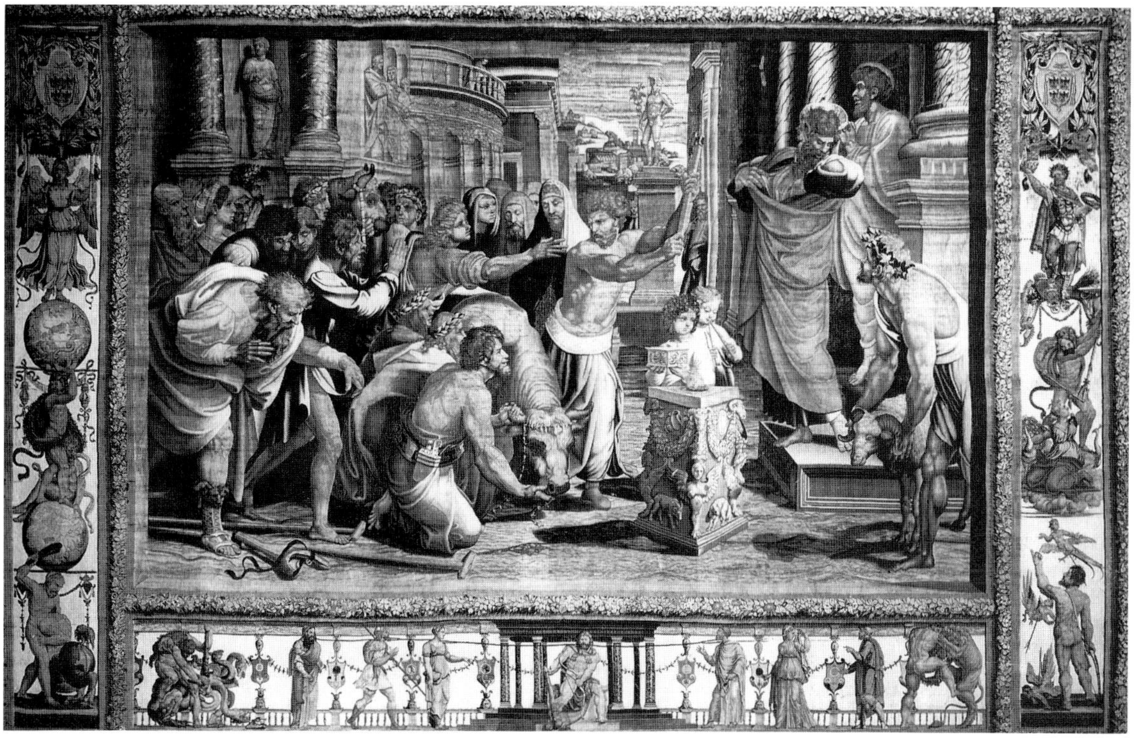

Fig. 35 *Acts of the Apostles: The Sacrifice at Lystra,* Brussels, workshop of Jan van Tieghem and others, before 1557. Mantua, Palazzo Ducale.

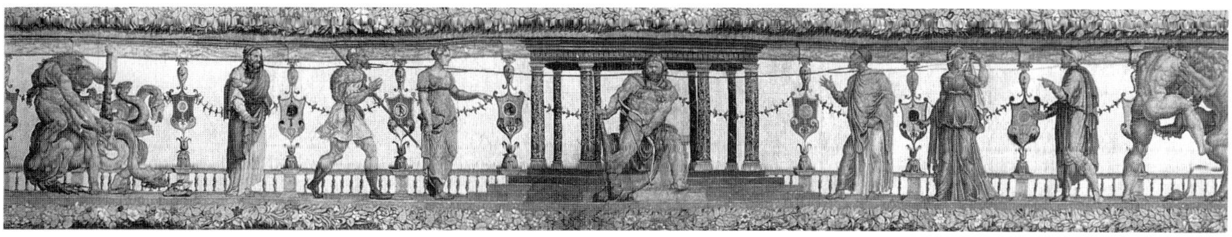

Fig. 36 Detail of *Hercules-Eloquentia* from the lower border of *The Sacrifice at Lystra* (Fig. 35).

lateral borders depict the Labors of Hercules, while Hercules as the personification of Eloquence is portrayed on the lower frieze (Figs. 36–37).

Four of the remaining tapestries (numbers 5, 6, 7, and 9) contain depictions of the Liberal Arts and the Virtues in their lateral borders. Similar figures, whose attributes are not always clear, appear in the lower frieze

5. *The Stoning of Stephen* (Fig. 38): The Trivium appears in the lateral borders,[25] while four of the Virtues are represented in the lower frieze.[26]
6. *The Conversion of Saul* (Fig. 39): The lateral borders depict the Quadrivium,[27] while the lower frieze contains the figures of Opportunity-Occasio surrounding

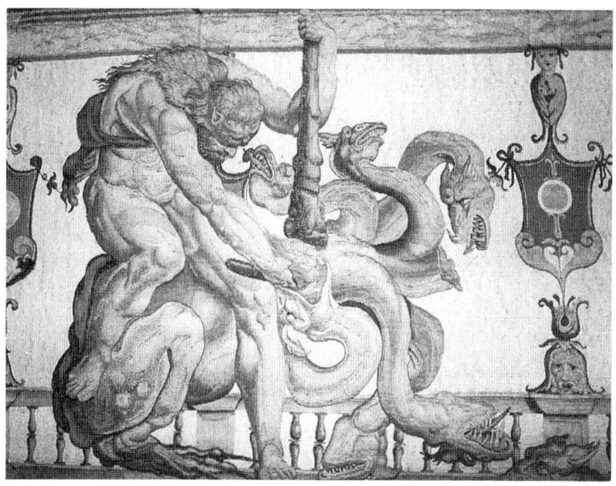

Fig. 37 Detail of *Hercules and the Lernaean Hydra* from the lower border of *The Sacrifice at Lystra* (Fig. 35).

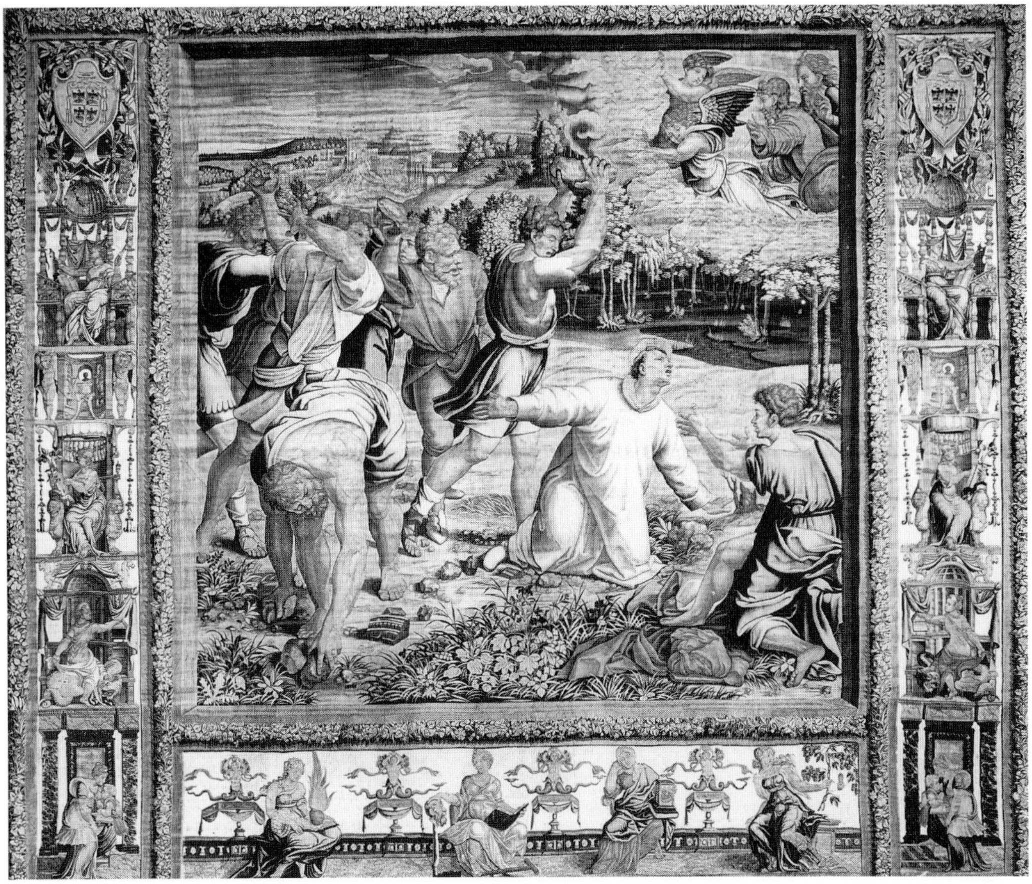

Fig. 38 *Acts of the Apostles: The Stoning of Stephen,* Brussels, workshop of Jan van Tieghem and others, before 1557. Mantua, Palazzo Ducale.

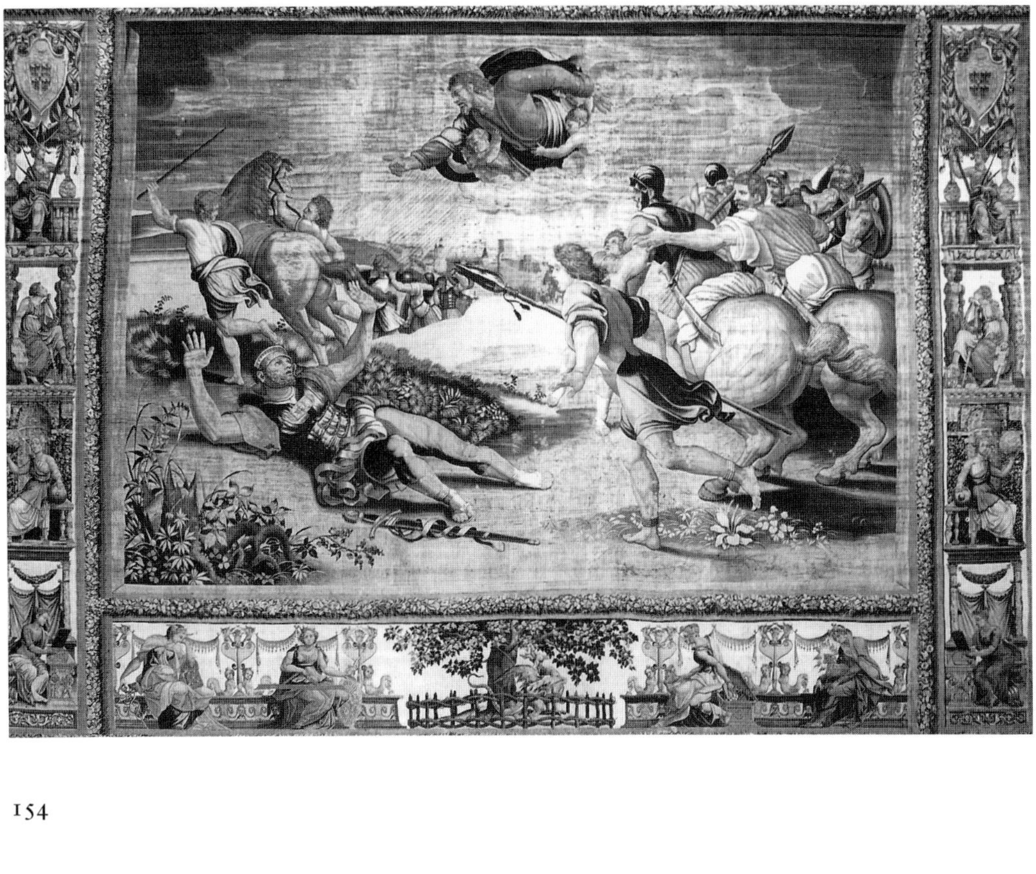

Fig. 39 *Acts of the Apostles: The Conversion of Saul,* Brussels, workshop of Jan van Tieghem and others, before 1557. Mantua, Palazzo Ducale.

the Dragon guarding the Garden of the Hesperides (Fig. 40).[28]

7. *The Conversion of the Proconsul* (Fig. 41): The Cardinal Virtues are in the lateral borders:[29] the Seven Virtues appear in the lower frieze.[30]
9. *Paul Preaching in Athens* (Fig. 42): The lateral borders depict the Theological Virtues,[31] while five allegorical figures appear in the lower frieze (Fig. 43).[32]

It is important to emphasize two aspects of the iconography of the lateral borders and the lower friezes. First, some of the allegorical female figures in the lower frieze of *The Conversion of the Proconsul* (Fig. 41) are directly inspired by the Virtues found in the *Los Honores,* woven in Brussels between 1520 and 1525, a set designed to serve as a woven mirror of the prince for the young Charles V. The third figure on the left is half nude and half armed. On the *Los Honores* tapestry (Segovia) of the *Triumph of Virtue over Vice,* she is identified as "Magnanimitas." The three women on the right of Hope are similarly borrowed by the *Los Honores* panel of the allegory of Prudence, according to Alanus de Insulis. They are (a) *Providentia* (woman with a globe and a lance), (b) *Cautio* (woman holding a monkey looking in a mirror), and (c) *Docilitas* (woman with a book and a bunch of rods on her lap).[33] Although based on medieval texts, these Virtues are all rendered in a Renaissance style.

It should be emphasized that the *Los Honores* set was woven by Pieter van Aelst, whose workshop was also responsible for the first edition of the *Acts of the Apostles.* If indeed Jan van Tieghem and his associates bought the cartoons of the *Acts* either from van Aelst or from his heirs, it may be that they also obtained access to drawings or models from the *Honores* that had been rewoven for Cardinal Erard de la Marck. The sketches and cartoons, because of the specific imperial iconography, were apparently considered crown property.[34]

A second link between van Aelst and van Tieghem is found in the Labors of Hercules seen in the borders surrounding the *Sacrifice at Lystra* (Figs. 36–37) The left lateral border of the Mantua set contains the figures of Fame, Hercules and Atlas, and Hercules and the Centaur, depictions that first appeared in the Vatican *Acts.*[35] A similar origin explains the right border with its scenes of a victo-

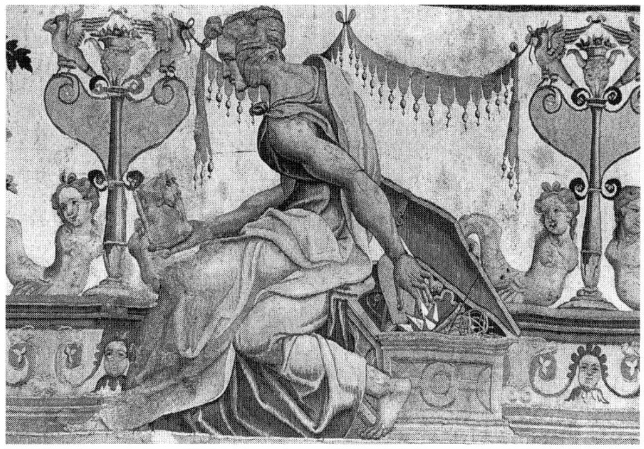

Fig. 40 Detail of *Occasio* from the lower border of *The Conversion of Saul* (Fig. 39).

rious king holding a crown in his hand (Victory as the counterpart of Fame at the right?), Hercules and Juno, and Hercules and the Stymphalian Birds. The lower frieze is even more remarkable. While the corner figures represent (left) Hercules wrestling with the Hydra and (right) the Nemean Lion, the central scene illustrates the story told by Lucan of Hercules holding men and women by chains fixed to his tongue and ears.

This representation of Hercules as Eloquence became widespread during the Renaissance, having been referred to by Erasmus (1506) and Budé (1508).[36] The original lateral Hercules border was related to *Paul Preaching at Athens.* Because of the connection made between Hercules' lion skin to the name of Pope "Leo," this image of Eloquence fit well in later editions of the tapestry. In the van Tieghem editions in Madrid and Mantua, the iconography is shifted to the *Sacrifice at Lystra.* It was perhaps first used for the edition delivered to Francis I by Bombeck-Dermoyen in 1534. The depiction of Hercules as Eloquence was claimed by the French humanists as the prototype of the "Hercules Gallicus," in contrast to the Libyan Hercules, which was linked to Charles V.[37] Thus it may be that the new lateral border on the right also had been determined by the edition for the French court. The king holding the laurel wreath of victory can be associated with Francis I, as well as serving as the counterpart of Fame on the left border. Hercules threatening Juno with a trident[38] may allude to Francis I's wars against the Hapsburg, as might Hercules' fight against the Stymphalian Birds. The link between the eloquence of

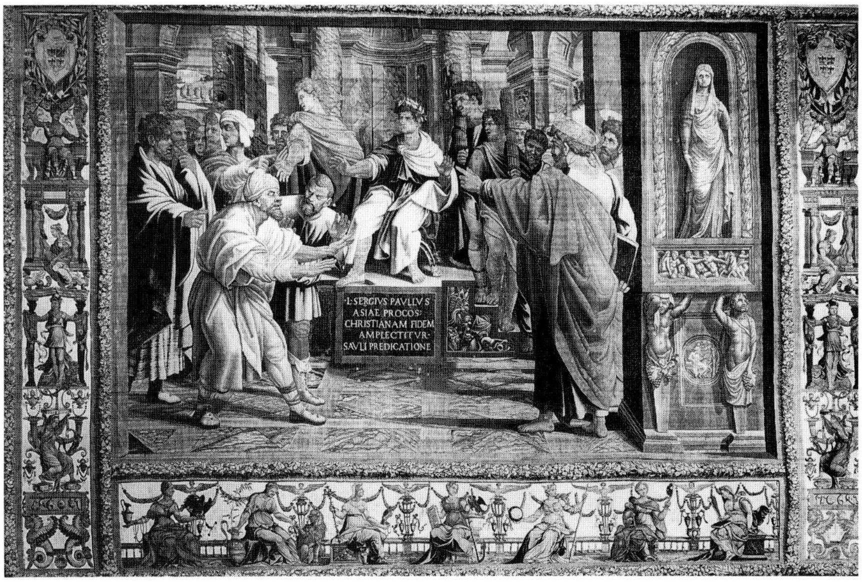

Fig. 41 *Acts of the Apostles: The Conversion of the Proconsul* or *The Blinding of Elymas.* Brussels, workshop of Jan van Tieghem and others, before 1557. Mantua, Palazzo

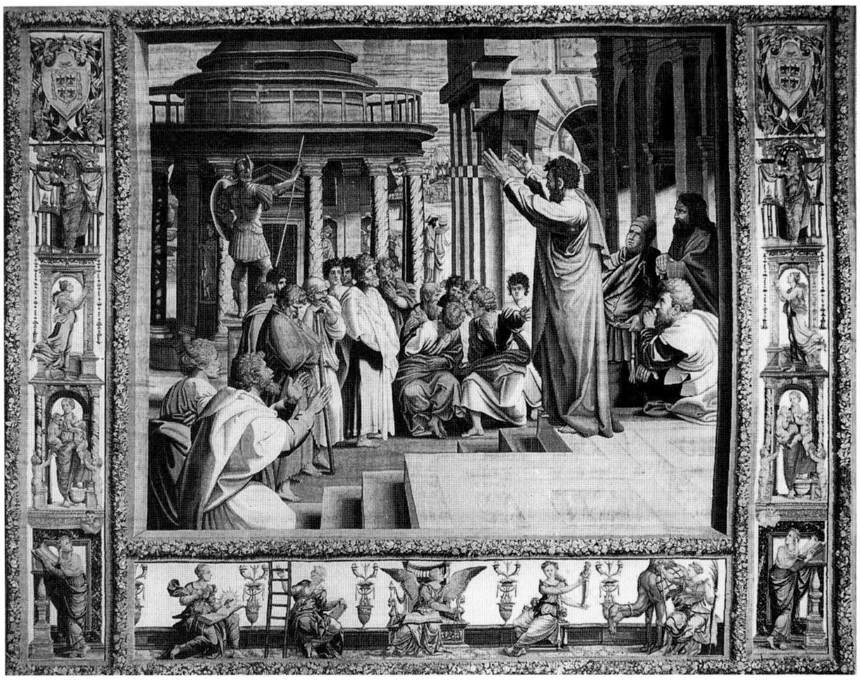

Fig. 42 *Acts of the Apostles: Paul Preaching in Athens,* Brussels, workshop of Jan van Tieghem and others, before 1557. Mantua, Palazzo Ducale.

Fig. 43 Detail of the allegorical figures from the lower border of *Paul Preaching in Athens* (Fig. 42).

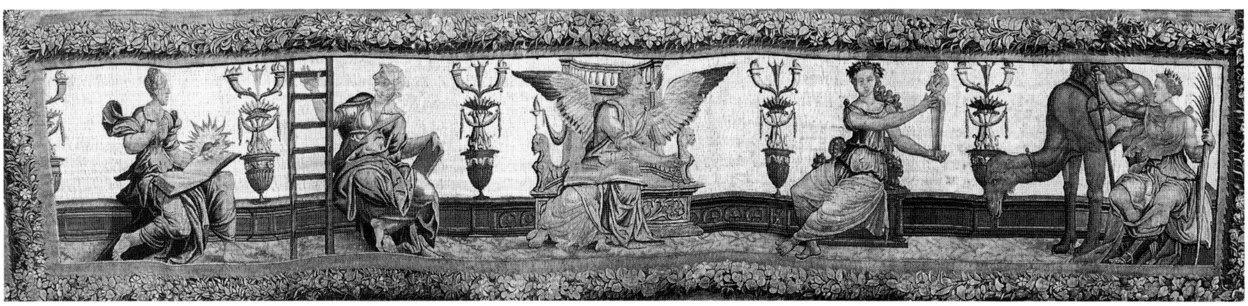

the Gallic Hercules and thus the king of France with the gospels of Saint Paul may have been too obvious, even embarrassing, for later patrons. Thus the weavers may have changed their disposition in subsequent editions.

The Hercules iconography has an obvious relationship to Ercole himself since it alludes to his own name.[39] If so, then this may point to the priority of the Mantua set over the Madrid edition, in which the same theme is developed in the same context.

NOTES

1. Information on the dimensions and materials (wool and silk) was provided by Birk, 1884, 214–15. See Kumsch, 1914, 13, for older comments as well as Luzio, 1913a, 1919. The most recent discussion of the *Acts* is by Viale, 1952, 48–49; Shearman, 1972, 144; and *Rome 1984,* 144. The set is fully reproduced in Corrain, 1986.

2. The arms are woven separately, in a finer weft than the rest of the tapestry, and then inserted by rewarping. This technical detail was confirmed by Anne Lievens, tapestry restorer, who examined the Mantua *Miraculous Draught of Fishes* in January 1988 after the exhibition in Ghent in 1988. See also Viale, 1952, 48–49.

3. Junquera, 1986, I, 63–72, series 12.

4. Shearman, 1972, 138–43.

5. See Catalogue 7.

6. Fenlon, 1980, 95ff.; *London 1981,* 90–91: "Planned as a dynastic temple on an imposing scale, the Basilica functioned partly as a private chapel, and partly as a state church."

7. Shearman, 1972, 140–41; *Rome 1984,* 144.

8. Schneebalg (1969, 309) suggests 1532 for the last mention of van Aelst. The Fugger bankers paid a debt to his heirs in 1533 (Poelnitz, 1958, I, 622). The eight pieces in Saragossa are not by van Aelst, as stated in Kumsch, 1914, 9, but by the Mattens workshop, Brussels, early 17th century (Steppe, 1956, 40–41).

9. Schneebalg, 1971, 261, 286.

10. Guiffrey, 1885, 293.

11. The Dermoyen workshop produced at least one set with a different border type. *The Stoning of Stephen* (Castle-Museum of Angers) is surrounded by a lavish border of the palm-trunk type, decorated with swags of fruit and flowers, with playing children. This type of ornament, initiated in the 1530s (see the *Foundation of Rome,* Madrid; Junquera, 1986, I, 93, series 14), was still in vogue in the 1540s, and it is found in the *Life of Joshua,* delivered to Mary of Hungary by Willem Dermoyen in 1544. For the reweaving in Vienna, see Halbturn, 1981, 19.

12. Kumsch, 1914, 12, series 4 and pl. 16; Shearman, 1972, 145, n. 65.

13. Madrid series 12 (Junquera, 1986, I, 63, etc.). This set was certainly not made for Margaret of Austria before 1528, as stated by Shearman (1972, 144).

14. Meoni, 1989, 57–66, pl. IIa. Van Tieghem's monogram is one of the few Flemish workshop marks authenticated by documentary evidence. Goebel, 1923, I, 327 (document of 1570).

15. Hefford, 1986, 86, with reference to the earlier literature.

16. This monogram has been successively attributed to van Herzeele (Mahl, 1967, 11–12), Frans Ghieteels (Schneebalg in Szablowski, 1972, 432–36), and Leo van den Hecke (Duverger, 1973, 76), who attributes three different marks at the same time to this workshop.

17. For Châteaudun, see under Ferrante's *Life of Moses* set (Catalogue 6); Madrid: Junquera, 1986, I, 163 and 354; Vienna: Mahl, 1967.

18. As can be deduced from the listings given by Szablowski (1972) from the 142 classified Flemish tapestries in the Wawel Castle collection, 89 bear workshop marks: no fewer than 76 belong to the here-cited group of weavers, namely, 25 to van Tieghem, 30 to the Geometric Master, and 21 to FNVG/Frans Ghieteels.

19. See Shearman (1972, 31, 37, 84–88) for the "reliefs" and 31, 43–44, 89, for the vertical borders. See also Romeo, 1990, 40ff.

20. These are also found on the Madrid *Moses,* the *Genesis* of the Bavarian collection (E. Duverger, 1973, 23–51), and the Vienna *Moses* set (Mahl, 1967, 18–21). They were reused later, probably after van Tieghem's flight to Protestant Germany in 1568, by other workshops, such as Willem de Pannemaker, for the *Mercury and Herse* set (Standen, 1971, 118–20, and Standen 1985, 87–99), and Cornelis de Ronde for his *Hannibal* editions, now in Florence and Munich (Delmarcel and Dumortier, 1986, 56–61).

21. As previously noted by Duverger (1973, 39).

22. In this, and in the notes that follow, mention is made of the identification of the allegories according to the former studies: M = Mahl 1967; D = Duverger 1973; S = Standen 1971.

The allegories at the inferior border of the *Healing of the Lame Man* are, from left to right: *Providentia* (M) or *Prudentia* (D); *Pax* (D), an antique soldier, crowned with laurels; *Abundantia* (M and D); *Fortuna,* with two faces as a Janus-like figure, reaching cups apparently filled with wine from the barrels behind her; a warrior bound on a column: an allegory of Christ (M) or Submission (D); a man making a gesture of repelling Fortune's gift, Deceit (M) or *Constantia* or *Fortitudo* (D).

23. Left from top to bottom: Jupiter (D), Clio (M) or Thalia (D), Calliope (M) or Euterpe (D), Polymnia (D). Right: woman with a scroll, Minerva (M), Erato(?) (M), Urania (M), Geography (M).

24. From right to left: Calliope (?), Euterpe (M), Fortitude or Melpomene (D), Terpsichore, Melpomene (M), or Thalia (D).

25. Identical figures in the two borders. From top to bottom: Allegory of Painting (D: *Grammatica*), *Rhetorica* (D), (M: *Sapientia*), *Dialectica* (D), (M: *Avaritia*), obviously *Grammatica*, (M: *Caritas;* D: "sagesse nourricière")

26. From left to right: *Caritas,* with burning heart (S), (M and D: *Fides*), *Fortitude, Temperance, Diligentia* (woman with hop shoots).

27. Identical on both sides. From top to bottom: *Geometria, Musica, Astronomia, Aritmetica.*

28. From left to right: Woman with a caduceus: Trade(?), Architecture, (M), the Dragon of the Hesperides, allegory of Vigilance, *Occasio* (Fig. 40) with her forelock, grasping in a chest containing instruments of geometry, woman with aureoled lamb on her knees.

29. Identical on both sides. From top to bottom: *Justitia, Prudentia, Fortitudo, Temperantia.*

30. From left to right: Woman holding an eagle and a vase, *Pax, Magnanimity* (M and D: *Victory*), *Spes, Providentia* (M: *Fortuna;* D: *Prudentia*), *Cautio* (M: *Luxuria,* D: *Vanitas*), *Docilitas* (D: *Obedientia*).

31. Identical on both sides. From top to bottom: *Fides, Spes, Caritas, Theologia* (M: *Poesia*).

32. From left to right: *Historia* (M) or "Fides in revelatione" (D), *Philosophia* (M) or "Fides in prophetas" (D), *Doctrina* (M) or *Oratio,* according to Ripa (D), *Sculptura* (?) (M) or *Constantia* (D), *Temperantia* (M) or "Foi des convertis" (D).

33. See Delmarcel, 1981, 345–52, already cited by Standen, 1985, I, 96. Tapestries reproduced in Delmarcel, 1979, pls. 2 and 3, and Junquera, 1986, I, 42 and 43.

34. For the La Marck set, see Steppe and Delmarcel, 1974, 41–42 and Figs. 4–8.

35. Shearman, 1972, 89–90.

36. Galinsky, 1972, 222–24.

37. Jung, 1966, 76–87.

38. Brommer, 1984, 107–8.

39. Surprisingly, Ercole apparently never owned a series with the *Labors of Hercules,* which was, after all, one of the most popular themes in Flemish tapestry during this period. See Delmarcel, 1982. In this regard (Document 38), it is important to recall Ercole's own words of caution against creating a frieze in his palace in Rome depicting the "Trionfo d'Hercole."

3. Ferrante's *Fructus Belli*

Ecouen, Musée de la Renaissance; West Dean, Chichester, West Dean College, Edward A. James Foundation; Brussels, Royal Museums of Art and History and location uncertain[1]
The Pay of the Soldiers. Ecouen (Inv. Ec. 101a): 437 × 823 cm (Color Plate II; Fig. 44)
The Artillery. West Dean: 360 × 750 cm (Fig. 47)
The Battlefield. West Dean: 360 × 562.5 cm (Fig. 48)
The Dinner of the Officers. Ecouen (inv. Ec. 101b): 442 × 817 cm (Color Plate III; Fig. 49)
The Triumphal Cortege. Brussels (inv. Tp. 14): 495 × 890 cm (Figs. 50–51, 56, 58–59, 68)
Reward and Punishment. West Dean: 360 × 345 cm. (Figs. 52–54) (The dimensions are not known for the lateral sections, which were on the Swiss art market in 1965)

Comparative Illustrations
The March and Encampment, workshop of Reymbouts, c. 1600 (Figs. 45, 55)
The Burning City, Gobelins, c. 1685–86 (Fig. 46)
Leone Leoni, bronze statue of Ferrante Gonzaga (Fig. 57)
G. Hendrickx, *Fructus Belli,* engraving, c. 1550 (Fig. 60)
Giulio Romano, *Trumphal Chariot of Scipio,* drawing, c. 1532–35 (Fig. 61)
Workshop of Giulio Romano, *Trophies* from the spandrels of the Sala di Troia, c. 1538 (Fig. 62)
Column of Trajan, Socle (Fig. 63)
Cartoon for *The Burning City* (Figs. 64, 69–70)
Cartoon for *The Artillery* (Figs. 65)
Cartoon for *The Triumphal Cortege* (Figs. 66–68)

This eight-piece set is documented in the Gonzaga collections from 1547 until 1709. The subject matter of each panel is recorded in Amadei's chronicle (Document 70).

1. *The Pay of the Soldiers:* "La paga che si dà a' soldati" (Fig. 44)
2. *The March and the Encampment:* "La marcia di un esercito" (Fig. 45).
3. *The Burning City:* "L'incendio di una città" (Fig. 46).
4. *The Artillery:* "L'assedio di una fortezza, batuta dal cannone" (Fig. 47)
5. *The Battlefield:* "una battaglia campale" (Fig. 48).
6. *The Dinner of the Officers:* "un convito alla militare" (Fig. 49)
7. *The Triumphal Cortege:* "Il Trionfo" (Fig. 50)
8. *Reward and Punishment:* "Il premio e la pena" (Figs. 52–54)

With the exception of numbers 2 and 3, all panels of the *editio princeps* have survived. *The Triumphal Cortege,* with its original borders, was acquired in 1977 by the Royal Museums of Art and History.[1] The Gonzaga arms with the chain of the Order of the Golden Fleece dates the edition to after December 1531. The other panels of the original set are missing their upper borders, although the jewel of the Golden Fleece is visible just below the upper frieze, proving that they come from the *editio princeps* (Fig. 51).[2] *Artillery, Battlefield,* and the central part of the *Reward and Punishment* are owned by the Edward A. James Foundation in West Dean, Chichester, while *Pay of the Soldiers* and *Dinner of the Officers* were recently bought by the Musée de la Renaissance (Ecouen) from a French private collection.[3] The lateral parts of *Reward and Punishment,* as well as their lateral borders, were on the Swiss art market in 1965.

At the time *The Triumphal Cortege* was exhibited in

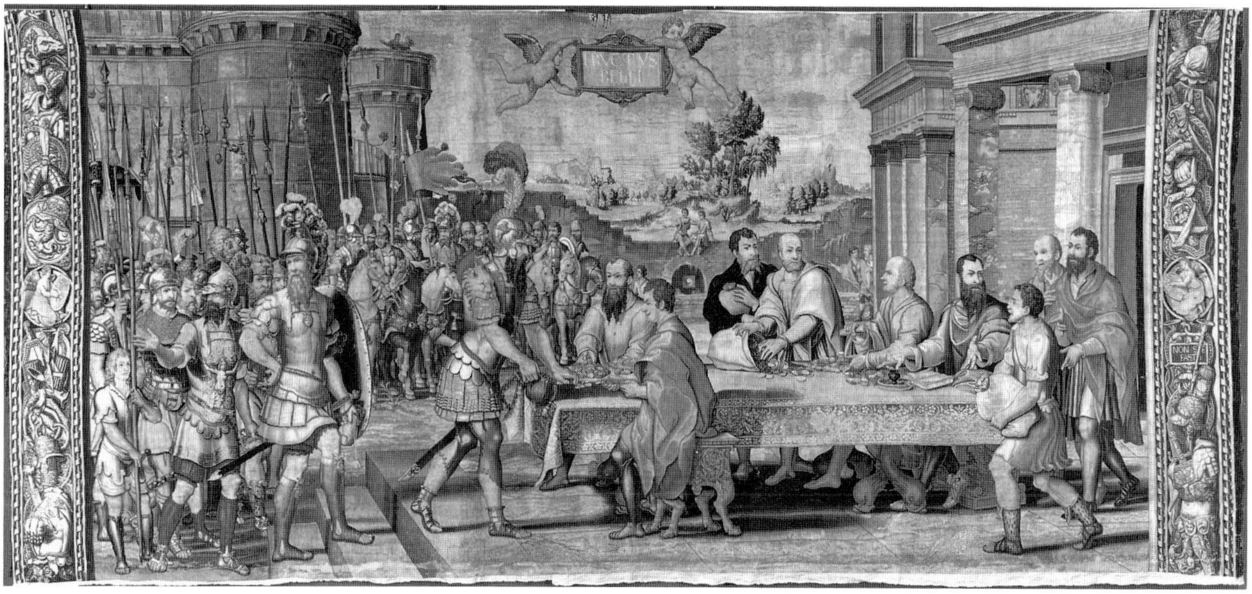

Fig. 44 *Fructus Belli: The Pay of the Soldiers,* Brussels, workshop of Jehan Baudouyn, c. 1545–47. Ecouen, Musée National de la Renaissance.

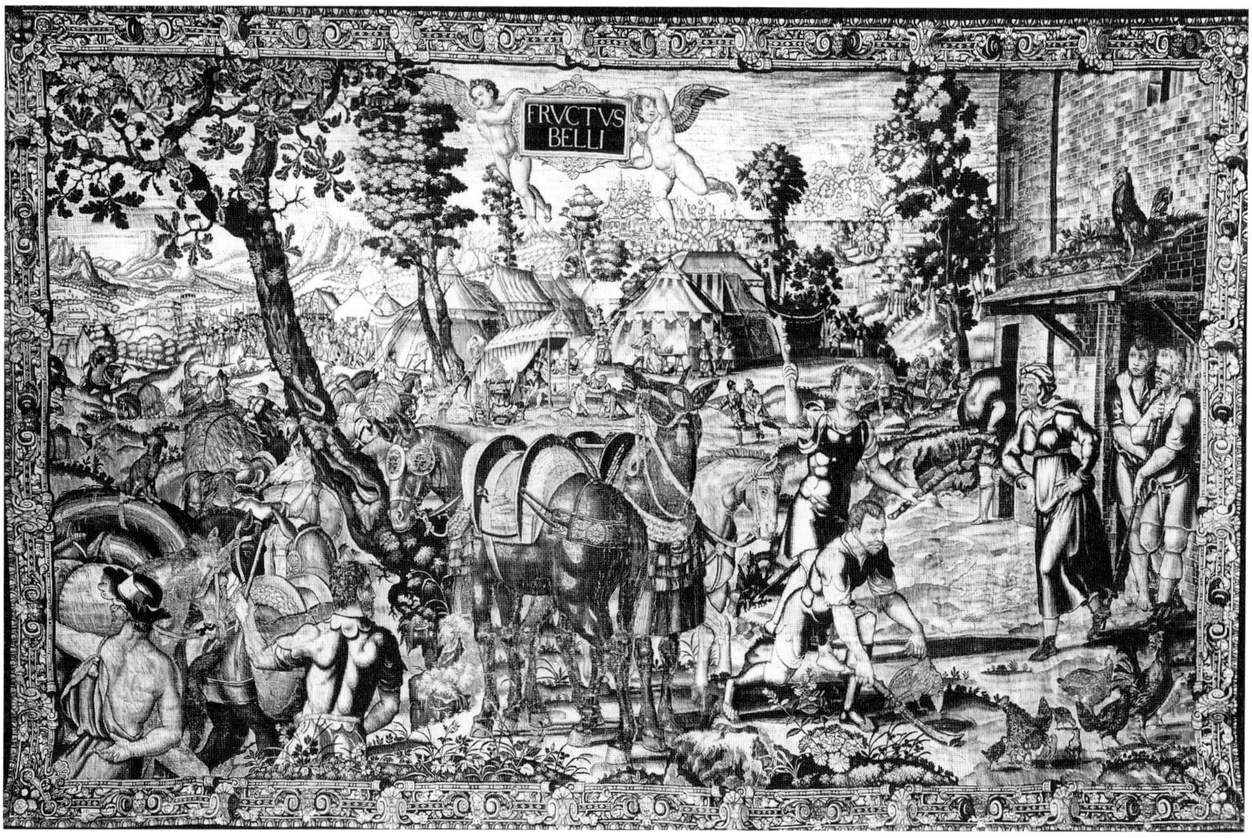

Fig. 45 *Fructus Belli: The March and the Encampment,* Brussels, workshop of Maarten Reymbouts, c. 1600. Vienna, Kunsthistorisches Museum.

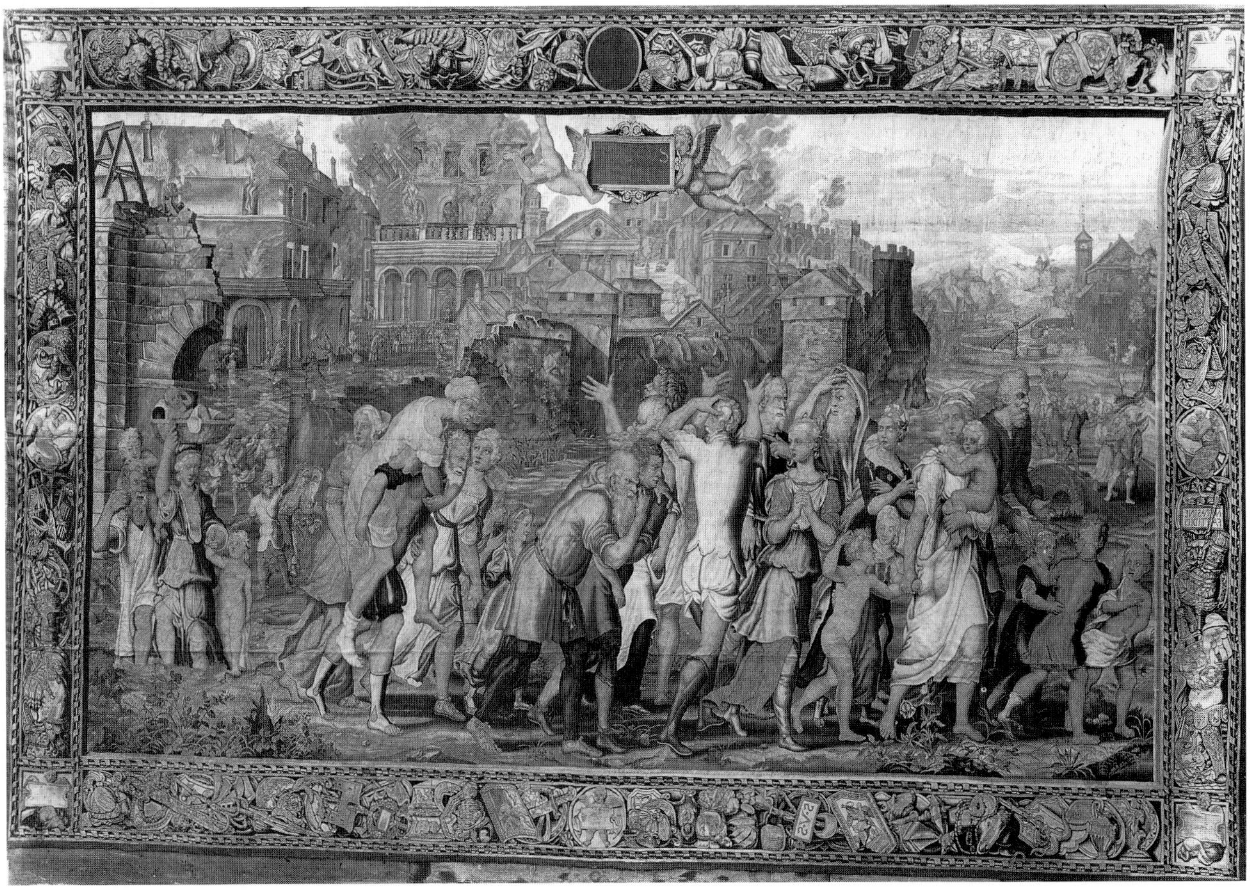

Fig. 46 *Fructus Belli: The Burning City,* Gobelins, c. 1685–86. Paris, Mobilier National.

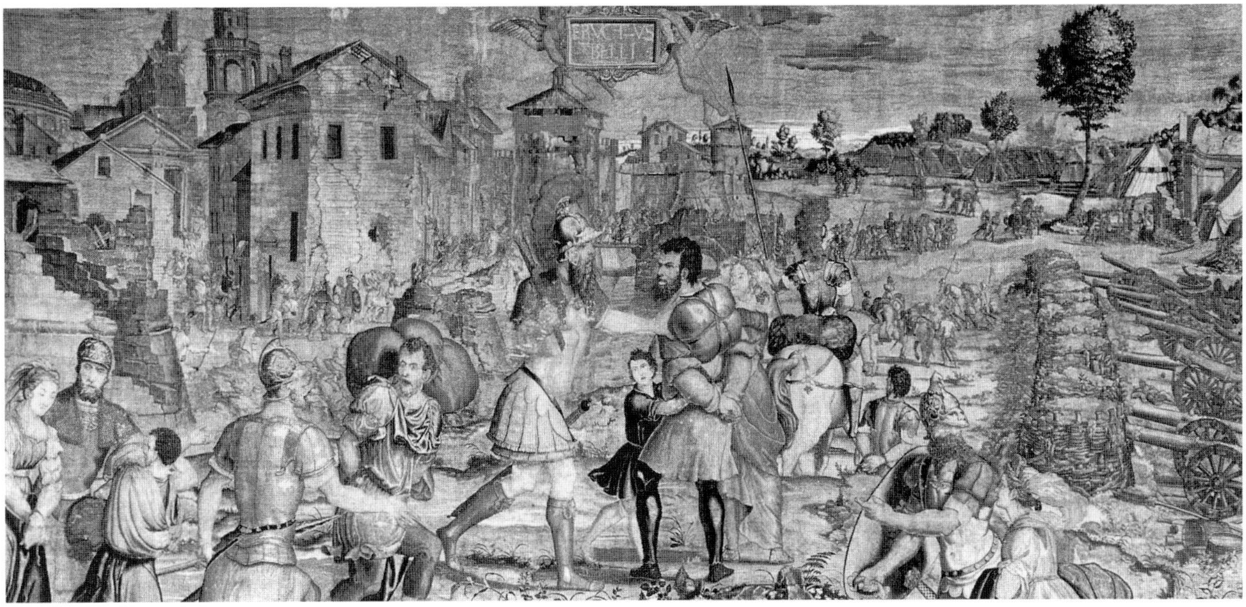

Fig. 47 *Fructus Belli: The Artillery,* Brussels, workshop of Jehan Baudouyn, c. 1545–47. West Dean, Edward James Foundation.

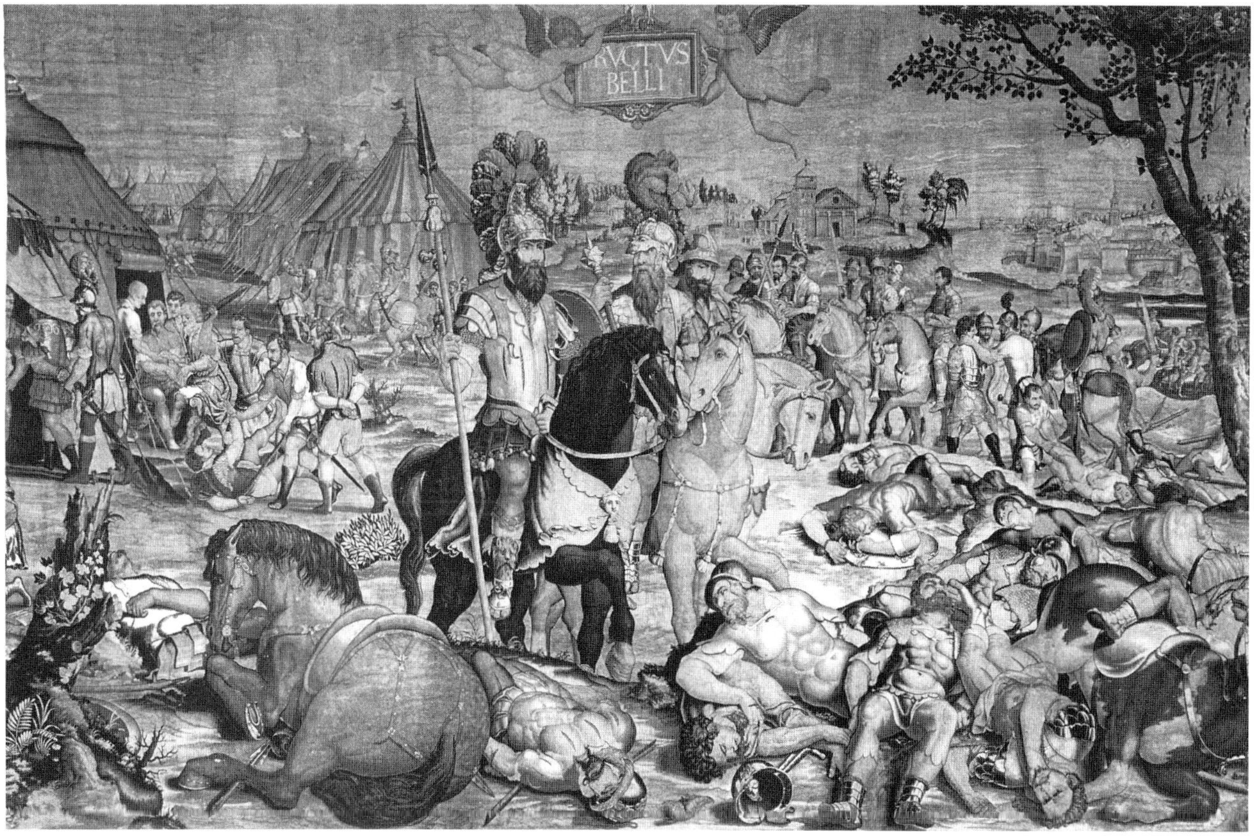

Fig. 48 *Fructus Belli: The Battlefield,* Brussels, workshop of Jehan Baudouyn, c. 1545–47. West Dean, Edward James Foundation.

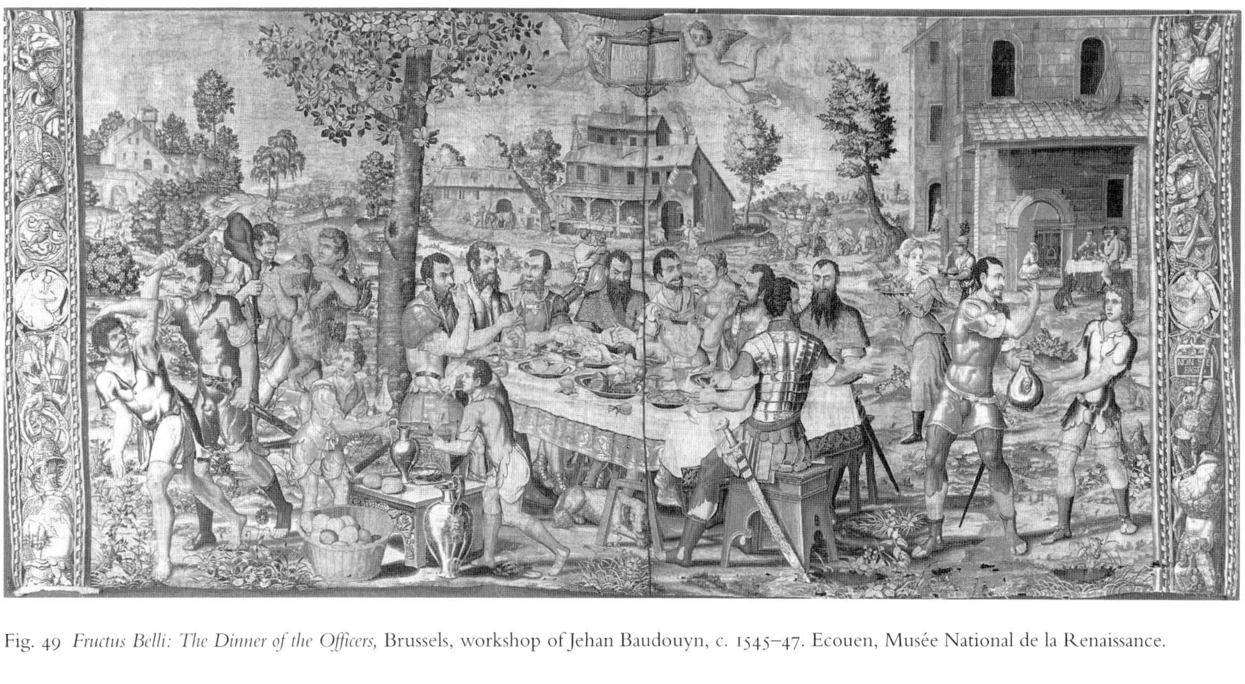

Fig. 49 *Fructus Belli: The Dinner of the Officers,* Brussels, workshop of Jehan Baudouyn, c. 1545–47. Ecouen, Musée National de la Renaissance.

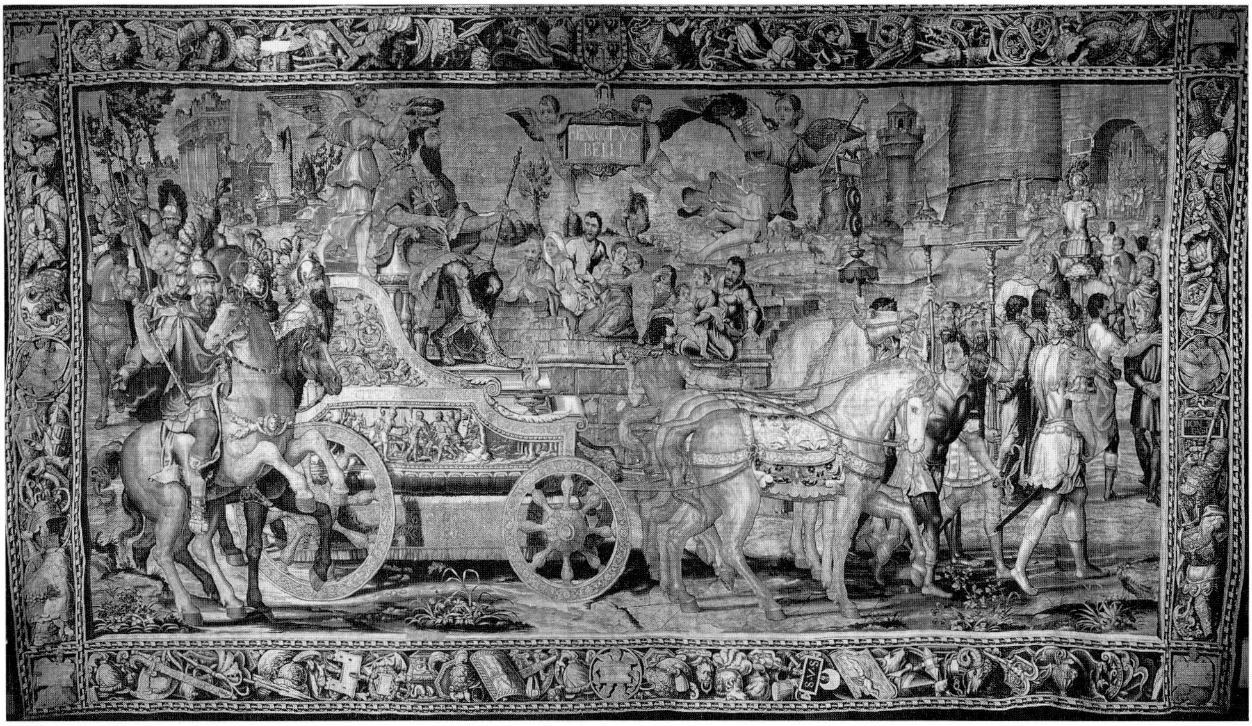

Fig. 50 *Fructus Belli: The Triumphal Cortege,* Brussels, workshop of Jehan Baudouyn, c. 1545–47. Brussels, Royal Museums of Art and History.

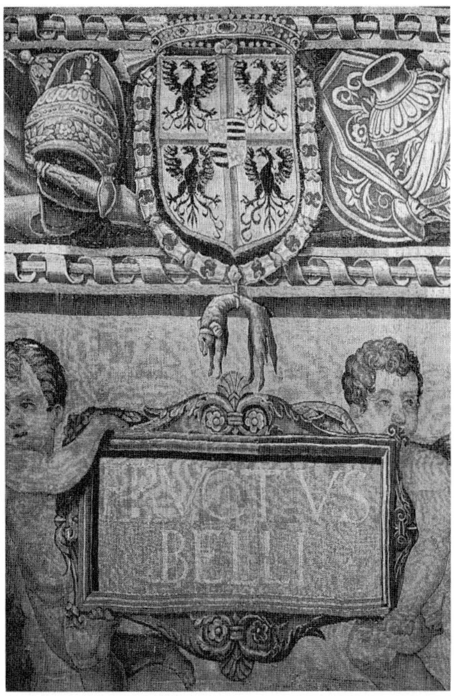

Fig. 51 Detail of the Gonzaga coat of arms and cartellino from the top of *The Triumphal Cortege* (Fig. 50).

Paris in 1865, Darcel identified the coat of arms as well as the cartoon in the Louvre. He also pointed out the mark of the city and of the weavers in the selvedges. Alphonse Wauters confirmed the city mark as that of Brussels and identified the weaver's monogram as comprising the letters IS.V.[4] Now lost, it was surely the workshop of Jehan Baudouyn, who is documented at work on the last panel of the set in the summer of 1547 (Document 12). Little is known about the activities of his atelier, but he must have had a good reputation as a weaver for Ferrante to have entrusted him with this commission, a commission that involved those intricate border designs about which Baudouyn complained in his letter. Variants of the IS.V monogram are found on other Brussels tapestries, including a scene of Roman history belonging to Giulio Romano's set of the *Rape of the Sabine Women*.[5] The monogram with the letters IS.B (IohanneS Baudouyn) is also found on the *Grotesques with Monkeys* in Madrid.[6]

As his letter of 31 August 1547 makes clear, Baudouyn had already completed seven of the eight pan-

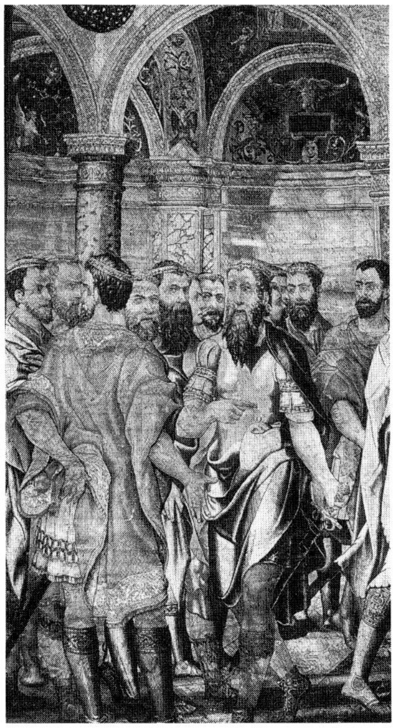

Fig. 52 *Fructus Belli: Reward and Punishment,* left lateral section, Brussels, workshop of Jehan Baudouyn, c. 1545–47. Location unknown.

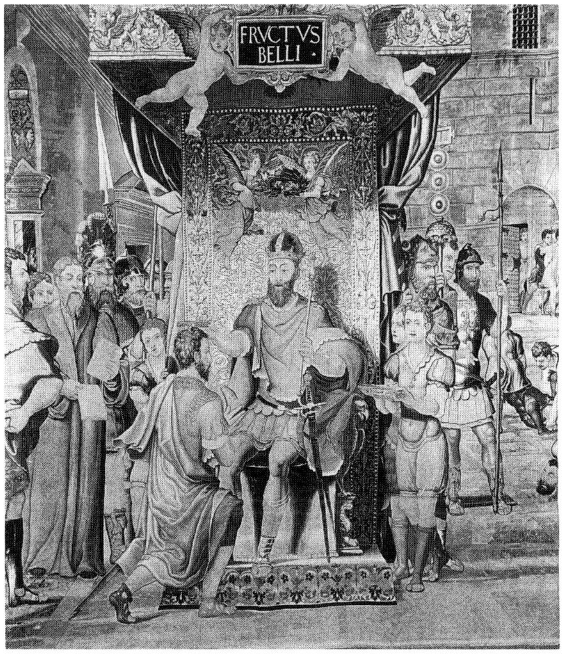

Fig. 53 *Fructus Belli: Reward and Punishment,* central section, Brussels, workshop of Jehan Baudouyn, c. 1545–47. West Dean, Edward James Foundation.

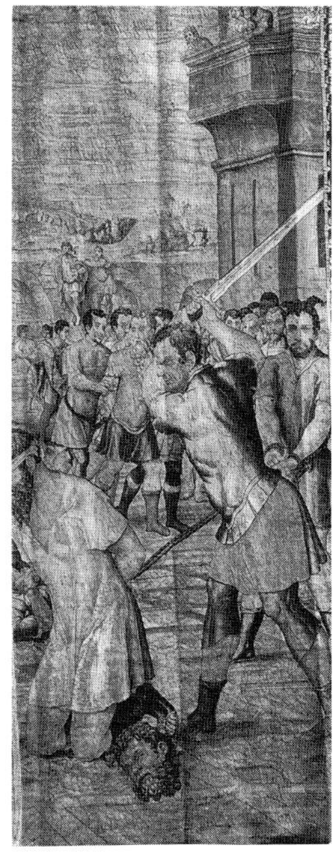

Fig. 54 *Fructus Belli: Reward and Punishment,* right lateral section, Brussels, workshop of Jehan Baudouyn, c. 1545–47. Location unknown.

els.[7] Estimating a weaving speed of some fifty centimeters a month, sixteen months would have been required for the weaving of the eight panels, which could have been worked on simultaneously on eight looms. Perhaps as much as twelve months would have been required for preparing the models, shipping them to Flanders, and creating the cartoons, all of which means that the project was probably initiated in the winter of 1544–45.[8] Thus it may be that Ferrante ordered the set when he was in the Low Countries in September 1544.

According to his letter, Ferrante had visited Baudouyn's workshop while the weaving was in progress and had given assurances of additional funds for unforeseen expenses. This visit must have occurred prior to Ferrante's departure in June 1546 for Milan. Baudouyn claimed that he had received an additional 250 *carolus* guilders from Anthoine Marco, but that he now estimated at three gold ducats *pro ell.*[9] It is not known whether he actually received the additional 200 ducats.

The *Fructus Belli* was expressly designed for Ferrante, whose coat of arms was woven in the upper borders. The arms are repeated on the blinkers of the horses of *March and the Encampment* and they were retained in the reedition by Reymbouts (Fig. 55). The Gonzaga banner floats from the building of *Dinner of the Officers.*[10] The profile of the victorious general in *Triumphal Cortege* was probably intended as a portrait of Ferrante (Figs. 56–57). A favorable comparison can be made between Leone Leoni's bronze statue in Guastalla and with written descriptions of Ferrante's features.[11]

The *Fructus* is first mentioned by Calvete de Estrella in his description of the banquet held on New Year's Day 1549 in honor of Philip II at Ferrante's suburban residence, the Villa Gualtiera, on the outskirts of Milan. The series is described as consisting of "rich pieces of tapestry on which, with subtle art and great skill, were represented all the facets of military life and the art of war and what usually happens to a warrior prince and a great captain" (Document 24). The inscription "FRVCTUS BELLI" is written on a *cartellino* held by winged *geniuses,* which is located on the upper part of each of the eight panels. Such "tituli" (clearly intended as a "motto" for

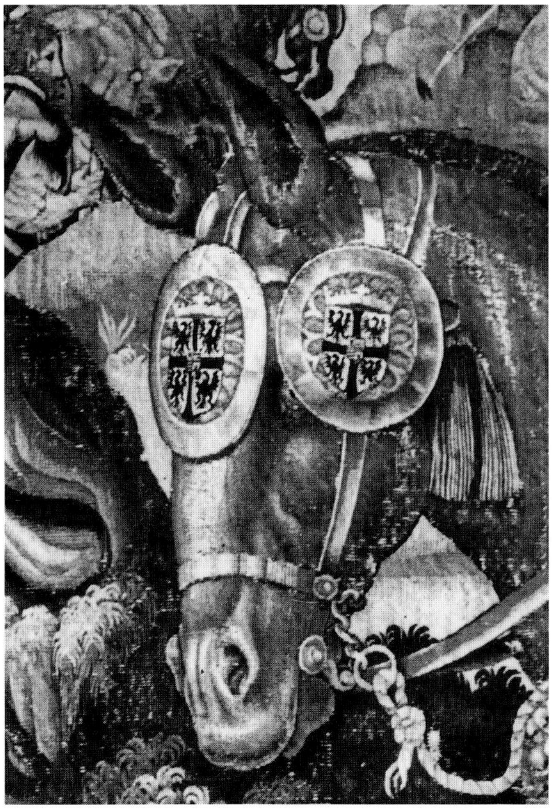

Fig. 55 Detail of the Gonzaga coat of arms on the blinkers of the horses from *The March and the Encampment* (Fig. 45).

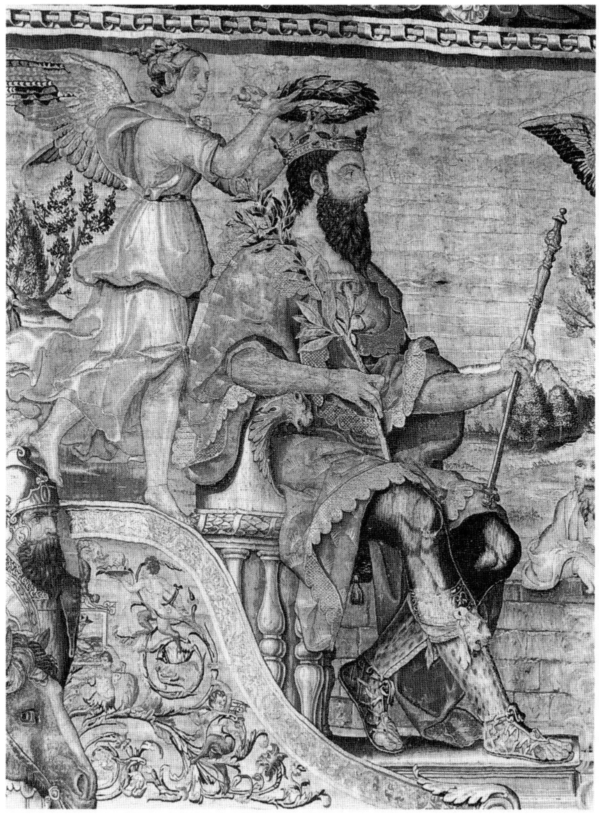

Fig. 56 The Triumphal General from *The Triumphal Cortege* (Fig. 50).

the entire set) are not uncommon as such in Flemish tapestries of the period, although it is unusual to find them located in the upper part of the composition. Rather than being conceived as a faithful rendering of a precise aspect of military life, the tapestries were intended to serve as an ironic and disenchanted commentary on the moment portrayed. The "fruits of war" consist not merely of the triumph of the victorious general but also of the wages given to the mercenary soldiers and officers, the soldiers who steal from the local farmers, the burning of houses, the persons displaced after the bombing of the town, the prisoners carried away after the artillery attack, the battlefield littered with dead bodies, the reveling officers ransoming the population, and the generals receiving their rewards while at the same time traitors are being beheaded. Other inscriptions woven in the borders of the panels confirm the pes-

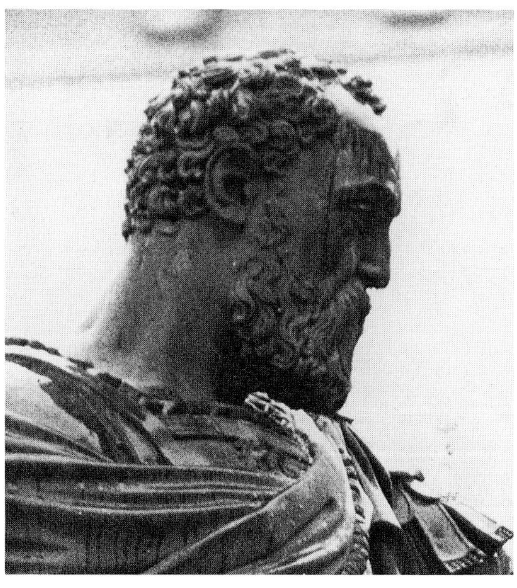

Fig. 57 Leone Leoni, bronze statue of Ferrante Gonzaga, detail. Guastalla, Piazza Maggiore.

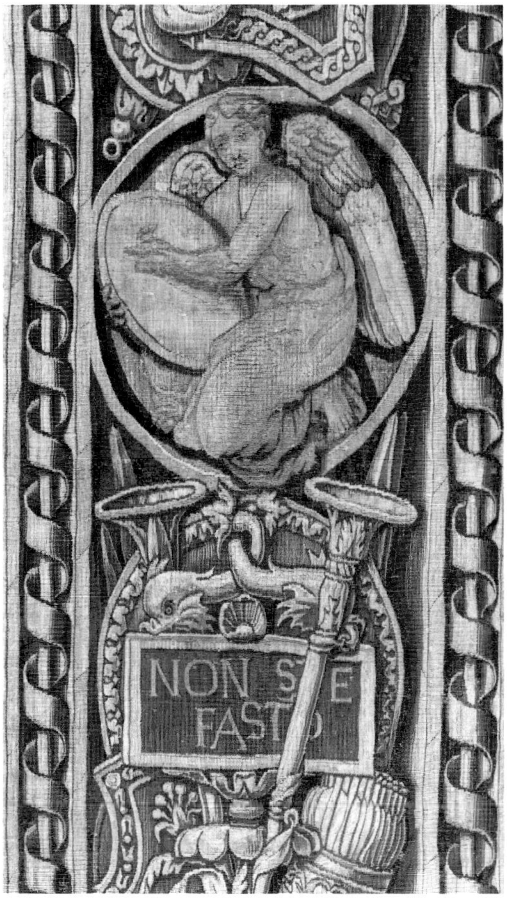

Fig. 58 Detail of the lateral border with the motto "NON S[IN]E FAST[IDI]O" from *The Triumphal Cortege* (Fig. 50).

Fig. 59 Detail of the lower border with the motto "S.V.S." from *The Triumphal Cortege* (Fig. 50).

simistic note that informs the *Fructus Belli* theme (Figs. 58–59). These include the phrase "NON S[IN]E FAST[IDI]O" ("not without aversion"), found in the right border, and the letters "S.V.S." woven on a pseudo-Roman military standard in the lower border, which probably stands for "sic victor/ultor sum" ("in such a way I am a winner/avenger").[12]

Ferrante ordered this set when he was at the apex of his military career as a commander-in-chief of the imperial troops. Having spent nearly twenty years of his life on the battlefields of Europe, he had become disenchanted by the horrors of war he had witnessed. Ferrante's fundamental attitude toward literature and toward military life seems to support this interpretation of the *Fructus Belli*. His biographer, Gosellini, noted that Ferrante was more inspired by contemporary events than by those of former times. For him the art of war was the major pastime of noblemen and as such was to be learned on the battlefield and not from books. This made Ferrante an authority on tactics and strategy.[13] Such an approach to military life may explain why the *Fructus Belli* scenes look so ahistorical, with soldiers clad in pseudo-antique armor and acting out their roles in a semi-antique, semi-Italian landscape. The pessimistic overtone, however, may have been suggested to Ferrante by such a contemporary text as the *Libro aureo de Marco Aurelio emperador,* a manual for the courtier written in Spanish in 1528 by Fray Antonio de Guevara and first translated into Italian in 1542. In a fictitious letter addressed to his friend Cornelius "nella quale ragiona de i travagli della guerra e della vanità del trionfo," Marcus Aurelius considers the prize and the offers that have been made in order to allow him to be celebrated on a triumphal chariot after his military victory. His compan-

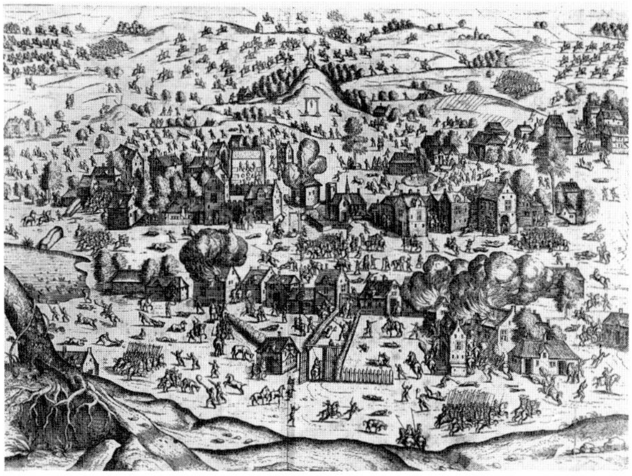

Fig. 60 G. Hendrickx, *Fructus Belli,* engraving, c. 1550. Brussels, Royal Library Albert I.

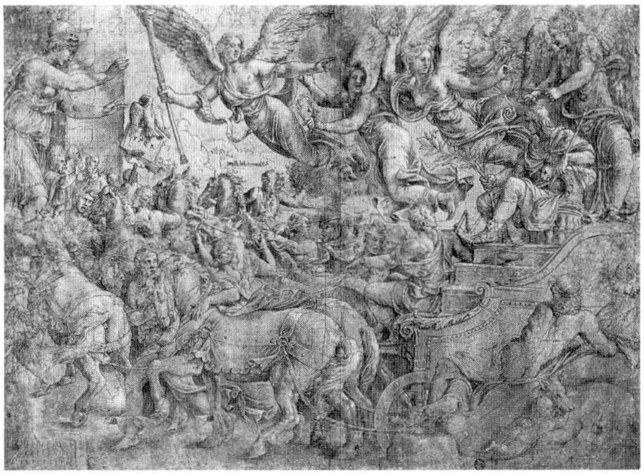

Fig. 61 Giulio Romano, *Triumphal Chariot of Scipio,* drawing, c. 1532–35. Paris, Musée du Louvre, Cabinet des Dessins.

ions lie dead on the battlefield, their widows and orphans live in sorrow, and civilians suffer from the damage caused by the mercenaries who stole their cattle and raped their women.[14]

Pleas for peace of course were common among the neo-Latin humanists, with Erasmus's *Querela Pacis* as the most notable example of the genre. Although none of these can be identified as the direct source for the program of the *Fructus Belli,* various parallels can be found, including the rejection of mercenary troops in favor of free citizens as described by Machiavelli in his *Libro dell'arte della guerra* (1521).[15] The "fruits of war," comprising only misery and disaster, were also illustrated in contemporary engravings (Fig. 60).[16] In any event, a moral and ahistorical visualization of war was not usual in the art of tapestry design. Earlier sets were devoted to specific victories, from the *Battle of Roozebeke,* delivered to Philip the Bold in 1387, to the *Battle of Pavia,* created for Charles V (1525–31), and the *Battle of Mühlberg,* commissioned by Ferrante's colleague and rival, the Duke of Alva.[17] It is hard to believe, therefore, that Ferrante decided not to represent any of his own military actions just because he was influenced by Guevara or Machiavelli. Was it simply a matter of natural modesty,[18] or must other factors be taken into account? Ferrante may have refused to personalize his military triumphs since they had all been conducted in the name of Charles V, with Ferrante merely serving as his representative. This is confirmed by Ferrante's *impresa,* the eagle feather amid other feathers and accompanied by the motto "Sic alias devorat una meas," meaning that the imperial eagle devours all others.[19] The *Fructus Belli* had been commissioned at the time when the imperial court ordered the *Siege of Tunis* tapestries.[20] Ferrante, then in residence at the court in Brussels, surely knew of this commission.[21] The *Tunis* set was the foremost celebration of Charles V's "fruits of war," and Ferrante therefore may have deliberately refrained from representing his own achievements, limiting himself in the *Fructus Belli* to a more generalized statement about military life, one fraught with pessimistic stoicism.

The designs for the *Fructus Belli* have traditionally been attributed to Giulio Romano, and indeed their morphology is deeply influenced by models related to Giulio's Mantuan *bottega.* A comparison with Giulio's drawing for the *Triumphal Chariot of Scipio* (Fig. 61) leaves no doubt about the artistic origins of the Brussels *Triumphal Cortege.* The *Scipio* tapestries, designed by Penni and Giulio Romano between 1528 and 1532, had been woven in Brussels for Francis I between 1532 and 1535.[22] Whereas the *Triumphal Cortege* can be considered a very formal quotation,[23] other panels in the *Fructus* set echo similar compositions from this older set.[24]

In addition to these parallels, a relationship exists between themes in the *Fructus* tapestries and those already worked out by Giulio at the Palazzo Te and the Ducal Palace. These had been created for Federico II, who was obsessed with imperial themes partially because of Charles's visit to Mantua.[25] Thus, for example, the

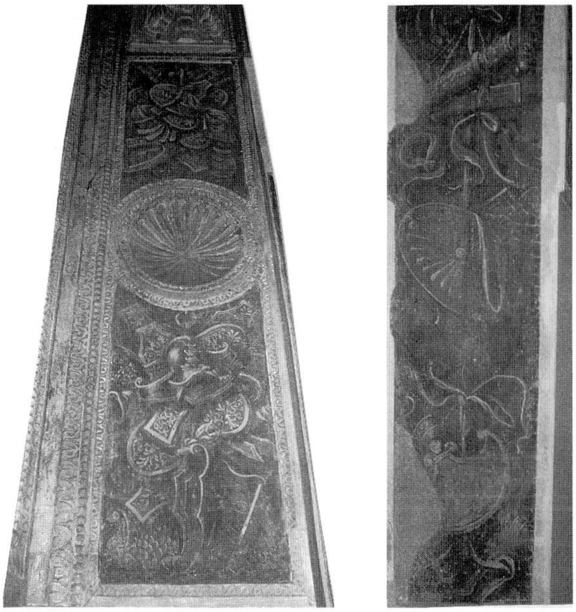

Fig. 62 Workshop of Giulio Romano, *Trophies* from the spandrels of the Sala di Troia, c. 1538. Mantua, Palazzo Ducale.

reliefs in the Sala degli Stucchi in the Palazzo Te are very close to the *Fructus* set. Both present the heroic military themes in the guise of a victorious antique army with soldiers bearing trophies and leading prisoners. The apotheosis of Mars and Hercules, surrounded by Victories, one of them writing the name CAROL(US) on a shield, is repeated in the lateral border of the Brussels *Fructus,* although it ultimately derives from a model provided by the column of Trajan in Rome.[26] Among the scenes from the lives of the Roman emperors painted between 1536 and 1538 for the Gabinetto dei Cesari in the Appartamento di Troia in the Ducal Palace are clear forerunners of compositions in the *Fructus* series. The foreground figures in *Nero Playing While Rome Burns* precede the crowds fleeing in the *Burning City*.[27] *The Triumph of Titus and Vespasian*, showing the two emperors standing in their chariot and crowned by a winged Victory, contains the same vivid movement and the same compositional scheme as the *Triumphal Cortege* in both the *Scipio* and the *Fructus* sets.[28]

The impressive borders of the *Fructus Belli,* consisting of *all'antica* trophies, also owe something to Giulio's workshop (Figs. 58–59). This type of ornamentation had been popular in representations of war themes since the second half of the fifteenth century,[29] and it was inspired from such antique examples as the carved piers of Santa Sabina in Rome (now in the Uffizi) and the frieze, with booty taken from the Dacians and the Raxolani, on the base of the Column of Trajan.[30] Specifically, however, the trophy borders in the *Fructus* can be traced to the ornaments painted in the window embrasures of the Sala di Troia (Fig. 62), which Giulio Romano's shop executed between 1538 and 1539.[31] The military implements are of a similar style and arrangement and both are colored to simulate bronze. Apparently invented by Giulio himself, this decor reappears in 1544 in the great "salone" of his own house.[32]

Like the trophy ornaments, so too the *cartellino* held by *putti* and containing the words "Fructus Belli" relate to the dedicatory inscription on the Column of Trajan (Fig. 63), which also provided the model for the winged female figure writing on a shield in the center of the lateral borders.[33] On the column, this figure, writing the names of the victorious warriors, is placed on the frieze between the end of the first and the beginning of the second Dacian war.[34] A more immediate precedent for the *Fructus tituli* is found in the dedicatory inscription about the entrance door of Andrea Mantegna's *Camera Picta*.[35] In Brussels tapestries, titles or inscriptions traditionally appear in the upper border, whereas in the *Fructus* they appear in the upper center of the visual field. Combined with the trophies, the *tituli* serve to

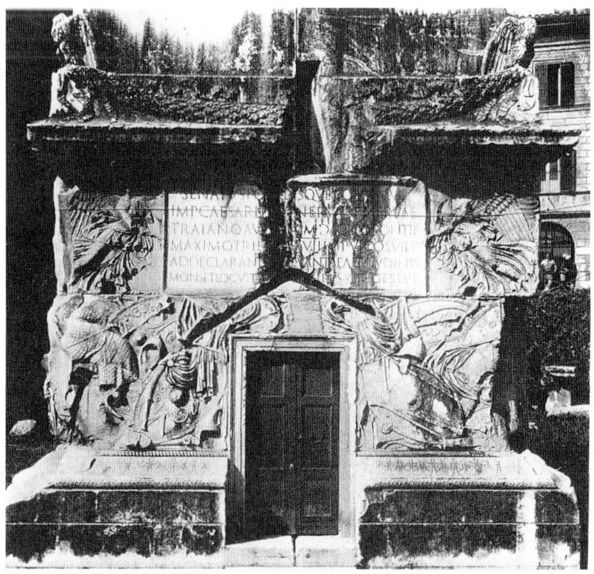

Fig. 63 Column of Trajan, socle, Rome, Trajan Forum.

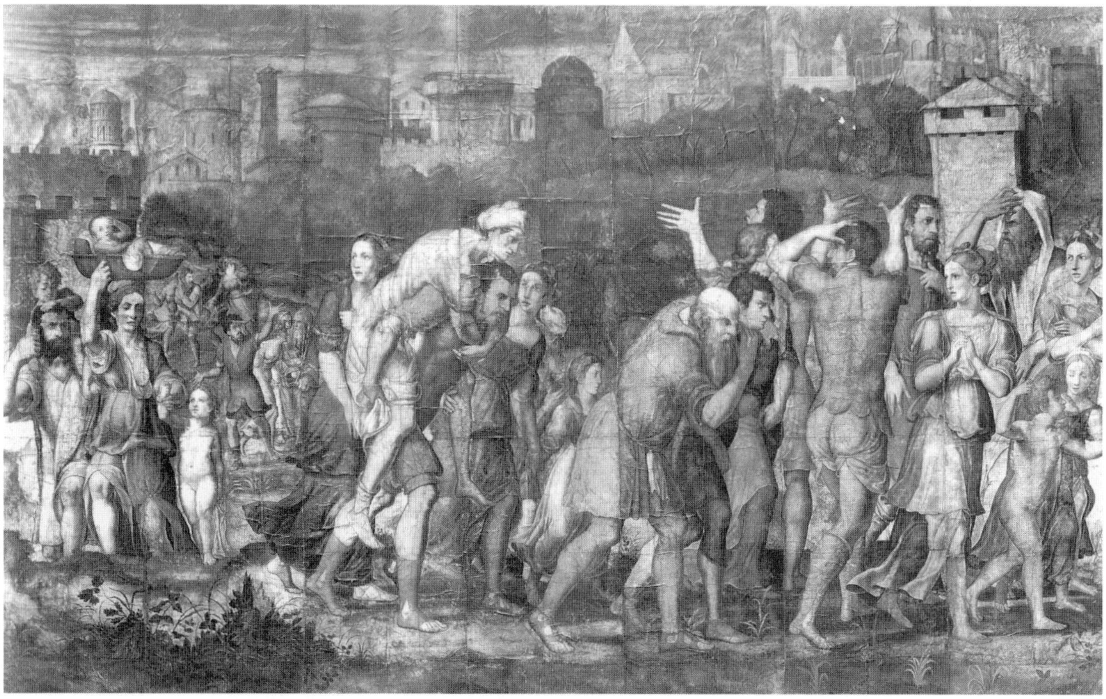

Fig. 64 *Fructus Belli:* cartoon for *The Burning City* (Fig. 46), body color on paper, Brussels(?), c. 1545. Paris, Musée du Louvre, Cabinet des Dessins.

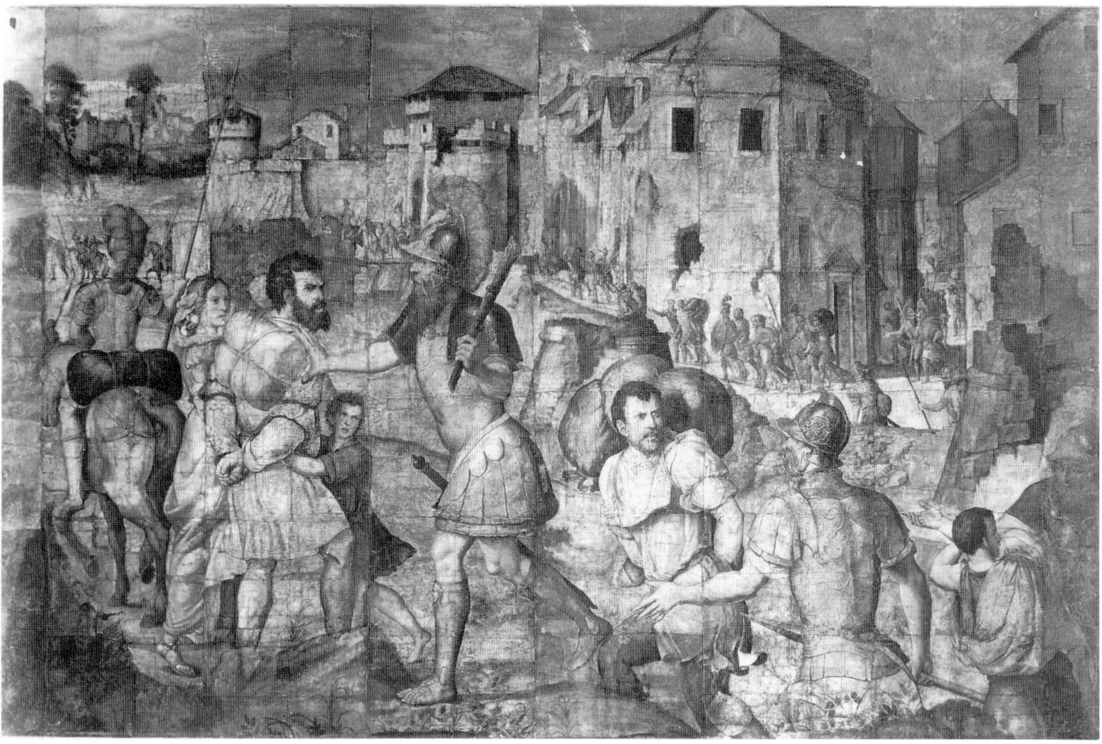

Fig. 65 *Fructus Belli:* cartoon for *The Artillery* (Fig. 47), body color on paper, Brussels(?), c. 1545. Paris, Musée du Louvre, Cabinet des Dessins.

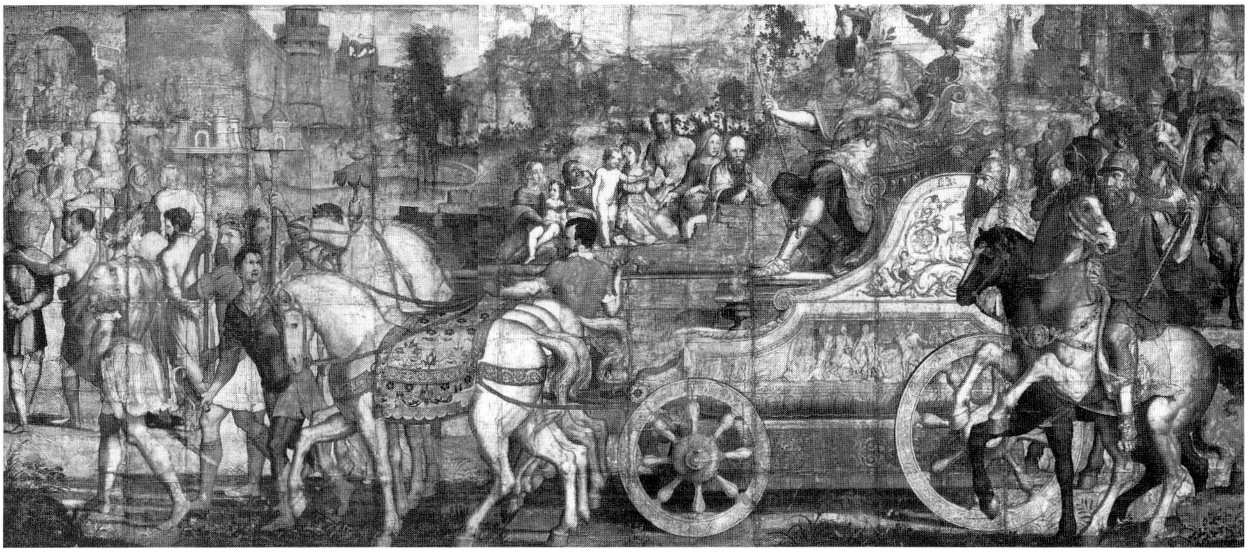

Fig. 66 *Fructus Belli:* cartoon for *The Triumphal Cortege* (Fig. 50), body color on paper, Brussels(?), c. 1545. Paris, Musée du Louvre, Cabinet des Dessins.

commemorate Ferrante's military triumphs.[36] Although the Flemish artists and weavers may have had some models of antique trophies at their disposal,[37] the general feel of the *Fructus* borders, as well as the combination of inscription and allegory of victory, points to models from Giulio Romano's workshop.

In contrast to Ferrante's *Puttini,* the cartoons for the *Fructus* were retained by the weaver who used them for the set presented by the King of Spain to Cardinal Mazarin at the Treaty of the Pyrenees (1659).[38] The series, which was subsequently owned by Louis XIV, disappeared at the time of the French Revolution. It is known, however, through a copy (Mobilier National) woven in the Gobelins *basse-lisse* workshop of de la Croix and Mozin in 1685–86.[39] Because the original cartoons were in Brussels, the French weavers had to rely on the Mazarin set. On 15 October 1692, the cartoons were described to the ambassador of the Duke of Savoy (Document 72). All eight cartoons of the "fructus belli ou fruict de la guerre" were then intact, although five subsequently disappeared. The surviving three (*Burning City, Artillery,* and *Triumphal Cortege*) were apparently purchased by the English painter Richard Cosway, who offered them to Louis XVI in 1786 (Figs. 64–66). Together with a cartoon from Giulio's *Scipio,* they are now preserved in the Cabinet des Dessins of the Louvre.[40] The cartoons represent the *Burning City,* the *Artillery,* and the *Triumphal Cortege,* the latter two giving the inverted image (because of the weaving on low-warp looms) of the original tapestries now in Brussels and West Dean.

Few sixteenth-century tapestry cartoons survive. Those that do provide a unique opportunity to study technique and the relationship that exists between cartoon and the woven design.[41] For the *Fructus* cartoons, charcoal was used to define the contour lines and pigment was used for the colored surfaces. At present, the paper sheets are glued on canvas. The paper sheets were originally glued to each other to provide the surface for the painted design. A split is clearly visible after each two sheets in width, which proves that these vertical paper strips were fixed in succession under the warp threads.[42] A comparison between the surviving tapestries and cartoons (Figs. 67–68) proves that the upper parts of the cartoons were largely overpainted and that paper strips and parts of the composition were lost on all four sides.[43] Despite these modifications and losses, the bulk of each scene has been remarkably well preserved. Some slight adjustments to the cartoon design are found in the tapestries of the first edition (Figs. 69–70). They should be viewed as "repentirs" by the cartoon painter, proving that the Louvre cartoons are the original ones and not later copies.

All aspects of the design were worked out in great detail. As there are few *pentimenti,* this presupposes a

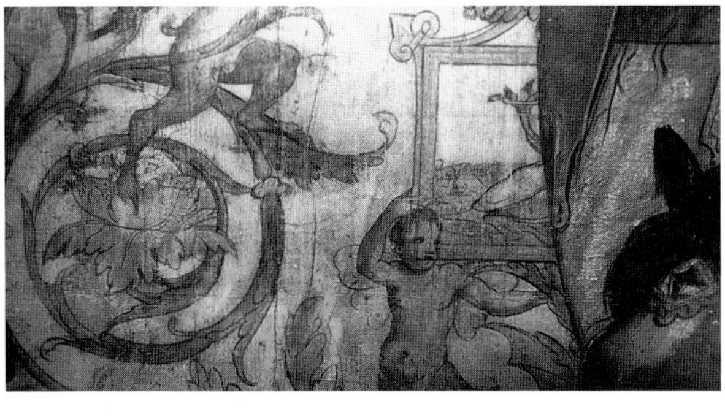

Fig. 67 Detail of sketch of the chariot with corrections from the cartoon for *The Triumphal Cortege* (Fig. 66).

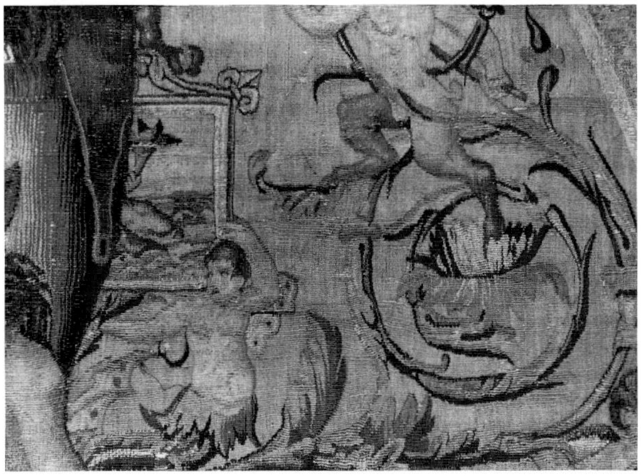

Fig. 68 Detail of the chariot from *The Triumphal Cortege* (Fig. 50).

considerable amount of preparatory work. The surfaces are colored in soft tones, with contrasts on details of the fabrics and specific objects such as the triumphal chariot. The artists who produced these cartoons were highly trained and the results are masterly. This helps to explain their survival, which may also be due to the names (Raphael and Giulio) attached to them.

Although the visual sources for the tapestries point to the shop of Giulio in Mantua, the cartoons were not painted in Italy. It is known that for the *Scipio* tapestries the cartoons were worked up in Brussels, as is proven by the trip made in 1532 by Primaticcio, who brought the small models from France to Brussels and who subsequently brought back to the French court the life-size cartoons.[44] When, for the *Oxen and Elephants* tapestry of the *Scipio,* one compares such an artistic creation on its three levels—model and design, cartoon, and tapestry—a clear loss of quality occurred between the "invenzione" and the surviving stages of cartoon painting (where the composition was both enlarged as well as being reversed) and the weaving.[45] This is particularly obvious when the cartoon was painted neither by the author of the "invenzione" nor under his immediate supervision.[46] Keeping this in mind, it is possible to accept Félibien's attribution of the models for the *Fructus Belli* to Giulio.[47] The heavy, even statuelike figures, compressed in blocked and compact compositions, correspond to Frederick Hartt's definition of Giulio's late style: "An increased austerity of composition restrains the groups to the foreground plane and to unusually compact configurations. A new gravity of demeanor inhibits the former violence of their action. Indeed the compositional forces are so strong as to compress the figures within block forms. The massiveness thus acquired is by no means restful. The figure rebels against compression, in the occasional twisted movement of limbs and extremities as in the overall linear tension carried out by the drapery."[48] Although it is doubtful that the identity of the painters will ever be known, the cartoons were apparently prepared under the supervision of an Italian artist familiar with Giulio's repertory, possibly by the "Jehan Baptiste painctre" mentioned in Jehan Baudouyn's letter of 1547 (Document 19). He is to be identified as Gianbattista Lodi da Cremona. In 1540 Gianbattista served as an expert to the court in Brussels regarding the value of compositions painted on four chimney mantelpieces by Frans Borreman, which suggest that he may have lived for some time in Brabant. One of his pupils affirmed that Johan Baptista was Italian and that he had lived in Brussels from 1540 to 1549. Thereafter he retired to the small town of Lier, near Antwerp, with Gian-Carlo Affaitadi, a Cremonese banker in Antwerp.[49] In 1552 Lodi served as Ferrante's agent in the commissioning of the *Puttini* in the Marzotto collection from Willem de Pannemaker, signing his letter from Lier as "Battista Lodi pittore" (Document 32).[50] Although his involvement with the *Fructus* cannot be proved, Lodi probably did not limit himself to inspecting Baudouyn's work in 1546–47. He surely supervised and perhaps even took part in the painting of the cartoons, which would explain the strong Italianate design of the figures and buildings.

Gianbattista Lodi da Cremona thus belongs to that

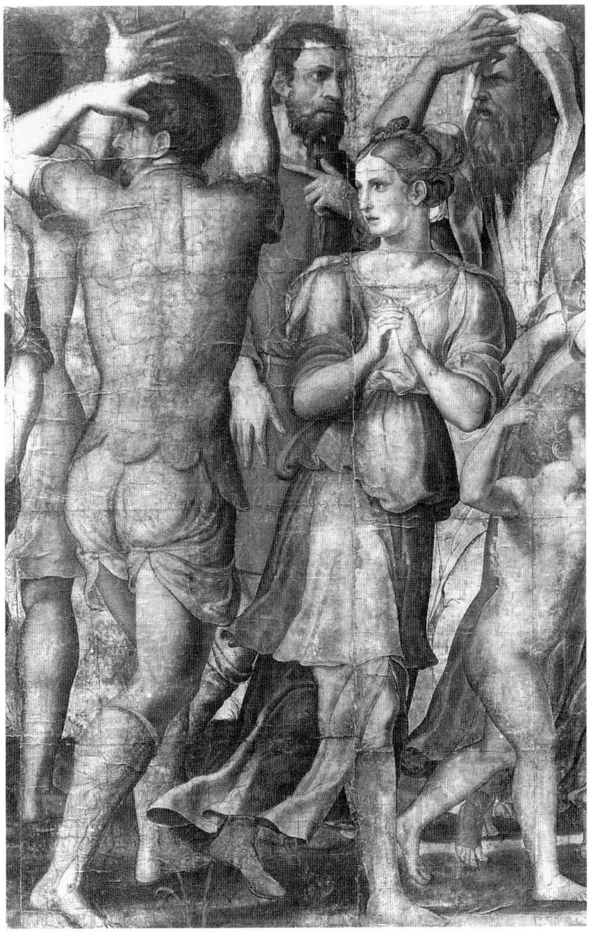

Fig. 69 Detail from the right-hand section of the cartoon of *The Burning City* (Fig. 64).

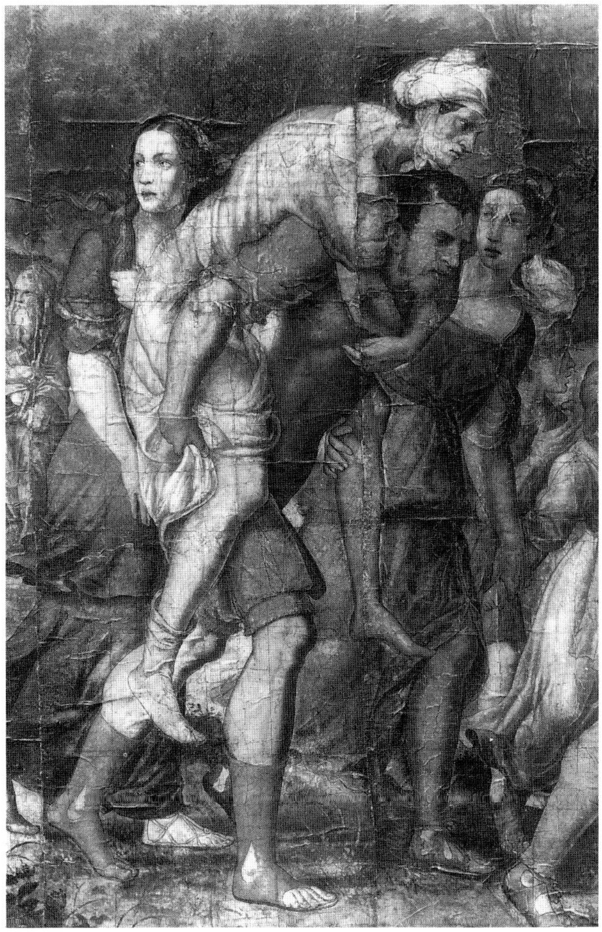

Fig. 70 Detail from the central section of the cartoon of *The Burning City* (Fig. 64).

group of Italian artists who, living in Brabant, transmitted transalpine models for the decorative arts, and especially for tapestries. Accordingly, he followed in the footsteps of Tommaso Vincidor da Bologna and Matteo del Nassaro.[51] A contemporary of Lodi, the Mantuan engraver Giorgio Ghisi lived and worked in Antwerp between 1549 and 1556, transmitting numerous models from Giulio's workshop to Flemish engravers. Although not documented, it is always possible that Ghisi also served as an adviser to Flemish cartoon painters.[52]

Mention should be made of the presumed collaboration of Jan Vermeyen, the painter of the cartoons for the *Siege of Tunis*. This hypothesis was recently set forth by Horn. Yet the similarity between the design of the horse at the far right in the *Fructus Triumph* cartoon and the one on the sixth *Tunis* cartoon is inadequate to prove Vermeyen's involvement in this project. Rather, this detail is probably due to some anonymous cartoon painter belonging to Vermeyen's "scavans et souffisans compaignons paintres des pays de par deça" and who could have worked for various weavers' workshops, including those of Pannemaker and Baudouyn in the same period.[53]

Ferrante's *Fructus Belli* was the first edition of these cartoons. Baudouyn apparently produced one other edition from the same cartoons, with identical borders but omitting the Gonzaga arms. This reedition came into the possession of Philip IV or his minister Don Luis de Haro and was presented to Cardinal Mazarin at the Treaty of the Pyrenees in 1659. Bequeathed to Louis XIV, it served as the model for the Gobelins copy (in reverse) in 1685–86 and was lost during the French

Revolution.[54] Toward 1600 the cartoons were reused in the Brussels workshop of Maarten Reymbouts, who produced at least two editions with less complicated borders than in the original. One of these reeditions is in Vienna; the other belonged to Louis XIV and disappeared during the French Revolution.[55]

NOTES

1. This set, and particularly the tapestry in Brussels, has been treated in detail by Delmarcel (1986, 1989). See also *Ecouen 1992*, 15–26. Thus the comments included here are by and large a summary of this material.

2. No later edition of the set has the chain of the Golden Fleece in its upper border. The two subjects lost from the first edition, no. 2 *The March and the Camp* and no. 3 *The Burning City*, are known from the original cartoon of no. 3 and from the later editions by Reymbouts (Brussels around 1600) and Gobelins.

3. *Ecouen 1992*, passim. The missing pieces, nos. 2–3, may eventually surface in some private collection.

4. Darcel, 1866, 75–76; Wauters, 1878, 122.

5. This tapestry was on the London art market in 1986. Franses, 1986, 18–22.

6. Junquera, 1986, I, 214–25 (series 30, monogram on tapestries 6 and 10). Junquera, 1986, I, 214–25 and idem 1973[A] (Brussels), 148–50, wrongly attributes this monogram to Seger Bombeck, whose mark comprises only S.B. See Standen 1985, II, 753. Bombeck left Flanders for Germany in 1543 and worked there until 1559. Goebel, 1934, III–24, 43–56.

7. "(. . .) il plaira à vostre illustre magnificence (. . .) me secourrir de quelque bonne somme de deniers pour pouvoir parachever et parfaire l'ouvraige de Vostre Excellence encommenchée. Dont ne reste àfaire que une seule pièche" (Document 19).

8. The surface of the first edition, now partially preserved, can be deduced from the faithful Brussels reedition, once in the possession of Cardinal Mazarin and later copied at the Gobelins factory. This edition comprised some 320 square meters. For an average width of some 8.10 m (but one Mazarin piece is 13 m) and a weaving speed of some O.5 m each month, the estimate of some twenty months from August 1547 is a valuable hypothesis. Many sets, such as the *Siege of Tunis* for Charles V, were woven in successive groups (Horn, 1989, I, 118–27). If this happened also with Ferrante's *Fructus Belli*, work may actually have begun around January 1544.

9. "Anthoine Marco" is actually Ferrante's secretary, Giovanni Antonio Mauro (see ASPr, b. 41, c. 1) and not the painter Antonio Moro, as stated by Hymans (1910, 23–25). According to the chronicle of Vicente Alvarez (1964, 41), the *Fructus Belli* represents "the entry [of Ferrante] into France at the time of the events at St. Dizier," thus during the wars of 1544. The buildings represented on the tapestry, however, are in the Italian style. Nonetheless, Alvarez's comment confirms the belief that the set was ordered in Brussels after the Treaty of Crépy.

10. Already noticed by Birk (1884, 176–77). As this Gonzaga heraldry appears in the later Reymbouts edition in Vienna, in which the original border was replaced by a neutral design without Ferrante's arms, the cartoons for the first edition no doubt were originally designed for the Gonzaga and that the weavers in Reymbouts's workshop forgot to remove them later on.

11. See under Ferrante circa 1529 in the Chronology for the descriptions by Ulloa and Gosellini.

12. The abbreviated inscription on the Brussels panel, "Non s(in)e fast(idi)o" (Fig. 58), is fully rendered as "non sine fastidio" in the Gobelins edition. The abbreviation "s.v.s." does not correspond to any motto in Gelli or Typotius. The closest parallel is the motto "sic immortalis sum," adopted by Ferrante's second son, Giovanni Vincenzo Gonzaga, after his participation in the "grand siege" of Malta in 1565 (Gelli, 1928, 453, no. 1588). It should be noted that tapestries nos. 1 and 6, now in France, bear the inscription "LABORVM MERCES," which was subsequently embroidered on the shield held by the Victory in the lateral borders.

13. Gosellini, 1574, 438–39 and 445.

14. Forti Grazzini, 1984, 32; *Mantua 1989*, 479; Guevara, 1559, 191; Delmarcel, 1989, 199. Fray Antonio de Guevara was preacher at the court of Charles V and "cronista" of the Siege of Tunis. Ferrante could have known and met him personally and, being fluent in Spanish, may even have read this book in the original edition (Ulloa, 1563, fols. 176–77). For the influence of Guevara's book, see Mezzatesta (1984, 624–25).

15. Buck, 1986, 1–12. In this book, based on antique authors such as Vegetius and Livy, Machiavelli rejected also the use of artillery, while the *Fructus* tapestries underline its effects.

16. Flemish engraving, around 1550, by G. Hendrickx; see Delmarcel, 1989, 182. In the illustrated German edition of Petrarch's *De remediis utriusque fortunae* (1532), "Military Victory" is represented as a warrior standing on the bodies of stabbed civilians (Raupp, 1984, 84–85).

17. For Alva's tapestry by Willem de Pannemaker (Palacio de Liria, Madrid), see Goebel, 1923, I, 312, and Delmarcel, 1988, 103.

18. Gosellini (1574, 439 and 442) insisted on Ferrante's modesty about his deeds of war. It is apparently more than a mere literary "topos."

19. Gelli, 1928, nos. 148 and 1833; De Boodt, 1603, 79 and 82; Delmarcel, 1989, 177, Fig. 16.

20. The contract for the painting of the cartoons by Jan Vermeyen was signed in June 1546, while the weaving by Willem de Pannemaker was executed between 1548 to 1554. The first ideas and models may therefore be dated early 1545 (Horn, 1989, 118–19 and 344).

21. The fact that the *Tunis* set was transferred from Antwerp to Brussels on Ferrante's request in July 1556 emphasizes his interest, for this famous military set was somewhat parallel to his *Fructus* series (Horn, 1989, 138).

22. For the *Scipio* set, see Hartt, 1958, I, 227–31; *Paris 1978;* and Forti Grazzini in *Mantua 1989*, 467–73.

23. The Mantuan prototype for the military triumph was the Mantegna *Triumph of Caesar*, now at Hampton Court Palace. All the elements of this triumph are repeated, sometimes in variants, in the *Triumphal Cortege* of the *Fructus Belli*. It should also be noted that these canvases were originally framed, in the Palazzo di San Sebastiano, with wooden pilasters ornamented with trophies, almost forerunners of the later borders of the *Fructus* set (Martindale, 1979, 35, 95 and pl. 87).

24. *The Burning City* (*Fructus Belli* no. 3) recalls the *Burning Camp* (*Scipio* no. 10); the guns on the *Artillery* (*Fructus Belli* no. 4) resemble the spears in the *Conquest of the Camp* (*Scipio* no. 8); the cortege of prisoners on the same, and of the citizens on *Fructus Belli* no. 3 rely on the Mocking of the Prisoners in *Scipio's Triumph* (*Scipio* no. 18); the *Dinner of the Officers* (*Fructus Belli* no. 6) is a variant of the *Dinner of Scipio and Syphax* (*Scipio* no. 7) and even more of *Scipio's Banquet* (*Scipio* no. 23). Finally, the emperor Charles V giving crowns to his generals (*Fructus Belli* no. 8) resembles Scipio's giving crowns after the siege of Carthagena (*Scipio* no. 4). For the *Scipio* set and its sequence, see *Paris 1978* and *Mantua 1989*, 467–73.

25. *London 1981*, 190.

26. Hartt, 1958, I, 147–49, and drawings in II, 312–20; Carpeggiani and Tellini, 1987, 89–92; *Mantua 1989*, 364–66 and 499.

27. Hartt, 1958, I, 173, and II, Fig. 375; *London 1981*, 190 and 191, no. 182. Both are of course reminiscent of Michelangelo's *Deluge* in the

Sistine Chapel, as well as of the left-hand group in the *Fire of the Borgo,* which was largely painted by Giulio (Hartt, 1958, I, 21–24).

28. Hartt, 1958, I, 174, and II, Fig. 177; *Paris 1983,* 121–23, no. P 2. A similar Winged Victory holding out a wreath was designed by Giulio for Charles's entry of 1530, and Fame and Victory holding wreaths or palm branches appear as bronze reliefs in the spandrels above Mercury and Minerva, painted by Giulio around 1544 in his Mantuan house (Hartt, 1958, pls. 492–93 and 523; Carpeggiani and Tellini, 1987, 135, 138, 139; *Mantua 1989,* 498).

29. For example, the Portals of War in the palace of Urbino, by Francesco di Giorgio and G. C. Romano; the Scala dei Giganti in the Ducal Palace of Venice, by Antonio Rizzo; book illustrations and engravings (for these, see Alexander 1977, 65, pl. 13; Hind, 1948 V, 50 and VI, pls. 554 and 555; Byrne, 1981, 82–83).

30. Martindale, 1979, 70–71 and pls. 212–18 and passim for the Trajan frieze and column; Delmarcel, 1989, 180 and 185.

31. Similar panels with trophies were also painted under the scenes of the Trojan War in his apartment, as they were designed by Andrea Andreasi (see B. Talvacchia in *Mantua 1989,* 406–11, and Harprath, 1984, 3–28). According to Talvacchia (personal communication), these ornaments cannot be attributed specifically to any member of Giulio's workshop.

32. Hartt, 1958, I, 240, and II, Fig. 489.

33. For this socle, see Zanker, 1970, 524 and 530, Fig. 46.

34. Lehmann-Hartleben, 1926, II, pl. 37; this allegory was inserted in the *Codex Escurialensis* (Egger, 1906, II, pl. 31), and Giulio had used her already in the Sala degli Stucchi at the Palazzo Te (see note 26 above).

35. *London 1981,* 118–19. Mantegna's room, painted in 1465–74, may have inspired Perugino (1499) in his similar use of cherubs holding tablets at the Collegio del Cambio in Perugia (Sparrow, 1969, 72, Fig. 27).

36. For Gonzaga arms on tapestries, see the Chicago *Annunciation,* Ercole's *Puttini* and *Acts of the Apostles* sets, and Guglielmo's *Moses* series. The Gonzaga as well as the d'Este arms, placed upon military trophies, are also woven on some contemporary Venetian velvets (Podreider, 1928, Fig. 238, and Santangelo, 1964, pl. 65).

37. See Frans Floris's sketches of several trophies from the base of the Column of Trajan, designed during his Roman stay in 1540–47 (Van de Velde, 1975, 338, and II, pls. 106, 108, and 109).

38. For the Mazarin inventory of 1661, mentioning the origin, see Mazarin, 1861, 159.

39. Fenaille, 1903, 285–86. For the most complete illustration of this set, see Vaucaire, 1917, 6–12. Louis XIV owned this set, as well as a Brussels edition by Maarten Reymbouts, having the same border as the set in Vienna, ser. LXII, and moreover the Gobelins copy of 1685–86. See Guiffrey (1885, 336, 338, 359) and Delmarcel (1984, 57).

40. For the detailed history of his gift, see Landon (1831, 19–20), Reiset (1887, 85–87), and Guiffrey (1879, 264–66). The *Scipio* cartoon is discussed in *Paris 1978,* 124–25. Cosway maintained that they were taken by the imperial troops during the siege of Mantua in 1629–30. This place of origin was apparently invented either by himself or by his supplier, a certain "chevalier Bonfield," in order to make the origin of the pieces sound more illustrious. Even though the cartoons were still in Brussels in 1692, neither these works nor the subsequent tapestries were ever related to the Gonzaga of Mantua. As the *Scipio* set was not woven in Brussels until 1675 or later, Cosway probably bought the cartoons here in the middle of the 18th century, when such compositions were considered totally out of date and when the decline of Brussels tapestry weaving and trade forced several shops to go out of business.

41. Few systematic studies of cartoons have been carried out, but Peter Cannon-Brookes is completing work on those from the 16th and 17th centuries.

42. The paper sheets are 58 cm in height and 38 to 42 cm in width. The strips of two sheets glued together total some 78 to 84 cm, which is indeed the maximum width reached by a weaver. Traces of nail holes are still visible on the edges of the strips, as they were nailed to a wooden lath under the warps. According to Rotraud Bauer, the same data can be observed on the *Tunis* cartoons in Vienna.

43. The cartoon of the *Burning City* can be compared with the Gobelins copy of the lost Brussels Mazarin tapestry. This set faithfully renders the original compositions, sometimes mutilated on their lateral sides in West Dean. As usual, the cartoons of the borders were made on separate sheets and they were not kept in later times.

44. *Paris 1978,* 13, and see also de Laborde (1877, II, 366).

45. Drawing: *Paris 1978,* 118; for the St. Petersburg cartoon, see Gourwitch, 1941; for the tapestry in Madrid, see Junquera, 1986, I, 183, and *Mantua 1989,* 470.

46. See Raphael's *Acts of the Apostles* or Vermeyen's *Siege of Tunis.* The quality of the design is better rendered by these cartoons made in the presence of the designer himself.

47. Félibien, 1685, I, 437.

48. Hartt, 1958, I, 235.

49. Schneebalg-Perelman, 1982, 279–80; Hymans, 1910, 36, 39, and 40; cited in *Cremona 1985,* 25–26.

50. Delmarcel and Brown, 1988, 120.

51. Dacos, 1980 (Vincidor); Sulzberger, 1960 (Nassaro).

52. *Brussels 1970,* VI, 28, 30, 58; *Vienna 1989,* 198–207.

53. For the definition of Vermeyen's assistants in the 1546 contract for the *Tunis* cartoons, see Horn (1989, II, 344). For the *Fructus Belli,* see Horn (1989, 46–47 and n. 104). The author agrees that the figure style is quite different from Vermeyen's, but he nevertheless believes that "numerous details are clearly related to comparable features in the cartoons for the *Conquest of Tunis* series." Since this study, the cartoons have been removed from the Palais de Tokyo and are now in storage in the Louvre. I now also believe, in contrast to my statement noted by Horn, 104 n. 479, that the thin black outlines are original and were not added later.

54. Mazarin, 1861, 159; Guiffrey, 1885, 336: set no. 22: "dessein de Julles Romain (. . .) bordure de trophees d'armes couleur de bronze"; Fenaille, 1903, 283; Delmarcel 1984, 42–43. See also Document 72, discussed above (doc. 1692). At an auction at Sotheby's, London, 13 December 1991 (auction cat. 8, entry 2), an old and worn-out fragment of a reedition of the *Battlefield* appeared, which may have been made on the cartoons with original borders. A borderless copy of the *Reward and Punishment,* apparently belonging to the same edition, was, according to Wendy Hefford, preserved in 1989 at Saltwood Castle, Hythe, Kent.

55. For the Vienna series LXII, together with a smaller set (ser. LXIII) of "entrefenêtres," see Birk (1884, 184, 176–78) and Baldass (1920, nos. 77–80). In the inventory of Louis XIV, this border is described as "un ornement fonds rouge, compartimens et roulleaux avec masques, fleurs et fueuillages" (Delmarcel, 1984[A], 42–43).

4. Federico II and Ercole's *Puttini*

Federico II: Mentana (Rome), Federico Zeri
Venus, a Satyr, and Playing Children: 410 × 450 cm (Fig. 72)

Ercole: Lisbon, Gulbenkian Museum; Milan, Poldi-Pezzoli Museum
The Barque of Fortune. Lisbon (inv. 29a): 360 × 420 cm (Figs. 73, 80–81)
The Ball Game. Lisbon (inv. 29b): 350 × 370 cm (Fig. 74)
The Dance. Lisbon (inv. 29c): 350 × 417 cm (Fig. 75)
The Fishermen. Lisbon (inv. 29d): 350 × 370 cm (Fig. 76)
The Cat. Lisbon (inv. 29e): 355 × 105 cm (Fig. 77)
The Dog. Lisbon (inv. 29f): 355 × 105 cm (Fig. 78)
The Dance. Milan (inv. 383): 341 × 107 cm (Fig. 79)

Comparative Illustrations
Giulio Romano, *Venus, a Satyr and the Playing Children,* drawing (Fig. 71)
Giulio Romano, *Fortune Leading the Chariot of State,* drawing (Fig. 82)
Giulio Romano, *Putto Leading the Chariot of State,* drawing (Fig. 83)

The *Puttini* is first documented in Ercole's collection in 1557. Called the "aulea illa sua in quibus alati pueri in viridarii ludentes variis inter sese modis intext sunt," the set was bequeathed to the Duke of Mantua (Documents 37 and 48).[1] According to the 1563 inventory (Document 49, no. 1), the set comprised ten large panels, two "portere," and two "sopraportiere."[2] The Gonzaga arms, surrounded with the tassels of Ercole's cardinal's hat, are seen in the surviving portions of the set in Milan and Lisbon (Fig. 81). Furthermore, the *cartellino* held by a *putto* in the foreground of the *Barque of Fortune* (Fig. 80) is inscribed with the words "HER[cules] EPISCOP[us] MAN [tovanus]."

It is generally believed that the *Puttini* was woven by Nicolas Karcher from models provided by Giulio Romano, from whose hand there exists a number of the drawings of the subject.[3] Karcher arrived in Mantua in 1539, at which time Federico II granted him a privilege that extended to the eleven members of his shop (Document 9). The text of his decree does not specify the subject matter of the tapestries Karcher was commissioned to weave. Conceivably these were a set of *Puttini* tapestries that was left unfinished when Federico II died on 28 June 1540. Shortly thereafter, the commission was apparently assumed by Ercole. Indeed Ercole's coat of arms, at least those found on the surviving portions in Lisbon and Milan, seems to have been added at the last minute, suggesting that either it was an addition to the cartoons or to the weavings themselves.[4]

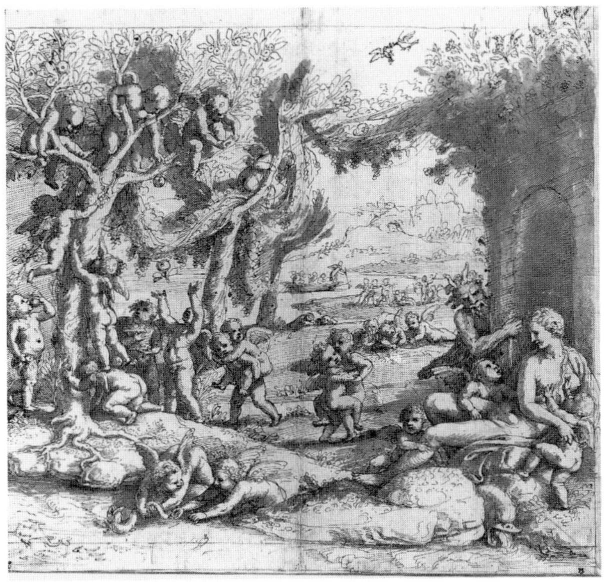

Fig. 71 Giulio Romano, *Venus, a Satyr, and the Playing Children,* drawing. Chatsworth, Devonshire Collection.

This sequence of events is confirmed by the discovery in 1989 of a *Puttini* tapestry bearing the arms and motto of Federico II (Fig. 72) and rendering in reverse the Chatsworth sketch of *Venus, a Satyr, and the Playing*

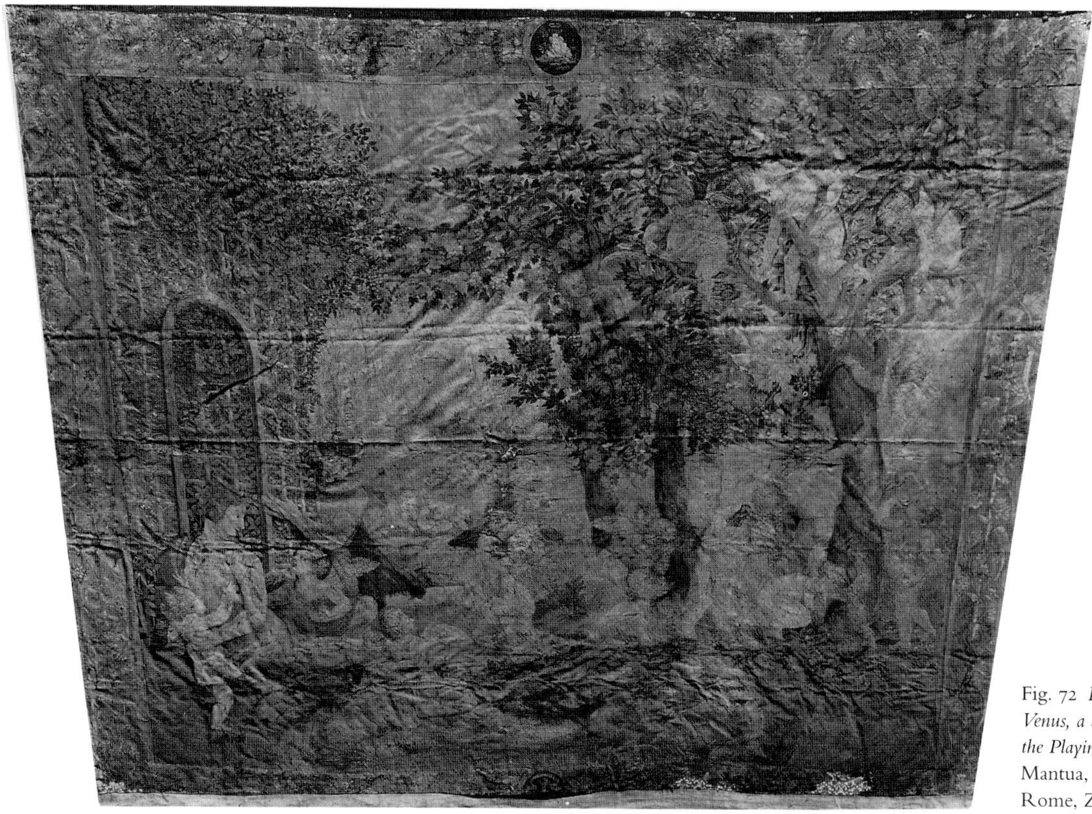

Fig. 72 *Puttini: Venus, a Satyr, and the Playing Children,* Mantua, 1539–40. Rome, Zeri.

Children (Fig. 71).[5] Federico II's tapestry in the Zeri collection is certainly the first subject of a set that was intended to unfold to the right. It is logical, therefore, to maintain that Karcher started with the first panel probably in November 1539 and that it was intended as a demonstration work of his skills.[6] Neither it nor other *Puttini* tapestries are cited in the January 1541 inventory (Document 9). This does not necessarily prove that the weavings were still on the loom, since four weavers working at the same time on a loom equal to the height of the tapestry would have been capable of making the Zeri weaving in six or seven months, that is, from November 1539 to June 1540.[7] Since Karcher's workshop included eleven weavers and himself, they could have started on at least two other pieces in Federico II's set. If such were created, then they were either subsequently lost or remain to be discovered.

Between the death of Federico II on 28 June 1540 and October 1545, when Karcher left for Florence, the weaver worked for Ercole, for whom he wove the *Moses in the Desert* (June 1540–January 1542), cited in the 1563 inventory (Documents 12 and 49, no. a).[8] The Lisbon-Milan *Puttini* was probably also made during this period from models supplied by Giulio Romano, who supervised the painting of the life-size cartoons. In July 1541 mention is made that Ercole had ordered tapestries "per suo passatempo" (Document 12). More likely than not, these were of a secular nature. Thus the reference may be to the *Puttini*. This hypothesis seems confirmed by the mention in the payments for supplies for Karcher. On 6 June 1542 Cortese was paid 71 libri for "lana tenta compra in Fiandra per far tappezzaria per Sua Signoria Reverendissima" (Document 12).[9] In contrast to the much coarser quality of the Zeri *Puttini* tapestry, one is struck by the outstanding quality of the colors of the wools and silks found in the Lisbon-Milan set. The coloristic effects of Ercole's *Puttini* are virtually identical to those of the best Brussels tapestries of the period. This can be explained only if the wool and the silk, available in Mantua, had been dyed in Brussels.[10]

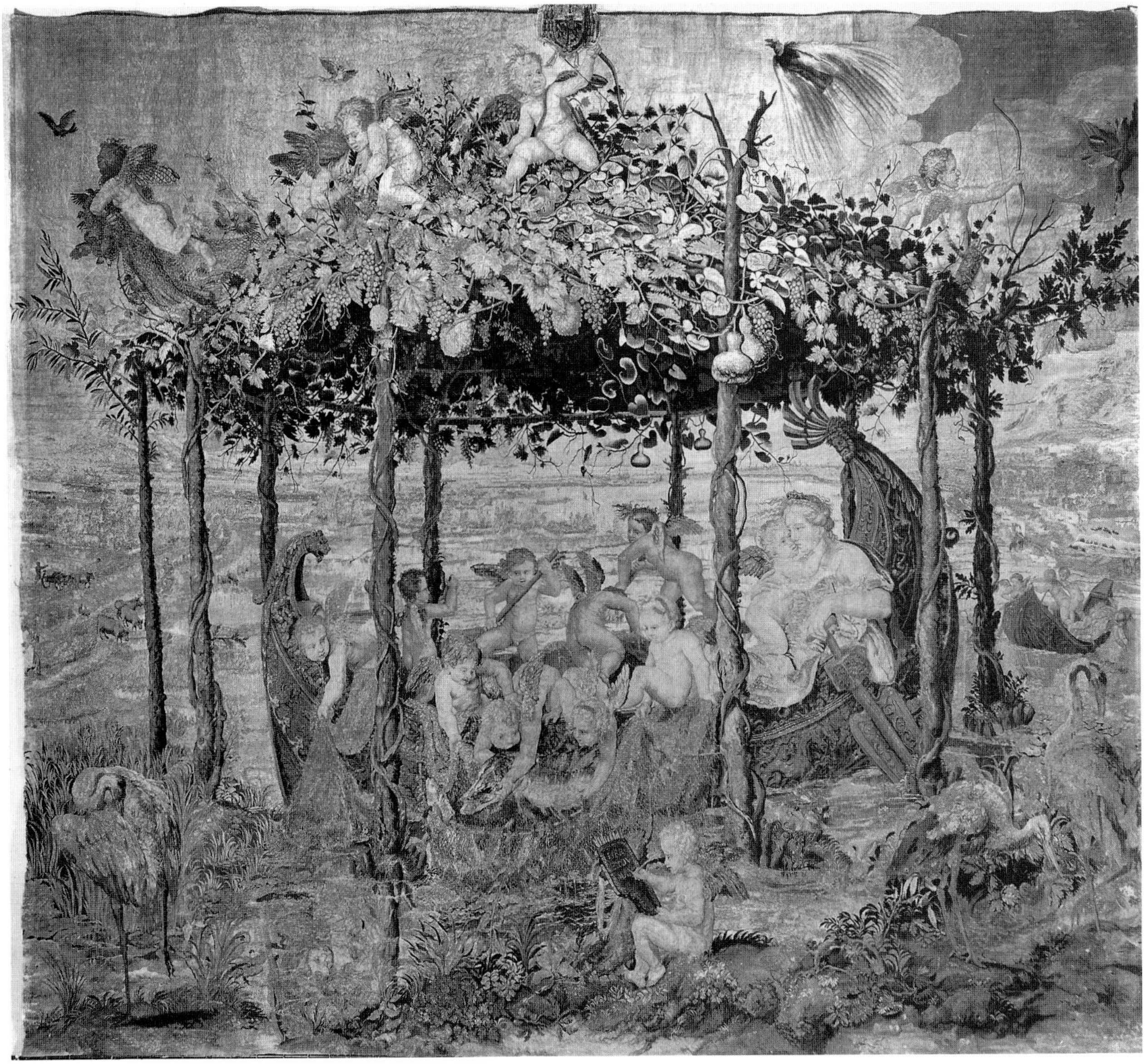

Fig. 73 *Puttini: The Barque of Fortune,* Mantua, workshop of Nicolas Karcher, 1540–45. Lisbon, Gulbenkian Museum.

To judge from the surviving portions of the set of ten, the tapestries were clearly developed from the "introductory" tapestry created for Federico II. The cartoons of the central visual field were the same size for both Federico II and Ercole's sets, although Ercole's never had a separate border.[11] The three surviving fragments from Ercole's set (two in Lisbon and one in Milan [Figs. 77–79]) are not *portiere* but fragments of larger panels. One of the fragments in Lisbon (inv. 29f) and the fragment in Milan include similar types of chestnuts. As the Milan fragment bears Ercole's arms, it was apparently the central section of a larger weaving, of which Lisbon inv. 29F originally may have been positioned on the left.[12]

Karcher's shop could have provided a set of ten large and five small tapestries in the five years and three months between June 1540 and October 1545. Four weavers were needed to accommodate the height of these tapestries and three panels could be woven simultaneously. To produce these panels, averaging 450 centimeters in width (the largest, the *Barque of Fortune* [Fig. 73], now measures

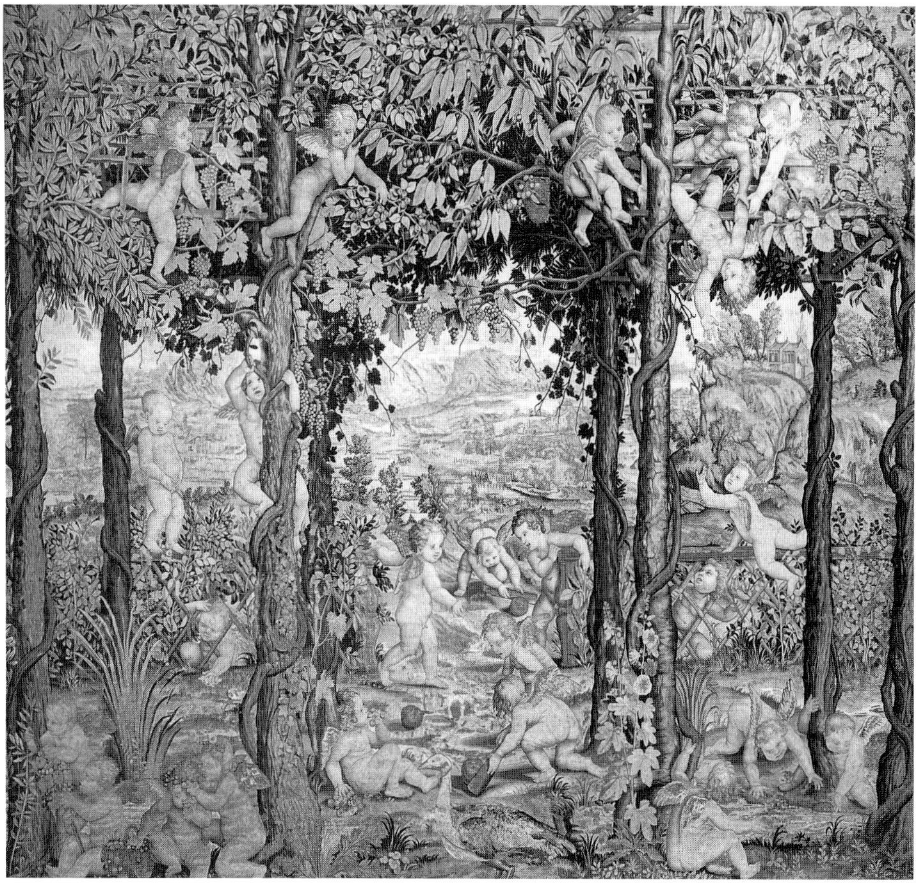

Fig. 74 *Puttini: The Ball Game,* Mantua, workshop of Nicolas Karcher, 1540–45. Lisbon, Gulbenkian Museum.

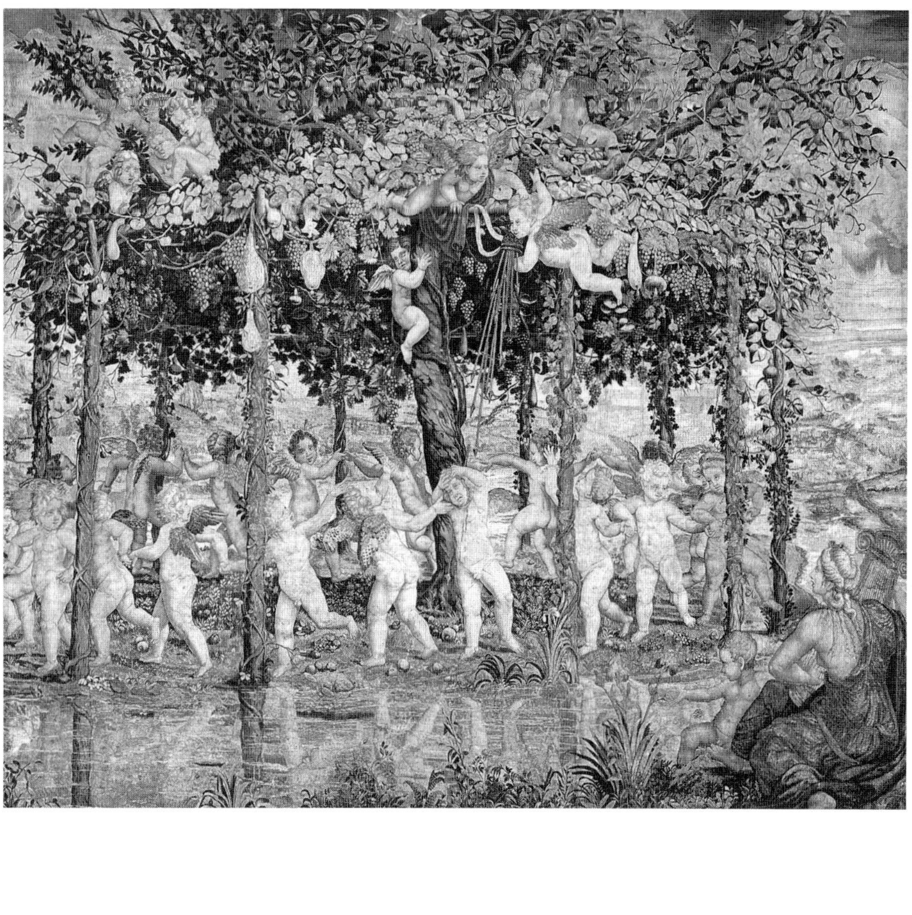

Fig. 75 *Puttini: The Dance,* Mantua, workshop of Nicolas Karcher, 1540–45. Lisbon, Gulbenkian Museum.

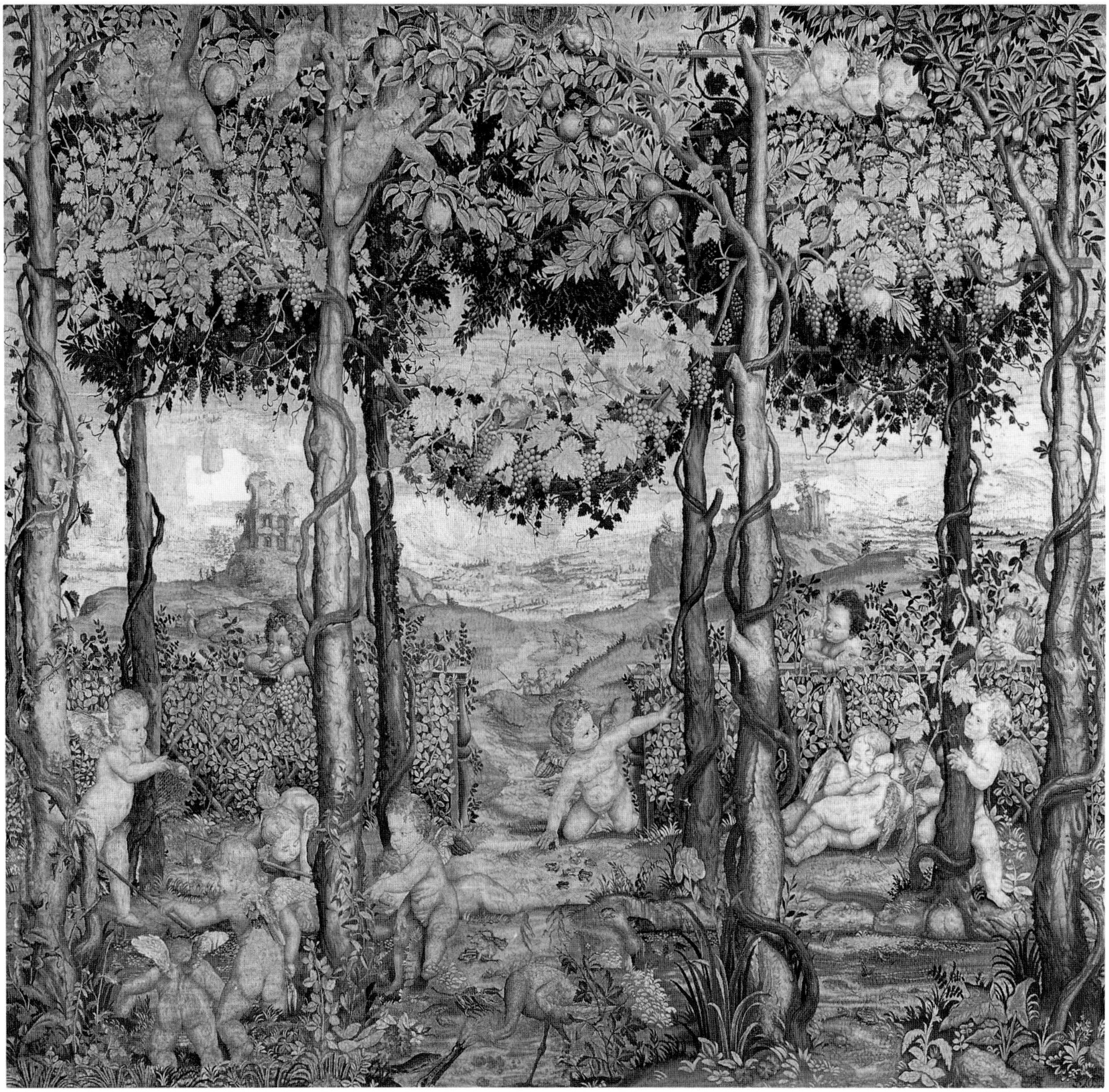

Fig. 76 *Puttini: The Fishermen,* workshop of Nicolas Karcher, 1540–45. Lisbon, Gulbenkian Museum.

420 cm), with an average production time being that of between 40 and 50 centimeters a month, forty to forty-two months (or three years and four to six months) were required. Even assuming that he was back in Ferrara between 1543 and 1544, Karcher could have finished the series before he left for Florence.

In view of the incomplete state of preservation of Ercole's *Puttini,* it is impossible to provide a detailed iconographic analysis.[13] Nonetheless, a great deal has been written about the meaning of these weavings. Forti Grazzini saw the set as the embodiment of the "aetas aurea" brought to Mantua by the Gonzaga clan, a time of peace and prosperity that began under Federico II and continued during the regency of Ercole and Ferrante.[14]

A chapter in Philostratos's *Imagines* served as the point of departure for these compositions. The Greek text was first translated into Italian toward 1511 for Isabella d'Este by Demetrius Moscus.[15] Philostratos's description of *Venus and the Playing Children* received its classical visualization with Titian's *Feast of Venus* (Madrid, Prado, 1518–19), a work done for the *camerino* of Alfonso d'Este.[16] Unlike Titian's painting, Ercole's *Puttini,* as well as the set subsequently woven for Ferrante, is not a literal translation of Philostratos's text, which seems to have been based on some now-lost variant devised by the likes of a Mario Equicola or a Battista Fiera.[17] Thus, for example, the Cupids are not gathering apples but rather pick grapes in a vineyard. The apples in the *Dance* tapestry are found in the trees supporting the vines, while cherries appear in the *Ball Player* and pomegranates in the *Fisherman.* A quiver with golden arrows hangs in the tree of the *Dance* as described by Philostratos, who says nothing about the boy injured by an arrow or about the boys fishing.[18] The most obvious change occurs in the choice of the picking of grapes rather than apples, a motif well known to Giulio, who used it in earlier works. Boys picking grapes are found on the twisted Salomonic columns in the cartoon for the Vatican *Healing of the Lame Man.*[19] The same motif occurs, but here as an allegory of Autumn, on the lateral border of the *Charge to Peter.*[20] Giulio inserted these columns in the *Donation* in the Sala di Costantino.[21] Furthermore, children playing in a vineyard appear several times in wall paintings by Giulio in the Palazzo Te, and thus it may be assumed that they were part of a common repertory of depictions of a "locus amoenus."[22]

In antiquity, vines inhabited by birds and children were an element of Dionysian symbolism. Subsequently taken over by the Church, the motif symbolized the vintage of the Lord.[23] This iconographic ambiguity may have fostered the use of this compositional type in a set that may originally have been ordered by Federico II for its pagan symbolism of the "aetas aurea" but that was adopted by Ercole, for whom the eucharistic symbolism of the vintage was clearly relevant. Ercole apparently ordered the *Puttini* for private use and it was in this sense that it was bequeathed to his nephew Guglielmo.[24] The original designation of Federico II's set remains to be determined. Might it have been intended for Margarita Paleologa's bedroom in the palazzino constructed beyond the Castello of the Palazzo Ducale? A drawing by Giulio showing a sketch for a bed canopy in the form of a vineyard suggests just such a use of the tapestries.[25]

With less than half of the ten tapestries extant, it is difficult to draw definitive conclusions regarding the iconography of the *Puttini.* Presumably, they were intended to be hung border to border, entirely covering the walls of a room, thus giving the spectator the illusion of sitting in the middle of a circular alley of trees with the flowing water of a river between them, a river that became a lake in the *Barque* or was interrupted by a specific motif, as in the *Dance.*

The *Barque* and the *Dance* deserve some additional comments. It has not previously been noted that the *Dance* is actually a visual paraphrase of Elysium as described by Virgil in his *Aeneid.* In the company of the Cumean Sibyl, Aeneas reached the field of eternal bliss where the souls were found to be dancing while Orpheus played on his lyre.[26] The *Dance* tapestry is clearly a variant on this theme, with the addition of the wounded *genius* as perhaps an allusion to the deceased Federico II. A near-contemporary Northern Italian precedent exists for this, namely, the bronze relief for the tomb of Girolamo and Marco Antonio della Torre (formerly in San Fermo Maggiore, Verona, and now in the Louvre), executed by Andrea Riccio between 1516 and 1521. In it the souls of the della Torre are inserted in the composition, which shows the blissful dancing to the accompaniment of Orpheus's lyre.[27]

The *Barque* is perhaps the most beautiful of the sur-

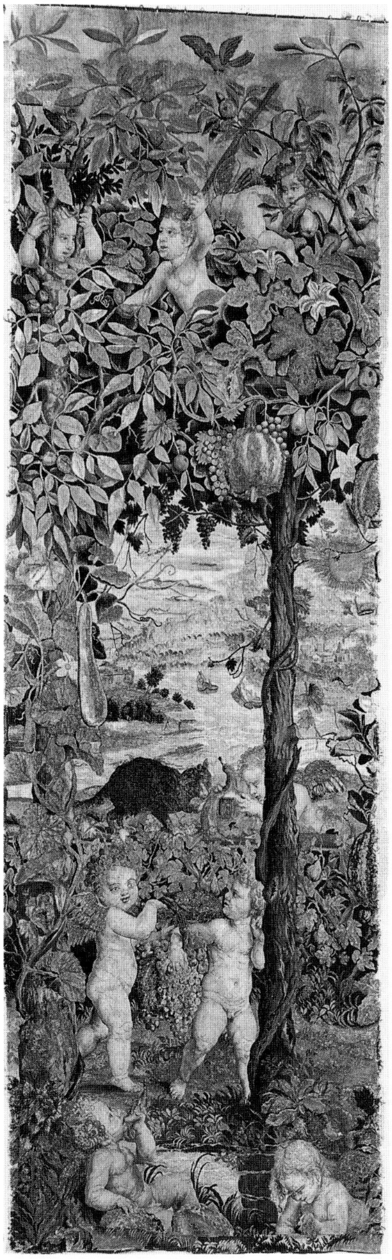

Fig. 77 *Puttini: The Cat,* fragment, workshop of Nicolas Karcher, 1540–45. Lisbon, Gulbenkian Museum.

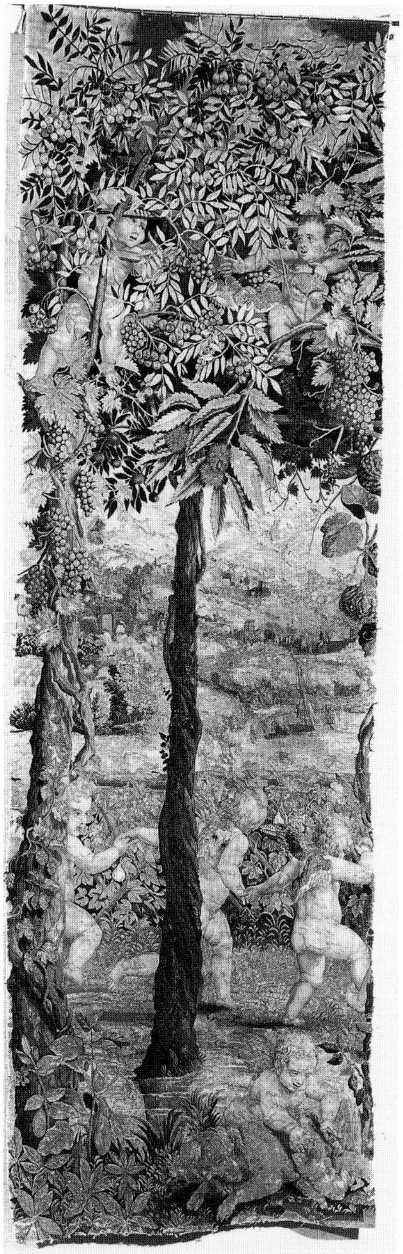

Fig. 78 *Puttini: The Dog,* fragment, workshop of Nicolas Karcher, 1540–45. Lisbon, Gulbenkian Museum.

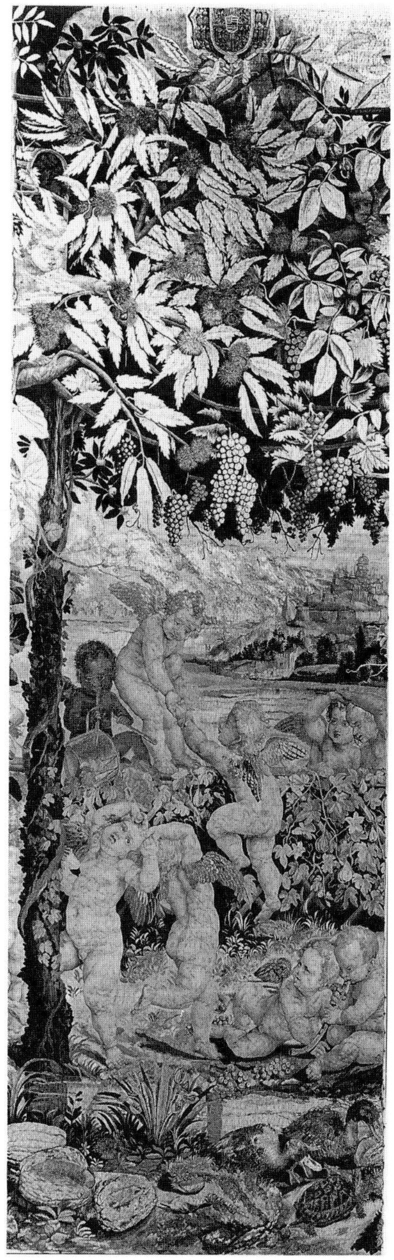

Fig. 79 *Puttini: The Dance(?),* fragment, workshop of Nicolas Karcher, 1540–45. Milan, Poldi Pezzoli Museum.

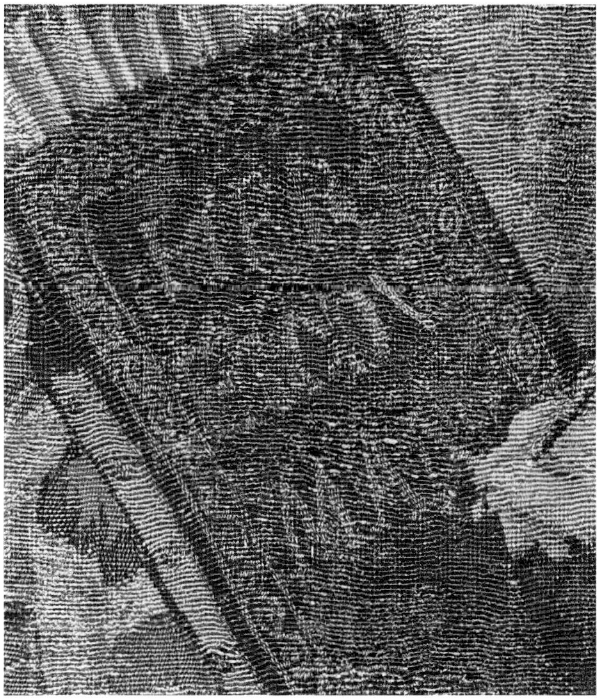

Fig. 80 *Cartellino* held by a *putto,* from *The Barque of Fortune* (Fig. 73).

viving sections of Ercole's *Puttini* (Fig. 73). Under a pergola in the water, the barque, under the guidance of a woman holding the rudder, is filled with winged *genii* who stroll and fish. Cranes engaged in searching for fish are located near the barque, while the *putto* seated on the shore in the foreground is engaged in writing Ercole's name and title on a *cartellino.* Commonly called the *Barque of Venus,* the tapestry should more correctly be interpreted as the *Barque of Fortune.*

On Federico II's *Puttini* panel, Venus was portrayed together with *genii* and a satyr. There is good reason, as was already noted, to see this as the first in a projected series of weavings based on the *Imagines* of Philostratos. If Ercole's tapestries were intended to complete this series, then it may be asked why Venus is twice repeated in the same set, although it should be noted that the *Barque of Venus* had already appeared in Flemish tapestries related to Raphael's workshop.

From the same workshop that produced the *Acts of the Apostles,* Leo X had ordered a set of *Grotesques* with Divinities from models provided by Giovanni da Udine. In Paul III's inventory of 1544, the tapestry with Venus is described as "uno panetto con la nave et trionfo de Venere."[28] Leo X's original edition is lost, but the design of his *Barque of Venus,* in which Venus is enthroned in a large ship filled with winged amorini and surrounded by *genii* riding on sea monsters, is known from a Brussels reedition of about 1570 and the Gobelins copy of 1684–95.[29]

In Ercole's tapestry, however, the female figure holds a rudder, the traditional attribute of Fortune. As such she appears in Giulio's drawing, now in Haarlem (Fig. 82), accompanied by the motto "Renovabitur ut Aquilae Ivventus" ["Youth will be renewed as the eagles": Psalm 103]. Clearly this refers to the gold era the Gonzaga clan promised to Mantua.[30] The Haarlem drawing and the related study in Chatsworth (Fig. 83), were clearly intended as models for tapestries in which the chariot of state, carried by Gonzaga eagles, is guided either by Fortune or by a winged *genius* similar to those found in Ercole's *Puttini.*

Considering their formal similarity to Ercole's *Puttini* tapestries, the Haarlem and Chatsworth drawings may have been models for the lost "portiere," although they could have served for the lost twelve *spalliere* (cited in the 1563 inventory, Document 49, no. 10) made in Flanders that represented "Fortuna condotta da quatro Aquile."[31] In any case, one can deduce from the Haarlem drawing that the woman holding a rudder in the *Barque* was intended to depict Venus as well as Fortune. Since late antiquity, Fortune had often been associated with the instability and dangers of the sea, and therefore her attribute became a rudder. The image of this marine

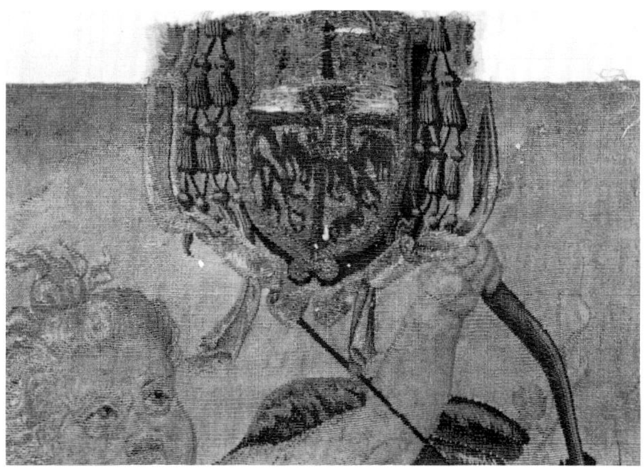

Fig. 81 Coat of arms of Cardinal Ercole from *The Barque of Fortune* (Fig. 73).

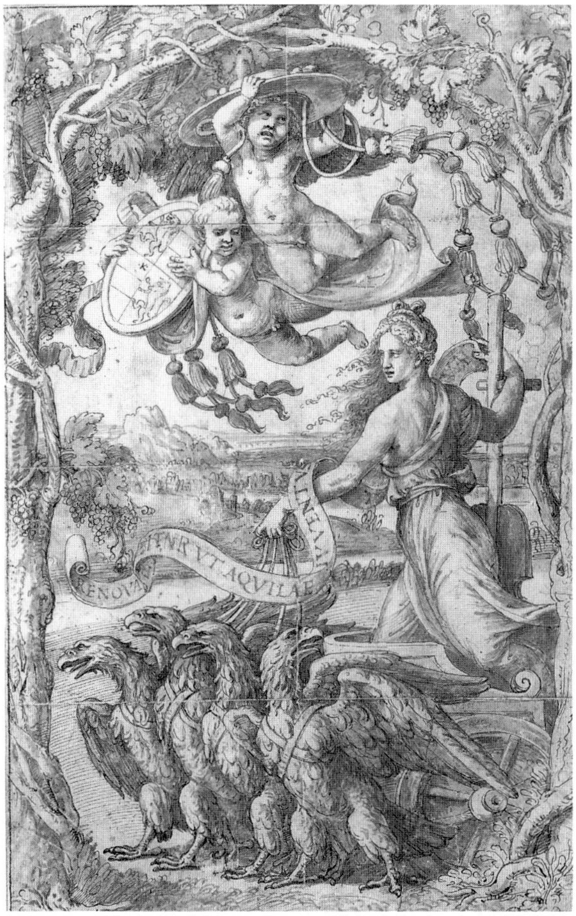

Fig. 82 Giulio Romano, *Fortune Leading the Chariot of State,* drawing, c. 1540. Haarlem, Teylers Museum.

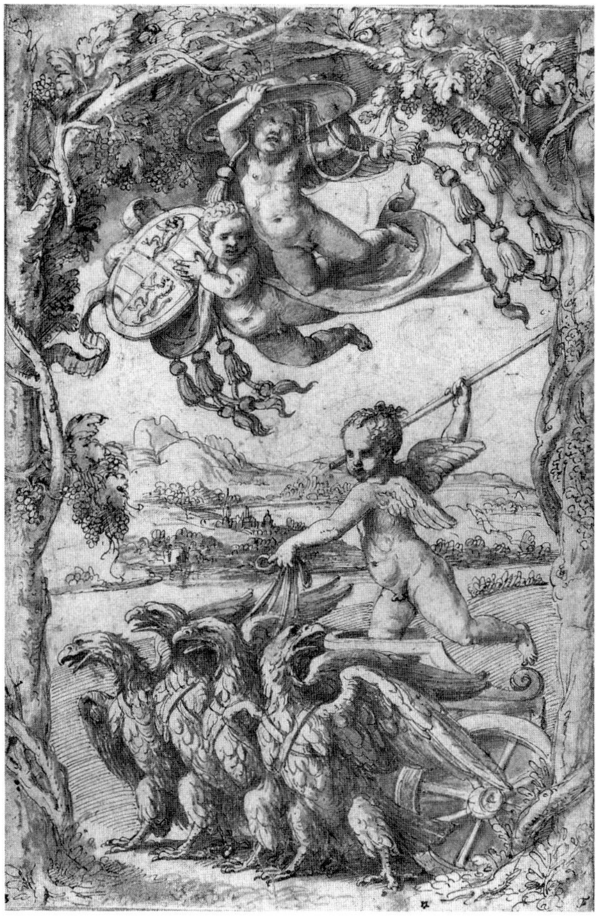

Fig. 83 Giulio Romano, *Putto Leading the Chariot of State,* drawing, c. 1540. Formerly Chatsworth, Devonshire Collection.

Fortune was used in the quattrocento, often with the goddess seen standing on a sphere or shell, holding a seal.[32] Moreover, in the quattrocento and beyond, Fortune was no longer considered to be a dangerous and fickle power but rather served as a model for man to direct his own fate, to steer the rudder of his own ship.[33]

If it is accepted that the woman holding the rudder in Ercole's tapestry is indeed Fortune, then other aspects of this weaving fall into place. The barque becomes a symbol of the Gonzaga state guided by Good Fortune and by Ercole himself, whose arms are woven about her pergola and whose name is written by the *genius* on the *cartellino* (Figs. 80–81). This last motif is to be associated with Fame and thus related to the well-known figure of Victory writing the name of a victorious commander on a shield as, for example, on the Column of Trajan or as on the border of Ferrante's *Fructus Belli*.[34] The formal aspect of this tapestry can indeed be associated with a famous model, one that also has cranes in the foreground: Raphael's *Miraculous Draught of Fishes*.[35] Might one also see in this parallel a reference to Ercole's ambitions for the papacy, especially when it is considered that he eventually acquired an early reedition of the *Acts of the Apostles?*[36] The *genii* here are a Christian motif, allegories of the Apostles, especially as the barque is set under the vine with its eucharistic connections. Such hypotheses can only be proved, however, when more is known about the genesis of these weavings.

NOTES

1. The Zeri tapestry contains only wool and silk, whereas the Lisbon and Milan pieces are woven with wool, silk, silver, and gold. The discussion of the *Puttini* is based on Delmarcel and Brown (1988, 109–21). It incorporates new data found in the catalogues of the Giulio Romano exhibitions in *Mantua 1989* and *Vienna 1989*. See also

Pecorari, 1991, 417ff.; Forti Grazzini, 1982, 76–79 and 161–87; Viale Ferrero, 1963, 21 and 54–55, and idem, 1984, 17–18.

2. Pecorari, 1991, 424 n. 67.

3. Hartt, 1958, I, 159 (no. 217), 302 (nos. 255–57), and II, figs. 354, 516; Wingfield Digby and Hefford, 1980, pl. 9; the best synthesis by Forti Grazzini is in *Mantua 1989*, 475–76, and also in *Vienna 1989*, 295, 296, 299.

4. Delmarcel and Brown, 1988, 111.

5. Forti Grazzini in *Mantua 1989*, 475, and Forti Grazzini, 1990, 10–11, for illustrations.

6. See Document 9 for the remark by Grossino on 14 November 1539 that the work had started on "li frisi"—meaning that the weavers had started the weaving on its lateral border, as was usual on a low-warp loom. A sample weaving was required of both Karcher and Jan Rost when they were working for Duke Cosimo I de' Medici in Florence (Adelson, 1983, 907–8).

7. With an average of 60 to 70 centimeters a month for such a tapestry containing no metal thread, four weavers on a loom with a minimum width of 410 cm (= height of tapestry) indeed needed six to seven months to weave a tapestry of 450 cm wide.

8. Despite Pecorari (1991, 418), this *Moses* weaving has nothing to do with the later *Moses* set (Catalogue 7). The seventeen Flemish square *ells* of the 1542 *Moses* tapestry represent a surface of 80.935 square centimeters, or an average tapestry of 287 by 287 cm square or 269 by 300 cm rectangle, which is far smaller than either any of the Milan *Moses* tapestries or of the Zeri *Puttini* (410 by 450 cm). The *Moses* tapestry cited in January 1542 as paid for and thus finished needed, if square, three weavers working for six months, each of them making some 45 centimeters weft per month for fine quality with gold and silver. Other pieces could thus have been woven by the twelve weavers of the Karcher's workshop during 1541.

9. Pecorari, 1991, 428, no. 2.

10. This conclusion derives from a close inspection of these tapestries during the Giulio Romano exhibition in Mantua in 1989 and a comparison with Giulio's *Scipio* tapestries, woven in the same period in Brussels (Madrid and Florence: Museo Stibbert).

11. These last ones, apparently slightly reduced in height and measuring actually 335 to 360 cm, correspond quite closely to the central field (without horizontal borders) of the Zeri tapestry, 345 cm high.

12. See Forti Grazzini (1982, 182, pls. 124–25), in which they are reproduced in the "right" order for this reconstitution.

13. It should be noted that the drawings, now in London at the British Museum, at the Victoria and Albert Museum, and in the Pouncey collection (see Wingfield Digby, 1980, pl. 95; *Mantua 1989*, 476; *Vienna 1990*, 296 and 299), are all focused on the play of children with swans and in presence of a stag. This theme is developed in the tapestry, with a border different from the Zeri piece, now in the Victoria and Albert Museum (Wingfield Digby and Hefford, 1980, pl. 94B), but not in the other remaining pieces of the Ercole set. See note 3 above.

14. *Mantua 1989*, 475. According to Forti Grazzini (in *Mantua 1989*, 477), an allusion to Federico's death may be found in the dancing child, injured by an arrow in the *Dance*.

15. See the transcription and comments by M. R. Fehl (in Marek, 1985, 124–33).

16. Delmarcel and Brown, 1988, 111 n. 10.

17. For the *Hymni Divini* (1515) of Fiera, see *London 1981*, 97, with further bibliography.

18. Philostratus the Elder, *Imagines*, Loeb edition, London, 1960, 20–29.

19. Shearman, 1972, Figs. 16 and 56–57, for this tapestry. The author is reluctant to accept Giulio's direct involvement in the painting of these cartoons (Shearman, 1972, 111, but mitigated on 114).

20. Shearman, 1972, Fig. 14. It is noteworthy that this border is connected to the *Healing of the Lame Man* in the Mantua reedition bought by Ercole himself.

21. Escher, 1909, 417.

22. Pagni was paid in 1532 "for painting putti in a room (. . .) with vine leaves on a blue ground" (Hartt, 1958, I, 159); children in vegetal scrolls are still visible in the Camera delle Imprese and in the Sala dei Cavalli (*Mantua 1989*, 202 and 237).

23. Ward-Perkins, 1952, 28.

24. Pecorari's statements (1991, 424 n. 67) are unsupported by any documents.

25. Thornton, 1991, 336–37.

26. Virgil, *Aeneid* VI.642–643: "Pars in gramineis exercent membra palaestris / contendunt ludo et fulua luctantur harena / pars pedibus plaudunt choreas et carmina dicunt / nec non Threicius longa cum ueste sacerdos / obloquitur numeris septem discrimina uocum / iamque eadem digitis, iam pectine pulsat eburneo."

27. Blume in *Frankfurt 1985*, 119 and 128 nn. 104–5.

28. Erkelens, 1962, 115–38. The inventory was cited by Darcel (1878, 1007).

29. Reproduced by Erkelens (1962, 125) and Viatte (in *Paris 1965*, 38 and 51, entry 28).

30. Martineau in *London 1981*, 204, no. 204; *Florence-Rome 1983–84*, 154–55, no. 66. For the rudder as an attribute of Fortune, see de Tervarent (1958, I, 203) and Cavallaro (1987, 158–59).

31. Forti Grazzini (*Mantua 1989*, 478–79) rejects the idea that these drawings were models for the "Spallere della Fortuna" (Delmarcel and Brown, 1988, 112), noting that their vertical size points toward door tapestries and not to *spalliere* (shoulder tapestries hung on the wall behind benches), which mostly are horizontal rectangles. According to the dimensions given in 1584 (Document 60), however, the *Fortuna* tapestries were vertical rectangles. their height was 4.25 *braccia*, or some 2.41/2.55 m, while the total width of the twelve pieces was 39 *braccia*, or 22 m, which, divided by 12, gives an average width of some 1.85/2.07 meters.

32. For literature, see Delmarcel and Brown (1988, 113 n. 21). The Renaissance "Fortuna velata" was recently analyzed by Pickering (1970, 219–20) and Verdier (1987, 52–54).

33. This by Alberti, Valla, Ficino, Pico della Mirandola, and especially Pontano, *De Fortuna libri tre* (Aldus Manuzio, 1518). See Cassirer, 1927, 81–92, and Warburg, 1932, 149–50.

34. See Catalogue 3 and Fig. 58.

35. See Fig. 30, also Delmarcel and Brown, 1988, 114.

36. See Catalogue 2.

5. Ferrante's *Puttini*

Trissino, Giannino Marzotto Collection
The City: 386 × 465 cm (Color Plate IV; Figs. 85, 96)
The Hare: 388 × 440 cm (Color Plate V; Figs. 84, 86, 95)
The Hobbyhorse: 387 × 415 cm (Color Plate VI; Fig. 87)
The He-Goat: 383 × 435 cm (Color Plate VII; Fig. 88)
The Winepress: 388 × 420 cm (Color Plate VIII; Fig. 89)
The Dance: 390 × 473 cm (Color Plate IX; Figs. 90, 93, 97)

Comparative Illustrations
Cupids at the Vintage, woodcut, Florence, 1460–70 (Fig. 91)
Cupids at the Vintage, woodcut from Colonna's *Hypnerotomachia Poliphili,* 1499 (Fig. 92)
Villa Gualtiera, engraving by Marc'Antonio dal Rè, 1726 (Fig. 94)

Ercole's *Puttini* tapestries were the source of inspiration for the set ordered in Brussels between 1552 and 1557 by Ferrante.[1] The "tappezzeria delle Puttini" are the only ones recorded in the 1590 inventory that contain gold and silver threads. The set is described as being in six pieces, each panel measuring five *ale* in height (Document 65, no. 13). Ferrante's *Puttini* was pledged in 1567 by Cesare Gonzaga to Venetian bankers (Document 53). They were placed for sale in 1579 by his son Ferrante II (Document 58), at which time Guglielmo Gonzaga and the ambassador of the Medici in Venice expressed interest in them. The Medici ambassador described the set as "lavorati a figure de putti ignudi che fanno giuoco intorno a viti." Ferrante II had a change of heart after the pieces were loaned back to him on the occasion of his marriage in 1587 (Document 61).

As noted in the Index to the Major Sets of Figurative Tapestries, the set was described as a "baccanali di Puttini che distaca uva e che scherza tra loro, indica l'Autunno" when it was owned by the Sagredo family (Document 77). It passed through a variety of hands before ending up in the Marzotto collection in Trissino, by which time its provenance had been forgotten. The key to determining the original owner of the set is provided in the correspondence between Cardinal Granvelle and his agents in the Netherlands in the years 1571 to 1574 (Document 55). During his stay in the Spanish Netherlands (1561–64), Granvelle became a passionate collector of tapestries (Document 46). After his exile in Madrid and his later nomination as viceroy of Naples in 1571, he started collecting again. The letters of his agents Viron and Morillon reveal that several lavish sets were ordered for the cardinal from Willem de Pannemaker, supplier to Charles V and other members of the imperial family.[2] On 16 February 1571, Viron informs Granvelle that Pannemaker did not have the cartoons of the "tapisserie des Vignes" (Document 55). Some days later, on 24 February, Viron mentions that Pannemaker found a fragment of the design for the border of the "tapisserie du Vignoble de don Fernand de Gonzaga."[3] The following year (June 1572) Viron traced the cartoons, which are described as "de la Vigne et des Petiz Enfants," to Ferrante Gonzaga's heirs. In 1573 Cesare Gonzaga agreed either to loan or to sell the cartoons in exchange for a payment of 400 or 500 *écus.* The reedition of the six pieces was virtually complete in July 1575, when five weavings were ready to be shipped to the cardinal.

Philip II acquired several tapestry sets from Granvelle's heirs and four of the "tapisseries de la Vigne et des Petiz Enfants" are still preserved in the Spanish royal collection.[4] These weavings are identical in all details with the Marzotto set and they also contain the marks of both Brussels and Willem de Pannemaker. Four of the Marzotto pieces were recorded in 1934 in the Donà dalle Rose collection in Venice.[5] The correspondence of Viron proves that Granvelle's set was copied from the cartoons ordered by Ferrante Gonzaga, and as

Ferrante's *Puttini* comprised six tapestries of gold and silver, which can be traced from 1561 to 1763 in the Gonzaga collections and afterward in other Northern Italian families (Documents 44 and 77), it is certain that the six *Puttini,* formerly in the Donà dalle Rose collection and now in Trissino, are identical to the set ordered by Ferrante Gonzaga. Moreover, the dimensions of the tapestries correspond to those cited in the documents.[6]

Granvelle's involvement with Willem de Pannemaker for the reedition of Ferrante's *Puttini,* and the presence of Pannemaker's weaver's mark on both his and the Marzotto sets (Fig. 84), leads to the conclusion that Pannemaker executed the original series for Ferrante Gonzaga. Another document very likely can be connected to the genesis of Ferrante's *Puttini,* namely, a letter sent by the painter Battista Lodi to Ferrante from Lier (near Antwerp) on 5 February 1552 (Document 32). In order to proceed with the commission, which had to be executed immediately ("da farse subito"), Lodi and a certain "Nicolas" contacted a Brussels weaver who employed many skilled workmen, who possessed silks of all colors, and who was in the process of weaving the *Siege of Tunis* for Charles V. This person is undoubtedly Willem de Pannemaker, who translated Vermeyen's cartoons of the *Siege of Tunis* into tapestries from 1548 onward, until April 1554.[7] He agreed to execute the "opera," according to the sketches or cartoons (already made?) for 14 guilders an *ell,* with gold and the finest silk, or for 8 guilders if the customer provided the gold. The object of these negotiations with the "miglior mastro che ivi si trove" was surely Ferrante's lavish *Puttini* set, as this is the only one with gold and silver threads recorded in the 1590 inventory.

Nothing more is known about the genesis of this set, and none of the preparatory drawings or cartoons has been preserved. The artist who designed the sketches and cartoons is unknown, as is the name or names of those responsible for the program. Starting with the cartoons, one immediately remarks that the similarity of Ferrante's *Puttini* with those of Ercole is limited to several formal aspects. Both sets present pergolas with vines, where naked children are playing and harvesting, and in both series Philostratos's *Imagines* was used as a general frame of reference for an antique source. Ercole's tapestries, woven in Mantua, clearly allude to the golden age brought by

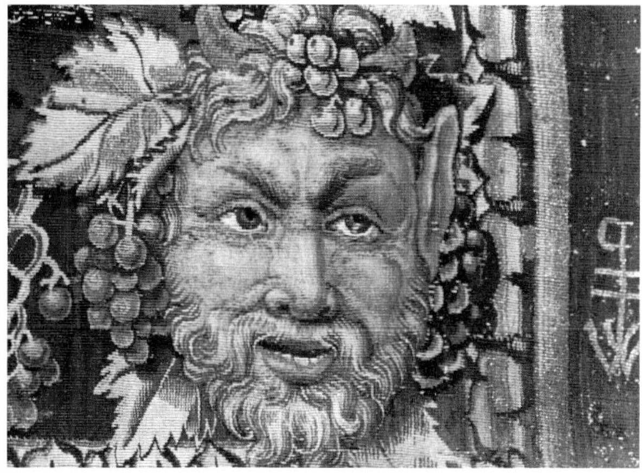

Fig. 84 Detail of the border with monogram of the weaver from *The Hare* (Fig. 86).

the Gonzaga to Mantua and to Ercole's good fortune as a regent of the duchy. The emphasis in Ferrante's *Puttini* is on the harvest of the grapes and the making of wine, and they belong to a more Dionysian genre.

The composition in each tapestry of the Ferrante series is divided in three parts by oak trees, disposed according to an axial symmetry and mutually linked by vine tendrils wound around their stems and branches and loaded with bunches of ripe grapes. These vineyards in pergolas are filled with naked boys who are playing and picking the grapes. Although no document lists or mentions the tapestries according to a specific order, the ideal sequence can more or less be deduced from the main activities of the figures and from the formal aspect of each weaving.

Four tapestries are dedicated to the harvest of the grapes, the fifth presents the pressing of the grapes, and the sixth and last one shows the dance after the work is completed. A formal progress for the reading is suggested by the increasing number of oak trees, namely, four in three weavings of the first group, six in a further one, then eight, and finally a whole alley. What follows appears to be the most logical sequence:[8]

1. *The City* (Fig. 85): In contrast to the other weavings, the background contains architectural decor, showing a street with palaces and a campanile, all in Italian Renaissance style. The boys in the foreground play leapfrog and ride on each others' backs, while others handle the picked grapes.

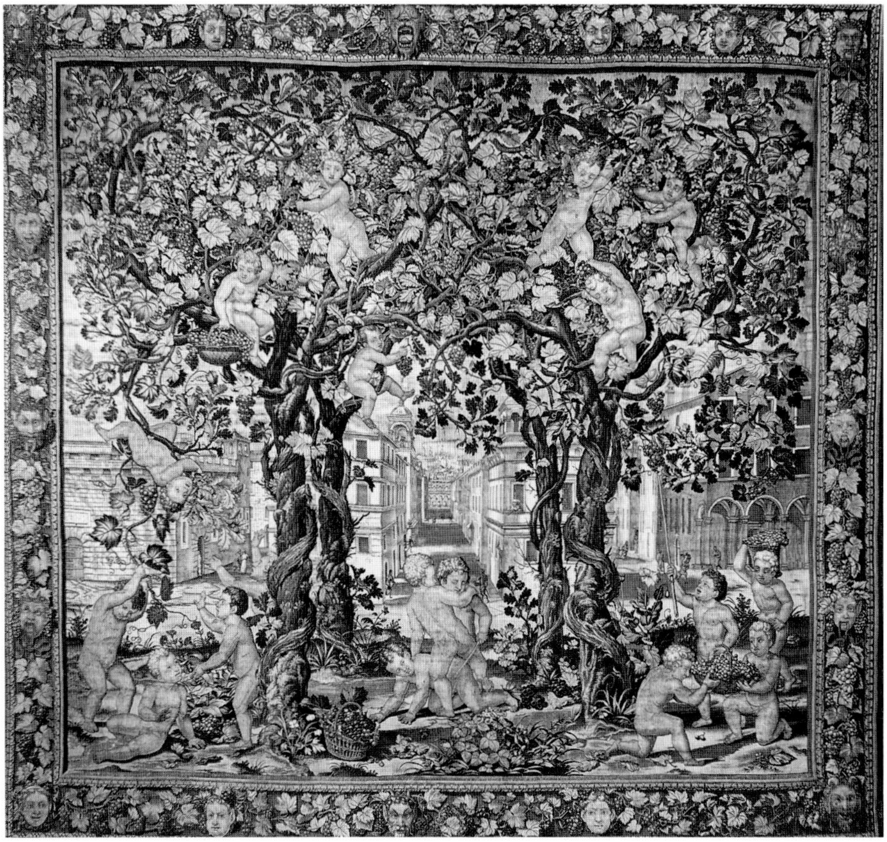

Fig. 85 *Puttini: The City,* Brussels, workshop of Willem de Pannemaker, 1552–57. Trissino, Marzotto.

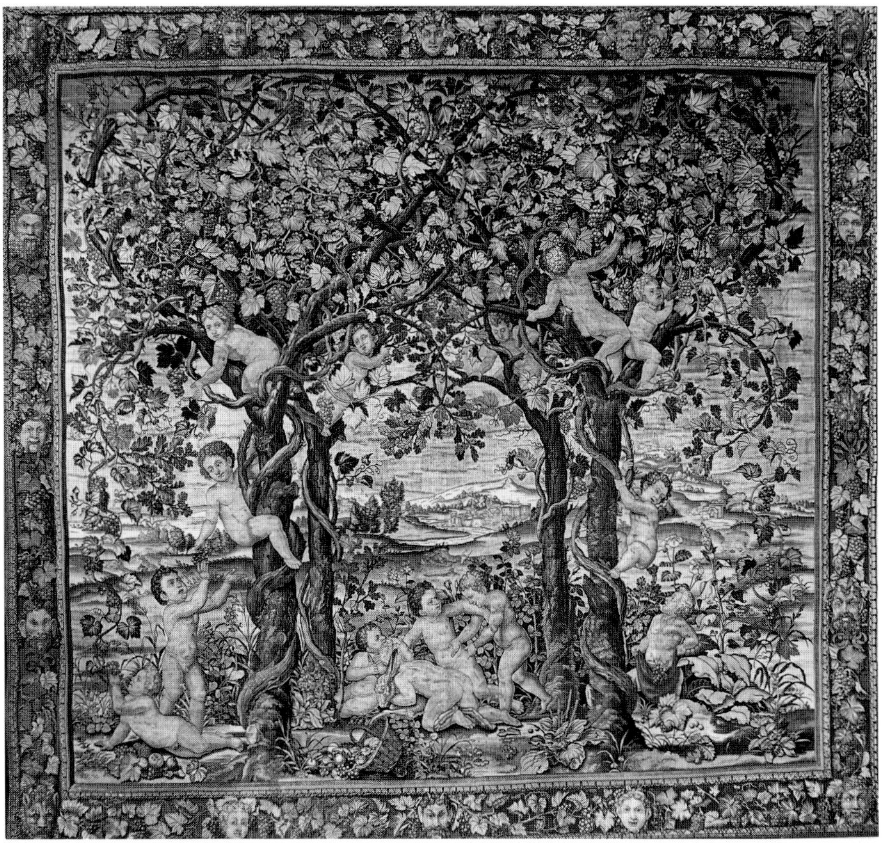

Fig. 86 *Puttini: The Hare,* Brussels, workshop of Willem de Pannemaker, 1552–57. Trissino, Marzotto.

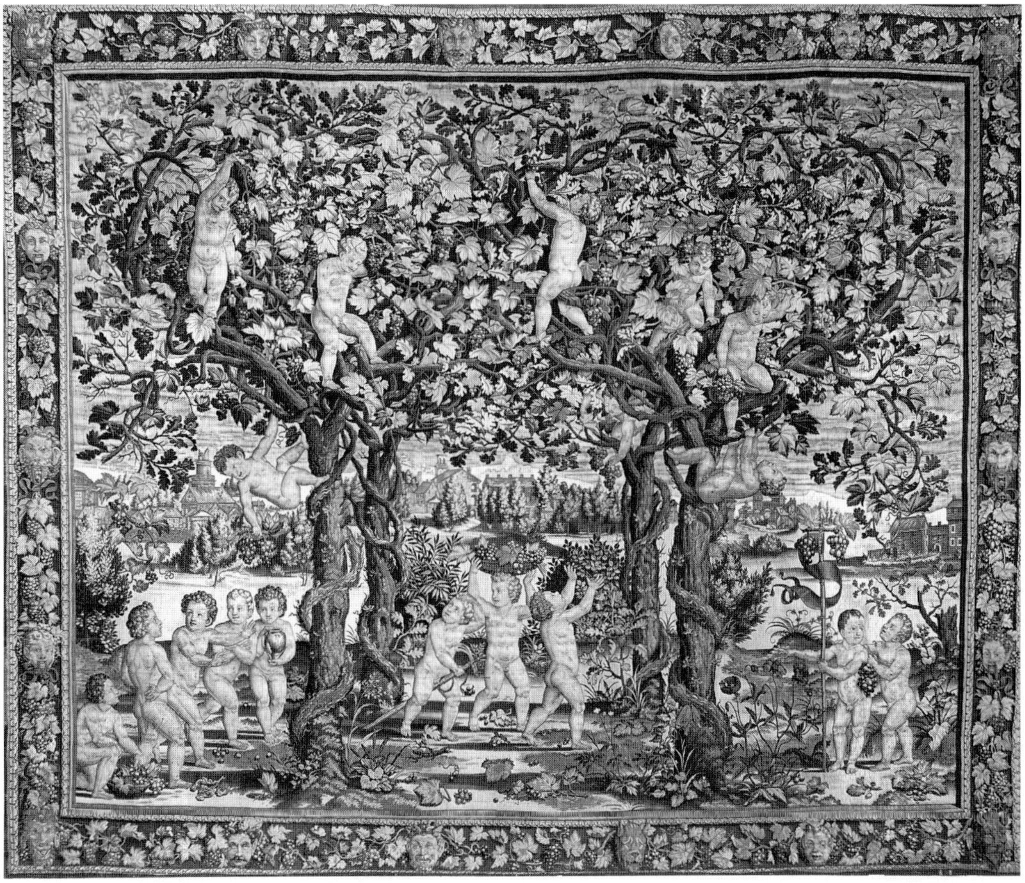

Fig. 87 *Puttini: The Hobbyhorse,* Brussels, workshop of Willem de Pannemaker, 1552–57. Trissino, Marzotto.

2. *The Hare* (Fig. 86). Four boys fight over the animal in the foreground, while the others harvest the grapes.
3. *The Hobbyhorse* (Fig. 87): A boy rides on a hobbyhorse next to others, while two boys on the left apparently discuss a vase, and one on the right holds a crossed banner.
4. *The He-Goat* (Fig. 88): Several children lead a he-goat in the foreground of this tapestry, also dedicated to the wine harvest.
5. *The Winepress* (Fig. 89): The young harvesters bring the grapes to the winepress, carrying them in baskets or on golden plates.
6. *The Dance* (Fig. 90): While some boys are still picking grapes in the treetops or while some rest, others dance under the pergola and some wrestle or carry away a tired (or injured) companion.

The Dionysian sense of the series also carries over to the borders. Between an inner frieze of acanthus leaves and on a golden background, the border is filled with vine tendrils and grapes, interrupted by heads of lions and satyrs (Fig. 84).

In Ercole's set, the emphasis of Philostratos's *ekphrasis* had shifted from a general paradisiac representation toward a symbolism of the vineyard, both in a Dionysian and Christian sense.[9] This shift is even more pronounced in Ferrante's set, in which the grape harvest and the wine pressing became the major theme.[10] The identification of the series as an allegory of autumn, as mentioned in the Sagredo inventory of 1762 (Document 77) is therefore on the mark. Ferrante seems, however, to have ordered a series that symbolizes more than just one season. He apparently wanted above all a representation of peaceful life, by a kind of paradise where eternal youth

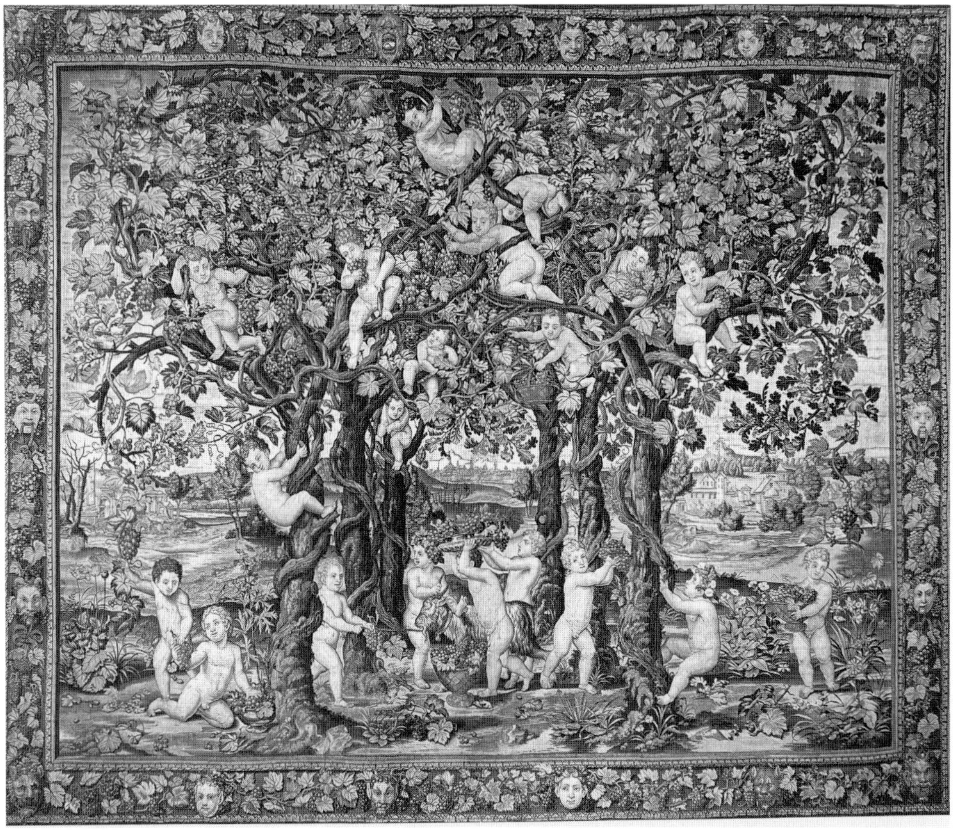

Fig. 88 *Puttini: The He-Goat,* Brussels, workshop of Willem de Pannemaker, 1552–57. Trissino, Marzotto.

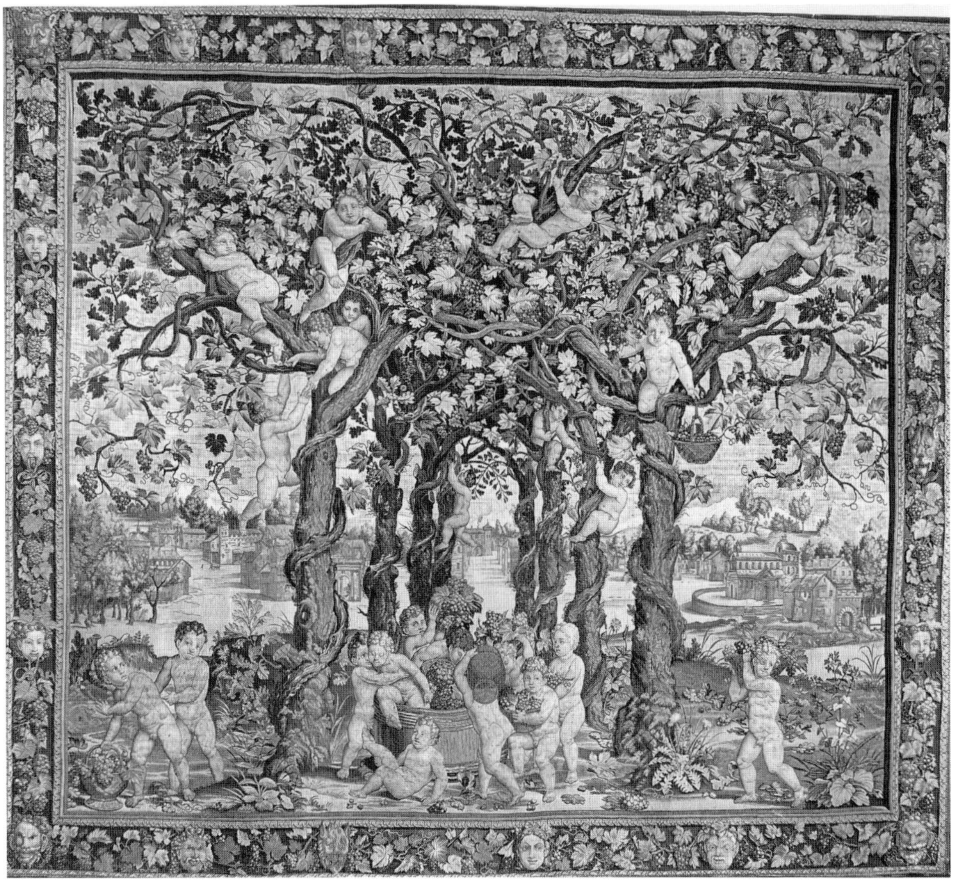

Fig. 89 *Puttini: The Winepress,* Brussels, workshop of Willem de Pannemaker, 1552–57. Trissino, Marzotto.

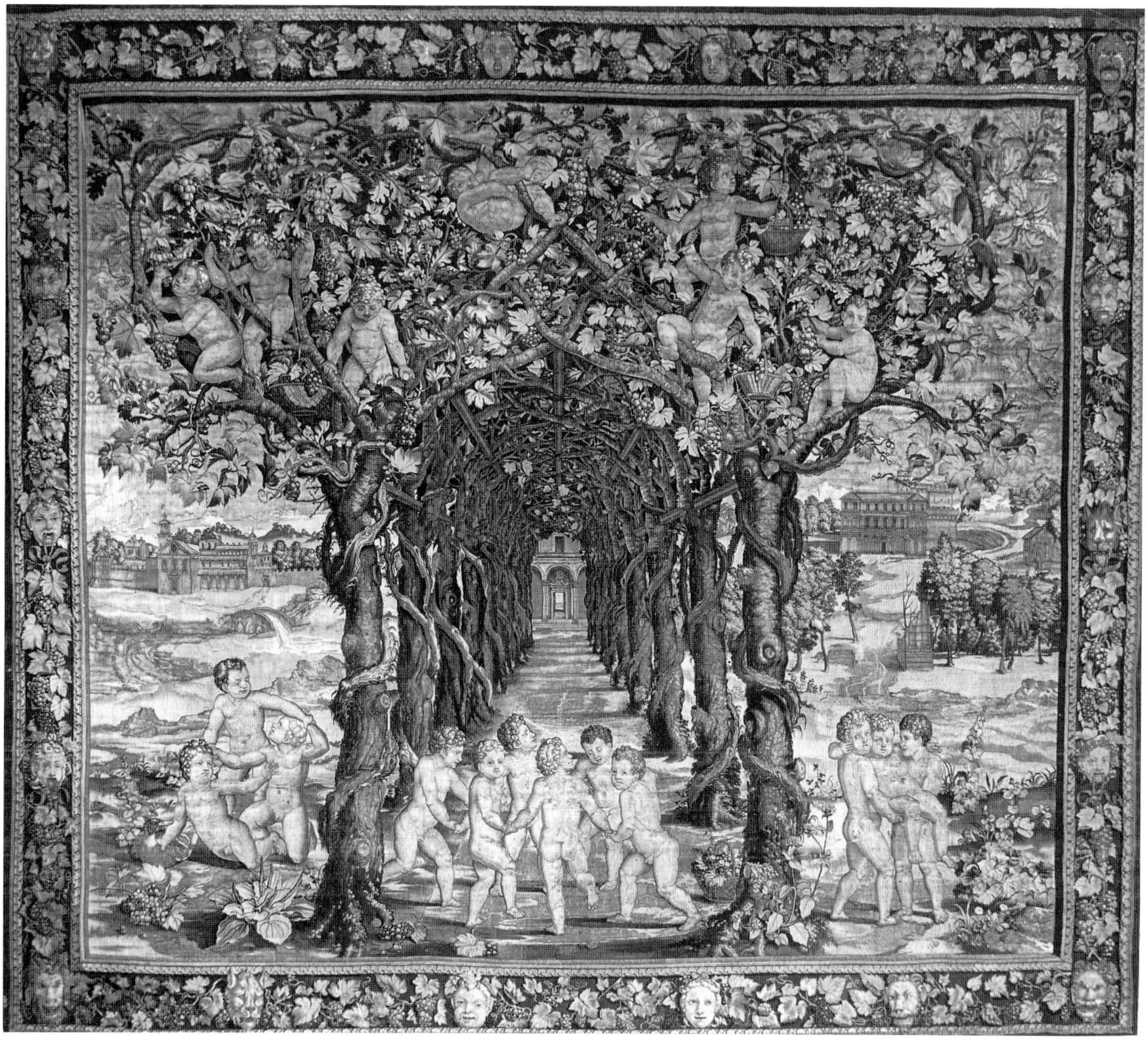

Fig. 90 *Puttini: The Dance,* Brussels, workshop of Willem de Pannemaker, 1552–57. Trissino, Marzotto.

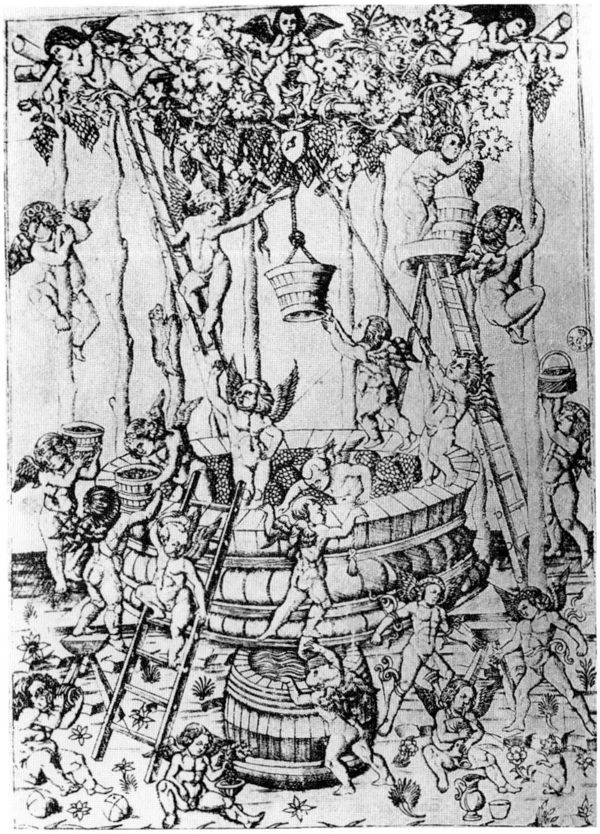

Fig. 91 *Cupids at the Vintage,* woodcut. Florence, 1460–70.

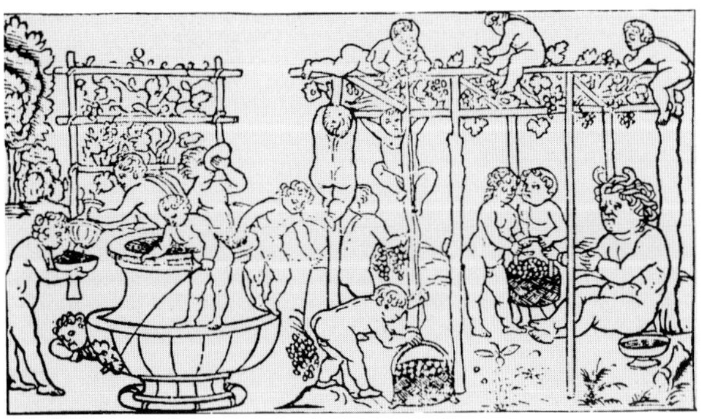

Fig. 92 *Cupids at the Vintage,* woodcut from Colonna's *Hypnerotomachia Poliphili,* 1499.

enjoys wine and play. In one of the panels the vines in the oak trees are located in front of an ideal city of the Renaissance, but otherwise in hilly landscapes. This evokes the "locus amoenus," the valley of *Tempe* as described by Aelian and Pliny.[11] The theme of *genii* working and reveling in the vineyard was well known in late *quattrocento* woodcuts (Figs. 91–92) of Northern Italy, which apparently were inspired by late antique reliefs and sarcophagi.[12] Such representations are connected with Roman funerary symbolism, in which wine was considered as having properties that could grant immortality.[13] A typical example of the former is found in Francesco Colonna's famous *Hypnerotomachia Poliphili* (Venice, 1499), in which a Bacchus-like figure presides over the wine harvest (Fig. 92). It illustrated the following description:

> Upon the other Anaglyph, I did behold a merrie and pleasant maiesticall personage, like a young fat boye, crowned with two folding serpents, one white and the other blacke, tied into a knot. Hee rested delightfullie vnder a plentifull vine tree full of grapes, and vpon the top of the frame there were little naked boies, climing up and sitting aloft gathering the ripe clusters: others offering them in a basket to the God, who pleasantly receiued them: other some lay fast a sleepe vpon the ground, being drunke with the sweet iuice of the grape. Others applying themselues to the worke of mustulent autumne: others singing and piping."[14]

As a personification of Youth and Peace, this set counterbalances Ferrante's *Fructus Belli,* which is an allegory of war. He may have wanted such a set after settling down in Milan in 1546 after his long, almost nomadic life on the battlefield. A personal association with Ferrante appears on the right part of *The Dance,* which is probably the last tapestry of the sequence. The lavish building in the background offers many similarities with Ferrante's Milanese residence (Figs. 93–94), the Villa Gualtiera (also called the Villa Simonetta), which was rebuilt and enlarged by Domenico Giunti from 1546 onward, the original design of which is recorded in later prints.[15]

This *Vineyard with Playing Children* was probably considered by Ferrante as a work of art for very personal and private use. This can be deduced not only from the absence of the Gonzaga coats of arms, so usual on other tapestry sets ordered by Ferrante and Ercole. In this regard it is also important to recall that the cartoons did not remain the property of the weaver but were handed over to the customer and remained in the family until Granvelle got them back for his reedition in 1573.

Ferrante ordered and paid for the cartoons and the preparatory sketches, which he obtained from an artist whose identity still remains unknown. As Giulio Romano, the designer of Ercole's *Puttini* tapestries, died in 1546, one can hardly believe that Battista Lodi still brought some of Giulio's unedited sketches to Willem de Pannemaker in 1552. Moreover, the style of these woven compositions, although from an unmistakable Italian origin, is not that of Giulio. This can be judged from the weavings, which were executed from cartoons painted in Brussels, and thus not made in Italy under direct supervision of an Italian artist, as had been the case for Ercole's *Puttini*. The anatomy of the young boys (Fig. 95) as well as the rendering of the flora clearly point to northern artists, while the Italian buildings presuppose an Italian inventor, presumably "Battista Lodi pittore," who apparently negotiated the weaving of this set with Pannemaker in 1552.[16] He can be identified as Giovanni Battista Lodi da Cremona, the same artist who was involved in the estimates of Ferrante's *Fructus Belli* tapestries, according to Baudouyn's letter of August 1547 (Document 19).[17] Unfortunately, no drawings or paintings are attributable to Lodi, but at the very least he must have supervised the translation of the Italian sketches into life-size cartoons by the specialized painters connected with Pannemaker's workshop.

If the creator of the sketches did not belong to the Mantuan *bottega* of Giulio Romano, he may have been active in Milan, where Ferrante resided from 1546 to 1554. Specialized painters were indeed at work on Ferrante's Milanese residence in 1547, when they are mentioned in relation to some "ispalliere" or dorsal tapestries (Document 18). A Milanese influence may be noted in the very dense design of the vine pergola (Figs. 96–97) and its trees with interwoven branches. They recall the Sala delle Asse in the Castello Sforzesco, painted by Leonardo between 1495 and 1498. Although the main theme of this room was a funerary evocation of Beatrice d'Este, the subsidiary motive of the Valley of Tempe has not been excluded.[18]

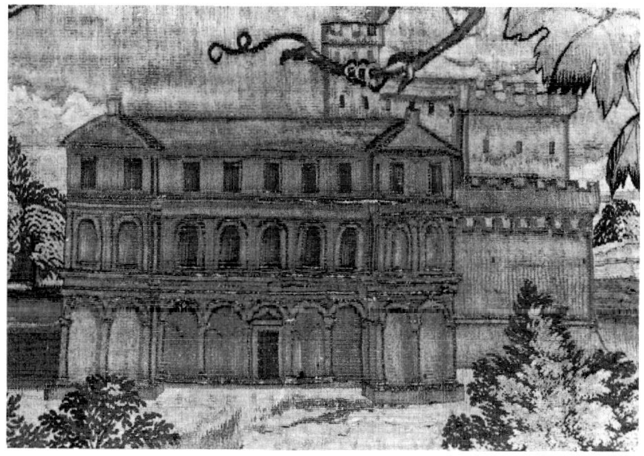

Fig. 93 Detail of the palace from *The Dance* (Fig. 90).

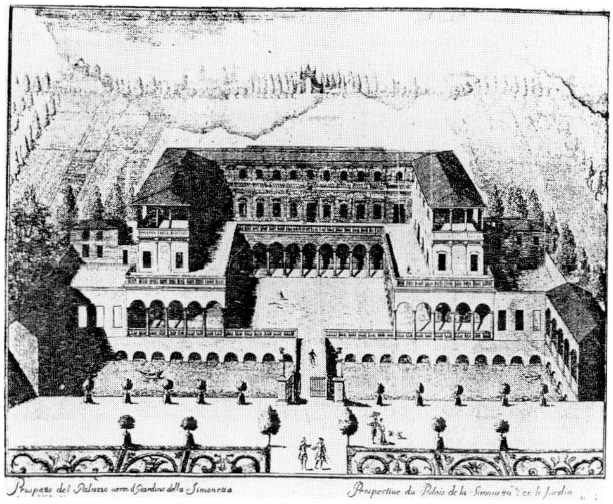

Fig. 94 Villa Gualtiera (also called Simonetta), *Prospetto del Palazo verso il Giardino della Simonetta,* engraving by Marc'Antonio dal Rè, 1726.

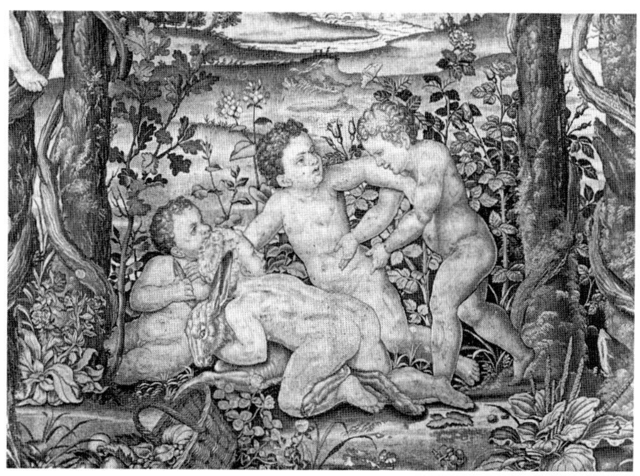

Fig. 95 Detail of the boys catching the hare from *The Hare* (Fig. 86).

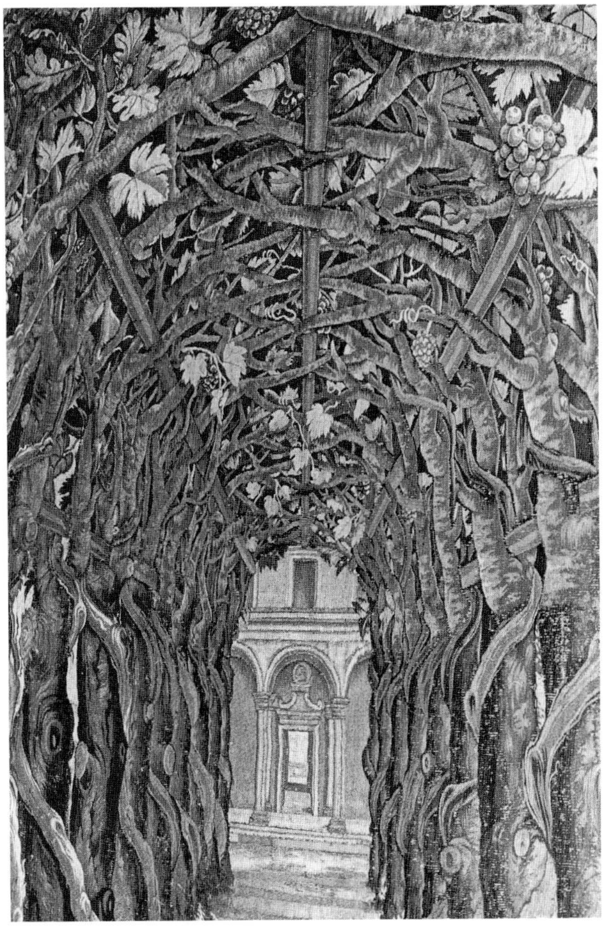

Fig. 96 Detail from the background of *The Dance* (Fig. 90).

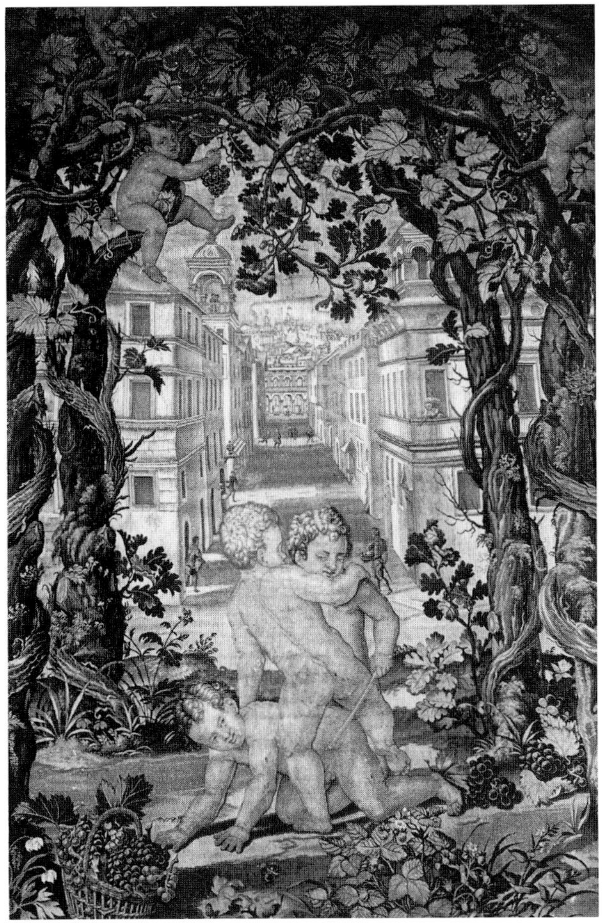

Fig. 97 Detail of the central section of *The City* (Fig. 85).

The several suggestions provided here regarding the iconography and style remain incomplete and hypothetical. The exceptional tapestry series therefore has not yet lost all its mysteries and this serves to enhance the charm of this textile environment, one of the most refined ever produced in the heyday of the most famous Brussels workshop, that of Willem de Pannemaker.

NOTES

1. The actual height varies from 383 to 390 cm, the widths from 415 to 473 cm (Delmarcel and Brown, 1988, 115–21).

2. For Granvelle and tapestry, see the basic study of Piquard, 1950, from which come the documents in Document 55. From Piquard's research it is known that Granvelle ordered three sets of *Garden Scenes* with galleries (one of which now in Vienna), an armorial set, a single tapestry of the *Siege of Tunis* (now in the town hall of Mechelen), and a copy of Ferrante's *Puttini*. Granvelle also tried, unsuccessfully, to obtain the cartoons for a reedition of the *Acts of the Apostles*.

3. Granvelle and Ferrante Gonzaga were closely connected in various political decisions (Van Durme, 1953, 30, 34, 108, 113, 240, and passim).

4. Junquera, 1986, I, 236–40, series 33, with the mark of W. de Pannemaker. In the 1598 inventory of Philip II, the set is described as comprising six pieces "de unas parras con unas figuras de unos niños desnudos," and the next mentioned set is "de unas galerias de jardines (. . .) que son los que por el mes de septiembre del año de 1587 se compraron de la almoneda del Cardinal Granvela" (Madrid, Archivo del Palacio Real, leg. 919, fol. 107). From the four actual pieces, two illustrate the same theme, the Hobbyhorse: it is probable, therefore, that one cartoon was lost when Viron got them from Cesare Gonzaga in 1573. This may also explain why a first shipment included only five tapestries, a second copy of the *Hobbyhorse* apparently having been sent later.

5. Lorenzetti and Planiscig, 1934, 69–70, nos. 341–42; Crick-Kuntziger in *Brussels 1935*, 83, no. 648.

6. According to the 1678 inventory (Document 71, no. 2), the set measured 5¾ "ale di Guastalla" in height, which is equivalent to 392 cm. The actual height varies from 383 to 390 cm and the width from 415 to 473 cm. The total width of 39⅙ *braccia*, or 26.68 meters, an average width of 4.44 meters, which corresponds to the dimensions of the Marzotto *Puttini*.

7. Junquera, 1986, I, 73, series 13. Horn, 1989, especially 125–28.

8. This proposal is by no means restrictive. Even in the first group (nos. 1–4), tapestries may be exchanged from location. The main subdivision, however remains: that is, four pieces with harvesting boys (nos. 1–4), one with the winepress (no. 5), and one with the dance after the work is completed (no. 6). On nos. 5 and 6, the boys in the trellis seem to rest, having (almost) finished the harvest.

9. See Catalogue 4.

10. Some elements of Philostratos's tale, however, seem to have survived, e.g., the hare and the wrestling and the dancing children.

11. Hoffmann, 1972, 56.

12. Hind, 1938, I–I, 68–69 and 258: A.II.13–15 and E.III.18, and I–II, pls. 98–110 and 410. Also Mesenzeva, 1983, 192–93. For the Roman sculpture, see Matz, 1969, III, 327, no. 178.

13. Schoutheete de Tervarent, 1956, 127–28.

14. Schoutheete de Tervarent, 1956, Fig. 16, from Colonna, 1976. For the description according to the English translation (probably by Sir Robert Dallington), in the edition printed for S. Waterson, London, 1592, see Colonna, 1976, 90r–v.

15. For the Marc'Antonio dal Rè engraving, see Castellano, 1984, 89, Fig. 93. If this tapestry indeed has to be "read" at the end of the set, it enhances the value of this representation of the patron's residence, as it is then located at the terminus of the sequence.

16. For example, the design and the *chiaroscuro* of the oak leaves, as well as several types of trees, appear in almost identical forms on the contemporaneous Brussels set of the *Genesis,* delivered to Cosimo de' Medici in Florence in 1551 (D'Hulst, 1960, 231–38; Adelson, 1983, 915; Meoni, 1989, passim).

17. See Catalogue 3, notes 49 and 50, for additional bibliography on Lodi.

18. Hoffmann, 1972, 51–62; Agghazy, 1978, 55–62; Moffitt, 1991–92, 76–90.

6. Ferrante's *Life of Moses*

Châteaudun Castle, Caisse des Monuments Historiques
Moses and the Burning Bush: 350 × 395 cm (Fig. 98)
Moses and Aaron before Pharaoh: 360 × 320 cm (Figs. 99, 112)
The Israelites Hand Over Their Silver Treasures to Moses: 350 × 340 cm (Color Plate X; Fig. 100)
The Passage through the Red Sea: 350 × 530 cm (Fig. 101)
The Israelites Praise the Lord: 350 × 465 cm (Fig. 102)
The Gathering of the Manna: 360 × 570 cm (Color Plate XI; Fig. 103)
Moses Striking the Rock: 350 × 470 cm (Fig. 104)
The Adoration of the Golden Calf: 350 × 465 cm (Fig. 105)
Moses Receiving the Tablets of the Law at Sinai: 350 × 405 cm (Fig. 106, 113)
The Raising of the Brazen Serpent: 350 × 450 cm (Fig. 107)
The Israelites Killing the Five Madianite Kings: 350 × 525 cm (Fig. 108)
The Abduction of the Madianite Women and Children: 350 × 400 cm (Figs. 109, 110, 114)

Comparative Illustration
The Abduction of the Sabine Women, Brussels, c. 1535–45 (Fig. 111)

This set, "sì per la bontà come per essere paramento raro" (Document 71, no. 5), was estimated in the 1678 inventory at 45,000 scudi (275,000 lire in Mantuan currency). It was second only to the *Fructus Belli,* which was assigned a value of 75,000 scudi (45,000 lire in Mantuan currency). In fact the *Moses* was actually the more valuable of the two for, in terms of the *braccio quadrato,* the *Moses* was worth 106.99 scudi per *braccio,* while the *Fructus Belli* was worth only 104.16 scudi.

Measuring 5 1/3 *braccia* in height, and with a total width of 79 1/4 *braccia,* the *Moses* weavings were first recorded in the 1590 Guastalla inventory. In all probability, however, the series came from the estate of Ferrante. The Guastalla *Moses* is last documented in 1749 (Document 76, nos. 1–2). The subsequent history of the weavings is difficult to trace, but they are probably to be identified with the ten panels said to come from the Episcopal palace in Genova,[1] purchased in 1955 for Châteaudun by the French government, which subsequently added the missing two panels, *The Israelites Hand Over Their Silver Treasures to Moses* and *The Gathering of the Manna.*[2] The Châteaudun set corresponds to the dimensions of the former Gonzaga set given in the 1679 inventory,[3] thus eliminating all doubt as to the origin of the series. Weavings from the original cartoons surviving in Madrid and in Vienna have been studied by Elisabeth Mahl, who concluded that the Châteaudun set must be the earliest (1545–50). She believed that the Madrid series, which has an arabesque border similar to the Châteaudun, was probably executed around 1550–55, while the Vienna series (with allegorical borders similar to those around Ercole's *Acts of the Apostles*) was most likely woven toward 1560.[4] This scenario fits perfectly with the assumption that the *editio princeps* was either commissioned or purchased by Ferrante Gonzaga during the years he served as governor of Milan (1546–54) and at the same time when he commissioned both the *Fructus Belli* and the *Puttini.* The subjects of the Châteaudun series, corresponding to the twelve pieces cited in the Gonzaga documents, are unique. The ten first pieces are the "classical" Moses scenes, borrowed from Exodus 3 (*Burning Bush*) to chapter 34 (*Moses Receiving the Tablets of the Law*), and Numbers 21 (*Raising of the Brazen Serpent*):

1. *Moses and the Burning Bush* (Exodus 3:1–14) (Fig. 98)
2. *Moses and Aaron before Pharaoh* (Exodus 7:12 and 8–10) (Figs. 99, 112)

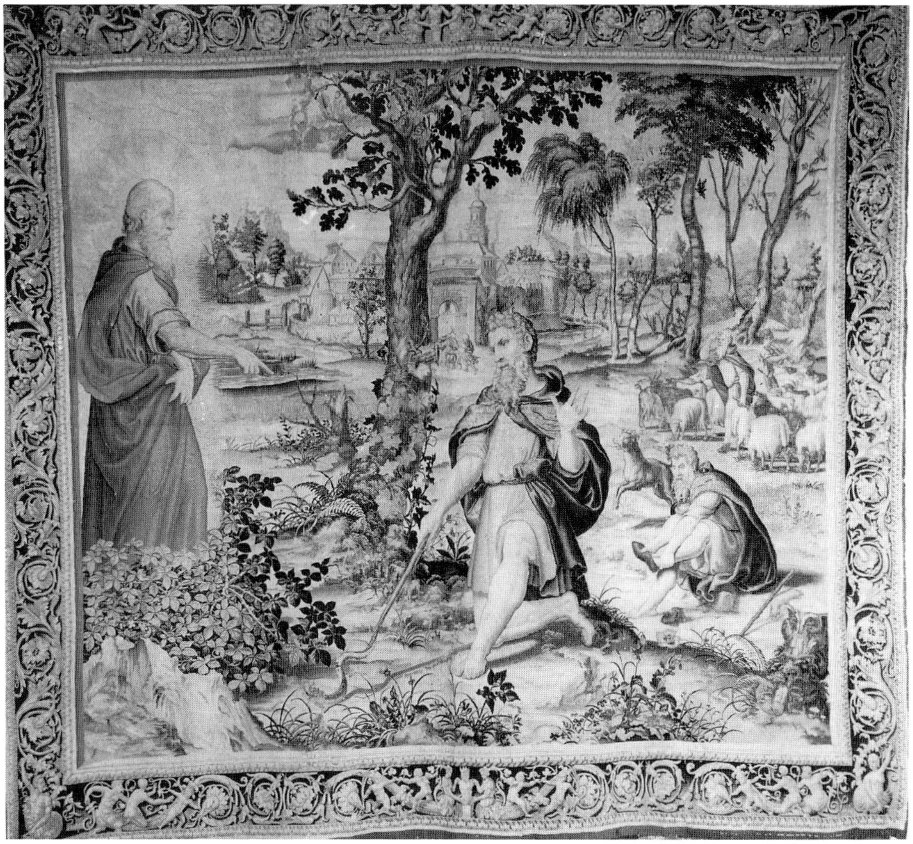

Fig. 98 *Life of Moses: Moses and the Burning Bush,* Brussels, workshop of Willem and Jan Dermoyen(?), 1545–50. Châteaudun Castle, Monuments historiques.

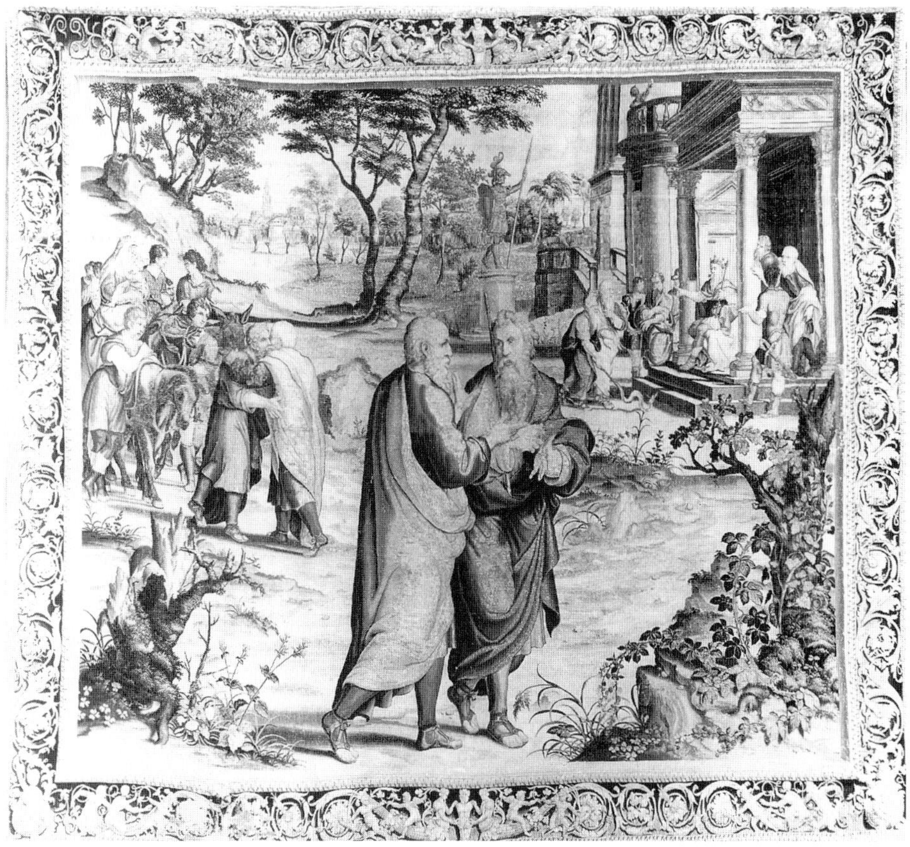

Fig. 99 *Life of Moses: Moses and Aaron before Pharaoh,* Brussels, workshop of Willem and Jan Dermoyen(?), 1545–50. Châteaudun Castle, Monuments historiques.

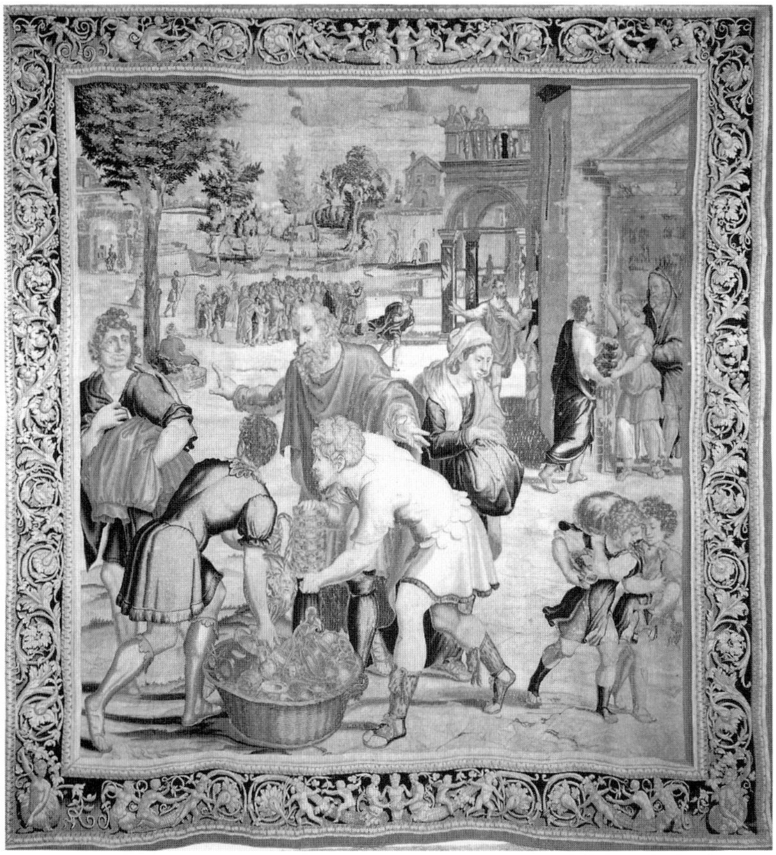

Fig. 100 *Life of Moses: The Israelites Hand Over Their Silver Treasures to Moses,* Brussels, workshop of Willem and Jan Dermoyen(?), 1545–50. Châteaudun Castle, Monuments historiques.

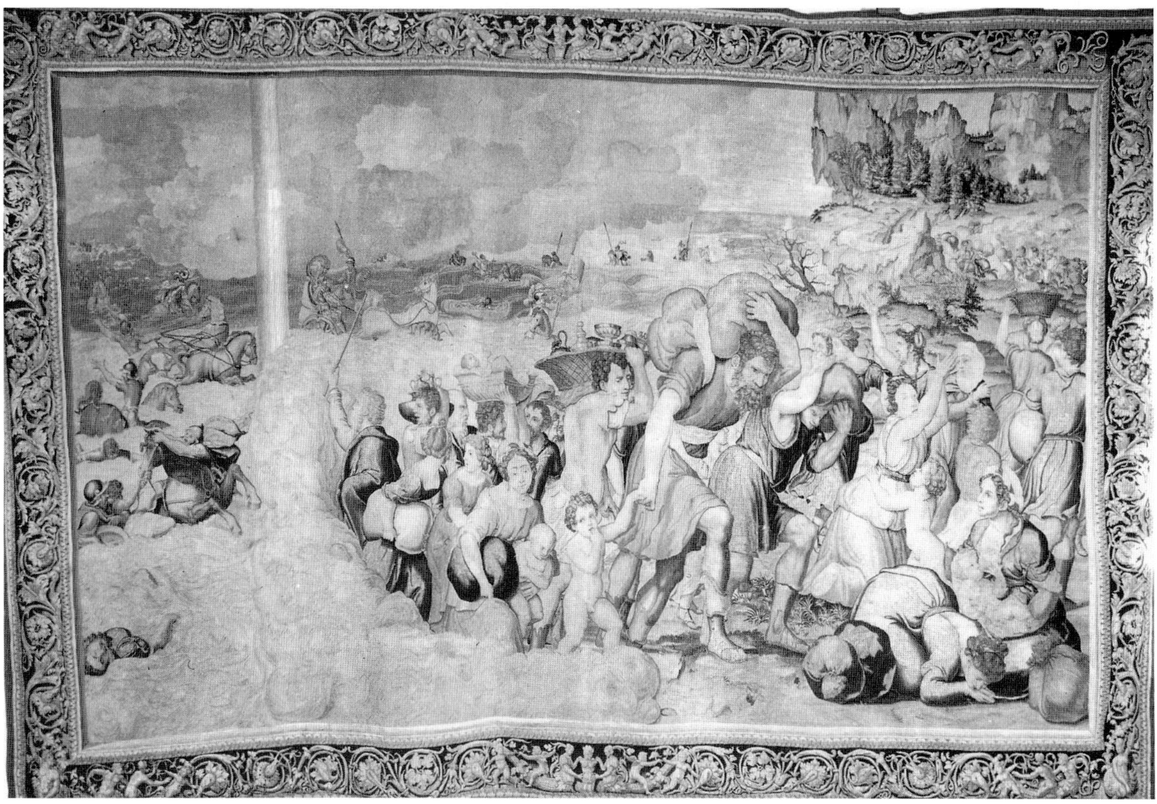

Fig. 101 *Life of Moses: The Passsage through the Red Sea,* Brussels, workshop of Willem and Jan Dermoyen(?), 1545–50. Châteaudun Castle, Monuments historiques.

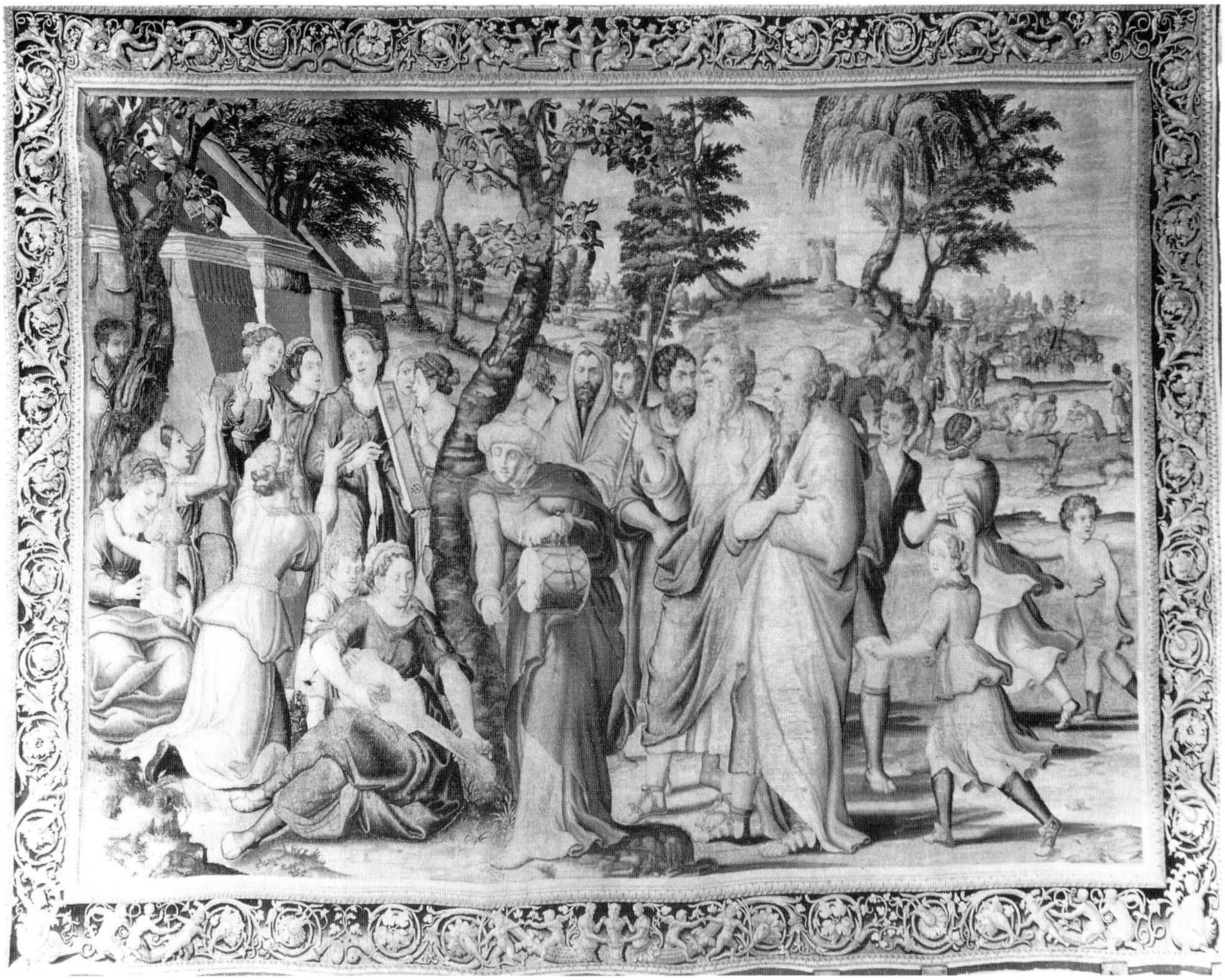

Fig. 102. *Life of Moses: The Israelites Praise the Lord,* Brussels, workshop of Willem and Jan Dermoyen(?), 1545–50. Châteaudun Castle, Monuments historiques.

3. *The Israelites Hand Over Their Silver Treasures to Moses* (Exodus 11:2) (Color Plate X; Fig. 100)
4. *The Passage through the Red Sea* (Exodus 14:22) (Fig. 101)
5. *The Israelites Praise the Lord* (Exodus 15:1–3) (Fig. 102)
6. *The Gathering of the Manna* (Exodus 16) (Color Plate XI; Fig. 103)
7. *Moses Striking the Rock* (Exodus 17:6) (Fig. 104)
8. *The Adoration of the Golden Calf* (Exodus 32) (Fig. 105)
9. *Moses Receiving the Tablets of the Law at Sinai* (Exodus 34) (Figs. 106, 113)
10. *The Raising of the Brazen Serpent* (Numbers 21:9) (Fig. 107)

The same subjects are also represented in the later editions now in Madrid and Vienna.

The Châteaudun set contains two unusual subjects: namely, *The Israelites Killing the Five Madianite Kings* (Numbers 31:7–8; Fig. 108) and *The Abduction of the Madianite Women and Children* (Numbers 31:9–12; Figs. 109, 110, 114).[5] The Madianite scenes seem to have been woven, if not actually conceived, separately from the ten other tapestries. The ornament of their borders differs slightly,[6] and they bear a different weaver's mark. Roethlisberger astutely observed that the design of the bodies and faces resembles those of the *Fructus Belli* tapestries.[7]

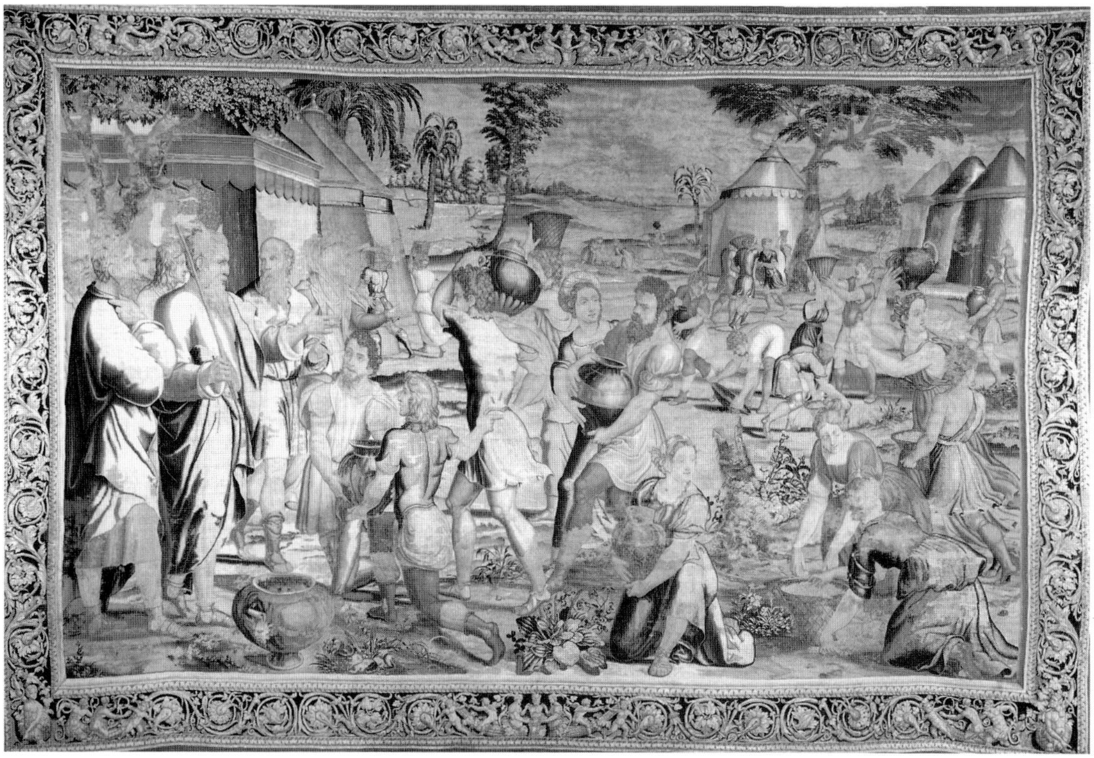

Fig. 103 *Life of Moses: The Gathering of the Manna,* Brussels, workshop of Willem and Jan Dermoyen(?), 1545–50. Châteaudun Castle, Monuments historiques.

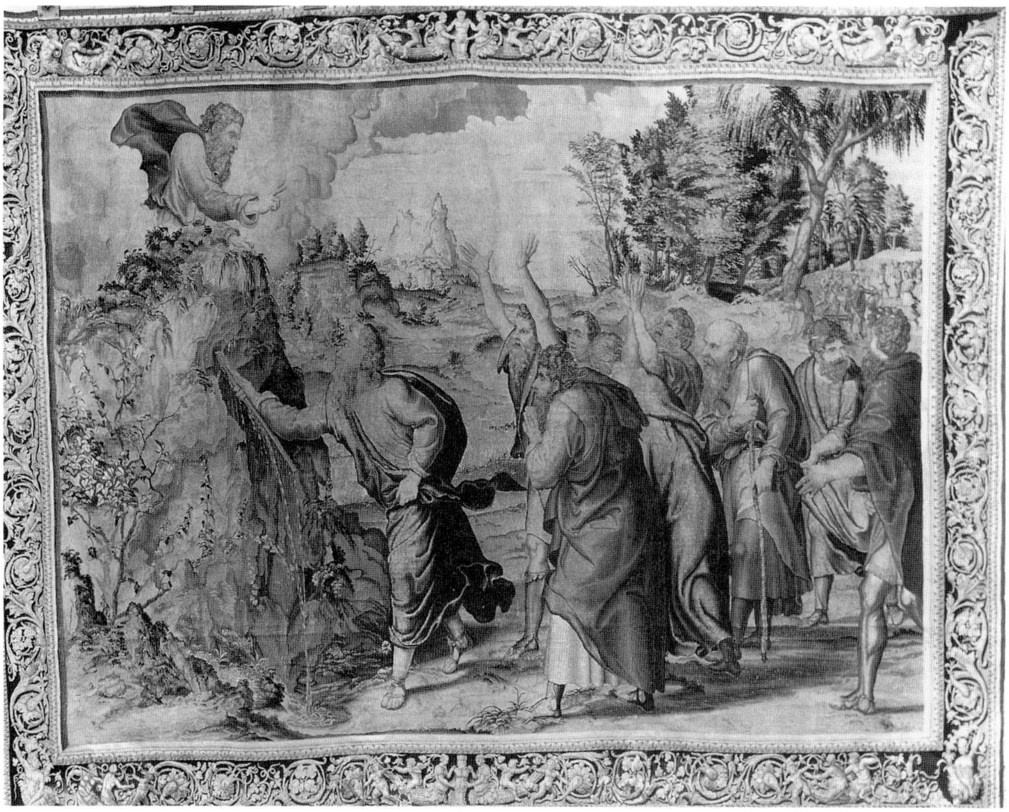

Fig. 104 *Life of Moses: Moses Striking the Rock,* Brussels, workshop of Willem and Jan Dermoyen(?), 1545–50. Châteaudun Castle, Monuments historiques.

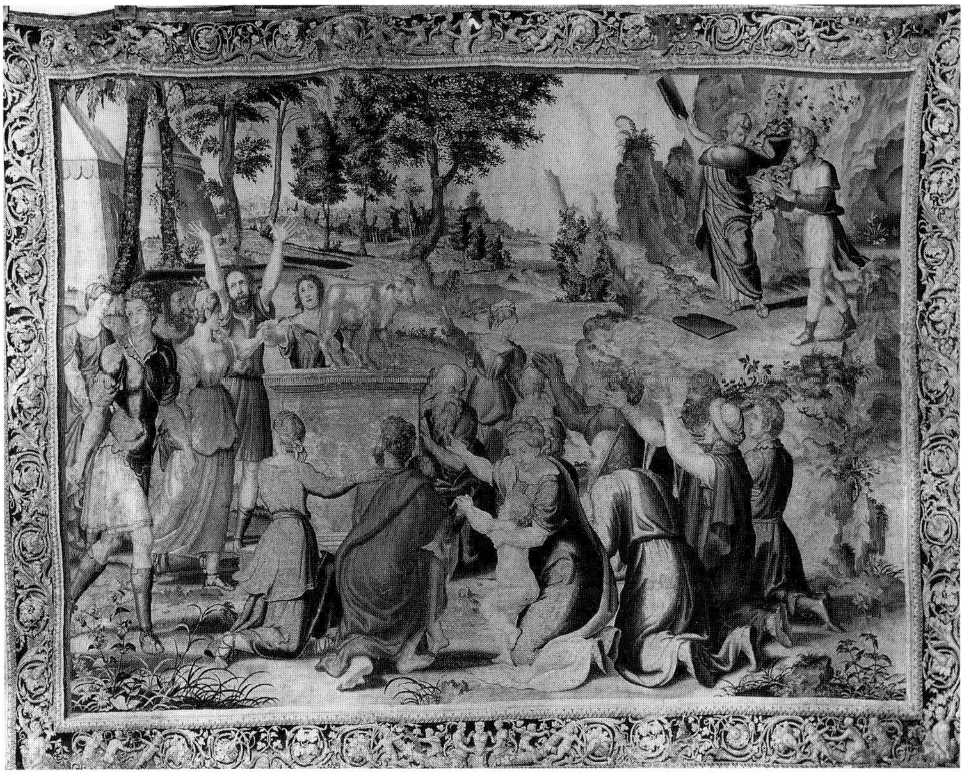

Fig. 105 *Life of Moses: The Adoration of the Golden Calf,* Brussels, workshop of Willem and Jan Dermoyen(?), 1545–50. Châteaudun Castle, Monuments historiques.

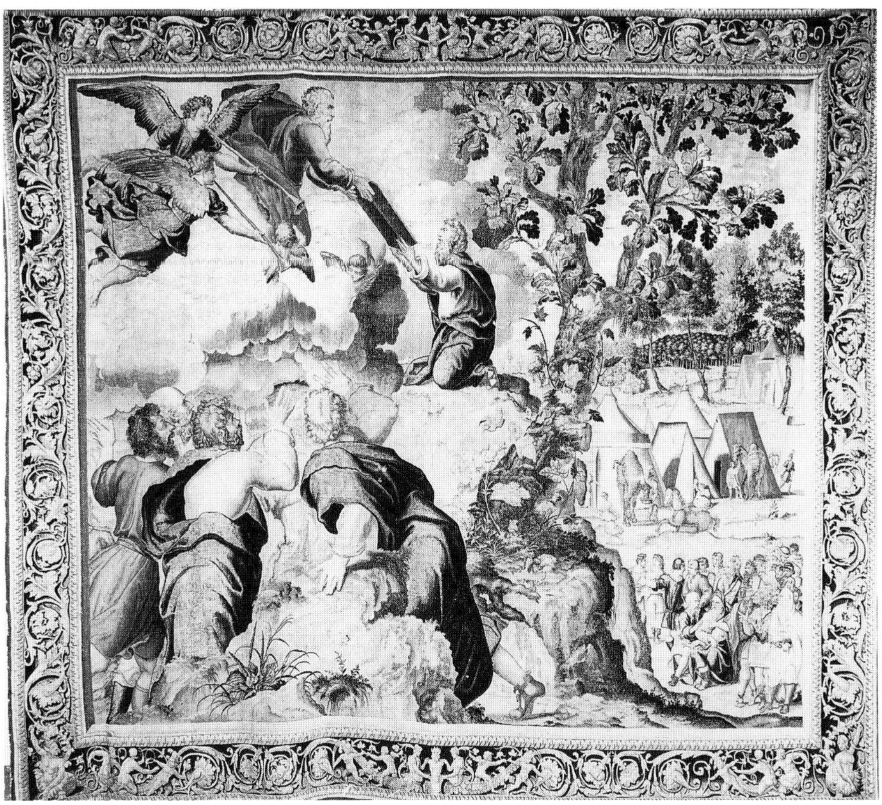

Fig. 106 *Life of Moses: Moses Receiving the Tablets of the Law at Sinai,* Brussels, workshop of Willem and Jan Dermoyen(?), 1545–50. Châteaudun Castle, Monuments historiques.

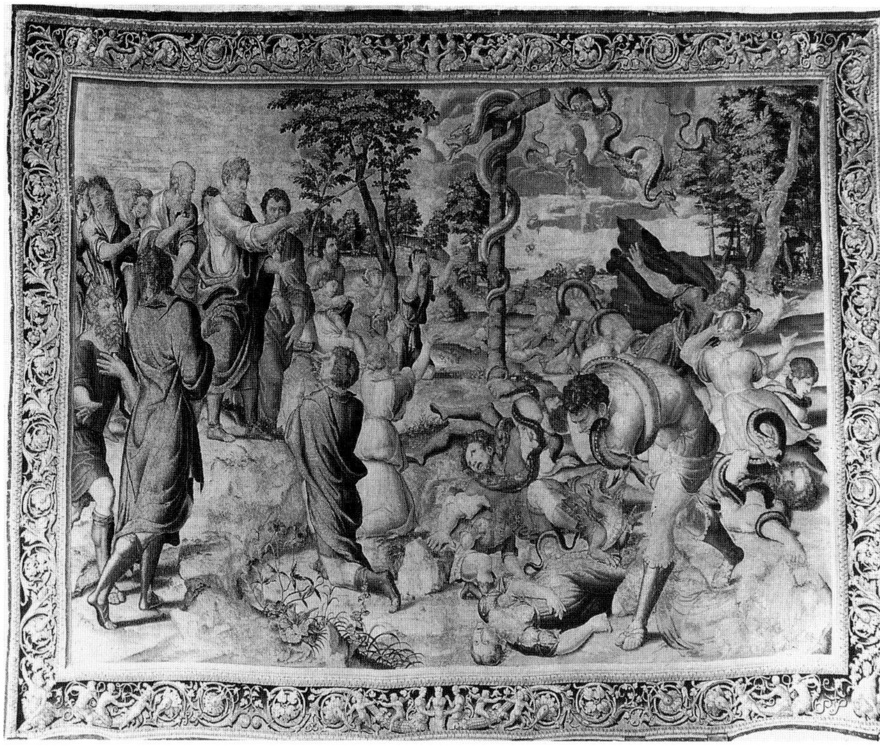

Fig. 107 *Life of Moses: The Raising of the Brazen Serpent,* Brussels, workshop of Willem and Jan Dermoyen(?), 1545–50. Châteaudun Castle, Monuments historiques.

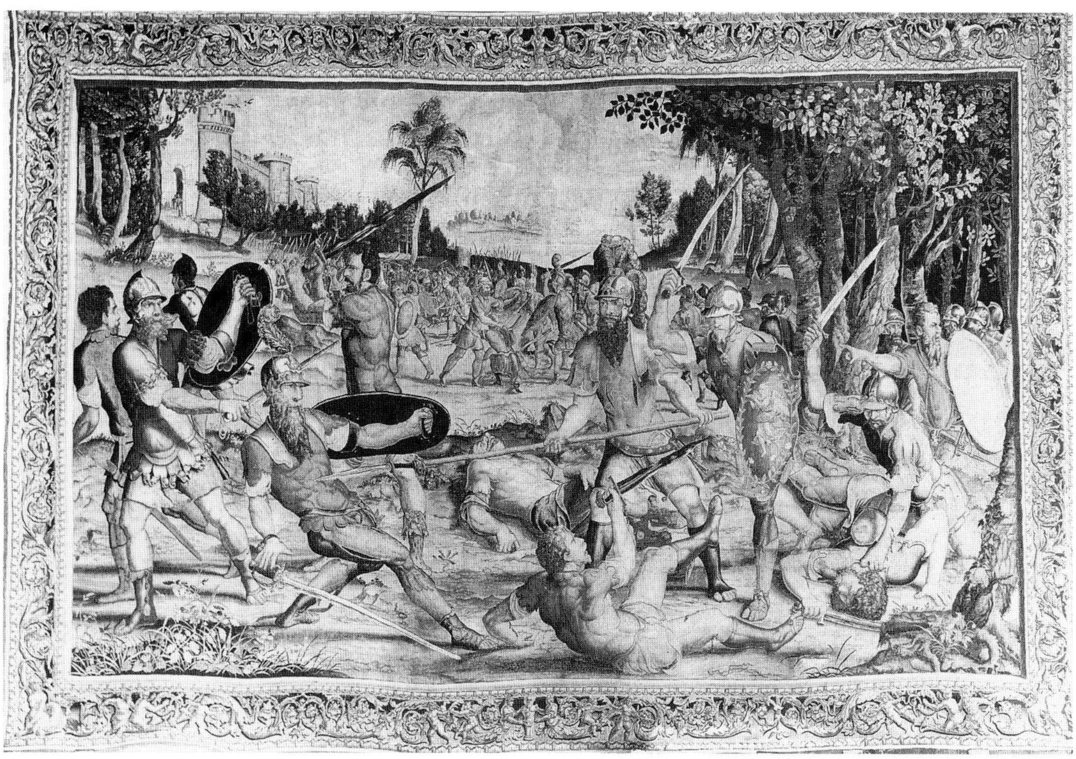

Fig. 108 *Life of Moses: The Israelites Killing the Five Madianite Kings,* Brussels, workshop of Peter van Oppenem(?), 1545–50. Châteaudun Castle, Monuments historiques.

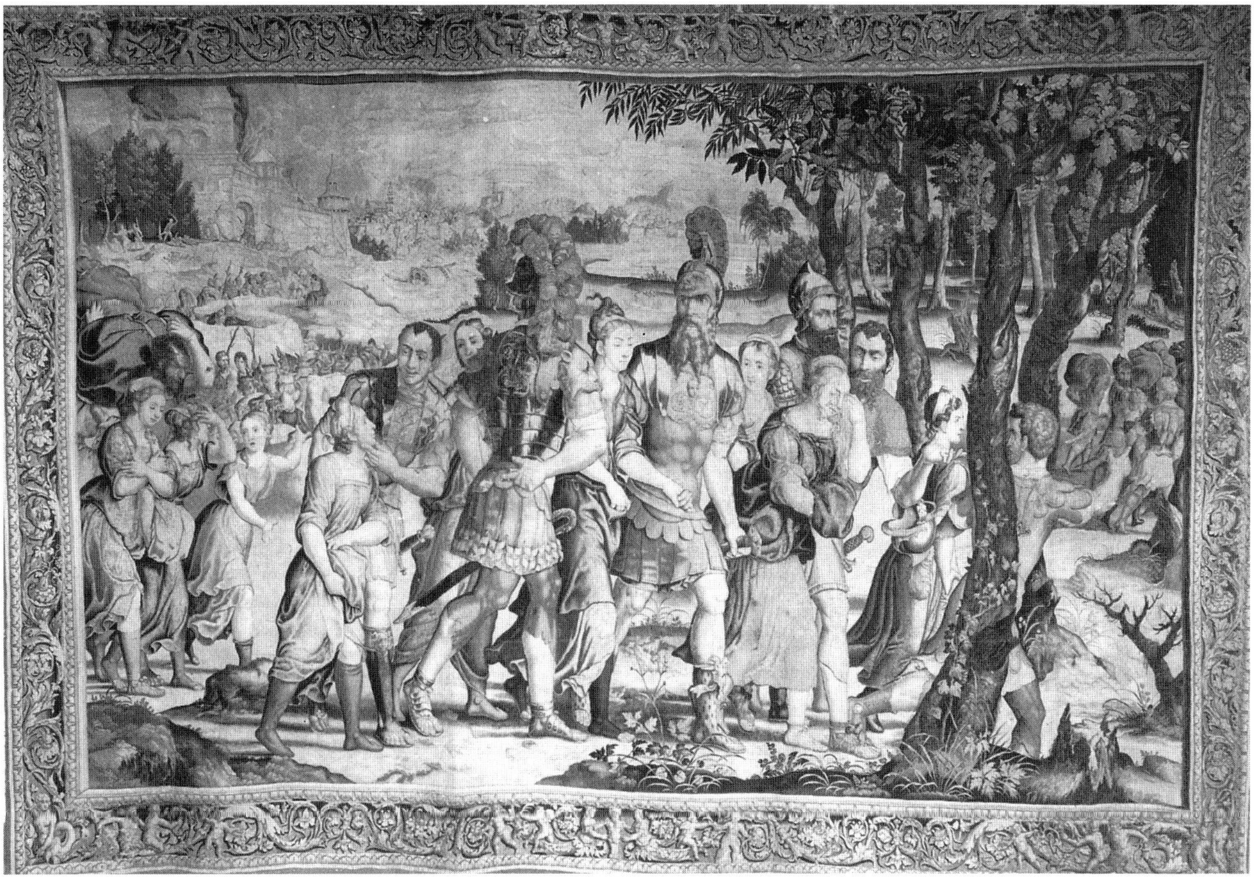

Fig. 109 *Life of Moses: The Abduction of the Madianite Women and Children,* Brussels, workshop of Peter van Oppenem(?), 1545–50. Châteaudun Castle, Monuments historiques.

Several other considerations confirm the date of the weaving and the connection with Ferrante. Mahl noted that the ten "classical" subjects of this *Moses* set relate to the style of Raphael's workshop, and that, accordingly, the original designs must have been made by an Italian artist rather than by a "romanized" Flemish painter such as Michiel Coxcie or others. The Art Institute of Chicago drawing for the *Raising of the Brazen Serpent* has been attributed to Tommaso Vincidor da Bologna, an artist who resided in the Low Countries, where he provided designs for tapestries from 1521 until his death sometime between 1534 and 1536.[8] Four other compositions of the *Moses* tapestries—those for *The Passage through the Red Sea, Moses Striking the Rock, The Adoration of the Golden Calf,* and *Moses Receiving the Tablets of the Law*—are directly borrowed from the frescoes in the Vatican Loggie.[9] The Châteaudun *Moses* and its derivative reeditions thus found their artistic roots in Raphaelesque models, which could have been transmitted to the Brussels cartoon painters by the Mantuan workshop of Giulio Romano. Such an artistic genesis seems acceptable, especially if it is assumed that Ferrante Gonzaga ordered this set. The style of the tapestries is indeed the result of the translation of Italian models by Flemish cartoon painters.[10]

This is particularly true for the two additional tapestries, for not only do they reflect the figurative style of the *Fructus Belli* series through their single protagonists, but they repeat some of the figure types (Fig. 110). The Israelites are not clad in "biblical" togas or robes, but they wear armor *all'antica* much like the warriors of the *Fructus* series; for example, the officers in the *Battlefield*

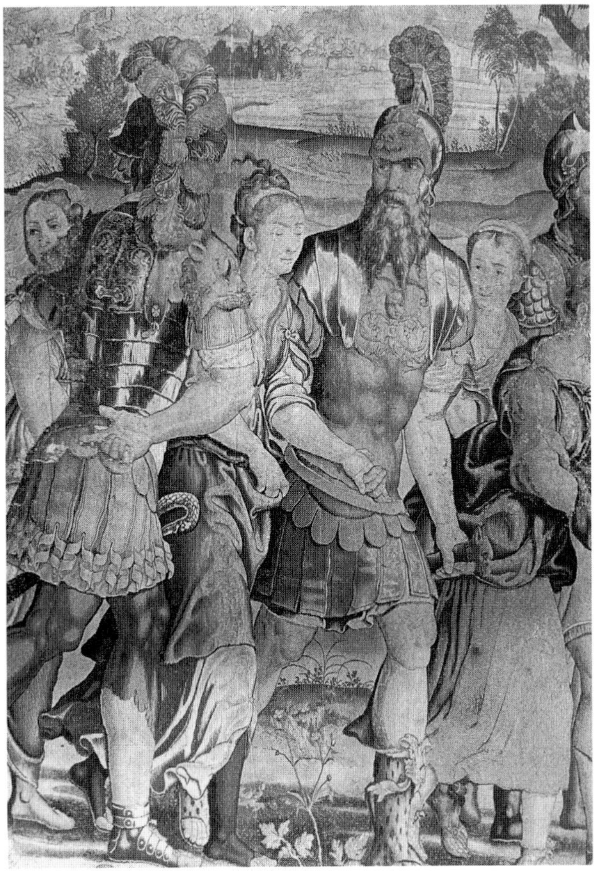

Fig. 110 Detail of *The Abduction of the Madianite Women and Children* (Fig. 109).

or the *Dinner of the Officers*. The rhythm of the cortege in the *Abduction* is similar to that of the *Burning City*. Thus, it seems evident that the cartoons of these pieces have been conceived and painted by the same artists who produced those of the *Fructus Belli*. This proves that both series were designed at the same time, between 1545 and 1550. It is always possible, however, that the ten "classical" *Moses* subjects may be slightly earlier.

Since they were woven in a different workshop and apparently added to the ten others, were these two tapestries originally conceived for the *Moses* set? They indeed may have been intended for other series. The two compositions may have fitted for the *Fructus* set, being other variants for the *Battlefield* or for the *Burning City*, then rejected in favor of the actual compositions of these themes, and eventually reused here in the *Life of Moses*. Such a hypothesis may explain the discrepancy of fashion noted above. In this case, we must presume that the design, if not the weaving, of the *Fructus Belli* set has been anterior to the *Moses* tapestries.

These two additional military scenes, however, may also have been intended for another series conceived by Giulio Romano, namely, *The Abduction of the Sabine Women* (Fig. 111). A Brussels set of six pieces has been attributed to Giulio since the inventory of Louis XIV (1663–73) as well as by Félibien. This edition is now lost, but three compositions of another Brussels sixteenth-century edition are preserved (Azay-le-Féron, Brussels Town Hall, and the Brussels Royal Museums of Art and History). Their style, which surely relied on models from Giulio's workshop, is also closely related to that of the additional battle scenes of the *Moses* set, which originally may have represented a battle between Romans and Sabines and the rape of the Sabine women.[11]

The two additional pieces do not disrupt the unity of style of the normal series of ten. All of them were issued from Giulio's workshop. As was the case for the *Fructus*, here too the design of the borders had been conceived by this workshop. The large arabesques of acanthus leaves are copied from antique models.[12] The decorative scheme, with figures issued from flowers in the corners and satyrs and *puttini* in the middle (Fig. 113), is almost identical to that of the upper frieze of the Sala di Ovidio in the Palazzo Te, painted from models by Giulio in 1527–28.[13] A striking similarity exists also with the horizontal borders of the *Battles and Triumphs of Scipio*, Giulio's main tapestry set first woven in 1533–35, as testified by the oldest editions preserved in Madrid and at the Museo Stibbert in Florence.[14] It emphasizes the tradition of arabesque borders, which often surrounded compositions from Italian or Italianate design on slightly older and contemporary Brussels tapestries,[15] but the cited examples of Giulio's workshops are the only very close and really convincing parallels or comparisons.

Some comments should be made about the workshops who produced this *Moses*. Besides the Brussels city mark, two different workshop monograms are still visible on these tapestries (Figs. 112–114). One manufacturer made the ten classical subjects, while another provided the two additional pieces. These last ones present a monogram consisting of a letter "P" in an "O" (Fig.

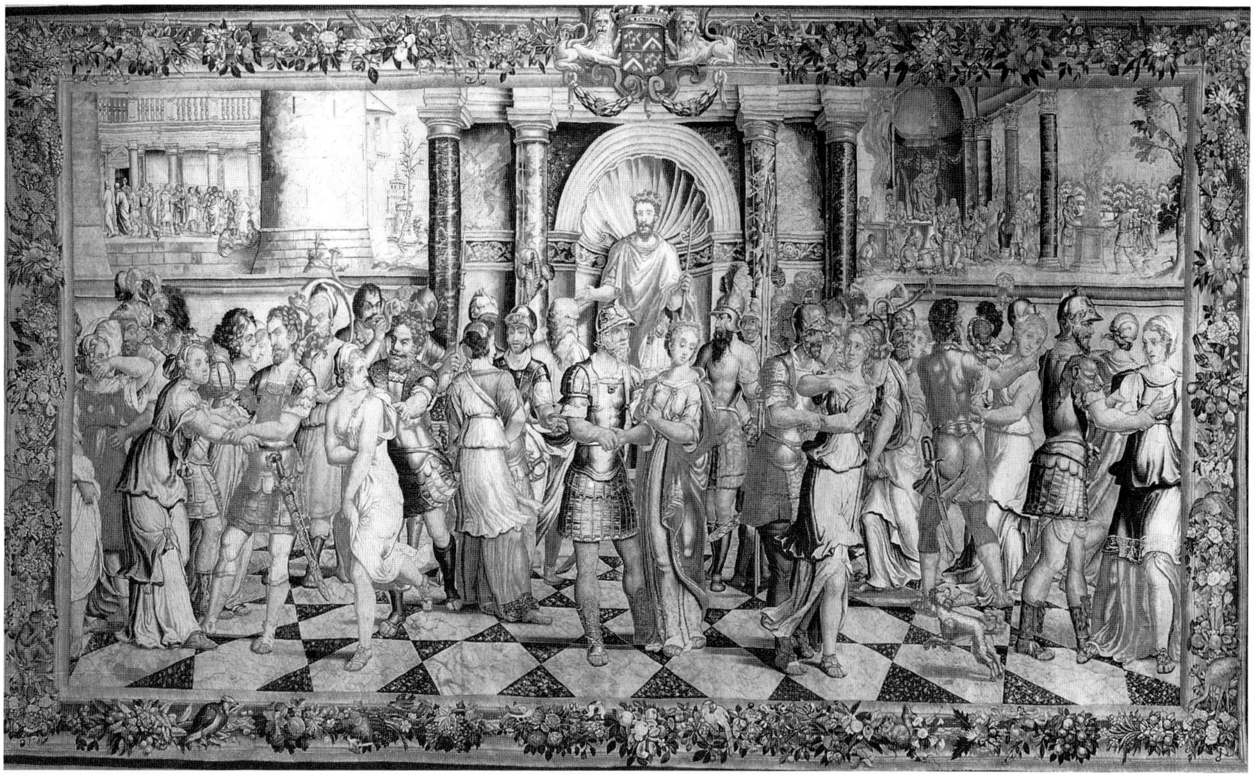

Fig. 111 *The Abduction of the Sabine Women,* Brussels, c. 1535–45. Castle of Azay-le-Féron.

114). This sign is also woven on two different editions of a *Life of Saint Paul* now in Madrid and Vienna, from cartoons by Pieter Coecke van Aelst and dated 1535–40.[16] It may point to Peter van Oppenem, a Brussels weaver mentioned in 1510 and 1529.[17] The monogram on four of the tapestries (Fig. 113) of the main group of ten consists of the letters "I" (isolated), "G," "V", and "W" (or reversed "M").[18] Although not firmly identified, it is most commonly attributed to Jan Gheteels, and the letters "I" and "G" may be his initials. Born around 1488, Ghieteels is cited as a tapestry manufacturer in Brussels from 1527 until 1556. No specific documents are known, however, for sets produced by this weaver.[19] Several outstanding Brussels series from this period still bear this monogram, and among them the *Hunts of the Emperor Maximilian* (Paris, Louvre), the *Battle of Pavia* (Naples, Museo di Capodimonte), and a set of the *Works of Hercules* (Madrid, Patrimonio Nacional, series 23). In archive documents that were partly overlooked until now, these tapestry sets are clearly related to another major Brussels workshop of this period, that of Willem (Guillaume) Dermoyen, or Van der Moyen, and his son, Jan. In August 1533 the Dermoyen firm provided samples of both the *Battle of Pavia* and the *Maximilian Hunts* to a German merchant, Jakob Rehlinger, who intended to sell the entire series to Süleyman the Magnificent in Istanbul.[20] The same weavers sold in 1535 a set of the *Works of Hercules* to Mary of Hungary, Regent of the Netherlands; this tapestry series is most probably identical to the series no. 23 in Madrid.[21] The Dermoyens are cited from 1539 to 1544, and Willem died around 1548. As the "Ghieteels" monogram on the Châteaudun *Moses* set can also be read as "Iohannes and Gugliemus or Guillaume Van (inverted "V") der Moyen (inverted "M")," a weaving of the *Moses* by the Dermoyen workshop before 1548 can be accepted.

Taking all factors into consideration, it may be concluded that most probably Ferrante Gonzaga bought, and possibly even ordered, a major set of ten *Moses* tapestries from models issued by Giulio Romano's work-

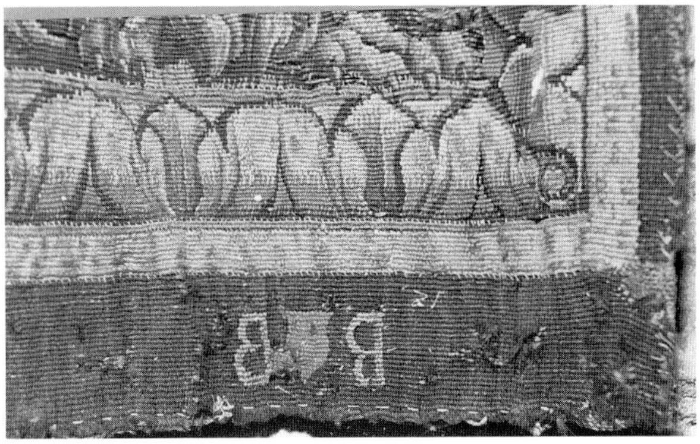

Fig. 112 Detail of the Brussels City mark from *Moses and Aaron before Pharaoh* (Fig. 99).

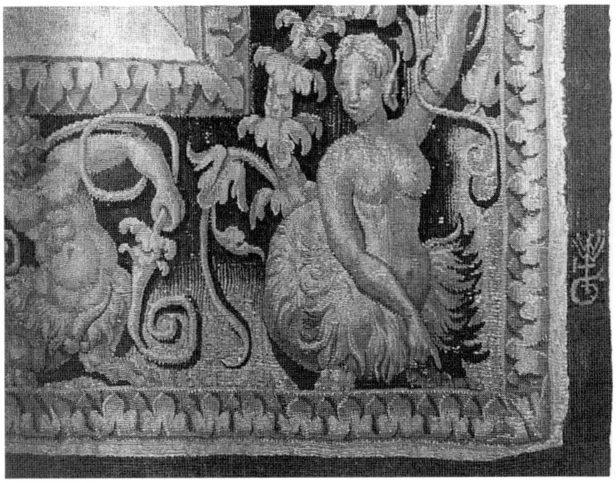

Fig. 113 Detail of the border and the weaver's monogram (here attributed to Dermoyen) from *Moses Receiving the Tablets of the Law at Sinai* (Fig. 106).

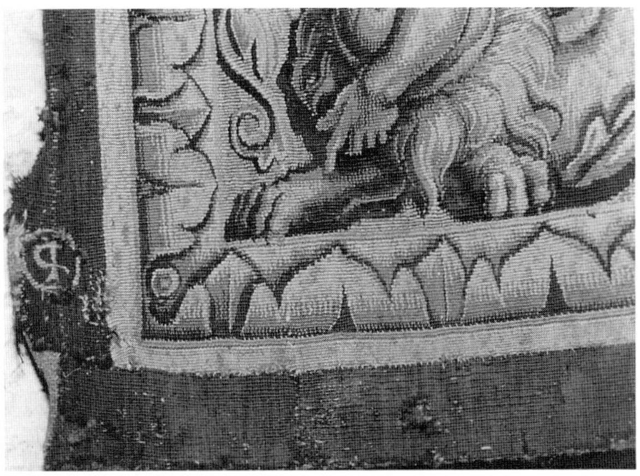

Fig. 114 Detail of the weaver's monogram (here attributed to van Oppenem) from *The Abduction of the Madianite Women and Children* (Fig. 109).

shop and woven in the major workshop of the Dermoyen, purveyors of the imperial court (such as Willem de Pannemaker for Ferrante's *Puttini* set) prior to 1548. For reasons that have been unclear until now, two other *Moses* tapestries, the cartoons of which were designed by the same artist as the previous ten, were woven in another Brussels workshop to form a set of twelve, now all exhibited in Châteaudun Castle. The two additional pieces may have been intended initially as subjects either for the *Fructus Belli* or for *The Abduction of the Sabine Women,* other Brussels sets conceived in the artistic entourage of the Mantuan workshop of Giulio.[22]

The role of Ferrante Gonzaga in defining the iconography of the *Fructus Belli,* and the relevance of these scenes to his career as military leader and civic ruler in the service of Charles V, has already been discussed. It remains to be determined what precisely interested him in commissioning a cycle dedicated to Moses, since the careers of the two men were never formally paralleled in the literature of the period. While various possibilities come to mind, the matter clearly requires further research.

NOTES

1. Acquired by the French government at the Sale Hôtel Drouot, Me Ader, Paris, 21 June 1955, no. 143. The set is woven with wool and silk.

2. This can be proved by the accurate identity of the borders: the design has been used only for this edition, and the dimensions, of both design and of the total width, are also identical to eight pieces of the set bought in 1955.

3. The actual average height of the tapestries is 3.50 to 3.60 meters: in 1679, the height was 5⅓ *braccia* di Guastalla, or 3.55 to 3.65 meters. The actual total length of the twelve tapestries comprises 52.85 meters: in 1679 it reached 79¼ *braccia,* or 53.17 to 54.00 meters. Tapestries tend to shrink in width after the traction of the loom on the horizontal warp threads has been released, and they may increase in height because, when hung vertically, sometimes for ages, the textile exerts weight on its finer weft threads.

4. Mahl, 1967, 38.

5. For a comparison of these subjects, see Mahl, 1967, 24. The last two pieces were identified by Roethlisberger, 1971, 108–9. No other *Moses* set of this period appears to have been composed of twelve pieces.

6. Mahl, 1967, 24: a red instead of a yellow shadow on the ornaments. It should also be noted that two *puttini* in the middle of the horizontal borders bear wings of a bat, instead of angels' wings, and that the entire border's width is some 1 to 1.5 cm smaller than on the other ten tapestries.

7. Roethlisberger, 1971, 109, n. 24.

8. Mahl, 1967, 33–37, with Vincidor's drawing on page 37, Fig. 35. Dacos (1980, 88 n. 111) does not consider it as an original drawing by Vincidor, but one influenced by him.

9. Hartt (1958) and Dacos (1977) attribute these four scenes as follows: *Passage through the Red Sea,* Perino del Vaga (Hartt)/Giulio (Dacos); *Moses Striking the Rock:* Giulio/Raffaello del Colle; *The Adoration of the Golden Calf:* Penni/Giulio; *Moses Receiving the Tablets of the Law,* Giulio/Perino del Vaga.

10. Such a deformation may also have been caused by copying prints from the Logge, where the original compositions were already altered. However, we could not find any such prints for the four Logge subjects considered here and that would reflect such a change.

11. *Paris 1965,* 37, and Asselberghs in *Culan 1971,* 16 (with previous literature); for Giulio as designer, see Delmarcel, in press.

12. *Vienna 1989,* 11, cat. 1/14.

13. *Mantua 1989,* 336–37. A similar type of ornamentation had earlier been employed by Pinturicchio in 1497 for the frieze in the Eroli Chapel in the Cathedral of Spoleto.

14. Madrid: Junquera, 1986, 1, series 26, 176, and *Mantua 1989,* 470; Florence: Viale, 1952, pl. 42.

15. See, for example, the *Spasimo di Sicilia* for Cardinal Bibbiena, Vatican; the Alva *Passion* set, now in Paris, New York, and Washington, D.C.; the *Coronation of the Virgin,* 1534–38, given to Pope Paul III by Cardinal Erard de la Marck, Vatican (Steppe and Delmarcel, 1974, 49, Fig. 11); the *Venus and Vulcan* set in the Biltmore House, Asheville, North Carolina.

16. The mark is on the lower left selvedge of the "Abduction." See also Bauer in *Halbturn 1981,* 37 and 51 (Vienna), and Junquera, 1986, 1, 355 (Madrid, series 32).

17. Goebel, 1923, 1, 308–9.

18. This mark appears on the selvedges of four of the ten pieces. See Goebel, 1923, 1; Marks pl. 4; and J. and E. Duverger, 1981, 241.

19. Concerning Jan Ghieteels, see the cited article by J. and E. Duverger (1981).

20. Kellenbenz (1965), mentioned and correctly interpreted by Necipoglu, 1989, but overlooked by all former tapestry historians, including Schneebalg, 1982. See Delmarcel, 1991, 122–23, and idem in Balis, De Jong, Delmarcel, and Lefébure, 1993, 39–43.

21. Pinchart, 1884, 88 (omitted by Junquera, 1986, 1, 155–56). Van den Boogert (*Utrecht 1993,* 295, 358 n. 72) published the document and maintained that the models for the set were provided by Giulio Romano.

22. Nello Forti Grazzini has suggested (in a personal communication) that the set was perhaps ordered from Giulio shortly before his death in 1546. This would explain why the *Moses* consists of two pieces based on designs of Giulio Romano and ten in a different style, but one based in part on frescos from the Raphael loggie. In his just published catalogue of the Quirinale tapestries (pp. 180–82), Forti Grazzini notes the affinity that exists between ten of the *Moses* weavings and the *Mercury and Herse.* He sees this as relating to the still to be documented style of Giovanni Battista Lodi. Forti Grazzini furthermore suggests that the differences in style between the two sections of the set may be explained both by the death of Giulio Romano and the death of the original weaver, Peter van Oppenem(?). According to this hypothesis, the remaining ten panels in the set would have been woven by a different firm and without the guidance of models provided by Giulio Romano. Showing how Giovanni Battista Lodi worked when left on his own, it also might explain why older models—those taken from the Raphael loggie—were selected.

7. Ercole and Guglielmo's *Life of Moses*

Milan, Museo del Duomo
The Passage through the Red Sea (inv. 191): 360 × 630 cm (Fig. 115)
Moses Receiving the Tablets of the Law (inv. 193): 373 × 265 cm (Fig. 116)
Raising of the Brazen Serpent (inv. 192): 377 × 380 cm (Fig. 117)
Moses and the False Magi before Pharaoh (destroyed 1906). (Fig. 118)
The Passover (destroyed 1906). (Fig. 119)
Gathering of the Manna (destroyed 1906). (Fig. 120)
Puttini with the Gonzaga Arms (inv. 190): 190 × 322 cm (Fig. 122)

Comparative Illustration
Angelo Bronzino, *The Passage through the Red Sea,* c. 1540 (Fig. 121)

Two of the scenes from the *Moses* cycle in the Museo del Duomo in Milan contain inscriptions ("GUGLIELMUS DUX MANTUAE" and "MARCHIO MONTIS FERRATI" [or: "MMF"] and all display the Gonzaga arms. They belong to a set of six weavings, three of which were destroyed by fire in 1906.[1] A gift from Guglielmo Gonzaga to Cardinal Carlo Borromeo, they are documented in Milan by 1566. Shortly thereafter, Borromeo sought to sell them in order to raise funds for various religious establishments. In 1568 it was suggested that Guglielmo might wish to buy them back (Document 66, Addenda C), but the following year, on 2 December 1569, they were donated by Borromeo to the Duomo of Milan.[2]

There is general agreement that Nicolas Karcher wove the Gonzaga-Borromeo-Milan *Moses* set, but it remains uncertain if the weaving was done in Ferrara or Mantua. Since the set was created between 1550 (when Guglielmo became duke) and 1566, when it was in the Borromeo collection, a Ferrarese origin is ruled out. Karcher left the city at the end of 1539. He was active in Mantua from 1539 to 1545 and was in Florence from 2 October 1545 at least until 21 October 1553. Karcher returned to Mantua in 1555 and remained here until his death on 1 October 1562 (Document 47). It is altogether possible that he worked on this set during his stay in Florence (1545–53).[3] According to his contract with Grand Duke Cosimo de' Medici of 17 November 1550, Karcher was allowed to work for other patrons, but until now proof that he actually exercised this option has been lacking.[4]

While in 1549 Karcher received payment for "una carpetta" (Document 27), the unspecified work mentioned in Ercole's letter of 1551 may well refer to the commissioning of the *Moses* set (Document 30). In this event the *Moses* tapestries with Guglielmo's arms could have been woven entirely or in part in Florence. Moreover, as Karcher was mentioned for the last time in Florence on 27 September 1553 (one month before his contract with Cosimo expired), he may have returned to Mantua in November 1553 in order to finish this set.[5]

A correct reading of the iconography of the Gonzaga-Borromeo-Milan *Moses* series serves to support this hypothesis. After all, the first work securely attributed to Karcher for Ercole was a "quadro di seta, oro, et argento di Moysis nel deserto" (Document 12), a work created just after he assumed the co-regency of Mantua after the death of Duke Federico II and at a time when he was preparing a major overhaul of the Mantuan diocese. The subject chosen for Karcher to weave seems therefore to have a strong biographical note—paralleling the mission of Moses to the burdens undertaken by Cardinal Ercole. Guglielmo was only twelve years old when he became duke on 24 April 1550, after the sud-

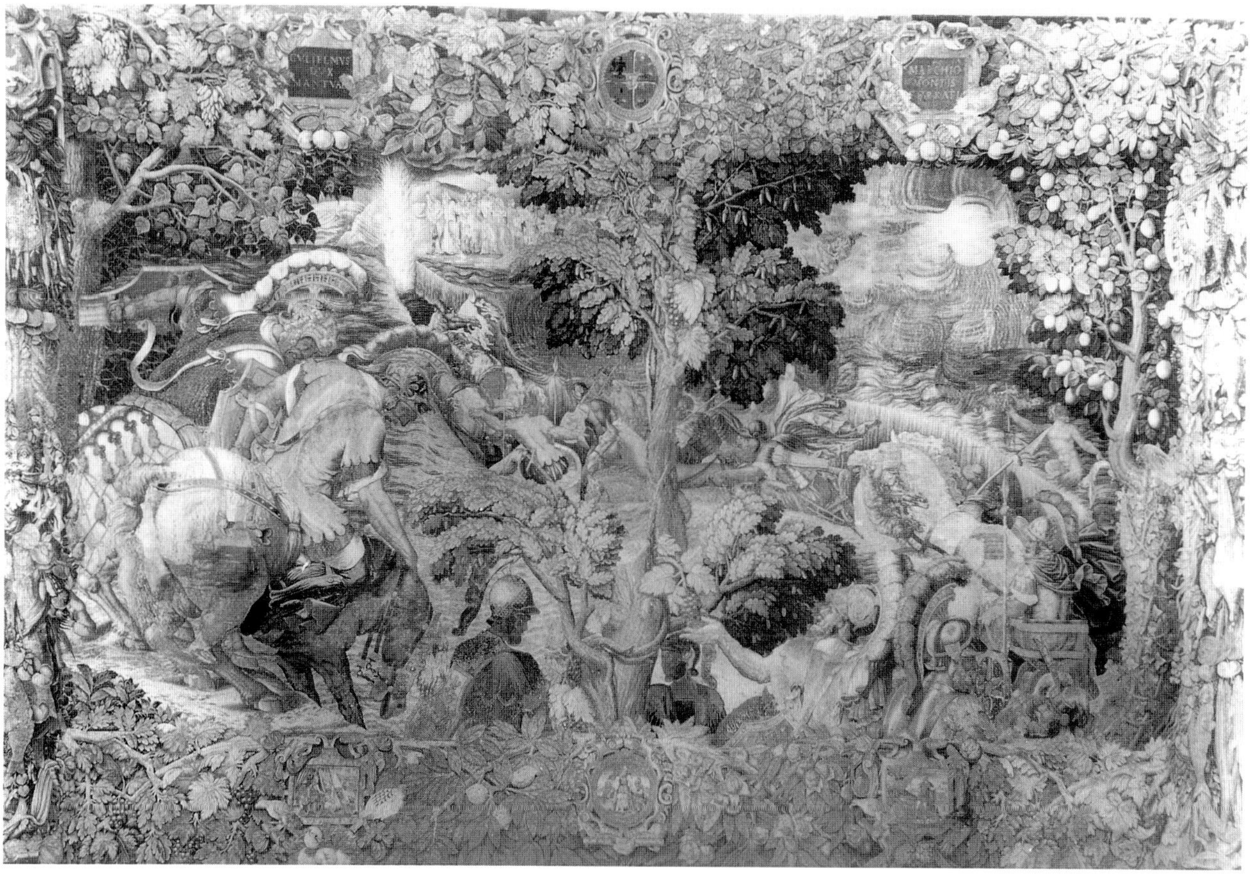

Fig. 115 *Moses: The Passage through the Red Sea,* Italian, workshop of Nicolas Karcher, 1553–62. Milan, Museo del Duomo.

den demise of his seventeen-year-old brother, Duke Francesco III. Since the death of their father, Federico II, in 1540, Mantua had been ruled by their mother, Margherita Paleologa, together with Ercole and Ferrante. The real authority resided, however, with Ercole, for Ferrante was rarely in residence and Margherita deferred in most matters to her brother-in-law. The Milan *Moses* set was therefore most probably ordered by Cardinal Ercole on behalf of Guglielmo rather than directly by the young duke himself. The subject matter of the series clearly reflects this political situation. Ercole may have desired tapestries that were representative both of his nephew and of himself and that referred to the circumstances in which Guglielmo came to the ducal power. Moses served first as an example of statemanship, leading his people to the promised land, as well as of religious leadership, being a prototype of Christ, as on the frescoed walls of the Sistine Chapel. The set could thus refer to the young secular duke as well as to his ecclesiastical uncle, who in fact continued to administer Mantua until Guglielmo's marriage in 1561, even though the duke gained the age of majority in 1556.[6]

The identity of the designer of the cartoons has not yet been established.[7] At first glance they seemingly belong to the *bottega* of Giulio Romano, since it is possible to identify several formal elements that had appeared already in sets conceived by Giulio. The *Passage through the Red Sea* (Fig. 115) relates to the *Battles of Scipio* of around 1535, while the now-destroyed *Gathering of the Manna* (Fig. 120) even contains some children picking apples in trees, a motif previously encountered in

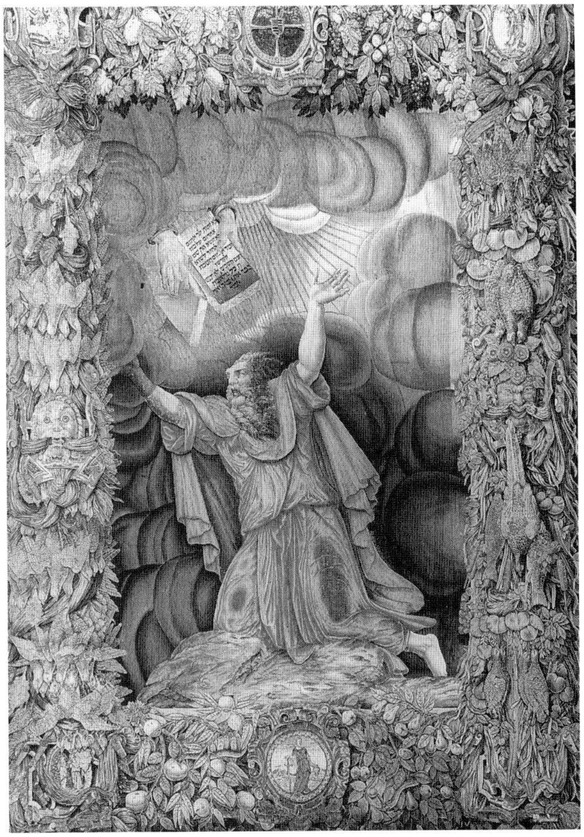

Fig. 116 *Moses: Moses Receiving the Tablets of the Law,* Italian, workshop of Nicolas Karcher, 1553–62. Milan, Museo del Opera del Duomo.

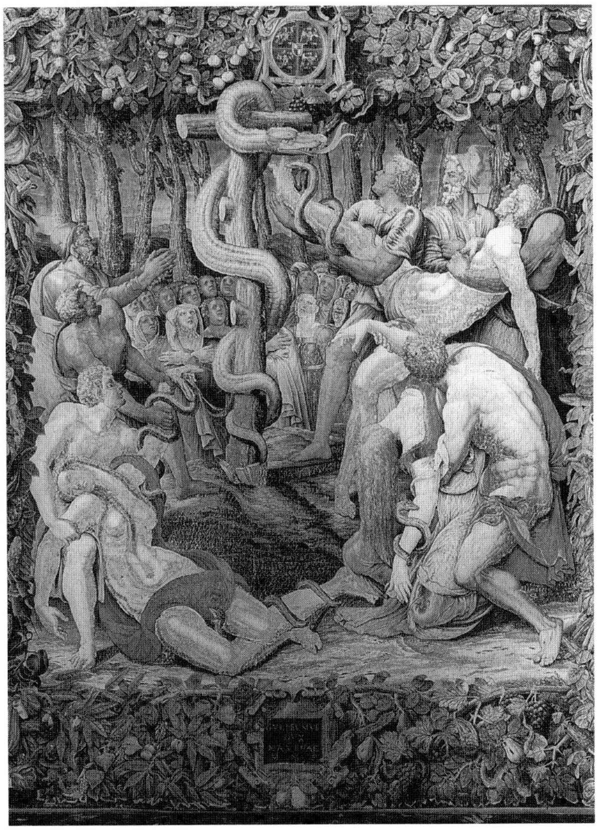

Fig. 117 *Moses: Raising of the Brazen Serpent,* Italian, workshop of Nicolas Karcher, 1553–62. Milan, Museo del Duomo.

Ercole's *Puttini* set of around 1540.[8] As Karcher may have started the weaving in Florence, before returning to Mantua toward 1553, it is not impossible that some of the models may have been provided by Florentine artists. The style of the four remaining tapestries is very different. Each weaving seems to have been conceived by a different master. Whereas *The Passage through the Red Sea* relates to ideas associated with Giulio Romano, the *Raising of the Brazen Serpent* (Fig. 117) is closer to the style of Bronzino, the Florentine master who was most actively involved in painting tapestry cartoons for Duke Cosimo I from 1545 to 1553.[9] Bronzino had earlier depicted this subject in the *Moses* cycle in the chapel of Eleonora of Toledo in the Palazzo Vecchio (Fig. 121). The manneristic design and the tense gestures and movements of the nude figures on the tapestry of the *Brazen Serpent* belong to the Bronzino types of erected and reclining figures in his *Passage through the Red Sea* fresco in Florence.[10] Candace Adelson's suggestion that some of these cartoons were designed by Benedetto Pagni da Pescia is therefore acceptable. Pagni was one of Giulio's asistants in Mantua and thereafter worked in Florence, where he was a rival of Bronzino.[11]

The borders of the Gonzaga-Borromeo-Milan set are distinctive, and the opulence of their design was a factor behind assuming their Ferrarese origin, or for an early intervention by Giuseppe Archimboldo.[12] And yet relevant stylistic comparisons can be made with the Florentine school. These essentially floral ornaments resemble those of the *Joseph* tapestries, probably created by Bronzino's pupils. The *mascheroni* of the Milan tapestry of *Moses Receiving the Law* (Fig. 116) can likewise be related to the *Joseph* series. Even the elongated forms of the *putti-ni* in the armorial piece of the Milanese set are very close

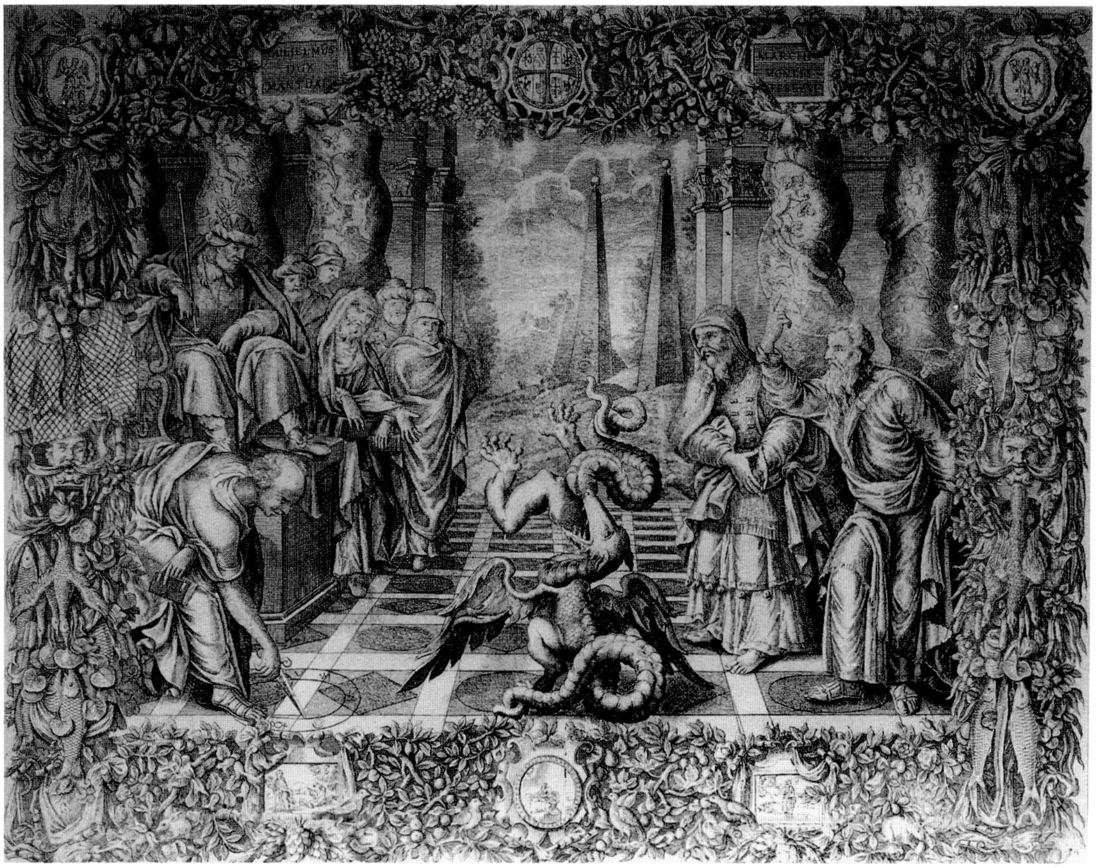

Fig. 118 *Moses: Moses and the False Magi before Pharaoh* (drawing), destroyed 1906, Italian, workshop of Nicolas Karcher, 1553–62. Milan, Museo del Duomo.

to the anatomy of Bronzino's figures in the Florentine tapestries.[13] The hunting trophies, with dead birds and fishes upon the reeds, remind one also of the fresco paintings in the Palazzo Vitelli a Sant'Egidio, in Città del Castello, executed by a collaborator of Vasari, Cristofano Gherardi, in the second quarter of the century.[14]

The subject matter of the Milan *Moses* tapestries was not unknown in Mantua.[15] The most striking and the best designed among the six compositions are the *Passage through the Red Sea* and the *Raising of the Brazen Serpent* (Figs. 115, 117). Related to the political realities in Mantua in 1550, they refer to "salvation from the water" and to "salvation from disease," thus referring by contrast to the young Duke Francesco III's death by drowning and by the subsequent fever that killed him, and containing some apotropaic wishful thinking for the future. Such a hypothesis would appear far-fetched were it not for the fact that other elements in these tapestries point toward such a historic metaphor. Until now, the borders of these weavings have been cited only for their decorative value. A detailed examination leads one to believe that they may contain a deeper iconographic sense. First, the border of each tapestry contains the Gonzaga arms, and some also contain one or two *cartellini* with the *titulus* of Guglielmo as Duke of Mantua and as Marquess of Monferrato. The coats of arms and the *tituli* are carefully integrated into the border design, and they were thus conceived and designed together with the other secondary scenes in medallions surrounded and sometimes even covered by the opulent vegetation. In other words, these secondary scenes are stylistically not only in a dialectical relationship to the central scenes of Moses' life but also to the identification of the patron or customer for whom the set was woven. Several of these cartouches

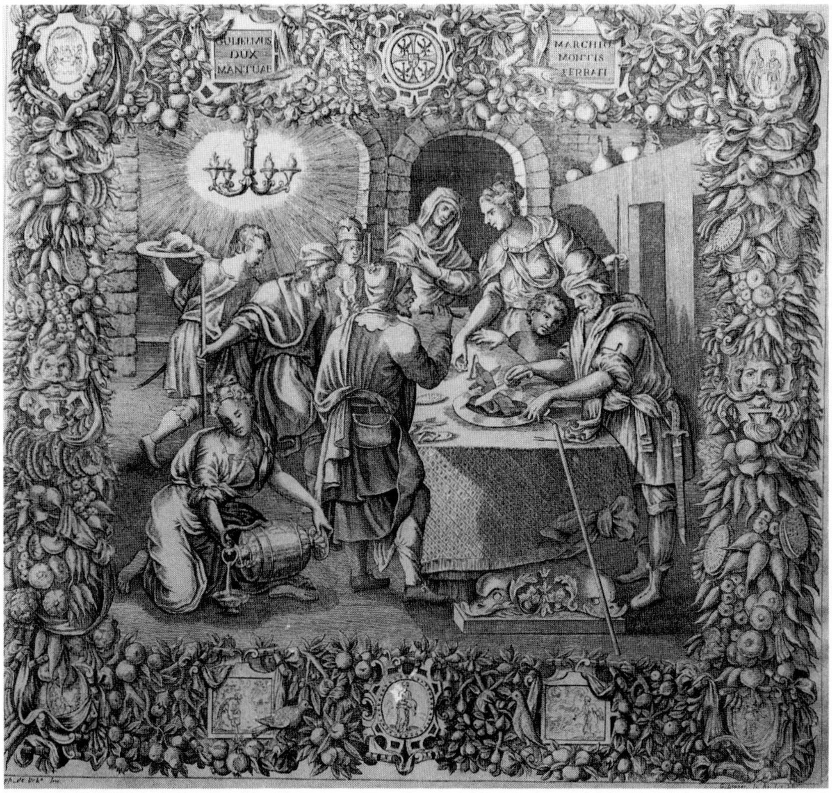

Fig. 119 *Moses: The Passover* (drawing), destroyed 1906, Italian, workshop of Nicolas Karcher, 1553–62. Milan, Museo del Duomo.

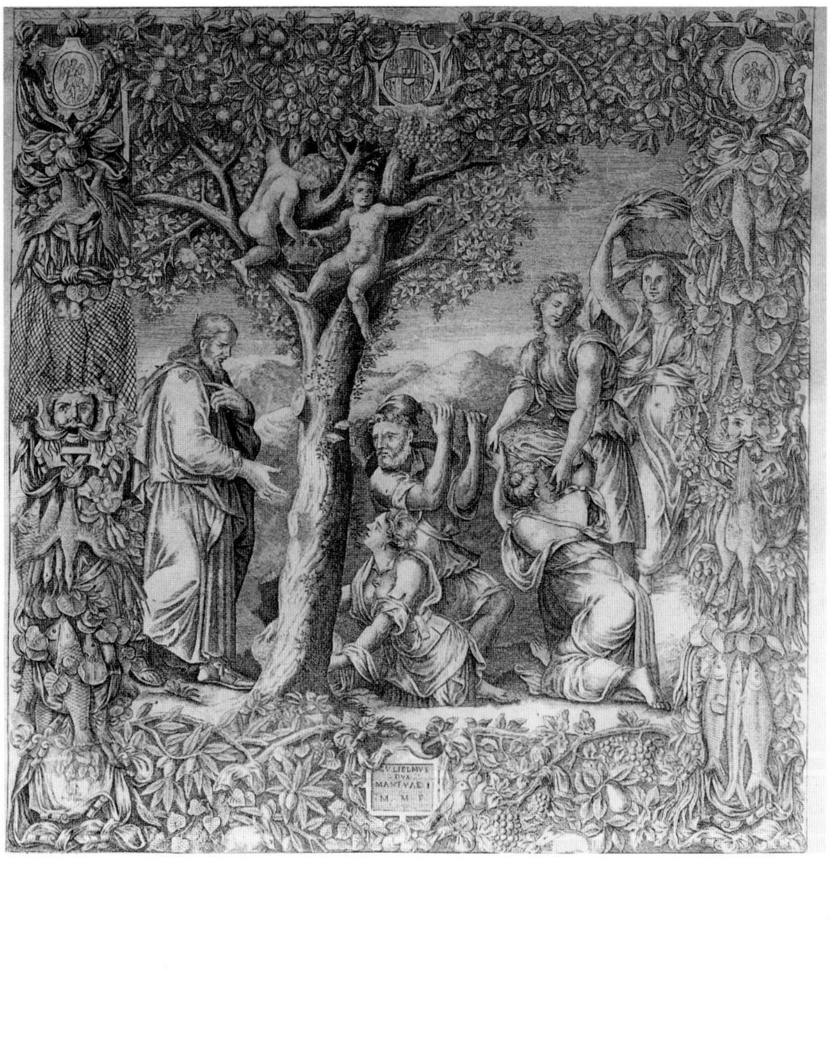

Fig. 120 *Moses: Gathering of the Manna* (drawing), destroyed 1906, Italian, workshop of Nicolas Karcher, 1553–62. Milan, Museo del Duomo.

and medallions contain episodes of Moses' life that are not represented in the main compositions.[16] Others contain personifications of virtues and scenes from two different biblical stories. The upper medallions of the *Brazen Serpent* (Fig. 117) present Charity and Justice, Moses' virtues illustrated in the central scene, but also the main virtues of any good ruler. Judith decapitating Holofernes and presenting his head to Israel is shown on the borders of the *Passage through the Red Sea* and of *Moses Receiving the Tablets of the Law*. It was copied in reverse from a woodcut by Bernard Salomon, published in Claude Paradin's *Quadrins historiques de la Bible,* in 1553.[17] This provides a *terminus ante quem non* for the tapestry. Judith is the model of Fortitude, another princely as well as cardinal virtue.

Several of the border scenes are borrowed from the life of Tobias: the young Tobias guided by the angel Raphael on the *Playing Children,* and the Cure of Tobit from the upper left corner of *Moses Receiving the Tablets of the Law* (Fig. 116) . This last scene has also been interpreted as "Jacob's Blessing of Joseph's Children."[18] Both "Raphael Guiding Tobias" and "Jacob's Blessing" clearly refer to Ercole's regency on behalf of Duke Francesco and Guglielmo, and the "Blessing of Jacob" may even recall that, as in this biblical episode, here also Federico's younger son finally, though forced, obtained God's blessing and the ducal crown. The scene of the Archangel Raphael guiding Tobias may even have been inserted as a direct "in memoriam" for the deceased Duke Francesco III. Indeed, the verso of a coin issued during Francesco's brief reign presents exactly the same scene of Raphael and Tobias, surrounded by the motto "Vias tuas Domine demonstra mihi."[19]

As apparently several scenes in the medallions allude to Ercole's regency and to the brief reign of Francesco III, second Duke of Mantua, we may wonder if the vegetal ornament of the border itself also relates to the events in the Gonzaga family around 1550. The main component of the vegetation is formed by bunches of reeds, as can be found in and around the lakes surrounding Mantua. Branches of reeds were already used as a specific ornament for the Gonzaga, as, for example, on the ceiling frescoes of the Loggia di Davide at the Palazzo Te, and as borders around the *Puttini* tapestry with the arms of Federico II (1539–40).[20] On the *Moses*

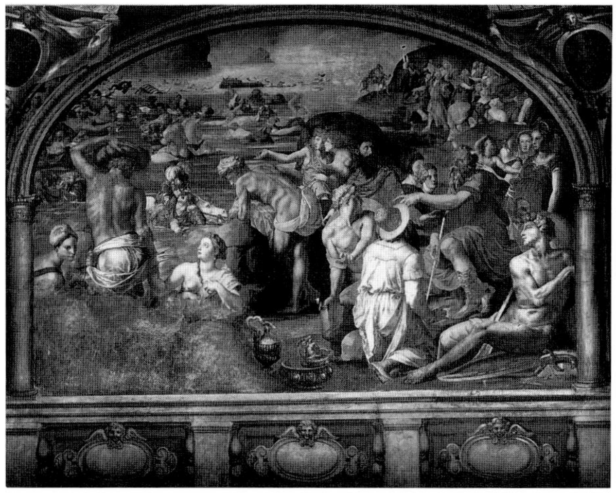

Fig. 121 Agnolo Bronzino, *The Passage through the Red Sea,* fresco, c. 1540. Florence, Palazzo Vecchio, Chapel of Eleonora of Toledo.

tapestries in Milan, they are intermingled with dead aquatic birds and rabbits, hanging as hunting trophies, but also with snakes. Do the snakes, symbols of disease and death in the composition of the *Raising of the Brazen Serpent,* allude to the death of Francesco III after his fall in the lake? Birds and vegetables may refer to the agricultural wealth of the fertile land surrounding Mantua, thus being an image for new life after death, and for a new "aetas aurea" under the new Duke Guglielmo.

The foregoing considerations are also valuable for any discussion of the related piece of the *Puttini with Gonzaga Arms,* owned by the Museo del Duomo in Milan (Fig. 122). This tapestry, ornated with a border identical to that of the *Moses* set, has undoubtedly been ordered and woven at the same time. The medallion cut at the inferior right side points to the loss of the inferior horizontal frieze, which probably contained a *cartellino* with Duke Guglielmo's name and title, such as on the *Brazen Serpent* or on the now-destroyed *Manna.* The medallions with Raphael and Tobias in the left and with Justice on the right emphasize once again Ercole's regency and the virtues of the ruler. Accordingly, it can be maintained that this tapestry formed part of the Guglielmo *Moses* set from its inception. This may explain why Fontana's letter of 1588 alluded to eight tapestries, while the donation of 1569 mentions only six pieces. The set may have consisted of eight pieces, six of them having scenes of Moses and two of playing chil-

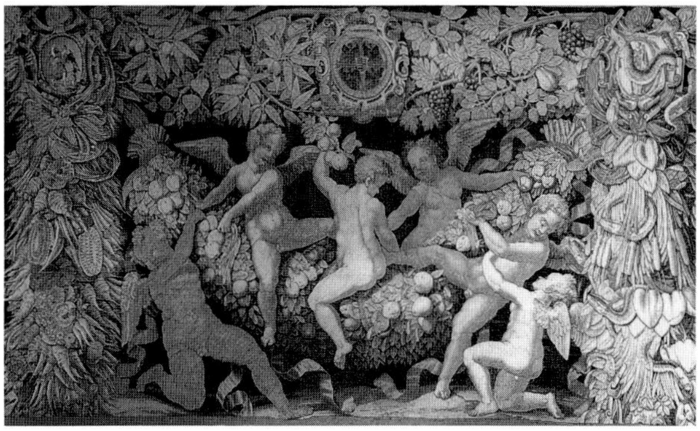

Fig. 122 *Puttini with the Gonzaga Arms,* Italian, workshop of Nicolas Karcher, 1553–62. Milan, Museo del Duomo.

dren (one of them then lost) around a swag, under the Gonzaga arms. In this case the *Puttini* tapestries could have been used as a "sopraporta" (their total height being apparently smaller than the *Moses* pieces), but also—and this is even more important—as a heraldic glorification of the Gonzaga family. It has indeed been noticed that the actual *Puttini* tapestry in Milan is a free interpretation of the Brussels *spalliere* made for Pope Leo X from designs by Giovanni da Udine and Tommaso da Vincidor.[21] This last set, however, was not a mere ornamental woven frieze, but a textile glorification of the heraldry and the emblems of Pope Leo X and the Medici family.[22] The Gonzaga *Puttini* tapestry in Milan is actually the oldest traceable woven adaptation of the Leonine set of 1521. By adapting such a tapestry devoted to papal heraldry, Ercole not only confirmed his regency in the duchy of Mantua but also his personal ambitions to the papacy, as will be explained below. The cartoon for this tapestry may have been painted by Anselmo Guazzi, who painted frescoes with *puttini* and festoons in 1549 for the Palazzo Vescovile in Mantua.[23]

At first sight, and considering the lack of documents, it is hard to understand why such a lavish set, woven with silk and gold, and containing apparently an implicit program referring to Ercole's regency, to the new young duke as well as to his unfortunate brother and predecessor, had been offered to Cardinal Borromeo almost immediately after its weaving. No document has provided evidence until now about the circumstances of this gift, but the relationships between the Gonzaga and Borromeo families in this period allow us understand how this translation has been achieved. Born in 1538, the son of Count Ghiberto Borromeo and of Margherita de' Medici, Carlo received his title of "doctor utriusque iure" on 6 December 1559. Three weeks later, on Christmas Day 1559, Margherita's brother, Giovanni Angelo de' Medici, was elected pope, as Pius IV. On 3 January 1560, Carlo was called by his uncle to Rome, on 31 January he was made cardinal deacon, and on 8 February he became Archbishop of Milan; but he resided at the Vatican, where he came in charge of the highest ecclesiastical responsibilities.[24] One month later, on 12 March 1560, Camilla Borromeo, sister of Carlo, married Cesare Gonzaga, lord of Guastalla, the eldest son of Ferrante and the nephew of Ercole.

From this alliance, important promotions resulted for several ecclesiastical members of the Gonzaga family. On 14 February 1561, Ercole was promoted as one of the five papal legates and as president of the Council of Trent, which had been reopened on 18 January. On 28 February 1562, Cesare's brother, Francesco, was made cardinal, and finally in 1563, a cardinal's hat was also given to Federico Gonzaga, brother of Guglielmo, second Duke of Mantua. Thus, plenty of reasons may have motivated the young Duke Guglielmo, and even more his powerful uncle Ercole, to offer the set to Cardinal Carlo Borromeo, who was, after all, their most powerful relative in the Church. The converging events of Borromeo's cardinalate and of the Gonzaga-Borromeo marriage at the beginning of 1560 make it very probable that Guglielmo's *Moses* set had been presented to Borromeo in this period. As Cardinal Carlo surely knew of the special value and of the recent creation of this set, he would particularly have appreciated such a gift.

It should not be overlooked that Ercole was a serious candidate for the papacy at the December 1559 conclave, which elected Pius IV Medici. Through the mediation of Cardinal Borromeo, Ercole recuperated part of his power in the Church, and he ensured for himself and his two nephews a lasting ecclesiastical career. No gift to Borromeo could be more representational than a rich set of tapestries of the Life of Moses. The initial programmatic intention of the set was thus deviated, in an appropriate way, in favor of another Prince of the Church who may enjoy the *exemplum* of

Moses as a religious leader of his people. Moreover, the *Puttini with the Gonzaga Arms* tapestry, which we consider an integral part of the *Moses* set and which clearly reflects Ercole's papal ambitions by its formal reference to Pope Leo X's tapestries of 1521, could also be perfectly appropriate for the pope's nephew, then residing at the Vatican. From the whole context of this princely gift, we can better understand Carlo Borromeo's reluctance to cede this set in 1566 and his decision to keep it for a while: Guglielmo's *Moses* tapestries surely got his special favor, both as a "family" present and as an inspiring weaving.

Exceptional as it was, Guglielmo's and Ercole's gift of an expensive set that had just been woven for them is not a unique fact in the history of tapestry. Almost the same scenario occurred in similar circumstances some sixty years later, when, in 1625, King Louis XIII of France offered to Cardinal Francesco Barberini, sent as legate by Pope Urban VIII, the first edition of Rubens's *Life of Constantine,* which had not yet been completed in the Parisian workshops. Here also, the set was offered to find favor with the pope's nephew.[25] This last one even founded the Roman Barberini workshop in order to finish the set, designed from cartoons by Pietro da Cortona. And in all the weaving centers here discussed, Florence and/or Mantua for Guglielmo's *Moses* and Paris and Rome for Rubens's and Cortona's *Constantine,* the splendor resulted from the skill of Flemish weavers.

NOTES

1. The tapestries are woven with wool, silk, and silver and gold threads. Bossaglia and Cinotti, 1978, 88–89, and Forti Grazzini, 1982, 79–80 and 189–204, pls. 135–52.

2. Forti Grazzini, 1982, 79. In exchange for the *Moses* set, the Capitolo del Duomo of Milan was required to pay 1,500 "scudi d'oro" toward the cost of building houses for the use of the clergy (*Annali della Fabbrica del Duomo di Milano dall'origine fino al presente,* Milan, 1881, IV, 65). See ibid., 104–5 and Viale Ferrero, 1982, 136 n. 31, for the letter of 9 March 1569 regarding the 3,000 scudi Borromeo hoped to realize through the sale of the *Moses* set. The foregoing references were kindly provided by Nello Forti Grazzini.

3. Karcher continued to execute or to offer to execute works for Margherita Paleologa as well as for Ercole (Documents 23, 27, 30–31).

4. Adelson, 1983, 909.

5. For this chronology, see Adelson, 1983, 913 n. 43. If the set was already on the loom in May 1551, then it may easily have been completed in Florence before October 1553.

6. Coniglio, 1967, 316–18.

7. As the set was surely conceived and woven between 1550 and 1566 at the latest, the former attribution of some models to Ippolito Andreasi (born 1548) around 1574 has to be rejected (see Harprath, 1984, 5 and 20, cat. 92, with former literature).

8. Forti Grazzini, 1982, 79; Bossaglia and Cinotti, 1978, pl. A28; Pecorari (1991, 418) repeats the suggestion of Tellini Perina that the tapestry *Moses Receiving the Tablets of the Law* may have been designed by Rinaldo Mantovano.

9. Adelson, 1991, 150. Sixteen of the twenty *Joseph* tapestries were designed by Bronzino.

10. Venturi, 1993, IX–6, 45, Fig. 26; *Florence 1980,* A87, no. 128; Adelson in *Florence 1985,* 20.

11. During his Florentine period Pagni created cartoons for the Medici (Adelson, 1992, 193–94).

12. Viale Ferrero, 1961, 25; Forti Grazzini, 1982, 79–80.

13. For the *Joseph* set, see Adelson (1985, 24–26) and Forti Grazzini (1982, 198–99).

14. Dacos, 1989, 64–67; Dacos (Fig. 59) does not relate the *Moses* borders but is inclined to believe that the weaver himself (i.e., Karcher) provided the design for this border, as well as for the *Life of Joseph,* for the Palazzo Vecchio (Florence).

15. Karcher delivered a *Moses* tapestry, now lost, to Ercole as early as 24 January 1542 (Document 12), and around 1545–50 Ferrante apparently ordered the *Life of Moses* in twelve pieces, now in Châteaudun (Catalogue 6).

16. *Moses and the Burning Bush, Moses and the Daughters of Jethro,* and *Moses Receiving the Tablets of Law.* As three of these medallions are largely covered by the flora of the borders, their themes remain unclear.

17. Forti Grazzini, 1982, 196, Fig. 142. The Salomon connection was kindly pointed out by Nicole de Reyniés.

18. Bossaglia and Cinotti, 1978, 89.

19. *Mantua 1974,* 83, no. 83. The coin is preserved in the Museo Nazionale Romano, Rome, with reference to the *Corpus nummorum italicum* (IV, 292, no. 12). For the device, see Gelli (1928, 517, no. 1778), who erroneously ascribed this device to Francesco Gonzaga, fifth Duke of Mantua (1586–1612). The error was repeated by Praz in *London 1981,* 67, despite the correct attribution in Typotius (1603) as given on page 69 in the same catalogue.

20. For the Loggia di Davide, see Carpeggiani and Tellini Perina (1987, 87, Fig. 52) and *Mantua 1989,* 221. For the *Puttini* tapestry in the Zeri collection, see *Mantua 1989,* 475, and Catalogue 4 (Fig. 72).

21. Forti Grazzini, 1982, 22.

22. Quednau, 1981; *Vatican 1984,* 357–58; *Vienna 1989,* 58 and 61.

23. Piva, 1985, 9ff. This was suggested by Nello Forti Grazzini, who also noted a possible connection with the payment to Guazzi in 1549 for cartoons for tapestries to be woven in Flanders (Document 25). A related frieze with *puttini* and festoons exists at San Benedetto Po (Piva and Del Canto, 1989, 123). See also under Document 25.

24. Mols, 1953, 486–534.

25. DuBon, 1964, 11ff.

Epilogue

> Be so kind as to ascertain if there are available any expertly woven wool and silk tapestries containing pleasing figures. I am not interested in those tapestries where figures have ill-formed faces and are otherwise inexpertly designed. The tapestries should be approximately five *ale* in height. I shall inform you of my decision as soon you provide me with the desired particulars regarding quality, beauty, subject matter, the number of pieces in the set and the price per *ale* (Document 42).

Each son of Francesco II Gonzaga and Isabella d'Este distinguished himself in the affairs of church and state, and each was also a leader in the cultural spheres in which the Italians excelled. That Federico II, Ercole, and Ferrante developed keen sensibilities for the arts surely owes a great deal to their having been brought up in a world defined by the remarkably lavish architectural and decorative programs devised by Francesco II for his villas in the Mantuan countryside at Marmirolo and Gonzaga, as well as for the suburban residence at San Sebastiano. They were no doubt also indebted to Isabella d'Este's *Studiolo* and *Grotta* in the Ducal Palace, as well as to the extraordinary works commissioned from Andrea Mantegna (the Camera degli Sposi and the *Triumph of Caesar*) and Leon Battista Alberti (the churches of San Andrea and San Sebastiano) by their great-grandfather, Ludovico II (d. 1478).[1]

The Mantua in which Federico II, Ercole, and Ferrante grew up had long been culturally preeminent because of its striking patronage of some of the leading humanists, architects, and painters of the Renaissance. It was the responsibility and privilege of the Gonzaga sons to carry that patronage a significant step further.

What would the later Renaissance have been had Federico II not brought Giulio Romano to Mantua and had Giulio not created for posterity those two influential monuments—the Palazzo Te and the Apartamento di Troia. It was also Federico II who bequeathed to his brother, and thus to posterity, the creations emanating from the fertile shop of Nicolas Karcher, who moved to Mantua from Ferrara and then back to Mantua from Florence.

Sadly the *Puttini* Karcher projected for Federico II was never fully realized. It did serve, however, as the model for the set commissioned by Ercole, a variant of which was subsequently created for Ferrante.

Since the Ferrante *Puttini* cartoons were subsequently copied for Cardinal Granvelle, the influence of what Federico II began, and what Ercole and Ferrante continued, spread throughout Europe. As is already clear, not only were the Gonzaga brothers in the forefront of those who patronized the looms of major weavers of the period, but the results of their costly expenditures have by and large survived to the present day. Equally remarkable, the documents related to these commissions and the inventories that record their movement from generation to generation, have survived in virtually unprecedented abundance.

Visitors to the Vatican who examine the *Cephalus and Procris* weavings are quite possibly seeing the very set that was loaned from the court of Ferrante to be displayed in Mantua in 1549 on the occasion of Duke Francesco III's marriage. Those who enjoy the *Moses* series at Châteaudun can well understand why it was passed on to Maria Vittoria Gonzaga of Guastalla in 1678 with a value of 45,000 scudi "si per la bontà come per essere paramento raro." So important was the *Puttini* to Ercole that he made special provisions for the set in his testament, bequeathing it to his nephew Duke Guglielmo, for whose palatine church Ercole also reserved the *Acts of the Apostles,* which is still preserved in the Ducal Palace in Mantua. As for the *Puttini,* although the set is only partially preserved (and not all in one place), the portions in Lisbon and Milan make it clear that Giulio Romano's designs were expertly realized using the finest threads. The *Puttini* set commissioned by Ferrante, on the other hand, can be enjoyed in its entirety in the special gallery constructed for it in the Villa Marzotto at Trissino. As for the copy made for Cardinal Granvelle, it is now found in Madrid.

Recently, two previously unknown panels from the original set of the Ferrante *Fructus Belli* were acquired for the Musée de la Renaissance at Ecouen. Some years earlier the *Triumphal Cortege* panel from this series was purchased by the Royal Museum of Art and History in Brussels. It was in fact the Brussels acquisition that motivated the research that led to this study.

All that has preceded this epilogue has been in the nature of a celebration of one of the major aspects of courtly life in Renaissance Italy, all of the major events of which, from births and marriages, to entertaining notable vistors, were staged in rooms covered with richly patterned figurative weavings. In addition to serving as a decorative backdrop, they also provided a rich legacy of meaning as, for example, in the highly personal statement Ferrante made in the iconographic underpinnings of his *Fructus Belli* tapestries.

The births of Federico II, Ercole, and Ferrante were anticipated but as yet unrealized back in 1490, when Francesco II Gonzaga took Isabella d'Este as his bride. He did so against the backdrop of the spectacular *Troy* tapestries, which were on loan from the Montefeltro court in Urbino.[2] At the time, perhaps neither parent realized the extent to which tapestries would play a dominant role in the lives of their three sons. While few particulars are known about Federico II's collection, it is not surprising that ecclesiastical subjects dominated Ercole's thinking, while the martial arts and secular themes were nearer and dearer to the interests of his brother Ferrante.

Each left his distinctive mark on one of the major and more costly aspects of Renaissance patronage. Federigo Amadei was clearly overly pessimistic in his appraisal regarding the unliklihood that future generations would be able to enjoy what was available to him (Document 70). Against all odds, Ferrante's *Fructus Belli, Puttini,* and *Moses* have survived. They are joined by some or all of the panels from the other major sets Ferrante and Ercole commissioned, including the *Acts of the Apostles* and the *Cephalus and Procis*. The generous and costly acts of patronage by Federico II, Ercole, and Ferrante have also left significant traces among the chancery records of their respective courts. Whereas previously the study of the art patronage of the Gonzaga brothers has largely been limited to matters pertaining to architecture, sculpture, and painting, this book suggests the need to expand the discussion to include figurative tapestries. They were arguably the most spectacular and visible expression of princely magnificence, serving as they did as the backdrop for all aspects of courtly life, and this perhaps nowhere more spectacularly than in 1530, when the bare walls of the Castello were covered "da ogni banda da alto a basso di finissime tapizerie" to honor Charles V (Document 9) or when, in 1587, the Raphael *Acts of the Apostles* was displayed on the facade of the Duomo on the occasion of the coronation of Vincenzo Gonzaga (Document 62).

Such occasions marked the auspicious beginning of a reign destined to fulfill the promise of the cultural preeminence of Mantua inaugurated in the quattrocento by Gian Francesco and Ludovico II Gonzaga. In the years leading up to the sale of the Gonzaga artistic patrimony to Charles I of England, and the Sack of the city of the imperial forces, Mantua, which had once hosted the talents of Antonio Pisanello, Andrea Mantegna, Leon Battista Alberti, and Giulio Romano, was transformed by the genius of Pieter Paul Rubens and Monteverdi. To the very end, and as evidenced both by the 1627 inventory (Document 67) and the 1670 marital agreement between Ferdinando Carlo, duke of Mantua, and Ferrante III, duke of Guastalla (Document 69), figurative tapestries played a substantial role in the life of the court.

Notes

1. The most recent publication on Isabella d'Este, with detailed bibliography, is *Vienna 1994*. Regarding Francesco II Gonzaga, see Brown, forthcoming.

2. For "la tapezaria sua de la historia troiana per poter metterla apparare la la sala dove se farà la festa," also referred to as "la tapezaria de la istoria troiana per metterla in apparamento de la sala dove se farà la festa, e così li suoi antiporti belli, e qualche tapete da terra," see ASMn, b. 2903, l. 134, c. 28r–v, and Luzio and Renier, 1893, 51–52, no. 1. Other correspondence with the Montefeltro is found in ASMn, b. 1066, cc. 196, 200, and ASMn b. 2903, l. 134, c. 28. For correspondence with other courts related to the loan of "drappi o brocate" and "tapezarie et argenti," see ASMn, b. 1307 (Pio da Carpi: 19, 20 December 1489, 5 February 1490); ASMn b. 2903, l. 134, cc. 17, 20v); ASMn b. 1184 (Sigismondo d'Este: 10 December 1489); ASMn, b. 1184 (Eleonora of Aragon: 6, 12 December 1489); ASMn, b. 2903, l. 134, cc. 28, 47v.; ASMn, b. 1143 (Giovanni II Bentivoglio: 21, 22 December 1489).

Bibliography

I: Books and Articles

Acqua, Marzio dall'. "Il dialogo con il Principe: Appunti per una cronaca dei primi anni di governo gonzaghescho a Guastalla." In *Il Tempo dei Gonzaga,* ed. Cinzia Bertoni and Fiorello Tagliavini. Guastalla, 1985, 35–58.

Adelson, Candace. "Cosimo de' Medici and the Foundation of Tapestry Production in Florence." In *Firenze e la Toscana dei Medici nell'Europa del '500, III: Relazione artistiche. Il linguaggio architettonico.* Florence, 1983, 899–924.

______. "Documents for the Foundation of Tapestry Weaving Under Cosimo I de' Medici." In *Renaissance Studies in Honor of Craig Hugh Smyth,* ed. Andrew Morrough. 2 vols. Florence, 1985, II, 3–17.

______. "Florentine and Flemish Tapestries in Giovio's Collection." In *Raccolta Storica, volume diciasettesimo: Società Storica Comense—Atti del Convegno Paolo Giovio, il Rinascimento e la Memoria,* ed. Stefano Della Torre. Como, 1985[A], 239–81.

______. "The Tapestry Patronage of Cosimo I de' Medici: 1545–1553," 4 vols. Ph.D. diss., New York University, 1990 (Ann Arbor, Xerox Microfilms, 1991).

______. "On Benedetto Pagni da Pescia and Two Florentine Tapestries: The Allegorical 'Portiere' with the Medici-Toledo Arms." In *Kunst des Cinquecento in der Toskana. Italienische Forschungen herausgegeben von Kunsthistorischen Institute in Florenz,* 3d series, XVII. Munich, 1992, 186–96.

______. *European Tapestries in the Minneapolis Institute of Art.* Minneapolis, 1994.

______, and Roberta Landini. "The Persian Carpet in Charles Le Brun's 'July' was a Sixteenth-century Florentine Table Tapestry." *Bulletin du CIETA,* LXVIII, 1990, 53–68.

Affò, Irene. *Vita di Luigi Gonzaga detto Rodomonte, Principe del sacro Romano Impero, Duca di Trajetto, Conte di Fondi, e Signore di Rivarlo.* Parma, 1780.

______. *Istoria della città e ducato di Guastalla.* 4 vols. Guastalla, 1785–87.

______. *Memorie di tre celebri Principesse.* Parma, 1787.

______. *Memorie degli scrittori e letterati parmigiani.* Vols. VI–VII by Angelo Pezzani. 7 vols. Parma, 1789–1833.

Agghazy, Marie G. "Locus amoenus et vinculum delictorum dans l'art de la Renaissance." *Bulletin du Musée hongrois des Beaux-Arts,* LI, 1978, 55–62.

Alberi, E. *Relazioni degli ambasciatori veneti al senato.* 15 vols. Florence, 1839–63.

Alexander, Jonathan James G. *Italian Renaissance Illuminations.* London, 1977.

Alvarez, Vicente. *Relation du beau voyage que fit aux Pays-Bas, en 1548, le prince Philippe d'Espagne,* trans. and ed. M. T. Dovillée. Brussels, 1964.

Amadei, Federigo. *Cronaca Universale della città di Mantova* (18th century), ed. Giuseppe Amadei and Ercolano Marani. 4 vols. Mantua, 1954–57.

Amadei, Giuseppe, and Ercolano Marani. *I Gonzaga a Mantova.* Milan, 1978.

______. *I ritratti gonzagheschi della collezione di Ambras.* Mantua, 1980.

Aretino, Pietro. *Lettere scritte al signor Pietro Aretino.* Venice, 1551.

______. *Lettere sull'Arte,* ed. Ettore Camescasca; commentary by Fidenzio Pertile. 3 vols. Milan, 1957–60.

Gli Arazzi del Cardinale: Bernardo Cles e il Ciclo della Passione di Pieter van Aelst, ed. Enrico Castelnuovo (with contributions by Marco Bellabarba, Guy Delmarcel, Nello Forti Grazzini, Michelangelo Lupo, and others). Trent, 1990.

Asselberghs, Jean-Paul, *Les tapisseries flamandes de la cathédrale de Zamora.* Ph.D. diss., Louvain, 1964.

______. "Les tapisseries tournaisiennes de la Guerre de Troie." *Revue belge d'archéologie et d'histoire de l'art,* XXXIX, 1970, 5–94.

______. "François Geubels et le tapissier bruxellois de l'histoire d'Hannibal." *Revue des archéologues et historiens d'art de Louvain,* IV, 1971, 165–74.

Baldass, Ludwig. *Die Wiener Gobelinssammlung.* Vienna, 1920.

______. "Tapisserieentwürfe des niederländischen Romanismus." *Jahrbuch der kunsthistorischen Sammlungen in Wien,* n.s. II, 1928, 247–66.

Balis, Arnout; Krista De Jonge; Guy Delmarcel; and Amaury Lefébure. *Les Chasses de Maximilien.* Paris, 1993.

Baratte, Sophie. "La collection de tapisseries du cardinal Hippolyte II d'Este." *Bulletin archéologique,* n.s. IX, 1973, 115–26.

Baroni, Costantino. *Documenti per la storia dell'Architettura a Milano nel Rinascimento e nel Barocco. Accademia Nazionale dei Lincei: Fonti e documenti inediti per la storia dell'arte.* Vol. II Rome, 1968.

Battle Huguet, Pedro. *Los tapices de la catedral primada de Tarragona.* Tarragona, 1946.

Baudi Di Vesme, Alessandro. *Schede Vesme: L'Arte in Piemonte.* 4 vols. Turin, 1982.

Beauvois-Faure, Lily. "Een nieuwe reeks met de geschiedenis van David naar een ontwerp van Barent van Orley." In *L'Age d'or de la tapisserie flamande. Colloque international 23–25 mai 1961.* Brussels, 1969, 29–39.

Beltrami, L. *Relazione di Don Ferrando Gonzaga in defesa delle progettata cinta dei bationi*. Milan, 1897.

Bennett, Anna G. *Five Centuries of Tapestry from the Fine Arts Museums of San Francisco*. San Francisco, 1976.

Bertolotti, Antonino. "Varietà artistiche e bibliografiche." *Il Bibliofilo*, v, 1884, 26–28 and passim through 163–66.

______. *Artisti in relazione coi Gonzaga, Duchi di Mantova nei secoli XVI e XVII*. Modena, 1885.

______. "Le arti minori alla corte di Mantova nei secoli XV, XVI e XVII: Ricerca storiche negli Archivi mantovani." *Archivio Storico Lombardo*, xv, 1888, 259–318, 491–590, 980–1075.

Berzaghi, Renato. "Committenze del Cinquecento: La pittura." In *I secoli di Polirone: Committenze e produzione artistica di un monastero benedettino*, ed. Paolo Piva. 2 vols. Quistello, 1981, i, 293–336.

______. "La Corte Vecchia del duca Guglielmo, tracce e memorie." *Quaderni del Palazzo Te*, iii, 1985, 43–64.

Birk, Ernst von. "Inventar der im Besitz des allerhöchsten Kaiserhauses befindlichen niederländer Tapeten und Gobelins." *Jahrbuch der Kunsthistorischen Sammlungen des Allerhöchsten Kaiserhauses*, i, 1883, 213–48; ii, 1884, 167–216.

Boccardo. "Fonti d'archivio per una storia degli arazzi a Genova." *Studi di Storia delle Arti: Genova*, v, 1983–85, 113–31.

Boettiger, John. *Tapisseries à figures des XVIe et SVIIe siècles appartenant àdes collections privées de la Suède*. Stockholm, 1928.

Bombe, Walter. "Raffaels Teppiche und Pieter van Aelst." *Repetorium für Kunstwissenschaft*, l, 1920, 15–29.

Boodt, Anselme Boèce de. *Symbola varia diversorum principum*. Vol. iii. Prague, 1603.

Borsieri, G. *Il Supplimento delle nobilità di Milano*. Milan, 1619.

Bossaglia, Renata, and Maria Cinotti. *Tesoro e Museo del Duomo*: I (Musei e Gallerie di Milano). Milan, 1978.

Braghirolli, Willelmo. *Sulle Manifatture di Arazzi in Mantova: Notizie storiche*. Mantua, 1879.

Brassat, Wolfgang. *Tapisserien und Politik. Funktionen, Kontexte und Rezeption eines repräsentatives Medium*. Berlin, 1992.

Brommer, Frank. *Herakles II: Die unkanonischen Taten des Helden*. Darmstadt, 1984.

Brown, Clifford M. "Lorenzo Costa in Mantua: Five Autograph Letters." *L'Arte*, xi–xii, 1970, 102–16.

______. "Pictures in the Ducal Palace in Mantua." *Zeitschrift für Kunstgeschichte*, xliv, 1981, 53–56.

______. "The Decoration of the Private Apartment of Federico II Gonzaga on the pianoterreno of the Castello di San Giorgio." In *Guerre, Stati e Città: Mantova e l'Italia Padana dal secolo XIII al XIX: Atti delle Giornate di Studio in omaggio ad Adele Bellù—Mantova 12–13 Dicembre 1986*, ed. Carlo Marco Belfanti, Francesca Fantini D'Onofrio, and Daniela Ferrari. Mantua, 1988, 315–43.

______. "Paintings in the Collection of Cardinal Ercole Gonzaga." In *Accademia Nazionale Virgiliana—Giulio Romano: Atti del Convegno Internazionale di Studi su Giulio Romano e l'espansione europea del Rinascimento*, Mantova, Palazzo Ducale, Teatro scientifico del Bibiena 1–5 Ottobre 1989 (with contributions by Orianna Baracchi, Eugenio Battisti, and others). Mantua, 1991, 203–26.

______. "Documents Regarding Duke Federico II Gonzaga's Interest in Flemish Art." *Source: Notes in the History of Art*, 1992, 17–20.

______. "Giovanni Battista Scultori and Cardinale Ercole Gonzaga." *Civiltà Mantovana*, iv, 1992[A], 25–29.

______. "Gifts from the Gonzaga Court for Ludwig and Wilhelm of Bavaria." *Civiltà Mantovana*, ix, 1994, 23–25.

______. "'Concludo che non vidi mai la più bella casa in Italia': Prolegomena to a Study of the Frescoed Decorations in Francesco II Gonzaga's Surburban Villa in the Mantuan Countryside at Gonzaga (1491–1496)." *Renaissance Quarterly*, xlix, 1996. Forthcoming.

______. "The Art Patronage of the Fourth Marquis of Mantua: Francesco II Gonzaga—Paintings by Lorenzo Costa, Dosso Dossi and Matteo di Bologna for the Palazzo di San Sebastiano" (1509–1512). *Quaderni di Palazzo Te*. Forthcoming.

______, and Gilberto Carra. "Francesco Bonsignori: Painter to the Gonzaga Court—New Documents." *Atti e Memorie dell'Accademia Virgiliana*, n.s. xlvii, 1979, 81–96.

______; Laurie Fusco and Gino Corti. "Lorenzo de' Medici and the Dispersal of the Antiquarian Collections of Cardinal Francesco Gonzaga." *Arte Lombarda*, xc–xci, 1989, 86–103.

______, and Anna Maria Lorenzoni. "Isabella d'Este e Giorgio Brognolo nell' anno 1496." *Atti e memorie dell'Accademia Virgiliana*, n.s. xl, 1973, 97–122.

______. *Our Accustomed Discourse on the Antique: Cesare Gonzaga and Gerolamo Garimberto: Two Renaissance Collectors of Greco-Roman Art*. New York and London, 1993.

Brunelli, Roberto. *Storia Religiosa della Lombardia: Diocesi di Mantova*. Brescia, 1986.

Buck, August. "Machiavelli's Dialog über die Kriegskunst." In *Krieg und Frieden im Horizont des Renaissancehumanisme*, ed. F. J. Worstbrock. Weinheim, 1986, 1–12.

Byrne, Janet S. *Renaissance Ornament Prints and Drawings*. New York, 1981.

Calvete de Estrella, Juan Cristóbal. *El felicisimo viaje del muy alto y muy poderoso principe Don Felipe*. Antwerp, 1552. Reprinted, Sociedad española de Bibliofilos, 2a época 8, Madrid, 1930.

Campori, Giuseppe. *Lettere artistiche inedite*. Modena, 1866.

Carpeggiani, Paolo. *Il Libro di Pietra: Giovanni Battista Bertani, architetto del Cinquecento*. In *Quaderni del Dipartimento di Conservazione e Storia dell'Architettura* (Politecnico di Milano, Facoltà di Architettura, i, 1992, 9–168.

______, and Chiara Tellini Perina. *Giulio Romano a Mantova*. Mantua, 1987.

Carreri, F. G. *Relazione delle cose di Sicilia fatta da D. Ferrando Gonzaga all'Imperatore Carlo V*. Palermo, 1896.

Cassirer, Ernst. *Individuum und Kosmos in der Philosophie der Renaissance,* Leipzig and Berlin, 1927.
Castellano, Aldo. "La 'villa' milanese nella prima metà del Cinquecento. Un prototipo inedito: La "Gualtiera-Simonetta." In *La Lombardia spagnola,* with contributions by Ada Annoni and others. Milan, 1984, 87–128.
Castelnuovo, Enrico. See under *Gli Arazzi del Cardinale.*
Cavallaro, Anna. "Pinturicchio a Roma: Il soffitto dei semidei nel palazzo di Domenico della Rovere." *Storia dell'Arte,* LX, 1987, 155–70.
Cavallo, Adolfo S. *Medieval Tapestries in the Metropolitan Museum of Art.* New York, 1993.
Chabod, Federico. *Lo Stato e la vita religiosa a Milano nell'epoca di Carlo V.* Turin, 1971.
Chambers, David. *A Renaissance Cardinal and His Worldly Goods: The Will and Inventory of Francesco Gonzaga.* In *Warburg Institute Survey and Texts,* XX. London, 1992.
Chastel, André. *Il Sacco di Roma 1527.* Turin, 1983.
Colonna, Francesco. *Hypnerotomachia Poliphili.* Venice, 1499. Reprinted in *The Renaissance and the Gods.* 2 vols. New York and London, 1976.
Comes, Natalis. *Mythologie ou Explication des Fables.* Paris, 1627. Reprinted in *The Renaissance of the Gods.* 2 vols. New York and London, 1976.
Coniglio, Giuseppe. *I Gonzaga.* Varese, 1967.
Corpus Nummorum Italicorum: Primo tentativo di un catalogo generale delle monete medievali e moderne coniate in Italia o da italiani in altre paesi. 20 vols. Rome, 1910–43.
Corrain, Lucia. *La Serie Mantovana degli Arazzi raffaelleschi.* Mantua, 1986.
Costa, E. *Registri di lettere di Ferrante Gonzaga.* In *Documenti pubblicati a cura delle Regia Deputazione di Storia Patria per le provincie parmensi,* I, 1889.
Cottafavi, Clinio. "Ricerche e documenti sulla costruzione del Palazzo Ducale: IV—Corte Vecchia." *Atti e Memorie dell'Accademia Virgiliana,* n.s. XXV, 1939, 203–26.
______. "Saggi inediti su edifici della Corte di Mantova (1939)," ed. E. Marani. *Atti e Memoria dell'Accademia Virgiliana,* n.s. XXXIV, 1963, 8–39.
Cox-Rearick, Janet. "Bronzino's Crossing of the Red Sea and Moses Appointing Joshua: Prolegomena to the Chapel of Eleonora di Toledo." *Art Bulletin,* LXIX, 1987, 45–67.
Crick-Kuntziger, Marthe. "Eine unveröfferentlichte Wandteppichfolge von Peter van Edingen, genannt van Aelst." *Pantheon,* XVII, 1936, 193–97.
______. "Note sur une tenture inédite de l'Histoire de Phaéton." *Revue belge d'archéologie et d'histoire de l'art,* XX, 1951, 127–37.
______. "La Cène de Léonard de Vinci et la tapisserie 'belge' aux armes de François Ier." *Revue belge d'archéologie et d'histoire de l'art,* XXI, 1952, 113–26.
______. *Musées royaux d'Art et d'Histoire de Bruxelles: Catalogue des tapisseries (XIVe au XVIIIe siècle).* Brussels, 1956.
Cugnoni, Giuseppe. "Agostino Chigi—il Magnifico." *Archivio della Società romana di Storia Patria,* II, 1879, 37–83, 209–26; III, 1880, 422–48; IV, 1881, 56–75, 195–216; VI, 1993, 139–72, 497–539.
Dacos, Nicole. *Le Logge di Raffaello: Maestro e bottega di fronte all'antico.* Rome, 1977.
______. "Tommaso Vincidor, un élève de Raphaël aux Pays-Bas." In *Relations artistiques entre les Pays-Bas et l'Italie à la Renaissance: Etudes dédiées àSuzanne Sulzberger* (Etudes d'histoire de l'art, publiées par l'Institut historique belge de Rome, VI). Brussels and Rome, 1980, 61–99.
______. "Alle fonti della natura morta italiana: Giovanni da Udine e le nature morte nei festoni." In *La natura morta in Italia,* I, ed. Federico Zeri. Milan, 1989, 55–68.
Darcel, Alfred. "Union centrale des beaux-arts appliqués à l'industrie. Musée rétrospectif. Le Moyen Age et la Renaissance. Emaux, miniatures, manuscrits et tapisseries." *Gazette des Beaux-Arts,* 1866, 48–77.
______. "Exposition Universelle de 1878: Le Moyen âge et la Renaissance au Trocadéro (Arts décoratifs)." *Gazette des Beaux-Arts,* 1878, 969–1010.
D'Arco, Carlo. *Delle Arti e degli Artefici di Mantova.* 2 vols. Mantua, 1857–59.
Davari, Stefano. *Federico Gonzaga e la famiglia Paleologa del Monferrato.* Genoa, 1891.
Davidson, Bernice. "The 'Furti di Giove' Tapestries Designed by Perino de Vaga for Andrea Doria." *Art Bulletin,* LXX, 1988, 424–50.
______. "The *Navigazione d'Enea* Tapestries Designed by Perino del Vaga for Andrea Doria." *Art Bulletin,* LXXII, 1990, 35–50.
Delmarcel, Guy. "Colecciones del Patrimonio Nacional. Tapices I. Los Honores," *Reales Sitios,* LXII, 1979, 39–48.
______. *Tapisseries 2. Renaissance et Maniérisme* Musées royaux d'Art et d'Histoire: Guide du visiteur. Brussels, 1979.
______. *Tapisseries anciennes d'Enghien.* Mons, 1980.
______. "De Brusselse wandtapijtreeks Los Honores (1520–1525). Een vorstenspiegel voor de jonge keizer Karel V," Ph.D. diss., Catholic University Leuven, Leuven, 1981.
______. "La Vie de la Vierge, deux nouvelles tapisseries du cardinal Erard de la Marck." In *Archivum Artis Lovaniense: Bijdragen tot de geschiedenis van de kunst der Nederlanden opgedragen aan Prof. Em. Dr. J. K. Steppe,* ed. M. Smeyers. Leuven, 1981[A], 225–37.
______. "Hercules en de Stymfalische Vogels: Een belangrijk Oudenaards wandtapijt van de zestiende eeuw voor de provincie Oost-Vlaanderen." *Kultureel Jaarboek van de provincie Oost-Vlaanderen. Bijdragen,* n.r. XVIII, 1982, 1–16.
______. "Les tapisseries des Chasses de Maximilien: Rêve et Réalité." *Revue belge d'archéologie et d'histoire de l'art,* LIII, 1984, 119–28.
______. "Fructus Belli, une tenture bruxelloise pour Ferrante Gonzaga." *Bulletin de Liaison du Centre International d'Etude des Textiles Anciens* (Lyon), LIX–LX, 1984[A], 42–53.
______. "La tenture des Guerres Judaiques à Marsala et l'atelier bruxellois C.T." In *La cultura degli arazzi fiamminghi di*

Marsala tra Fiandra, Spagna e Italia: Atti del convegno internazionale, 7–9 luglio 1986, ed. Maria Giulia Aurigemma and Maria Azzarello. Palermo, 1988, 95–107.

______. "Fructus Belli: Brusselse wandtapijten en Italiaanse Renaissance bij de Gonzaga's." *Bulletin des Musées royaux d'Art et d'Histoire Bruxelles,* LX, 1989, 159–201.

______. "A propos de deux tentures bruxelloises d'après Bernard van Orley. *Revue belge d'archéologie et d'histoire de l'art,* LX, 1991, 121–23.

______. "Giulio Romano and Tapestries at the Court of Mantua: The Present State of Research." In *Gonzaga in the Age of Andrea Mantegna and Giulio Romano.* Acts of the International Conference co-sponsored by the London School of Historical Studies and the Royal Academy of Art. In *Europa delle Corte,* ed. Robert Oresko and Cesare Mozzarelli. In press.

______. See under *Gli Arazzi del Cardinale.*

______, and Clifford M. Brown. "Les Jeux d'Enfants, tapisseries italiennes et flamandes pour les Gonzague." *RACAR (Revue d'art canadienne/Canadian Art Review),* XV, 2, 1988, 109–21.

______, and Claire Dumortier. "Cornelis de Ronde, wandtapijtwever te Brussel (+ 1569)." *Revue belge d'archéologie et d'histoire de l'art,* LV, 1986, 41–67.

______, and Erik Duverger. *Bruges et la tapisserie.* Mouscron-Bruges, 1987.

De Poorter, Nora. *The Eucharist Series.* In *Corpus Rubenianum Ludwig Burchard.* Part II. Brussels, 1978.

Dhanens, Elisabeth. "Vlaamse tapijtwerken te Bergamo." *Bulletin de l'Institut historique belge de Rome,* XXVIII, 1953, 333–42.

D'Hulst, Roger A. *Tapisseries flamandes du XIVe au XVIIIe siècle.* Brussels, 1960.

Dictionnaire d'histoire et de géographie et ecclésiastique, ed. R. Aubert. Paris, 1912–.

Donesmondi, Ippolito. *Dell'istoria ecclesiastica di Mantova.* 2 vols. Mantua, 1613–16.

Donnet, Fernand. "Les tapissiers de Bruxelles, Enghien et Audenaerde pendant la Furie Espagnole (1576)." *Annales de la Société royale d'archéologie de Bruxelles,* VIII, 1894, 442–76.

______. "Documents pour servir à l'histoire des ateliers de tapisserie de Bruxelles, Audenarde, Anvers etc. jusqu' à la fin du XVIIe siècle." *Annales de la Société royale d'archéologie de Bruxelles,* XI, 1897, 48–84 and 354–69.

Doursther, Horace. *Dictionnaire universel des poids et mesures anciens et modernes.* Brussels, 1840.

DuBon, David. *Tapestries from the Samuel H. Kress Collection at the Philadelphia Museum of Art: The History of Constantine the Great Designed by Peter Paul Rubens and Pietro da Cortona.* Aylesbury, 1964.

Dussler, Luitpold. *Raphael: A Critical Catalogue of His Pictures, Wall-Paintings, and Tapestries.* London and New York, 1971.

Duverger, Erik. "Tapijtwerk uit het atelier van Frans Geubels." In *L'Age d'Or de la tapisserie flamande: Colloque international 23–25 mai 1961.* Brussels 1969, 91–204.

______. "Tapijten naar Rubens en Jordaens in het bezit van het Antwerps handelsvennootschap Fourment—Van Hecke." *Artes Textiles,* VII, 1971, 119–73.

______. "Tapisseries de Jan van Tieghem représentant l'Histoire des Premiers Parents, du Bayerisches Nationalmuseum de Munich." *Bulletin des Musées royaux d'Art et d'Histoire, Bruxelles,* XLV, 1973, 19–63.

Duverger, Jozef. "Notes concernant les tapisseries du seizième siècle au château du Wawel." *Bulletin des Musées royaux d'Art et d'Histoire, Bruxelles,* XLV, 1973, 65–76.

Duverger, Jozef, and Erik Duverger. "Aantekeningen betreffende de zestiende-eeuwse Brusselse tapijtwever Jan Ghieteels." In *Archivum Artis Lovaniense: Bijdragen tot de geschiedenis van de kunst der Nederlanden opgedragen aan Prof. Em. Dr. J.K. Steppe,* ed. M. Smeyers. Louvain, 1981, 239–47.

Duverger, Jozef, and J. Versyp. "Religieuze voorstellingen in Oudenaardse tapijten." *Cultureel Jaarboek der provincie Oostvlaanderen,* I, 1951, 259–73.

Egger, Hermann. *Codex Escurialensis. Ein Skizzenbuch aus der Werkstatt Domenico Ghirlandaios.* 2 vols. Vienna, 1906.

Eikemeier, Peter. "Der Gonzaga—Zyklus des Tintoretto in der Alte Pinakothek." *Münchner Jahrbuch der bildenden Kunst,* XX, 1969, 75–142.

L'Entrata della Serenissima et Illustrissima Signora Caterina d'Austria Sposa del Eccellentissimo Duca di Mantova (. . .) nella detta sua Città con l'ordine di Tornei, Giostre, Banchetti, Comedie, Musiche, et altri sontuosi apparecchi fatti per la venuta sua, Mantova, Ottobre 1549. Mantua, November 1549.

Erkelens, A. M. L. E. "Rafaeleske Grotesken op enige Brusselse wandtapijtseries." *Bulletin van het Rijksmuseum,* X, 1962, 115–38.

Escher, Conrad. "Die columnae vitineae in St. Peter in Rom im Werk eines französischen Künstlers." *Monatshefte für Kunstwissenschaft,* II, 1909, 413–19.

Fabbi, Paolo. *Gusto Scenico a Mantova nel tardo Rinascimento.* Padua, 1974.

Félibien, André. *Entretiens sur les vies et sur les ouvrages des plus excellens peintres anciens et modernes.* Paris, 1685.

Fenaille, Maurice. *Etat général des tapisseries de la Manufacture des Gobelins. II: Période Louis XIV.* Paris, 1903.

Fenlon, Ian. *Music and Patronage in Sixteenth-Century Mantua.* 2 vols. Cambridge, 1980.

Ferrari, Daniela. "L'inventario dei beni dei Gonzaga (1540–1542)." *Quaderni di Palazzo Te,* I, 1994, 101– 15.

Ferrero, Giuseppe Guido, ed. *Pauli Iovii Opera.* 6 vols. Rome, 1956–.

Ferrero Viale. See Viale Ferrero.

Follino, Federico. *Descrittione delle solenni cerimonie, fatte nella Coronatione del Serenissimo signore il Signor Duca Vincenzo Gonzaga IIII Duca di Mantova et di Monferrato II et cetera* (published together with the *Descriptione dell'infermità, morte e funerali di Guglielmo Gonzaga III duca di Mantova et cetera*). Mantua, 1587.

Forti Grazzini, Nello. *L'Arazzo ferrarese.* Milan, 1982.

______. *Museo d'arti applicate: Arazzi* (Musei e Gallerie di Milano). Milan, 1984.

______. "Disegni di Giulio Romano per gli Arazzi Estensi." *Arte Tessile,* I, 1990, 9–21.

______. "Leonello d'Este nell'autunno del Medioevo: Gli arazzi delle 'Storia di Ercole.'" In *Le Muse e il Principe: Arte di corte nel Rinascimento padano, Saggi* (intro. by G. A. Dall'Acqua). Modena, 1991, 53–62.

______. "Un contesto per l'arazzo con 'Enea davanti a Didone' delle Civiche Raccolte d'Arte Applicata." *Rassegna di Studi e Notizie, Castello Sforzesco.* XVII, 1993, 99–146.

______, ed. *Il Patrimonio artistico del Quirinale: Gli Arazzi.* 2 vols. Milan, 1994.

Franses, Simon. *European Tapestries, 1450–1750: A Catalogue of Recent Acquisitions.* London, 1986.

Friedensburg, Walter. "Der Briefwechsel Gasparo Contarini's mit Ercole Gonzaga." *Quellen und Forschungen aus Italienischen Archiven und Bibliotheken,* II, 1899, 161–222.

Galinsky, Karl G. *The Herakles Theme: The Adaptations of the Hero in Literature from Homer to the Twentieth Century.* Oxford, 1972.

Gaye, Giovanni. *Carteggio inedito d'Artisti dei secoli XIV, XV, XVI,* 3 vols. Florence, 1839–40.

Gelli, Jacopo. *Divise, Motti e imprese di famiglie e personaggi italiani.* 2d ed. Milan, 1928.

Giovio, Paolo. *Gli Elogi: Vite brevemente scritte d'huomini illustri di Guerra, Antichi et Moderni,* tradotte per Lodovico Dominichini. Venice, 1558.

Giulio Romano: Repetorio di fonti documentarie (Pubblicazioni degli Archivi di Stato, Fonti XIV—Archivio di Stato di Mantova), ed. Daniela Ferrari, intro. by Amadeo Belluzzi. 2 vols. Rome, 1992.

Goebel, Heinrich. *Wandteppiche: I. Die Niederlände.* 2 vols. Leipzig, 1923.

______. "Die Wandteppichmanufakturen von Mantua" *Der Cicerone,* XVI, 1924, 585–96.

______. *Wandteppiche II: Die Romanischen Länder.* 2 vols. Leipzig, 1928.

______. *Wandteppiche: III. Die Germanischen und Slawischen Länder.* 2 vols. Berlin, 1933–34.

Golzio, Vincenzo. *Raffaello,* Vatican City, 1936 (repr. 1971).

Gombrich, Ernst H. "The Early Medici as Patrons of Art: A Survey of Primary Sources." In *Italian Renaissance Studies: A Tribute to the Late Cecilia M. Ady,* ed. E. F. Jacob. London, 1961, 279–311.

Gosellini, Guliano. *Vita del prencipe don Ferrando Gonzaga in tre libri divisa.* Milan, 1574.

Gould, Cecil. *Correggio.* London, 1976.

Gourwitch, N. "A Cartoon of Giulio Romano at the Hermitage." In *Musée de l'Ermitage: Travaux du département de l'art européen,* II, 1941, 1–38.

Grandi artisti in una piccola corte dei Gonzaga-Per un museo della Città: 450° anniversario dello Stato gonzaghesco di Guastalla (with contributions by Franco Bonilauri, Marzio Dall'Acqua, and others). Viadana, 1990.

Grassi, Maria Giustina. "La Deposizione con il Cardinal Ercole Gonzaga in S. Egidio a Mantova." *Civiltà Mantovana,* XXVIII, 1993, 44–61.

Grunzweig, A. *Correspondance de la filiale de Bruges des Medici.* Brussels, 1931.

Guasti, C. "Intorno alla vita e alle opere di Domenico Giuntalodi." In Giorgio Vasari, *Le Vite de più eccellenti pittori, scultori, ed architettori,* ed. Gaetano Milanesi. 6 vols. Florence, 1878–81, VI, 31–53.

Guevara, Antonio de. *Vita, gesti, costumi, discorsi e lettere di Marco Aurelio Imperatore.* Venice, 1559.

Guicciardini, Lodovico. *Descrittione di tutti i Paesi Bassi, altrimenti detti Germania inferiore.* Antwerp, 1588.

Guiffrey, Jules. "Cartons de Jules Romain pour la tenture de Scipion, offerts au roi Louis XVI par le peintre anglais Richard Cosway (août-septembre 1786)." *Nouvelles Archives de l'art français,* 2d series, I, 1879, 263–68 (also Frederic Reiset, 465–68).

______. *Inventaire général du Mobilier de la Couronne sous Louis XIV.* Paris, 1885.

Harprath, Richard. "Ippolito Andreasi as a Draughtsman." *Master Drawings,* XXII, 1984, 3–28.

Hartt, Frederick. *Giulio Romano.* 2 vols. New Haven, 1958.

Haverkamp-Begemann, Egbert. *The Achilles Series.* In *Corpus Rubenianum Ludwig Burchard.* Part X. Brussels, 1975.

Hefford, Wendy. "Another Aeneas Tapestry." *Artes Textiles,* XI, 1986, 75–86.

Heinz, Dora. *Europäische Wandteppiche. I: Von den Anfängen der Bildwirkerei bis zum Ende des 16. Jahrhunderts. Bibliothek fur Kunst-und Antiquitätenfreunde.* Vol. XXXVII. Braunschweig, 1963.

Hill, George Francis. *A Corpus of Italian Medals of the Renaissance Before Cellini.* 2 vols. London, 1930.

Hind, Arthur M. *Early Italian Engraving.* 7 vols. London, 1938–48.

Hirst, Michael. "Sebastiano's Pietà for the Comendador Mayor." *Burlington Magazine,* CXIV, 1972, 585–89.

______. *Sebastiano del Piombo.* Oxford, 1980.

Hoffmann, Volker. "Leonardos Ausmalung der Sala delle Asse im Castello Sforzesco." *Mitteilungen des Kunsthistorischen Institutes in Florenz,* XVI, 1972, 51–62.

Hoogewerff, G. J. "Prelaten en Brabantsche Tapijtwevers." *Mededelingen van het Nederlandsch Historisch Instituut te Rome,* III, 1923, 209–22.

Hope, Charles. *Titian.* London, 1980.

______. "Artists, Patrons, and Advisors in the Italian Renaissance." In *Patronage in the Renaissance,* ed. G. F. Lytle and S. Orgel. Princeton, 1981, 298–302.

Horn, Hendrik J. *Jan Cornelisz Vermeyen: Painter of Charles V and His Conquest of Tunis,* 2 vols. Doornspijk, 1989.

Hunter, George L. "The Gonzaga Annunciation Tapestry." *Art in America,* II, 1914, 147–52.

Hurtubise, Pierre. "La table d'un cardinal de la Renaissance." *Mélanges de l'Ecole française de Rome,* XCII, 1980, 249–82.

Hyginus. *Hygini Fabulae,* ed. H. I. Rose. Leiden, 1967.

Hymans, Henry. *Antonio Moro, son oeuvre et son temps.* Brussels, 1910.

Intra, Gian Battista. *Nozze e Funerali alla Corte dei Gonzaga, 1549–1550.* Mantua (1896), 1974.

Jansen, Dirk J. "Jacopo Strada et le commerce d'art." *Revue de l'Art,* LXLXXVIII, 1987, 11–21.

Jarry, Madeleine. "Unknown Tapestries at the Mobilier National." *Burlington Magazine,* CVIII, 1966, 16–20.

Jedin, Hubert. "Il figlio di Isabella d'Este: Il cardinale Ercole Gonzaga." In *Chiesa della Fede, Chiesa della Storia: Saggi scelti,* intro. by G. Albergio. Brescia, 1972, 499–529.

Jestaz, Bertrand. "L'exportation des marbres de Rome de 1535 à 1571." *Mélanges d'archéologie et d'histoire,* LXXV, 1963, 415–66.

Joubert, Fabienne. *La tapisserie médiévale au Musée de Cluny.* Paris, 1987.

Jung, Marc-René. *Hercule dans la littérature française du XVIe siècle: De l'Hercule courtois à l'Hercule baroque.* Geneva, 1966.

Junquera de Vega, Paulina. "Los tapices de la catedral de Cuenca." *Archivo espanol de Arte,* CLXXXI, 1973, 1–11.

______. "Les séries de tapisseries de Grotesques et l'Histoire de Noé de la Couronne d'Espagne." *Bulletin des Musées royaux d'Art et d'Histoire, Bruxelles,* XLV, 1973[A], 143–71.

______, Concha Herrero Carretero, and Carmen Dias Gallegos. *Catalogo de Tapices del Patrimonio Nacional.* 2 vols. Madrid, 1986 (cited as Junquera, 1986).

Kellenbenz, Hermann. "Jakob Rehlinger, ein Augsburger Kaufmann in Venedig." In *Beiträge zur Wirtschafts- und Stadtgeschichte. Festschrift für Hektor Ammann,* ed. Hermann Aubin and Edith Ennen. Wiesbaden, 1965, 362–79.

Keniston, Haywood. *Francisco de los Cobos, Secretary of the Emperor Charles V.* Pittsburgh, 1958.

Kolsky, Steven. *Mario Equicola: The Real Courtier.* Geneva, 1991.

______. "Lelio Manfredi traduttore cortigiano: Intorno al *Carcer d'Amore* e lo *Tirante il Bianco.*" *Civiltà Mantovana,* X, 1994, 45–69.

Knecht, Robert Jean. *Renaissance Warrior and Patron: The Reign of Francis I.* Cambridge, 1994.

Kumsch, Ernst. *Die Apostel-Geschichte: Eine Folge von Wandteppichen nach Entwürfen von Raffael Santi.* Dresden, 1914.

Laborde, Léon de. *Les comptes des Bâtiments du Roi.* 2 vols., Paris, 1877–80.

La Farina, Giuseppe. *Messina ed i suoi monumenti.* Messina, 1840.

Lando, Ortensio. *Sette Libri de Cathaloghi a varie cose (. . .).* Venice, 1553.

Landon, Charles Paul. *Annales du Musée, ou Recueil complet de Gravures: Ecoles italiennes.* Vol. VI. 2d ed. Paris, 1831.

Lavin, Irving. "Cephalus and Procris: Transformations of an Ovidian Myth." *Journal of the Warburg and Courtauld Institutes,* XVII, 1954, 260–87.

Lehmann-Hartleben. Karl. *Die Trajanssäule: Ein römisches Kunstwerk zu Beginn der Spätantike.* Berlin and Leipzig, 1926.

Leydi, Silvio. *Le cavalcate dell'ingegnero: L'opera di Gianmaria Olgiati, ingegnere militare di Carlo V.* Modena, 1989.

Lippencott, Kirsten, and Rodolfo Signorini. "The 'Camera dello Zodiaco' of Federico II Gonzaga." *Journal of the Warburg and Courtauld Institutes,* LIV, 1991, 244–47.

Lorenzetti, Giulio, and Leo Planiscig. *La Collezione dei Conti Donà dalle Rose a Venezia.* Venice, 1934.

Luzio, Alessandro. "Federico Gonzaga ostaggio alla Corte di Giulio II." *Archivio della R. Società Romana di Storia Patria,* IX, 1886, 509–82 (1–78 in extract).

______. "Ercole Gonzaga allo Studio di Bologna." *Giornale Storico della letteratura italiana,* VIII, 1886[A], 374–86.

______. *Pietro Aretino nei primi anni a Venezia e la Corte dei Gonzaga.* Turin, 1888.

______. "Tre lettere di Tiziano al Cardinale Ercole Gonzaga." *Archivio Storico dell'Arte,* III, 1890, 207–9.

______. "A proposto d'arazzi." *Gazetta di Mantova,* XXIX, no. 249, 19–20 September 1891.

______. "Isabella d'Este ne'primordi del paato di Leone X e il suo viaggio a Roma nel 1514–1515." *Archivio Storico Lombardo,* VI, 1906, 99–188, 454–89.

______. "Isabella d'Este e il Sacco di Roma." *Archivio Storico Lombardo,* X, 1908, 5–107, 361–425.

______. "La prammatica del Cardinal Ercole Gonzaga contro il lusso (1551)." In *Scritti varii di erudizione e di critica in onore di Rodolfo Renier.* Turin, 1912, 65–78.

______. *La Galleria dei Gonzaga venduta all'Inghilterra nel 1627–1628.* Milan, 1913.

______. "Contributo alla storia delle suppellettili del Palazzo Ducale di Mantova: Gli arazzi raffaelleschi." *Atti della R. Accademia Virgiliana, Mantova,* VI, 1914, 71–112.

______. *Gli Arazzi dei Gonzaga restituiti dall'Austria.* Bergamo, 1919.

______. *L'Archivio Gonzaga di Mantova, vol II: La corrispondenza familiare, amministrativa e diplomatica dei Gonzaga.* Verona, 1922.

______, and Rodolfo Renier. *Mantova e Urbino: Isabella d'Este ed Elisabetta Gonzaga nelle relazioni familiari e nelle vicende politiche.* Turin and Rome, 1893.

______. *La coltura e le relazioni letterarie di Isablla d'Este Gonzaga.* Turin, 1903 (reprinted from *Giornale storico della letteratura italiana,* XXXIII–XLII, 1899–1903).

Mahl, Elisabeth. "Die 'Mosesfolge' der Tapisseriensammlung des Kunsthistorischen Museums in Wien." *Jahrbuch der Kunsthistorischen Sammlungen in Wien,* LXIII, 1967, 7–38.

Mantova, La storia, ed. Giuseppe Coniglio, Leonardo Mazzoldi, Renato Giusti, and Rinaldo Salvadori; *Le lettere,* ed. Emilio Faccioli; *Le arti* ed. Giuseppe Paccagnini, Ercolani Marani, and Chiara Perina. 9 vols. Mantua, 1958–61.

Marek, Michaela J. *Ekphrasis und Herrscherallegorie: Antike Bildbeschreibungen im Werk Tizians und Leonardos.* Worms, 1985.

Margonari, Renzo and Attilio Zanca. *Il Santuario della Madonna della Grazie presso Mantova.* Mantua, 1973.

Martindale, Andrew. *The Triumphs of Caesar by Andrea Mantegna in the Collection of Her Majesty the Queen at Hampton Court.* London, 1979.

Matz, Friedrich. *Die antiken Sarkophagreliefs. IV: Die dionysischen Sarkophage.* 4 vols. Berlin, 1968–69.

Mayer, Christa C. *Masterpieces of Western Textiles from The Art Institute of Chicago.* Chicago, 1969.

Mazarin. *Inventaire de tous les meubles du Cardinal Mazarin, dressé en 1653, et publié d'après l'original, conservé dans les archives de Condé.* London, 1861 (repr., Geneva, 1973).

Mendonca, Maria José de. *Inventario de tapeçarias existentes em museus e palacios nacionais.* Lisbon, 1983.

Meoni, Lucia. "Gli Arazzieri delle 'Storie della Creazione' medicee." *Bollettino d'Arte,* LVIII, 1989, 57–66.

Meroni, Ubaldo, ed. *Mostra dei Codici gonzagheschi.* Mantua, 1966.

______, ed. *Fonti per la Storia dell a Pittura, IV, Serie Documentaria: Lettere e Altri Documenti Intorno alla Storia della Pittura raccolte di Quadri a Mantova nel Sei-Settecento.* Monzambano, 1976.

Mesenzeva, Charmian. "Zum Problem: Dürer und die Antike: Albrecht Dürers Kupferstich 'Die Hexe.'" *Zeitschrift für Kunstgeschichte,* XLVI, 1983, 187–202.

Mezzatesta, Michael P. "Marcus Aurelius, Fray Antonio de Guevara and the Ideal of the Perfect Prince in the Sixteenth Century." *Art Bulletin,* LXVI, 1984, 620–33.

Moffit, J. "Leonardo's Sala delle Asse and the Primordial Origins of Architecture." *Arte Lombarda,* XCIV, 1991–92, 76–90.

Mols, R. "St Charles Borromée." In *Dictionnaire d'histoire et de géographie ecclésiastiques,* ed. R. Aubert. Paris, XII, 1953, col. 486–534.

Morrogh, Andrew. "The Medici Chapel." In *Michelangelo Drawings,* ed. Craig Hugh Smyth. Hanover and London, 1992, 143–61.

Moscardo, Ludovico. *Historia di Verona.* Verona, 1668.

Mozzarelli, Cesare. "I Gonzaga a Guastalla." In *Il Tempo dei Gonzaga,* ed. Cinzia Bertoni and Fiorello Tagliavini. Guastalla, 1985, 11–33.

Muentz, Eugène. *Les arts à la cour des Papes* (Bibliothèque des Ecoles françaises d'Athènes et de Rome, série I, vols. 4, 9, 28). 3 vols. Paris, 1878–82.

______. "La tapisserie à Rome au XVe siècle." *Gazette des Beaux-Arts,* XIV, 1878, 173–79.

______. *Les collections des Médicis au XVe siècle.* Paris, 1888.

Necipoglu, Gülru. "Süleyman the Magnificent and the Representation of Power in the Context of Ottoman-Hapsburg-Papal Rivalry." *Art Bulletin,* LXXI, 1989, 401–27.

Nelson, Kristi. "Jordaens and Three Alexander Tapestries at the Ringling Museum." *Ringling Museum of Art Journal,* 1983, 204–19.

Nordenfalk, Carl. "Queen Christina's Roman Collection of Tapestries." *Analecta Regenensia,* I–III, 1966, 266–95.

Orbaan, J. A. F. "Parmezaansche Gegevens." *Oud Holland,* XL, 1923–24, 250–57.

Ovid. *Metamorphoses,* ed. and trans. Frank J. Miller. 2 vols. London and Cambridge, Mass., 1964–66.

Paccagnini, Giovanni. *Il Palazzo Ducale di Mantova.* Turin, 1969.

Patricolo, Achille. "Gli Arazzi del Duomo di Mantova." *Rassegna d'Arte,* IV, 1904, 113–22.

Pecorari, Giuseppe. "Il Palazzo del cardinale Francesco Gonzaga." *Civiltà Mantovana,* IX, 1985, 9–29.

______. "Gli Arazzi a soggetto biblico appartenuti al Cardinale Ercole Gonzaga," In *Accademia Nazionale Virgiliana—Giulio Romano: Atti del Convegno Internazionale di Studi su Giulio Romano e l'espansione europea del Rinascimento,* Mantova, Palazzo Ducale, Teatro scientifico del Bibiena 1–5 Ottobre 1989 (with contributions by Orianna Baracchi, Eugenio Battisti, and others). Mantua, 1991, 417–30.

Philostratus. *Imagines,* ed. and trans. Arthur Fairbanks. London, 1960.

Pickering, Frederick P. *Literature and Art in the Middle Ages.* London, 1970.

Pilati, Renata. "I Feudi Gonzagheschi nel Regno di Napoli." *Vespasiano Gonzaga e il Ducato di Sabbioneta,* ed. Ugo Bazzotti, Daniela Ferrari, and Cesare Mozzarelli. Mantua, 1993, 327–55.

Pinchart, Alexandre. *Histoire générale de la tapisserie. III: Pays-Bas.* Paris, 1884.

Piquard, Maurice. "Le cardinal de Granvelle, amateur de tapisseries." *Revue belge d'archéologie et d'histoire de l'art,* XIX, 1950, 111–26.

Piva, Paolo. "Un intervento inedito dell'équipe giuliesca: Le stanza di Ercole Gonzaga in vescovato." *Quaderni del Palazzo Te,* II, 1985, 9–17.

______. *L'altro Giulio Romano: Il Duomo di Mantova, la Chiesa di Polirone e la Dialettica col Medioevo.* Quistello, 1988.

______, and E. Del Canto. *Dal Correggio a Giulio Romano: La committenza di Giulio Cortese.* Mantua, 1989.

Plon, Eugène. *Benvenuto Cellini.* Paris, 1883.

______. *Leone Leoni, sculpteur de Charles-Quint, et Pompeo Leoni sculpteur de Philippe II.* Paris, 1887.

Podreider, P. *Storia dei tessuti d'arte in Italia.* Bergamo, 1928.

Poelnitz, Georg von. *Anton Fugger. I. 1453–1535.* Tübingen, 1958.

Pollard, Graham. *Italian Renaissance Medals in the Museo Nazionale of the Bargello.* 3 vols. Florence, 1984–85.

Quazza, Romolo. *La Guerra per la successione di Mantova e del Monferrato.* 2 vols. Mantua, 1926.

Quednau, Rolf. *Die Sala di Constantino im Vatikanischen Palast: Zur Dekoration der beiden Medici Päpste Leo X und Clemens VII.* Studien zur Kunstgeschichte, XIII. Hildesheim and New York, 1979.

______. "Zeremonie und Festdekor: Ein Beispiel aus dem Pontifikat Leos X." In *Europäische Hofkultur im 16. und 17. Jahrhundert. Kongress 1979.* Vol. II. Hamburg 1981, 349–58.

Rabanos Faci, Carmen. *Los tapices en Aragon.* Saragossa, 1978.

Raupp, Hans-Joachim. "Die Illustrationen zu Francesco Petrarca 'von der Artzney Bayder Glueck des Guten und Widerwertigen' (Augsburg 1532)." *Wallraf-Richartz-Jahrbuch* XLV, 1984, 59–112.

Reiset, Frederic. *Notice des dessins, cartons, pastels, miniatures et émaux exposés dans les Salles du 1er et du 2e étage au Musée National du Louvre. Première partie: Ecoles d'Italie, Ecoles Allemande, Flamande et Hollandaise,* 2d ed. Paris, 1887.

Rezzaghi, Roberto. *Il 'Catecismo' di Leonardo de Marini nel contesto della riforma pastorale del Cardinale Ercole Gonzaga.* Rome, 1968.

Rhodes, Dennis E. "A Book from the Gonzaga Library at Mantua." *Journal of the Warburg and Courtauld Institutes,* XVII, 1954, 377–80.

Roethlisberger, Marcel. "Deux tentures bruxelloises du milieu du XVIe siècle." *Oud Holland,* LXXXVI, 1971, 88–115.

Romano, Giacinto. *Cronaca del soggiorno di Carlo V in Italia.* Milan, 1892.

Romeo, Ilaria. "Raffaello, l'antico e le bordure degli arazzi vaticani." *Xenia,* XIX, 1990, 40–86.

Ronchini, Armadio. "Leone Leoni d'Arezzo." *Atti e Memorie della R.R. Deputazione di Storia patria per le provincie modenesi e parmensi,* III, 1865, 9–41.

Rossi, Umberto. "Commedie Classiche in Guazzuolo nel 1501–1507." *Giornale storico della letteratura italiana,* XIII, 1889, 305–15.

______. "Jehan Baudouyn, arazziere fiammingho." *Archivio Storico dell' Arte,* II, 1889, 252–53[A].

Rostagno, E. "Il Monumentum Gonzagium di Giovanni Benevoli o Buonavaglia." *La Bibliofilia,* I, 1899, 135–68, 186–89.

Rotondi, Pasquale. *Il Palazzo Ducale di Urbino,* Milan, 1951.

Saintenoy, Paul. "Les tapisseries de la cour de Bruxelles sous Charles V." *Annales de la Société royale d'archéologie de Bruxelles,* XXX, 1921, 5–31.

Salza, El-Kader. *Luca Contile—uomo di Lettere e di negozi del secolo XVI.* Florence, 1903.

Santangelo, Antonio. *The Development of Italian Textile Design.* London, 1964.

Sanvito, Paolo. "Collezionismo imperalregio e collezionismo a Sabbioneta: L'influenza del modello Asburgico." In *Vespasiano Gonzaga e il Ducato di Sabbioneta,* ed. Ugo Bazotti, Daniela Ferrari, and Cesare Mozzarelli, Mantua, 1993, 181–205.

Schaeffer, Emil. "Der 'Triumph des Federico Gonzaga' von Lorenzo Costa." *Monatshefte fuer Kunstwissenschaft,* I, 1908, 162ff.

Schmitt, Ursula. "Francesco Bonsignori." *Münchner Jahrbuch der Bildenden Kunst,* XII, 1961, 72–152.

Schneebalg-Perelman, Sophie. "Un grand tapissier bruxellois: Pierre d'Enghien, dit Pierre van Aelst." In *L'âge d'or de la tapisserie bruxelloise. Colloque international,* 23–25 May 1961. Brussels, 1969, 279–323.

______. "Le rôle de la banque de Medicis dans la diffusion des tapisseries flamandes." *Revue belge d'archéologie et d'histoire de l'art,* XXXVIII, 1969[A], 19–41.

______. "Richesses du garde-meuble parisien de François Ier: Inventaires inédits de 1542 et 1551." *Gazette des Beaux-Arts,* CXIII, 1971, 253–304.

______. *Les Chasses de Maximilien: Les énigmes d'un chef-d'oeuvre de la tapisserie.* Brussels, 1982.

Schoutheete de Tervarent, Guy de. "L'origine des fontaines anthropomorphes." *Académie royale de Belgique. Bulletin de la Classe des Beaux-Arts,* XXXVIII, 1956, 122–29.

Schrenck von Nozing, Jacob. *Augustissimorum imperatorum (. . .).* Joannes Agricola, 1601.

Scotti, Aurora. "Per un profilo dell'architettura milanese (1535–1565)." In *Omaggio a Tiziano: La cultura artistica milanese nell'età di Carlo V,* ed. Mercedes Garberi. Milan, 1977, 97–121.

Scuderi, Vincenzo. "La storia di Enea negli arazzi Whitaker." *Kalos: Arte in Sicilia,* V, 1993, 6–15.

Segarizzi, Arnaldo. *Relazioni degli Ambasciatori Veneti al Senato,* 4 vols. Bari, 1912–16 (repr., 1968).

Segre, Arturo. *Un Registro di Lettere del Cardinale Ercole Gonzaga.* Turin, 1912.

Seznec, Jean. *The Survival of the Pagan Gods: The Mythological Tradition and Its Place in Renaissance Humanism and Art.* New York, 1961.

Sheard, Wendy Stedman. *Antiquity in the Renaissance.* Northhampton, Mass., 1979.

Shearman, John. *Raphael's Cartoons in the Collection of Her Majesty the Queen and the Tapestries for the Sistine Chapel.* London, 1972.

______. "Giulio Romano and Baldassare Castiglione." In *Accademia Nazionale Virgiliana. Giulio Romano: Atti del Convegno Internazionale su "Giulio Romano e l'espansione europea del Rinascimento."* Mantova, Palazzo Ducale, Teatro scientifico del Bibiena 1–5 Ottobre 1989 (with contributions by Orianna Barocchi, Eugenio Battisti, and others). Mantua, 1991, 293–301.

Signorini, Rodolfo. *Opus Hoc Tenue: La Camera Depinta di Andrea Mantegna: Lettera storica, iconografica, iconologica.* Mantua, 1985.

______. *Lo Zodiaco di Palazzo d'Arco in Mantova.* 2d ed. Mantua, 1988.

Siple, Ella S. "A Flemish Set of Venus and Vulcan Tapestries." *Burlington Magazine,* LXXIII, 1938, 212–20.

Smit, Hillie. "The Tapestry Collection of Pope Julius II: Notes by Marcantonio Michiel in 1519." *Bulletin du CIETA,* LXXI, 1993 (published 1994), 49–60.

Smith, Marc Hamilton. "François Ier, L'Italie et Le Châtreau de Blois." *Bulletin Monumental,* CXXXXVIII, 1989, 307–23.

Soldini, N. "Strategie del dominio: La cittadella nuova di Piacenza (1545–1556)." *Bollettino Storico Piacentino,* LXXXVI, 1991, 11–69.

Solmi, Edmondo. "La Fuga di Bernardino Ochino secondo i documenti dell'Archivio Gonzaga di Mantova." *Bullettino Senese di Storia Patria,* XV, 1908, 3–78 (in extract).

Sorbelli, Albano. *Guastalla.* In *Inventari dei Manoscritti delle Biblioteche d'Italia,* founded by Giuseppe Mazzatini. Vol. LXIII. Florence, 1937.

Sparrow, John H. A. *Visible Words: A Study of Inscriptions in and as Books and Works of Art.* London, 1969.

Standen, Edith A. "Some Sixteenth-Century Flemish Tapestries Related to Raphael's Workshop." *Metropolitan Museum Journal,* IV, 1971, 115–21.

______. "Romans and Sabines: A Sixteenth-Century Set of Flemish Tapestries." *Metropolitan Museum Journal,* IX, 1974, 211–28.

______. *European Post-Medieval Tapestries and Related Hangings in The Metropolitan Museum of Art.* 2 vols. New York, 1985.

Steppe, Jan-Karel. "Vlaamse wandtapijten in Spanje: Recente feiten en gebeurtenissen." *Artes Textiles,* III, 1956, 27–66.

______. and Guy Delmarcel. "Les tapisseries du cardinal Erard de la Marck prince-évêque de Liège." *Revue de l'Art,* XXV, 1974, 35–54.

Stettler, Michael. "Das Trojanische Pferd. Ein Brüsseler Wandteppich." In *Artes Minores: Dank an Werner Abegg,* ed. Michael Stettler and Mechthild Lemberg. Bern, 1973, 229–62.

Sulzberger, Suzanne. "Matteo del Nassaro et la transmission des oeuvres flamandes en France et en Italie. *Gazette des Beaux-Arts,* LV, 1960, 147–50.

Szablowski, Jerzy, ed. *The Flemish Tapestries at the Wawel Castle in Krakow.* Brussels, 1972.

Tamalio, Raffaele. *Ferrante Gonzaga alla Corte Spagnola di Carlo V nel carteggio privato con Mantova (1523–1526).* Mantua, 1991.

___. *Federico Gonzaga alla Corte di Francesco I di Francia nel carteggio privato con Mantova (1515–1517).* Paris, 1994.

Tanzi, Marco. "Comprimari e comparse nell'équipe giuliesca a San Benedetto Po: Fermo Ghisoni, Anselmo Guazzi, Francesco Maria Castaldi." In *Dal Correggio a Giulio Romano: La Committenza di Gregorio Cortese,* ed. Paolo Piva and E. Del Canto. Mantua, 1989, 133–42.

Tarchi, Ugo. *La Villa detta "La Simonetta" nel Suburbio di Milano.* In *I Monumenti italiani,* ser. II, fasc. II. Rome, 1953.

Tellini Perina, Chiara. "Teodoro Ghisi: L'immagine fra Maniera e Controriforma." In *La Scienza a Corte. Collezionismo eclettico, natura e immagine a Mantova fra Rinascimento e Manierismo* (with contributions by Dario Franchini, R. Margonari, and others). Rome, 1979, 239–68.

Tervarent, Guy de. *Attributs et symboles dans l'art profane de la Renaissance.* 2 vols. Geneva, 1958.

Thornton, Peter. *The Italian Renaissance Interior, 1400–1600.* London, 1991.

Thorpe, W. A. "The 'Plus Oultra' Cabinet at South Kensington." *Connoisseur,* CXXVIII, 1951, 24–28, 56.

Tiraboschi, Girolamo. *Storia della letteratura italiana.* 9 vols. in 16. Milan, 1822–26.

Torra de Arana, Eduardo, and others. *Los Tapices de la Seo de Zaragoza.* Saragossa, 1985.

Typotius, Jacobus. *Symbola divina et humana (. . .).* Prague, 1601–3.

Ulloa, Alfonso. *Vita dell'Invittissimo Imperator Carlo Quinto.* Venice, 1562.

______. *Vita del valorosissimo e gran capitano Don Ferrante Gonzaga principe di Molfetta etc.* Venice, 1563.

Valenti, Filippo. *Artigianato e oggetti di artigianato a Modena dal 1650 al 1800.* Modena, 1986.

______. *L'Inventario 1771 dell'arredo del Palazzo Ducale di Modena.* Modena, 1986[A].

Van de Velde, Carl. *Frans Floris (1519/20–1570). Leven en Werk (Verhandelingen van de Koninklijke Academie voor Wetenschappen, Letteren en Schone Kunsten van België. Klasse der Schone Kunsten,* jaargang XXXVII, 30). 2 vols. Brussels, 1975.

Van Durme, Maurice. *Antoon Perrenot, bisschop van Atrecht, kardinaal van Granvelle, minister van Karel V en van Filips II: 1517–1586 (Verhandelingen van de Koninklijke Academie voor Wetenschappen, Letteren en Schone Kunsten van België. Klasse der Lettern,* jaargang XV, 18). Brussels, 1953.

Van Tichelen, Isabelle. "La manifattura di Martin Reymbouts." In *Arazzi per la Cattedrale di Cremona: Storie di Sansone, Storia della vita di Cristo,* ed. Loretta Dolcini. Milan, 1987, 54–55.

Vasari, Giorgio. *Le vite de'più eccellenti pittori, scultori e architettori,* ed. Gaetano Milanesi. Florence, 1878–85.

Vaucaire, Maurice. "Fructus Belli, tapisseries d'après les cartons de Jules Romain." *Les Arts,* no. 159, 1917, 6–12.

Venturi, Adolfo. *Storia dell'arte italiana. IX: La Pittura del Cinquecento.* Part 6. Milan, 1933.

______. *Storia dell'arte italiana. X: La scultura del Cinquecento.* Part 3. Milan, 1937.

Verdier, Philippe. "Sur trois oeuvres de Léonard Limousin." *Revue de l'Art,* LXXVII, 1987, 51–61.

Verheyen, Egon. "Jacopo Strada's Mantuan Drawings." *Art Bulletin,* XLIX, 1967, 62–70.

______. *The Palazzo del Te in Mantova: Images of Love and Politics.* Baltimore and London, 1977.

Versyp, Jacqueline. "Zestiende-eeuwse jachttapijten met het wapen van de Vidoni." *Artes Textiles,* VII, 1971, 23–46.

Viale, Mercedes, and Vittorio Viale. *Arazzi e Tappeti antichi.* Turin, 1952.

Viale Ferrero, Mercedes. *Arazzi italiani del Cinquecento.* Milan, 1961.

______. *Arazzi italiani del Cinquecento.* 2d ed. Milan, 1963.

______. "Nouveaux documents sur les tapisseries de la maison de Savoie." In *Miscellanea Jozef Duverger: Bijdragen tot de Kunstgeschiedenis der Nederlanden,* ed. Jacqueline Versyp and A. Monballieu. 2 vols. Ghent, 1968, II, 806–18.

______. "Quatre tapisseries inédites de l'Histoire de Troie." *Artes Textiles,* X, 1981, 183–92.

______. "Arazzo e pittura." In *Storia dell'arte italiana,* ed. P. Fossati. Vol III-4. Turin, 1982.

______. "Arazzi." In *Museo Poldi-Pezzoli: Arazzi-Tappeti-Tessuti Copti-Ricami-Ventagli* (Musei e Gallerie di Milano). Milan, 1984.

Virgil. *Aeneid,* ed. and trans. H. R. Fairclough. 2 vols. London, 1966–67.

Volckaert, An. "De Meester van de Verloren Zoon en de Brusselse wandtapijtkunst." *Jaarboek Koninklijke Museum voor Schone Kunsten Antwerpen,* 1987, 93–106.

Wace, Alan. *The Marlborough Tapestries at Blenheim Palace and Their Relation to Other Military Tapestries of the War of Spanish Succession.* London and New York, 1968.

Warburg, Aby. *Gesammelte Schriften.* Vol. I. Leipzig and Berlin, 1932.

Ward-Perkins, John Bryan. "The Shrine of St. Peter and Its Twelve Spiral Columns." *Journal of Roman Studies,* XLII, 1952, 21–33.

Wauters, Alphonse. *Les tapisseries bruxelloises.* Brussels, 1878.

Wethey, Harold. *The Paintings of Titian.* 3 vols. London, 1969–75.

Wingfield Digby, George, and Wendy Hefford. *Victoria and Albert Museum: The Tapestry Collection. Medieval and Renaissance.* London, 1980.

Wojno Kiefer, Geraldine A. "Mid-Sixteenth-Century Veronese Painting in the Duomo of Mantua." *Antichità Viva,* XXVI, 1987, 34–43.

Zanker, Paul. "Das Trajansforum in Rom." *Archäologischer Anzeiger,* IV, 1970, 499–543.

Zupko, Ronald E. *Italian Weights and Measures from the Middle Ages to the Sixteenth Century.* Philadelphia, 1981.

II. Exhibition Catalogues

Brussels 1935:
Exposition universelle et internationale de Bruxelles 1935, Bibliothèque royale Albert I. Cinq siècles d'art. Tome II. Dessins et tapisseries, ed. Marthe Crick-Kuntziger. Brussels, 1935.

Brussels 1951:
Le siècle de Bourgogne, 1951.

Brussels 1970:
Hieronymus Cock, prentenuitgever en graveur, ed. Lydia De Pauw-De Veen. Brussels, 1970.

Brussels and London 1972:
Dessins flamands du dix-septième siècle-Collection Frits Lugt. Institut Neérlandais, Paris, ed. Carlos van Hasselt. London, Paris, Bern, Brussels, 1972.

Brussels 1974:
Musées royaux d'Art et d'Histoire. Acquisitions nouvelles, 1964–1973. Brussels, 1974.

Cremona 1985:
I Campi e la Cultura cremonese del Cinquecento, Cremona, Santa Maria della Pietà and other venues, ed. Mina Gregori (with contributions by Giulio Bora, Ciovanni Vigo, and others). Milan, 1985.

Cremona 1987:
Arazzi per la Cattedrale di Cremona: Storie di Sansone, Storie della vita di Cristo, Cremona, Santa Maria della Pietà 15 April–5 July 1987, ed. Loretta Dolcini (with contributions by Antonio Paolucci, Giovanni Rodella, and others, including Guy Delmarcel). Milan, 1987.

Culan 1971:
Chefs-d'oeuvre de la tapisserie flamande: Onzième exposition du château de Culan, 12 June–12 September 1971, ed. Jean-Paul Asselberghs. Bourges, 1971.

Ecouen 1992:
Autour des Fructus Belli: Un tapisserie de Bruxelles du XVIe siècle, Musée national de la Renaissance, Château d'Ecouen, Val d'Oise, 18 June–21 September 1992 (with contributions by Guy Delmarcel, Julien Guilbault, and others). Paris, 1992.

Florence 1980:
Firenze e la Toscana dei Medici nell'Europa del Cinquecento. Palazzo Vecchio: Committenza e collezionismo medicei, Firenze, Palazzo Vecchio, ed. Paola Barocchi and Giovanna Gaeta Bertelà. Florence, 1980.

Florence, 1980[A]:
Firenze e la Toscana dei Medici nell'Europa del Cinquecento: Il Primato del Disegno, Firenze, Palazzo Strozzi, intro. Luciano Berti (with contributions by Luciano Bellosi and others). Florence, 1980.

Florence and Rome 1983–84:
Disegni italiani del Teylers Museum Haarlem provenienti dalle collezioni di Cristina di Svezia e dei principi Odescalchi (Bert W. Meijer, C. van Tuyll). Florence, 1983; Rome, 1984.

Florence 1985:
Gli Arazzi della Sala dei Duecento: studi per il restauro. Firenze, Palazzo Vecchio. Modena, 1985.

Frankfurt 1985:
Natur und Antike in der Renaissance. Frankfort am Main, Liebieghaus Museum alter Plastik, 5 December 1985–2 March 1986, ed. Herbert Beck and Dieter Blume. Frankfurt am Main, 1985.

Ghent 1987–88:
Tapisseries flamandes du château du Wawel à Cracovie et d'autres collections européennes: Vlaamse wandtapijten uit de Wawelburcht te Krakau en uit andere Europese verzamelingen, Sint-Pietersabdij, Centrum voor Kunst en Cultuur, 12 December 1987–14 February 1988 (with contributions by Maria Hennel-Bernasikova, Erik Duverger, and others). Ghent, 1987–88.

Halbturn 1981:
Tapisserien der Renaissance nach Entwürfen von Pieter Coecke van Aelst, Rotraud Bauer and Jan Karel Steppe, Schloss Halbturn, 15 May–26 October 1981.

London 1965:
Exhibition of Important Tapestries, 480–1780, V. Stenberg and C. Sternberg. London, 1965.

London 1980:
Princely Magnificence: Court Jewels of the Renaissance, 1500–1630, London, Victoria and Albert Museum, 15 October 1980–1 February 1981, ed. A. G. Somers Cocks (with contributions by Peter Burke, E. A. Jobbins, and others). London, 1980.

London 1981:
Splendours of the Gonzaga, London, Victoria and Albert Museum, 4 November 1981–31 January 1982, ed. David Chambers and Jane Martineau (with contributions by Ilaria Toesca, Rodolfo Signorini, and others). Milan, 1981.

Mantua 1972:
Pisanello alla corte dei Gonzaga. ed. Giovanni Paccagnini, Mantova, Palazzo Ducale. Mantua, 1972.

Mantua 1974:
Tesori d'arte nella terra dei Gonzaga, Mantova, Palazzo Ducale, intro. by Ciro Ferrari (with contributions by Lionello Giorgio Boccia, Luigi Boscio, and others). Milan, 1974.

Mantua 1979:
La Scienza a Corte: Collezionismo eclettico natura e immagine a Mantova fra Rinascimento e Manerismo, Mantova, Palazzo Ducale (with contributions by Dario Franchini, Renzo Margonari, and others), in *Centro Studi "Europa delle Corti," Biblioteca del Cinquecento,* no. 7. Rome, 1979.

Mantua 1989:
Giulio Romano, Mantova, Palazzo Te and Palazzo Ducale, 1 September–12 November 1989 (with contributions by Ernst H. Gombrich and others, including Nello Forti Grazzini). Milan, 1989.

Milan 1977:
Omaggio a Tiziano: La cultura artistica milanese nell'età di Carlo V, Milano, Palazzo Reale, 27 April–20 July 1977 (with contributions by Mercedes Garberi, Pinin Brambilla Barcilon, and others). Milan, 1977.

Paris 1865:
Union Centrale des Beaux-Arts appliqués à l'industrie. Exposition de 1865, Paris, Palais de l'Industrie. Musée rétrospectif, Paris, 1865.

Paris 1965:
Le XVIe siècle européen. Tapisseries, Paris, Mobilier National. Paris, 1965.

Paris 1978:
Jules Romain. L'Histoire de Scipion. Tapisseries et dessins, Bertrand Jestaz and Roseline Bacou, Paris, Grand Palais. Paris, 1978.

Paris 1981:
Les chevaux de Saint-Marc, Paris, Grand Palais. Paris, 1981.

Paris 1983:
Autour de Raphaël, Paris, Musée du Louvre, ed. Roseline Bacou and Sylvie Beguin. Paris, 1983.

Rome 1937:
L'antico tessuto d'arte italiano, ed. Luigi Serra. Rome 1937.

Rome 1984:
Aspetti dell'Arte a Roma prima e dopo Raffaello, Rome, Palazzo Venezia, 22 March–13 May, intro. by Dante Bernini (with contributions by Roberto Cannatà, Claudio Strinati, and others, including Alia Englen). Rome, 1984.

Trent 1993:
I Madruzzo e l'Europa 1539–1658: I Principi vescovi di Trento tra Papato e Impero, Trento, Castello del Buonconsiglio, 10 July–31 October 1993, ed. Laura Dal Prà. Milan and Florence, 1993.

Utrecht 1993:
Maria van Hongarije, koningin tussen keizer en kustenaars: 1505–1558, ed. A. M. Koldeweij. Utrecht and s'Hertogenbosch, 1993.

Vatican 1984:
Raffaello in Vaticano, Città del Vaticano, preface by Carlo Pietrangli, intro. by Fabrizio Mancinelli. Milan, 1984.

Vienna 1983:
Tapisserien im Zeichen der Kunst Raffaels, ed. R. Bauer, Vienna, Messepalast. Vienna, 1983.

Vienna 1989:
Fürstenhöfe der Renaissance: Giulio Romano und die Klassische Tradition, Wien, Neue Burg, December 6 1989–February 18 1990, ed. Sylvia Ferino Pagden, Konrad Oberhuber, and Nikolai Dobrowolskij. Vienna, 1989.

Vienna 1994:
La Prima Donna del Mondo: Isabella d'Este Fürstin und Mäzenatin der Renaissance, Wien, Kunsthistorisches Museum, ed. Sylvia Ferino Pagden. Vienna, 1994.

Index

Listings have not been provided for the three principals (Federico II, Ercole, and Ferrante Gonzaga) or for modern (post-17th-century) authors. Cities are recorded only when they contain specific works of art. Family names have not always been easy to determine, as for example in the case of the "Francischo," who is described by Nicolas Karcher as "mio genero," and where the spelling is given as "Fransischo" (Document 31). Accordingly, such individuals are listed precisely as they appear in the archival records. **Bold** is used to identify the major references to the tapestries.

PHOTOGRAPHY CREDITS

Unless otherwise noted, the photographs were provided directly by the owners of the works of art.

Brussels: A.C.L. (Archives photographiques de l'Institut du Patrimoine artistique: Figs. 18, 29–30, 43, 50, 53–54, 56, 58–59. Royal Library Albert I: Fig. 60. Speltdoorn: Color Plate XI and Fig. 103. **Florence:** Alinari, Fig. 121. **Frankfurt-am-Main:** Edelmann, Fig. 27. **Hamburg:** Kiemer, Fig. 19. **Leuven:** Delmarcel, Figs. 17, 32, 37, 40, 51–52, 57, 62, 67–68, 84, 95–97, 112–14. **London:** British Museum, Fig. 14. Courtauld Institute: Figs. 71, 83. **Mantua:** Archivio di Stato, Fig. 8. Giovetti, Color Plates IV–IX and Figs. 6, 11, 16, 31, 33–35, 38–39, 41–42, 84–89. Soprintendenza per i Beni artistici e storici di Mantova, Color Plate I and Fig. 28. **Milan:** Museo del Duomo, Figs. 115–20, 122. Forti Grazzini, Fig. 72. **Paris:** Archives Photographiques, SPADEM, Figs. 98–99, 101–2, 104–8. Caisse Nationale der Monuments Historiques, Figs. 46, 109–11. Galerie Chevalier, Color Plate X and Fig. 100. Réunion des Musée Nationaux (RMN), Figs. 44, 49, 61, 64–70. **Rome:** Anderson, Fig. 26. **Vienna:** Bildarchiv der Oesterreichische Nationalbibliothek, Fig. 45.

Photographs taken from publications: Fig. 12 (*Trent 1993,* 114); Fig. 7 (Amadei and Marani, 1975, 272); Fig. 63 (Zanker, 1970, fig. 46); Fig. 91 (Hind, 1938–48, II, pl. 98); Fig. 92 (Colonna, 1976); Fig. 94 (Castellano, 1984, 89, fig. 93).